Metodi e approcci archeologici: l'industria e il commercio nell'Italia antica

Archaeological Methods and Approaches: Industry and Commerce in Ancient Italy

Edited by

Eric C. De Sena
Hélène Dessales

BAR International Series 1262
2004

Published in 2016 by
BAR Publishing, Oxford

BAR International Series 1262

Metodi e approcci archeologici / Archaeological Methods and Approaches

ISBN 978 1 84171 620 6

BAR Publishing is the trading name of British Archaeological Reports (Oxford) Ltd. British Archaeological Reports was first incorporated in 1974 to publish the BAR Series, International and British. In 1992 Hadrian Books Ltd became part of the BAR group. This volume was originally published by Archaeopress in conjunction with British Archaeological Reports (Oxford) Ltd / Hadrian Books Ltd, the Series principal publisher, in 2004. This present volume is published by BAR Publishing, 2016.

Printed in England

BAR
PUBLISHING

BAR titles are available from:

BAR Publishing
122 Banbury Rd, Oxford, OX2 7BP, UK
EMAIL info@barpublishing.com
PHONE +44 (0)1865 310431
FAX +44 (0)1865 316916
www.barpublishing.com

Table of Contents

Eric C. DE SENA, Hélène DESSALES, *Preface* .... iii-iv

Margarita GLEBA, *Textile production in protohistoric Italy : The Use of Implements in Reconstructing a "Missing" Craft* 1-11

Laurent HUGOT, *Aire sacrée ou atelier de tissage? A propos des deux monuments cylindriques de via fondazza à Bologne* 12-24

Christine MACHEBOEUF, *Fabrication et commerce de la pourpre en Italie romaine* ... 25-37

Martine LEGUILLOUX, *L'identification des tanneries antiques par l'archéologie et l'archéozoologie* 38-48

Jacopo BONETTO, Andrea Raffaele GHIOTTO, *Linee metodologiche ed esempi di approccio per lo studio dell'artigianato tessile laniero nella Venetia et Histria* 49-62

Renato PERONI, *Sistemi ponderali nella circolazione dei metalli in europa tra lo scorcio del* II *e l'inizio del* I *millennio a.C.* 63-79

Andrea CARDARELLI, Marco PACCIARELLI, Paolo PALLANTE, *Pesi e bilance nell'età del bronzo italiana: quadro generale e nuovi dati* 80-88

Daniel ISTRIA, *Les échanges commerciaux entre la Corse et l'Italie septentrionale au* XIVe *siècle: méthodes d'investigation et interprétation des données* 89-95

Sara Tiziana LEVI, Andrea SCHIAPPELLI, *I pithoi di ispirazione egea del tardo Bronzo nell'Italia meridionale: tecnologia, contenuto, immagazzinamento, circolazione* 96-108

Francesco DI GENNARO, Cristiano IAIA, *Evidenze relative alla produzione ceramica a Fidene nella prima età del ferro* 109-119

Alessandra PIERGROSSI, Silvia TEN KORTENAAR, Valeria ACCONCIA, *Lo sviluppo e la circolazione della ceramica di impasto rosso in Etruria meridionale e nel Lazio* 120-132

Valeria ACCONCIA, *La tecnologia del bucchero : alcune considerazioni sulle produzioni dell'Etruria meridionale e settentrionale* 133-143

Diego ELIA, *Nuovi dati sulla produzione e sulla circolazione della ceramica italiota a figure rosse nel iv secolo a.C. a Locri Epizefiri* 144-158

Franca CIBECCHINI, Jordí PRINCIPAL , *Per chi suona la Campana B ?* 159-172

Gloria OLCESE, *Anfore greco-italiche antiche : alcune osservazioni sull'origine e sulla circolazione alla luce di recenti ricerche archeologiche ed archeometriche* 173-192

Alessandra BOUSQUET, Sabrina ZAMPINI, *Note preliminari per una tipologia delle ceramiche comuci dell'etruria meridionale ("Tiber valley project")* 193-201

Archer MARTIN, *Considerazioni su un confronto tra gruppi funzionali in quattro contesti ceramici del V sec. d.C.* 202-204

Massimiliano DI FAZIO, *Note sulla presenza di bolli laterizi nel territorio di Fondi (LT)* 205-213

Francesca DELL'ACQUA, *L'industria vetraria di san Vincenzo al Volturno tra IX e XII sec.: il bilancio di un ventennio di studi* 214-218

Gabriele CIFANI, *Recenti approcci e metodi per lo studio dell'edilizia antica : il caso della Roma arcaica* 219-225

Maria Teresa D'ALESSIO, *La villa dell'auditorium e la questione agraria : tra le riforme di Servio Tullio e la serrata del Patriziato* 226-235

Evelyne BUKOWIECKI, Paola CIANCHI, *Raccolta e progetto di catalogo dei bolli anepigrafici su bessales d'epoca imperiale (Roma ed il suo territorio)* 236-242

Filippo DEMMA, *Anfiteatro Flavio di Pozzuoli, la decorazione marmorea nella storia edilizia : tipologia e stile, restauri, officine e artigiani* 243-261

Paolo BARRESI, *Anfiteatro flavio di Pozzuoli, portico in summa cavea : una stima dei costi* 262-267

Elisabetta BIANCHI, *Produzioni laterizie e cantieri edilizi traianei* 268-290

Nicolas MONTEIX, *Amedeo Maiuri et les boutiques d'Herculanum : approche historiographique* 291-299

Paolo GULL, *Tra continuità e rottura. Le associazioni medievali di mestiere nel pensiero storico e politico tra fine del XIX e XX secolo* 300-305

PREFACE

Eric C. DE SENA *(American Academy in Rome; John Cabot University)*
Hélène DESSALES *(Fellow École française de Rome 2000-03 ; Ecole Normale Supérieure)*

This volume represents the final product of a three-day conference organized by the editors and sponsored by the American Academy in Rome and the École Française de Rome. *Archaeological Methods and Approaches: Ancient Industry and Commerce in Italy*, April 18-20, 2002, involved 29 papers authored or co-authored by 43 scholars from 24 institutions.

The impetus for this conference was twofold: to reinforce the importance of reflecting upon archaeological methods and approaches in research endeavors, and to create a forum in which industry and commerce in pre-modern Italy could be discussed with virtually no temporal boundaries (2nd millennium BC and the early 2nd millennium AD). The organizers, both classical archaeologists, maintain that too many scholars work within super-specialized solar systems of research that often do not merge into galaxies of knowledge.[1] By calling together Prehistorians, Etruscologists, Romanists and Medieval archaeologists, each of whom necessarily relies upon very different research strategies in their work due a reliance upon different bodies of evidence (and who rarely compare notes),[2] the organizers hoped to promote greater communication between the fields of study.

Traditionally, scholars have discussed the industry and commerce of specific cultures and periods of time with few attempts to trace the development of productive and distributional systems in Italy for so vast a period. We are well informed, for example, about many classes of Etruscan, Roman and Medieval pottery, but our knowledge of how ceramic production and distribution evolved between these periods is inadequate. The AAR/ÉFR conference was intended to narrow these gaps and most attendees found that there was more common ground than anticipated.

The conference papers were organized thematically rather than chronologically in order to facilitate methodological and historical comparisons: Textile Production, Supply of Foodstuffs, Commercial Systems, Production and Exchange of Pottery, Production of Glass and Metal, Organization of the Building Industry and Historiographic Studies. The articles in this volume follow the same order. Two papers discuss the standardization of units of weight for metal and stone in Italy and central Europe during the late Bronze Age (Peroni, Cardarelli et al.). Several papers are concerned with the manufacture and exchange of craft goods in specific times and places ranging from the South Italian Bronze Age to Molise in the high Middle Ages (Levi and Schiapelli, di Gennaro, Piergrossi et al., Acconcia, Elia, Cibecchini and Principal, Hugot, Bousquet and Zampini, Dell'Acqua). Many other papers considered the organization of the textile, brick and construction industries (Gleba, Macheboeuf, Leguilloux, Bonetto and Ghiotto, di Fazio, Cifani, Bukowiecki and Cianchi, Bianchi, Barresi, Demma). A small number of articles take a regional approach, sometimes highlighting the striking variation of production and consumption patterns among geographically associated sites (Istria, Martin). One paper discussed the recent excavation of an archaic farm in the immediate suburbs of Rome (D'Alessio). Two papers (Monteix, Gull) considered how past and modern scholars viewed aspects of the ancient economy in light of political, social and scientific agendas. Olcese discussed the relevance (and irrelevance) of using archaeometric techniques in the study of ceramic production, exchange and utilization. The authors of two conference papers opted not to contribute to this volume.

It is admitted that the majority of the papers deal with the question of archaeological methods implicitly in their descriptions and interpretations, while only a few participants presented their research strategies at great length. We learned that most scholars make use of information technology, yet research still boils down to excavation, optical analysis of artifacts and architectural features, the development of typologies, distributional analysis and statistics. Less than a third of the studies made use of scientific instrumentation (e.g., petrography, chemical analysis). Not surprisingly, considering the "science-like" paradigm in which we are currently working, none of the papers took a clearly school-oriented approach (e.g., Processualist, Post-P, Marxist), although the prehistorians were certainly the most unified in terms of their methods and results. What is important is that

[1] Cf. recently, Shiffer 2000, who stresses the importance of "bridge-building".
[2] Perhaps the only exception is the International Conference on Italian Archaeology.

research does not become mechanical and that we consciously reflect upon the nature of our bodies of evidence, the development of realistic objectives and the procedures used to achieve valid conclusions.

The editors wish to thank the American Academy in Rome and the École Française de Rome, and in particular Dr. Lester Little (Director, AAR), Dr. André Vauchez, Dr. Michel Gras (Directeur, ÉFR), Dr. Ingrid Rowland (Mellon Professor for the Humanities, AAR), Dr. Stéphane Verger (Directeur des études, section Antiquité, ÉFR), Dr. Archer Martin (Archaeology Supervisor, AAR), and Véronique Séjournet (Secrétaire de la section Antiquité, ÉFR). We are indebted to Dr. Jean Pierre Brun (Centre Jean Bérard, Naples), Dr. Roberto Meneghini (Sovraintendenza Comunale di Roma), Dr. Carlo Pavolini (University of Tuscia, Viterbo), Dr. Renato Peroni (University "La Sapienza" of Rome) and Dr. Andrea Zifferero (University of Siena), who served admirably as moderators for the sessions and reviewed many of the papers for this volume. The editors are also indebted to Dr. François Bougard (Directeur des études, section médiévale, ÉFR), Dr. Paolo Carafa (Università degli Studi di Cosenza), Dr. Wolfgang David (Ludwig-Maximilians-Universität München), Dr. Jacopo De Grossi Mazzorin (Laboratorio de Archeozoologia, Soprintendenza Archeologica di Roma), Dr. Janne P. Ikäheimo (University of Oulu, Finland), and Dr. Stéphane Verger (ÉFR) who also served on the review committee. Finally, we thank the authors for their interest in the conference, their contributions and their patience with our editing and review procedures.

TEXTILE PRODUCTION IN PROTOHISTORIC ITALY: THE USE OF IMPLEMENTS IN RECONSTRUCTING A "MISSING" CRAFT

MARGARITA GLEBA
(Bryn Mawr College)

ABSTRACT: Throughout antiquity, textile manufacture was an industry of great cultural and economic importance and has to be factored into any balanced assessment of the ancient economy. However, due to the extremely poor preservation of archaeological textiles, discussions of textile production have been practically absent from all studies of ancient industry and commerce in ancient Italy. The great quantity of implements associated with textile manufacture can be used to study the craft and its technological and economic aspects in the absence of actual textiles. A tool-based approach to the textile studies can be used to start reconstructing the craft that has been "missing" in the context of the early Italic economy.

INTRODUCTION

Throughout antiquity, textile manufacture was practiced on all levels of society and was one of the most labor-intensive of occupations (Barber 1991: 4). As such, it was an industry of great cultural and economic importance and has to be factored into any balanced assessment of the ancient economy. However, discussions of textile production have been practically absent from all studies of ancient industry and commerce in ancient Italy. This is especially true for the Early Iron Age and the beginning of the historic period, or, for the purposes of this paper, the tenth through seventh centuries BCE, a time when textile craft reached a technically sophisticated stage.[1] The main reason for this significant gap is the extremely poor preservation of fabrics. In contrast to the products of other crafts, such as pottery production or metallurgy, textile materials and products rarely survive in the archaeological record of ancient Italy.

The extant textiles come predominantly from burial contexts and are often simple cloths that had been used for wrapping objects or cremated ashes. Most of the surviving fragments are small, preserved as pseudomorphs on metal surfaces.[2] Some of the most spectacular finds are known from Sasso di Furbara (Mamez and Masurel 1992) and Verucchio (Stauffer 2002). The recent discoveries of textiles in the Orientalizing cemetery at Casale Marittimo (Esposito 1999: 93-94) and clothing articles found frozen at Vedretta di Ries in the Aurine Alps (Dal Ri 1996) add significantly to our knowledge about textiles of Iron Age Italy. These textile products are of high technical and aesthetic quality, as attested by the variety in their weight and design, as well as their polychromy. A greater problem than the scarce textile finds, however, is the lack of publication and synthetic work on the few that do survive.[3]

The depictions in the painted tombs of Tarquinia and other representations of ancient clothing in Italy give an idea of the appearance of these textiles, even though they come from chronologically later contexts.[4] Nevertheless, apart from general observations, the representations of dress offer little information about the technical aspects of ancient Italian textiles.[5]

Despite these objective difficulties, ancient iconography is of great importance to our understanding and reconstruction of textile technology for illustration of production activities. Two objects are of particular significance.

From the area of Bologna, in northern Italy, comes one of the most important depictions of textile production in the ancient world, a so-called bronze *tintinnabulum* found in tomb 5 ("Tomba degli Ori") of Bologna's Arsenale Militare necropolis (Morigi Govi 1971, Kossack 1999: 67-68) (Figure 1). It is dated to the second half of seventh century BCE. Four scenes depict various stages of textile manufacture. The bottom scene of side A depicts two women seated in throne-like chairs dressing the distaffs for spinning. The top scene of side A shows a woman at the task of spinning. Side B of the *tintinnabulum* shows activities associated with weaving. The bottom scene has not been given a satisfactory explanation. The most likely interpretation has been put forward independently by Stage (1985: 56) and Barber (1991: 116), who suggest that the scene represents the weaving of the starting border necessary for the warp-weighted loom. Such an explanation would fit in with the sequence of production, since the last scene provides a rendering of a warp-weighted loom. This representation is unique as it shows the only two-storied loom known from antiquity.

Another important object, also from northern Italy, is the wooden throne found in Tomb 89 of Verucchio (Figure 2), the shape of which closely resembles the chairs on the *tintinnabulum* (Gentili 1987: 207-263). The throne, extraordinary for the conservation of material, has been dated to the end of the eighth – beginning of the seventh century BCE (von Eles 2002, 273-275). The scenes intricately carved on the inner side of the back illustrate the cycle of wool production, including rearing and shearing of sheep, washing of wool, spinning, weaving and, finally, garment manufacture (Torelli 1997: 63-86; Kossack 1995, 1999: 64-68).

The Bologna *tintinnabulum* and the Verucchio throne are of great value for our understanding of textile-making activities, especially the phases of the production process. Apart from these two objects, however, we are left to rely on archaeological material in attempting to learn about textile production in Iron Age Italy. The great quantity of implements associated with textile manufacture, can be used to study the craft and its technological and economic aspects. This paper will outline a methodology of studying textile manufacture through some of these implements.

Spinning and weaving implements

Spinning and weaving implements constitute the single most important and plentiful type of evidence for assessment of the scale of production and technology of the weaving industry in ancient Italy. The implements to be considered include tools associated with various stages of textile manufacture: preparation of the fibers, spinning of the yarn, weaving of the fabric, and secondary processes like sewing of the fabric together to create a garment and embroidery and other decoration techniques. Not all of these stages leave clear physical traces in the archaeological context, since many tools, especially those used in the preparation of fibers, could be made of perishable materials such as wood or bone, and have not survived time and the elements. Extant implements are most frequently made of fired clay. These include spindle whorls, loom weights and "spools".[6] Metal tools, such as needles and, sometimes, distaffs and spindles are also among the documented finds.

In pre-Roman Italy, weaving implements occurred in three contexts: funerary, votive, and settlement. Starting in the ninth century BCE, the textile craft became a symbol of the female sphere of life, and women's contribution to the community as textile workers was expressed by the deposition of spinning and weaving tools in their burials (Bartoloni 1989, Torelli 1997, Toms 1998, Nielsen 1998, Jannot in preparation). Spindle whorls, spindles, distaffs, "spools", and, less frequently, loom weights and needles, are found in burials dating to the Villanovan and early periods of Etruscan culture (Gleba 1999: 31-35). The symbolic value of these objects in female tombs has been a subject of attention in recent scholarship.[7] The social implications of spinning and weaving activities are also underlined by the occurrence of weaving implements in votive deposits (Gleba 1999: 35-37).

However, the primary function of these objects, that of being used in textile production, can only be inferred from settlement contexts. A study of the number, distribution, and morphology based on the statistical analyses of physical parameters of preservation, size, weight, use wear of artifacts, provides valuable information about technology, scale of production and importance of textile production for the particular site, as well as the raw materials and the final products. On a broader scale, these implements can be used to track both chronological and technological developments in textile production, while through a diachronic approach it is possible to examine some of the economic and social aspects of the craft, such as the development of workshops from household production. Excavated habitation sites with well-documented finds are *conditio sine qua non* for a systematic study of this kind.

In the remaining part of this paper I will focus on several specific classes of implements and the information that can be derived from their examination. Then, as an example of the application of this type of approach to a concrete situation, I will examine the material from the site of Poggio Civitate (Murlo).

Since basically no implements used in fiber preparation survive for this period, I will start by examining tools used for spinning. These include a distaff and a spindle.

Distaffs

The distaff served to keep together a certain quantity of fiber during spinning. It was usually made of wood and not a single example of this instrument is known from ancient Italic settlement sites. Instead, numerous objects identified as distaffs made of luxury materials including bronze, amber, and ivory, have been found in wealthy tombs dated to the Villanovan and Orientalizing periods (Bartoloni 1989: 42-44). These instruments, inspired by the functional types, probably took on a symbolic significance that alluded to the role of a woman in the domestic sphere. Pliny the Elder (*NH* VIII, 194) records that the distaff and wool of Tanaquil, wife of Tarquinius Priscus, the first Etruscan king of Rome, was displayed for centuries in a temple erected, according to tradition, in 466 BCE. Later still, Roman brides carried a spindle and a distaff during wedding processions (Torelli 1984: 131-133; Nielsen 1998: 73). Distaffs found in early tombs, thus, most likely represented status symbols and need not have been used in spinning. They are useful, however, in estimating the size and shape of working distaffs, which could exceed a meter in length.

SPINDLES AND SPINDLE WHORLS

Considerably more information is known about the spindles. Their shafts were usually made of wood and a few exceptional examples have in fact survived in the archaeological record. For example, four spindle shafts have been excavated in the Forum Boarium in Rome (Castagnoli *et al.* 1981: 147) and one was found during underwater excavation of Early Iron Age settlement of Gran Carro in Lago di Bolsena (Tamburini 1995: 169, Fig. 51). These surviving implements are instructive for the reconstruction of the shape and size of ancient spindles. Thus, the estimated average length of a spindle was *ca.* 20-30 cm.

A much more commonly found part of the spindle, however, is the spindle whorl, a symmetrical, centrally pierced object, often made of fired clay, stone, bone or wood, that was attached to the lower part of the spindle shaft.[8] The hole for the spindle shaft is an important feature of a whorl since it has to be large enough to accommodate the shaft. The expected range of the hole diameter for spindle whorls is 0.3 to 1 cm, which helps in distinguishing them from larger beads, which have a piercing of smaller average size.

Spinning involves drawing out and twisting the fibers (Barber 1991: 42). In order to achieve control over fineness and evenness of the thread, the fibers must be drawn and twisted simultaneously and with the same speed. A whorl provides weight and tension for this action. Hence, the weight of the whorl is its most important feature and can indicate the quality of the thread produced. For particular types of yarn, spindle whorls fall within a certain range of weights.[9] For spinning long-staple wool, heavy spindles are used, ranging 100-150 g. Even heavier implements are utilized for spinning full-length flax or for plying wool yarns. On the other hand, short wool, flax tow or cotton, are spun with a light spindle. The weight of the spindle used for short fine wool is about 8 g, while for the medium to heavy wool it is about 33 g. Thus, statistical analysis of this parameter can help in determining what kind of fiber was used in antiquity in a particular settlement.

Another important aspect of a spindle whorl is its shape, which influences the speed of spinning and, thus, the tightness of the thread twist. A smaller diameter will cause the whorl to rotate faster and, therefore, to produce tighter twist than could be accomplished with a wider whorl of the same weight. The proportion of whorl diameter to its height produces a coefficient of rotation speed, which indicates the twist tightness. Thus, a coefficient above one, as in disc-shaped spindle whorls, would indicate loose twist, while a coefficient below one, typical for biconical whorls, would show a tight one. The most common whorl shape on Italian sites appears to be the truncated cone, which is suitable to make thread of medium tightness. Since tightness of twist influences the strength and flexibility of the yarn, whorl shape analysis may help in establishing the quality of the yarn produced at a site.

LOOM WEIGHTS

The next stage of textile production is weaving. The loom used in Italy before Roman times was of the vertical warp-weighted kind, formed by two vertical supports joined by horizontal beams. The warp threads were suspended from the top beam and were kept taught by loom weights during the weaving process. Loom weights constitute the only archaeologically retrievable part of the loom, the rest having been made of wood and disintegrated.

The main forms of loom weights in the ancient world were cylindrical, donut, discoid, conical and trapezoidal. The cylindrical weights are characteristic of Bronze Age contexts. The trapezoidal shape seems to have been prevalent from the Early Iron Age on and varies from pyramidal to almost cuboid. In Northern Italy donut-shaped weights were also common. Conical weights may have been introduced to Italy by Greek settlers and occur mostly in the south of the peninsula, as do the discoid ones.

The manner in which the weights were attached to the warp is still debated. Most likely the threads were tied, not to the loom weight itself, but to an intermediary device such as a metal ring, a cord, or a bar, which also attached the loom weights to each other to keep them organized.

The degree of uprightness and the height of a warp-weighted loom, as well as the distribution of the weights must be considered when attempting to suggest its possible position. Archaeological and representational evidence suggests that the main upright portion of the loom was probably braced at an angle by a wall or a post from behind, an arrangement that uses gravity, with a bar at the bottom to separate the threads into a shed. The height is more problematic, since although the normal loom would not be much higher than human height, the Bologna *tintinnabulum* and Verucchio throne indicate that very large, even two-storied looms were used.

A set of loom weights is typically composed of six to thirty implements, although it could reach as many as eighty (Barber 1991: 104). The evidence for these numbers is provided by ethnoarchaeology and by the configuration of loom weights occasionally found *in situ*, having fallen to the ground when the warp to which they were originally attached was destroyed. Such loom weight series also permit reconstruction of the exact orientation and the width of the loom, which, in turn, can be used to speculate about the size and quality of the textile being woven. Distribution of the loom weights can also be useful in providing information about the location of textile producing activities within the settlement.

Based on the maximum possible width of the putative loom, the number of the loom weights found at the site, and the mean maximum bottom width per weight, the possible number of looms present at a site may be calculated (Barber 1991: 103). The weight of a loom weight is thus its most important physical parameter. Fewer loom weights would be needed if they were heavy and more if they were light. Heavier weights were used for fabrics with simple weaves, and lighter ones for finer and more complex material.[10]

"Spools"

"Spools" are cylindrical objects, often with flaring ends, approximately 5-6 cm in length and 40-60 grams in weight. Their function has been debated for some time but for the most part these objects have been connected to textile production. Many excavators believe that "spools" functioned for storing spun yarn.[11]

"Spools" occur in female burials and only in a small percentage of them, usually in multiples. The numbers range from 3 to over 40, some burials having over 100.[12] In the majority of cases, these groups contain "spools" that are very close in weight and size, and often bear the same decoration. Some tombs contain two or more groups of "spools" of different sizes. This suggests that "spools" were used in sets, like loom weights.

I have argued elsewhere that these spools were in fact used as small weights to produce narrow patterned strips of cloth (Gleba 1999, Gleba 2000, 79). Lise Ræder Knudsen has demonstrated quite convincingly that they may have been utilized as weights for the sets of threads passing through the tablets used to make the borders on the Verucchio textiles (Ræder Knudsen 2002, 228-229).[13]

The tension for each set of threads was provided by one "spool" as suggested by their mean weight. The concave portion of the shaft may have been used to store the excess thread in the initial stages of production. Information on the distribution and position of "spools" found in primary contexts of settlements would be crucial to testing the theory of them having been used as loom weight analogs since it could help reconstruct their function in the same fashion that loom weights have been used to recover the information about the size and location of warp-weighted looms.

The fabrics obtained in the process of weaving could have been dyed or decorated in some way. Unfortunately, for the moment, there is insufficient data on other textile activities such as washing, fulling, or dying in the protohistoric period in Italy. There is, however, one more class of instruments to be examined, needles.

Needles

Needles are not frequently mentioned among published excavation finds, and their analyses are few (Macnamara 1976: 146-147). Unlike other tools, needles seldom occur in tombs and hoards and are more commonly found on habitation sites, although due to their small size both conservation and recovery rate are poor. Bronze gives strength and thinness, which is advantageous for fine stitching of cloth and leather. More often, however, needles were probably made of bone, a material that is cheaper, but also less likely to survive. Bone needles are usually shorter and thicker than the bronze ones, to prevent breakage. It is impossible to know whether needles made of different materials were used for different types of fabrics or different functions.

Although in antiquity clothes were usually woven in one piece and not tailored, the paintings in Tarquinian tombs show garments with stitches, demonstrating one of the uses of a needle.[14] Another use was probably embroidery. The same paintings in the tombs of Tarquinia show dresses of semitransparent material, interpreted as linen, adorned with small decorative elements. Since linen is extremely difficult to dye, such decoration had to be added while weaving or with embroidery technique, hence with a needle. These decorative ornaments may have also been made of other materials, such as bronze, amber and golden plaques as well as glass beads that were sewn onto the garments – in which case needles would have been used as well. Undoubtedly, needles were also used for mending, as attested by the textiles of Vedretta di Ries (Dal Ri 1996: 372-375).

At this point I would like to consider a specific case in order to demonstrate how the approach described in this paper can be applied to obtain information about textile production at a given settlement.

Poggio Civitate (Murlo)

At Poggio Civitate (Murlo), an Etruscan settlement in the province of Siena, spinning and weaving implements have turned up almost every season since the excavations began in 1966 (Figure 3).[15] More than thirty years of excavation and study have shown two distinct chronological phases of the site, the Orientalizing, spanning 650-625 BCE, and Archaic, dated to 600-530 BCE. The Archaic phase consists of a large square building measuring approximately 61 m on each side, with a courtyard in the center. The preceding Orientalizing phase is currently represented by three structures, the Lower Building, the Southeast Building, believed to have been a workshop structure, and the recently excavated Orientalizing Complex 3.

The Orientalizing structures appear to have been destroyed by a violent fire, after which the site was leveled and the new, Archaic structure was built. This so-called Upper building was also destroyed sometime after 530 BCE (Edlund-Berry 1994; de Grummond 1997). It should be noted that the precise dating of artifacts is often problematic because of the destruction, leveling, and later dismantling of the structures, which created mostly mixed contexts for all objects not sealed within the earlier buildings. As a result, the archaeological date of many artifacts, including the implements relevant to this discussion falls between 650 and 530 BCE, the broad period of occupation of Piano del Tesoro.

Nevertheless, the distribution and decoration style of the spinning and weaving implements at Poggio Civitate may be taken to indicate that most of them were probably associated with the Orientalizing phase, and hence, were manufactured and/or used over the period of about a quarter of a century.[16] Although scattered by the destruction and leveling of the site, the tools for textile production appear to be concentrated in just two areas, both associated with seventh-century structures. One is in the northern part of the Lower Building. Another area in which implements are concentrated is around the so-called Southeast Building. This structure has been identified as a workshop, because of deposits of the debris of ivory and bronze-working, as well as the presence of unfired tiles (Nielsen 1998: 98-99). The distribution of spinning and weaving implements not only confirms the functional identification of this structure but also suggests that textile manufacture was as important as the production of other types of materials and goods, mostly luxury in nature.

Judged by the number of spinning and weaving implements alone, Poggio Civitate appears to have been a significant textile-producing center. In 1998 the catalogued finds included 441 spindle whorls, 69 loom weights, 580 "spools", as well as 13 needles. The results of the analyses of these implements support some generalizations about textile production on the site.[17]

The great number of spindle whorls at Poggio Civitate (Figure 4), especially in comparison to other sites for which information is available, indicates that the scale of yarn production was large. The mean weight of spindle whorls at Poggio Civitate is 9.6 grams, which is appropriate for spinning short, fine wool.[18] This suggests that a large quantity of very fine yarn was manufactured at the site. Ninety three percent of the whorls are of truncated conical shape, suitable for spinning yarn of medium twist, with biconical, ovoid, conical and globular shapes also represented. The very uniform proportions of the whorls suggest that spinning was both organized and specialized. The concentration of the large quantity of very uniform implements in specific areas of the site suggests a workshop situation: spinning seems to have been one of the major crafts on the site.

The number of loom weights at Poggio Civitate seems to be small in comparison to the quantity of spindle whorls and "spools" (Figure 5). At the contemporary site of Lago d'Accesa, for example, the number of loom weights is at least four times higher than the number of spindle whorls (Camporeale 1997: 199, 205-9).

The weight of Murlo loom weights ranges from 34 to 795 grams.[19] This is a very broad range in comparison to loom weight size at contemporary sites. For example, at Acquarossa, in Latium, loom weights fall into three distinct groups of approximately 300, 400, and 500 grams (*Architettura Etrusca* 1986: 112, 125). Over 90 loom weights found at Lago d'Accesa, near Massa Marittima, vary between 125 and 450 grams (Camporeale 1997: 199). At Ficana, however, the range is much wider with groups of 250-310 grams, 310-370 grams, and 900-1400 grams. The broad weight range suggests that textiles of various quality and complexity was being produced at Poggio Civitate.

Although not all parts of the site have been excavated, for the moment the numbers suggest that the amount of spun yarn significantly exceeded the quantity of fabric that was being produced at the site. This inconsistency may be explained by the extraordinary quantity of "spools" on the site (Figure 6). Their number (over 580) is higher even than the quantity of spindle whorls and, if the hypothesis that their function was analogous to that of loom weights is correct, may indicate that the workshop specialized in the production of fine patterned textiles strips, as confirmed by the functional analysis of the whorls and the "spools".[20]

Finally, 13 fine bronze and bone needles found at Murlo should be mentioned. Not only do they indicate that sewing was practiced on the site, they also suggest that several workers could have been sewing simultaneously.

From this brief summary it is clear that textiles were manufactured at Poggio Civitate on a scale significantly larger than what would be considered production for domestic consumption. In fact, the evidence of spinning and weaving implements points towards Poggio Civitate having played a significant role in production and possibly even exchange in the Orientalizing period. Thus, despite the total absence of textiles at the site, it is possible to draw some conclusions about their role in the economy of the settlement.

CONCLUSIONS

The fact that few textiles have survived from the protohistoric and early historic period in Italy should not detract from our understanding of their production. In the absence of actual fabrics, a tool-based approach to textile studies can be used to start reconstructing this craft, which until now has been missing in the context of the study of Early Iron Age and Archaic economy in Italy. The feasibility of such an approach hinges on the publication of necessary data by the excavators and I would like to underline the importance of publishing of physical parameters of excavated objects in archaeological reports. Until now, the weight values have been published only rarely for loom weights and basically never for spindle whorls and "spools". Even more important is the stratigraphic information since, textile craft being conservative by nature, the most reliable way of dating implements is through their association with other material. Artifact distributions are also essential for a study of this type since concentrations of implements reflect the areas of activity. When found *in situ*, they can provide specific information about the location and the size of tools, parts of which were made of perishable materials and thus do not survive in the archaeological record.

Before a more integrated study of textile production in Italy is possible through consideration of the textiles themselves, implements used in their production, literary and epigraphic evidence, comparative archaeology with European, Near Eastern and Egyptian cultures, as well as ethnographic and experimental data, each kind of evidence has to be examined in its own right. Implements associated with textile manufacture constitute by far the most numerous and the most understudied area of textile studies in Italy. They are anything but spectacular, yet they can be of great value in beginning to reconstruct this craft that so far has been "missing" in the studies of the early Italian economy.

ENDNOTES

1 This is a lamentable gap in ancient textile studies, especially in comparison to the state of affairs in Central and Northern Europe; See Hald 1980, Bender Jorgensen 1991, Teržan 1996, Stegmann-Rajtár 1998, and Banck-Burgess 1999, all of which contain exhaustive bibliographies. The situation is slightly better for the Italian Bronze Age period; see Barber 1991, 174-175, and Rast-Eicher 1997, 545-553.

2 See Gillard *et al.*, 1994, for discussion of the mineralization of textile fibers in burials with relevant bibliography.

3 See, however, Bonfante 1975, Stage 1991, Barber 1991, 194-195, and Gleba 2003 for short summaries of extant Etruscan textile fragments.

4 Etruscan iconographic material has been analyzed by Bonfante 1975.

5 See, however, Granger-Taylor 1982, for an excellent discussion of some of the later techniques of Mediterranean clothing manufacture based on surviving textiles and depiction of clothing in Etruscan and Roman art.

6 I put the word "spool" in quotation marks because, as will be discussed later, the term suggests a function, which, in my opinion, is unlikely.

7 Based on the material from Osteria dell'Osa, Bietti Sestieri 1992, 102, has proposed a differentiation between "spinners", defined by a single spindle whorl, originally associated with a wooden spindle and, sometimes, a distaff, and "weavers", whose burial assemblages included several spindle whorls and numerous "spools". Also see Bartoloni 1989, 42.

8 The spindle used in Italy was the low-whorl kind. See Barber 1991, 53-57.

9 The following numbers are given by Barber 1991, 52.

10 More complex weaves require the warp to be divided into multiple sheds with fewer threads attached to each loom weight. The loom weighs, thus, need to be lighter and smaller.

11 This interpretation is unlikely because most *"spools"* have too small a taper to have provided an efficient way to store yarn. Being made of terracotta, they are heavy and are prone to break easily. Finally, their production requires the expenditure of time, energy, and resources that are not easily justifiable by their function to store yarn, when any wooden stick, or, in fact, the spindle shaft on which the spun yarn was wound during spinning could have been used for the purpose. The latter theory is especially attractive since leaving spun yarn on a spindle would have saved the time needed to transfer the yarn onto a spool and the spindle shaft could have been then used as a shuttle during weaving.

12 In the so-called Isis Tomb at Vulci, there were at least 131 "spools", while the tomb Lippi 18 at Verucchio had 144; for the latter see von Eles 1995.

13 One would expect to find the tablets as well but because these were most likely of wood or bone, they have not survived in the archaeological record.

14 In fact, see Bonfante 1975, 92: "Unlike Greek garments woven in one piece, Etruscan clothes were often sewn up from several pieces."

15 See Phillips 1993, and De Puma and Small 1994, for information on excavations at the site and bibliography.

16 The database of all Poggio Civitate finds is currently in the making, which will render possible creation of much more precise chronological and geographical distribution maps allowing for a revision of the analysis of this material. I hope, however, that it will not alter significantly the conclusions presented in this paper.

17 The following is a brief summary of a more extensive study, which has been undertaken as research for a thesis written by the author in fulfillment of the requirements for the degree of Master of Arts at Bryn Mawr College, Pennsylvania (Gleba 1999). See also Gleba 2000.
18 The median was 8, range 2-48, standard deviation 7.79, standard error 0.41. No clear clusters are present, the distribution being bell-shaped and slightly skewed towards the lower end of the range.
19 Here the distribution is too wide and the sample is too small to have a meaningful mean weight, especially since many weights are fragmentary. However, clusters seem to occur around several groups: 34g; 66-184g; 220-260g; 292-444g; 572-585g; and one item over 795g.
20 Given the popularity of patterned borders on garments depicted in contemporary figurative representations (Bonfante 1975) and actual such borders found at Verucchio (Stauffer 2002) and Sasso di Furbara (Mamez and Masurel 1992), it is tempting to suggest that the Murlo workshop specialized in production of these elements, which, in addition to being decorative, were also indicators of status (Stauffer 2002, 192, 208). See Gleba forthcoming.

BIBLIOGRAPHY

Architettura Etrusca nel Viterbese. Ricerche svedesi a San Giovenale e Acquarossa 1956-1986, *1986, Roma.*

Banck-Burgess, J., 1999, *Hochdorf IV, Die Textilfunde aus dem späthallstattischen Fürstengrab von Eberdingen-Hochdorf (Kreis Ludvigsburg) und veitere grabtextilien aus hallstatt- und latenezeitlichen Kulturgruppen*, Stuttgart.

Barber, E.W., 1991, *Prehistoric Textiles. The Development of Cloth in the Neolithic and Bronze Ages*, Princeton.

Bartoloni, G., 1989, Marriage, Sale and Gift: A proposito di alcuni corredi femminili dalle necropoli populoniesi della prima età del ferro, in *Le donne in Etruria* (ed. A. Rallo), 35-54, Roma.

Bender Jørgensen, L., 1991, *North European Textiles until AD 1000*, Aarhus.

Bietti Sestieri, A., 1992, *The Iron Age Community of Osteria dell'Osa*, Cambridge.

Bonfante, L., 1975, *Etruscan Dress*. Baltimore & London.

Camporeale, G., 1997, *L'abitato Etrusco dell'Accesa*, Roma.

Castagnoli, F., *et al.*, 1981, *Enea nel Lazio: archeologia e mito* (Catalogo della Mostra), Roma.

Dal Ri, L., 1996, I ritrovamenti presso il rifugio Vedretta di Ries/Rieserferner nelle Alpi Aurine (2850 m s.l.m.). Notizia preliminare, *Rivista di Scienze Preistoriche*, XLVII, 367-388.

de Grummond, N.T., 1997, Poggio Civitate: a Turning Point, *Etruscan Studies*, 4, 23-40.

De Puma, R.D. and J.P. Small, 1994, *Murlo and the Etruscans: Art and Society in Ancient Etruria*, Madison, Wisconsin.

Edlund-Berry, I.E.M., 1994, Ritual Destruction of Cities and Sanctuaries: The "Unfounding" of the Archaic Monumental Building at Poggio Civitate (Murlo), in *Murlo and the Etruscans: Art and Society in Ancient Etruria* (eds. R.D. De Puma and J.P. Small), 16-28, The University of Wisconsin Press.

Esposito, A. M., 1999, *I principi guerrieri. La necropolis etrusca di Casale Marittimo*, Milano.

Gentili, G.V., 1987, Verucchio, in *La formazione della città in Emilia Romagna* (ed. G. Bermond Montanari), 207-263, Bologna.

Gleba, M., 1999, *Textile Production in Etruria: the Case of Poggio Civitate (Murlo)*, Masters thesis, Bryn Mawr College.

Gleba, M., 2000, Textile Production at Poggio Civitate (Murlo) in the 7th c. BC", in *Archéologie des textiles des origines au Ve siecle, Actes du colloque de Lattes*, oct. 1999, (eds. D. Cardon and M. Feugère), 75-80, Monographies Instrumentum 14, Montpellier.

Gleba, M., 2003, Etruscan Textile Studies, *Etruscan News* 2: 8-9.

Gleba, M., forthcoming, Textile Production in Protohistoric Italy: the "Missing" craft, in *Ancient Textiles: Production, Craft and Society* (ed. E. Andersson, B. Burke, C. Gillis, and M.-L. Nosch).

Gillard, R.D. *et al.*, 1994, The mineralization of fibres in burial environments, *Studies in Conservation*, 39, 132-140.

Granger-Taylor, H., 1982, Weaving Clothes to Shape in the Ancient World: The Tunic and Toga of the Arringatore, *Textile History*, 13 (1), 3-25.

Hald, M., 1980, *Ancient Danish Textiles from Bogs and Burials*, Kopenhagen.

Jannot, J.-R., In preparation, Assemblées de femmes: une survivance clusienne des valeurs familiales archaïques.

Kossack, G., 1992, Lebensbilder, mythische Bilderzählung und Kultfestbilder. Bemerkungen zu Bildszenen auf einer Thronlehne von Verucchio, in *Festschrift zum 50jähringen Bestehen des Institutes für Ur- und Frühgeschichte der Leopold-Franzens-Universität Innsbruck, Universitätsforschungen zur Prähistorischen Archäologie* 8, 231-246, Bonn.

Kossack, G., 1999, *Religiöses Denken in dinglicher und bildlicher Überlieferung Alteuropas aus der Spätbronze- und frühen Eisenzeit (9.-6. Jahrhundert v. Chr. Geb.)*, Bayerische Akademie der Wissenschaften. Phil.-Hist. Klasse. Aabhandlungen N.F., Heft 116, München.

Macnamara, E., 1976, Chapter III: The Small Finds, in *A Faliscan Town in South Etruria. Excavations at Narce 1966-71* (ed. T.W. Potter), 127-178, London.

Mamez, L. and H. Masurel, 1992, Étude complémentairrre des vestiges textiles trouvés dans l'embarcation de la nécropole du Caolino à Sasso di Furbara, *Origini*, XVI, 295-310.

Morigi Govi, C., 1971, Il tintinnabulo della "Tomba degli Ori" dell'Arsenale Militare di Bologna, *ArchCl*, 23, 211-35.

Nielsen, E., 1998, Bronze Production at Poggio Civitate (Murlo), *Etruscan Studies*, 5, 95-107.

Nielsen, M., 1998, Etruscan Women: A Cross-Cultural Perspective, in *Aspects of Women in Antiquity* (eds. L. L. Lov•n and A. Strömberg), 69-84, Jonsered.

Phillips, K.M., Jr., 1993, *In the Hills of Tuscany: Recent Excavations at the Etruscan Site of Poggio Civitate (Murlo, Siena)*, Philadelphia.

Ræder Knudsen, L., 2002, La tessitura con le tavolette nella tomba 89, in *Guerriero e sacerdote. Autorità e comunità nell'età del ferro a Verucchio. La Tomba del Trono*, (ed. Von Eles), 220-234, Firenze.

Rast-Eicher, A., 1997, Tessuti dell'età del bronzo in Europa, in *Le Terremare. La più antica civiltà padana* (eds. M. Barnabò Brea, A. Cardarelli and M. Cremaschi), Modena.

Stage, J.C., 1985, *Etruscan Textile Arts: The Literary and Archaeological Evidence* (MA thesis), Tallahasse: The Florida State University.

Stage, J.C., 1991, Extant Etruscan Textiles: A Working List, *SteMat*, 6, 146-150.

Stauffer, A., 2002, I tessuti, in *Guerriero e sacerdote. Autorità e comunità nell'età del ferro a Verucchio. La Tomba del Trono* (ed. von Eles), 192-220, Firenze.

Stegmann-Rajtár, S. 1998. Spinnen und Weben in Smolenice-Molpír. Ein Beitrag zum wirtschaftlichen und religi◇s-kultischen Leben der Bewohner des Hallstattzetlichen "Fürstensizes." *Slovenská Archeológia* XLVI-2: 263-287.

Tamburini, P., 1995, *Un abitato villanoviano perilacustre. Il "Gran Carro" sul lago di Bolsena (1959-1985)*, Roma.

Teržan, B., 1996, Weben und Zeitmessen im südostapinen und westpannonischen Gebiet, in *Die Osthallstattkultur. Akten des Internationalen Symposiums, Sopron, 10.-14. Mai 1994*, 507-536, Budapest.

Toms, J., 1998, The construction of Gender in Early Iron Age Etruria, in *Gender and Italian Archaeology: Challenging the Stereotypes* (ed. R.D. Whitehouse), Accordia Specialist Studies in Italy 7, 157-179, London.

Torelli, M., 1984, *Lavinio e Roma*, Roma.

Torelli, M., 1997, *Il rango, il rito e l'immagine. Alle origini della rappresentazione storica romana*, Milano.

von Eles, P., 1995, *Verucchio, Museo Civico Archeologico*, Rimini.

von Eles, P., 2002, Guerriero e sacerdote. Autorità e comunità nell'età del ferro a Verucchio. La Tomba del Trono, Firenze.

Fig. 1. Tintinnabulum from Bologna, Arsenale Militare, "Tomba degli Ori", bronze, late 7th century BCE: a) side A, b) side b. Archivio del Museo Civico Archeologico di Bologna.

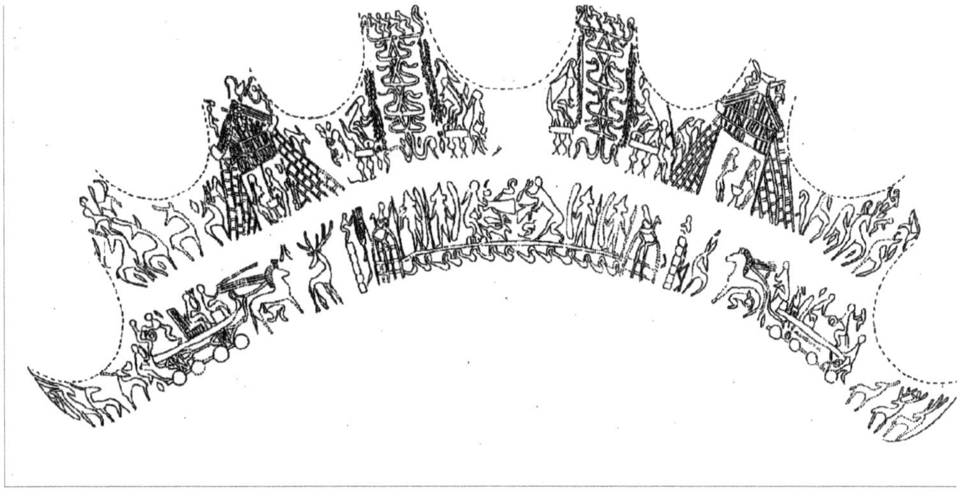

Fig. 2. Throne from Verucchio, Rocca Malatestiana Tomb 89, wood and bronze, late 8th century BCE. Details of scenes illustrating textile production. From Kossack 1999, fig. 44.

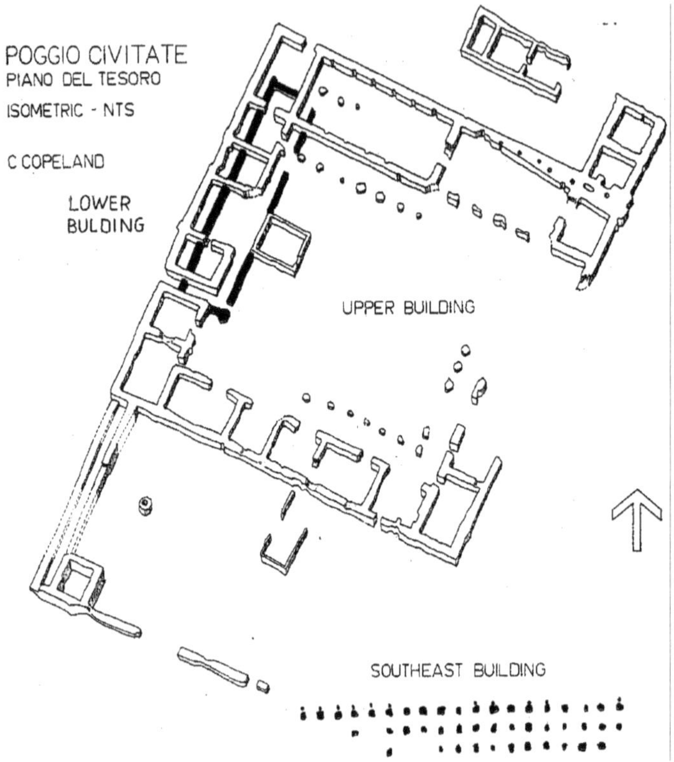

Fig. 3. Poggio Civitate (Murlo). Site plan.

Fig. 4. Spindle whorls from Poggio Civitate (Murlo), fired clay, late 7th – early 6th century BCE (Courtesy of Anthony Tuck).

Fig. 5. Loom weights from Poggio Civitate (Murlo), fired clay, late 7th – early 6th century BCE (Courtesy of Anthony Tuck).

Fig. 6. "Spools" from Poggio Civitate (Murlo), fired clay, late 7th – early 6th century BCE (Courtesy of Anthony Tuck).

AIRE SACREE OU ATELIER DE TISSAGE ? A PROPOS DES DEUX MONUMENTS CYLINDRIQUES DE VIA FONDAZZA À BOLOGNE

LAURENT HUGOT

ABSTRACT: The two large sandstone cylinders discovered below via Fondazza in Bologna and dated to the end of the 7th century BC are generally interpreted as religious or funerary monuments. Toutefois, en reprenant les données des fouilles, en faisant de new comparaisons and utilizing the symbolic sources at our disposal, it appears that these monuments pertain to the material culture of the Etruscan Orientalizing phase. They appear to be associated to the production of wool and textiles située près d'une demeure aristocratique.*

Voici quelques années, d'une manière humoristique, Ian Morris[1] imaginait la découverte d'une chambre d'hôtel du XXième siècle par des archéologues dans le futur. Ces derniers, voyant une télévision dans la pièce, l'analysaient comme étant liée à une divinité et les restes de repas retrouvés dans la chambre étaient perçus des offrandes sacrées. Cet ouvrage provocateur a eu le mérite de mettre l'accent sur l'intérêt fondamental des réflexions méthodologiques dans les études archéologiques pour éviter d'aller vers de mauvaises interprétations. Ceci est d'autant plus vrai dans le monde étrusque que ceux-ci nous ont laissé bien peu de textes. Avec Tite Live, nous pensons que les Etrusques étaient sinon "les plus religieux des hommes" au moins des hommes très religieux. C'est souvent vrai, mais ne nous laissons nous pas parfois guider par ce présupposé ? N'analysons nous pas le résultat de certaines fouilles en partant, peut-être parfois à tort, de ce postulat[2] ?

C'est dans cette optique que nous avons souhaité réétudier les deux énormes cylindres de pierre qui trônent majestueusement dans le musée de Bologne. L'originalité de ces deux gros cylindres de pierre, leur taille imposante, mais aussi le soin apporté à leur confection et à leur décoration rendent fascinante ces deux masses sculptées avec un raffinement que l'on conçoit difficilement à l'aube de la civilisation étrusque. C'est pour ces raisons qu'on a rapidement supposé le caractère religieux de ces monuments. Nous souhaitons montrer comment, en reprenant les données des fouilles, en faisant de nouvelles comparaisons et en utilisant les sources symboliques à notre disposition il est possible de proposer une nouvelle analyse des monuments de Via Fondazza.

1. LES PREMIERS AUTELS ETRUSQUES ?

1.1 Des objets uniques dans l'espace méditerranéen[3]

Les deux énormes cylindres de grès trouvés enterrés sur le site sont des objets uniques dans l'art étrusque (Figs. 2, 3). Ils sont datés de la fin du VIIième siècle avant JC. Personne n'a à ce jour pu établir de comparaisons strictes, iconographiques ou structurelles, avec d'autres monuments ou représentations[4]. On peut toutefois observer que leur décor rappelle des motifs connus dans l'aire nord syrienne. Il est d'ailleurs possible que ces monuments furent taillés par des artisans orientaux dont quelques uns ont très certainement émigré en Italie du Nord où leur art était particulièrement prisé[5]. La qualité des gravures, très largement supérieure à ce que l'on connaît dans cette région à la même époque, est un argument important à l'appui de cette hypothèse.

Une fois mis en place, ces blocs avaient une hauteur d'un mètre vingt à un mètre soixante-dix, leur diamètre étant d'environ un mètre. La réflexion de F. H. Massa-Pairault qui affirme que de tels objets n'ont pu être fait que dans une société hiérarchisée nous semble particulièrement pertinente. Mais quelle pouvait être la fonction de ces monuments ?

1.2 La fonction des monuments de Via Fondazza

Ce ne sont pas des cippes funéraires car aucune tombe ne se trouve dans la zone[6]. Cela aurait été étonnant car il n'existe pas de cippes funéraires semblables dans cette région. Ce ne sont pas plus des bases de statues car la face supérieure ne dispose pas de trous de fixation. De plus la table des monuments n'est pas lisse, il aurait été impossible de faire tenir une statue dessus. Pourtant, les deux cylindres ont été enterrés avec un soin très particulier, les morceaux brisés ont été utilisés pour les caler dans des fosses[7]. En faisant un parallèle avec la destruction et l'ensevelissement religieux des restes de l'édifice de Murlo, on peut penser que ce soin particulier était apporté à cause de leur nature sacrée et que ces monuments avaient une fonction religieuse encore au milieu du Vième siècle, au moment de leur enterrement.

C'est la raison pour laquelle on a pensé qu'ils étaient des autels ou des tables pour déposer des offrandes[8]. Les deux "autels" ont été décrits comme ouraniens car ils ne sont pas percés d'un canal central pour apporter le liquide vers le sol : ils ne sont donc ni chtoniens, ni "funéraires à libation". De plus, leur forme rappelle l'autel figuré sur l'une des fameuses plaques Campana (fig. 4) conservées au musée du Louvre[9]. L'autel peint, presque contemporain des monuments de Via Fondazza, peut en effet être circulaire. Il est également, comme les monuments de Via Fondazza, constitué d'un module répété (fig. 5).

Ces monuments pourraient être un couple d'autels sacrificiels près d'une aire de culte qui furent religieusement enterrés en marge de cette "aire sacrée". L'hypothèse selon laquelle "les autels de via Fondazza marquent une étape de l'évolution politique de la cité" a également été émise (Pairault-Massa 1989). La consécration de ces monuments aurait été un acte officiel de la cité et de ses magistrats, ils traduiraient la présence à cette époque d'une cité unitaire à deux parties (populi, gentes). Le culte, assumé par des gentes qui ont connu un déclin, aurait cessé vers le milieu du Vième siècle, date où ces monuments sont enterrés. Ce sanctuaire à ciel ouvert aurait été en rapport avec un culte des eaux.

1.3 Les limites des interprétations

On ne peut pas décrire ces monuments comme un couple d'autels car ces deux monuments ne sont pas contemporains, le monument A est très probablement légèrement plus ancien que le B[10]. De plus, J. Ortalli a montré que le grès utilisé provient d'une carrière locale (Ortalli 1998). S'il témoigne d'une société organisée, il n'est pas la preuve d'une société très fortement hiérarchisée[11].

Ensuite, la qualification d'autels pour ces monuments est discutable. Les auteurs sont d'ailleurs de plus en plus prudents pour qualifier ces monuments (voir note 7).

De plus, nous disposons à ce jour d'un corpus de plus de 500 représentations d'autels étrusques et aucun autel ne ressemble de près ou de loin aux cylindres de Via Fondazza. Les quelques autels de pierre connus pour cette époque sont des autels funéraires, le plus souvent à libation, d'aspect assez fruste[12]. De plus, le premier autel figuré sur un vase daté des années 590-570 est un grand autel construit au sommet duquel on parvient grâce à un escalier[13], il est donc fondamentalement différent des monuments de Bologne. Le seul autel avec lequel il pourrait être judicieux d'établir un parallèle avec les monuments de Via Fondazza est l'autel, presque contemporain, peint sur une plaque Campana. Cependant, l'autel de la plaque Campana est clairement un autel fabriqué en briques et non un bloc de pierre et il n'est pas décoré. De plus, il n'y a pas de trace de feu sur la partie supérieure des "autels" de Bologne alors que sur la plaque Campana un feu brûle sur la table de l'autel. Enfin, une comparaison entre les modules des ces monuments (fig. 6) prouve que la comparaison n'a pas lieu d'être : les profils sont en fait très différents. Il n'existe que deux points communs non significatifs entre les monuments de Via Fondazza et l'autel de la plaque Campana : leur taille qui pouvait être identique[14] et la répétition d'un module, différent pour chaque cas, dans la construction.

Ces monuments avaient une vocation ostentatoire car J. Ortalli a relevé des traces d'enduits blancs sur le monument B. Ceci prouve qu'il était peint. On peut aisément imaginer que cet enduit était recouvert par les couleurs flamboyantes caractéristiques des premières peintures étrusques[15]. Par contre, ceci exclut que l'on ait pu faire du feu sur l'autel car celui-ci aurait très rapidement détruit ces décors. Ainsi, il est peu probable que ces monuments soient des autels. Le contexte archéologique dans lequel ces monuments ont été retrouvés est-il au moins un contexte religieux ?

2. PRESENTATION DU SITE

L"aire sacrée de Via Fondazza", fut découverte à la faveur de fouilles de sauvetage en milieu urbain, à Bologne, entre avril et juin 1985 (Fig. 1). Les opérations furent dirigées par G. Bermond Montanari.

Les archéologues ont seulement pu fouiller la zone de 70 mètres carrés que les travaux avaient dégagée. Il ne leur a pas été possible de mettre au jour des structures complètes. De plus, toute la partie centrale de l'espace fouillé avait été totalement détruite par les travaux avant le passage des archéologues. Malgré ces difficultés et le caractère urgent des fouilles qui ne devaient pas excéder trois mois, le travail effectué est remarquable, les données à notre disposition sont nombreuses et de qualité.

On comprend aisément que la lecture de la zone soit difficile. Il a toutefois été possible de déterminer trois phases d'occupation avant la conquête romaine.

2.1 Les phases d'occupation du site.

Une présence humaine est attestée sur ce site pendant une longue période, de la seconde moitié du VIIième siècle (phase IV B du villanovien à Bologne) à la fin du IVième siècle. Quelques traces anthropiques sont même décelables à partir de l'âge du fer. L'occupation du site n'est pas intense mais elle est continue.

2.1.1 Les deux premières phases d'occupation

Ce sont en fait deux étapes d'une même phase. Dans un premier temps, à l'extrémité ouest du site, un canal orienté Sud-Nord a été creusé. Une sédimentation lente, fine et importante prouve que ce canal a été utilisé pendant une longue période.

On distingue aussi plusieurs autres structures fonctionnelles ; un petit puits près d'une grande cavité pas entièrement découverte par les fouilles et qui pose un important problème d'interprétation mais qui doit être un fond de cabane (une première cabane de forme indéterminée a été dans une seconde phase transformée en cabane rectangulaire) ; plusieurs trous de poteaux ont également été découverts mais il a été impossible de déterminer précisément leur rôle. Des restes carbonisés, des ossements d'animaux et de la céramique (impasto) ont aussi été récoltés dans la zone mais en faibles quantités.

Dans une seconde étape, le canal a été bouché et remplacé par deux autres ayant la même orientation nord-sud. Dans le secteur est, on remarque des trous de poteaux de dimensions différentes ainsi qu'une fosse de fondation orientée est-ouest. Un petit puits semble être en activité.

L'occupation du site est donc prolongée, constante mais pas très importante ; le matériel archéologique est rare (quelques fragments de céramique attique ont été trouvés).

2.1.2 La troisième phase d'occupation
Cette longue occupation s'interrompt brusquement vers le milieu du Vième siècle. C'est à cette époque que l'on creuse deux fosses pour mettre les monuments cylindriques (figs. 2-3-5-13). Les fosses, à la juste mesure des cylindres de pierre, ont des orientations différentes (sud-sud/est | nord-nord/ouest pour le monument B et est-sud/est | ouest-nord/ouest pour le monument A). Ces monuments n'ont pas été transportés sur une longue distance à cause de leur taille et de leur fragilité. En effet, un long déplacement aurait été dangereux pour leur intégrité. Pourtant, on ne connaît pas l'emplacement originel des deux monuments. Il est certain qu'ils n'étaient pas dressés à l'intérieur des fosses où on les a découverts car celles-ci ne sont pas assez profondes. On peut affirmer qu'ils n'étaient pas installés à l'origine dans l'espace fouillé.

2.2 L'abandon du site
La fin de la fréquentation du site semble couvrir la fin du Vième siècle et une partie du IVième siècle. Les canaux sont bouchés. Si on a récolté peu de matériel, celui-ci est particulièrement intéressant. On a effectivement mis au jour quelques fragments d'ex-voto anatomiques. Ceci confirme la nature sacrée du site[16] pendant cette période. Cependant, la rareté du matériel est l'expression d'un sanctuaire d'importance secondaire.

3. Une aire sacrée ?

3.1 La position du site
Bologne connaît dès le VIIIième siècle une période de forte croissance démographique. On sait que l'agglomération villanovienne, formée de plusieurs villages, est constituée dès le début du VIIIième siècle. Pourtant, une partie de la population est encore très dispersée sur le territoire. Si les chercheurs pensent que le site de Via Fondazza se situait en zone périurbaine, on ne peut exclure la présence d'un village ou d'une habitation dans son voisinage immédiat. Les trous de poteaux peuvent aussi bien être les traces d'une habitation ou de l'annexe d'une habitation[17] que d'un édifice à vocation religieuse. La présence de tuiles ne prouve pas la présence d'un édifice religieux mais simplement celle d'un bâtiment d'importance[18].

3.2 Les canaux, la preuve d'un sanctuaire lié à l'eau ?
L'hypothèse de la fonction religieuse des canaux ne nous semble pas pertinente. En effet, c'est plus le sens de la pente vers l'ouest que la position des étoiles qui a déterminé l'orientation de ces canaux[19] ! Ceux-ci sont situés en bas de la pente et devaient servir de drains. Ils ne sont pas la preuve d'une utilisation de l'eau à des fins religieuses ou thérapeutiques mais de la volonté de contrôler l'écoulement de l'eau.

Les structures adjacentes aux cylindres de pierre (traces de bâtiments et canaux) ne permettent pas de supposer une fonction religieuse de ce secteur. L'identification de cette zone avec une "aire sacrée" ne repose que sur la nature des deux monuments cylindriques identifiés à des autels.

La qualification d' "aire sacrée" ne repose pas sur des arguments solides. En premier lieu, les deux cylindres de grès n'étaient pas à l'origine installés sur la zone fouillée. De plus, la présence des canaux peut très bien être un aménagement assurant la salubrité du lieu, d'autant plus que le matériel est caractéristique d'une zone proche d'un habitat[20]. Il faut ajouter que les ex-voto ne sont attestés qu'au IVième siècle et que rien ne prouve qu'auparavant cet espace était consacré[21].

Cette aire n'avait pas une fonction religieuse, seule une nouvelle analyse des monuments et de nouvelles comparaisons doivent nous permettre d'aller plus loin dans notre réflexion sur la nature des monuments de Via Fondazza.

4. Une nouvelle analyse de la bande inférieure incisée sur le trône de Verucchio[22]

Une nouvelle voie de recherche a été ouverte grâce à Mario Torelli[23]. Dans son étude récente sur le trône de Verucchio, celui-ci a justement fait remarquer que nos monuments ressemblent étonnement à deux sortes de piliers moulurés et surmontés chacun d'un personnage, incisés sur le dossier du désormais fameux trône daté de la première moitié du VIIième siècle (fig. 8).

La comparaison entre nos monuments et les piliers du trône de Verucchio est pertinente, mais techniquement pas plus que celle effectuée avec la plaque Campana (figs. 6 et 7)[24]. Le profil des monuments incisés sur le trône de Verucchio est trop simplifié pour que nous puissions en tirer des conclusions. Seule une étude contextuelle doit pouvoir nous permettre de comprendre la fonction des piliers incisés sur le trône de Verucchio et s'il y a lieu d'établir une comparaison plus que formelle avec les monuments de Via Fondazza.

4.1 Analyse de la bande inférieure du trône de Verucchio[25]

Il n'est pas ici question de remettre en cause la lecture de la bande supérieure du trône qui représente deux fois la même scène. Il s'agit du tissage, du cardage de la laine et de sa teinte ou du lavage de la laine près d'une maison de bois[26]. Ces scènes liées au travail de la laine, ont été bien décrites[27]. Ce magnifique trône de bois était certainement un trône féminin. Nous connaissons quelques représentations de tels sièges sur le tintinnabule de Bologne (625-600)[28] sur lequel sont figurées les activités féminines liées au travail de la laine.

Cependant, il est nécessaire de se pencher une nouvelle fois sur l'analyse de la bande inférieure de ce trône. Cette décoration est identifiée à un échange dans une zone de confins consacrée, lors d'un mariage (Torelli 1997). La scène centrale (fig. 9) qui se déroule sur une estrade est constituée de deux hommes face à face, de part et d'autre d'un élément indéterminé. Le personnage de gauche tient un long couteau dans l'une de ses mains. Cette scène ne représente pas un sacrifice (Kossack 1992, p. 236), mais il ne s'agit pas non plus d'une scène d'échange car on ne voit pas dans ce contexte l'utilité du couteau. Plutôt qu'une scène de découpe de viande qui serait aberrante par rapport aux autres activités incisées sur le trône, il faut plutôt y voir une scène de tonte de mouton. En effet, le personnage de droite tient l'animal, sommairement représenté, ou plus probablement récolte la laine détachée du corps de l'animal par son voisin. Le long couteau du premier personnage dont la forme est proche d'une *makaïra* est encore utilisé par quelques bergers d'Afrique du Nord pour tondre leurs moutons par raclage ou par rasage de la peau des animaux. C'est d'ailleurs la meilleure technique pour récolter la laine en l'absence des ciseaux à laine inconnus au VIIième avant JC dans la plaine du Pô[29]. Cette scène centrale est donc une scène de récolte de la laine. Le couple de guerriers placé de chaque côté de la scène témoigne de l'importance de cette matière première qu'il était nécessaire de protéger mais témoigne également d'une société structurée et hiérarchisée. De plus, les deux chariots (fig. 10) placés aux extrémités de la bande figurée et qui convergent vers le centre ne démontrent pas obligatoirement un contexte matrimonial[30]. Les comparaisons faites jusqu'alors utilisent fâcheusement des documents parfois postérieurs de plusieurs siècles au trône de Verucchio. Il ne faut pas oublier que ce moyen de transport, s'il était celui utilisé pour les mariages, était celui de la vie quotidienne pour ces aristocrates. Ces chariots dont on ne sait s'ils avaient quatre ou huit roues sont conduits par un aurige. Derrière cet homme, un autre personnage masculin qui tient un insigne est assis sur un trône. Le vase situé à l'arrière de la carriole et au-dessus duquel deux personnages s'affairent est comparable à celui de la scène inférieure de la face A du tintinnabule de Bologne (fig. 11) qui représente une scène de cardage de la laine[31]. C'est très certainement une scène semblable qui se déroule sur ces chariots. Ces deux scènes représentent des aristocrates qui apportent la laine ou qui viennent la chercher pour le cardage[32] et qui sont accompagnés de leurs "ouvriers"[33].

Il est plus difficile de comprendre la nature et la fonction des personnages situés de part et d'autre de l'estrade et qui sont tournés vers celle-ci (fig. 12). Ceux à gauche de l'estrade sont presque effacés mais ils étaient identiques à ceux situés en face. Le personnage au pied de l'estrade est assis sur un siège juché au sommet d'une construction de bois (petite tour carrée) constituée de quatre poteaux, maintenus verticaux malgré le poids du personnage, grâce à plusieurs renforts horizontaux qui relient les poteaux les uns aux autres et consolident ainsi cette construction. M. Torelli pense qu'il pourrait s'agir d'une tour de surveillance. Pourtant, ce personnage est penché en avant vers un fil qui descend devant lui et qui se termine, à la hauteur de l'estrade, par une grosse masse. Le doute n'est pas permis, il s'agit d'un personnage qui tisse comme sur le tintinnabule de Bologne (fig. 11, face B, haut). La masse terminale représente les pesons utilisés pour maintenir les fils tendus verticalement. Cette représentation est un peu différente de celles incisées sur la bande supérieure mais la technique utilisée est identique. Trois fils descendent aussi devant le second personnage qui est accroupi sur une base moulurée dont nous avons noté la ressemblance avec les monuments de Via Fondazza. Son activité est également liée au travail de la laine et c'est aussi le tissage qui est représenté et plus précisément le tissage de bandes qui étaient ensuite assemblées pour faire de grandes tentures. Pourquoi employer deux structures différentes pour une même activité ? On peut apporter plusieurs réponses à cette question. D'une part, ce sont des personnages assis sur des trônes qui utilisent les structures de bois ("les tours"), ceci témoigne probablement d'une différence de statut social avec les personnages debout sur les bases. De plus, on pouvait tisser des ouvrages beaucoup plus larges sur les bases, espace ouvert, qu'à l'intérieur de ces grandes tours (des couvertures et des tentures). Ensuite, ces grandes bases moulurées pouvaient avoir plusieurs utilisations : le tissage certes, mais aussi la préparation du fil de trame comme sur le tintinnabule de Bologne (fig. 11, face B, bas) ainsi que le filage d'un fil beaucoup plus solide (en premier lieu le fil de chaîne).

4.2 La représentation d'une fête

La description sommaire que fait W. Kruta du trône (Torelli 1997, p. 84, note 59) est tout à fait pertinente. Celui-ci parle d'une scène de la vie quotidienne. Ce n'est en fait pas réellement le cas, il faut plutôt penser que nous sommes devant la représentation d'une fête où le monde divin n'était probablement pas absent. La tonte des animaux est saisonnière (avril-juin), cette opération était

pratiquée lors de la période de mue des animaux et cet évènement devait certainement donner lieu à des festivités ; c'est ce que représente la décoration incisée sur le trône de Verucchio. Il fallait certainement que cette tonte fût effectuée par des mains "consacrées" et que celles-ci tondent tous les moutons de la communauté, la laine était par la suite partagée entre les propriétaires des animaux. Ceci expliquerait d'une part la présence des deux chariots avec "un personnage trônant" différent sur chacun d'eux[34] et d'autre part la présence des guerriers assurant le bon déroulement des opérations.
Toutes les scènes représentées sur ce trône sont liées au travail de la laine. Notre relecture de la bande incisée du trône de Verucchio peut apporter une explication satisfaisante à l'"énigme de Via Fondazza".

5- Vers une résolution de "l'énigme de Via Fondazza"

5.1 Ré-interprétation des monuments de Via Fondazza.
Un élément de la description des monuments cylindriques a selon nous été injustement négligé, pourtant celui-ci rend encore la comparaison entre les piliers du trône de Verucchio et les monuments de Via Fondazza plus pertinente. En effet, les inventeurs du site ont remarqué une usure différenciée et mécanique sur la face supérieure du monument B (Ortalli 1998, fig. 6) ; le monument A est trop détérioré pour que nous puissions faire de telles constatations (fig. 13). L'usure est beaucoup plus prononcée au centre du monument que sur les bords décorés de rosaces gravées, même si dans un endroit le décor est usé sur une vingtaine de centimètres et les rosaces ne sont presque plus visibles. Selon J. Ortalli, l'usure "sembrata frutto di una qualche azione meccanica indotta artificialmente, per sfregamento o rotatura, più che di semplice consunzione da esposizione agli agenti atmosferici" (Ortalli 1998, p. 53 : dernier paragraphe). Une telle usure, si elle ne s'explique pas par l'exposition aux agents atmosphériques, ne peut pas s'expliquer non plus par le dépôt d'offrandes sur ce monument ni à plus forte raison par la présence d'une statue le couronnant. Il est légitime de penser qu'une telle usure différenciée a été causée par des hommes ou des femmes qui ont marché pendant une longue période sur ces monuments. Ces actions répétées sur la table l'ont poli. La fonction des monuments de Bologne était donc identique à celle représentée par deux fois sur le trône de Verucchio où un personnage accroupi sur une haute base moulurée s'affaire sur des fils tendus devant lui. L'usage des monuments de Bologne est donc magnifiquement illustré sur ce trône de bois. Sur le monument B, on peut même reconstituer l'endroit où se trouvaient tendus les fils de laine car comme nous l'avons vus, le décor de rosettes sur la bordure de la table est usé à l'endroit où, penché sur son ouvrage, l'artisan se rapprochait du bord et donc des fils qu'il travaillait[35].

La découverte d'objets liés au tissage sur le site, il s'agit au moins d'une fusaïole et d'une canette, renforce encore notre hypothèse (Ortalli 1986, p. 24 et p. 25 fig. 2).

Les bases qui servaient au tissage de la laine étaient le plus souvent en bois. Mais dans le cas qui nous intéresse l'aristocrate local a décidé de commander un, puis un second objet de pierre. Ces monuments soigneusement gravés et probablement peints devaient être particulièrement esthétiques.

Les traces de poteaux qui ont été relevés sur le site sont peut-être les traces des petites tours de tissage en bois que l'on retrouve à la fois sur le trône de Verucchio, de part et d'autre de l'estrade et sur le tintinnabule de Bologne (face B, haut).

5.2 D'autres représentations semblables
On pourrait nous opposer le fait que la représentation du trône de Verucchio n'est pas très claire et que nous ne pouvons en tirer de telles conclusions. Ceci serait exact si d'autres preuves n'existaient pas. S'il n'a pas été possible de faire des rapprochements avec le monde grec, d'autres représentations existent ailleurs. D'une part, dans l'Egypte ancienne, il existe au moins une représentation intéressante pour notre propos mettant en scène la préparation du tissage (fig. 14). Sur cette représentation, deux personnages sont installés sur une petite base pour préparer les fils qui seront ensuite utilisés. L'utilisation de base est donc attestée et utile pour le filage, cette technique était connue et utilisée depuis fort longtemps dans le monde Méditerranéen. C'était peut-être l'une des utilisations des bases de Via Fondazza mais ce n'est pas celle qui est représentée. D'autre part, une scène beaucoup plus proche des bases de Verucchio existe sur une urne découverte à Odenburg en Hongrie[36] (fig. 15) et qui est contemporaine ou presque contemporaine (période de Hallstatt) des monuments de Via Fondazza. Cette représentation d'inspiration géométrique met en scène trois personnages. Le premier est une femme de profil droit dont le corps est représenté par un triangle, convention bien connue pour la représentation des femmes dans l'art géométrique, est en train de filer la laine. On voit très nettement son bras levé devant elle avec un fil qui tombe de sa main avec au bout du fil une petite masse représentant le fuseau. Puis, une femme identique est occupée au tissage, devant elle sont tendus verticalement quatre gros et longs fils lestés de poids. On voit en haut de l'ouvrage que le travail est déjà commencé. Les fils descendent beaucoup plus bas que les pieds de cette femme, celle-ci est debout sur une base ou sur une estrade. A droite de l'ouvrage, un joueur de cithare de profil gauche qui est probablement de sexe masculin. Les similitudes entre la scène centrale et les scènes représentant un personnage sur une base sur le trône de Verucchio est saisissante et on ne peut mettre y en doute la représentation du tissage. C'est au nord est de la plaine du Pô qu'une technique semblable existait à la

même période, on connaît les relations qui existaient depuis fort longtemps entre les populations de l'Italie du nord et celle de l'Europe Centrale.

5.3 Pourquoi une telle mise en scène du travail de la laine ?

L'activité principale des femmes aristocrates d'Etrurie du Nord était la production de vêtements de laine, de tentures et de couvertures comme dans bien d'autres régions méditerranéennes. Cette activité était extrêmement valorisante et valorisée. Ceci n'était pas une simple occupation, ces dames fabriquaient les gros manteaux dans lesquels les aristocrates Etrusques aimaient à se faire représenter aux VIIième-VIième siècle. Le vêtement et les grandes pièces d'étoffes[37] était naturellement une marque visible de richesse et de pouvoir[38]. Disposer de vêtements particuliers et de grandes couvertures témoignait de l'art de la femme du maître, mais également de la richesse de celui-ci qui possédait des animaux à laine et qui disposait des moyens techniques de faire fabriquer ces tissus. Il ne faut pas sous estimer l'importance de la fabrication de vêtements et de tentures au VIIième siècle[39]. Cette activité était tout aussi essentielle que la guerre ou que le commerce et participait à la pompe du pouvoir. Des monuments comme ceux de Bologne ne sont donc pas incongrus dans ce contexte. L'aire de Via Fondazza témoigne une fois encore de l'opulence de certains aristocrates de la région de Bologne durant la période orientalisante[40].

Nous savons qu'il devait exister des constructions importantes pour travailler la laine. Les documents archéologiques sont rares car ces constructions de bois ne nous sont parvenues qu'illustrées sur quelques objets exceptionnels, qu'il s'agisse du trône de Verucchio ou du tintinnabule de Bologne[41].

A Via Fondazza, les deux piliers de bois ont été remplacés par de gros cylindres de pierre dans le but d'affirmer une richesse et un pouvoir important mais aussi de pérenniser ces constructions. C'est cette même volonté qui a conduit les aristocrates étrusques à utiliser des matériaux plus solides dans la construction de leur demeure et à faire de leurs tombes des constructions familiales monumentales. Les monuments de Via Fondazza sont l'expression d'une stratégie familiale d'appropriation d'un l'espace en y installant des objets qui sont presque impossible à déplacer ; c'est une volonté d'immortalité de la part de cette famille. La découverte de cet ensemble archéologique exceptionnel et les interrogations qu'il suscite montre que leur but a été atteint au-delà de leurs espérances.

6. Conclusion.

L'aire de Via Fondazza n'est donc pas une "aire sacrée des confins". Les structures mises au jour et le matériel dégagé montrent qu'il s'agissait au départ et durant une assez longue période d'une zone d'habitat. Bermond Montanari a dégagé les abords d'une demeure aristocratique extrêmement importante pour cette époque[42] et plus précisément l'aire de production de la laine et du tissage située près de cette demeure. Les deux monuments de Via Fondazza étaient des objets qui avaient plusieurs utilisations possibles : le filage, le tissage ainsi que la préparation du fil de trame. Mais ils étaient peut-être et surtout des symboles, des constructions qui avaient un but idéologique, celui d'affirmer la puissance du maître des lieux et de sa famille. Les deux cylindres de pierre sont restés en place pendant une longue période puis, les hommes ont oublié leur fonction première et ont cru qu'il s'agissait de monuments religieux, impressionnés comme nous le sommes par la taille et l'aspect de ces monuments. Ils les ont enterrés comme tels. Par la suite, tardivement, cette zone est devenue une petite aire religieuse où quelques uns ont déposé des ex-voto.

NOTES

* Cet article est dédié à Germaine OUVRARD. Je tiens à remercier Messieurs JR Jannot, D. Frère et T. Piel ainsi que Mesdames S. et N. Monqid, L. Bodiou et MR. Hugot.
1 Morris Ian, *Death-ritual and social structure in classical antiquity*, Cambridge, 1992.
2 Depuis quelques années, plusieurs études ont montré que des monuments ou des objets qui avaient tout d'abord été analysés comme des témoignages religieux étaient plus certainement des témoignages de la culture matérielle (ré-interprétation du "*mundus*" d'Artena comme un foyer lié à une structure thermale (Jolivet V., recension de l'ouvrage de R. Lambrechts, *RA*, 1999) ; dans le même esprit, la fameuse maison aux Bacchanales de Bolsena n'est peut-être qu'une simple citerne (De Cazanove O., *Cahier Glotz*, 2000).
3 Monument A (fig. 2) Inv. : 67302. Bologne, Museo Civico Archeologico. H : 1,90 m ; diam. : 1 m. Monument B (fig. 3) Inv. : 67301. Bologne, Museo Civico Archeologico. H : 1,90 m ; diam. : 0,90 m.
4 Les deux monuments sont de forme cylindrique ; la partie supérieure du monument A est détériorée. Les cylindres se composent d'un haut fût (la moitié du monument environ) avec une frise de méandres interrompus en haut. La partie supérieure a été évidée en partie pour mettre en relief la mouluration. Elle est composée d'un même module répété. Le profil de chaque module est composé d'un bec de corbin renversé, d'une baguette entre ovolo renversés et d'un large bandeau. La face des bandeaux est décorée d'une théorie de sphinges vers la gauche sur le monument A et d'une frise de fleurs de lotus et palmettes et fleurs de lotus alternées.
5 Sur cette question, voir Colonna G., Novità sui culti di Pyrgi. Ancora sul culto etrusco di Apollo, *Rend. Pont. Acc.*, 57, 1984-1985, p. 57 ss. Il suggère la présence d'artisans syriens en Etrurie avec des arguments très convaincants. Voir également Colonna G., Von Hase F. W., Alle origini della statuaria etrusca : la tomba delle statue presso Ceri, *SE*, LII, 1986 [1986], pp. 13-59.
6 On a émis l'hypothèse que ces cippes marquaient l'entrée d'une voie menant à une nécropole. Cette hypothèse est intéressante mais selon nous artificielle. Il s'agit d'une tentative pour expliquer pour quelle raison des monuments que l'on pense être des cippes funéraires se trouvent hors d'une zone de nécropole! La grande voie qui traversait la ville est en fait assez éloignée du site (Ortalli, Bermond Montanari 1986, fig. 6. Ortalli 1998, fig. 15).
7 Il est possible qu'ils aient été brisés lors de leur déplacement mais il est beaucoup plus probable qu'on ait choisi de les ensevelir à cause de leur état de dégradation.
8 L'évolution sémantique pour qualifier ces monuments est révélatrice. On a commencé par les qualifier d'autels (Massa 1989. Montanari 1988), puis de cippes et enfin de monuments (Ortalli 1998). M. Marchesi les nomme cippes et reste distante par rapport à l'interprétation traditionnelle de l'aire sacrée (Bologne 2000), pp. 340-341, n° 449-450.
9 Daté des années 650-625 et provenant de Cerveteri (nécropole de la Banditaccia). Paris, le Louvre. Collection Campana (inv. : S.4034). Orientation bibliographique : Neppi Modona A., Pitture etrusche arcaiche. Le lastre fittili policrome ceretane, *Emporium*, LXVII 7, 1928, p. 97-106, fig. 8. Roncalli F., *Le lastre dipinte da Cerveteri*, Florence, 1965, tav. III.
10 Les analyses effectuées par Ortalli 1998 montrent que le monument a été soumis plus longtemps aux agents atmosphériques. De plus les décors des deux monuments sont différents : théorie de sphinge pour A et frise végétale pour B.
11 Ces monuments sont importants mais ils ne sont pas gigantesques, leur construction nécessitèrent pas un nombre important d'ouvrier mais simplement quelques artisans d'un haut niveau technique pour cette époque.
12 Par exemple celui de la tombe Campana I de Cerveteri (Nécropole de Monte Abatone). 625-600. Voir Prayon F., *Frühetrüskische Grab- und Hausarchitektur*, Heidelberg, 1975, pp. 112-113, taf. 62-63 et Steingräber S., Le culte des morts et les monuments de pierre des nécropoles étrusques, *"Les plus religieux des hommes" 1992*, la documentation française 1997, Paris, pp. 101-102 et 104.
13 Sur ce cratère du peintre "delle Code Annodate" conservé à Cerveteri (Museo Archeologico, inv. 19539), voir Martelli M., *La ceramica degli Etruschi. La pittura vascolare*, Ed. Istituto Geografico de Agostini, Novare, 1987, n°85, pp. 289-291, fig.85, p. 132 (avec bibliographie antérieure).
14 Même si l'hypothèse selon laquelle la partie non moulurée des monuments bolognais devait être enterrée nous semble discutable et n'est pas prouvée ! Cette similitude de taille n'est donc pas assurée.
15 L'enduit blanc servait de support pour appliquer la peinture. Le résultat est de meilleure qualité que si on applique la peinture directement sur la pierre. Cette technique est pourtant peu employée au VIième siècle. Dans les premières tombes peintes étrusques la couleur est le plus souvent directement appliquée sur la paroi. Ceci est encore un argument pour souligner, s'il en était besoin, le caractère exceptionnel des cylindres de Bologne.
16 Pour les ex-voto voir Gentili 1988. Ce sanctuaire est alors devenu semblable à la majorité des sanctuaires étrusques de la même époque qui avant leur abandon se transforment en sanctuaires liés à des "divinités guérisseuses".
17 Le matériel trouvé sur le site avant le IVième siècle rappelle celui que l'on retrouve dans les zones proches d'habitations.
18 On trouve de nombreuses tuiles à la Castellina sul Marangone qui, au moins jusqu'à l'époque hellénistique, est un site d'habitat.
19 Ortalli 1998, p. 47. "le due più antiche fasi di vita erano testimoniate da canalette idriche orientate astronomicamente".

20 La céramique est très fragmentaire (comme dans les sites d'habitat) et constituée presque essentiellement avant le IVième siècle de céramiques qui étaient utilisées dans la vie quotidienne. Aucun dépôt votif n'a été mis en évidence avant le IVième siècle.
21 C'est peut-être même la redécouverte d'un de ces monuments au IVième siècle qui est à l'origine de la vocation religieuse, d'ailleurs très secondaire, du lieu. En effet la fosse dans laquelle le monument A a été enterré n'était pas assez profonde (ce qui explique qu'il est très dégradé) et il devait légèrement affleurer. Ce phénomène est fréquent, songeons par exemple à l'idée que les Grecs se faisaient de l'origine des ruines des palais mycéniens. Plus près de nous, de nombreuses églises ont été construites sur les ruines de villas gallo-romaines qu'on pensait être d'anciennes églises.
22 Je remercie le Professeur Peroni de m'avoir informé d'une publication définitive en 2002 ou 2003 de la tombe où fut découvert le trône de Verucchio.
23 Torelli 1997, pp. 67-68. Ce chercheur pense que le site de Via Fondazza était un sanctuaire de confins, les monuments auraient alors marqué une limite sacrée entre deux espaces et les figures sommitales seraient soit de petites statues, soit les images de divinités (nous avons montré plus haut que cette hypothèse ne peut être retenue). On pourrait alors parler d'*horos*. Il faudrait donc comparer ces monuments aux cippes étrusques qui comportent l'inscription "tular". On sait par ailleurs que les Etrusques délimitaient les "espaces" (humain / sauvage ; territoires civiques…) avec un soin très particulier. L'hypothèse de M. Torelli est reprise par Ortalli 1998 qui la considère comme valable tout en réaffirmant la probabilité que ces monuments soient des autels. Nous ne connaissons à ce jour aucun cippe comparable ni en Etrurie ni dans les régions voisines. Sur les cippes en Etrurie : Steingräber S., Etruskische Monumentalcippi, Miscellanea etrusca e italica in onore di M. Pallottino, Rome, 1992 (*=ArchClass, 43, 1991 [1992]*), vol 2, pp. 1079-1102. Candida B., Altari e cippi nel Museo Nazionale Romano, Rome, 1979. Blumhofer M., Etruskische Cippi, Vienne, 1993.
24 Les piliers de Verucchio sont constitués d'une base lisse et de la répétition d'un module, comme à Via Fondazza.
25 Sur cet objet et les lectures de son décor figuré, *Ocnus* IV, p. 263, Tav. 1. (pour le dessin complet de la décoration figuré sur le trône découvert par Gentili). Voir aussi Gentili 1988 ; Torelli 1997, pp. 52-86.
26 Ce n'est en fait pas la même scène répétée. Les deux scènes sont en réalité symétriques par rapport au centre du dossier.
27 La lecture de Gentili a été affinée par Torelli.
28 Sur cet objet, Torelli 1997, figs. 47 et 48 ; mais également Torelli M. (dir.), *Gli Etruschi*, Catalogue de l'exposition de Venise, Ed. Bompiani, 2000, fig. p. 134. Le tintinnabule était un bijou féminin. Son utilisation devait être religieuse mais nous ne disposons pas d'éléments précis sur son utilisation. Il semble qu'il devait produire un son particulier lorsque la femme bougeait la tête.
29 Les cisailles ou forces ont été inventées vers 1000 av JC mais on les retrouve surtout au second âge du fer et encore plus fréquemment à l'époque romaine. Avant l'invention de cet outil il fallait attendre la saison de la mue pour pratiquer l'épilation, le plus souvent à l'aide d'un peigne. C'est cette épilation qui est représentée ici à l'aide d'un long peigne qui à la forme d'un grand couteau ou un rasage à l'aide de l'animal à l'aide d'un grand couteau.
30 Cette hypothèse est également contestée par Piel T., *Principes Etruriae : Recherches sur les représentations et la nature du pouvoir en Etrurie (VIIième-I^ier^ siècle avant JC), vol II, analyse (A)*, Thèse de doctorat, Université de Nantes, 2000, p. 493 et note 89 avec une argumentation très convaincante.
31 Il s'agit tout simplement d'une situle.
32 Le cardage de la laine sur un tel chariot devait tenir de l'exploit mais l'essentiel n'était sans doute pas là et devait être de nature symbolique. On retrouve des scènes comparables encore à la fin du IVième siècle sur la céramique à figure rouge (Del Chiaro M. A., *Etruscan Red-Figured Vase-Painting at Caere*, Berkeley, 1974, pl. 18).
33 Le décor du trône de Verucchio montre des femmes mais aussi des hommes participaient aux activités textiles. Une partie des opérations était probablement effectuée par des esclaves, par exemple la teinte de la laine qui est une activité éprouvante à cause de l'odeur dégagée par les produits utilisés.
34 Il s'agirait non d'une seule scène et non d'une scène répétée symétriquement.
35 Les moulurations des monuments ne sont peut-être pas seulement décoratives. Si l'on observe la scène inférieure de la face B du tintinnabule de Bologne, on remarque qu'un pilier est utilisé pour tendre la laine lors de la préparation de la trame. Ce pilier est situé devant la femme assise sur le trône (fig. 11).
36 Représentation dans Forbes 1964, p. 226, fig. 34 (bibliographie, p. 223, note 31).
37 L'ouvrage de référence sur ce sujet est celui de Bonfante L., *Etruscan Dress*, Londres-Baltimore, 1975, particulièrement le chapitre I. On peut aussi voir Bartoloni G., *La donna del Principe*, Bologne, 2000, pp. 272-274.
38 Songeons à l'importance du vêtement en Grèce comme à Rome et à la codification très stricte de leur utilisation. Pour anecdote, une loi oubliée, interdisant le port du pantalon pour les femmes, existe encore en France.
39 Jean René Jannot, lors d'une journée d'étude à Nanterre, vient de faire une étude magistrale de plusieurs représentations dites de mariage sur des cippes de Chiusi. Il démontre que ces scènes sont exclusivement féminines et qu'il s'agit de la présentation de cérémonies de présentation d'étoffes lors des funérailles des aristocrates clusiennes. Les aristocrates s'extasient et touchent les étoffes faites par la défunte.
40 Pour se rendre compte de l'opulence et surtout de leur volonté d'ostentation voir Catalogue de l'exposition de Bologne (2000), on peut par intérêt et par plaisir regarde le beau catalogue de Emiliozzi A., *Carri da Guerra e Principi Etruschi*,

Catalogue de l'exposition de Viterbe, Palazzo dei Papi, 24 mai-12 octobre 1997, L'Erma, 1997. L'Iliade et l'Odyssée sont pleins d'anecdotes montrant l'importance des tissus et la place des femmes aristocrates dans leur fabrication.
41 Le même constat dans Moscati S. (coord), *Les Celtes. Catalogue de l'exposition. Les Celtes au Palazzo Grassi, Venise*, 1991, Paris, Stock, 1997, Les textiles, p. 262.
42 Comme nous l'avons montré, le contexte archéologique montre qu'il ne s'agissait pas d'une zone religieuse mais d'une zone d'habitat.

BIBLIOGRAPHIE

Le site de Via Fondazza :

Bologne, 2000, *Principi etruschi tra Mediterraneo ed Europa*, Bologne, pp. 340-341, n° 449-450.

Montanari, G.B., 1988, L'area sacra di via Fondazza, *La formazione della città in Emilia Romagna*, Bologne, Museo Civico, 26 septembre 1987-24 janvier 1988, vol II, pp. 81-88.

Ortalli, J. and Bermond Montanari, G., 1986, Il complesso monumentale protofelsineo di Via Fondazza a Bologna, *SE*, LVI, pp. 15-45.

Ortalli, J., 1998, Nuove osservazioni sui monumenti orientalizzanti bolognesi di via Fondazza, *AEmil*, 2, Nr.1, pp. 47-59.

Pairault-Massa, F.H., 1989, Bologne, Chronique d'étruscologie, *RA*, 2, pp. 321-323.

Le trône de Verucchio :

Gentili, G.V., 1998, Verucchio. Tomba 89, 93 a-b. Il trono ligneo, *Montanari 1988*, pp. 243-246.

Kossack, G., 1992, Lebensbilder, mythische Bilderzählung und Kultfestbilder. Bemerkungen zu Bildszenen auf einer Thronlehne von Verucchio, *Universitätsforschungen zur prähistorischen Archäologie aus dem Institut 8. Festschrift zum 50jährigen Bestehen des Institutes für Ur und Frühgeschichte des Universität Innsbruck.*

Torelli, M., 1997, *Il rango, il rito e l'immagine. Alle origini della rappresentazione storica romana*, Milan, Electa, pp. 52-86.

Le travail de la laine :

Breniquet, C. and Mintsi, E., 2000, Le peintre d'Amasis et la glyptique mésopotamienne pré-et protodynastique, *REA*, tome 102, n°3-4, pp. 333-360.

Cardon, D. and Feugère, M., 2000, *Archéologie des textiles des origines au V*ième *siècle*, Actes du colloque de Lattes, octobre 1999, Lattes.

Forbes, R.J., 1964, *Sudies in Ancient Technology*, Volume IV, Leiden, E. J. Brill.

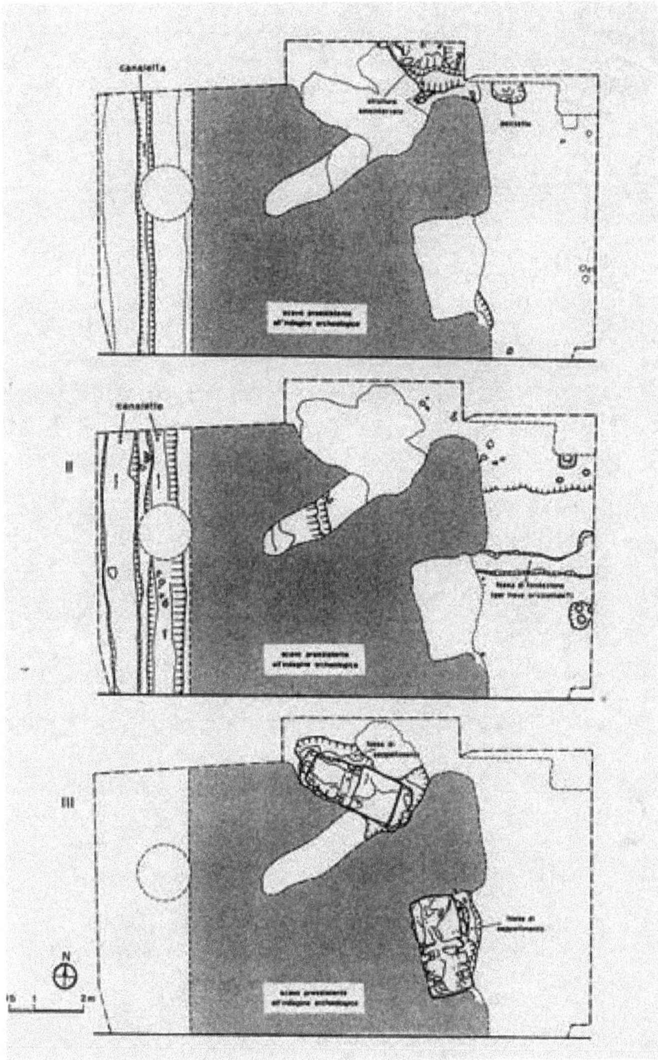

Fig. 1. Via Fondazza. Les trois phases d'occupation (Ortali 1998, fig. 3).

Fig. 2. Via Fondazza, Monument A (Montanari 1998, fig. 53).

Fig. 3. Monument B (Pairault-Massa 1989, fig. 8).

Fig. 4. Plaque Campana, Musée du Louvre (A.J. Pfiffig, *Religio Etrusca* (Graz 1975), abb. 19).

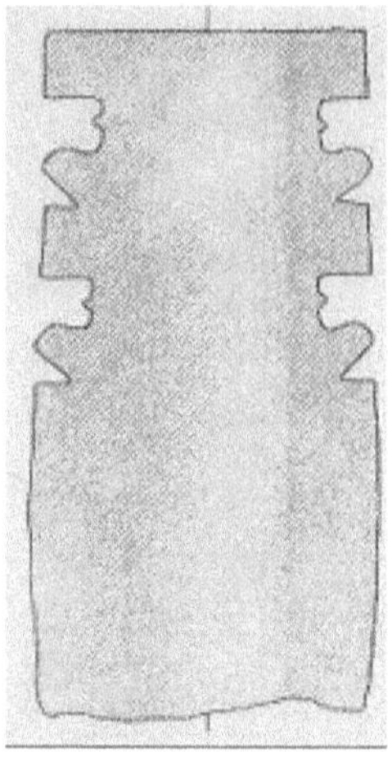

Fig 5. Profil du monument B (Ortali, Bermond Montanari 1986, fig. 9).

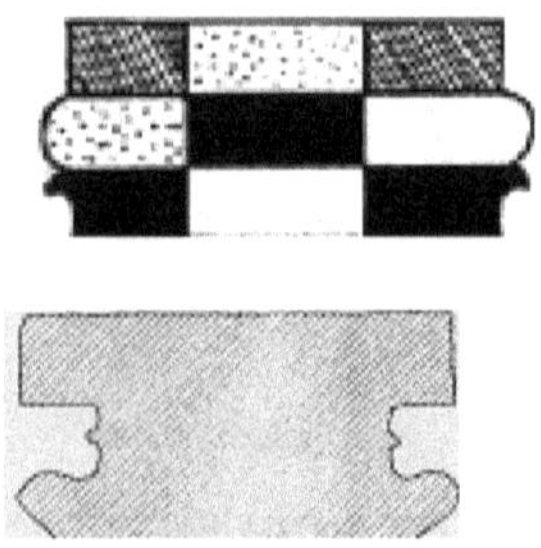

Fig. 6. Comparison entre les modules des figs. 4 et 5.

Fig. 7. Monument du trône de Verucchio (détail de fig. 8).

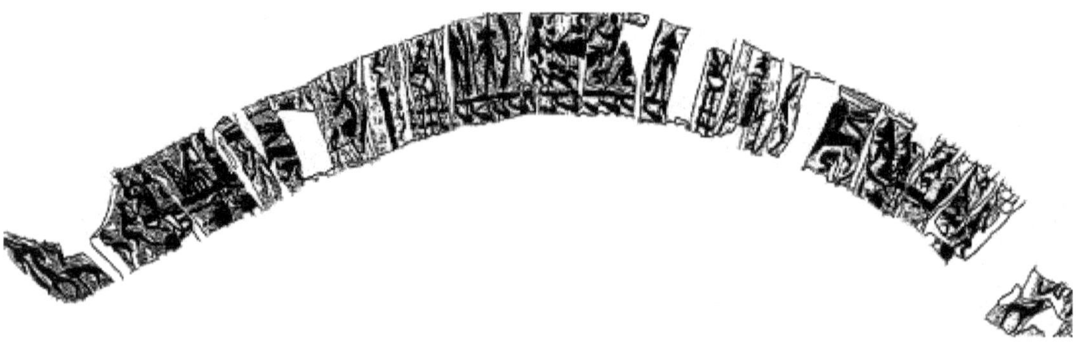

Fig. 8. Frise inférieure du trône de Verucchio.

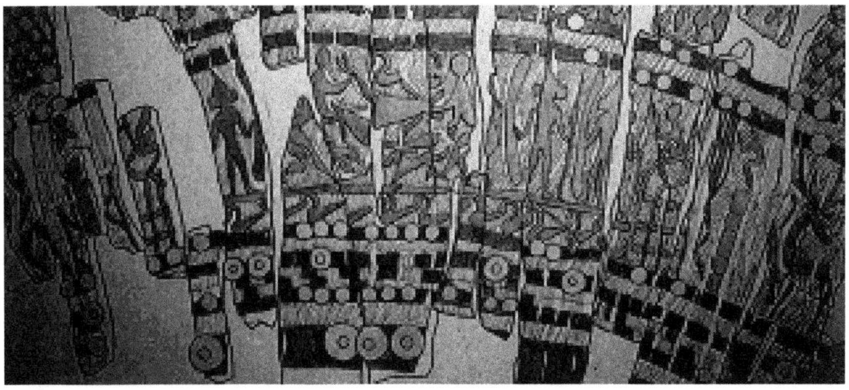

Fig. 9. Détail fig. 7 (scéne central) (Torelli 1997, p. 66, fig. 55).

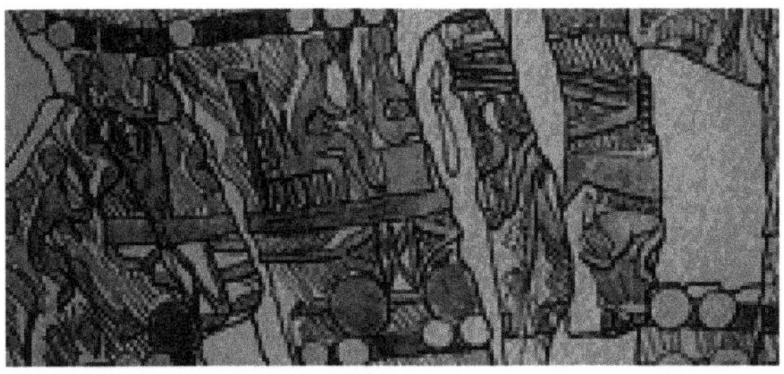

Fig. 10. Détail fig. 7 (chariot) (Torelli 1997, p. 62, fig. 50).

Fig. 11. Tintinnabule de Bologne (Torelli 1997, p. 60, figs. 47-48).

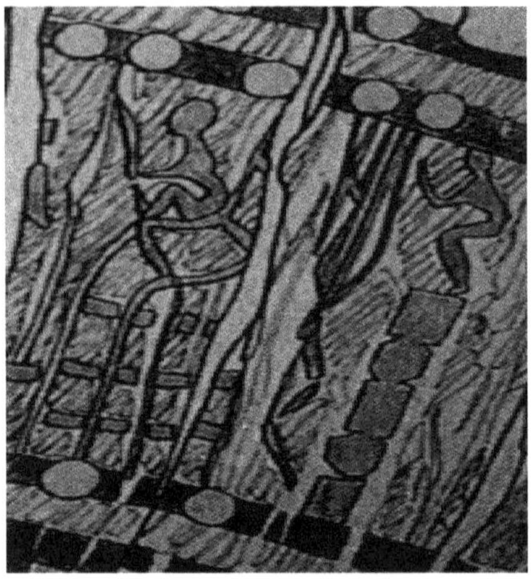

Fig. 12. Détail fig. 8 (travail de la laine).

Fig. 13. Table du Monument B de Via Fondazza (Ortali 1998, fig. 6).

Fig. 14. Filage et préparation di chaînage (Beni Hassan) (Forbes 1964).

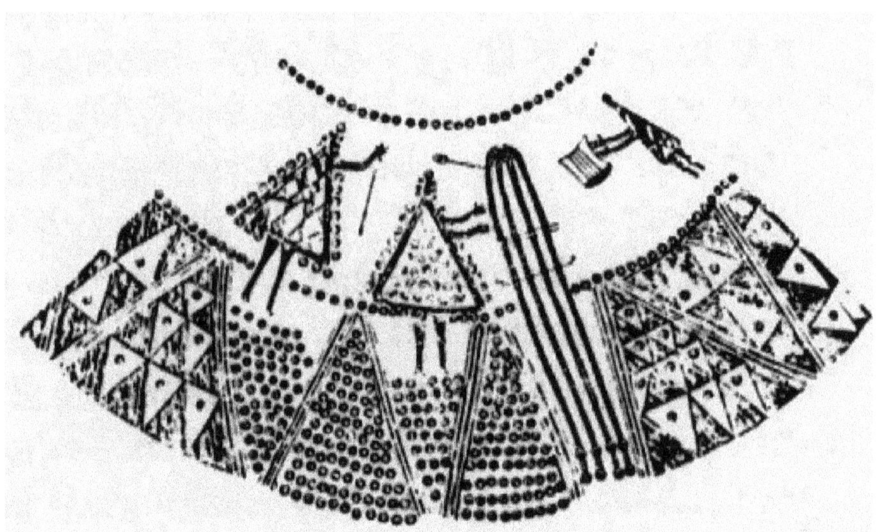

Fig. 15. Représentation di tissage et filage de la laine. Urne, Hongrie (Odenburg/Sopron). Hallstatt (Forbes 1964).

FABRICATION ET COMMERCE DE LA POURPRE EN ITALIE ROMAINE

CHRISTINE MACHEBOEUF
(Université du Littoral, Boulogne-sur-mer)

ABSTRACT: The production or *purpura* and its trade is a vast subject whose study requires a rigorous methodological approach. Thanks to systematic surveys of literary and archaeological sources, as well as work done in the subdiscipline of experimental archaeology, there is ample avidence for the existence of a *purpura* industry in Italy and Sicily. The current study examines literary, epigraphic and iconographic sources in order to investigate the more nuanced questions regarding the commerce of *purpura*.

La couleur pourpre qui désignait, dans l'Antiquité, toute une série de teintes allant du rose au violet très sombre, était depuis les débuts de Rome un symbole de pouvoir puisque, si l'on en croit Plutarque, Romulus portait déjà cette couleur qui deviendra l'emblème des sénateurs et des empereurs (*Romulus*, 14).

Les Romains appréciaient tout particulièrement la pourpre marine élaborée à partir de la glande de certains coquillages. Celle-ci était considérée comme la pourpre par excellence. Etant d'un prix très élevé, elle fut l'objet de bien des imitations grâce à de savants mélanges de végétaux, comme la garance ou l'orcanette, avec d'autres substances, comme le vitriol ou la chaux (R. Halleux, 1981).

Pour l'obtention de la pourpre marine que nous évoquerons seulement ici, trois coquillages furent principalement utilisés : le *murex brandaris*, le *murex trunculus* et le *purpura haemastoma* (*RE, s.v. Purpura*). Mais de quelle manière était-elle plus précisément fabriquée ? A-t-elle été produite dans des ateliers d'Italie et de Sicile ? Comment pouvaient être organisés la production et le commerce de cette précieuse teinture ?

LA FABRICATION DE LA POURPRE MARINE

L'apport de l'archéologie expérimentale aux sources littéraires

La fabrication de la pourpre marine nous est connue grâce aux témoignages d'Aristote (*Histoire des Animaux*, V, 15), de Vitruve (*De Architectura*, VII, 3) et de Pline l'Ancien (*Histoire Naturelle*, IX, 126). La description de Pline l'Ancien est de loin la plus complète. Nous en reprendrons donc ici les grands points tout en gardant une vision critique des écrits du naturaliste qui, pour la pourpre, s'est vraisemblablement davantage inspiré des écrits d'Aristote que de sa propre expérience.

La première opération est « l'extraction des glandes » qui doit se faire impérativement sur « des pourpres vivants, parce qu'ils évacuent leur suc en expirant » (*Histoire Naturelle*, IX, 126 *: vivas capere contendunt, quia cum vita sucum eum euomunt.*) Selon Pline, il existe deux façons d'extraire ces glandes selon que le coquillage est gros ou petit. Lorsque les coquillages sont gros, on tire les mollusques hors de leur coquille sans briser cette dernière, comme on le fait habituellement pour les consommer (*Histoire Naturelle*, IX, 126 : *Et maioribus quidem purpuris detracta concha auferunt)*. Lorsque les coquillages sont petits, on les écrase *« vivants, avec leur coquille »* (*HN*, IX, 126 : *minores cum testa uiuas frangunt*), afin d'accéder plus facilement à la glande. Ces deux procédés ne résistent pas cependant à l'expérimentation. Le premier s'est révélé totalement irréalisable, car il est impossible d'extirper un *murex* vivant de sa coquille tant il y est fortement attaché. Le second n'a très certainement pas été pratiqué, car casser entièrement la coquille risquerait de crever la glande tinctoriale (C. Macheboeuf, thèse en cours).

En fait, nous avons constaté qu'il était très facile d'extraire les glandes des coquillages, en donnant un coup sec sur la coquille à l'endroit opposé à l'ouverture. Un morceau de la coquille se brise alors au niveau de la dernière et de l'avant-dernière spire et découvre ainsi la partie du corps du *murex* comportant la glande tinctoriale. Il reste ensuite à détacher la glande du corps. Les ouvriers utilisaient, selon Vitruve, des outils de fer *(De l'Architecture,* VII, 13, 3) qui devaient être contondants. En effet, nos expériences ont montré qu'il suffisait de disposer d'un objet coupant tel qu'une lame de couteau pour pouvoir séparer la glande du reste du corps (C. Macheboeuf, thèse en cours).

La seconde opération décrite par Pline consisterait à faire macérer les glandes dans du sel : « on ôte ensuite la veine dont nous avons parlé ; il est nécessaire d'y mettre du sel, environ un setier par centaine de livres » (*HN*, IX, 133 :

eximitur postea uena quam diximus, cui addi salem necessarium, sextarios ferme centenas in libras). En réalité cette macération qui devait durer trois jours, n'est en aucun cas nécessaire à l'élaboration de la substance tinctoriale à en juger d'après l'expérience que nous avons menée avec I. Boesken-Kanold (que nous remercions ici vivement) et le recours au sel est un point qui reste encore à élucider (C. Macheboeuf, thèse en cours). Munies de glandes tinctoriales et d'eau nous avons pu passé directement à l'opération décrite par Pline à l'étape suivante.

Ce dernier a en effet raison de remarquer qu'il fallait faire chauffer les glandes « à feu modéré » pendant plusieurs jours (*HN, IX, 133 : ...aequari ad modico vapore torreri et ideo longinquae fornacis cuniculo).* Cette opération s'effectuait dans des cuves de plomb. Il ne s'agissait pas d'une cuisson, mais plutôt d'une fermentation. Le terme de « feu modéré » a ici toute son importance : le contenu de la cuve doit être chauffé à une température constante de 50°. Il ne doit absolument pas être exposé à de hautes températures, car il fournit alors non plus une couleur violette, mais une couleur brunâtre voire même grisâtre qui ne présente plus aucun intérêt (C. Macheboeuf, thèse en cours.).

Au bout du dixième jour environ, on procédait au filtrage du contenu des cuves et à un premier essai de teinture en y trempant « une laine nettoyée *» (vellus elutriatum).* Ici encore, l'opération de filtrage décrite par Pline semble superflue : les glandes et dépôts de chair restent en effet dans le fond de la cuve (C. Macheboeuf, thèse en cours).

Nous avons nous-même préparé une cuve de colorant avec 50 *murex trunculus* grâce à l'aide d'I. Boesken-Kanold, et nous tenterons bientôt de déterminer combien de centimètres carrés de laine peuvent être teints avec une telle quantité. Mais d'ores et déjà une expérience réalisée l'été dernier en Crète par des chercheurs de l'Université américaine de Winnipeg nous permet d'en savoir plus (D. Ruscillo, 2002, p. 252). En effet, ceux-ci ont procédé à la reconstitution d'un atelier de pourpre et à la fabrication de la teinture dans les conditions décrites par les auteurs anciens. C'est ainsi que 825 *murex* ont permis de faire 6 bains différents de teinture pourpre dans lesquels 40 bouts de tissus d'environ 15 cm sur 15 cm ont pu être teints (D. Ruscillo que nous remercions ici pour ce renseignement oral).

L'apport des fouilles archéologiques aux sources littéraires

L'étude archéologique des sites de Délos et de Djerba (*Meninx*) est venue compléter de façon significative l'apport des sources textuelles en mettant notamment en évidence des caractéristiques propres aux ateliers de pourpre.

Tout d'abord les dépôts de *murex* recueillis sur ces sites se composent de coquilles brisées et de coquilles entières percées d'un trou latéral d'un diamètre variant de 1 à 2 cm selon la taille des coquillages. Cette cassure est faite à l'endroit de la glande tinctoriale et relève sans aucun doute du procédé que nous avons décrit plus haut (supra p. 2). De fait, nous pensons que tous les *murex* étaient cassés de la même façon. Les coquilles retrouvées brisées aujourd'hui ont simplement subi l'action du temps et le passage des nombreux pêcheurs ou promeneurs qui les ont piétinés.

Ce qui frappe ensuite est la présence de très importants gisements de *murex*, une caractéristique de tous les sites producteurs de pourpre, où elle est un indice certain d'atelier, et que l'on retrouve par exemple à Mogador, l'une des îles purpuraires sur lesquelles le roi de Maurétanie Juba II a fait produire la célèbre pourpre de Gétulie (A. Jodin, 1967).

On comprend mieux de tels amoncellements, longs parfois de plusieurs kilomètres, si l'on sait qu'un *murex* ne fournit qu'une dose infime de substance tinctoriale comme le soulignait déjà Pline (*HN*, IX, 126 : *liquoris hic minimi est*). Des expériences ont été réalisées sur des *murex* afin de déterminer avec précision la quantité de teinture contenue par coquillage (C. Minitti, 1999). L'une d'elles, effectuée au début du siècle dernier, avait conclu que 12000 *murex brandaris* fournissaient 1,5 gramme de colorant pur (P Friedlander, 1907, p.765). Or le colorant ne peut être utilisé seul. Il n'est qu'un composant d'une teinture dans laquelle se mêlent d'autres éléments comme les chairs des mollusques, l'urine dans le cas des couleurs conchyliennes (Pline, Histoire Naturelle, IX, 138) et surtout la substance colorante d'un autre mollusque. D'ailleurs, ce résultat est aujourd'hui remis en question, car le *murex brandaris* ne contient pas l'enzyme nécessaire à l'obtention de la substance tinctoriale : il est indispensable de le mélanger avec quelques *murex trunculus* afin que le colorant pourpre renfermé dans sa glande tinctoriale se révèle et donne alors sa couleur à l'étoffe (J. Doumet, 1999).

Quoi qu'il en soit, ces expériences ont prouvé que, même si le nombre de *murex* utilisé pour fabriquer la teinture est beaucoup moins important que ce que l'on croyait jusqu'alors, il n'en est pas moins considérable. L'expression de « shell mount » pour désigner les coquilles de *murex* qui se sont amoncelées à Sidon sur une hauteur d'environ 18 mètres et sur une largeur de 6 mètres ne paraît pas exagérée (A. H. Cooke, 1909).

Une autre particularité propre à un atelier de pourpre est la présence de billots (en granit à Délos) destinés à casser les coquillages. On en a découvert six à Délos (Bruneau, 1969, p. 768), un à Djerba (A. Drine, 2000, p. 93 ; fouilles en cours). Leurs dimensions (entre 60 et 90 cm de hauteur et 70 à 80 cm de diamètre à Délos) expliquent qu'on les retrouve rarement.

Mais ce qui retient immédiatement l'attention ce sont surtout les grands bassins et les cuves découverts dans ces ateliers. A Délos, ce sont deux « cuves » et un « bassin » qui ont été mis au jour (selon les mots employés par P. Bruneau, 1969, p. 770) ; à Djerba, ce sont deux « cuves » et deux « bassins » (selon les mots employés par A. Drine, 2000). Quelle définition peut-on donner à chacun de ces deux termes ? Malgré des dimensions qui nous font défaut, le tableau comparatif ci-dessous montre que nous avons bien affaire à deux types de contenant et qu'il convient peut-être de corriger leur dénomination.

D'après ce tableau, il semble que les « bassins » de Djerba correspondent en fait aux « cuves » de Délos. Bien que leurs dimensions ne soient pas identiques, ces structures ont en commun une forme rectangulaire, un trou d'écoulement et une profondeur comprise entre 0, 65 m et 0, 70 m. Inversement, les « cuves » de Djerba pourraient correspondre au « bassin » de Délos : ce sont des structures de forme ronde (Délos) ou de forme rectangulaire à angles arrondis (Djerba) ; elles sont plus petites, mais plus profondes que les précédentes et elles ne possèdent pas de trou d'écoulement.

Quelle pourrait être la fonction de ces deux types de structures ? Les sondages archéologiques effectués près des cuves ont révélé des traces de combustion. On pourrait alors imaginer que dans ces cuves en pierres étaient encastrées les cuves de plomb dans lesquelles était chauffée la substance tinctoriale qui permettait d'obtenir la couleur pourpre. La forme arrondie de ces cuves était sans doute indispensable, mais nous n'en connaissons pas encore les raisons. Quant aux bassins ils étaient peut-être des sortes de viviers dans lesquels les *murex* étaient conservés vivants (*supra* p. 2) jusqu'à ce qu'ils fussent utilisés. En effet, si les pêcheurs ramenaient quelques centaines de kg voir quelques tonnes de *murex* en une seule campagne, on peut penser que ces derniers n'étaient pas tous utilisés en même temps. Ainsi, on possédait des réserves de *murex* frais à disposition. Les trous d'écoulement serviraient alors à changer régulièrement l'eau des bassins afin que les mollusques ne manquent pas d'oxygène.

Enfin la localisation en bordure de côte est aussi une constante de la plupart des ateliers actuellement attestés : il était en effet plus commode de teindre à proximité des lieux de collecte des *murex*. De plus l'atelier devait disposer d'une plage suffisamment grande pour permettre aux pêcheurs de décharger leurs nombreuses cargaisons. A Délos, les deux ateliers de pourpre étaient situés sur le rivage Est, sous les vents dominants qui emportaient la mauvaise odeur des coquillages en décomposition (P. Bruneau, 1969, p.790). Cela aussi pouvait accessoirement caractériser l'implantation d'une fabrique.

Les autres sites producteurs de pourpre de l'Empire romain ne sont malheureusement pas aussi représentatifs que ceux de Délos et de Djerba. Il est en effet extrêmement rare de trouver des cuves ou des billots, pour la simple raison que l'action de la mer et l'urbanisation souvent intense des grands ports ont fait disparaître nombre d'installations. Pourtant grâce à la découverte d'amas de *murex,* nous savons que la pourpre a été exploitée au Proche-Orient (à Sidon, Tyr), en Libye (Berenice, Leptis Magna, Tobrouk) en Grèce (à Cos, Délos, Erétrie), en Tunisie (à Carthage et à Djerba), au Maroc (à Mogador), en Espagne (aux îles Baléares et Carteia), enfin en Gaule (à Narbonne et Toulon).

L'Italie et la Sicile productrices de pourpre

Qu'en est-il en Italie et en Sicile ? Dans l'état actuel des recherches sont attestés, pour la péninsule italienne, sept sites spécialisés dans la production de pourpre à grande échelle: Ancône, la région du Monte Circeo ainsi que les villes de Pouzzoles, Canusium, Tarente, Satureum et Hydruntum. En Sicile, la ville de Syracuse a sûrement produit de la pourpre et peut-être celles d'Etna, Nétum, Hélore, Ségeste et Lilybée.

Les sites italiens

- Les sites attestés par les sources textuelles : Ancône, Pouzzoles, Canusium, Satureum et Hydruntum.

Ancône, sur la côte adriatique, est citée dans l'œuvre de Silius Italicus pour la beauté de sa pourpre qui égale celle d'Orient : « *là se tient sous les armes la ville dont les laines teintées ne sont pas inférieures aux pourpres de Sidon ni à celles de la Libye, Ancône, celle qu'arrose le Vomanus* » (*La Guerre Punique*, VIII, 435).

La production de pourpre à Pouzzoles est célèbre grâce à un passage de Pline sur le *purpurissum* : « [...] *on le fabrique en imprégnant de teinture de la craie à polir l'argent en même temps que les étoffes à teindre en pourpre et la craie absorbe cette couleur plus vite que la laine* » (*Histoire Naturelle,* XXXV, 44). En effet, ce grand port de l'Italie romaine a fabriqué une pourpre destinée d'une part à teindre des vêtements, d'autre part à teindre la craie appelée *creta argentaria.* Cette substance qui était de la « farine fossile » (S. Augusti, 1961, p. 126) servait généralement à polir l'argenterie. Mais elle pouvait aussi être trempée dans de la pourpre et sous le nom de *purpurissum* servait alors en peinture. Le *purpurissum* de Pouzzoles, continue Pline, est préféré à *ceux de Tyr, de Gétulie ou de Laconie d'où viennent les pourpres les plus précieuses* » (*HN,* XXXV, 45). L'on ne s'étonnera pas que Pouzzoles ait livré aussi deux inscriptions mentionnant deux *purpurarii* : un dénommé

Lucius Plutius Hermippus ainsi qu'un certain Numerius Haius Doryphorus (*C.I.L.*, X, 540).

Comme nous le dit Pline dans ce même passage, la ville de Canusium fabriquait aussi du *purpurissum*, de moindre prix toutefois (*HN*, XXXV, 45) : « *La variété la moins chère vient de Canusium* ». Cette ville se trouvait à environ 25 km de la côte, le long du fleuve Aufidus. On peut tout à fait supposer que de la pourpre y a été produite sur les plages situées à l'embouchure du fleuve. En effet, il n'était pas rare, dans l'Antiquité, que des villes aient leur centre politique et religieux installé en retrait de la côte et leurs activités commerciales et industrielles situées au bord de mer. Rappelons ici un célèbre passage d'Aristote qui préconisait ce type d'implantation urbanistique dont Alexandrie, Athènes et bien sûr Rome fournissent des exemples notoires : « *Mais nous voyons aujourd'hui même beaucoup de territoires et de cités disposer de mouillages et de port naturellement si bien situés par rapport à la ville, que sans faire partie du centre lui-même, ils sont cependant maîtrisés par des remparts ou d'autres fortifications du même genre; il est donc évident que, si quelque avantages résulte de la liaison ville-port, la ville profitera de cet avantage...* » (*La Politique*, VII, 6, 5).

Il semble qu'un site voisin de Tarente nommé Satureum (Satyrion) ou plus précisément « l'*oppidum* » de Satureum ait également produit cette teinture comme le signale Servius : « *en effet à côté de Tarente, il y a des ateliers de pourpre dans lesquels on teint la laine* » (*Commentaire de Virgile*, IV, 335 : *a Satureio oppido : iuxta Tarentum enim sunt baphia, in quibus tinguitur lana*).

Au début du Ve siècle, sous le roi Théodéric, la ville d'Hydruntum, l'actuelle Otrante dans le promontoire du Salentum, était le siège d'un atelier de pourpre impérial et sa pourpre était réputée : « *...les coquillages de pourpre de la mer d'Hydronte (...) cet amas de Neptune qui toujours produit une pourpre éclatante...* » (Cassiodore, *Variae*, I, 1, 2).

- Un site attesté par l'archéologie : le promontoire du *Mons Circeum*

Sur la côte tyrrhénienne, des ateliers de pourpre se sont installés au voisinage du Monte Circeo. On sait que l'un des projets de Jules César était de détourner les eaux du Tibre vers le Mons Circeum afin d'assainir et d'urbaniser le Champ de Mars, que Néron, reprenant cette idée à son compte, avait commencé à faire creuser un canal entre le Mons Circeum et la capitale. Les travaux furent interrompus à sa mort (A. Balland, 1965, pp. 349-393), mais ces essais d'aménagement ont peut-être favorisé l'installation d'ateliers de pourpre sur ces plages. En tout cas aujourd'hui encore, à moins de 500 m du rivage, des amas de *murex trunculus* jonchent la route sur 60 m de long et 50 cm d'épaisseur (A. C. Blanc, 1962, p. 188). Une telle concentration de *murex trunculus*, dont certaines coquilles sont trouées sur le coté, ne peut correspondre qu'à la présence d'ateliers de pourpre. D'après une datation au radiocarbone, le promontoire du Monte Circeo a produit de la pourpre de la fin du Ier siècle après J.-C. jusqu'à la 1ère moitié du IIe siècle après J.-C. (A. C. Blanc, 1962, p. 193).

- Tarente : un site attesté par les sources textuelles et l'archéologie

Citons maintenant la plus célèbre ville productrice de pourpre de la péninsule italienne : Tarente. Cette dernière produisait certainement déjà de la pourpre sous la domination grecque, comme le montre un statère d'argent de Tarente à l'effigie de Taras, dieu fleuve éponyme de Tarente, portant un *murex* dans le champ (époque de Kléonimos, dernier tiers du IVe siècle avant J.-C. ; Head, 1911, n° 69). Dès l'époque républicaine, la pourpre de Tarente était célèbre pour son éclat : « *Qu'est-ce donc qu'on admire ? Cette laine où la teinture de Tarente imite la couleur des violettes.* » (Horace, *Epîtres*, II, 207-209). De même, Pline l'Ancien fait dire à Cornélius Népos : « *Au temps de ma jeunesse, la pourpre violette était en vogue [...] Peu de temps après ce fut la pourpre écarlate de Tarente* » (Pline l'Ancien, *HN*, IX, 137). Cette production s'est prolongée sur plusieurs siècles puisque la *Notitia Dignitatum* qui date de la première décade du Ve siècle après J.-C. atteste la présence d'un procurateur de la pourpre à Tarente (Seeck, Occ., 65 : *procurator bafii Tarentini, Calabriae*). De plus, des vestiges archéologiques sont venus corroborer les écrits anciens puisque des restes de fabriques et des amas de *murex* étaient encore présents à la fin du siècle dernier sur les bords du *Mare Piccolo*, « *un peu au- delà de Collepazzo, en dehors de la muraille d'enceinte hellénique, au lieu nommé Fontanella* » (F. Lenormand, 1881, p. 107). Nous pouvons encore observer de nos jours, à ce même endroit, le « monte cociolli » dont le nom est bien révélateur (F.G. Lo Porto, 1971, p. 358).

Les sites siciliens

La pourpre s'est aussi bien sûr fabriquée en Sicile (T. Frank, 1959, III, p. 349).

Cicéron, dans sa deuxième plaidoirie contre Verrès (*Verrines*, II, 2, 59-60), accuse le propréteur de Sicile d'avoir pris part à des affaires financières et commerciales (au mépris bien sûr de la *Lex Claudia* de 218 avant J.-C.). Verrès qui fournissait la pourpre demandait à des amis de fabriquer des tapis et des étoffes de pourpre qu'il revendait au prix fort. L'avocat énumère à cette occasion six villes dans lesquelles Verrès avait fait tisser des étoffes pourpre : Etna, Syracuse, Nétum, Hélore, Ségeste et Lilybée. Cela ne fait pas à priori de ces villes des sites producteurs de pourpre, mais des lieux de production textile. Pourtant, il est fort probable que Verrès ait fait produire de la pourpre au moins à Syracuse qui était, selon la *Notitia Dignitatum* (Seeck, Occ., 68) le lieu de résidence d'un procurateur de la pourpre

(*Procurator bafii Syracusani, Siciliae*) et dont la production pourrait avoir duré au moins jusqu'au début du Ve siècle après J.-C.

Mais de plus, la plaidoirie du célèbre orateur fait apparaître cinq sites potentiels de production de pourpre : celui d'Hélore qui se situe en bordure de mer ainsi que celui de Lilybée qui était déjà productrice de pourpre sous la domination carthaginoise, comme le suggère la découverte d'une monnaie de la 2e moitié du Ve siècle avant J.-C. représentant un *murex* devant un cheval (A. Holm, 1906, p. 128, n°19). Comme à Tarente, les Romains auraient pu reprendre pour leur compte un site déjà exploité avant eux. Les sites de Nétum, Etna et Ségeste qui ne sont qu'à vingt-cinq km environ de la côte, pourraient être des exemples de « villes doubles » (*supra*, p. 7). Sur chacun de ces sites la production de pourpre pouvait être associée à celle du textile (*supra*, p. 11).

Après avoir recensé les villes productrices de pourpre, intéressons-nous maintenant aux hommes. Voyons comment ils ont organisé le commerce de la pourpre.

Remarques sur l'organisation de la fabrication et du commerce de la pourpre

Une laine teinte à l'atelier

Nous savons que la teinture pourpre est obtenue après macération (non obligatoire selon nous, *supra* p. 10) puis lente fermentation des glandes tinctoriales de *murex* dans une cuve de plomb chauffée à une température constante d'environ 50°. Une fois le processus de fermentation terminé, on procède ensuite, d'après Pline, à la teinture de la laine et à son cardage. Selon lui en effet, le cardage se fait à la suite d'un premier bain : « La laine trempe cinq heures ; après avoir été cardée, elle subit un second bain jusqu'à ce qu'elle soit saturée. » (*HN*, IX, 133 : *quinis lana potat horis rursuque mergitur carminata, donec omnem ebibat saniem*). Carder (*carminare*) consiste à démêler les fibres de la laine, à faire disparaître les inégalités et les nœuds. Il convient ensuite de peigner (*pectere*) la laine, c'est-à-dire d'épurer et de trier les fibres avant le filage. Ces deux opérations sont assez similaires. Mais, il est difficile d'admettre que les ouvriers aient teint de la laine encore sale et pleine de nœuds. Nous pensons que la laine destinée à être teinte était au minimum peignée, voir même filée. Si une opération avait lieu entre deux bains de teinture, c'était peut-être uniquement un rinçage afin peut-être d'atténuer l'odeur pestilentielle de la substance tinctoriale.

En tout cas, dans la description de Pline, les ateliers qui fabriquaient la pourpre procédaient aussi à la teinture de la laine, alors que leur tâche aurait pu se limiter à la fabrication de la teinture pourpre (C. Macheboeuf, thèse en cours). Il n'est donc pas étonnant que, dans la péninsule italienne et en Sicile, les centres producteurs de pourpre aient été en même temps des centres producteurs de laine, et que les ateliers de pourpre aient été alimentés par des laines locales.

L' Apulie était une région spécialisée dans la production lainière et textile (F. Grelle, 2001). La laine de Tarente, sur laquelle nous possédons plus de 24 références textuelles était aussi célèbre que sa pourpre (J.-P. Morel, 1978, p. 100) et Pline mentionne aussi bien la laine que la pourpre de Canusium (*HN*, VIII, 190).

La Campanie était également connue pour sa production lainière (Moeller, 1976) et ainsi Pouzzoles a très certainement reçu les laines de son arrière-pays.

La Sicile est décrite, par de nombreux auteurs, en particulier Aristote (*Histoire des Animaux*, 3, 17) et Athénée (*Deipnosophistes*, 396a) comme une terre couverte de pâturages et de moutons. Aux dires de Strabon les moutons de la région d'Etna étaient même tellement gros qu'il fallait les saigner de temps en temps afin qu'ils ne suffoquent pas (*Géographie*, 6, 2, 3). Ce n'est pas la seule ville où Verrès aurait pu associer une production de pourpre et de tissu (*supra* p. 12). Syracuse était notoirement un centre producteur de pourpre et un important centre de tissage (T. Frank, 1959, III, p. 290).

Pour la péninsule italienne et la Sicile, production de laine et production de pourpre semblaient donc aller de pair. Les ateliers de pourpre n'étaient jamais isolés, mais ils étaient au contraire liés à la présence d'un artisanat du textile et plus précisément de la laine. Peut-être même ateliers de pourpre et ateliers de tissage étaient-ils parfois structurellement associés, comme à Erétrie où les fouilles archéologiques ont révélé la présence de pesons à proximité de l'atelier producteur de pourpre (S. G. Schmid, 1999). Mais venons-en maintenant aux hommes qui s'occupaient de fabriquer et de vendre la pourpre.

Les purpurarii *: des teinturiers ou des gens de commerce ?*

- L'apport de l'épigraphi*e*

Pour tenter de répondre à cette question, nous nous sommes essentiellement appuyée sur les témoignages épigraphiques, c'est-à-dire sur les 22 dédicaces et inscriptions funéraires retrouvées en Italie, qui évoquent des purpuraires. Quelle était exactement la tâche de ces derniers ? Il est aisé de répondre que Eius Civis à Rome et Murrius Zetus Placentinus à Aquinum en pays Samnite, ville réputée accessoirement pour sa pourpre végétale (Horace, *Epîtres*, I, X, 27) faisaient du commerce : le premier était un « *negocians purpurarius* » (*C.I.L.*, VI, 33888), le second un « *mercator purpurarius* » (*AE*, 1972, 74, Aquinum). Il s'agit probablement de deux inscriptions impériales, car les inscriptions républicaines ne précisent jamais la nature des affaires du *mercator* et du *negociator* (Rougé, 1966, pp. 281 et 289). Quelle différence existe-t-il entre ces deux termes ? Le *negocians* ou *negociator,* qui était sous la République un grand brasseur d'affaires, devient sous l'Empire un grand commerçant, étroitement lié au commerce maritime, possédant un ou plusieurs bateaux. C'est ainsi que Eius Civis à Rome pourrait s'être spécialisé dans le commerce en gros de la pourpre marine. Bien qu'il puisse avoir le sens de « petit commerçant », notamment sous la République, le mot *mercator* peut désigner sous l'Empire un commerçant voyageur, et plus particulièrement un commerçant qui allait se ravitailler loin de son lieu de résidence. C'est ce sens que nous retenons pour Murrius Zetus qui avait fondé une société et qui pouvait avec son associé (*socius)* Murrius Eros avoir pratiqué aussi un commerce d'importation et d'exportation de la pourpre. Dans ce domaine comme dans d'autres, ces deux catégories d'hommes d'affaires semblent en effet avoir pratiqué le même métier. Seule changeait l'importance des affaires traitées : le *negociator* faisait un commerce de gros, le *mercator* de demi-gros (Rougé, 1966, pp. 274-291), mais ils devaient être tous deux des intermédiaires entre les ateliers de pourpre et les commerçants détaillants.

La plupart de nos inscriptions évoquent ensuite des hommes ou des femmes désignés uniquement comme *purpurarii.* Ceux-ci étaient-ils des commerçants ou des teinturiers ? Remarquons tout d'abord que 9 *purpurarii* sur les 28 répertoriés sur le sol italien ont exercé leur activité à l'intérieur des terres : à Truento (*C.I.L.*, IX, 5276), à Capoue (*C.I.L.*, X, 1, 3973), à Parme (*C.I.L.*, XI, 1069a), à Clusium (*C.I.L.*, XI, 2136), à Sassina Mevaniola (*C.I.L.*, XI, 6604), à Marino (*C.I.L.*, XIV, 2433), à Marcianise (*A.E.*, 1967, 88) et à Aquinum (*AE*, 1972, 74). La distance d'au moins 40 km séparant ces villes de la mer rend tout simplement une production de pourpre peu rentable en raison des coûts de transport. Ces 8 *purpurarii* sont donc très probablement versés dans le commerce de la pourpre.

Il semble que ce soit aussi le cas des 16 *purpurarii* de l'*Urbs*. L'inscription du *CIL*, VI, n° 37820 nous montre en effet que certains *purpurarii* de Rome ne pouvaient être des teinturiers. Veturia et ses compagnons sont *purpurarii* près des *monumenta Mariana,* qui se situaient soit sur l'Esquilin (M. Cima, 1986, p. 37), soit à proximité du Forum romain (F. Coarelli, 1983, p. 101). Or l'installation de teintureries de pourpre à Rome dans l'un ou l'autre de ces deux endroits est difficile à imaginer, quand on sait que dès le début de l'Empire on assiste à l'éloignement progressif du centre de la Ville des métiers « polluants » et que ceux-ci cèdent la place aux métiers de luxe (J.-P. Morel, 2001, p. 321 ; C. Macheboeuf, 2000). Il y a donc lieu de croire que ces *purpurarii* ne faisaient que vendre la teinture et qu'ils n'étaient pas à la fois teinturiers et commerçants, comme le veut G. L. Gregori (1992, p.740). Certes, un *purpurarius* exerçait son activité dans le Trastevere (*C.I.L.*, VI, 9847) qui était alors le quartier où se concentraient les industries polluantes comme les tanneries, mais si Rome avait dû posséder un atelier de pourpre, il faudrait plutôt le chercher sur le littoral, aux environs d'Ostie, même si, pour le moment, nous n'en possédons aucun indice.

Qu'en est-il maintenant des *purpurarii* ayant exercé leur activité dans des villes côtières, c'est-à-dire de Plutius Hermippus, de Haius Doryphorus, *purpurarii* à Pouzzoles (*C.I.L.*, X, 540-1952), et de Nonnius Stephanus, *purpurarius* à Ostie (*C.I.L.*, XIV, 473) ? La présence certaine ou probable d'ateliers de pourpre dans ces deux villes invite à la prudence. Si, comme on l'observe dans d'autres secteurs, ce sont les fabricants qui vendent eux-mêmes leurs produits (Loane, 1938, pp. 69-79), les *purpurarii* pourraient être ici des entrepreneurs-commerçants. Mais ce n'est pas certain. Seule une enquête plus large, que nous ne sommes pas encore en mesure d'entreprendre, sur les noms donnés aux teinturiers et aux autres acteurs de la production de pourpre pourrait nous aider à y voir plus clair.

A l'heure actuelle, même si tous les *purpurarii* devaient posséder un atelier, y compris ceux des villes intérieures, ils nous apparaissent principalement comme des commerçants et plus spécialement comme des commerçants détaillants, ainsi que nous le montre la stèle funéraire de C. Puppius Amicus à Parme.

- La stèle de C. Puppius Amicus : la confrontation du texte et de l'image

La stèle de C. Puppius Amicus (*CIL*, IX, 1069a) conservée au Musée archéologique de Parme, constitue en effet un témoignage indéniable : on y voit représentés, bien qu'ils ne soient pas tous à la même échelle, les outils de travail nécessaires au travail d'un *purpurarius* (Fig.1). Au centre de la stèle se trouve une balance romaine qui supporte à chaque extrémité un écheveau de laine. A côté d'elle figurent deux paquets de six et quatre écheveaux de laine munis d'anneaux de préhension. Sur la gauche de la stèle un objet en forme de pince peut être identifié avec une *regula*, règle destinée à mesurer la laine (C. Macheboeuf, 2002, pour une analyse plus détaillée de la stèle). Mais surtout, ce qui attire l'attention est la représentation de trois bouteilles ou flacons, en particulier celle d'un flacon muni d'un bouchon élégant. De toute évidence ces récipients ne pouvaient que contenir une substance liquide permettant de teindre en pourpre. Cette représentation vient éclaircir, selon nous, un passage de Suétone qui nous explique que Néron fit vendre quelques onces (*paucula̲s uncias*) de pourpre améthyste ou tyrienne un jour de foire (*Néron*, 32). Sachant qu'une once est égale à 27,28 grammes, quelques onces représentent une petite quantité de pourpre, peut-être 100 à 120 grammes (C. Macheboeuf, 2000). Le texte de Suétone ne nous dit pas comment la pourpre était conditionnée. Mais si on le rapproche de la stèle de Parme, il ne fait guère de doute que la pourpre était vendue sous forme liquide dans des flacons. Le flacon le plus élégant de la stèle de Parme ressemble à un *unguentarium*, ce petit vase dans lequel on conservait habituellement les essences et les parfums. Ces flacons sont certes très communs et très souvent retrouvés en fouille, mais la découverte de flacons analogues sur les sites de Mogador (Jodin, 1967, p. 185) et d'Ibiza (M. Astruc, 1978, pl. XXXVIII) qui ont également produit de la pourpre n'est peut-être pas fortuite.

Mais le *purpurarius*, on l'a vu, ne vendait pas seulement une substance tinctoriale liquide, il recevait et vendait également des écheveaux de laine très certainement déjà teints en pourpre à l'atelier. La stèle de Parme rejoint ici le texte de Pline (*HN*, IX, 133) qui dit clairement que la laine était déjà teinte dans les ateliers.

L'analyse de tissus retrouvés à Palmyre, au cours de fouilles (Pfister, 1940, p.15), nous permet de comprendre l'usage de ces écheveaux. Il apparaît, en effet, que les étoffes retrouvées jusqu'ici n'étaient jamais teintes entièrement en pourpre. Les étoffes de lin comme de laine y étaient seulement brodées de fils pourpres. Les écheveaux que le marchand vendait dans son échoppe étaient donc vendus en petites quantités, et étaient très certainement destinés à de telles broderies (C. Macheboeuf, 2002).

Certes, nous savons grâce à d'autres témoignages littéraires que des robes ou des manteaux étaient entièrement teints en pourpre (en particulier Martial, *Epigrammes*, V, 13). Le tissu était alors très certainement immergé directement dans les cuves des ateliers. Mais, cela relève d'une organisation du travail qui n'est pas celle qui est mise en évidence par la stèle de Parme.

Conclusion

Grâce à l'étude et au recoupement d'un certain nombre de sources textuelles, épigraphiques et archéologiques, nous savons désormais que l'Italie romaine et la Sicile ont produit de la pourpre dans 13 villes réparties sur ses trois façades littorales, dont la plus importante est indéniablement Tarente. Notons également l'importance de Syracuse qui fut tout de même le lieu de résidence d'un procurateur de la pourpre.

Nous savons ensuite qu'aussi bien en Italie qu'en Sicile, les régions productrices de pourpre étaient aussi des régions productrices de laine et que ces deux industries étaient sans doute étroitement liées.

Bien sûr, des zones d'ombre subsistent quant à l'organisation du travail et du commerce de la pourpre : atelier de pourpre et atelier textile étaient-ils économiquement associés ? Quel était le rôle exact des *negociatores* et des *mercatores purpurarii ?* Certains *purpurarii* possédaient-ils leurs propres ateliers ? Mais d'ores et déjà, le recoupement des témoignages épigraphiques nombreux qu'ont livrés l'Italie et la Sicile et du relief figuré de la stèle de C. Puppius Amicus à Parme, montre que le *purpurarius* était directement en contact avec la clientèle et qu'il pouvait vendre de la « pourpre liquide », fait qu'il est souvent de bon ton de contester.

Choix d'inscriptions

C.I.L, I, 1413 = I.L.S, 9428: Rome
V(ivus) D(ecimus) Veturius D(ecimi) l(ibertus) Diog(enes) / □ (mortuus) D(ecimus) [Veturius] D(ecimi) l(ibertus) Nicepor / v(iva) Veturia D(ecimi) l(iberta) Fedra de sua pecunia faciund(um) coir(avit) / sibi et patrono et conlibert(o) / et liberto / Nicepor conlibertus v(ixit) mecum annos XX / purpurari(i) a Marianeis[1]*/ viv(us) D(ecimus) Veturius D(ecimi) l(ibertus) Philarcur(us)*[2]
De son vivant, Decimus Veturius Diogène affranchi de Decimus. Decimus [Veturius] Nicépor décédé, affranchi de Decimus. De son vivant Veturia Fedra, affranchie de Decimus a pris soin de faire cela sur ses ressources, pour elle, son patron, son compagnon d'affranchissement et son affranchi. Nicépor mon compagnon d'affranchissement a vécu 20 ans avec moi. Les purpuraires [du quartier des] Marianae. De son vivant Decimus Veturius Philarcurus, affranchi de Decimus.

C.I.L., VI, 9844 : Rome
D(iis) m(anibus) / L(ucio) Pl(utio) Her / Mippo purp(urario)
Aux dieux Mânes de Lucius Plutius Hermippus, purpuraire.

C.I.L., VI, 9845 : Rome
L(ucius) Venonius / Hospes / purpurarius
Lucius Venonius Hospes, purpuraire.

C.I.L, VI, 9846 : Rome

N(umini) N(eronis) l(ibens) a(nimo) / Viciria A(ugusti) l(iberta) [---] / Viciria N(eronis) l(iberta) t[---] / Viciria N(eronis) l(iberta) Nice / Viciria A(ugusti) l(iberta) Creste / purpurar(iae)
Au numen de Néron de bon coeur. Viciria [---] affranchie impériale. Viciria T[---] affranchie de Néron. Viciria Nice affranchie de Néron. Viciria Chreste affranchie impériale. Purpuraires.

C.I.L., VI, 9847 : Rome
[...] P[urp]urar(io) / a [Tr]anstiberim et / Sontiae [R]estitutae / coniugi eius et / libertis libertabus / posterisque eius / fecit / Attia Delphis / coiunx
A [...] purpuraire du Trastevere et à Sontia Restituta son épouse, à ses affranchis et affranchies, et à sa descendance. L'épouse Attia Delphis a fait cela.

C.I.L, VI, 9848 : Rome
Ap(pii) Clodi(i) Philonici Euraniae Mu(sae) purpurari(ae) de vico
A Eurania Musa, (esclave d') Appius Clodius Philonicus, purpuraire du quartier.

C.I.L., VI, 33888 : Rome
Eius Ci[vis] / [ne]gotia(n)s pur[purarius] / [...]
Eius Civis, négociant purpuraire

Année épigraphique, 1994, 283 : Rome
L(ucius) Beniu[s---] / purpu[rar(ius)] / L(ucius) Ben[nius---] / L(ucius) Be[nnius---] / ----
Lucius Bennius, purpuraire. Lucius Bennius [---]. Lucius Bennius [---].

C.I.L., IX, 5276: Truentum
C(aius) Marcilius / Eros purpura(rius) / V vir Truenti
Caius Marcilius Eros, purpuraire, quinquevir de Truentum.

C.I.L., X, 1, 1952 : Pouzzoles
D(iis) m(anibus) / L(ucio) Pl(utio) Her / Mippo pur(purario)
Aux dieux Mânes de Lucius Plutius Hermippus, purpuraire.

C.I.L., X, 1, 3973 : Capoue
C(aio) Minati(o) C(aii) l(iberto) Philodami(o) purpur(ario) / Minatia (Caii) l(iberta) Fausta fecit sibi et patro(no)
A Caius Minatius Philodamius, affranchi de Caius, purpuraire. Minatia Fausta, affranchie de Caius, a fait cela pour elle et son patron.

C.I.L., XI, 1069a : Parme
C(aius) Pupius C(aii) l(ibertus) Amicus / purpurarius / vivos fecit / sibi et suis / in f(ronte) p(edes) XII in a(gro) p(edes) XX
Caius Pupius Amicus, affranchi de Caius, purpuraire. Il a fait cela de son vivant pour lui et les siens. De face 12 pieds, en profondeur 20 pieds.

C.I.L., XI, 2136: Clusium, en Etrurie
P(ublius) Vettius D(ecimi) l(ibertus) Antioc(hus) / purpurarius
Publius Vettius Antiochus, affranchi de Decimus, purpuraire.

C.I.L., XI, 6604 : Sassina Mevaniola (Santa Sofia)
M(arcus) Saellius Q(uinti) [f(ilius)] / Stel(latina tribu) Marcellus [pu] / rpurarius sex vi[r] / sibei et Muronia[e/ ...] / l(ibertae) Primae viv(o)s fec(it)
Marcus Saellius Marcellus, fils de Quintus, de la tribu Stellatina, purpuraire sevir, a fait cela de son vivant pour lui et pour Muronia Prima affranchie de [...].

C.I.L., XIV, 2433 : Marino, en Campanie
L(ucio) Plutio L(ucii) L(iberto) Eroti / purpurario de vico Tusco / Plutia L(ucii) l(iberta) Auge / fecit sibi et Veturiae c(oniugi) C(aii) l(ibertae) Atticae
A Lucius Plutius Eroti, affranchi de Lucius, purpuraire du quartier Tuscus. Plutia Auge, affranchie de Lucius, a fait cela pour elle et pour Veturia Attica son épouse à lui, affranchie de Caius

Année Epigraphique, 1923, 59 : Rome
D(ecimus) Veturius D(ecimi) l(ibertus) Atticus / purpur(arius) de vico Iugar(io) / Veturia D(ecimi) l(iberta) Tryphera / arbitratu
Decimus Veturius Atticus, affranchi de Decimus, purpurarius du quartier Iugarius. Veturia Tryphera, affranchie de Decimus, de son plein gré.

Année Epigraphique, 1967, 88 : Marcianise, près de Pompéi
A(ulo) Oppei(o) A(uli) l(iberto) Glauciae / purpurarei(o) ossa heic sita / sunt
A Aulus Oppeus Glaucia, affranchi de Aulus, purpuraire. Ici reposent ses ossements.

Année Epigraphique, 1972, 74, Aquinum
[P(ublius). M]urrius P(ubliorum duorum) l(ibertus) Zetus / [Plac]entinus mercator / [pur]purarius, hic situs est ; / [uiator] consiste et casus hominum cogita : / annorum natu(s) XXXV arbitror fuissem / [quom] plurimi fui et florebam maxume, / [et ce]cidi longe ab domo et meis amantib[us]. / P(ublius) Murrius P(ubliorum duorum) li(bertus) Eros / [con]libertus et socius uiuus / hoc monumentum fecit ossaque [tran]stulit Placentiam
Ici se trouve Publius Murrius Zetus de Plaisance, affranchi des deux Publius, négociant purpuraire ; voyageur, arrête-toi et pense au sort malheureux des hommes : je devais avoir 35 ans quand j'étais dans la fleur de l'age et que je prospérais au mieux, et je suis mort loin de chez moi et des miens qui m'aimaient. Publius Murrius Eros, affranchi des deux Publius, son compagnon d'affranchissement et associé survivant a fait construire ce monument de son vivant et a transféré ses ossements à Plaisance.

NOTES

1 Nous avons choisi l'interprétation de G. L. Grégori, *Epigrafia della produzione e della distribuzione*, p. 321, non celle du CIL et du Dessau (*purpuraria marianeis*).
Les Marianae sont un quartier où furent élevés des monuments à la gloire de Marius lors de sa victoire contre les Cimbres et les Teutons. Ce quartier se situerait près du Forum ou sur l'Esquilin.
2 Il s'agit sans doute de l'affranchi de Veturia Fedra dont le nom aurait dû figurer après celui de Nicépor dans l'énumération des deux premières lignes.

SOURCES ET BIBLIOGRAPHIE

Sources épigraphiques
C.I.L, I, 1413 = *I.L.S*, 9428: Rome; *C.I.L*, VI, 2, 9843; *C.I.L.*, VI, 9844; *C.I.L.*, VI, 9845; *C.I.L*, VI, 9846; *C.I.L.*, VI, 9847; *C.I.L*, VI, 9848; *C.I.L.*, VI, 32454; *C.I.L.*, VI, 33888; *C.I.L.*, IX, 5276; *C.I.L.*, X, 1, 540 ; *C.I.L.*, X, 1, 1952 ; *C.I.L.*, X, 1, 3973 ; *C.I.L.*, XI, 1069a ; *C.I.L., XI, 2136; C.I.L., XI, 6604 ; C.I.L.*, XIV, 473 ; *C.I.L.*, XIV, 2433 ; *AE*, 1923, 59 ; *AE*, 1967, 88 ; *AE*, 1972, 74 ; *AE*, 1973, 140 ; *AE*, 1975, 233 ; *AE*, 1984, 207 ; *AE*, 1990, 461 ; *AE*, 1994, 283 ; *AE*, 1996, 715.

Sources littéraires
Aristote, *Politique*, VII, 6, 5
Histoire des Animaux, III, 17 ; V, 15
Athénée, *Deipnosophistes*, XI, 396a
Cassiodore, *Variae*, 468
Cicéron, *Verrès*, II, 2, 59-60
Code Théodosien, IX, 45, 3 ; X, 20, 5, 17; XIII, 4, 2
Horace, *Epîtres*, I, X, 27; II, 207-209
Histoire Auguste, *Alexandre Sévère*, 40, 6
Martial, *Epigrammes*, V, 23
Pline l'Ancien, *Histoire Naturelle*, IX, 122 ; IX, 133 ; XXVI, 44 ; XXXV, 44
Plutarque, *Romulus*, 14
Silius Italicus, *La Guerre Punique*, VIII, 435
Strabon, *Géographie*, 6, 2, 3
Suétone, *Néron*, XXXII
Vitruve, *De Architectura*, VII, 3

Bibliographie

M. Astruc, La necropolis de Villaricos, *CGEA, Informes y Memorias*, n° 25, Madris 1951, pl. XXXVIII, n° 26.

S. Augusti, Sui Colori degli Antichi. Il purpurissum. *Rendiconti della Academia di Archeologia, Lettere e Belle Arti, nouv. ser.*, 36, Napoli 1961, pp. 123-130.

S. Augusti, *I colori Pompeiani*, Roma 1967.

A. Balland, Nova Urbs et Neapolis. Remarques sur les projets urbanistiques de Néron, *MEFRA*, **77**, 1965, pp. 349-393.

A. C. Blanc, Residui di manufatture di porpora a Leptis Magna e al Monte Circeo, *Bolletino del Centro di Studi per la Storia dell'Architettura*, n°12, 1958, pp. 187-210.

H. Blümner, *Technologie und Terminologie der Gewerbe und Künste*, **I**, 1912.

I. Boesken-Kanold, The Purple Fermentation Vat, Dyeing or Painting Parchment with Murex Trunculus, *Dyes in History and Archaeology*, 20th Meeting in Amsterdam 2001, sous presse.

F. Bruin, Royal Purple and the Dye Industries of the Mycenians and the Phoenicians, *International Conference of Maritime History*, Beirut, 5-10 septembre 1966, pp. 77-85.

Ph. Bruneau, Documents sur l'industrie délienne de la pourpre, *B.C.H*, **XCIII**, 1969, pp. 759-791.

Ph. Bruneau, Fabrication de pourpre à Délos, *B.C.H,* **CII**, 1978, pp. 110-114.

D. Cardon, *Guide des teintures naturelles*, Delachaux et Niestle, Lausanne 1990.

D. Cardon, *Teintures précieuses de la Méditerranée*, Catalogue du Musée de Carcassonne, 1999.

M. Cima, Dagli scavi dell'Esquilino all'interpretazione dei Monumenti, in *Le tranquille dimore degli dei,* Roma 1986, p. 139.

F. Coarelli, *Il Foro Romano, I. Periodo arcaico*, Roma 1983.

A. H. Cooke, On the Shell-Mound at Sidon, *Proceedings of the Malacological Society of London*, 1909, pp. 34-36.

C. Daremberg et E. Saglio, *Dictionnaire des antiquités grecques et romaines, s.v. creta et purpura.*

J. Doumet, *A Study of the Ancient Purple Colour*, Beyrouth 1980.

J. Doumet, De la teinture en pourpre des Anciens par l'extraction du produit colorant des *murex trunculus*, *brandaris* et des *purpura haemastoma*, *National Museum News*, n° 9, 1999.

A. Drine, Les fouilles de Méninx. Résultats des campagnes de 1997 et 1998, *Geografi, viaggiatori, militari nel Maghreb: alle origine dell'archeologia nel Nord Africa, L'Africa romana*, 13, 1, 2000, pp. 87-94.

G. Fabre, *Libertus : recherches sur les rapports patron-affranchi à la fin de la République romaine,* Ecole Française de Rome 1981.

T. Frank, *An Economic Survey of Ancient Rome*, III, Sicily, New Jersey 1959.

J. M. Frayn, *Sheep-rearing and the wool Trade in Italy during the Roman Period*, Liverpool 1984.

P Friedlander, Zur Kenntnis des Farbstoffs des antiken Purpurs aus Murex Brandaris. *Monatsheft Feuer Chemie*, 28, 1907, pp. 10-12.

E. Furnari, Nuovi contributi all'identificazione del litorale antico di Pompei in *Neapolis Temi Progettuali*, II, Rome 1994, pp. 219-291.

G. L. Gregori, *Purpurarii* in *Epigrafia della Produzione e della Distribuzione*, Actes de la 7e rencontre franco-italienne sur l'épigraphie du monde romain, Rome, 5-6 juin 1992, Rome 1994, pp. 738-742.

F. Grelle, M. Silvestrini, Lane apule e tessuti canosini, *Epigrafia e territorio. Politica e societe*, **VI**, Bari 2001, pp. 124-138.

R. Halleux, *Les alchimistes grecs*, Les Belles Lettres, Paris 1981.

B.V. Head, *Historia Numorum*, éd. Oxford, 1911.

A. Holm, *Storia della monetazione siciliana,* Turin 1906.

B. S. J. Insserlin et *al*, Motia, a phoenician-Punic Site near Marsala, Sicily, Preliminary report of the Leeds-London Fairleigh Dickinson excavations, 1961-1963, *Annual of Leeds University Oriental Society*, 1962-1963 pp. 84-131.

A. Jodin, *Les établissements du roi Juba II aux îles purpuraires*, Tanger 1967.

S. R. Joshel, *Work, identity, and legal status at Rome*, Londres 1992.

F. Lenormand, *La Grande Grèce*, I, Paris 1881.

H. Loane, *Industry and Commerce of the City of Rome (500 BC-200 AD)*, New-York 1938.

A. Locard, *Histoire des mollusques dans l'Antiquité*, Lyon-Paris 1884.

F. G. Lo Porto, Topografia antica di Taranto, in *Taranto nella civilta della Magna Grecia, Atti del X Convegno intern. Di studi sulla Magna Grecia* (Tarente 1970), Naples 1971, pp. 343-382.

O. Longo (éd.), *La Porpora. Realta e immaginario di un colore simbolico*, 1998.

C. Macheboeuf, Contribution des femmes à l'industrie textile à Rome, in *Colloque Femme et Sociétés* organisé par le C.E.R.C.L.E, Université du Littoral, 20-22 mai 2000, sous presse.

C. Macheboeuf, Les étoffes pourpres, *Colloque Teintures et Textiles de la Méditerranée romaine*, Ibiza 08-10 nov. 2002, sous presse.

C. Macheboeuf, *Exploitation et commercialisation de la pourpre dans l'Empire romain*, thèse de doctorat en cours.

U. Mannering, The Roman Tradition of Weaving and Sewing: a Guide to Function, *Textile Newsletter*, vol. 30, pp.79-87.

C. Minitti, L'utilizzazione dei molluschi nell'età del Bronzo di Coppa Nevigata, *19e Convegno sulla Preistoria-Protostoria e Storia della Daunia*, San Severo 1999, pp. 40-52.

W. Moeller, *The Wool Trade in Ancient Pompei*, Leiden 1976.

J.-P. Morel, La laine de Tarente, *KTEMA*, n° 3, 1978, pp. 93-110.

J.-P. Morel, La topographie de l'artisanat et du commerce sous la Rome antique, *L'Urbs, Espace urbain et histoire (Ier siècle avant J.-C.- IIIe siècle après J.-C.) Actes du Colloque International de Rome*, 1987, pp. 127-155.

H. Parkins, C. Smith, *Trade, Traders and the Ancient City*, London 1998.

L. Pareti, Sui primi commerci e stanziamenti fenici nei paesi méditerranei e specialmente in Sicilia, *Archivio Storico per la Sicilia Orientale*, XII, 1934, pp. 3-28.

R. Pfister, *Textiles de Palmyre,* Paris 1940.

G. Radwin, Murex shells of the world: an illustrated guide to the Muricidae, Stanford 1976.

Realencyclopädie Pauly-Wissova, K. Schneider, s.v. *Purpura*, XXIII, 2, 2000-2020, 1959.

D. Reese, The Méditerranean Shell Purple Dye Industry, *American Journal of Archaeology*, 90, (2), 1986, pp. 184-193.

M. Reinhold, On Status Symbols in the Ancient World, *Classical Journal*, 64, 1964, pp. 134-156.

M. Reinhold, History of Purple as a Status Symbol in Antiquity, coll. *Latomus*, 116, Bruxelles 1970.

J. Rougé, *Recherche sur l'organisation du commerce maritime en Méditerranée sous l'Empire romain*, Paris 1966.

M. Ruggiero, Del sito di Pompei e dell'antico lido del mare, in *Pompei e la regione sotterata dal Vesuvio nell'anno 79*, Naples 1979, pp. 5-32.

D. Ruscillo, To Dye for: Reconstructing Murex Dyeing Techniques in the Bronze Age Aegean, American *Journal of Archaeology*, vol. 106, 2002, p. 252.

T. Schreiber, *Kulturhistorischer Bilderatlas*, vol. I, 1888.

S. G. Schmid, Decline or prosperity at Roman Eretria ? Industry, purple dye work, public buildings and gravestones, *Journal of Roman Archaeology* 12, 1999, pp. 55-68.

O. Seeck, *Notitia digninatum*, éd O. Seek, Frankfort 1962.

N. Tiberi, Le conchiglie pompeiane, in *Pompei e la regione sotterata dal Vesuvio nell'anno 79*, Naples 1979, pp. 96-104.

S. Treggiari, *Roman Freedmen during the Late Republic*, Oxford 1969.

A. Vigili, *Vita e costumi antichi : acconciature e maquillage*, Rome 1989.

L. Virno Bugno, M. Barronio Sura e l'industria della porpora ad Aquino, *Atti della Accademia Nazionale dei Lincei*, Rendiconti, XXVI, 1971, pp. 685-695, pl. I-IV.

M. G. Vogelsang-Eastwood, *A Brief Guide to the Cataloguing of Archaeological Textiles*, 1984.

P. Walton Rogers, L. Bender Jorgensen et al., *The Roman Textile Industry and its Influence*, 2001.

Djerba		**Délos**	
Cuve 1	Longueur : 7, 20 m; Largeur : 2, 24 m	Cuve 1	Longueur : 3, 35 m; Largeur : 1, 37 m; Profondeur : 0, 70m; Trou d'écoulement Cubage : 3m³
Cuve 2	Longueur : 5, 80 m; Largeur : 1,45 m; Profondeur : 1, 45m; Cubage : environ 12m³	Cuve 2	Longueur : 2, 50 m; Largeur : 1, 23 m; Profondeur : 0, 65m; Trou d'écoulement Cubage : environ 2m³
Bassin 1	Longueur : 11, 20m; Largeur : 2,90 m Trou d'écoulement	Bassin 1	Diamètre : 1, 15m
Bassin 2	Longueur : 9, 55m; Largeur : 2, 90m; Profondeur : 0, 65m; Trou d'écoulement Cubage : environ 18m³		

Tableau 1. Djerba et Délos au confrontation.

Fig. 1. Stèle de C. Pupius Amicus, *purpurarius*, Musée de Parme.

L'IDENTIFICATION DES TANNERIES ANTIQUES PAR L'ARCHÉOLOGIE ET L'ARCHÉOZOOLOGIE

MARTINE LEGUILLOUX
(Centre archéologique du Var)

ABSTRACT: Leather played an important role in the daily life of ancient cultures, yet tanneries of the classical period are poorly understood. The main reason for this lacuna lies in the fact that tanneries were often located on the periphery of villas, areas that are rarely explored. Thus, archaeologists lack the knowledge of how to identify them. Five types of evidence have been considered for this study: epigraphical, architectural (plans), ethno-archaeological (more recent workshops where *chaîne opératoire* can be observed), archaeological (tools and facilities) and archaeozoological. The study is based upon the analysis of faunal remains and other archaeological and architectural evidence from the best preserved ancient tanneries in the Roman world, namely those at Pompeii.

On ne peut nier la place fondamentale du cuir dans la vie quotidienne des populations antiques. La rareté des découvertes d'objets en peau a longtemps fait sous-estimer l'importance de l'industrie du cuir dans l'économie d'une cité ou d'une communauté. Or le cuir était un des matériaux les plus largement utilisés ; il était omniprésent dans les activités économiques et dans la vie quotidienne, sous forme d'outres, de chaussures, de sangles, etc. Les installations pour le traitement des peaux et leur transformation en cuir devaient donc être très répandues dans les villes et dans le monde rural. Et pourtant, l'archéologie peine à les découvrir.

La raison d'une telle méconnaissance est vraisemblablement liée à la difficulté d'en identifier les vestiges. La découverte de fragments de cuir est limitée à des conditions très particulières, en milieux humides ou arides. En dehors de ces cas, seuls les vestiges archéologiques et le matériel non périssable permettent de reconnaître une activité artisanale de tannerie.

Les aménagements destinés au travail du cuir ne sont pas toujours aisément identifiables. Les divers équipements qui sont utilisés pour le traitement sont en effet peu spécifiques, qu'il s'agisse par exemple des cuves de trempage en bois ou creusées à même la terre, ou encore des jarres de type *dolia*. Les principales caractéristiques du travail du cuir, les gestes, les outils, et souvent même les équipements et les produits n'ont évolué que très peu avant les procédés modernes. Les pratiques dans les tanneries du Moyen Age et du début de l'époque moderne sont donc proches de celles de l'Antiquité et dans certains pays, notamment du Maghreb, ces méthodes traditionnelles sont encore employées (mais elles sont en voie de disparition).

Ainsi la détermination doit-elle s'appuyer sur un faisceau d'indices et doit-elle les croiser. Les indications sont de plusieurs ordres. Épigraphiques : la présence d'inscriptions ou de graffiti. Architecturales : l'organisation du plan, l'existence de cuves, d'établis, de canalisations d'adduction et d'évacuation d'eau. Ethno-archéologiques : la connaissance de la chaîne opératoire employée dans les tanneries traditionnelles encore en fonction au Maghreb est fondamentale pour comprendre l'agencement des vestiges antiques.Archéologiques : la découverte d'amphores servant au transport de l'alun et d'outils métalliques ou osseux utilisés par les tanneurs. Archéo-zoologiques : certaines proportions de restes osseux, tels que les bas de pattes et les cornes, sont typiques des tanneries.

Pour illustrer chacun de ces critères, nous prendrons des exemples connus et avérés de vestiges de tanneries d'époques romaines fouillées récemment, avec comme point de référence avant tout, la tannerie de Pompéi, la plus complète connue à ce jour. Certains points pourront être illustrés par des exemples sélectionnés dans des modèles de tanneries de diverses périodes, médiévale et moderne, voire contemporaine lorsqu'il s'agit de techniques utilisées dans des sociétés traditionnelles.

L'ÉPIGRAPHIE

Jusqu'à présent, une seule installation a livré un texte susceptible d'assurer son identification : dans la pièce d'entrée de la tannerie de Pompéi (*regio* I, *insula* 5, maison 2), un graffito écrit au charbon de bois indiquait : X / LMICORARIANO, dans lequel on trouve la racine de *coriarius,* le tanneur (*C. I. L.* IV, 4014).

LE PLAN

Le second élément à prendre en compte pour l'identification d'une tannerie est le plan et l'emplacement des équipements. Lorsque le plan d'une tannerie est suffisamment conservé, il apparaît clairement une organisation spatiale typique. La disposition des espaces de travail est en effet liée aux techniques de transformation des peaux, selon un ordre respecté dans l'Antiquité comme au Moyen Age et jusqu'à la période préindustrielle.

Les techniques de transformation des peaux comptaient trois phases (le travail de rivière, le tannage proprement dit, le corroyage ou finition). Pour l'Antiquité, les sources évoquent en effet chacune de ces étapes, parfois de façon indirecte, en précisant les produits utilisés. La reconstitution des procédés indique que les tanneurs antiques connaissaient et pratiquaient cette division du tannage en trois phases (*Dictionnaire archéologique des techniques* 1963 ; Forbes 1966), principe qui sera repris au Moyen Age et jusqu'à l'époque moderne.

La première de ces trois phases est celle que l'on nomme aujourd'hui le « travail de rivière » ; elle est destinée à éliminer les poils et les résidus graisseux. Théophraste (*H. P.* 9, 20, 3), Pline (XVII, 51 ; XXIII, 22 et 140) et Martial (VI, 93) mentionnent certains produits utilisés : les excréments, l'urine, seule ou associée à des végétaux comme les feuilles de mûriers reviennent régulièrement et sont encore employés dans les tanneries traditionnelles en Afrique du Nord (Jemma 1971). Les matières fécales y sont utilisées pour éliminer les poils : les peaux macèrent dans des fosses remplies de fiente de pigeons, à laquelle sont ajoutés parfois tous les résidus de la tannerie (chute de cuirs, poils). Cette macération entraîne une fermentation et un début de décomposition qui facilite l'élimination du pelage.

Cette étape était suivie par le tannage proprement dit, à l'alun, au sel, à la graisse ou au tanin d'écorce (Théophraste *H. P.* 3, 9, 1 ; Pline XIV, 98 ; XVI, 26 et 124 ; XXIV, 91 ;) ou de fruits (Pline XIII, 55, 63 et 113 ; XXIII, 107 ; XXIV, 91 ; XXIV, 109 ; Théophraste *Hist. pl.* 3, 18, 5). Dans les tanneries traditionnelle, le tannage végétal à l'aide d'écorce ou de fruits à haute teneur en tanin reste la pratique principale car il apporte une meilleure qualité au cuir.

La troisième phase, la finition, est appelée corroyage. Elle était éventuellement précédée de la teinture des cuirs. Pour la finition, l'alun était parfois employé pour « parfaire les cuirs » (Pline XXXV, 183 et 184). Le tannage végétal à l'écorce est toujours pratiqué en Afrique du Nord mais, pour les cuirs les plus souples, les finitions se font parfois à l'aide d'alun mélangé à des matières grasses, de l'huile généralement (Jemma 1971)

Cette organisation du travail influence nécessairement le plan des tanneries, les peaux devant subir ces trois étapes successivement afin d'être correctement tannées, le schéma de circulation des peaux à l'intérieur de la tannerie doit donc être conçu de façon à permettre de limiter les temps de manipulation et il doit être agencé de façon à faciliter le passage des peaux dans les différentes zones de traitement.

L'ordonnance des tanneries du Moyen Age et d'époque moderne se faisait selon ce principe : on y trouve trois zones distinctes. Cette caractéristique revient régulièrement dans les manuels de tannage de l'époque moderne et dans l'*Encyclopédie* de d'Alembert et Diderot (fig. 1.1). La tannerie idéale de l'époque moderne était installée en bordure de rivière où se déroulaient les premières opérations, d'élimination des poils. La zone située au-delà de cet espace était consacrée à la mise en cuve de tan, enfin le troisième espace comportait les ateliers de finition près de la sortie (Diderot, D'Alembert 1751-1758: 856).

Les tanneries pré-industrielles et traditionnelles d'Afrique du Nord présentent le même schéma, par exemple celles de Marrakech au Maroc (fig. 1.2). Les peaux arrivent pour les premières opérations dans une zone située près de l'entrée, mais dans ce cas, localisée dans une cour ; puis elles circulent ensuite dans plusieurs zones en périphérie notamment dans les cuves à tan, pour revenir dans les ateliers de corroyage, également situés près de l'entrée, dans de petits espaces de travail, face aux espaces prévus pour le travail de rivière (Jemma 1971: 68–75).

Le même principe régissait l'organisation de l'espace dans les tanneries pré-industrielles grecques (fig. 1.3). Une étude de K. Zarkia sur les tanneries abandonnées dans la première moitié du XXe siècle à Dimitsana dans le Péloponnèse, un grand centre de production de cuir (Zarkia 1997). Les complexes de très petites tailles, comportaient seulement deux ou trois pièces ; il était donc primordial que le plan soit agencé de façon optimale afin de limiter les temps de manipulation. Un plan de cheminement plus ou moins circulaire répondait parfaitement à ces exigences : les peaux arrivaient pour les premières opérations dans une zone située près de l'entrée, elles passaient ensuite dans plusieurs zones en périphérie pour revenir dans les ateliers de corroyage, situés aussi près de l'entrée.

Ce principe planimétrique se retrouve dans la tannerie de Pompéi, qui a conservé intacts son plan et son équipement. Elle est située dans l'*insula* V de la *regio* I, à l'intérieur de la ville mais en bordure immédiate du rempart, où elle occupe la presque totalité de l'îlot. Les dégagements de la fin du XIXe siècle (Mau 1874, 1875, Sogliano 1874, Viola, 1879) ont mis à jour un vaste espace consacré à l'industrie du cuir, divisé en trois zones par leur fonction et leurs équipements (fig. 2) :

1° La première zone était localisée dans le péristyle de l'ancienne maison occupée par la tannerie. On y accédait par l'entrée donnant sur la rue, elle était bordée sur deux côtés par un portique. Dans cette zone, les peaux fraîches subissaient les premières opérations de traitement, c'est l'espace destiné au travail de rivière, un secteur où fut retrouvé des outils caractéristiques de cette phase.

2° Une deuxième zone était destinée au tannage, une grande salle caractérisée par une batterie de cuves. Les peaux qui y étaient transportées devaient rester pendant un temps relativement long pour subir les différentes opérations de tannage.

3° Pour finir les peaux quittaient la salle de tannage et on les transportait à nouveau vers le portique de la cour, où se déroulaient les opérations de finition des cuirs, le corroyage : le battage, l'étirage, éventuellement la teinture. La zone destinée au finition du cuir, divisée par des murets transversaux, contenait les équipements utilisés pour les finitions, *dolia* de foulage et de rinçage, établi, cuves.

L'ethno-archéologie et les équipements liés à la chaîne opératoire

Les études ethnologiques fournissent un cadre pour restituer l'enchaînement des opérations dans la tannerie. Chaque étape doit pouvoir trouver une traduction matérielle susceptible d'être retrouvée par l'archéologie.

Le travail de rivière

Le travail de rivière, qui comme son nom l'indique, se faisait à l'époque médiévale et moderne en bordure de rivières car elle comportait un trempage en eau claire (la trempe) destiné à éliminer les résidus comme le sang et les poils, laisse généralement peu de traces d'équipements. Le trempage des peaux dans des produits corrosifs (urines : Pline XVII, 51 ; *Géop.* 2, 22, 1 ; dans des bains d'urine et de feuilles de mûrier : Pline XXIII, 140) ou qui entraîne une dégradation des tissus (excréments : Michnâh *Keth.* VII, 10) pouvaient se faire dans des baquets en bois ou dans des fosses comme dans les tanneries préindustrielles d'Afrique du Nord et ne laisser en conséquence aucune trace visible lors d'une fouille. Aussi aucun équipement lié à ce type de travail n'a été identifié jusqu'à présent pour les périodes antiques.

Pourtant elle devait être systématiquement effectuée et cette première phase est attestée par les sources dès la période classique grecque, cette opération était semble-t-il alors confiée à un artisan indépendant, chargé de nettoyer les peaux pour le tanneur (Aristophane *Ploutos,* 167–168).
Aucun équipement n'est même nécessaire en cas « d'échauffe naturelle », pratique élémentaire qui consistait à empiler les peaux les unes sur les autres pour les amener à la limite de la putréfaction. Cette technique simple avait certainement cours dans l'Antiquité, comme le suggère un pamphlet du poète Martial (VI, 93) qui évoque les peaux aux odeurs nauséabondes que convoitent les chiens dans le Trastevere, quartier des tanneurs.

À la fin de cette première phase, les peaux sont prêtes à recevoir le passage du couteau à lame semi-circulaire, outil spécialisé qui permet l'élimination du pelage.

Le travail de tannage

Il en va autrement de la phase de tannage proprement dite. Le tannage consiste à mettre les « peaux vertes » en contact avec des produits fortement tanniques. Par osmose, le tanin imprègne les fibres dermiques et assure leur imperméabilité et leur imputrescibilité. Les produits les plus couramment utilisés étaient des végétaux à forte concentration d'acide tannique, comme la noix de galle, les écorces d'arbres, certains fruits (voir la liste des produits utilisés et des références dans Forbes 1966), mais peut-être aussi l'alun (Pline XXXV, 183 et 184 : ce texte, peu clair, suggère plutôt son emploi pour la finition des cuirs et non pour le tannage proprement dit) et la graisse (Caton *Agr.* 135, 3 : pour les courroies de pressoirs).

Pour l'immersion des peaux dans des bains de tanins, des équipements étaient nécessaires, des cuves généralement : celles-ci pouvaient être en bois, de forme carrée, comme dans le fortin romain de Vindolanda en Bretagne (Birley 1977). Elles pouvaient être creusées dans la terre sous le niveau de la nappe phréatique, comme dans la tannerie du *vicus* de Liberchies, en Belgique où les parois sont en osier (Dewert, Severs 1989). Ailleurs, les cuves étaient bâties : en briques comme à Saepinum où elles sont tronconiques (De Caro 1991) ou en moellons enduits de mortier de tuileau comme à Pompéi. Dans ce dernier cas, elles sont de grande taille (1,30 m à 1,60 m) et forment des cylindres plus ou moins réguliers, profonds d'un mètre et demi environ.

Il faut également souligner que les cuves de trempage peuvent être absentes des petites unités de production où l'on pouvait les remplacer par des jarres. Aucune référence archéologique ne permet de l'affirmer, mais l'iconographie égyptienne le suggère. Quelques fresques représentent le travail des peaux à l'époque pharaonique et montrent ce détail (Davis N. G. 1943 [reed. 1973] ; Junker 1957), la fresque la mieux conservée est celle de la tombe d'un noble nommé Rekhmiré, du Nouvel Empire, XVIIIe dynastie, entre 1500 et 1300 av. J.-C.).

Le travail de corroyage ou de finition des cuirs

La finition consistait à battre les cuirs, les oindre de graisse ou d'alun, pour les assouplir ou encore, à les lustrer avec un outil à lame sans tranchant (l'étire). Dans la tannerie de Pompéi, de nouvelles campagnes de fouilles entreprises depuis l'automne 2001 ont permis de mieux cerner l'utilisation de certaines zones et en particulier celle où se pratiquait le corroyage (Leguilloux 2002). Elle était équipée de structures destinées à la finition des cuirs, les plus représentatifs sont des *dolia* alimentés par une arrivée d'eau et un établi.

Le rinçage des peaux est nécessaire à de nombreuses étapes du traitement, en particulier après le tannage afin d'éliminer le surplus de tan et assouplir les peaux. La tannerie de Pompéi est équipée de trois *dolia* probablement destinés à cette activité de rinçage. Chacun d'eux était alimenté par des arrivées d'eau pour assurer un remplissage régulier (fig. 3). Ce type de structure est jusqu'à présent unique, mais il existe un équipement que l'on retrouve à la fois dans les tanneries modernes et à Pompéi : un établi pour battre le cuir, l'oindre de graisse ou d'alun (fig. 3). À Pompéi, il est placé dans la zone consacrée au corroyage : il s'agit d'une pierre monolithe calcaire de forme rectangulaire, posée sur des matériaux de récupération.

On retrouve le même type d'équipement dans la tannerie moderne (fig. 4). Dans les ateliers de corroyage des tanneries du XVIIIe siècle, un établi servait toujours à battre les cuirs qu'on assouplissait avec des maillets, après leur sortie des bains de tan et le rinçage. Dans les planches de l'*Encyclopédie* de Diderot et d'Alembert sont représentés les outils et les équipements composant une tannerie au XVIIIe siècle. Parmi ces équipements se trouve un établi en bois sur lequel étaient manipulés les cuirs subissant les opérations de corroyage, notamment le battage au maillet (Diderot, D'Alembert 1751-1758: 858).

Les outils et les conteneurs

Un quatrième critère d'identification se fonde sur les vestiges mobiliers. L'outillage du tanneur comportait peu d'instruments, mais très spécifiques et adaptés à chaque étape du processus. Un certain nombre de ces outils ont été retrouvés sur des sites de tanneries antiques. L'ensemble le plus complet provient de Pompéi : un lot de trois outils a été abandonné dans la cour du péristyle (fig. 5.1) : un couteau à lame métallique arquée, un outil à lame métallique rectangulaire et un couteau à lame semi-circulaire.

1° Le couteau à lame arquée était utilisé pour la première phase du traitement des peaux, le travail de rivière. Il servait à éliminer le pelage des peaux. Son emploi n'a pas changé entre l'Antiquité et l'époque moderne. On posait la peau sur un tronc d'arbre scié dans sa longueur et posé sur des tréteaux asymétriques afin de former un angle par rapport au tanneur qui se tenait debout. On passait le couteau sur la peau en mouvements de va et vient, pour éliminer les poils, les graisses et les chairs. Les gestes et les outils sont parfaitement illustrés dans l'*Encyclopédie* de Diderot et d'Alembert (fig. 5.2). Des outils métalliques aux formes très proches ont été découverts, à Mayence parmi des débris de peaux. Dans le camp militaire de Vindonissa, près de Bâle, ces couteaux ronds, en fer, ne possédaient qu'une seule poignée (Gansser-Burckhardt, 1942: fig.14). Ces couteaux n'étaient pas forcément en métal : on pouvait les fabriquer en os ou en bois, comme les quatorze demi-disques trouvés dans la tannerie du début du IIe siècle après J.-C. à Vindolanda (Birley 1977: fig. 36). Ces objets ont en effet été identifiés par les fouilleurs comme des ustensiles destinés à l'élimination des poils ; ils étaient associés à un grand peigne en bois destiné au peignage des toisons. Sur le site de Liberchies, des côtes de bovins découvertes en grand nombre présentent des traces de polissage sur leur face interne, ce qui suppose leur utilisation pour l'épilation.

2° Le deuxième outil, à lame rectangulaire, est dénommée aujourd'hui étire ; il était encore utilisé au XIXe siècle pour parfaire les cuirs. On passait cette lame sans tranchant sur la surface du cuir, généralement au préalable enduit de graisse pour allonger les fibres du cuir et l'assouplir. C'est un outil de corroyage.

3° Le troisième outil servait aux tanneur et au cordonnier à découper des pièces de cuir. Il s'agit d'un outil très ancien que l'on retrouve dans des fresques du Nouvel Empire en Egypte. En complément à la fresque des tanneurs, dans la tombe de Rekhmiré, une autre fresque montre le travail des cordonniers et l'utilisation du couteau semi-circulaire (Davis 1943). Le même couteau était utilisé par les cordonniers de la Grèce antique, il est représenté sur des vases à figures noires puis à figures rouges qui montrent ces artisans au travail (Junker 1957).

À ces instruments spécifiques, il faut ajouter les amphores. Philippe Borgard a montré dans sa thèse que les amphores Richborough 527 largement répandues dans l'occident romain, notamment en Bretagne, étaient fabriquées à Lipari et qu'elles avaient servi à transporter l'alun natif récolté sur cette île volcanique (Borgard 2001). L'alun était principalement utilisé pour mordancer les fibres textiles et fixer les couleurs ; la présence d'amphores de Lipari dans une installation artisanale est donc un indice fort qu'il s'agit d'une teinturerie. Mais l'alun étant aussi employé pour tanner et pour corroyer les cuirs, les amphores de Lipari peuvent signaler une tannerie. De fait, plusieurs amphores de Lipari ont été trouvées dans un remblai déposé après le tremblement de terre de 62 après J.-C. dans la rue longeant la tannerie de Pompéi.

Les restes osseux

Un dernier critère est fourni par l'étude des ossements trouvés en fouille. Les os rejetés par les tanneurs correspondent aux déchets du travail des peaux et la prédominance de certains types d'ossements est caractéristique de cette activité.

Aucun texte antique ne signale cette particularité de l'activité du tanneur, mais les analyses archéozoologiques de ces dernières années ont permis de fixer un certain nombre de critères permettant de distinguer un dépôt contenant des déchets de tannerie. Les bouchers qui abattaient les animaux laissaient, sur les peaux, les extrémités de l'animal : les pieds, les cornes, parfois les queues. Ainsi le tanneur achetait ces peaux en sachant le sexe, l'age, ou l'espèce de l'animal.

C'était une pratique connue encore aux époques post-médiévales, au XVIe siècle dans la tannerie allemande par exemple (fig. 6) : une gravure sur bois montre un tanneur en train de retirer le pelage d'une peau disposée sur un chevalet ; derrière lui, des peaux fraîches attendent d'être préparées ; les os des membres et les crânes des animaux leur sont encore attachés.

La pratique qui consiste à laisser les extrémités sur les peaux est confirmée par l'archéozoologie et l'étude de restes osseux découverts dans des zones de tanneries post-médiévales en Hollande et en Angleterre, mais aussi à Marseille pendant l'Antiquité Tardive (Ve siècle après J.-C.) (fig. 7). Enfin pour confirmer les méthodes de dépouillage spécifique des peaux destinées aux tanneurs, on dispose désormais de données recueillies dans la tannerie de Pompéi. Un petit dépotoir qui avait échappé aux dégagements du XIXe siècle a été retrouvé dans la cour, scellé par les *lapili* de l'éruption. Il contenait des fragments osseux appartenant à part égale à des moutons et des chèvres. Ces restes se composaient à 90 % d'os de pieds : métacarpes, métatarses, carpes, tarses et phalanges, qui correspondent aux sabots (3e phalanges).

Selon les dépôts, on retrouve une prédominance d'ossements des pieds, c'est-à-dire les phalanges et les métapodes, ou bien les os des pieds et les cornes.

Laisser les extrémités sur les peaux impliquait des techniques de dépouille et de découpe particulière. La découpe au niveau des pieds et plus particulièrement des carpes et des tarses laisse peu de traces de découpe, en revanche lorsque les chevilles osseuses sont attachées aux peaux, les coups de tranchet sont bien visibles sur la corne, la dépouille restant attachée au fragment d'os crânial, comme à Marseille au Ve siècle ap. J.-C. (fig. 8).

Ces méthodes de dépouillage ont été très longtemps employées : elles sont attestées, par exemple, par les restes osseux trouvés dans une tannerie du IXe siècle à Huy en Belgique ; le résultat est significatif pour les os de moutons et de chèvres (fig. 9).

Le dépouillage des bovins était différent : on laissait sur la dépouille, le haut du crâne, le frontal sectionné au niveau des orbites et les cornes. Ce type de découpe a été observé dans le matériel de Marseille (Leguilloux 1998) et dans des dépôts de la tannerie de Liberchies en Belgique.

L'archéologue dispose donc de cinq types d'indices pour identifier une tannerie : l'épigraphie, le plan, les installations telles que les cuves, le mobilier archéologique (outils, amphores) et la structure très particulière de la faune. Les conditions sont désormais réunies pour que, à l'occasion de fouilles extensives aux abords des villes antiques, le long de cours d'eau par exemple, de nouvelles installations de tannage soient identifiées.

BIBLIOGRAPHIE

Baxter I. L., 1998, Late medieval tawyer's waste and pig skeletons in early post-medieval pits from Bonners Lane, Leicester, England, U.K, *Anthropozoologica*, 1998, 28, p. 55-63.

Birley R., 1977, *Vindolanda. A Roman frontier post on Hadrian's Wall,* London, Thames and Hudson, 184 p.

Borgard P., 2001 *L'alun de l'Occident romain*, Aix-en-Provence (Thèse dactylographiée).

Davis N. G., 1943 [rééd. 1973], *The tomb of Rekh-mi-Rê at Thèbes*, New York, Metropolitan Museum, 188 p., 122 pl.

De Caro S., 1991, Une conceria a Saepinum, *in* : *Samnium*, p. 250-251.

Dewert J.-P., Severs L., 1989, Une tannerie gallo-romaine dans un quartier artisanal aux "Bons-Villers"-Liberchies (Ht), *Actes du Congrès de Namur, 18-21 Aoû t1988*, Namur, p. 147-152.

Dictionnaire archéologique des techniques, 1963, Paris, Éditions de l'Accueil.

Diderot D., D'Alembert J. D., 1751-1758, *Encyclopédie ou dictionnaire raisonné sur les sciences, les arts libéraux et les arts méchaniques*, 6, Paris.

Forbes R. J., 1966, *Studies in ancient technology,* 5, Leiden, E. J. Brill.

Gansser-Burckhardt A., 1942, *Das Leder und seine Verarbeitung im römischen Legionslager Vindonissa*. Basel.

Gautier A., 1992-1993, Notes sur deux assemblages archeozoologiques de la période médiévale à Huy, *Vie archéologique*, 40, p. 44-48.

Jemma D., 1971, *Les tanneurs de Marrakech*. Mémoires du Centre de Recherches Anthropologiques Préhistoriques et Ethnographiques, XIX, Alger.

Junker H., 1957, *Weta und das LederKunsthandwerk im Alten Reich*, Österreichische Akademie der Wissenschaften, 231/1.

Leguilloux M., 1998, La faune tardive du port de Marseille (Ve s. - VIIe s. ap. J.-C.) d'après les fouilles de la Bourse (1980-1981), *Revue Archéologique de Narbonnaise*, 31, p. 233-253.

Leguilloux M., 2002, Techniques et équipements de la tannerie romaine : l'exemple de l'*officina coriaria* de Pompéi, *in* : Beyries A., Audoin-Rouzeau F. — *Le travail du cuir de la préhistoire à nos jours. Actes des 22e rencontres internationales d'archéologie et d'histoire d'Antibes*. Antibes, ADPCA, p. 268-282.

Mau A., 1874, 1875, *Scavi di Pompei*, Napoli.

Prummel W., 1978, Animal Bones from tannery pits of s'-Hertogenbosch, *Berichten van de Ryksdienst voor het Oudheid Kundig Bodem-onderzoek*, 28, p. 399-422.

Serjeantson D.,1989, Animal remains and the tanning trade, *in* : Serjeantson, D. , Waldron, T. (eds.), *Diet and crafts in towns,* Oxford, BAR British series 199, p. 129-146.

Sogliano A., 1874, Notizia dei Nuovi scavi, *in* : Fiorelli, G., *Giornale degli scavi di Pompei,* 3, col 49-52, Napoli.

Viola M., 1879, *Pompei e la regione soterrata dal Vesuvio*, Napoli.

Zarkia K., 1997, *Preindustrial tanning in Greece*. Athens, The ETBA Cultural foundation, 45 p.

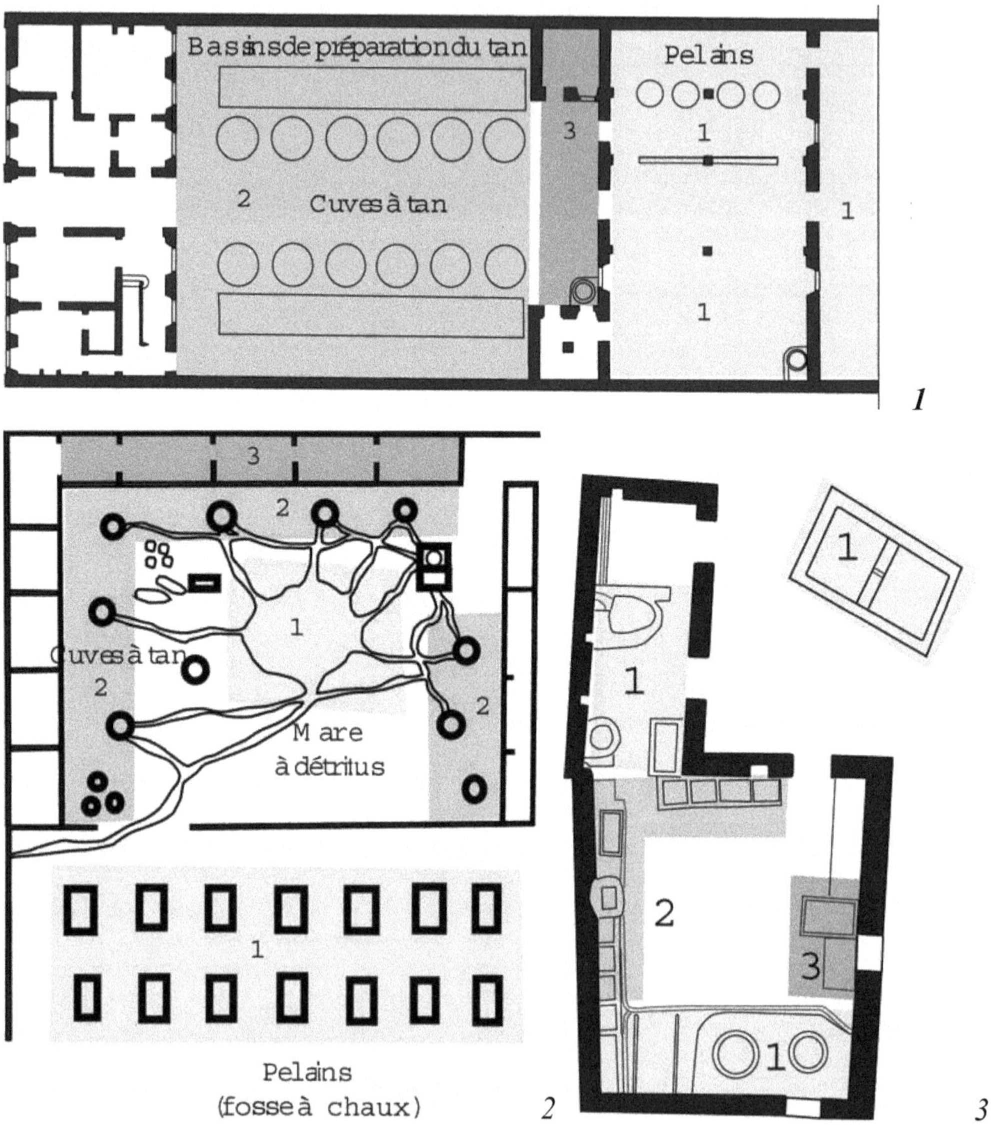

Fig. 1. *1°* Le plan d'une tannerie d'époque moderne (d'après l'*Encyclopédie* de Diderot et d'Alembert 1751-1758, pl. I du chapitre sur les tanneurs). *2°* Plan des tanneries traditionnelles modernes grecques (d'après Zarkia 1997, fig. 6). *3°* Plan d'une tannerie traditionnelle à Marrakech (d'après Jemma 1971, fig. 32).

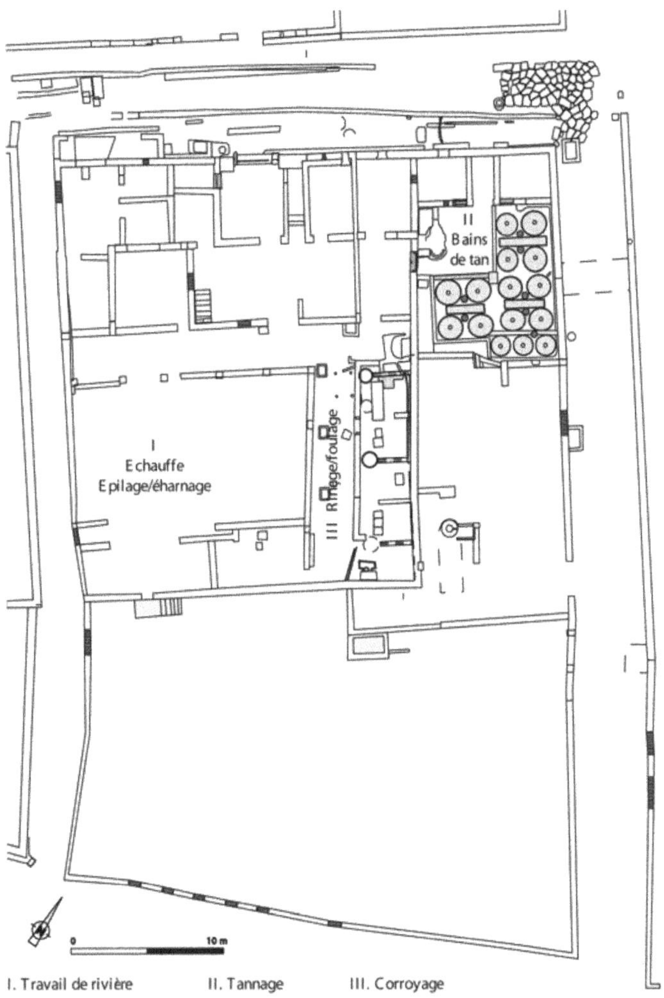

Fig. 2. Plan de la tannerie de Pompéi et les trois zones de travail (fond de plan établi en 2002 par le Centre Jean Bérard).

Fig. 3. La zone de corroyage de Pompéi avec *dolium* et établi.

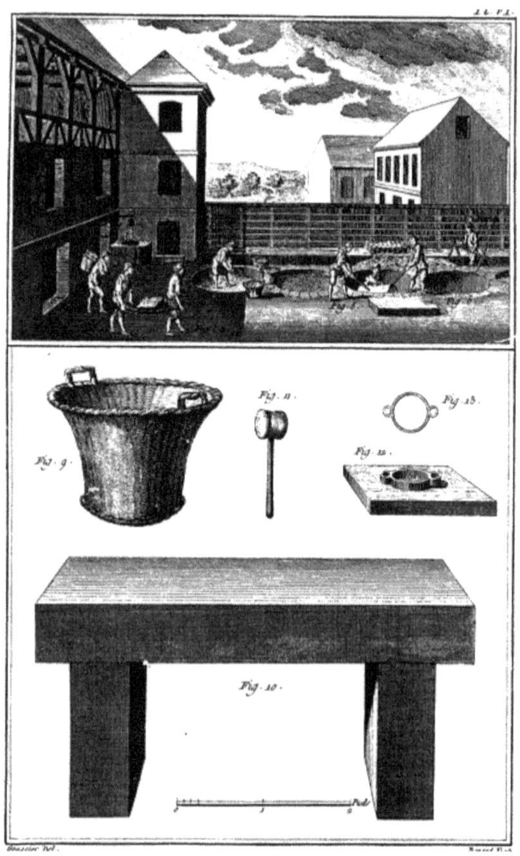

Fig. 4. Comparaison avec l'établi de l'*Encyclopédie* de Diderot et d'Alembert 1751-1758, (pl. VI du chapitre sur les tanneurs).

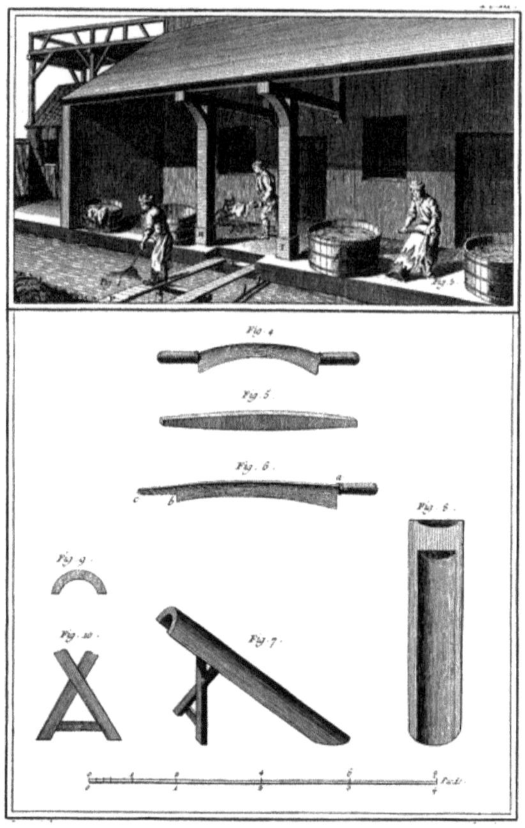

Fig. 5. Le travail de rivière et le travail de cuves et les outils du tanneur analogues à ceux de Pompéi (d'après l'*Encyclopédie* de Diderot et d'Alembert 1751-1758, pl. III du chapitre sur les tanneurs.

Fig. 6. Une gravure allemande du XVIe siècle (d'après Searjantson 1989).

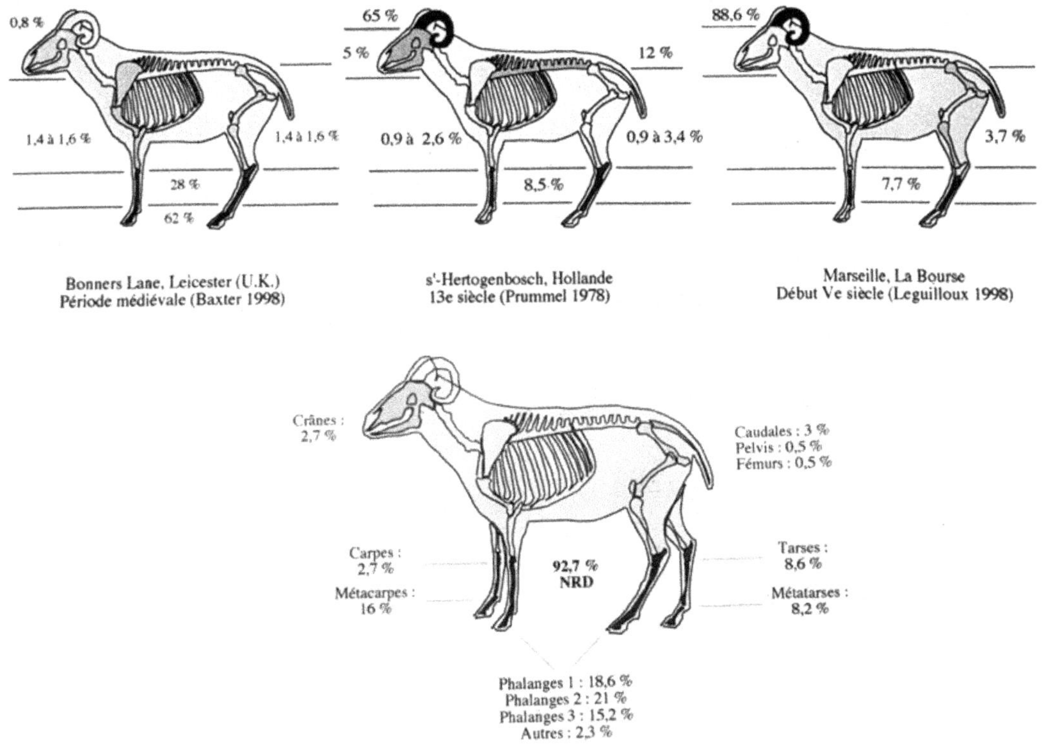

Fig. 7. Découvertes de restes osseux dans des zones de tanneries antiques, médiévales et postmédiévales.

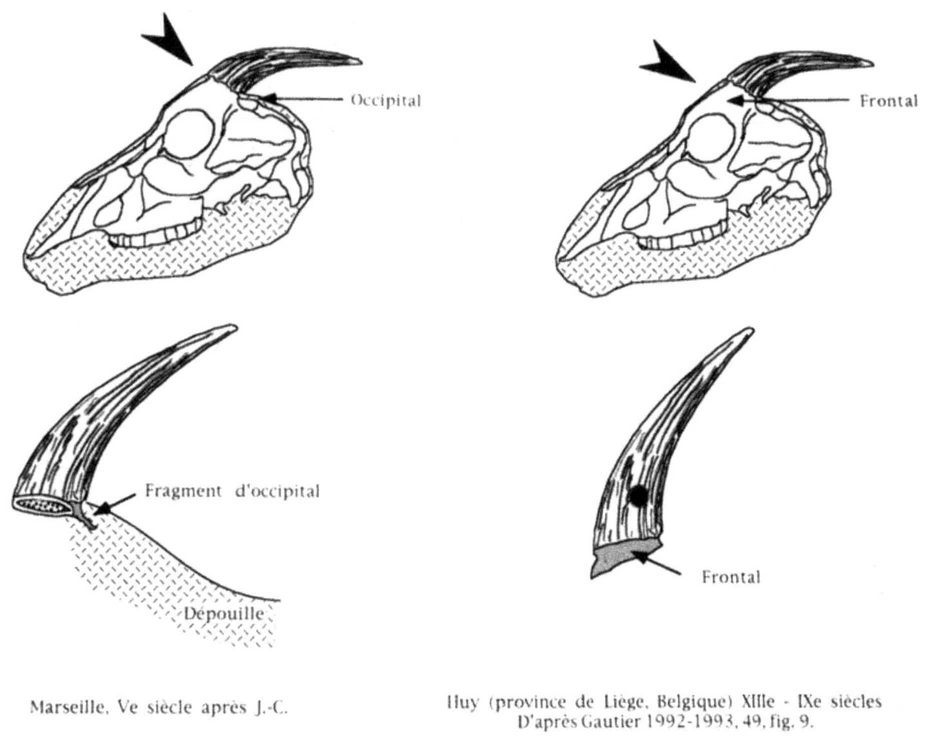

Fig. 8. Technique de découpe des chevilles osseuses de petits ruminants.

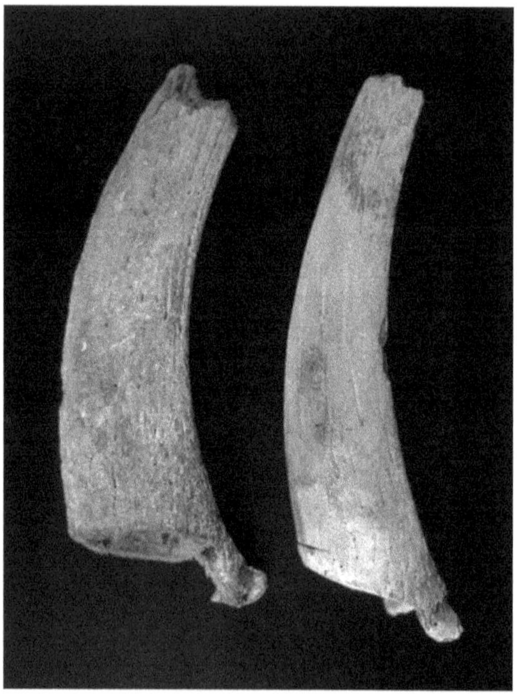

Fig. 9. Les traces sur les ossements : chevilles osseuses de chèvres (Marseille, Bourse, Ve siècle ap. J.-C.).

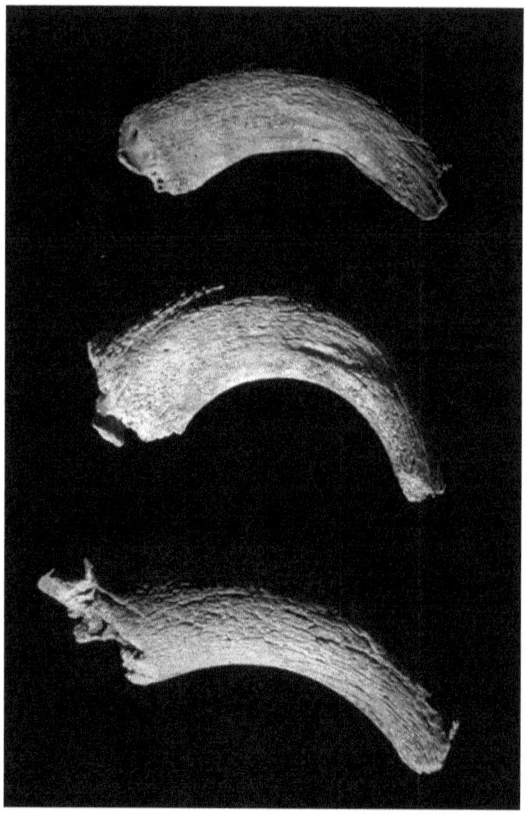

Fig. 10. Les traces de découpe sur les ossements : chevilles osseuses de brebis (Marseille, Bourse, Ve siècle ap. J.-C.).

Linee metodologiche ed esempi di approccio per lo studio dell'artigianato tessile laniero nella *Venetia et Histria*

Jacopo Bonetto - Andrea Raffaele Ghiotto
(Università di Padova)

Abstract: The theme of the wool-textile industry in the Veneto region, very well developed in the Roman period, requires a more holistic type of survey. A correct approach to the material, theorized in this paper, requires scholars not only to consider literary and epigraphic sources, but a detailed examination of archaeological evidence as well. The evidence from Altino and Padova, when compared, allow us to reconstruct quite specifically the different economic dynamics of these two important centers of wool production. Based upon the evidence at hand, the first section concerns the commercio of high-quality wool from Altino, while the second part of this study focuses upon the sale of finished products (*gausapa*).*

Verso una metodologia integrata

Fin dai primi studi sull'economia pastorale antica nella *Venetia* compiuti presso l'Istituto di Archeologia dell'Università di Padova da parte di A. Marchiori agli inizi degli anni '90 (Marchiori 1990), l'approccio metodologico è apparso orientato verso una forma di stretta integrazione delle più diverse fonti di informazioni.

Questo indirizzo di ricerca è stato condiviso e ribadito in modo sempre più marcato nei successivi lavori relativi all'argomento (Bonetto 1997) e appare attualmente come la linea guida più appropriata entro cui procedere con le ulteriori fasi di un'articolato programma di indagine che, partito dallo studio dell'allevamento migratorio nel territorio di *Patavium* (Bonetto 1997; c.s.a), si sta da un lato gradatamente allargando verso le regioni limitrofe (Bonetto 1999a; 1999b; Modugno 1999; Rosada 1999; Ghiotto 2000; Modugno 2000; 2000-2001; c.s.) e dall'altro va ad affrontare sia la lettura di altre forme di conduzione del bestiame e il loro rapporto con l'agricoltura (Bonetto c.s.b) sia lo studio del rilievo economico dei prodotti derivati (Bonetto 2002: latte e formaggio), primo fra tutti la lana (Bonetto 2001; Basso, Bonetto, Ghiotto c.s.), che costituisce l'oggetto di queste brevi note.

Il viatico più consono ad una comprensione del fenomeno pastorale e delle dinamiche economiche connesse alle produzioni derivate come la lana appare quello di una metodologia integrata che punti sia a far dialogare le più tradizionali fonti storiche (epigrafi e testi letterari) con i dati archeologici e le informazioni provenienti da altri campi disciplinari (la geomorfologia, la botanica, la zoologia), sia ad aprirsi verso la ricchissima documentazione medievale e moderna sui fenomeni pastorali (Borgherini 1964; Panciera 1996; Bonetto 1997: 173-181; Demo 2001)[1] per trarne rigeneranti indizi e chiavi di lettura degli assetti antichi.

Un tale approccio "aperto", tanto in senso disciplinare quanto in quello cronologico, mira a far convergere sullo stesso piano di analisi e discussione esperienze e competenze tradizionalmente divise tra l'archeologo e lo storico, l'epigrafista e il medievista, lo zoologo e l'esperto di assetti vegetativi del territorio, come di altri specialisti ancora, abitualmente poco portati al pieno dialogo. La prospettiva epistemologica è evidentemente quella della più radicale multidisciplinarietà, che appare nella letteratura corrente tanto reclamata quanto disattesa, con il fine di ricondurre ad unità interpretativa gli aspetti della realtà antica spesso poco compresi perché appunto frammentati secondo logiche d'indagine monosettoriali.

Questo percorso è apparso peraltro da subito complesso e rischioso, perché ha comportato da parte di singoli studiosi di antichistica l'impegno di unificare risultati di ricerche provenienti da settori assai diversificati, ma al contempo risulta di massima efficacia nel cogliere in profondità fenomeni solo in parte comprensibili se letti attraverso un filtro ermeneutico singolo, sia esso archeologico, storico-epigrafico, topografico-territoriale, etnografico o di altro genere.

Oltre che nella selezione delle fonti, la linea metodologica attualmente seguita punta anche ad innovare il modo di affrontare l'argomento stesso oggetto di interesse. La lana è infatti divenuta oggetto di interesse per l'intero suo ciclo, dal momento dell'allevamento degli animali fino al commercio dei prodotti tessili finiti, passando in rassegna, come in una catena di eventi consequenziali e collegati in forma sistemica, tutte le fasi che interessano il trattamento della materia prima, dei tessuti e dei capi finiti, senza privilegiare o escludere nessuna di esse.

La terza scelta importante sul piano metodologico è stata quella di prendere in considerazione il "fenomeno lana" all'interno di un preciso e coerente quadro di riferimento territoriale, che nel caso specifico è quello della regione nord-adriatica compresa tra il lago di Garda e la penisola istriana. Questa si caratterizza in modo molto unitario non solo per le vicende storico-culturali che ne hanno segnato l'evoluzione dall'età del Ferro fino ad epoca Medievale, ma pure sotto il profilo geografico, climatico e vegetativo, fattori questi fortemente condizionanti l'allevamento e le derivate produzioni. Tale accentuata unitarietà storico-ambientale della regione, che al tempo stesso ne marca la differenza su quelle contermini, ha generato nei diversi centri urbani e nei settori territoriali che la compongono fenomeni produttivi e commerciali fortemente simili tra loro, così da far apparire l'analisi unitaria del nord-est della Penisola non solo come la più idonea, ma pure come assolutamente necessaria.

Questa complessiva impostazione della ricerca tesa ad ampliare lo spettro delle fonti di conoscenza e gli orizzonti di indagine entro un quadro geografico unitario costituisce nel panorama degli studi sull'argomento un elemento di almeno parziale novità.

Così infatti, per quanto riguarda l'utilizzo delle fonti, nei lavori più approfonditi sull'argomento inerenti l'ambito cisalpino, tra cui sono da ricordare almeno quelli di G.E.F. Chilver (1941), di F. Sartori (1964), di E. Noé (1974), di E. Buchi (1987), di M. Verzár-Bass (1987), di A. Giovannini (1993) e di F. Vicari (1994; 2001), la precisione documentaria e l'ampia lettura socio-economica dei fenomeni tendono a basarsi in via prevalente sulla documentazione epigrafica, con analisi meno serrata del patrimonio documentario letterario e menzioni spesso cursorie della documentazione archeologica; del tutto marginali e di semplice corredo documentario sono poi i riferimenti alle forme di continuità medievale dei fenomeni, lasciando così poco spazio all'integrazione tra diversi dati utili. Sulla stessa linea, pur nella feconda varietà di approcci, appaiono altri studi sulla lana compiuti in ambito italico, come nei casi dell'analisi della produzione urbana di H. Loane (1938), di quella apula di F. Grelle e M. Silvestrini (2001) e di quella pompeiana di W. O. Moeller (1976).

Inoltre i lavori citati hanno rivolto l'attenzione, spesso a seconda delle fonti impiegate, solo su uno o su alcuni dei momenti che compongono l'intero ciclo produttivo della lana; in rapporto poi al quadro territoriale considerato, gli studiosi hanno preso in esame comprensori molto ampi come l'intera Cisalpina, mentre in altri casi lo studio è stato affrontato solo entro i limiti di una regione amministrativa moderna (Veneto) o di un'area geografica definita (Istria), ma in nessun caso si è preso in esame il comprensorio dell'antica *Venetia et Histria* nella sua omogeneità ed esclusività.

Va in ogni caso notato come a fronte di queste osservazioni, che vogliono essere esclusivamente uno spunto di discussione sul piano del metodo, tutti gli studi citati hanno ottenuto risultati basilari sul piano delle conoscenze relative alla produzione, lavorazione e commercio della lana in età antica. E da queste basi infatti si è recentemente ripartiti con quell'approccio metodologico "multispettrale" cui si è fatto riferimento al fine di cogliere nuovi elementi interpretativi su un fenomeno economico sicuramente tra i più importanti della regione per il periodo antico.

La ricerca, che è tuttora in corso di svolgimento, ha preso le mosse da una raccolta sistematica di tutte le epigrafi edite o in corso di edizione e dei passi letterari che fanno riferimento alle produzioni laniere dell'Italia nord-orientale (Basso, Bonetto, Ghiotto c.s.). Fin dalla prima lettura del sostanzioso *corpus* di iscrizioni e di passi di autori è emersa la necessità di definire le modalità d'uso e distinguere le potenzialità informative di ogni categoria di documenti. È già stato in altra sede notato come le fonti epigrafiche e letterarie costituiscano in effetti un filtro di lettura della realtà antica da usare con estrema cautela e in modo differenziato a seconda dei casi (Jongman 2000: 189).

Una prima distinzione netta è opportuno creare tra le fonti letterarie e quelle epigrafiche, poiché originate da contesti diversi e non dotate del medesimo valore informativo. Un'epigrafe, nell'assoluta maggioranza dei casi, ci attesta l'esistenza di un artigiano o di un collegio di operatori e vale sostanzialmente come riferimento ad una situazione unica o circoscritta nello spazio e nel tempo. Quelle epigrafiche sono così fonti che potremo definire "analitiche". Al contrario le fonti letterarie costituiscono una fonte "di sintesi", perché la notizia riferita da un autore relativa alla produzione di lana o di vesti di un'area o di una città ha origine da una raccolta di una pluralità di notizie e non può essere mai frutto di attestazioni sporadiche o occasionali. La menzione di un prodotto grezzo o lavorato nella letteratura poetica o tecnico-scientifica diventa così il segno di una sua affermazione, per periodi non brevi, non solo sul mercato locale delle aree d'origine, ma pure su quello esterno fino a raggiungere i contesti urbani dove solitamente operavano gli autori di età romana che ne recano l'eco. Inoltre gli stessi autori, soprattutto nel caso dei componimenti poetici, dovevano prestare attenzione ad utilizzare riferimenti a luoghi e prodotti "familiari" al pubblico cui era destinata l'opera; pertanto quanto è menzionato doveva vantare una notorietà e una diffusione stabile. E tutto questo presuppone, a monte, contesti d'origine del prodotto formati da plurime unità produttive, organizzazioni commerciali rodate e sistemi economici floridi connessi.

In sintesi se un'epigrafe può ricordare quasi sempre l'esistenza di una singola unità produttiva o commerciale, una fonte letteraria può provare l'esistenza di decine di unità produttive e un solido apparato commerciale di diffusione.

All'interno poi delle stesse fonti letterarie è però anche importante distinguere tra le diverse voci, in particolare tra quelle a carattere tecnico (come Varrone e Columella) le cui informazioni hanno superato un vaglio critico da parte degli stessi e costituiscono un'informazione puntuale e di alta affidabilità, da quelle più evidentemente poetiche o narrative (Marziale, Orazio, Virgilio e altri), la cui aderenza alla realtà dei fatti è invece molto più sfumata e debole.

La seconda parte del lavoro è consistita nella raccolta della documentazione archeologica[2], per la quale è necessario un discorso a parte; questo tipo di dati, sulla base della distinzione più sopra operata, può essere considerato una fonte "analitica" e non "di sintesi". Esiste però una netta sproporzione, tutta a svantaggio del ricercatore, tra il valore dei documenti archeologici per risolvere questioni tecniche e socio-economiche e la modestia numerica e qualitativa degli stessi, dovuta a diversi fattori: primo fra tutti vi è il disinteresse manifestato fino a pochi decenni fa dall'archeologia classica nei confronti di materiali di carattere "povero" (pesi da telaio, fusaiole, etc.); ma a ingigantire la carenza documentaria contribuisce in modo netto la natura stessa delle attività pastorali e di trattamento della lana, per lo più legate a strumenti, strutture e materiali provvisori e deperibili, privi quindi di visibilità nel record archeologico (Barker 1989; 1991; Basso, Bonetto, Ghiotto c.s.).

Dopo le fonti antiche e i documenti archeologici un altro grande bacino di acquisizione di informazioni utili è costituito dalla documentazione medievale. È universalmente riconosciuto e oggettivamente evidente che l'allevamento ovino con le derivate forme produttive siano fenomeni di "lunga durata", ma non è per nulla chiaro agli studiosi, in perenne dibattito su questo punto e divisi tra "continuisti" e "discontinuisti" (Quilici 1987; Giardina 1989: 97-98; Corbier 1991, con bibliografia di riferimento alla nota 6; Gabba 1994: 174-176), quali e quanti siano stati i mutamenti nelle forme di conduzione e sfruttamento del bestiame nel passaggio tra l'età del Ferro e il periodo romano, o, ancor più, nell'arco della difficile e complessa transizione tra l'epoca romana e il Medioevo, quando transumanza e mercato dei prodotti derivati tornano ad assumere contorni dimensionali ed economici di tutto rispetto.

In chi scrive è forte la convinzione che sia impossibile evidenziare forme di continuità diretta o di frattura assoluta nel corso delle varie fasi storiche, o ancora di trasferire modelli economici e di sfruttamento territoriale dal medioevo all'età antica, ma che sia invece corretto credere a fluttuazioni di periodo negli aspetti quantitativi dello sviluppo del fenomeno pastorale. È altrettanto chiara inoltre la convinzione che sia lecito selezionare ed isolare alcuni temi fondamentali o "elementi strutturali" primari che connotano e interessano il fenomeno allevatorio in qualsiasi epoca e ne costituiscono le chiavi di lettura diacroniche basilari. Per accennare ai più importanti si può indicare almeno: a) i rapporti con l'agricoltura; b) i sistemi infrastrutturali legati al movimento del bestiame; c) i rapporti con le risorse del territorio; d) i centri urbani di riferimento; e) le dimensioni del fenomeno; f) l'impatto economico sul territorio e le città; g) i tempi e le stagioni dell'allevamento e della transumanza; h) i prodotti derivati.

Si tratta di aspetti di base, dipendenti da fattori inalterati nel tempo (come il quadro geografico/climatico e il sistema insediativo principale) e perciò fortemente conservativi pur nel mutare delle forme politiche ed economiche delle regioni. Per il loro riproporsi ciclicamente o continuativamente in forme assai simili nelle epoche storiche più diverse, è quindi possibile, pur con grande cautela e attenzione, utilizzare la documentazione loro relativa di età alto o basso medievale per ricostruire assetti di età antica. Si realizza così un esame comparativo diacronico all'indietro nel tempo sfruttando l'insostituibile ricchezza documentaria post-antica per illuminare e congiungere i radi tasselli sopravvissuti della documentazione antica.

Un peso importante è stato infine dedicato allo studio di aspetti ambientali e zoologici legati al ciclo biologico degli ovini. Spesso infatti si dimentica, paradossalmente, che la lana è un prodotto della pecora e che dal suo regime nutrizionale e allevatorio dipende la qualità e la quantità della lana prodotta. È divenuto così fondamentale comprendere le necessità alimentari dell'animale, la qualità del foraggio delle diverse aree, la disponibilità di foraggio durante l'anno in rapporto al clima, la cura da prestare agli animali durante le diverse stagioni, le diverse tipologie di razze di ovini in relazione alle produzioni derivate, etc.

Seguendo le linee metodologiche fin qui tracciate si cercherà nelle pagine seguenti di affrontare i casi urbani più esemplificativi per il ciclo produttivo della lana in età antica, partendo dalla fase di fornitura della materia prima dall'allevamento ovino per seguire quindi i processi di trasformazione in capi d'abbigliamento e di commercializzazione degli stessi.

(J. B.)

L'INDUSTRIA E IL COMMERCIO DELLA LANA: I CASI DI PADOVA E ALTINO

Le testimonianze dell'attività laniera nella *Venetia et Histria* appaiono ampiamente distribuite nel territorio regionale[3], interessando a vario titolo quasi tutte le principali città venete e istriane[4]. Una vasta documentazione letteraria, epigrafica e archeologica testimonia tuttavia come l'allevamento ovino e la produzione della materia prima fossero gestiti in prevalenza dai grandi poli urbani di Altino e di Padova (da ultimo, Vicari 2001: 39-41) (Fig. 1).

Il primato di questi due centri sulle altre realtà della *X Regio*, con la sola eccezione di Aquileia, trova spiegazione nella loro favorevole collocazione geografica a diretto contatto con le migliori aree prative di pianura e, al tempo stesso, a breve distanza (km 40-60) dagli estesi pascoli estivi offerti dalle Prealpi venete (Bonetto 1999b). Inoltre gli stessi centri disponevano anche del controllo amministrativo e commerciale sulle frange lagunari produttrici di sale, sostanza fondamentale per l'allevamento ovi-caprino ed elemento "marcatore" di tutti i grandi contesti pastorali antichi (agri laziali, Tavoliere delle Puglie, Foci del Rodano)[5].

L'importanza del fenomeno allevatorio, che nel contesto territoriale veneto trovò le prerogative ideali per il suo pieno sviluppo, è stata chiarita grazie a recenti studi che hanno riletto in chiave funzionale come veri e propri "tratturi" per la transumanza (sino a poco tempo fa noti soltanto in Italia centrale) le due grandi direttrici stradali dell'"Arzeron della Regina" (Bonetto 1997) e della cosiddetta "via Claudia Augusta altinate" (Maschio 1999-2000; Rosada 2001), le quali, all'inizio del I sec. d.C., vennero a collegare le periferie di Padova e Altino[6] con le pendici prealpine.

Per quanto riguarda Altino, numerose sono le fonti letterarie che attestano l'eccellente qualità della produzione laniera e la continuità della pratica allevatoria nel corso dei primi secoli dell'Impero (Columella (VII, 2, 3), Marziale (XIV, 155: *Lanae albae*), Plinio il Giovane (ep. II, 11, 25) e Tertulliano (pall. III, 6)). In particolare, i passi di Columella e di Marziale rivelano che, nella seconda metà del I sec. d.C., la lana bianca di Altino era considerata una tra le più pregiate nel contesto dell'intero Mediterraneo e trovava confronto in Italia solamente nella produzione di Taranto (e dell'*Apulia* in genere), di Parma e di Modena.

Una conferma dell'ottima fama di cui godeva la lana altinate in età imperiale si trova nella straordinaria testimonianza offerta dall'Editto dei Prezzi di Diocleziano (301 d.C.). Tra le varie qualità di lane (*Edict. Diocl.*, ed. Giacchero, 25, 1-6), la fonte epigrafica ricorda infatti proprio quella di Altino come la seconda in ordine di prezzo per tutto l'Impero, preceduta soltanto da quella di Modena. In un altro passo dell'Editto, dedicato ai salari per i *lanarii* (*Edict. Diocl.*, ed. Giacchero, 21, 1-4), la lana altinate appare come una delle quattro produzioni (con quelle di Modena, Taranto e Laodicea di Frigia) degne della "denominazione d'origine", nettamente distinte dalle lane di minor pregio.

Più limitate sono invece le testimonianze archeologiche relative alla fase produttiva della materia prima. Esse sono costituite da alcune iscrizioni graffite su un vaso fittile e su diverse laminette plumbee impiegate come etichette per balle di lana (perlopiù non lavorata)[7], nonché da alcune cesoie da tosatore rinvenute in contesti tombali[8].

Circa il trattamento della lana grezza dopo la tosatura i dati non sono del tutto concordi. Nell'Editto dei Prezzi la lana altinate è una tra le poche ad essere indicata senza la qualifica di "lavata". Questo fatto induce a ritenere che la fibra fosse in genere commercializzata con il rivestimento di grasso naturale (*lana sucida*)[9], mantenuto probabilmente per agevolare la filatura a mano o per consentire la realizzazione di vesti più resistenti per i climi rigidi e umidi delle regioni settentrionali (Frayn 1984: 143-144). Di contro, la prova che almeno una parte della produzione doveva subire un primo trattamento di pulitura sul posto è costituita da un'attestazione epigrafica, risalente alla prima metà del I sec. d.C., nella quale è ricordato il locale collegio dei *lanar(ii) purg(atores)* (AE 1987, 443; Tirelli 1997: 198-202)[10], cui spettava proprio il compito della prima depurazione della materia grezza (Fig. 3).

Tuttavia, nella stessa città perilagunare, a questo ruolo di assoluto rilievo nella produzione laniera non sembra corrispondere un altrettanto sviluppato interesse imprenditoriale nei confronti delle operazioni di lavorazione della fibra. In questa prospettiva è ancora altamente istruttivo il testo dell'Editto dei Prezzi che, pur riconoscendo l'eccellente qualità della materia prima, non menziona alcun genere di vestiario confezionato ad Altino (in particolare nel capitolo 19, dedicato ai vari tipi di vesti), elencando invece nel dettaglio la produzione di Modena e Laodicea di Frigia.

A memoria delle attività di lavorazione laniera svolte nella città veneta restano infatti solamente un paio di attestazioni epigrafiche e il rinvenimento di vasche e di grandi pesi da telaio fittili riferibili probabilmente a un laboratorio tessile privato[11], oltre ad alcune anfore per il trasporto dell'allume[12], un materiale spesso utilizzato come mordente nella tintura della lana[13].

Dalle due fonti epigrafiche pervenuteci siamo a conoscenza dell'attività svolta dai *lotor(es)* (AE 1931, 98), addetti al lavaggio dei tessuti in laboratori forse dislocati appena al di fuori dell'abitato (Buonopane c.s.; cfr., invece, Sartori 1964: 41-42), e dal *col(legium) cent(onariorum)* (CIL, V, 2176 = ILS, 8369), nel quale si è generalmente riconosciuta "un'associazione di straccivendoli addetti alla raccolta degli avanzi della lavorazione della lana e al riciclaggio di oggetti e indumenti usati, ma anche alla confezione di vestiti destinati alla popolazione più povera e di stoffe grossolane di poco prezzo, da cui si ricavavano coperte di vari pezzi e colori (*centones*); intervenivano volontariamente, per lo più in cooperazione con i collegi dei fabbri e dei dendrofori, nello spegnimento dei frequenti incendi" (Buchi 1987: 136-137)[14].

In sostanza, dopo circa quarant'anni, si può tuttora asserire con F. Sartori (1964: 41; cfr., invece, Noè 1974: 925) che "quasi nulla, e comunque assai dubbia, è la documentazione di attività tessili in Altino", tanto nelle testimonianze materiali quanto in quelle scritte. L'insieme dei dati porta così a vedere in questa città un centro provvisto di una fiorente attività allevatoria, garantita da un favorevole contesto naturale, capace di fornire in abbondanza una lana bianca il cui pregio era riconosciuto in tutto il mondo antico. Emerge però chiaramente che la lana di produzione altinate non era lavorata *in loco*, ma veniva almeno in larga parte esportata verso altri poli manifatturieri sia della *Venetia* sia di altre aree del Mediterraneo, anche molto lontane, come provato dalla menzione di specifici *lanarii in lana Altinata* nell'Editto dioclezianeo (ed. Giacchero, 21, 2), un calmiere utilizzato in tutto l'Impero.

Su questo punto della differenziazione tra luoghi di produzione e luoghi di lavorazione della lana ha operato un'attenta riflessione J.-P. Morel (Morel 1978; cfr. Vicari 2001: 24-26), affrontando il caso di Taranto in età romana. In questo contesto, che pur sembra aver conosciuto un certo fervore di attività tessili in epoca preromana (Mele 1997), le fonti antiche ricordano di frequente l'eccellente produzione laniera, ma in nessun caso lasciano trasparire l'eventualità che nel centro apulo avessero luogo le fasi di trasformazione della materia prima, dando adito all'ipotesi che la lana tarantina fosse venduta ed esportata verso altri centri di lavorazione. Come già ricordato, anche nel caso di Taranto, in piena analogia con quanto attestato per Altino, lo stesso Editto dei Prezzi menziona la città apula come uno dei principali centri produttori di materia prima di tutto l'Impero, senza tuttavia accennare all'eventuale esistenza di una seppur limitata attività tessile. Altrove, simili esempi di città solitamente equivocate come poli manifatturieri, ma ricordate in genere dalle fonti per la sola produzione di lana, sembrano essere *Pollentia*, in *Liguria* (*IX Regio*), e Mileto, in Asia Minore (Jongman 2000: 190).

Ad Altino, questa netta prevalenza della vocazione produttiva e commerciale su quella manifatturiera potrebbe ora trovare una più precisa definizione in alcuni straordinari documenti epigrafici rinvenuti presso la periferia settentrionale dell'abitato lungo il corso del Siloncello, uno dei canali navigabili della città antica. Si tratta di alcune laminette plumbee graffite, cui si è già fatto riferimento in più occasioni[15], le quali, molto probabilmente, erano in origine utilizzate come etichette legate a balle di lana perlopiù non lavorata[16]. Sebbene la loro lettura epigrafica sia piuttosto difficoltosa e ancora incerta, è probabile che in alcune di esse siano ricordate Taranto e Modena (in forma aggettivale abbreviata), città che possono essere plausibilmente interpretate come luogo di provenienza della merce importata presso il centro perilagunare[17].

Questa interpretazione, se confermata, aprirebbe orizzonti insospettati nella ricostruzione dei traffici commerciali relativi al mercato della lana nell'Italia antica. Si profila così l'eventualità che ad Altino venisse importata materia prima da altri grandi centri di produzione, per essere poi ulteriormente smerciata per la lavorazione verso altri luoghi dell'Italia e dell'Impero grazie all'efficiente rete di comunicazioni terrestri, fluviali, lagunari e marittime in cui era inserita la città veneta.

Inoltre, la possibilità di un transito di lana tarantina attraverso Altino assume tratti di maggiore verosimiglianza se si richiama non solo la tradizione di Taranto come grande centro di esportazione laniera, ma soprattutto se si ricorda l'esistenza di un intenso flusso commerciale di prodotti lanieri tra l'*Apulia* e le province galliche attraverso le rotte adriatiche e la rete fluviale padana, vie di comunicazione assai sviluppate, nelle quali la città perilagunare era attivamente inserita sia dal punto di vista infrastrutturale sia da quello commerciale (Grelle, Silvestrini 2001: 99-100).

Né va tralasciata, nell'ottica diacronica indicata come potenzialmente molto promettente nell'introduzione metodologica di J. Bonetto, la massiccia importazione di lane pugliesi a Venezia in età moderna, sulla spinta di una tradizione che affondava le sue radici in epoche ben più remote (Panciera 1996: 161-165, 354-355; cfr. Demo 2001: 43).

Nel territorio della *Venetia* la lana smerciata da Altino doveva essere in buona parte esportata nella vicina Padova, nota alle fonti letterarie come centro di primaria importanza nel campo della trasformazione della fibra per la produzione di tessuti e di vesti, così come per la loro commercializzazione su scala extraregionale. Per questo suo ruolo di principale polo manifatturiero dell'intera *Venetia et Histria*, cui si affiancava Aquileia nell'estremo settore altoadriatico (Giovannini 1993; Modugno 2000-2001), è possibile che nel capoluogo euganeo confluisse anche parte della materia prima proveniente da altri centri veneti minori (come Este e Vicenza).

Va da sé che, per mantenere competitive le proprie manifatture e per meglio ammortizzare i costi di produzione, Padova non poteva certo fare affidamento unicamente sull'acquisto di lana dalle città limitrofe, ma doveva basare il suo successo nel ramo tessile soprattutto su un'abbondante disponibilità di materia prima di produzione propria. Come nel caso di Altino, questa era garantita da un'affermata tradizione allevatoria, sviluppatasi in un territorio caratterizzato da grandi risorse pascolative distribuite tra la Laguna e le Prealpi e da una solida organizzazione infrastrutturale appositamente adattata alle necessità di questo settore economico (Bonetto 1997).

Circa le dimensioni del fenomeno dell'allevamento e della produzione di lana le fonti letterarie sono tuttavia piuttosto carenti. Se si eccettua un fugace accenno alla "mollezza" delle pecore euganee da parte di Giovenale (VIII, 15), pressoché isolata è la testimonianza di Strabone (V, 1, 12), il quale collega esplicitamente le produzioni tessili patavine a un tipo di lana di qualità intermedia tra quella pregiata di Modena e quella scadente prodotta nel territorio dei Liguri e dei Simbri.

Maggiore è invece il numero di occasioni in cui le fonti letterarie si soffermano a celebrare i tessuti e le vesti di produzione patavina. Particolarmente rinomati erano i *trilices* (tessuti molto resistenti a tre fili) (Mart. XIV, 143: *Tunicae Patavinae*) e soprattutto i *gausapa*, un genere di stoffe in lana molto spessa e villosa con le quali si confezionavano coperte e vesti di notevole pesantezza, particolarmente adatte ai climi rigidi (Strab., V, 1, 12; Mart. XIV, 152: *Gausapum quadratum*).

Ma fra tutte, la testimonianza più rilevante dal punto di vita storico-economico è quella offerta ancora una volta da Strabone nel secondo decennio del I sec. d.C. Dopo aver ricordato la ricchezza straordinaria raggiunta da Padova, al punto da risultare, insieme con Cadice, una delle due città più ricche dell'Impero dopo la sola Roma (Strab., III, 5, 3), in un passo di fondamentale importanza egli collega strettamente questo sviluppo economico proprio alla industriosità del centro euganeo nel settore delle manifatture laniere, portando come prova la gran quantità di "vestiario di ogni tipo" inviata verso il mercato dell'Urbe (Strab., V, 1, 7).

Nel leggere questa fonte, in primo luogo si osserva l'aspetto quantitativo del fenomeno: nella prima età imperiale, Padova poteva vantare una produzione tessile di portata eccezionale nel contesto della *Venetia* centrale, al punto da presentarsi come il polo manifatturiero prevalente nell'intera area (cfr. Jongman 2000: 189-190, 193). È molto probabile quindi, ancorché non documentato, che il lanificio patavino si basasse su una disponibilità di stabilimenti produttivi e di "forza lavoro" propria di un'organizzazione di tipo "industriale", ben diversa dallo standard delle manifatture a conduzione familiare di altri centri minori (Chilver 1941: 164-165; cfr., da ultimo, Vicari 2001: 41).

La commercializzazione delle vesti verso il mercato di Roma, oltre a ribadire la potenzialità produttiva della città, le cui "eccedenze" superavano evidentemente la richiesta locale e persino regionale, tradisce poi l'esistenza di una sviluppata capacità organizzativa dei meccanismi commerciali e, seppur implicitamente, dei cospicui guadagni derivanti dall'operazione di scambio, che doveva garantire l'ammortizzamento dei costi di trasporto della merce oltre l'Appennino.

Stranamente, l'indubbio primato manifatturiero di Padova, tanto celebrato dalle fonti letterarie, non trova però una conferma altrettanto solida né nella documentazione materiale né, soprattutto, in quella epigrafica, che sembra limitarsi a una menzione del locale *collegi(um) centonariorium* (CIL, V, 2864 = ILS, 5406)[18].

Si deve tuttavia ricordare che, dal punto di vista archeologico, la conoscenza di Padova romana appare assai gravemente lacunosa, tanto più se si considera l'assoluta rilevanza assunta dal centro nella prima età imperiale. Ad ogni modo, alcune testimonianze materiali permettono di ribadire con convinzione le considerazioni sinora espresse.

Infatti, recenti scavi condotti dalla Soprintendenza Archeologica per il Veneto in Via C. Battisti hanno portato in luce un piccolo vano a pianta quadrata di mq 4 ca., con un pavimento interamente costituito da pesi di telaio fittili di forma troncopiramidale, disposti appaiati in una maglia geometrica assai regolare, caratterizzata da file alternativamente verticali e orizzontali (Bianco *et al.* 1996-1997: 20-23)[19] (Fig. 4). La pavimentazione si data alla metà del I sec. d.C. Tenuto conto del rinvenimento di un'altra decina di pesi da telaio nei pressi di questo ambiente, si può ipotizzare che nell'area sorgesse "un'officina di un fabbricante di pesi da telaio"[20] oppure, forse più plausibilmente, un piccolo laboratorio di tessitura, dal quale proverrebbero i manufatti reimpiegati integri nel piano pavimentale (Basso, in Basso, Bonetto, Ghiotto c.s.).

A conferma dell'attitudine commerciale della città euganea sta poi una preziosa testimonianza epigrafica relativa ad alcuni tessuti, di origine quasi certamente patavina, esportati presso il celebre emporio del Magdalensberg, in Carinzia. In una laminetta plumbea rinvenuta nella località del Norico (Fig. 5), risalente alla seconda metà del I sec. a.C., appaiono citati gli stessi *gausapa* celebrati dalle fonti letterarie come il prodotto più caratteristico dell'"industria laniera" patavina, contestualmente a un gentilizio di probabile ascendenza veneta (Bonetto 2001: 155-161).

Inoltre, un'attestazione indiretta dell'esistenza di alcune tintorie può essere dedotta dal ritrovamento in città di un deposito di una settantina di anfore ad impasto grezzo (Fig. 6), datato entro la metà del I sec. d.C. Sulla base dei confronti tipologici e delle analisi archeometriche, si è ipotizzato che tali contenitori siano stati utilizzati per trasportare allume proveniente da Milo, uno dei principali centri estrattivi di questa sostanza, impiegata come mordente nella tintura della lana (Cipriano, De Vecchi, Mazzocchin 2000).

Sul piano storico è opportuno evidenziare come il predominio patavino nel quadro della produzione e della lavorazione della lana sembri circoscritto tra l'età della romanizzazione e il I sec. d.C., mentre sembrano mancare testimonianze relative alle epoche successive, quando la città conobbe una fase di sensibile declino (Sartori 1981: 186-189). Emblematico di questo stato di cose è, ad esempio, il già citato Editto dei Prezzi di Diocleziano, nel quale la produzione laniera e tessile di Padova non figura in alcun modo, tanto meno tra i centri cisalpini considerati produttori di lana o di capi d'abbigliamento di un certo pregio, quali Altino e Modena.

Per concludere, si può solo accennare al fatto che l'importanza assunta da Padova, a fianco di Altino, nel settore dell'allevamento ovino e della manifattura laniera nel contesto della *Venetia* romana può essere maggiormente compresa attraverso il confronto con la realtà medievale. Dopo il Mille, superata la fase critica dell'età altomedievale, Padova tornò infatti a ricoprire un ruolo di rilievo nella produzione e nella lavorazione della lana in ambito veneto, per quanto inferiore a quello rivestito da altre città quali Verona e Vicenza (Demo 2001).

Probabilmente sin dal Basso Medioevo - ma non si può escludere che la sua origine sia più antica - si andò selezionando nel territorio patavino una razza specifica di ovini (le "pecore gentili") (Fapanni 1823; Pastore, Legume, Carazzolo 1999: 34-37), nota per la produzione di lana pregiatissima ed esportata in varie regioni europee con il fine di migliorarne le specie locali. Da queste pecore, allevate perlopiù in forme stanziali, derivava una quantità assai considerevole di materia prima che andava ad alimentare la manifattura cittadina secondo le regole dettate dall'"Università della lana", una potente corporazione dei lanaioli, provvista di propri Statuti, che svolgeva un ruolo imprescindibile nell'economia comunale (Borgherini 1964; cfr. Bonetto 1997: 176, con bibliografia).

(A.R.G.)

ENDNOTES:

* Il presente lavoro è frutto di una comune riflessione da parte dei due autori; nello specifico, a J. Bonetto si deve la stesura del paragrafo 1, ad A.R. Ghiotto quella del paragrafo 2.

1 Il rilievo della tradizione medievale e moderna nel campo dell'allevamento ovino e della lavorazione e commercio della lana per la regione veneta è straordinario; le informazioni recuperabili attraverso documenti d'archivio sono di grande interesse. Lo studio di questo panorama documentario è stato avviato anche attraverso la collaborazione con la cattedra di Storia economica dell'Università di Padova (prof. G.L. Fontana; prof. W. Panciera; dott. E. Demo; dott.ssa E. Novello) che da tempo si occupano dell'economia pastorale e laniera nel Medioevo e in età moderna.

2 La documentazione archeologica è in corso di studio da parte di P. Basso che in questa sede ringraziamo per il consueto spirito di collaborazione con cui ha messo a disposizione i suoi dati e le sue idee (cfr. Basso, in Basso, Bonetto, Ghiotto c.s.).
3 Nel contesto dell'Italia romana, la *Venetia et Histria* ha restituito una quantità di testimonianze epigrafiche sulle attività laniere inferiore solamente a quella di Roma e della *I Regio* (*Latium et Campania*), nel cui numero rientra però la straordinaria mole di iscrizioni proveniente dall'Urbe e da Pompei (cfr. Grelle, Sivestrini 2001: 126-129) (Fig. 2).
4 Per una prima raccolta sistematica delle testimonianze letterarie, epigrafiche e archeologiche relative alla produzione, alla lavorazione e al commercio della lana nella *Venetia*, cfr. Basso, Bonetto, Ghiotto c.s.
5 I territori municipali di Padova e Altino si estendevano sino a comprendere vaste parti della Laguna di Venezia, dove anticamente, come ricorda Cassiodoro (var. XII, 24), assai abbondante era la produzione di sale. Sul rapporto tra il sale e l'allevamento ovino cfr. Bonetto 1997: 130-131 (con nota 73), 137-138 (con note 104-113).
6 Nella periferia di Altino, in località Canevere, sorgeva un'importante area santuariale legata ad attività "emporiche", ubicata all'inizio della cosiddetta "via Claudia Augusta" (Cresci Marrone 2001: 141-146).
7 Queste preziosissime testimonianze sono state recentemente presentate da A. Buonopane al III Convegno di Studi Altinati *Produzioni, merci e commerci in Altino preromana e romana* (Venezia, 12-14 dicembre 2001). Si tratta di un frammento di coppa in ceramica sigillata italica con breve iscrizione graffita nella quale compare il vocabolo *lan(arius)*, che il relatore reputa riferibile alla professione oppure al *cognomen* del personaggio citato, e di una serie di laminette plumbee, pure graffite, nelle quali sembrano ricorrere, tra l'altro, sia alcuni termini tecnici relativi al prodotto laniero commercializzato sia, probabilmente, la provenienza della merce (Buonopane c.s.; cfr. *infra* nota 17). Cogliamo l'occasione per esprimere il nostro ringraziamento nei confronti di A. Buonopane per la consueta disponibilità.
8 Di tali cesoie è stata data notizia al III Convegno di Studi Altinati (Venezia, 12-14 dicembre 2001), i cui Atti sono attualmente in corso di stampa (Zaccaria, Cottica c.s.).
9 In una delle etichette plumbee citate compare la dizione *suc(ida) (*scilicet *lana)*; cfr. *supra* nota 7.
10 Un'indicazione simile proviene da una delle laminette plumbee citate che riporta la dicitura *purgat(a) (*scilicet *lana)* o, meno probabilmente, *purgat(ores)*; cfr. *supra* nota 7.
11 Lo scavo è stato condotto dall'Università di Venezia (prof.ssa A.P. Zaccaria Ruggiu) e dalla Soprintendenza Archeologica per il Veneto (dott.ssa M. Tirelli) nel biennio 2000-2001. Alcuni dati sono stati presentati in dattiloscritto al III Convegno di Studi Altinati (Venezia, 12-14 dicembre 2001) e saranno prossimamente editi nei relativi Atti (Zaccaria, Cottica c.s.).
12 Le anfore sono in corso di studio da parte di S. Pesavento Mattioli e S. Cipriano, che ringraziamo per la preziosa segnalazione.
13 Plin. nat. XXXV, 52; Cipriano, De Vecchi, Mazzocchin 2000: 195.
14 Secondo Kneissl (1994: 141-143), i *centonarii* sarebbero stati invece addetti esclusivamente allo spegnimento degli incendi; secondo Vicari (1994: 252), i *centonarii* sarebbero "solo una struttura della vita municipale, più che un reale riflesso di gruppi significativi di lavoranti tessili" (cfr. Vicari 2001: 12-13).
15 Cfr. *supra* nota 7.
16 Sulle laminette plumbee e sulla loro relazione abituale con imballaggi di fibre, tessuti o capi d'abbigliamento cfr. Römer-Martijnse 1990; Bassi 1996; Bonetto 2001.
17 In questo caso le etichette, giunte ad Altino, sarebbero state staccate dalle balle di lana, e quindi gettate, una volta conclusa la loro funzione. Meno verosimilmente esse potrebbero essere state legate a una partita di merce in partenza che, mai inviata, rimase abbandonata sul posto.
18 Molto incerta è l'attestazione di una *sarcinatrix* (rammendatrice) in CIL, V, 2881.
19 Nella stessa Padova, un pavimento realizzato in modo analogo, tuttora inedito, è stato rinvenuto nella centrale Via dei Livello (Bianco *et al.* 1996-1997: 23, nota 16).
20 Possibili "tracce di una piccola fornace" sono state riconosciute immediatamente a Sud di questo vano (Bianco *et al.* 1996-1997: 21).

BIBLIOGRAFIA

Barker, G., 1989, The archaeology of the Italian shepherd, *ProcCambrPhilSoc*, 215, 1-19.

Barker, G., 1991, Archaeological survey and ethnoarchaeology in the Cicolano Mountains, Central Italy. Preliminary results, in *Archeologia della Pastorizia nell'Europa meridionale, Atti della tavola rotonda internazionale (Chiavari 22-24 settembre 1989)* (eds. R. Maggi, R. Nisbet e G. Barker), estratto da *RStLig*, anno LVII, nn. 1-4, Bordighera (Im), 109-121.

Bassi, C., 1996, Tre *lamellae perforatae* da Savazzona-Quistello (Mantova), *Epigraphica*, LVIII, 207-216.

Basso, P., Bonetto, J. e Ghiotto, A.R., c.s., Produzione, lavorazione e commercio della lana nella *Venetia* romana: le testimonianze letterarie, epigrafiche e archeologiche, in *La lana: prodotti e mercati (XIII-XX secolo), Atti dell'Euroconferenza (Schio, Valdagno, Follina, Biella, 24-27 ottobre 2001)* (eds. G.L. Fontana e G. Gayot), Padova.

Bianco, M.L. *et alii* 1996-1997, Lo scavo urbano pluristratificato di via C. Battisti 132 a Padova, *AVen*, XIX-XX, 7-150.

Bonetto, J., 1997, *Le vie armentarie tra* Patavium *e la montagna*, Dosson (Tv).

Bonetto, J., 1999a, L'allevamento degli ovi-caprini nel Veneto centrale: alcune note sull'età antica, in *L'allevamento ovi-caprino nel Veneto. Analisi e prospettive future di un settore ricco di storia* (eds. E. Pastore e L. Fabris), Verona, 167-177.

Bonetto, J., 1999b, Gli insediamenti alpini e la pianura veneto-friulana: complementarietà economica sulle rotte della transumanza, in *Studio e conservazione degli insediamenti minori romani in area alpina, Atti dell'Incontro di studi (Forgaria del Friuli, 20 settembre 1997)* (ed. S. Santoro Bianchi), Bologna-Imola, 95-106.

Bonetto, J., 2001, Mercanti di lana tra *Patavium* e il Magdalensberg, in *Carinthia Romana und die römische Welt. Festschrift für Gernot Piccottini zum 60. Geburtstag*, Klagenfurt, 151-161.

Bonetto, J., 2002, Latte e formaggio tra Prealpi venete e pianura nell'Antichità e nel Medioevo, in *Lac d'amour. Il latte e i suoi derivati, Atti del VII Colloquio interuniversitario "Homo Edens" (Vicenza, 14-16 marzo 2001)* (eds. O. Longo e P. Scarpi), Padova, 257-281.

Bonetto, J., c.s.a, La transumanza lungo il Brenta tra pianure e montagne, in *Il Brenta* (ed. F. Vallerani), Verona.

Bonetto, J., c.s.b, Economia agricola e economia pastorale nella Cisalpina romana, in *Pecus. Man and animal in Antiquity, Swedish Institute in Rome (11-15 september 2002)*, Rome.

Borgherini, M., 1964, *L'arte della lana in Padova durante il governo della Repubblica di Venezia, 1405-1797*, Deputazione di Storia Patria per le Venezie, Miscellanea di studi e memorie, X, Venezia.

Buchi, E., 1987, Assetto agrario, risorse e attività economiche, in Il Veneto in età romana, I, Storiografia, organizzazione del territorio, economia e religione (ed. E. Buchi), Verona, 103-184.

Buonopane, A., c.s., La produzione tessile ad Altino: le fonti epigrafiche, in Produzioni, merci e commerci in Altino preromana e romana, Atti del III Convegno di Studi Altinati (Venezia, 12-14 dicembre 2001) (eds. G. Cresci Marrone e M. Tirelli).

Chilver, G.E.F., 1941, Cisalpine Gaul. Social and economic history from 49 b.C. to the death of Trajan, Oxford.

Cipriano, S., De Vecchi, G.P. e Mazzocchin, S., 2000, Anfore ad impasto grezzo con ossidiana a Padova: tipologia, impasti, provenienza, in *Produzione ceramica in area padana tra il II secolo a.C. e il VII secolo d.C.: nuovi dati e prospettive di ricerca, Atti del Convegno internazionale (Desenzano del Garda, 8-10 aprile 1999)* (eds. G.P. Brogiolo e G. Olcese), Mantova, 191-197.

Corbier, M., 1991, La transhumance entre le Samnium et l'Apulie: continuités entre l'époque républicaine et l'époque impériale, in *La romanisation du Samnium aux IIe et Ier siècles av. J.-C., Actes du colloque (Naples 4-5 novembre 1988)*, Naples, 149-176.

Cresci Marrone, G., 2001, La dimensione del sacro in Altino romana, in *Orizzonti del sacro. Culti e santuari antichi in Altino e nel Veneto orientale* (eds. G. Cresci Marrone e M. Tirelli), Roma, 139-161.

Demo, E., 2001, *L'"anima della città". L'industria tessile a Verona e Vicenza (1400-1550)*, Milano.

Fapanni, A., 1823, *Della coltivazione delle pecore padovane*, Padova.

Frayn, J.M., 1984, *Sheep-rearing and the wool trade in Italy during the Roman period*, Liverpool.

Gabba, E., 1994, La transumanza nell'Italia romana. Evidenze e problemi. Qualche prospettiva per l'età altomedievale, in Gabba, E., *Italia romana*, Como, 167-176 (già in *Settimane di Studio del Centro Italiano di Studi sull'Alto Medioevo*, XXXI, *L'uomo di fronte al mondo animale nell'Alto Medioevo*, I, Spoleto 1985, 373-389).

Ghiotto, A.R., 2000, Il Monte Summano e la pastorizia a Santorso e in Val d'Astico in età antica, *QuadAVen*, XVI, 165-172.

Giardina, A., 1989, Uomini e spazi aperti, in *Storia di Roma, IV, Caratteri e morfologie*, Torino, 71-99.

Giovannini, A., 1993, L'allevamento ovino e l'industria tessile in Istria in età romana. Alcuni cenni, *AttiMemIstria*, n.s. XLI, 7-34.

Grelle, F. e Silvestrini, M., 2001, Lane apule e tessuti canosini, in *Epigrafia e territorio. Politica e società. Temi di antichità romane VI*, Bari, 91-136.

Jongman, W., 2000, Wool and the textile industry of Roman Italy: a working hypotesis, in *Mercati permanenti e mercati periodici nel mondo romano, Atti degli Incontri capresi di Storia dell'economia antica (Capri, 13-15 ottobre 1997)* (ed. E. Lo Cascio), Bari, 187-197.

Kneissl, P., 1994, Die *fabri, fabri tignuarii, fabri subaediani, centonarii* und *dolabrarii* als Feuerwehren in den Städten Italiens und der westlichen Provinzen, in E fontibus haurire. *Beitrage zur römischen Geschichte und zur ihren Hilfswissenschaften*, Paderborn-München, 133-146.

Loane, H., 1938, *Industry and commerce of the city of Rome*, Baltimore.

Marchiori, A., 1990, Pianura, montagna e transumanza: il caso patavino in età romana, in *La* Venetia *nell'area padano-danubiana. Le vie di comunicazione, Atti del convegno internazionale (Venezia 6-10 aprile 1988)*, Padova, 73-82.

Maschio, M., 1999-2000, *La questione della Claudia Augusta. Funzionalità della rete stradale tra Altino e la media valle del Piave*, tesi di laurea, Università di Padova, rel. prof. G. Rosada.

Mele, A., 1997, Allevamento ovino nell'antica *Apulia* e lavorazione della lana a Taranto, in *Schiavi e dipendenti nell'ambito dell'*"oikos" *e della* "familia", *Atti del XXII Colloquio GIREA (Pontignano, 19-20 novembre 1995)* (eds. M. Moggi e G. Cordiano), Pisa, 97-104.

Modugno, I., 1999, La viabilità aquileiese tra fascia rivierasca e montagne: la questione della transumanza. Una nota preliminare, *JAT*, IX, *Atti del Terzo congresso di Topografia antica. La viabilità romana in Italia (Roma, 10-11 novembre 1998)*, I, 51-66.

Modugno, I., 2000, Alcune considerazioni sul culto di Ercole nel territorio di Aquileia tra protostoria ed età romana con particolare riferimento al fenomeno della transumanza, *AquilNost*, LXXI, 57-76.

Modugno, I., 2000-2001, *Le direttrici stradali aquileiesi di età romana tra fascia rivierasca e montagne, con particolare riferimento al fenomeno della transumanza*, tesi di dottorato, rel. prof. G. Rosada.

Modugno, I., c.s., "... pascua que sunt inter Ysoncium et Wipaum et Ortaona atque iuga Alpium...": le strade dei pascoli tra Aquileia e l'Istria, in *Pecus. Man and animal in Antiquity, Swedish Institute in Rome (11-15 september 2002)*, Rome.

Moeller, W.O., 1976, *The wool trade of ancient Pompeii*, Leiden.

Morel, J.-P., 1978, La laine de Tarente, *Ktema*, III, 93-110.

Noè, E., 1974, La produzione tessile nella Gallia Cisalpina in età romana, *RendIstLomb*, CVIII, 918-932.

Panciera, W., 1996, *L'arte matrice. I lanifici della Repubblica di Venezia nei secoli XVII e XVIII*, Treviso.

Pastore, E., Legume, B. e Carazzolo, A., 1999, Le razze allevate, in *L'allevamento ovi-caprino nel Veneto. Analisi e prospettive future di un settore ricco di storia* (eds. E. Pastore e L. Fabris), Legnaro (Pd), 33-83.

Quilici, L., 1987, La transumanza nell'Italia centrale in età moderna e medioevale come contributo alla conoscenza di quella antica, in *Atti del XX Convegno di Studi Maceratesi*, 143-164.

Römer-Martijnse, E., 1990, *Römerzeitliche Bleietiketten aus Kalsdorf, Steiermark*, Denkschr. Österr. Akademie Wiss. Phil.-hist. Kl., 205, Wien.

Rosada, G., 1999, La viabilità nella *X Regio* (*Venetia et Histria*). Strade di collegamento e strade di sfruttamento territoriale, *JAT*, IX, *Atti del Terzo congresso di Topografia antica. La viabilità romana in Italia (Roma, 10-11 novembre 1998)*, I, 81-106.

Rosada, G., 2001, Sessant'anni dopo. Per "capire" una strada, postfazione a *La via Claudia Augusta altinate*, ristampa anastatica dell'opera edita nel 1938, Venezia, XI-XXXI.

Sartori, F., 1964, Industria e artigianato nel Veneto romano, in *Atti dell'Assemblea del 14 giugno 1964 della Deputazione di Storia Patria delle Venezie*, Padova, 13-46.

Sartori, F., 1981, Padova nello stato romano dal sec. III a.C. all'età dioclezianea, in *Padova antica. Da comunità paleoveneta a città romano-cristiana*, Sarmeola di Rubano (Pd)-Trieste, 97-189.

Tirelli, M., 1997, *Horti cum aedificiis sepulturis adiuncti*: i monumenti funerari delle necropoli di Altinum, in *Monumenti sepolcrali romani in Aquileia e nella Cisalpina*, Antichità Altoadriatiche, XLIII, Trieste, 175-210.

Verzár-Bass, M., 1987, A proposito dell'allevamento nell'alto adriatico, in *Vita sociale, artistica e commerciale di Aquileia romana*, Antichità Altoadriatiche, XXIX, I, Udine, 257-280.

Vicari, F., 1994, Economia della Cispadana romana: la produzione tessile, *RStorAnt*, XXIV, 239-260.

Vicari, F., 2001, *Produzione e commercio dei tessuti nell'Occidente romano*, BAR International Series 916, Oxford.

Zaccaria, A.P. e Cottica, D., c.s., La lana: il ciclo della lavorazione, in *Produzioni, merci e commerci in Altino preromana e romana, Atti del III Convegno di Studi Altinati (Venezia, 12-14 dicembre 2001)* (eds. G. Cresci Marrone e M. Tirelli).

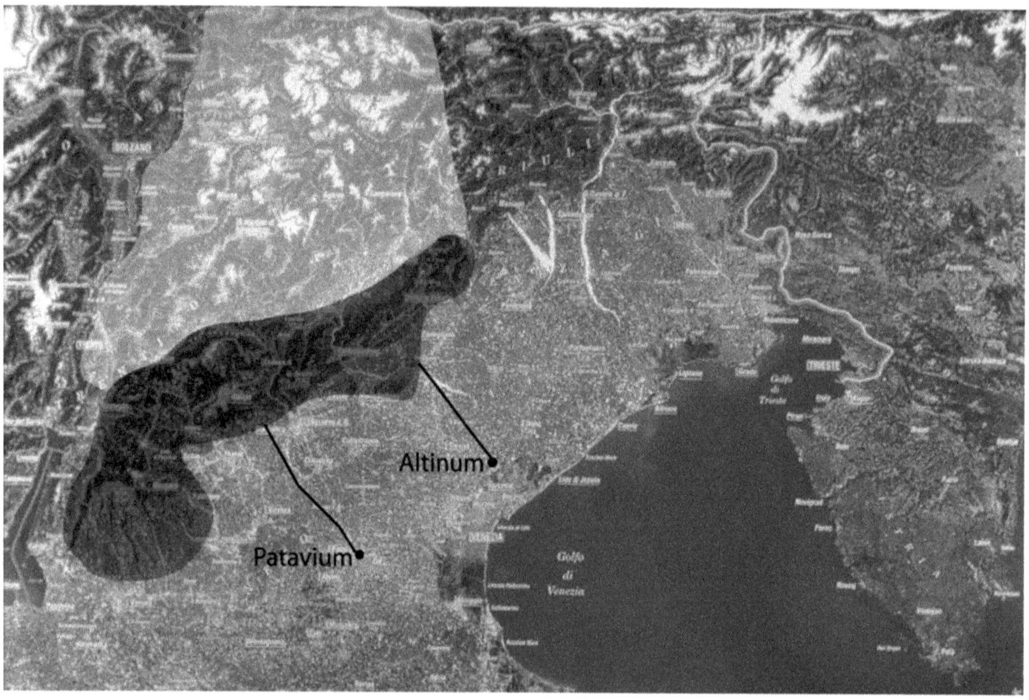

Fig. 1 Il territorio della *Venetia* centrale in età romana, con indicazione degli importanti centri lanieri di Altino e di Padova.

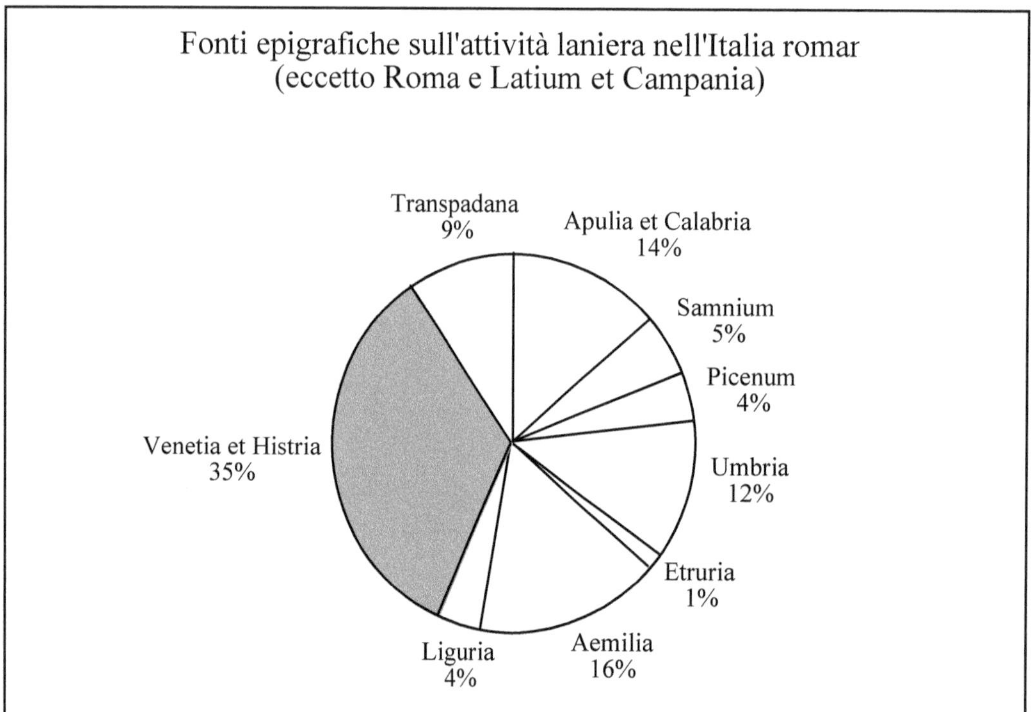

Fig. 2 La predominanza delle fonti epigrafiche sull'attività laniera nella *Venetia et Histria* nel contesto dell'Italia romana, con l'eccezione di Roma e *Latium et Campania* (sulla base dei dati raccolti in Grelle, Silvestrini 2001:126-129).

Fig. 3 L'iscrizione del collegio dei *lanar(ii) purg(atores)* di Altino (AE 1987, 443; da Buchi 1987: 137).

Fig. 4. Il pavimento in pesi da telaio fittili disposti in maglia regolare rinvenuto in Via C. Battisti a Padova (da Bianco *et al.* 1996-1997: 21).

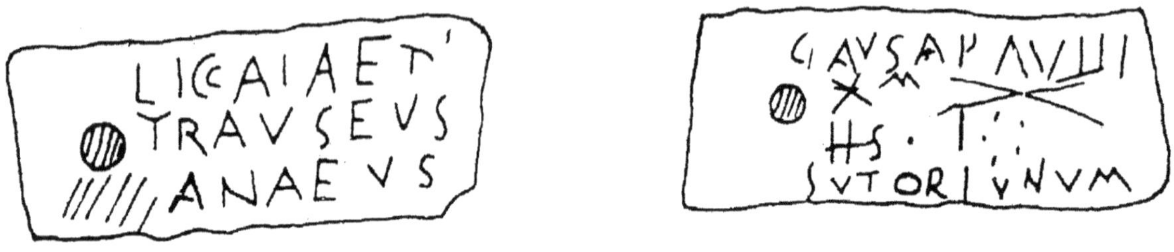

Fig. 5. Disegno della laminetta plumbea rinvenuta nell'emporio del Magdalensberg, in Carinzia, che attesta il commercio di *gausapa* di produzione probabilmente patavina (da Bonetto 2001: 156).

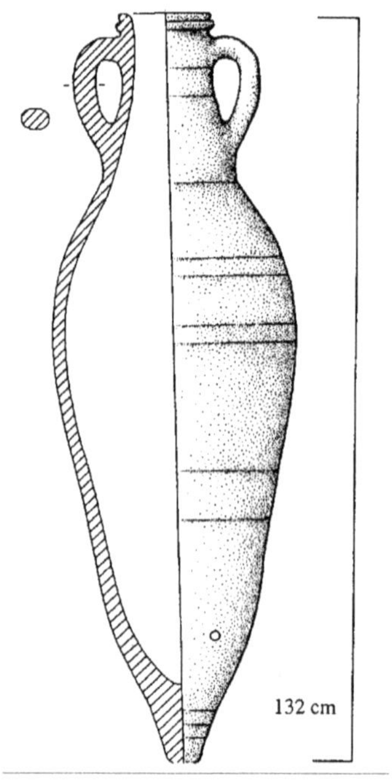

Fig. 6. Disegno di un'anfora ad impasto grezzo per il trasporto di allume rinvenuta a Padova (da Cipriano, De Vecchi, Mazzocchin 2000: 191).

SISTEMI PONDERALI NELLA CIRCOLAZIONE DEI METALLI IN EUROPA TRA LO SCORCIO DEL II E L'INIZIO DEL I MILLENNIO A.C.

RENATO PERONI
(Università di Roma "La Sapienza")

ABSTRACT: This paper demonstrates that despite significant socio-political inequalities among the various cultures which inhabited central Europe, Italy and the Aegean during the late Bronze Age, a strong interest in trade led to the establishment of a more or less standardized system of weighs throughout this broad region. Trade according to a standard system of weights served to facilitate trade between cultures which may have had very different socio-economic structures.

La grande maggioranza degli storici dell'economia considera anacronistico parlare di commercio -inteso come una forma di scambio gestita professionalmente- a proposito di società preurbane. Tuttavia, vedremo che certe attività di scambio attraverso l'Europa attestate tra lo scorcio del II e l'inizio del I millennio a.C. presentano inequivocabili elementi di professionalità[1].

Molto notevole è la varietà delle forme di scambio in Europa e nel Mediterraneo durante questo periodo: traffici terrestri e marittimi, a breve e a lunga distanza, riguardanti materie prime e prodotti finiti, con un complicato accavallarsi delle diverse combinazioni tra queste alternative.

Prendiamo ad esempio le rotte dei navigatori egei verso l'Italia meridionale, la Sicilia e la Sardegna. Il loro percorso verso Ovest è segnato dalle importazioni di ceramiche micenee (Vagnetti 1999: 156, Map 1), mentre nella direzione opposta prescindendo dalla Sardegna dobbiamo postulare un flusso di rame grezzo proveniente almeno dalle altre due regioni; ma a questo si collegava un altro itinerario (cfr. ad es. Giardino 1995: 236, fig. 116), quello lungo il quale manufatti in bronzo prodotti nella penisola iberica (dove del resto importazioni micenee sono pure attestate) raggiungevano Sicilia e Sardegna. Volendo, queste due tappe possono essere considerate alla stregua di traffici a distanza non troppo lunga: ma la prospettiva cambia del tutto se le vediamo inserite nella 'via dello stagno' che dalla Cornovaglia, seguendo la costa atlantica dell'Europa Occidentale, si riallacciavano al Mediterraneo o facendo il giro di Gibilterra, o tagliando direttamente per la terraferma a Nord dei Pirenei.

Non meno complesso è il quadro che ci si presenta se consideriamo l'altra grande via -o meglio rete-transcontinentale, quella detta 'dell'ambra', che convogliava il prezioso materiale (la cui circolazione ci è peraltro documentata essenzialmente sotto la forma di manufatti finiti) dai giacimenti lungo il Mare del Nord e il Baltico (Champion *et al.* 1984: 218 s.), risaliva i grandi fiumi che vi sboccano -Elba, Oder, Vistola- e valicava i Carpazi occidentali, per poi penetrare nelle Alpi orientali e di lì sfociare nel Carnaro, o piuttosto -fu questa l'alternativa preferita nel periodo in discorso- raggiugere la Val d'Adige e percorrerla fino all'Adriatico, costeggiare quindi la riva occidentale di questo e attraversare il Canale d'Otranto, per toccare alla fine le isole ioniche della Grecia (Piggott 1976: 143, fig. 75; von Hase 1995: 245, Abb. 5). Solo quest'ultimo tratto, dal Salento alla Bassa padana, è segnato da rinvenimenti di ceramiche micenee (Vagnetti 1999: 161, Map 5), mentre i manufatti in bronzo di produzione italica e danubiana giungevano fino alla cerchia nordica (Piggott 1976: 160, fig. 88); e il rame grezzo dei Carpazi e lo stagno dei Monti Metalliferi (=*Erzgebirge*) tra Boemia e Sassonia discendevano sia il ramo settentrionale della strada, rifornendo la Scandinavia -la cui ricchissima produzione metallurgica sembra non potesse attingere a fonti locali, sia quello meridionale.

Sarà opportuno limitarsi alla sola menzione degli altri grandi percorsi attorno e attraverso il continente (Mazzeo *et al.* 1999: 289): la via tra Isole Britanniche e Scandinavia passando per il Mare del Nord, quella che da questo risaliva la valle del Reno per collegarsi al Mediterraneo Occidentale discendendo verso Sudovest il Rodano e verso Sud-Est il Ticino, quella che dall'Egeo risaliva il Vardar e il Danubio fino a riallacciarsi nuovamente al Mare del Nord, e quella che dal Mar Nero seguiva il Dnestr per collegarsi ai Paesi Baltici.

Attraverso questa rete si propagò, dall'Atlantico ai Carpazi, dalla Scandinavia alla Sicilia, a Creta, a Cipro, quell'insieme di tipi di armi, di ornamenti, di utensili di vastissima diffusione variamente sovrapposta (*Terram.*: 598, figg. 345, 346), ma solo per pochi di essi estesa all'intero continente, che va sotto il nome di*koinè* metallurgica europea; un fenomeno ben noto che esula del tutto dal nostro argomento.

A questi traffici di materia prima e manufatti metallici si legano due aspetti che invece in questa sede ci interessano: la tesaurizzazione e la comparsa di forme premonetali.

In tutta l'Europa questo periodo è caratterizzato da una crescita dei ripostigli di bronzi, sia per quanto concerne il loro numero, sia per quantità di pezzi e complessità di composizione. Indipendentemente dal non facile problema di come si possano distinguere i ripostigli in senso stretto, quelli cioè motivati da finalità mondane, dalle deposizioni cultuali, è chiaro che gli uni come gli altri costituiscono forme di tesaurizzazione.

Frequentissima è la presenza nei ripostigli deposti durante o attorno a questo periodo, accanto ai manufatti interi o in frammenti, di materia prima grezza in pani, in lingotti, in oggetti-lingotto non funzionali, anche questi interi o in frammenti (*aes rude*). Le forme vanno dai pani 'a focaccia' (Pare 1999: fig. 38, 3; Primas 1998: 36, Abb. 9, 1) o 'a piccone' (Pare 1999: fig. 38, 1,2) ai lingotti 'a pelle di bue' *(ox-hide)* di tipo egeo (Primas 1998: 39, Abb. 10, 2b), a quelli 'a barretta', (Primas 1998: 55, Abb. 20) ai lingotti ovali (Primas 1998: 53, Abb. 19) o a forma di lama d'ascia (Primas 1998: 51, Abb. 18), ai falcetti-lingotto (Sommerfeld 1994: Taf. 3, 4).

Si conoscono anche lingotti di ridotte dimensioni, come quelli 'a cuscino' dalla Croazia e dall'Ungheria (Pare 1999: 494, fig. 37A), che richiamano certi lingotti 'a pelle di bue' in miniatura da Cipro (Pare 1999: 494, fig. 37B).

In certi minuscoli lingotti parallelepipedi, spesso rastremati alle estremità, rinvenuti per lo più in sepolture di guerrieri eminenti diffuse nei territori di Repubblica Ceca, Ungheria, Germania, Svizzera e Francia, di recente Christopher Pare ha convincentemente proposto di individuare dei veri e propri pesi da bilancia (Pare 1999: 422 ss., figg. 10-19) , e di estendere tale diagnosi ad alcuni oggettini decorati a sottili, fitte e marcate costolature trasversali, ricavati dal riciclaggio di frammenti, appartenuti per lo più a spilloni (Pare 1999: 443 ss., fig. 17, 6,7). Queste ipotesi appaiono avvalorate dalla circostanza che in altre analoghe sepolture, tutte localizzate in Francia (Pare 1999: 443 ss., fig. 17, 6,7), come pure in un contesto abitativo, quello di Bordjos in Serbia (Pare 1999: 452, fig. 22B; Hänsel (a cura di) 1995: 213, fig. 4), sono stati rinvenuti dei gioghi appartenenti a piccole bilance di precisione del tipo a bracci simmetrici. Ora, mentre gli esemplari francesi non risultano associati a pesi, quello da Bordjos era accompagnato da un *set* di ciottolini non lavorati, differenziati per dimensioni, in cui lo scavatore riconobbe subito una serie di pesi (Hänsel (a cura di), 1995: 211 ss., fig. 2), sulla quale si tornerà più avanti.

Di dimensioni di gran lunga maggiori, e sicuramente relative a bilance di tipo del tutto diverso, sono le due classi -con scanalatura e con appiccagnolo- di pesi in pietra, non di rado pregiata, dalle Terremare del Bronzo medio e recente, (ma anche da un'area che va dall'Italia meridionale alla zona del Garda), individuate e indagate da Andrea Cardarelli e Marco Pacciarelli, e più recentemente integrate da Paolo Bellintani (*Terram.*: 629 ss.; Bellintani 2001) con i reperti dalla celebre stazione del Bronzo finale di Frattesina di Fratta Polesine presso Rovigo. Analoghi, ma appartenenti ormai tutti al Bronzo finale, sono i pesi in pietra, bronzo e piombo dalle palafitte della Svizzera e delle regioni vicine (Pare 1999: 500 ss.).

Se, come tutto incoraggia a ritenere, la principale funzione di questi pesi era la pesatura del metallo, appare degna della massima attenzione la circostanza, ampiamente documentata, che i frammenti di pani, lingotti e oggetti d'uso rinvenuti nei ripostigli risultano essere assai spesso il prodotto di una frammentazione intenzionale. Questo procedimento può trovare le più diverse spiegazioni, dalla pratica della frattura rituale alla riduzione delle dimensioni dei pezzi per agevolarne la rifusione. L'ipotesi che la frammentazione fosse invece mirata all'ottenimento di pezzi portatori di determinati valori di peso -certo finalizzati anche al raggiungimento della predeterminata quantità di metallo richiesta dalla matrice di fusione- e di una precisa valenza premonetale fu formulata per la prima volta verso la fine dell'Ottocento da Michele Stefano De Rossi (1886), e ripresa ottant'anni più tardi e oltre trent'anni addietro dallo scrivente (Peroni 1966: 190 ss.), con un' accoglienza piuttosto scettica (Sorda 1975) fino a qualche tempo fa, quando le evidenze e le opinioni favorevoli hanno incominciato a moltiplicarsi.

L'esame di molti ripostigli attesta che frammenti di *aes rude* e rottami di oggetti finiti furono spesso conservati a lungo, talvolta per secoli, e pervennero in molti casi in luoghi lontanissimi da quelli di fabbricazione. Il ripostiglio di S. Francesco di Bologna, deposto alla fine dell'VIII secolo, ha ad esempio restituito addirittura un pugnaletto risalente al Bronzo antico (Bianco Peroni 1994: n. 279), e quello assai più antico di Oberwilflingen nel Württemberg ha dato quattro frammenti di lingotti 'a pelle di bue' in rame cipriota (Primas 1998), ivi pervenuti o attraverso il l'Egeo e il Mar Nero, risalendo poi il corso del Danubio, o più verosimilmente lungo le rotte mediterranee fino alla Sardegna, che ne ha restituito un gran numero (Lo Schiavo 1989), e di qui alla Pianura Padana, al Ticino e all'Alto Reno. Questi pezzi poterono dunque e essere oggetto di tesaurizzazione, e circolare ampiamente con funzione di mezzo di scambio.

L'analisi ponderale di tutte queste categorie di oggetti, pani, lingotti e manufatti d'uso interi e frammentari, come pure pesi di vario genere e materiale, ha portato all'individuazione (Fig. 1) di un'ampia gamma di valori ponderali ricorrenti (per i riferimenti ai singoli dati ponderali, per i relativi elenchi e per la bibliografia di dettaglio sui vari contesti, cfr. Pizzitutti 1995; Peroni e

Pizzitutti 1997; Peroni 1998, 2001), collegati tra loro da una fitta rete di corrispondenze e correlazioni, che consentono di raggrupparli ed ordinarli in due serie ponderali, ciascuna costituita da un concatenamento di multipli e sottomultipli. Ambedue queste serie risultano ampiamente rappresentate (Fig. 2), sia nel Mediterraneo orientale, sia in quello centro-occidentale, sia sul continente europeo fino alla Scandinavia. Mentre però in alcune situazioni una delle due serie appare esclusiva o prevalente, in altre esse sembrano equilibratamente coesistere. La serie che ho denominato *A*, per la quale ho preso convenzionalmente come base un valore di 27 gr. circa, risulta esclusiva nel ripostiglio ungherese del Bronzo medio di Férégyhàza, ma è attestata anche in altri contesti danubiani della stessa epoca (oggetti in oro da ripostigli ungheresi dell'orizzonte detto di Opaly), del Bronzo recente (pani dal ripostiglio rumeno di Craciunesti), e del passaggio al Bronzo finale (lingotti - o forse pesi - 'a cuscino'); è di nuovo esclusiva in un esteso campione di oggetti dall'area scandinava, appartenenti a diversi periodi dell'età del bronzo nordica a partire dagli inizi del Bronzo medio, e che dunque vi attestano una tenace continuità di tradizione ponderale; compare anche nelle Isole Britanniche, dove però è documentata solo in età avanzata (lingotti di piombo e di stagno); sembra quasi esclusiva nei lingotti 'a pelle di bue', rinvenuti in gran prevalenza sia a Cipro, sia a Creta, sia in Sardegna, ma che in buona parte sono costituiti da rame cipriota. La serie *B*, con valore-base di gr. 62 (di cui però, proprio come in ambito miceneo, esistono due varianti, l'una 'leggera' e l'altra 'pesante'), appare invece da sola in un gruppo di ripostigli del Bronzo recente (=III periodo nordico) dalla Germania orientale (Berlin-Kaulsdorf) e dalla Polonia (Lubsko, Wilenko), nei piccoli pesi parallelepipedi di ampia diffusione centroeuropea studiati da Christopher Pare, e in una forma di fusione per lingotti a barretta dalla palafitta di Zurigo-Alpenquai; nel ripostiglio di S. Francesco di Bologna, che come abbiamo visto è stato deposto in età parecchio successiva, ma conteneva anche materiali molto più antichi, la serie *B* è prevalente rispetto ad altri valori ponderali, qui peraltro assai differenziati e articolati. Le due serie compaiono insieme anche nell'ampia raccolta di pesi da bilancia venuta in luce in contesti molto antichi, dell'inizio dell'età tardominoica ad Ayia Irini nelle Cicladi. Resta tuttavia per ora incerto se già là e allora fosse stata creata tra esse una qualche forma di connessione, che li riconducesse ad un insieme in qualche modo unitario.

Ciò avvenne invece sicuramente nel bacino danubiano durante il Bronzo recente, e in quello padano già un pò prima.

E' possibile dimostrare (Hänsel (a cura di) 1995: 213 ss.; Peroni 1998: 219; 2001: 23) che i ciottolini rinvenuti a Bordjos in associazione con il ricordato braccio di bilancia, e subito interpretati come un gruppo di pesi da bilancia, costituiscono in effetti un *set* unitario, completo e conchiuso; inoltre che nell'ambito di tale *set* le due serie ponderali sono state adattate l'una all'altra, e collegate così tra loro da formare quasi un unico sistema ponderale.

Una volta posto -sulla base di un'equazione ovviamente arbitraria e approssimativa- un rapporto di 7:16 tra le due unità di base *A1* e *B1*, le due serie vennero tradotte l'una nell'altra, e ciò consentì di interpolare e combinare tra loro i rispettivi valori. La somma complessiva dei valori di Bordjos equivale infatti ad un decuplo di *B1* .

Un procedimento analogo si coglie anche nel caso dei pesi da bilancia in pietra, provenienti soprattutto dalle Terramare emiliane. Delle due principali fogge individuate, l'una è lenticolare biconvessa per lo più con una scanalatura perimetrale continua, l'altra globulare con appiccagnolo ad occhiello.

Soprattutto nell'ambito dei pesi lenticolari (*Terram.* : 632 ss.; Cardarelli e Pacciarelli 2001: 42 ss.; Peroni 1998: 219 ss.; 2001: 23 s.) si rilevano da una parte una netta graduazione, dall'altra una notevole regolarità di ricorrenze e uniformità di valori. Salta subito agli occhi che si tratta per la maggior parte di multipli dell'unità di base *A1* di 27 grammi. Per i pesi con appiccagnolo (*Terram.* : 635 ss.; Cardarelli e Pacciarelli 2001: 38 ss.; Peroni 1998: 219 ss.; 2001: 23 ss.) il quadro potrebbe sembrare alquanto diverso: la graduazione dei valori si presenta più articolata, con distanze minori. In realtà, tuttavia, se si ordinano insieme le due fogge in un unico diagramma logaritmico a scala 3,1% (Fig. 3), sul quale si evidenziano bene le principali concentrazioni, corrispondenti ai diversi valori ponderali, risulta chiaro l'ampio coincidere dei valori che si riferiscono all'una e all'altra (Peroni 1998: 220, Abb. 3; 2001: fig. 3). Non è pertanto possibile parlare a questo proposito di due sistemi ponderali fondamentalmente diversi. Se è infatti vero che, mentre tra i pesi con appiccagnolo sono prevalenti i valori ponderali della serie*B*, tra quelli lenticolari le due serie si bilanciano, va sottolineato che esse risultano comunque strettamente intrecciate tra loro (Peroni 1998: 221, Abb. 4; 2001: fig. 4) (Fig. 4 : notare anche qui lo sdoppiamento tra un valore 'leggero' ed uno 'pesante' di *B10*). Occorre dunque ammettere che nelle Terramare le due serie ponderali erano state ricondotte ad un sistema in qualche modo unitario. Come si è accennato, ai pesi dalle Terramare si riallacciano quelli dalle palafitte della Svizzera e delle regioni vicine, appartenenti ormai al Bronzo finale e a fasi coeve della prima età del ferro italiana; l'affinità non sta solo nelle forme, ma anche nel sistema ponderale, pure esso composito.

Anche in Italia la sopravvivenza di tale sistema misto almeno fino al Bronzo finale è attestata dalla serie -sulla quale torneremo più analiticamente in seguito- di ripostigli, per lo più con pani a piccone, sparsi da Piano di Tallone nel Grossetano a Madriolo in Friuli. Con quest'ultimo rinvenimento ci veniamo a trovare in contiguità non solo geografica, ma anche cronologica e metrologica -questa attestata da diverse e suggestive comunanze (valori *A2, A3, B1, B3*)- con il contesto della bilancia di Bordjos. A fare ancor più strettamente da ponte provvede poi il gruppo dei ripostigli sloveni del Bronzo recente e finale.

E' tuttavia interessante rilevare che da una parte la diffusione dei pani a piccone (Bietti Sestieri 1997: 389, fig. 5) risulta geograficamente assai più estesa, dalla Slovenia all'Est della Francia, dall'altra gli esemplari integri noti rientrerebbero, secondo un'ipotesi ponderale di Pare, forse un pò azzardata dato che presuppone valori multipli del 9 altrimenti non documentati, tutti ed esclusivamente nella serie ponderale *A* .

Tornando al sistema misto, esso si estese anche all'Europa centro-settentrionale, come dimostrano i valori registrati nel ripostiglio di Weißig in Sassonia.

Anche nei ripostigli sardi del Bronzo finale e primo Ferro -Flumenelongu (Lo Schiavo 1976), S. Antine di Torralba (Lo Schiavo 1988), Ittireddu, Nuraghe Funtana (GALLI 1984, 1985), S. Anastasia di Sardara (UGAS 1986), Pattada, M. Ottinnera[2]-, come pure in quelli coevi della penisola iberica (questi però costituiti da oggetti aurei interi, soprattutto braccialetti: Galàn e Ruiz-Gàlvez 1996: 153 ss.) le due serie ponderali appaiono organicamente connesse in un sistema unico.

Per quanto riguarda il possibile rapporto tra le due serie ponderali considerate come entità separate, va detto che tale impostazione è stata fatta propria anche da Christopher Pare nel suo, più volte citato, recente lavoro (1999: 481 ss.). Secondo Pare, tuttavia, il rapporto tra di esse sarebbe di natura essenzialmente cronologica: la serie *B* sarebbe la più antica, e deriverebbe da un sistema ponderale miceneo, diffusosi sul continente europeo durante il Bronzo medio, e affermatosi definitivamente col Bronzo recente; la serie *A* ,sviluppatasi da un sistema ponderale cipriota-levantino, avrebbe preso piede in Europa con il passaggio al Bronzo finale (per l'esattezza, traducendo la sua in terminologia italiana, con il Bronzo recente avanzato).

Paradossalmente, questa tesi di Pare appare inconciliabile proprio con i dati da lui stesso selezionati e utilizzati, oltre che con gli altri dati qui esposti. Una revisione dei valori ponderali di Ayia Irini (Alberti 1995, 1999) ha mostrato che, fin dagli inizi dell'età tardominoica, accanto al sistema cd. 'miceneo' vi era già presente quello cd. 'cipriota'. Le due serie ponderali coesistevano anche nei pesi delle Terramare, in uso fin dal Bronzo medio e poi nel Bronzo recente. Viceversa, i dati relativi all'area danubiana e alla Scandinavia ci documentano durante il Bronzo medio in quelle regioni solo l'esistenza della serie *A*. Significativo sembra anche il fatto che la serie *B* non sia a quanto pare mai arrivata ad affermarsi nell'area scandinava. Dal Bronzo recente in poi i due sistemi o si combinano assieme, o perdurano separatamente in aree o in contesti diversi.

Al gruppo dei ripostigli italiani del Bronzo finale, con - Manciano (Peroni 1961, 1966), Madriolo, Redipuglia (Borgna 1992), Villamarzana (Bellintani 1994)- o senza - Piano di Tallone (Peroni 1961), loc. ignota al Mus. Pigorini (Pellegrini 1987-88), Pulfero di Celò (Borgna 2000-2001: 317 ss.)[3]- pani a piccone, si accosta il grandioso ripostiglio di S. Francesco di Bologna (Zannoni 1888; Sorda 1975), che è molto più tardo, della fine dell'VIII secolo; ed è con riferimento a quest'ultimo, cui va aggiunto il ripostiglio di Ardea presso Roma (Peroni 1966, 1967), di poco più antico, che più sopra si è accennato alla presenza di più serie ponderali differenziate tra loro, caratteristica peraltro comune a tutti questi contesti.

Il quadro d'insieme dei valori ponderali attestati in questa serie di ripostigli è qui stato reso sotto forma di tabella analitica (Fig. 5). Esso mostra una notevole varietà di raggruppamenti di pesi, nel cui ambito è possibile individuare e distinguere l'uno dall'altro in modo sufficientemente chiaro singoli valori ponderali, soprattutto in base ai valori medi e ai valori dei rispettivi punti di massima concentrazione. Tali valori rientrano in quattro diverse serie, due delle quali si possono ricollegare rispettivamente alle nostre serie *A* e *B*, mentre per ora le altre due costituiscono per noi qualcosa di nuovo. Va tuttavia rilevato che la prima di esse, la serie che chiamiamo *C* , non è probabilmente altro che una derivazione dalla serie *B,* visto che la sua unità-base (*C1*), di poco più di 40 g., equivale ai 2/3 dell'unità *B1*; mentre l'unità-base della serie *D* (*D1*), di quasi 70 g., equivale ad 1/4 dell'unità *A10.*

Appare dubbio che si possa qui legittimamente parlare di una graduale evoluzione nell'ambito del lungo spazio di tempo che va dal XII all'VIII sec. Tutte e quattro le serie ponderali in discorso risultano in effetti ampiamente rappresentate già nei più antichi ripostigli del gruppo, ma lo sono altrettanto nei più recenti.

Sembra comunque certo che le due nuove serie ponderali -o forse addirittura sistemi indipendenti?- siano proprio quelle cui si sarebbe poi venuto ad aprire un ulteriore sbocco. Due dei valori riportati sulla tabella meritano in particolare la nostra attenzione. L'uno, siglato *D4*, è di circa 267 g., l'altro, siglato *C8* , di circa 340 g. Ora, si dà il caso che dai depositi votivi del VI-VII secolo del santuario arcaico di Satricum, che dista pochi chilometri da Ardea, provengano, assieme a parti di bilance, due pesi da bilancia in piombo, rispettivamente proprio di 267 e 340 g. (Nijboer 1994: 1 ss., figg. 3, 4). In termini metrologici sono stati definiti l'uno come una libbra romano-osca, l'altro come una libbra romano-attica (Nijboer 1994: 3 ss.).

In un'ottica fondata sui dati italiani sembrerebbe dunque proponibile l'ipotesi che il passaggio dalla generale uniformità alla frammentazione dei sistemi ponderali sia da collocare poco dopo la fine dell'età del bronzo recente, in corrispondenza della svolta tra la *koiné* metallurgica europea e la sua successiva disgregazione in cerchie culturali locali (Peroni 1996: 278 ss., 384 ss.). Tuttavia, almeno nell'ambito del territorio italiano continuarono a sussistere ampie unità geografiche in campo metrologico. Ad esempio, i menzionati ripostigli, aventi in comune le quattro serie ponderali che abbiamo definito, si distribuiscono su ampie zone dell'Italia centro-settentrionale; e almeno tre di quelle serie ricorrono nel deposito siciliano del Mendolito presso Adernò (Albanese Procelli 1993: 109, con i dati ponderali), coevo di S. Francesco e di Ardea. Solo successivamente dovette aver luogo, in concomitanza o forse in conseguenza del processo di differenziazione in un gran numero di gruppi regionali culturali ed etnici, la formazione di quelle unità metrologiche locali per lo più minori, che all'inizio dell'età storica ci sono documentate dalle fonti scritte e dalle evidenze numismatiche (Cfr. da ultimo Parise 1989: 581 ss.).

Poiché è nello spirito di questo incontro di studio trattare, oltre ai problemi relativi all'economia antica sia produttiva che di scambio, anche i percorsi metodologici seguiti nell'affrontarli, aprirò ora una breve parentesi per illustrare, con riferimento ad un campione di contesti particolarmente adatto per la sua coerenza cronologica e geografica, che abbraccia i ripostigli italiani del Bronzo finale con o senza pani a piccone insieme a quelli sloveni coevi o non troppo più antichi, le procedure analitiche seguite per l'analisi di contesti per i quali sia ipotizzata ma ancora da dimostrare la presenza di valori ponderali ricorrenti.

Il modello di rappresentazione grafica più adatto all'individuazione e delimitazione di aggregazioni e rarefazioni di valori è ovviamente quello dell'istogramma, che evidenzia il numero di esemplari che vengono a cadere in ciascuno degli intervalli di una scala graduata appositamente predisposta. Poiché però l'approssimazione di ciascuna misura, e con essa l'intervallo tra i valori formati dall'aggregazione delle misure, tende sempre a variare in modo proporzionale all'entità della misura stessa, in altre parole secondo un rapporto percentuale con essa, una scala a graduazione fissa non può non presentare seri inconvenienti: in essa i valori più bassi appariranno troppo fitti e tenderanno a confondersi, quelli più alti si presenteranno rarefatti e dispersi. Nel caso della frammentazione intenzionale di pani, lingotti e rottami di manufatti in bronzo, poi, c'è da attendersi un margine di approssimazione particolarmente alto. Spesso si procedeva per tentativi successivi, come mostrano le frequenti tacche o incisioni preparatorie, traccia di pentimenti o di prove fallite. Ora, in una scala graduata logaritmica gli scarti tra un valore e l'altro sono proporzionali al valore di partenza: in una scala al 3%, ad esempio, col raddoppiare del peso raddoppierà anche lo scarto, e il valore successivo al 100 sarà di 103, ma il valore successivo al 200 sarà di 206, e via di seguito.

In un diagramma ponderale logaritmico le aggregazioni di pesi più caratteristiche e significative sono segnalate da *picchi* con andamento a doppio spiovente che richiama una curva gaussiana, nei quali il fatto che la concentrazione, più densa in mezzo, tenda a disperdersi ai lati denota il suo gravitare attorno ad un valore centrale, e che dunque essa è il prodotto di un procedimento intenzionale.

Una volta riconosciuta la presenza di un valore, si tratta però di individuarlo e di delimitarlo il più precisamente possibile.

Per quanto riguarda il primo problema, il caso ideale di determinazione più certa e precisa è quello in cui nell'ambito di un'aggregazione di pesi il valore apicale, ossia il punto di massima concentrazione indicato dal picco sull'istogramma, coincide o tende a coincidere con il valore medio. Più aumenta lo scostamento, più si fa incerta la lettura del diagramma. Tuttavia, può essere ritenuto fisiologico il fenomeno per cui il valore medio è spesso moderatamente inferiore al valore apicale -che dunque è quello giusto-, dato che chi pesa, pur mirando soprattutto alla precisione, se proprio deve sbagliare tende umanamente a sbagliarsi un pò più spesso in meno che in più: qual'è il bottegaio che, magari inconsciamente, non ruba ogni tanto un pochino sul peso? Nel caso opposto, invece, quello più problematico in cui il valore medio risulta superiore a quello apicale, è ragionevole supporre che quest'ultimo sia inaffidabile perché statisticamente deformato da un errore del caso, e che il primo si avvicini un pò di più al vero.

Più complesso è il secondo problema, quello della delimitazione del campo di oscillazione di un valore di peso, in altre parole della determinazione dei suoi limiti minimo e massimo. Accade infatti che la distanza tra i due limiti tenda a crescere in proporzione con l'altezza del *picco*, vale a dire con la consistenza del campione statistico; e che con l'aumento di questo le basi di due *picchi* diversi tendano a incontrarsi, fondersi e confondersi tra loro. Teoricamente questo problema non consente soluzione: abbiamo paragonato l'andamento a doppio spiovente di un *picco* ad una curva gaussiana, ma com'è noto questa non ha termine, perché tende a perdersi, sia pure in un misura statisticamente irrilevante, all'infinito. Mettendo il discorso in un altro modo, l'artefice che faceva a pezzi un pane o un manufatto in bronzo da riciclare mirando a ricavarne determinati valori di peso, procedeva, per quanto fosse bravo, in modo approssimativo, tendendo cioè a mantenersi all'interno di una data banda di oscillazione, e magari riuscendoci quasi sempre; ma ogni tanto inevitabilmente si sbagliava, a volte anche di brutto. In pratica, il problema si risolve assumendo a una prima lettura come limiti del campo di oscillazione del valore che si vuole delimitare i margini estremi della base del *picco*, o, quando questa incontri quella di altri *picchi*, le selle che li separano; e confrontando a una seconda lettura tra loro gli istogrammi relativi a contesti diversi, ma in cui ricorra lo stesso valore, in modo da paragonarne i limiti, così da rilevarne costanti e scarti.

Ma veniamo ora al merito di questa sezione della nostra ricerca, la comparazione tra i valori ponderali individuati in due gruppi di ripostigli: da una parte quelli italiani del Centro e del Nord-Est elencati più sopra, caratterizzati fra l'altro dalla presenza di frammenti di pani, in parte del tipo a piccone, e databili in prevalenza alla fase piena del Bronzo finale (BF2), dunque anteriori al 1000 a.C., dall'altra i ripostigli sloveni di composizione spesso analoga, risalenti alle prime fasi dell'età dei Campi di Urne, equivalenti all'intero nostro Bronzo recente e finale (Terzan (ed.) 1995)[4]. La comparazione è stata effettuata sia (Fig. 6) accostando tra loro specularmente i due istogrammi ponderali logaritmici relativi rispettivamente ai ripostigli italiani (in alto) e sloveni (in basso), sia (Fig. 7) mediante una tabella analitica, in cui sono messe a confronto in parallelo una per una le rispettive aggregazioni ponderali, con l'indicazione volta a volta dei singoli valori (S.), delle coppie (SS.), e delle serie di valori, per ciascuna delle quali ultime sono riportati: i due valori estremi (da - a), o anche diverse coppie di valori quando la serie presenti delle discontinuità, la media (M.), il valore apicale o di massima concentrazione (C.). Mentre però negli istogrammi tali aggregazioni sono ovviamente ordinate secondo la progressione numerica, nella tabella in esse vengono individuati valori noti come pertinenti ad una delle quattro serie ponderali (A, B, C, D) di cui si è parlato prima, indicati dalla sigla sulla destra, e per serie esse vengono ordinate. La comparazione mostra un parallelismo complessivamente assai stretto tra i due gruppi: in grandissima prevalenza i valori delle serie A e B presenti nei ripostigli italiani trovano riscontro anche in quelli sloveni, e ancor più viceversa, anche se spesso valori rappresentati negli uni da numerosi esemplari lo sono in misura assai minore negli altri. Di gran lunga minoritarie, soprattutto in quanto rappresentate da una esigua gamma di valori, risultano in entrambi i gruppi le serie C e D -sebbene a rigore dovremmo annoverare tra queste anche i valori che esse hanno in comune con le serie *A* e *B* : *C1* equivalente di *B2/3* , *D4* equivalente di *A10* e *D8* equivalente di *A20* -, confermando l'impressione che la loro maggiore fortuna risalga alla prima età del ferro, per la quale però disponiamo solo di evidenze italiane.

Per tornare a quanto si è anticipato all'inizio, è dunque senz'altro legittimo riconoscere elementi di professionalità, anzi di professionalità transculturale nelle attività di scambio praticate durante il Bronzo recente attraverso il Mediterraneo e il continente europeo. Secondo Pare (1999: 476, 510), i capi guerrieri deposti nelle tombe da lui studiate utilizzavano davvero personalmente per la pesatura di oro, ambra ed altre materie preziose, proprio come avveniva in ambito miceneo, le loro bilance di precisione ed i relativi *set* di piccoli pesi, come documentano gli appositi astucci, in cui il tutto veniva riposto assieme a cianfrusaglie di uso personale, come ami da pesca e altro. Ma che cosa determinava questo singolare accostamento tra potere politico-militare e professionalità di tipo mercantile?

Sempre a Pare (1999: 511 ss.) si deve la suggestiva proposta di annoverare quella europea dell'età del bronzo tra le società non urbane o protourbane (come quella del tardo La Tène, quella merovingia, quella vichinga) ad economia di circolazione fondata sulla pesatura dell'equivalente. I pesi delle Terramare e delle palafitte e la massa enorme di metallo grezzo o in rottami a frammentazione intenzionale mirante all'ottenimento di determinati valori ponderali conservata nei ripostigli ci dimostrano tuttavia che, oltre e più che dall'oro, questa funzione di equivalente era assolta dal bronzo.

Resta però da chiedersi se questa funzione di circolante avesse luogo solo all'interno del traffico del metallo - se insomma il bronzo (come materia prima) fungesse solo da equivalente di sé stesso (come manufatto) - o se piuttosto non investisse anche altre attività economiche.

Dobbiamo a Luigi Bernabò Brea e a Madeleine Cavalier (1980: 738 s.) una implicita presa di posizione in questo senso, formulata come molte altre volte con straordinaria naturalezza. Parlando dei frammenti di *aes rude* e dei rottami di oggetti d'uso dal ripostiglio di Lipari, essi li definiscono "pezzi che hanno lungamente circolato come mezzo di scambio a guisa di moneta", ma poi aggiungono: "...lo stesso significato hanno d'altronde i numerosi frammenti, spesso informi, di metallo, che abbiamo raccolto sparsi nei livelli della tarda età del bronzo dell'acropoli di Lipari....", dove questa circolazione è evidentemente vista come un fenomeno piuttosto comune, non legato in modo esclusivo a situazioni molto particolari.

La stessa suggestione di quotidianità quasi banale emana dal borsellino di Neuwühren (Sommerfeld 1994: 406, Taff. 12, 22,23; 13, 1), nella Germania nord-occidentale al confine della Danimarca. Rinvenuto in una tomba maschile con spada del III periodo nordico, coevo del nostro Bronzo recente, esso era in cuoio, tenuto assieme da stringhe, era racchiuso in una scatola di truciolato di legno rivestito di pelliccia, e conteneva a sua volta due frammenti di lama di falcetto ed uno di coltello, come quelli che si rinvengono in grandi quantità nei ripostigli della stessa età nella stessa zona.

E' fin troppo ovvio che, per quanta importanza le si voglia attribuire, un'economia di scambio fondata sulla pesatura del circolante metallico non è che un settore assai limitato e secondario dell'economia *tout court* di una popolazione. Se tuttavia mi sono soffermato tanto a lungo su questo argomento, è perchè questo costituisce l'unico elemento unificante nell'ambito di strutture economiche per il resto del tutto difformi da zona a zona del continente europeo.

Durante l'età del bronzo recente, procedendo da Sud verso Nord vediamo ll'Europa attraversata da grandi formazioni economico-sociali strutturalmente assai differenziate (Peroni 1996: 3-43): quella palaziale nell'Egeo; quella gentilizio-clientelare nell'Italia centro-meridionale e nel Sud della penisola balcanica; quella delle grosse comunità a base funzionale e territoriale nell'Italia del Nord e nella fascia temperata a Nord delle Alpi, tra l'Atlantico e i Carpazi; quella nordica, articolata in comunità più piccole, di norma residenti in fattorie isolate, in Scandinavia. Rispetto a dislivelli tanto marcati, l'economia di scambio ad equivalente pesato, che su ciascuna delle forme socio-economiche coinvolte, nessuna esclusa, esercitava una lenta, quasi impercettibile azione disgregante, veniva a creare una sorta di varco, diciamo una specie di rampa che raccordava le acropoli alla steppa. Quella rampa convogliò, assieme ai traffici, tutta una serie di manifestazioni che, per il fatto di non essere strutturalmente condizionate, risultavano compatibili con le diverse forme di organizzazione economico-sociale. Non solo transculturali, dunque, ma interstrutturali, destinate ad esercitare anch'esse una progressiva azione disgregante, ma al tempo stesso aggregante.

NOTE

1 Questa ricerca deve molto alla collaborazione di due persone, la dott.ssa Geraldine Pizzitutti che l'aveva incominciata assieme a me anni fa, e poi purtroppo ha passato la mano, e il dott. Luca Alessandri che l'ha incominciata in questa occasione -a lui si devono in gran parte le illustrazioni-, e al quale mi piacerebbe passare la mano, prima o poi. Li ringrazio entrambi.
2 Devo alla cortesia dell'amica F. Lo Schiavo, che desidero qui ringraziare vivamente per questa, come pure per tante altre informazioni e suggerimenti, il seguente elenco di valori ponderali: gr. 20; 21,5; 61,6; 62; 62; 67; 79; 104,7; 163; 212; 237; 264; 266; 285,6; 334;
553; 661; 686; 879; 970; 1406; 1507; 1588,5; 2777.
3 Ringrazio le amiche Serena Vitri per la cortese autorizzazione ad effettuare la pesatura dei pezzi, e Paola Guida Càssola per la segnalazione di questo ripostiglio, e per il gentile aiuto prestatomi nella circostanza. Ne ho ricavato il seguente elenco di valori ponderali: gr. 1,8; 5,6; 8,8; 9,4; 11,3; 11,8; 59,2; 68,8; 73,2; 76,2; 77,6; 78,8; 84,4; 97; 97,2; 110; 112; 114; 117; 117; 193; 215; 225; 261; 261. 310; 423; 469; 487; 635; 789; 839; 897, con segno di un taglio chiaramente finalizzato ad una frammentazione a caldo; 919, con taglio; 1374; 1451; 1731; 2315, con taglio; 2573; 2593; 2835; 3200; 6560; peso complessivo del ripostiglio gr. 34342.
4 Per la paziente trascrizione dei valori ponderali riportati nell'opera citata ringrazio Maja Gori, laureanda in Protostoria Europea appunto con una tesi sui ripostigli sloveni.

BIBLIOGRAFIA

Albanese Procelli, R.M., 1993, *Ripostigli di bronzi della Sicilia nel Museo Archeologico di Siracusa,* Palermo.

Alberti, M.E., 1995, Ayia Irini: les poids de balance dans leur contexte, *Quad. ticinesi di numismatica e antichità classiche,* XXIV, 9-27.

Alberti, M.E., 1999, Il sistema ponderale egeo tra omogeneità e flessibilità: continuità e discontinuità tra il mondo minoico e quello miceneo, in *Epì pònton plazò menoi, Simposio italiano di studi egei dedicato a L. Bernabò Brea e G. Pugliese Carratelli* (a cura di V. La Rosa, D. Palermo e L . Vagnetti), Roma, 339-350.

Bellintani, P., 1994, Un ripostiglio di bronzi contenente pani a piccone nell'abitato protoveneto di Villamarzana - Campagna Michela (Rovigo),*Civiltà Padana,* V, 7-16.

Bellintani, P., 2001, Osservazioni su alcuni pesi di Frattesina, in Cardarelli e Pacciarelli, 2001, 44-45.

Bernabò Brea, L., Cavalier, M., 1980, *Meligunì s - Lipàra IV ,* Palermo.

Bianco Peroni, V., 1994, *I pugnali nell'Italia continentale,* P.B.F. VI, 10, Stuttgart.

Bietti Sestieri, A. M., 1997, Italy in Europe in the Early Iron Age, *Proceedings of the Prehistoric Society,* 63, 371-402.

Borgna, E., 1992, *Il ripostiglio di Madriolo presso Cividale e i pesi a piccone del Friuli Venezia Giulia,* Roma.

Borgna, E., 2000-2001, I ripostigli del Friuli: proposta di seriazione cronologica e di interpretazione funzionale, *Rivista di Scienze Preistoriche,* LI.

Cardarelli, A., e Pacciarelli, M., 2001, Pesi e bilance dell'età del bronzo italiana, in *Pondera. Pesi e misure nell'Antichità* (a cura di C. Corti e N. Giordani), Campogalliano, 33 ss.

Champion, T., Gamble, C., Shennan, S., Whittle, A., 1984, *Prehistoric Europe,* London.

De Rossi, M. S., 1886, Pezzi di *aes rude* di peso definito e le asce di bronzo adoperate come valore monetale, *Dissertazioni della Pontificia Accademia Romana di Archeologia,* S. 2, 2, 454 ss.

Galàn, E., e Ruiz-Gàlvez Priego, M., 1996, Divisa, dinero y moneda. Aproximaciòn al estudio de los patrones metrològicos peninsulares, *Complutum Extra,* 6 (II).

Galli F., 1984, Scavi nel nuraghe Funtana di Ittireddu (Sassari), *Nuovo Bullettino Archeologico Sardo,* 1.

Galli F., 1985, Nota preliminare sulla terza e quarta campagna di scavo al nuraghe Funtana (Ittireddu - Sassari), *Nuovo Bullettino Archeologico Sardo,* 2.

Giardino, C., 1995, *Il Mediterraneo Occidentale tra XIV ed VIII secolo a. C. Cerchie minerarie e metallurgiche,* B.A.R. I.S. 612, Oxford.

Hänsel, B. (a cura di), 1995, *Handel, Tausch und Verkehr im bronze- und früheisenzeitlichen Südosteuropa,* München - Berlin.

Lo Schiavo, F., 1976, Il ripostiglio del nuraghe Flumenelongu, *Quaderni della Soprintendenza di Sassari e Nuoro,* 2.

Lo Schiavo, F., 1988, Il ripostiglio della Capanna 1, in *Il Nuraghe S. Antine nel Logudoro-Meilogu* (a cura di A. Moravetti), Sassari.

Lo Schiavo, F., 1989, Early Metallurgy in Sardinia: Copper Ox-Hide Ingots, in *Archäometallurgie der Alten Welt* (a cura di A. Hauptmann, E. Pernicka, G. A. Wagner), Bochum, 33 ss.

Mazzeo, R., Negroni Catacchio, N., Raposso, B., Le perle di ambra, in *Ipogei della Daunia* (a cura di A. M. Tunzi Sisto), Foggia, 289 ss.

Nijboer A., 1994, A pair of early metallic monetary units from Borgo Le Ferriere (Satricum), *The Numismatic Chronicle,* CLIV.

Pare, Chr. F. E., Weights and weighing in Bronze Age Central Europe, in *Eliten in derBronzezeit* (AA. VV.), Mainz, 421 ss.

Parise, N., 1989, Economia e società. Libbre e bronzo librale nell'Italia antica, in *Italia omnium terrarum parens* (a cura di G. Pugliese Carratelli), Milano.

Pellegrini, E., 1987-88, Un ripostiglio del Bronzo finale inedito dalle collezioni del Museo Pigorini, *Studi Etruschi,* 55.

Peroni, R., 1961, *Ripostigli dell'età dei metalli. Ripostigli del Grossetano,* Inventaria Archaeologica, Italia, 2, I. 4.

Peroni, R., 1966, Considerazioni ed ipotesi sul ripostiglio di Ardea, *Bull. Paletn. Ital.,*

75,175 ss.

Peroni, R., 1967, *Ripostigli dell'età dei metalli. Ripostiglio di Ardea,* Inventaria Archaeologica, Italia, 4, I. 9.

Peroni, R., 1994, *Introduzione alla protostoria italiana,* Roma - Bari.

Peroni, R., 1996, *L'Italia alle soglie della Storia,* Roma - Bari.

Peroni, R., 1998, Bronzezeitliche Gewichtssysteme im Metallhandel zwischen Mittelmeer und Ostsee, in*Mensch und Umwelt in der Bronzezeit Europas* (a cura di B. Hänsel), Kiel, 217 ss.

Peroni, R., 2001, Sistemi ponderali nella circolazione dei metalli dell'età del bronzo europea, in *Pondera. Pesi e misure nell'Antichità* (a cura di C. Corti e N. Giordani), Campogalliano, 21 ss.

Peroni, R., e Pizzitutti, G., 1997, recensione a Chr. Sommerfeld, *Gerätegeld Sichel,* in *Prähistorische Zeitschrift* , 72, 2, 257 ss.

Pizzitutti, G., 1995, *Dati e problematiche interpretative su sistemi metrologici ponderali a carattere premonetale nell'Italia protostorica,* Tesi di laurea inedita in Protostoria Europea, Università di Roma 'La Sapienza'.

Piggott, S., 1976, *Europa antica,* Torino.

Primas, M., 1998, Der Depotfund von Oberwilflingen, *Germania,* 76, 1, 25 ss.

Sorda, S., 1975, I 'ripostigli' di bronzi protostorici dell'Italia centrale, *Suppl. Annali Istit. Ital. Numismatica,* 22, 61 ss.

Sommerfeld, Chr., 1994,*Gerätegeld Sichel,* Berlin - New York.

Terram., 1997,*Terramare, la più antica civiltà padana* (a cura di M. Bernabò Brea, A. Cardarelli, M. Cremaschi), Milano.

Terzan, B. (ed.), 1995, *Hoards and individual metal finds from the Eneolithic and Bronze Ages in Slovenia,* I-II, Catalogi et monografiae Narodni Muzej Ljubljana.

Ugas, G., 1986, Nuovi scavi nel santuario nuragico di S. Anastasia di Sardara, in *La Sardegna nel Mediterraneo tra il II e il I millennio a. C. - Atti del II Convegno di Studi,*

Selargius.

Vagnetti, L., 1999, Mycenaean pottery in the central Mediterranean: imports and local production in their context, in*The complex past of pottery, Proceedings of the ARCHON internat. conference 1996* (a cura di J.P. Crielaard, Vl. Stissi, G.J. van Vijngaarden), Amsterdam, 137 ss.

von Hase, F.W., 1995, Ägäische, griechische und vorderasiatische Einflüsse auf das tyrrhenische Mittelitalien, in*Beiträge zur Urnenfelderzeit nördlich und südlich der Alpen, Ergebnisse des Kolloquiums* (AA. VV.), Bonn, 239 ss.

Zannoni, A., 1888, *La fonderia di Bologna scoperta e descritta,* Bologna.

Serie B	Peso (gr.)	Serie A	Serie B	Peso (gr.)	Serie A
B1/12	5.2		B6	372.0	
B1/8	7.8			432.0	A16
	9.0	A1/3	B8	496.0	
B1/6	10.3			540.0	A20(D8)
B1/4	15.5		B10	620.0	
B1/3	20.6		B12	744.0	
	27.0	A1		864.0	A32
B1/2	31.0		B15	930.0	
B3/5	37.2		B16	992.0	
B2/3(C1)	41.3			1080.0	A40(D16)
	54.0	A2	B20	1240.0	
B1	62.0			1350.0	A50
	81.0	A3	B24	1488.0	
B1 1/2	93.0			1620.0	A60
	108.0	A4		1728.0	A64
B2	124.0		B30	1860.0	
	135.0	A5(D2)		2160.0	A80
	162.0	A6	B40	2480.0	
B3	186.0			2700.0	A100
	189.0	A7	B48	2976.0	
	216.0	A8		3240.0	A120
B4	248.0			6480.0	A240
	270.0	A10(D4)		27000.0	A1000
	324.0	A12		32400.0	A1200

Fig. 1. Le serie ponderali *A* e *B*.

	Férégyhaza	Opalyi e Cracunesti	Scandinavia	Gran Bret.	Pelle di bue	Ling. a cuscino	Ayia Irini	Weissig	Bordjos	Terramare (e Frattesina)	Rip. italiani BF	Ripostigli sloveni	Pani a piccone	Sardegna	Spagna BF	S.Francesco	Pal. svizzere	Zurig.	P. a prisma	Berlino	
											5.15 (M.)	5.2 (M.)									B1/12
A1/3											9(M.)	9, 9 (S. S.)									
											11.3, 11.8	11.2 (M.)									B1/6
							15, 15.9 (S. S.)		16.95 (S.)		15, 16 (S.S.)								15.3		B1/4
							20.25, 20.35 (S. S.)					21(M.)		20, 21.5					20.4		B1/3
A1		27.25 (M.)					28.1, 28.6 (S. S.)				24.6 (M.)	24.5(M.)									
							30.35, 31.6 (S. S.) da 30.35 a 35.8				31.3(M.)	31.4(M.)						31 (S.)		31.5 (M.)	B1/2
										36.5, 36.6 (S. S.)	36.6(M.)	36(M.)									B3/5
							da 38.7 a 42.3			43.2* (S.)	43.2(M.)	40.5(M.)							40.9		B2/3
A2	55.21 (S.)		53.3 (M.)				da 53.3 a 55.75	57 (S.)	51.18 (S.) 54.37 (S.) 55.70 (S.)		52.3(M.)	47.1(M.)		53.3 (M.)							
							58.9, 65.55 (S. S.)		62.72 (S.)		60.7(M.)	61.6(M.)		62 (M.)	60(S.)			62 (S.)	61.3	66 (M.)	B1
A3			80.3 (M.)				83.05, 85.7 (S. S.)		86.72 (S.)		81.5(M.)	83.2(M.)		76, 79 (S.S.)							
							91.9 (S.)				93.8(M.)	93.2(M.)		89.5 (M.)			98.3 (S.)			91 (M.)	B1
A4			107.07 (M.)	112.3 (S.)							105.3(M.)	103.5(M.)		109.5 (M.)	110.45(S.)	110 (M.)	102 (S.)				
							121 (S.)		122.17 (S.)		117(M.)	120.3(M.)		123.1 (M.)	120.7(M.)	125.5 (M.)		124		124	B2
A5			133.84 (M.)					138 (S.)						140 (M.)							
A6				158 (S.)		158, 158 (S. S.)						158.4(M.)		164 (M.)	158.2, 167.3 (S.S.)						
A7			187.37 (M.)						183.7 (S.)		183.6(M.)	192(M.)		184 (M.)	196.1(M.)	191.3 (M.)	195 (S.)				B3
A8	211.45 (S.)					da 211 a	219.2 (S.)			206 (S.)	220.4(M.)	213.4(M.)		215.1 (M.)	230.9(S.)	224 (M.)	210 (S.)				
										251 (S.)	237(M.)	245(M.)		248 (M.)		245.1 (M.)				254	B4
A10				256, 262							281(M.)	276(M.)		267 (M.)							
A12	331.25 (S.)									301.7 (M.)	307(M.)	309.7(M.)		333.3 (M.)		307 (M.)					
							390.6 (S.)			376.6 (M.)	375(M.)	(392.3 M.)		356.5 (M.)	380(M.)	396 (M.)	386, 389				B6
A16		432 (S.)								427.9 (M.)	420.3(M.)	448(M.)		436.2 (M.)	461(S.)	434 (M.) 436					
							506.6 (S.)	492 (S.)		487.4 (M.)	483.5(M.)	486.8(M.)				481 (M.)					B8
A20								da 534 a 560		537.6 (M.)	557.3(M.)	537(M.)		536.6 (M.)			530 (S.)				
							626 (S.)	625, 630 (S. S.)	633.51**	628 (M.)	608(M.)	602,1(M.)		613 (M.)	583(M.)	617 (M.)	613.77 (S.)				B10
											776.8(M.)	754.2(M.)		735 (M.)	750(S.)		da 727 a				B12
A32					852 S. (S.)					862.8 (M.)		854(M.)		865 (M.)			848, 870				
											921.4(M.)						da 920 a				B15
											976.2(M.)			971 (M.)	950(S.)						B16
A40												1064(M.)		1073.5 (M.)			1052 (S.)				
											1171(M.)			1188, 1229	1256.5(S.)						B20
A50					1316 S. (M.) 1346.4, 1411.8 O. (S. S.)						1357, 1374(S.S.)	1308,1358 (S. S.)		1317.3 (M.)							
											1425, 1451(S.S.)	1526(S.)	1425 (S.)	1473 (M.)							B24
A60											1606(S.)			1595 (M.)							
A64					1671 S. (M.) 1682.8 O. (S.)		1695 (S.)				1702(M.)			1695.6 (M.)							
					1871 S. (M.)						1810(S.)	1818(S.)		1871.5 (M.)	1950,						B30
A80											2170(S.)	2175(S.)		2153 (M.)							
											2315, 2385(S.S.)		da 2370 a 2388		2300(S.)						B40
A100											2573, 2593(S.S.)			2740, 2777 (S.S.)							
											2835(S.)	2955(S.)	2840, 2844 (S.S.)								B48
A120					3254.2 O. (S.)						3200(S.)										
A240											6560(S.)										
A1000					da 27000 a 27900 C. 27100 S. (S.)																
A1200					32000 H.T. (S.) 32100 E. (S.) 33300 S. (S.)																

Fig. 2. Principali localizzazioni e contesti europei con attestazioni delle serie ponderali *A* e *B* . *Abbreviazioni* : (S.) valore singolo; (S.S.) due valori singoli; (M.) valore medio; (C.) concentrazione principale.

NOTA

una versione completa della tabella nella pagina precedente è disponibile come download da www.barpublishing.com/additional-downloads.html

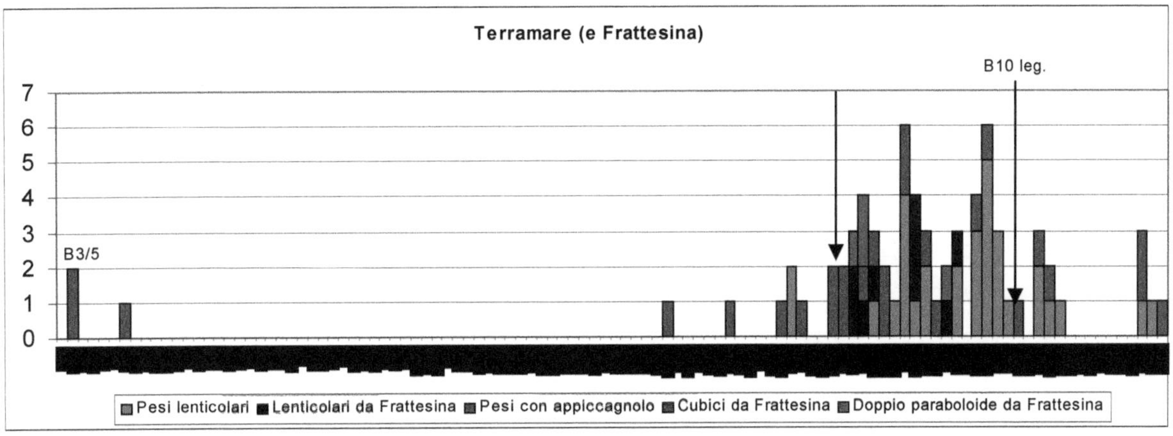

Fig. 3. Distribuzione graduata su scala logaritmica dei valori ponderali relativi a pesi in pietra, con le maggiori concentrazioni individuate riferite alla serie ponderali *A* e *B*.

TERRAMARE (e Frattesina)

	LENTICOLARI	APPICCAGNOLO	
		36.5, 36.6	B3/5
		43.2	B2/3(=C1)
A12	**299, 304**	da 295 a 309	
		da 340 a 348	B16/3(=C8)
	da 361 a 388	da 376 a 392	B6
A16	**da 415 a 443**	417, 420	
		453, 461	?
	da 483 a 494		B8
A20	**da 520 a 559**	524, 539	
	580	590	B10 leggero
	da 630 a 664	636, 641	B10 pesante
A32	**850, 876**	842, 848	

Fig. 4. Corrispondenze tra i valori ponderali relativi alle due distinte classi di pesi in pietra, riferiti alle serie ponderali *A* e *B*.

Manciano	Mus. Pigorini	Pulfero	Madriolo	Villamarzana	Piano di Tallone	Redipuglia	S. Francesco	Ardea	Valore ponderale
da 23 a 25 24 (M.), 24.5 (C.)				24 (S.)					A1
da 48 a 57 52 (M.), 51.5 (C.)			da 53 a 56 54.3 (M.), 53.5 (C.)	55 (S.)					A2
da 107 a 108, da 112 a 121; 107.5 (M. e C.), 116 (M.), 118 (C.)	104, 110 (S.S.)		da 101 a 116 109.2(M.)				da 106.4 a 114.7 110 (M. e C.)		A4
	153, 162 (S.S.)		da 149 a 161 154.2 (M.), 149 (C.)						A6
da 223 a 237 229 (M.), 225 (C.)		215, 225(S.S.)	223, 237 (S. S.)				da 213.9 a 231.4 224 (M.)	228 (S.)	A8
		310(S.)	319(S.)		da 307 a 321 314 (M. e C.)		291.5 a 319.7 307 (M.)	306, 313 (S.S.)	A12
		423(S.)	424, 436 (S.S.)			430 (S.)	da 415 a 453 434 (M.), 436 (C.)	432, 435 (S.S.)	A16
		1374(S.)	1357(S.)						A50
		1731(S.)							A64
		2573, 2593(S.S.)							A100
		3200(S.)							A120
		6560(S.)							A240
da 60 a 63 61.3 (M.), 62 (C.)		59.2(S.)	da 61 a 62 61.6 (M. e C.)		da 58 a 62 59.5 (M.), 59.2 (C.)				B1
da 95 a 98 96.2 (M.)		97, 97.2(S.S.)							B1 1/2
da 126 a 128 127 (M.)	da 123 a 133 126.7 (M.)	da 110 a 117 114(M.)					da 121.3 a 129.5 125.5 (M.)		B2
da 191 a 195 192.5 (M. e C.)	180, 200 (S.S.)	193(S.)	da 179 a 195 187 (M. e C.)	191 (S.)	da 187 a 199 192.5 (M.)		186.9 a 197.4 191.3 (M.), 189 (C.)		B3
da 245 a 261 254 (M.), 258.5 (C.)	da 238 a 248 244.3(M.)	261, 261(S.S.)					da 240.5 a 251.8 245.1 (M.), 243 (C.)	245 (S.)	B4
da 370 a 404 384 (M. e C.)	381 (S.)		384, 389 (S.S.)		da 383 a 414 396.6 (M.), 387.5 (C.)		388 a 401.5 396 (M. e C.)		B6
482 (S.)		469, 487(S.S.)			484 (S.)		da 476 a 483.5 480.6 (M. e C.)	487 (S.)	B8
		635(S.)			602, 605 (S.S.)		599.4 a 631.3 617 (M.)	da 603 a 611 607 (M. e C.)	B10
		789(S.)	da 779 a 813 796.5 (M. e C.)	782 (S.)		720 (S.)		da 764 a 773 767 (M.)	B12
			da 967 a 1015 987.6 (M.), 974 (C.)		958 (S.)	940, 960 (S.S.)			B16
		2315(S.)							B40
		2835(S.)							B48
da 85 a 91 88.2 (M.), 90.3 (C.)		84.4(S.)	da 85 a 93 89.2 (M.), 89.5 (C.)	85 (S.S.)					C2
da 171 a 177 175 (M.), 173 (C.)					174, 177 (S.S.)		da 165.4 a 183 175 (M.), 177 (C.)		C4

			338 (S.)		da 336 a 350 341 (M.), 336.5 (C.)		338.6 a 343.6 341 (M.)		C8
			da 656 a 690 673.6 (M.), 682.5 (C.)				da 664.6 a 676.6 671 (M. e C.)	da 666 a 704 685 (M.), 691 (C.)	C16
da 73 a 74 74 (M. e C.)	72, 75 (S.S.)	da 68 a 78.8 74.9(M.)	da 68 a 71 69.4 (M.), 68.6 (C.)	71 (S.)	da 71 a 75 73.7 (M.), 74.6 (C.)				D1
da 137 a 141 139 (M. e C.)			da 134 a 138 136 (M. e C.)	da 135 a 140 136.6 (M.)	147 (S.)				D2
			da 263 a 275 266 (M.), 263 (C.)					da 267 a 273 270 (M.), 268 (C.)	D4
567 (S.)			da 540 a 571 557.6 (M.), 566.5 (C.)				da 539.1 a 562.6 549 (M.), 557 (C.)	da 532 a 550 542 (M. e C.)	D8

Fig. 5. Le serie ponderali *A* , *B* , *C* e *D* attestate nei ripostigli italiani del Bronzo finale e primo Ferro. *Abbreviazioni*: (S.) valore singolo; (S.S.) due valori singoli; (M.) valore medio; (C.) concentrazione principale.

Ripostigli italiani	Ripostigli sloveni	
da 8.8 a 9.4 9(M. e C.)	9, 9 (S. S.)	A1/3
	da 16.4 a 17.5 17(M.) 17.5 (C.) 18.6, 19(S. S.) (M. compl. 17.5)	A2/3
da 23 a 27 24.6(M.) 24(C.)	da 23 a 23.9 23.3(M.) 23.2(C.) da 24.8 a 26.1 25.4(M.) (M. compl. 24.5)	A1
da 48 a 49 48.75(M.) 49(C.) da 51 a 56 53.5(M.) 55(C.) (M. compl. 52.3)	da 44.4 a 54.3 47.1(M.) 48.5(C.)	A2
da 80 a 82 81.5(M.) 82(C.)	da 77.5 a 87.8 83.2(M.) 86(C.)	A3
da 101 a 107 105.3(M.) 107(C.)	da 99.7 a 106.2 103.5(M.) 104(C.)	A4
	da 149.9 a 159.1 154.2(M.) 154(C.) da164.8 a 166.1 165.3 (M.) 164.8(C.) (M. compl. 158.4)	A6
da 210 a 215 212.5(M.) da 223 a 231 225.8(M.) 223(C.) (M. compl 220.4)	da 201 a 225 213.4(M.) 222(C.)	A8
da 275 a 287 281(M.) 284(C.)	da 263 a 283 276(M.) 275(C.)	A10 (D4)
da 292 a 321 307(M.) 319(C.)	da 289.3 a 331.6 309.7(M.) 320(C.)	A12
da 404 a 436 420.3(M.) 424(C.)	da 472.2 a 458 448(M.) 445(C.)	A16
530, 540 (S.S.) da 562 a 574 568.5(M.)	da 523.9 a 554.6 537(M.) 538(C.)	A20(D8)
	da 804.4 a 916.9 854(M.) 851(C.)	A32
	da 1019.2 a 1103.8 1064(M.)	A40
1357, 1374 (S.S.)	1308,1358 (S. S.)	A50
1606(S.)		A60
da 1677 a 1731 1702(M.)		A64
2170(S.)	2175(S.)	A80
2573, 2593(S.S.)		A100
3200(S.)		A120
6560(S.)		A240
da 5 a 5.6 5.15(M.)	da 5 a 5.6 5.2 (M.)	B1/12

Ripostigli italiani	Ripostigli sloveni	
da 41 a 45 43.25(M.)	da 38.5 a 42 40.5(M.) 41.5 (C.)	B2/3 (C1)
da 58 a 63 60.7(M.) 62(C.)	da 57.3 a 59.4 58.9 (M.) 59.3(C.) da 61.3 a 66.5 64.1(M.) 65.5(C.) (M. compl. 61.6)	B1
da 89 a 98 93.8(M.) 97(C.)	da 90.1 a 96.3 93.2(M.) 92(C.)	B1 1/2
da 108 a 123 115(M.) 117(C.) da 126 a 128 127(M.) (M. compl. 117)	da 108.2 a 131.8 120.3(M.) 119(C.)	B2
da 177 a 202 183.6(M.) 192(C.)	da 183.1 a 198.2 192(M.) 196(C.)	B3
da 237 a 238 237(M. e C.) da 245 a 263 256(M.) 261(C.) (M. compl. 252.8)	da 230.5 a 254.7 245(M.) 251(C.)	B4
da 350 a 392 375(M.) 385(C.)	da 372 a 376.1 373.5 (M. e C.) da386.8 a 414 408(M.) (M. compl. 392.3)	B6
da 453 a 489 474.7(M.) 476(C.) da 502 a 517 507.7(M.) (M. compl. 483.5)	da 474.7 a 491.8 486.8(M.) 490(C.)	B8
da 595 a 635 608(M.)	da 581.5 a 624.5 602,1(M.) 590(C.)	B10
da 749 a 789 776.8(M.) 780(C.)	da 714.8 a 785.8 754.2(M.) 777(C.)	B12
da 897 a 940 921.4(M.) 924(C.)		B15
da 958 a 1015 976.2(M.) 967(C.)		B16
da 1108 a 1225 1171(M. e C.)		B20
1425, 1451(S.S.)	1526(S.)	B24
1810(S.)	1818(S.)	B30
2315, 2385(S.S.)		B40
2835(S.)	2955(S.)	B48
da 84.4 a 85 84.9(M.) 85(C.)		C2
da 158 a 175 168(M.) 174(C.)	da 168 a 176.9 173.3 (M.) 176(C.)	C4
da 332 a 338 335.2(M.) 336 (C.)	da 343.4 a 359 354(M.) 351(C.)	C8
da 656 a 690 673.6(M.) 682.5(C.)		C16
da 68 a 78.80 73.4(M.) 75(C.)	da 68.2 a 76 72.4(M.) 74(C.)	D1

	7.6 (S.)	B1/8	da 133 a 153 140.2(M.) 138(C.)	da 136.4 a 146.3 142(M. e C.)	D2
11.3, 11.8 (S.S.)	da 10 a 12.1 11.2 (M.) 11.1 (C.)	B1/6			
15,16 (S.S.)		B1/4			
	da 19.5 a 22.4 21(M.) 20.6(C.)	B1/3			
da 31 a 32 31.3(M.) 31(C.)	da 29.4 a 33.5 31.4(M.) 32.4(C.)	B1/2			
da 36 a 38 36.6(M.) 36(C.)	da 35.2 a 36.7 36(M.) 36.2(C:)	B3/5			

Fig. 7. Corrispondenza tra i valori ponderali delle serie *A* , *B* , *C* e *D* attestati nei ripostigli italiani e sloveni. *Abbreviazioni* : (S.) valore singolo; (S.S.) due valori singoli; (M.) valore medio; (C.) concentrazione principale.

PESI E BILANCE NELL'ETÀ DEL BRONZO ITALIANA : QUADRO GENERALE E NUOVI DATI

ANDREA CARDARELLI (Museo archeologico etnologico di Modena),
MARCO PACCIARELLI (Museo Comunali di Imola)
PAOLO PALLANTE (Museo Comunali di Imola)

ABSTRACT: This paper indicates that by the 13th century BC the system of weights and measures throughout Bronze Age Italy and neighboring regions to the north was highly standardized. These finding yield further evidence for medium-distance trade along sea and inland routes.*

Una delle questioni che sono state a lungo al centro del dibattito sull'età del bronzo dell'Europa "barbarica" riguarda il carattere dei processi di produzione e scambio. È ben noto come nell'età del bronzo si assista ad un incremento della produzione metallurgica e come l'impiego della lega di rame e stagno di per sé configuri una affermazione più consistente degli scambi anche a lunga distanza, come del resto confermato anche dalla ampia circolazione di altre materie prime "rare", come l'ambra e l'oro. È altrettanto evidente come a partire dal Bronzo B e C (Bronzo medio) e in modo più consistente dal Bronzo D (Bronzo recente) la produzione metallurgica raggiunga vertici mai toccati prima, sia in termini quantitativi, sia per l'ampliamento della gamma dei prodotti, sia infine per l'affermarsi in gran parte d'Europa e nell'area Egea di una "koinè" metallurgica, chiara testimonianza di un incremento della rete di contatti fra varie cerchie artigianali, favoriti con ogni probabilità da un consistente aumento del volume dei traffici (Carancini e Peroni 1997). La domanda che molti autori si sono legittimamente posti è dunque se a questa evidenza corrisponda una economia di scambio in buona parte non più legata a forme di reciprocità ma invece organizzata attraverso forme convenzionali di quantificazione (Cardarelli *et al.* 2001). In questa prospettiva riveste un'importanza centrale il dibattito sull'eventuale esistenza di sistemi ponderali, che possano confermare una diffusa utilizzazione della pesatura mediante bilancia, da tempo già in uso in area Egea.

Per quanto riguarda le comunità di villaggio dell'età del bronzo italiana ed europea, sebbene ricorrenze ponderali siano state proposte fin dalla fine del XIX secolo, la serrata critica di ascendenza sostantivista ha sostenuto, soprattutto a cavallo fra gli anni '70 e '80 del novecento, che la circolazione dei beni nelle società della protostoria fosse da comprendere in buona parte all'interno del modello della reciprocità. Tale modello presuppone forme di scambio organizzate in base soprattutto a principi qualitativi, ben diverse da quelle basate su una quantificazione oggettiva del valore, che si sarebbero sviluppate solo nell' ambito delle prime società urbane. A livello teorico si può però ipotizzare che è assai più verosimile pensare ad un'affermazione progressiva del sistema di scambio mediante valori quantificati, piuttosto che a una sua subitanea affermazione in corrispondenza dell'età urbana. Anzi la prospettiva andrebbe semmai rovesciata, considerando l'evoluzione dei sistemi di scambio come una delle condizioni fondamentali che hanno condotto alla crisi delle società di villaggio e all'emergere di quelle protourbane e poi urbane.

All'interpretazione sostantivista deve aver certo contribuito il fatto che la ricerca di sistemi ponderali si sia basata in passato quasi esclusivamente sull'evidenza dei ripostigli di lingotti, o di oggetti finiti aventi funzione di lingotti, per l'antica età del bronzo, e di oggetti frantumati per le fasi più avanzate. Mancavano infatti, o comunque erano estremamente scarse, testimonianze incontrovertibili di un sistema di pesatura, vale a dire la concomitante attestazione di bilance e di pesi ordinati secondo una riconoscibile sequenza ponderale. La ricerca di questi ultimi anni sembra invece dar forza all'ipotesi che i sistemi di scambio nelle società della protostoria europea fossero in parte regolati da forme di transazione economica diverse da quelle ascrivibili al modello polanyano della reciprocità. In estrema sintesi dai lavori di vari autori (Eiwanger, Lenerz De Wilde, Malmer, Peroni, Primas, Sommerfeld ecc.; cfr. Cardarelli *et al.* 2001: 33-35) emerge l'uso durante il Bronzo antico di accumulare metallo secondo quantità predefinite sotto forma sia di manufatti finiti (collari e asce), sia di lingotti di varia forma che sembrano in buona parte seguire rapporti ponderali costanti anche se approssimativi. A partire dalla fine del Bronzo antico i lingotti divengono tendenzialmente più piccoli e progressivamente si diffonde la circolazione di oggetti frammentati intenzionalmente, pratica che raggiunge il suo apice a partire dal XIII secolo, e che secondo la Primas (1997) corrisponderebbe all'affermarsi dello scambio mediante pesatura.

Il nostro contributo al problema dell'esistenza di sistemi ponderali nell'Italia del Bronzo medio e tardo ha preso avvio nel 1996 escludendo i frammenti di manufatti, evidentemente oggetto della pesatura, e concentrandosi invece sugli strumenti di pesatura e cioè bilance e soprattutto pesi

(Cardarelli *et al.* 1996), approccio seguito successivamente anche da Christian Pare in un ampio lavoro dedicato all'Europa centrale (Pare 1999)[i]. Ricordiamo che fino a poco tempo fa l'esistenza di piccole bilance al di fuori del mondo egeo sembrava limitata alla Sicilia, mentre negli ultimi anni bilance a bracci uguali sono state identificate anche in contesti dell'età del bronzo della Serbia e della Francia, e noi stessi abbiamo indicato alcuni possibili esempi per l'Italia (Cardarelli *et al.* 2001).

In particolare la nostra analisi si è rivolta verso due tipi di pesi litici, uno di forma lenticolare, l'altro di forma globulare o piriforme con appiccagnolo, ben attestati in area padana, spesso realizzati con materie prime non locali ed entrambi in genere accuratamente modellati e levigati. Questi pesi non avevano, se non in un caso, di cui comunque discuteremo più avanti, evidenze di contrassegni che potessero connotare una loro identificazione all'interno di un sistema ponderale, come avviene frequentemente in età storica e anche nel mondo Egeo; ciò ha rappresento un condizionamento oggettivo della ricerca, di cui abbiamo dovuto tener conto.

Nell'affrontare lo studio delle due classi di pesi abbiamo in primo luogo analizzato le caratteristiche della produzione, la sua cronologia e il suo areale di fabbricazione e circolazione. Successivamente ci siamo posti il problema di verificare l'esistenza delle seguenti condizioni, da noi considerate necessarie per il riconoscimento di un sistema ponderale:

a. L'identificazione di almeno alcuni significativi punti di addensamento statistico dei pesi;
b. L'esistenza di intervalli regolari o almeno modulari tra i principali addensamenti;
c. Il riconoscimento di un sistema di valori riconducibile ad un'unità fondamentale per ciascuno dei due tipi di pesi, esteso alla quasi totalità degli esemplari;
d. La possibilità di identificare una plausibile progressione di valori multipli dell'unità.

Ci siamo poi dati, quale ulteriore parametro di convalida, la ricerca di un rapporto con le serie ponderali coeve già note, in primo luogo con quelle dell'Egeo e successivamente con quelle ipotizzate per l'Europa continentale.

A proposito dell'analisi ponderale va premesso che è da presupporre una certa oscillazione dell'unità di riferimento e quindi ancor più dei suoi multipli, come è ben dato riconoscere anche in sistemi ponderali evoluti e dotati di contrassegni, come quello Egeo, o come quello della città etrusca di Marzabotto (Cattani 2001). In quest'ultimo, pur evidenziandosi un addensamento attorno al valore di 370 grammi, l'unità può oscillare fino al 10% in più o in meno rispetto al valore centrale.
Al fine di restringere il campo della ricerca, ci siamo tuttavia dati come obiettivo quello di considerare valide solo oscillazioni contenute di norma entro il 4% rispetto al valore centrale.

Presupponendo che ciascuna delle due classi di pesi potesse avere avuto una caratterizzazione specifica, vista anche la loro almeno parziale contemporaneità, abbiamo operato inizialmente una analisi differenziata, sottoponendo poi a confronto i risultati.

PESI LENTICOLARI

Forma e materiale

La classe di pesi quantitativamente più attestata è quella di forma lenticolare biconvessa, dotata di norma di una scanalatura perimetrale (Fig. 1). Insieme ai 42 esemplari di forma canonica abbiamo considerato anche tre pesi affini provenienti da Frattesina caratterizzati da uno spigolo sul margine e da una doppia concavità sulle due facce, ed anche un singolo esemplare dallo stesso sito privo di scanalatura e con protuberanze centrali (Cardarelli *et al.* 2001: fig. 16).

L'86% dei pezzi è fabbricato con arenarie e talvolta calcari di origine appenninica reperibili entro qualche decina di chilometri dagli insediamenti, mentre il restante 14% è di provenienza extraregionale, come nel caso dei pesi attestati nelle terramare emiliane e realizzati in porfidi atesini o marmi della Val D'Ossola.

Diffusione e cronologia

Per quanto riguarda la diffusione possiamo affermare che in Italia questa classe di pesi è per ora attestata esclusivamente nella pianura padana, in un territorio in larga misura coincidente con la zona terramaricola; fuori dall'Italia la classe dei pesi lenticolari è attestata in Svizzera e in Croazia (Cardarelli *et al.* 2001).

Per quanto riguarda la cronologia l'attestazione di molti di questi pesi nei complessi terramaricoli scavati lo scorso secolo costituisce un generico riferimento cronologico all'età del bronzo media o recente; l'unica indicazione cronologica precisa proviene da un peso rinvenuto a S. Rosa di Poviglio in un contesto del Bronzo recente (Cardarelli *et al.*2001: 37) Nei contesti svizzeri (Hauterive-Champréveyers e Auvernier Nord) i pesi lenticolari rinvenuti sono riferibili ad un periodo compreso fra l'XI e il IX secolo a.C.; per quello di Kalnik in Croazia, trovato assieme a varie forme di fusione, è possibile una attribuzione cronologica compresa fra il XII e il IX secolo a.C. Una datazione simile potrebbero avere gli esemplari di Frattesina, trovati non in contesto di scavo. Per i pesi lenticolari attestati in Italia possiamo dunque ragionevolmente proporre una cronologia compresa fra almeno l'inizio del Bronzo recente e un momento per ora non precisabile del Bronzo finale.

Analisi ponderale

I pesi lenticolari italiani sono perlopiù compresi fra 299 e 876 grammi ma esaminando la distribuzione dei valori ponderali risultano immediatamente evidenti due concentrazioni (fig.2). La prima è costituita da ben 15 esemplari, distribuiti fra 415 e 445 grammi, con una media di 429,3; la seconda da 13 pesi distribuiti fra 520 e 559 grammi, con una media di 540,3. I valori medi delle due concentrazioni sono pertanto separati da un intervallo di 111 grammi. Un intervallo analogo è riscontrabile con un'altra serie costituita da quattro pesi distribuiti fra 630 e 664 grammi, il cui valore mediano è di circa 645. Sembra dunque riconoscibile l'esistenza di tre concentrazioni ponderali con intervalli medi compresi fra 106 e 111 grammi. Tuttavia l'esistenza di altri pesi che si collocano a distanze pari all'incirca alla metà di questi valori rende plausibile l'esistenza di un'unità ponderale di circa 53,5 grammi, entro i multipli della quale sono compresi, se si considera un'oscillazione massima pari al 4% , quasi tutti i pesi lenticolari, compresi quelli che si concentrano attorno al valore significativo di 16. In questa progressione l'unica eccezione può essere rappresentata dai due pesi attorno a 300 grammi, su cui torneremo. Abbiamo inoltre considerato a parte due piccoli pesi lenticolari di circa 41 grammi, dei quali tratteremo più avanti.

Confronto con i sistemi coevi

Quest'unità ponderale di 53,5/ 54 grammi ca. sembra avere vari confronti con l'ambito egeo-orientale e con l'Europa. In particolare possiamo notare come essa sia coincidente con un unità Egea definita ***W***, pari a circa 53 grammi, multiplo 10 dell'unità egea di precisione ***w***, pari circa a 5,5 grammi (Alberti 1999). Quest'unità sembra attestata già in contesti antichi del Tardoelladico, come dimostra ad esempio la presenza di un peso di piombo a disco di 54,4 grammi e di alcuni multipli di tale unità nella tomba di Vapheio (Kilian Dirlmaier 1987).

Un'altra importante coincidenza ponderale è riscontrabile con l'unità A1 individuata da Renato Peroni in ambito europeo, mediterraneo ed egeo (Peroni 2001), il cui peso di 26 grammi circa corrisponderebbe ad ½ dell'unità ponderale dei nostri pesi lenticolari.

PESI AD APPICCAGNOLO

Forma e materiale

I pesi appartenenti a questo tipo direttamente controllati e pesati sono 28. Sono poi attestati altri esemplari che non abbiamo inserito nei diagrammi perchè molto frammentati o in corso di lavorazione (cfr. Moscosi di Cingoli: Pignocchi 1999). La forma generale di questi pesi è globulare, ma esistono anche esemplari piriformi, tutti sono comunque forniti di un'appicagnolo forato, funzionale alla sospensione (fig. 3). Un esemplare dopo la rottura (casuale o intenzionale) dell'appiccagnolo è stato rifunzional-izzato grazie ad una scanalatura diametrale. Sono tutti pesi litici, ad eccezione di uno, proveniente da Peschiera, realizzato in piombo. Differentemente dalla classe dei pesi lenticolari, che come si è visto sono prevalentemente realizzati in pietra locale, questi sono per la maggior parte (68%) costruiti con pietra alloctone, distanti anche varie centinaia di chilometri dal luogo di rinvenimento. In gran parte tali pesi sono realizzati con litotipi del settore dei Lessini e dei Berici, oppure in marmi della Val d'Ossola (Cardarelli *et al.* 2001: 49-55).

Importante notare che fra questa tipologia di pesi, accanto alla maggior parte che è compresa fra i 300 e gli 850 grammi circa, esistono tre pesi molto piccoli (grammi 36,5-36,6 - 43 ca.), realizzati tutti con litotipi alloctoni. Uno è in marmo, presumibilmente di Candoglia, uno è in alabastro, verosimilmente dell'area toscana, e infine uno è in barite microcristallina di provenienza alpina.

Diffusione e Cronologia

La diffusione di questa classe di pesi è prevalentemente padana e segnatamente è ben attestata in ambito terramaricolo, ma sono attestati pesi con appiccagnolo lungo la fascia adriatica, a Coppa Nevigata (Puglia settentrionale) e a Moscosi di Cingoli nelle Marche; in area tirrenica è attestato un unico esemplare a Grotta Nuova (VT) (Cardarelli *et al.* 2001). Fuori dall'Italia questa classe di pesi sembra per ora attestata in Svizzera, dove sono presenti esemplari in piombo e in pietra (Pare 1999; Cardarelli *et al.* 2001). Sul piano cronologico l'attestazione in numerosi contesti terramaricoli fa presupporre una datazione generica al Bronzo medio o al Bronzo recente. La recente scoperta di due esemplari dalla terramara di Gaggio di Castelfranco (MO) in un contesto di Bronzo medio 2 permette di far risalire a tale fase l'apparizione del tipo, mentre il ritrovamento a Moscosi in un contesto ben datato di vari esemplari in corso di lavorazione dimostra il suo perdurare fino al Bronzo recente (Pignocchi 1999). In ogni caso per ora non vi sono evidenze in Italia di attestazioni di pesi ad appiccagnolo oltre il Bronzo recente, come sembrerebbe dimostrare ad esempio l'assenza di questa classe fra gli esemplari di pesi trovati a Frattesina.
In Svizzera questi pesi sembrano invece databili nel loro complesso fra XI e IX secolo a.C.

Analisi ponderale

Nel costruire il grafico che illustra la distribuzione ponderale del tipo ad appiccagnolo abbiamo separato i pesi più piccoli (quelli cioè al di sotto dei 100 grammi) dalla serie più consistente di pesi compresa fra i 295 e gli 850 grammi circa (fig. 4).

Analizzando i più piccoli si può verificare che essi possono facilmente essere spiegati con un'unità ponderale di 6,1 grammi, con la quale coincidono in modo quasi perfetto. Infatti due pesano rispettivamente 36,5 e 36,6 grammi, cioè 6 volte l'unità indicata, un terzo pesa all'incirca 43 o 43,5 grammi cioè 7 volte 6,1, mentre un quarto esemplare da Mörigen (Svizzera) pesa 98,3 grammi, cioè circa 16 volte 6,1.

Accantonando per ora il problema del peso di circa43 grammi, il cui valore 7 suscita qualche perplessità per la sua anomalia rispetto alla norma dei sistemi ponderali preclassici, e sul quale torneremo fra poco, proviamo a verificare se questo stesso sistema ponderale può essere usato per gli esemplari più pesanti.

Significativamente i primi esemplari della serie più pesante si riferiscono al multiplo 50 di 6,1 (6,1 x 50 = 305). L'intervallo medio riconoscibile fra i vari gruppi di pesi è di 36,9 grammi corrispondente al peso di 36,6 grammi dei due pesi più piccoli. Le classi di peso individuate sembrano progredire dunque per classi di 36,6 grammi con un'oscillazione che non supera il 3,5 %. I pesi dunque non sarebbero semplicemente multipli di 36,6, bensì ancora multipli dell'unità teorica di 6,1 grammi, organizzati però secondo una scansione corrispondente a sei volte il suo peso.

Confronto con i sistemi coevi

La base di 6,1 grammi corrisponde ad un decimo dell'unità fondamentale Egea, che secondo Petruso (1978) nella sua versione prevalente equivale a 61 grammi. Il valore 36,6 oltre ad essere pari a 6 volte 6,1 costituisce in area Egea un'unità a se stante riservata specificamente alla pesatura dei tessuti (Alberti 1999). A queste evidenze che riportano costantemente all'ambito egeo si deve aggiungere che i valori ponderali riscontrati da C. Pare (1999) per i pesi ad appiccagnolo della Svizzera si concentrano in buona parte su valori compatibili anch'essi con un piede di grammi 6,1 o 12,2, o forse almeno in parte direttamente con l'unità fondamentale di 61 grammi. Si noti in particolare la notevole concentrazione di pesi attorno alla media di 732, 9 grammi, corrispondente a 12 volte tale unità. Inoltre un sistema ponderale articolato per frazioni dell'unità di 61 grammi è stato riconosciuto da Pare anche per un'altra tipologia di piccoli pesi metallici da bilancia diffusi in area transalpina soprattutto nel XIII secolo a.C.

CONSIDERAZIONI SUI RAPPORTI FRA LE DUE CLASSI DI PESI

Benchè i due tipi di pesi esaminati corrispondano sostanzialmente a due diversi sistemi ponderali rimangono da spiegare alcuni aspetti: il confronto fra i due istogrammi rivela differenze ma anche alcune significative concordanze. Il *range* ponderale è del tutto analogo per entrambe le classi. I pesi maggiori sono distribuiti in entrambi i casi fra 300 e 650 grammi circa e attorno a 850 grammi. Ciò sottende analoghe esigenze di pesatura. Un confronto più analitico condotto mediante istogramma con evidenziate le due classi di peso a confronto (Fig. 5) mostra tuttavia come i maggiori picchi di pesi lenticolari si discostino sostanzialmente rispetto alla scansione dei pesi globulari, i quali a loro volta in almeno due casi sono totalmente discordanti rispetto a quelli lenticolari. Ciò conferma che le due classi hanno un ordinamento sostanzialmente distinto. Rimane comunque aperta la possibilità indicata da Renato Peroni (2001) di forme di contaminazione e convertibilità fra le due serie. Può essere il caso ad esempio di due pesi lenticolari prossimi a grammi 300, che corrisponderebbero meglio con il valore di 50 volte l'unità di grammi 6,1. In quest'ottica segnaliamo inoltre la recentissima identificazione di due piccoli pesi lenticolari il cui peso si aggira attorno ai 41 grammi uno rintracciato nelle raccolte storiche del Museo Pigorini, e di un esemplare del tutto simile rinvenuto nella terramara di Montale fra la terra di risulta degli scavi ottocenteschi. Un valore non molto diverso è quello del pesetto globulare ad appiccagnolo in barite sempre da Montale di 43/43,5 grammi. Quest'ultimo presenta 25 o 26 linee incise verticali e un segno a V coricato. Tali pesetti, prossimi o di poco superiori ai 40 grammi, appaiono relazionarsi meglio con l'unità fondamentale Egea di 61 grammi, di cui rappresenterebbero i 2/3. Più precisamente potrebbero equivalere al doppio della c.d. unità egea K di circa 21 grammi, corrispondente ad 1/3 dell'unità fondamentale.

Come si è visto l'insieme dei pesi italiani qui esaminati può agevolmente essere inquadrato nell'ambito dei sistemi ponderali di ascendenza egea, che attraverso l'Italia e in particolare l'area padana avrebbero raggiunto nel Bronzo recente le regioni transalpine.

Secondo Pare (1999) e altri autori a partire dal XII secolo sarebbe riscontrabile in Egeo e in Europa l'introduzione di sistemi ponderali diversi di origine levantina, basati sullo shekel di valore compreso fra 8,7 e 9 grammi. Su questa base si sarebbero costruiti, secondo Pare, valori di 26-27 e 52,8 grammi circa, pari a tre e sei shekel, e una mina di 475,2 grammi, riscontrabile nei pani a picconi, pari a 9 volte 52,8 grammi. Tali valori sono tuttavia affini a quello di circa 53,5 grammi riscontrato per i pesi lenticolari, nonché all'unità A1 di Peroni di 26-27 grammi, come si è visto entrambi preesistenti al XII secolo a.C.

A tale affinità potrebbe essere sottesa una forma di continuità tra i sistemi ponderali del Bronzo medio e recente di ascendenza egea e quelli del BF almeno in parte agganciabili ai sistemi orientali. E' difficile al momento dire se l'aggancio tra l'unità di circa 53-54 grammi e i sistemi di ascendenza orientale possa risalire già al Bronzo medio-recente, oppure se sia avvenuto a posteriori nel Bronzo finale, tuttavia il quadro prospettato in ogni caso sembra presupporre l'esistenza di forme di convertibilità fra le unità ponderali europee di origine egea e quelle di ascendenza orientale.

A tale proposito è utile riprendere in considerazione il piccolo pesetto globulare ad appiccagnolo in barite da Montale del peso di circa 43 grammi, il quale presenta 25 o 26 linee verticali incise e un segno a V coricato. Si è già detto che tale peso possa essere considerato il multiplo 7 dell'unità egea di 6,1, ma anche il doppio dell'unità egea K che a sua volta rappresenta 1/3 dell'unità fondamentale egea di 61 grammi, di cui il pesetto da Montale rappresenterebbe dunque i 2/3. Tuttavia questo piccolo peso globulare può essere ricompreso anche nella scala ponderale dell'unità riconosciuta per i pesi globulari di 53,5 grammi di cui rappresenterebbe i 4/5. Appare in questo senso interessante ricordare che sono noti due pesetti lenticolari (uno da Montale e l'altro da Castione dei Marchesi) con un peso assai prossimo (circa 41 grammi) al pesetto ad appiccagnolo da Montale. Tale analogo valore ponderale, rispondente alle due diverse scale e rappresentati da entrambe le forme dei due tipi di peso potrebbe sottintendere che tali piccoli pesi potessero essere usati nell'ambito di rapporti di conversione ponderale.

Resta tuttavia da spiegare il senso delle incisioni sul pesetto ad appicagnolo. Il suo valore ponderale (circa 43 grammi) e l'unità dei pesi lenticolari da noi proposta (53,5 grammi ca.) potrebbero entrambi essere considerati multipli di uno shekel di circa 8,7-8,9 grammi. Moltiplicando tale unità ponderale per le linee verticali incise, presumibilmente 25, si ottiene il valore di 218 grammi che appare significativamente coincidere con 5 volte il peso di 43,5 grammi, 4 volte il peso di 53,5 grammi e 6 volte il peso di 36,6. Sembrerebbe dunque evidenziabile una possibile rapporto di equivalenza ponderale tra le varie serie ponderali attorno ai 218 grammi. Il punto debole di tali ipotesi è tuttavia la mancanza di attestazioni di pesi proprio attorno a questo valore. Un valore attorno al quale si concentra invece un notevole numero di pesi lenticolari è invece quello di circa 430 grammi, equivalente al rapporto 8, 10, 12 delle suddette unità, che potrebbe corrispondere anche a 50 shekel.

I pesi litici di Frattesina, presumibilmente per lo più riferibili al Bronzo finale, sono in gran parte assimilabili alla forma del peso lenticolare, sebbene con alcune peculiarità tipologiche non attestate nell'ambito terramaricolo-padano del Bronzo medio e recente. Anche dal punto di vista ponderale tali pesi sono inquadrabili nel sistema ipotizzato per i pesi lenticolari con base di 53,5 grammi. Un buon numero di pesi sembra tuttavia rientrare sia in questo sistema, sia in uno a base 36,6 grammi, sia forse in uno a base 43,5 grammi (Bellintani; cfr Cardarelli *et al* 2001). Sono infatti attestati vari pesi attorno alla media di 369 gr. (10 volte 36,6) e attorno alla media di 436 (10 volte 43,5; cfr. pesetto globulare con segni incisi). Si potrebbe dunque ritenere che a Frattesina durante il Bronzo finale sia oramai in uso un sistema ponderale principale con base 53,5, ma che all'interno di questo sistema siano attestati anche altre unità ponderali attestate nell'area padana durante il Bronzo medio e recente, sebbene esclusivamente con alcuni valori significativi convergenti ponderalmente con il sistema principale. La continuità attestata a Frattesina potrebbe peraltro rappresentare un possibile aggancio per spiegare l'origine della presenza in ambito adriatico di un'unità ponderale preromana di 370-379 grammi (Parise 1989).

CONCLUSIONI

1. La prima attestazione sicura di un bilancino di precisione in Europa al di fuori dell'area egea è da collocarsi in Sicilia ai tempi della facies di Castelluccio (Cardarelli *et al.* 2001), ambiente che intrattenne intensi rapporti con il mondo egeo già dal Tardo Elladico I-II. Allo stato delle conoscenze non sappiamo se queste prime esperienze di pesatura si siano diffuse anche in Italia meridionale, dove pure abbiamo evidenze di precoci contatti con il mondo egeo. Il recente rinvenimento nei livelli del Bronzo medio 2 della terramara di Gaggio di pesi globulari ad appiccagnolo, legati a un sistema di pesatura basato sull'unità egea di 61 grammi, dimostra che già almeno dal XV secolo a.C. questo tipo di pesi era utilizzato nella pianura padana. La presenza di pesi globulari ad appiccagnolo in contesti che comprendono anche le prime fasi della media età del bronzo in Italia meridionale adriatica (Coppa Nevigata) e sul versante medio tirrenico (Grotta Nuova) potrebbe tuttavia suggerire l'ipotesi che l'Italia centro-meridionale abbia giocato un ruolo nella trasmissione di unità ponderali e sistemi di pesatura già in una fase iniziale del Bronzo medio, quando rapporti diretti fra mondo egeo ed Italia settentrionale non sembrano attestati da altre classi di fonti archeologiche.

2. I pesi lenticolari, in Italia per ora presenti solo in area padana, in base ai dati a disposizione risultano databili a partire dal Bronzo recente, e si configurano dunque come una innovazione cronologicamente successiva, propria dell'Italia settentrionale. Poiché i pesi lenticolari sono connessi a un sistema ponderale diverso, basato su un'unità di 53-54 grammi, vi è la possibilità che tale sistema sia giunto attraverso vie e vettori distinti rispetto a quelli legati alla circolazione dei pesi globulari.

3. Al momento appare altamente verosimile che la massima diffusione dei pesi litici si collochi durante il Bronzo medio 3 e il Bronzo recente, età alle quali risale con ogni probabilità gran parte dei numerosi esemplari rinvenuti nel territorio padano, e segnatamente terramaricolo. La massiccia presenza di pesi in quest'ultima area può forse corrispondere ad una sproporzione accidentale dei ritrovamenti, ma più probabilmente è correlata ad un carattere e ad un ruolo particolare di quell'ambito storico-geografico. Le elevatissime densità demografiche, il grande potenziale produttivo e l'alta specializzazione artigianale delle comunità terramaricole sono fattori che hanno certo favorito un intenso flusso di materie prime e manufatti. Ci si può anche chiedere se non sia proprio la connotazione sociopolitica comunitaria di tali gruppi ad aver stimolato il radicamento di una vasta e diffusa rete di scambi regolata da convenzioni ponderali. Beninteso la struttura comunitaria e "aperta" della società terramaricola non esclude affatto la possibilità di ipotizzare che alcune precise figure sociali abbiano svolto il ruolo di protagonisti dello scambio . Vi è anzi motivo di credere che tra queste figure oltre agli artigiani, vi fossero i maschi adulti armati. Ciò è indirettamente confermato da corredi funerari di guerrieri dell'Europa centrale in cui sono stati trovati sia bilance che pesi (Pare 1999).

4. Nel corso del XIII secolo a.C. nell'Europa transalpina si diffondono sistemi ponderali basati sull'unità di 61 grammi propria del mondo egeo, utilizzando però piccoli pesi metallici diversi da quelli italiani. È possibile che tale unità di peso si sia diffusa a partire dall'Italia (ma in questo caso ci si deve chiedere perché vi si associno

diverse forme di pesi) ma non si può escludere una provenienza diversa, ad esempio per il tramite dell'Europa orientale.

5. Tra l'XI e il IX secolo nella Svizzera e almeno in parte in Croazia si riscontra la presenza di pesi litici e unità ponderali di tipo fortemente affine a quelli presenti in area terramaricola nei secoli precedenti. L'ipotesi più verosimile è che tali sistemi di pesatura siano stati acquisiti in area circumalpina a partire almeno dalla metà del XII secolo a.C., cioè alla fine del Bronzo recente, attraverso contatti con il mondo terramaricolo. Si osservi a tale proposito che i pesi globulari, ampiamente attestati in Svizzera, sono presenti nelle comunità padane e medioadriatiche fino al Bronzo recente, mentre invece risultano assenti nel Bronzo finale.

6. La notevole presenza di pesi litici lenticolari nel grande centro del Bronzo finale di Frattesina dimostra come il grande sviluppo dei traffici e delle attività artigianali che si verificò durante il Bronzo finale nell'area prossima al delta del Po si ponga in un chiaro rapporto di continuità con i sistemi economici e di scambio propri del mondo terramaricolo. L'unità di 53-54 grammi propria di tali pesi appare almeno potenzialmente relazionabile con le unità ponderali di origine levantina che circolano durante il Bronzo finale nell'area circum-adriatica; qualora in futuro si raccolgano ulteriori elementi a sostegno di tale possibilità, rimarrebbe da stabilire se tale rapporto sia frutto di un adattamento *a posteriori* o se invece si sia andato configurando già dall'età precedente.

* Gli autori desiderano ringraziare la dott.ssa Maria Antonietta Fugazzola Delpino Soprintendente alla Soprintendenza speciale per la Preistoria e l'Etnografia per l'autorizzazione a esaminare e riportare i valori ponderali di alcuni pesi lenticolari ed appiccagnolo conservati nelle raccolte del Museo Nazionale Preistorico Etnografico- Luigi Pigorini. La segnalazione dell'esistenza di tali pesi ci è stata segnalata dalla dott.ssa Alessandra Serges, dipendente dello stesso Museo alla quale va la nostra riconoscenza.

BIBLIOGRAFIA

Alberti, M.E., 1999, Il sistema ponderale egeo tra omogeneità e flessibilità: continuità e discontinuità tra il mondo minoico e quello miceneo, in Epì Pònton Plazòmenoi, *Simposio Italiano di studi egei dedicato a L. Bernabò Brea e G. Pugliese Carratelli* (eds. V. la Rosa, D. Palermo e L. Vagnetti), Roma, 339-350.

Carancini, G.L. e Peroni, R., 1997, La koinè metallurgica, in *Le Terramare. La più antica civiltà padana*, (eds. M. Bernabò Brea, A. Cardarelli e M. Cremaschi), Milano, 595-601.

Cardarelli, A., Pacciarelli, M. e Pallante, P., 1997, Pesi da bilancia dell'età del bronzo?, in *Le Terramare. La più antica civiltà padana*, (eds. M. Bernabò Brea, A. Cardarelli e M. Cremaschi), Milano, 629-642.

Cardarelli, A., Pacciarelli, M. e Pallante, P., 2001, Pesi e bilance dell'età del bronzo italiana, in *Pondera. Pesi e misure nell'antichità* (eds. C. Corti e N. Giordani), Campogalliano, 33-58.

Cattani, M., 2001, I pesi in pietra in Etruria padana, in *Pondera. Pesi e misure nell'antichità* (eds. C. Corti e N. Giordani), Campogalliano, 89-94.

Kilian Dirlmaier, I., 1987, Das Kuppelgrab von Vapheio, *Jahresbericht Zentralmuseums Mainz* **24/I**, 197 ff.

Pare, C., 1999, Wheights and wheighing in Bronze Age Central Europe, in *Eliten in der Bronzezeit, Ergebnisse zweier Kolloquien in Mainz und Athen*, 421-514.

Parise, N.F, Economia e società: Libbre e bronzo librale nell'Italia Antica, in *Italia omnium terrarum parens* (eds. G.Pugliese Carratelli), Milano, 581-599

Peroni, R., 2001, Sistemi ponderali nella circolazione dei metalli dell'età del bronzo europea, in *Pondera. Pesi e misure nell'antichità* (eds. C. Corti e N. Giordani), Camogalliano, 21-27.

Petruso, K.M., 1978, *Systems of Weight in the Bronze Age Aegean*, Indiana University, PhD thesis.

Pignocchi, G., 1999, Quattro pesi ponderari, in *I Piceni: Popolo d'Europa*, Roma.

Primas, M., Bronze Age Economy and Ideology: Central Europe in Focus, *Journal of European Archeology* **5**, 115-130.

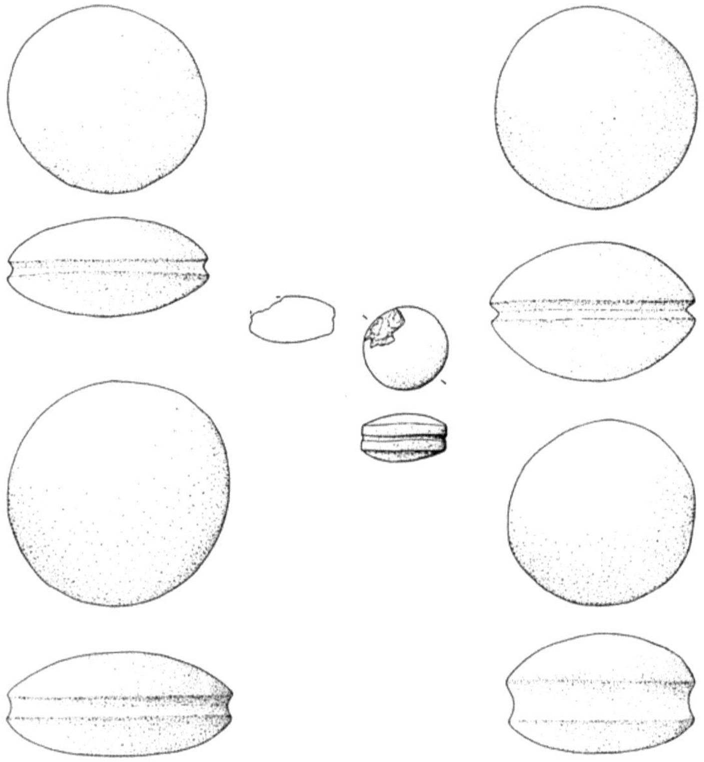

Fig. 1. Pesi lenticolari: 1. in marmo da Montale (429 g); 2. in arenaria da Gazzade (533 g.); 3. in arenaria da S.Rosa di Poviglio, superficie (545 g.); 4. in porfido da Scandiano (436 g); 5. in arenaria da Montale (36,5 g.; ricostruito ca. 41 gr.)

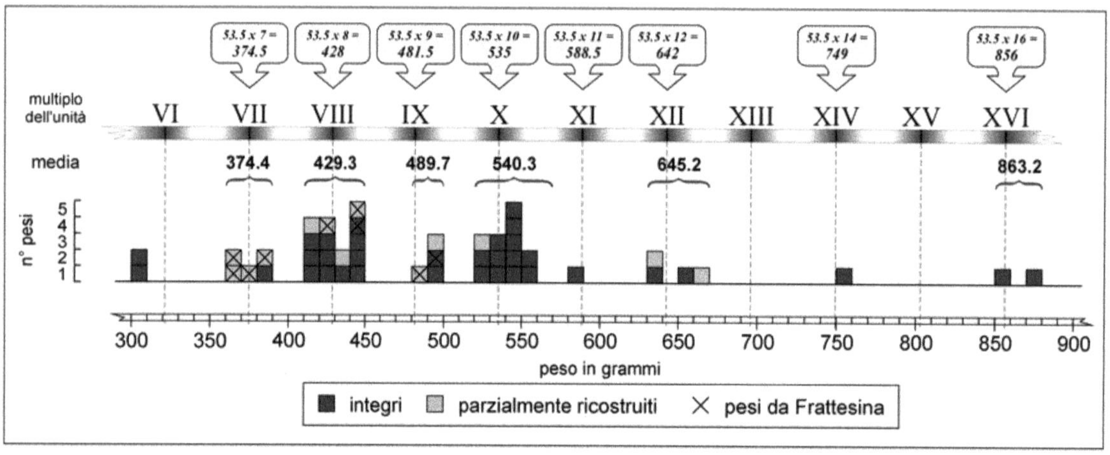

Fig. 2. Istogramma dei pesi lenticolari con indicazione delle classi di peso multiple di 53,5 g. Provenienze dei pesi: Basilicanova 299g; Peschiera 304g.; Frattesina 361, 362, 376, 385g; Montale 388g; Peschiera 415; Savana di Cibeno 416g; Montale 417g; Casaroldo 419g; Bellanda 424g; Montale 428, 429g; Frattesina 429g; Scandiano 436g; Ognissanti 437g; Frattesina 440, 440 g; Montale 442g; Peschiera 443g; Castellaro di Gottolengo 445g; Frattesina 483, 490g; Redù 492; Cornocchio 494g; Montale 520, 520g; Cella T.Cassoli 525g.; Gazzade 535g.; Montale 538, 539g; Redù 542g; Poviglio 545g; Casinalbo 546g; Castelfranco 548g; Redù 549g; Gazzade 559g; Castellazzo di Fontanellato 560g; Savana di

Cibeno 580g; Montale 630g; Gazzade 633g; Montale 650g; Casinalbo 664; Castelgoffredo 755g; Montale 850g; Gazzade 876g.

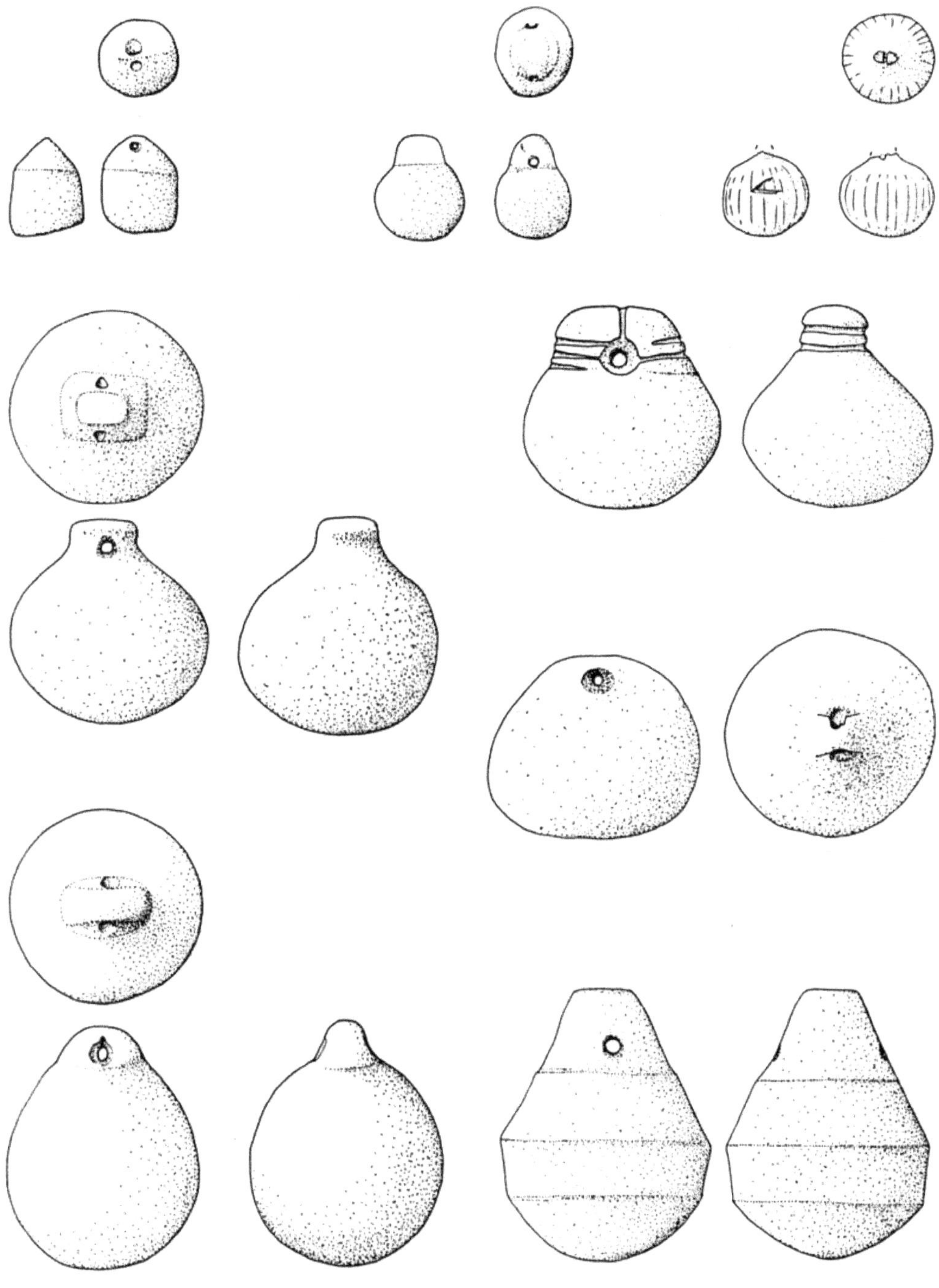

Fig 3. Pesi ad appiccagnolo: 1. in marmo da Gaiato (36,6 g); 2. in alabastro da Montale (36.6 g); 3. in barite da Montale (ca. 43 g) ; 4. in rosa ammonitico da Montale (392 g.) ; 5. in calcare da Quingento (340 g); 6. in calcareniite da S.Giuliano di Toscanella (420 g.); 7. da Gaggio (450 g); 8. in arenaria di Bismantova da Gorzano (391 g)

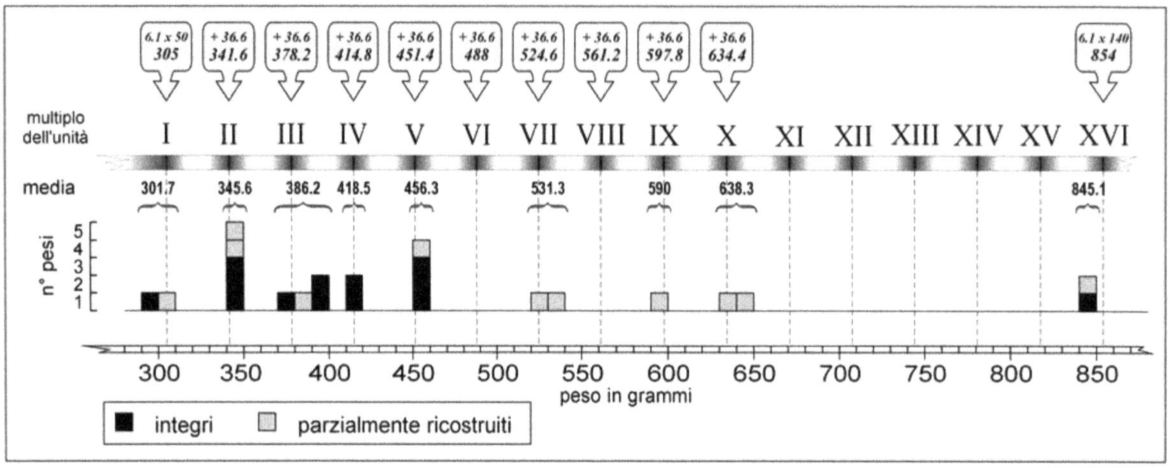

Fig. 4. Istogramma dei pesi ad appicagnolo con indicazione delle classi di peso con intervalli di 36,6 g. Provenienze dei pesi: Montale 295, 308g; Quingento 340g; Servirola S.Polo 343, 347g; Gaggio di Castelfranco 346g; M.Barello 348g; Peschiera 376G;;Redù 385g; Gorzano 392g; Montale 392g; Peschiera 417g; Toscanella Imolese 420g; Gaggio di Castelfranco 451g; Grotta Nuova 453g; Castelgoffredo 460g Montale 460g; Reggiano 524g; Coppa Nevigata 539g; Monte Barello 590g; Reggiano 636g; Reggiano 641g; Reggiano 842g.

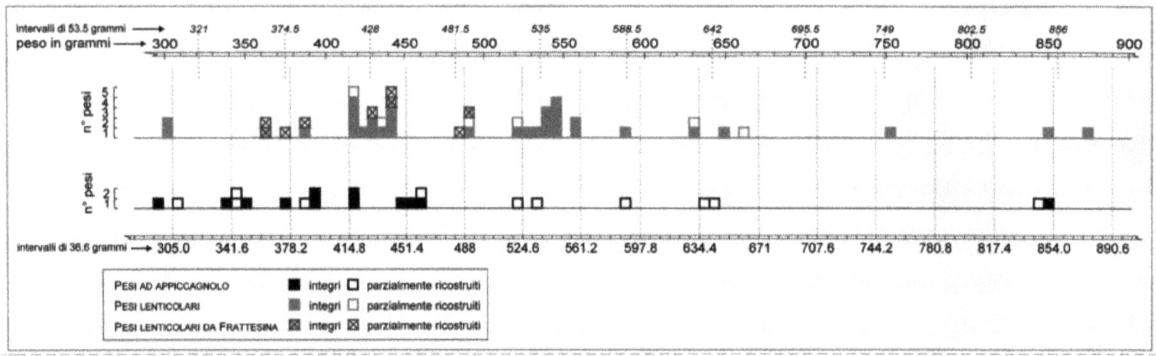

Fig. 5. Raffronto fra gli istogrammi delle due classi di peso.

Les echanges commerciaux entre la Corse et l'Italie septentrionale au XIVe siecle : methodes d'investigation et interpretation des donnees

Daniel Istria
(École Française de Rome)

Abstract: This paper presents the preliminary results of a team project on archaeological sites in Mugliunaccia and Rostino, two *castra* in the mountainous region of northern Corsica, allowing us to address the problem of comparing written and archaeological sources. This is also an opportunity to highlight the importance of studying animal bones, particularly of caprine/suine/bovine assemblages, and comparing them to craft goods like pottery. Only by a complete linkage of archaeological finds will we be able to reconstruct a more nuanced economic history of the Middle Ages.

La Corse, par sa situation géographique au croisement des grandes routes maritimes et par son histoire, étroitement liée durant tout le Moyen Age à celle de deux puissantes cités commerçantes, Pise et Gênes, est un terrain d'investigation privilégié pour l'analyse de l'évolution des savoir-faire et des échanges. Pourtant, l'étude des relations commerciales entre l'île et l'Italie septentrionale du XIIe au XIVe siècle soulève un problème d'interprétation lié, essentiellement, à la nature de la documentation disponible.

Dès le début du XIIIe siècle, la colonie génoise de Bonifacio draine une importante partie de la production agricole du sud de la Corse. Les blés et les produits dérivés de l'élevage (fromages, laine, peaux) achetés dans les ports de la côte sud-ouest de l'île font en effet l'objet d'un commerce international orchestré par les marchands ligures installés dans la ville. En revanche, la documentation écrite concernant la moitié nord de la Corse (actuel département de Haute-Corse), est beaucoup moins abondante. Néanmoins, elle atteste l'existence d'un commerce entre cette région Pise et Gênes dès le XIIIe mais surtout au XIVe siècle. Ainsi, registres de gabelle, contrats de *societates maris* ou notices relatives à des litiges entre commerçants pisans et insulaires, nous renseignent sur la vente en Toscane et en Ligurie de froment, d'orge, de poissons séchés, de laine, d'animaux de boucherie mais surtout de quantités importantes de vin du Cap Corse.

Pourtant, ces textes ne nous apprennent rien sur la nature exacte, la chronologie, l'importance et la fréquence de ce commerce, ni même sur les conséquences que ces échanges ont pu avoir sur l'économie locale. Se pose alors le problème récurrent de la représentativité de ces documents. Reflètent-ils des situations exceptionnelles ou sont-ils, au contraire, les seuls témoins conservés après la destruction d'une partie des archives, d'une réalité bien plus complexe, c'est-à-dire de l'existence d'un véritable système commercial ? L'évolution des méthodes de recherche, sous l'impulsion des pré- et protohistoriens et grâce à l'apport des sciences naturelles, laisse penser qu'aujourd'hui l'archéologie peut apporter quelques éléments de réponse[1]. Mais, quels types d'informations peut-elle fournir ? Dans quelle mesure ces données archéologiques peuvent-elles être confrontées aux sources écrites et contribuer à une meilleure connaissance de l'histoire économique ?

Pour tenter de répondre à cette interrogation, nous avons choisi de présenter brièvement quelques résultats issus d'un travail d'équipe[2] sur les sites archéologiques de la Mugliunaccia et de Rostino, deux *castra* de montagne du nord de la Corse (département de Haute-Corse).

Le castrum de la Mugliunaccia

La Mugliunaccia est un *castrum* perché entre 610 et 654 m d'altitude, sur un éperon calcaire très escarpé. Il est situé en haute Balagne (commune d'Olmi-Cappella), dans un secteur montagneux de la dépression centrale, ouvert sur l'intérieur de l'île mais coupé du littoral par une chaîne de montagnes qui s'élève rapidement à plus de 1000 m au-dessus du niveau de la mer.

Le village fortifié est divisé en deux parties, haute et basse. La première est caractérisée par la présence de quatre structures (A, B, C et D) construites à l'extrémité de l'éperon, entre deux arêtes rocheuses très saillantes formant rempart, perpendiculaires à la ligne de sommet de l'interfluve. Une petite tour dominait l'ensemble du site. Dans la partie basse, quatorze maisons ont été individualisées. Elles se trouvent sur la pente particulièrement abrupte, au sud-est du relief, et sont protégées par une enceinte et une succession d'à-pics rocheux. Ce village, fondé au tournant des XIIIe et XIVe siècles, est abandonné vers les années 1350-60.

Les quatre campagnes de fouilles archéologiques qui se sont déroulées entre 1995 et 1998, ont permis d'explorer dans leur totalité cinq maisons ainsi que la tour (Istria et Comiti 2000 ; Istria 2000).

LE CASTRUM DE ROSTINO

Le château de Rostino (commune de Castello-di-Rostino) est aujourd'hui le mieux connu grâce aux fouilles archéologiques qui y sont conduites depuis 1999 (Istria 2000, 2002). Au XIIIe siècle, il est considéré comme la forteresse principale des marquis de Massa et de Corse et commande un réseau de six ou sept fortifications qui permettent le contrôle de cinq *pievi* du nord de la Corse. Il est implanté à 610 m d'altitude sur un éperon rocheux aux versants escarpés d'où il domine la vallée du Golo, principal axe de pénétration vers l'intérieur de l'île depuis la côte nord-orientale. Barrière à la fois naturelle et artificielle, le site se présente aussi comme une sentinelle au centre d'un semis d'habitats dispersés et d'églises rurales, toujours isolées, enracinés sur les pentes des montagnes couvertes de maquis, de châtaigniers et de pins.

Les quatre campagnes de fouilles ont permis d'explorer la totalité de la *rocca*. Celle-ci s'implante au sommet de l'éperon constitué d'un petit plateau terminé par des à-pics importants et surmonté à l'est par un petit mamelon rocheux d'environ 6 m de hauteur. C'est sur celui-ci que fut érigée une tour entre 1139 et 1150 environ.

Au XIIIe siècle, la défense de la plate-forme est renforcée par la construction d'un rempart maçonné et d'un mur en pierres sèches contre lequel est appuyée une maison de bois. Mais, c'est surtout vers la fin du XIIIe ou le tout début du XIVe siècle que l'espace est totalement réorganisé. La nouvelle fortification couvre alors une superficie d'environ 850 m^2. Toutes les structures sont détruites à l'exception de la tour contre laquelle est construite une porte permettant l'accès à la plate-forme sommitale, désormais entièrement protégée par une enceinte. Un nouveau donjon, de dimensions plus importantes (5 x 3 m), est érigé à l'extrémité ouest. Autour de lui s'organisent les bâtiments résidentiels constitués de quatre pièces desservies par un large couloir. Probablement au même moment, un village fortifié se développe au pied du château.

Comme la Mugliunaccia, Rostino est abandonné vers le milieu du XIVe siècle, consécutivement à une destruction violente (Istria 2000).

Les problématiques qui ont motivé les fouilles archéologiques de ces structures d'habitats, ont imposé la mise en œuvre de méthodes particulières aussi bien dans le cadre des opérations de terrain pour une collecte la plus exhaustive possible des informations, que dans celui des études en laboratoire (Vigne et Ruas 1995). Si tous les types de vestiges archéologiques sont en mesure d'apporter des informations utiles à la connaissance de l'histoire économique de l'île, nous ne présenterons ici que l'analyse de ceux qui ont été retrouvés en très grande quantité : les céramiques et les ossements d'animaux.

LES CERAMIQUES

Entre la fin du XIe et le XIIIe siècle, de la céramique fine fabriquée en Grèce, au Proche-orient, en Egypte, en Tunisie, dans le Sud de l'Espagne, en Sicile, dans le Latium ou encore en Ligurie, est importée dans l'île par l'intermédiaire des marchands pisans puis génois. Dès le XIIe siècle, elle est diffusée en quantité encore modeste mais dans toute l'île, jusque dans les villages de montagne comme Rostino.

À partir de l'extrême fin du XIIIe et surtout durant la première moitié du XIVe siècle, cette céramique d'importation devient beaucoup plus abondante mais aussi beaucoup moins diversifiée. Les majoliques archaïques produites à Pise dominent alors largement, mais sont aussi parfois accompagnées de cruches et d'amphores de type *acroma depurata*, de vases à décor bleu et brun sur émail stannifère blanc fabriqués dans la région de Florence et encore de marmites de production ligure ou provençale[3]. Dans les contextes de la première moitié du XIVe siècle des sites de la Mugliunaccia et de Rostino, ces objets constituent respectivement 33 et 40 % du total des fragments de céramique découverts, mais dans les niveaux d'occupation les plus récents de certaines structures – milieu XIVe siècle -, ce taux peut atteindre près de 60 % (Fig. 1).

Or, dans les sites comparables de Toscane, de Ligurie, du Var ou encore du Languedoc (Gambaro 1987 ; Colin et *al.* 1996 ; Ribot 1985 ; Boldrini, Roncaglia 1984), où les importations sont extrêmement rares, la céramique fine n'apparaît qu'au XIVe siècle. Dans le village de Montarrenti, situé à quelques kilomètres de Sienne, elle reste réservée aux villageois les plus aisés jusque vers les années 1350 (Boldrini, Roncaglia 1984).

Cette confrontation amène à faire deux remarques. Tout d'abord, il faut souligner que la céramique fine, ou de table, occupe en Corse une place très importante dans le vaisselier de la maison rurale ; place comparable à celle qu'elle occupe ailleurs dans les milieux urbains (Démians d'Archimbaud, Vallauri 1998 : 105). D'autre part, ce mobilier est constitué uniquement d'objets importés, fabriqués pour l'essentiel dans les ateliers pisans qui comptent, alors, parmi les plus grands producteurs de terre cuite du bassin nord-occidental de la Méditerranée. Les études conduites par G. Berti (1997a ; 1997b ; Berti et *al.* 1986) montrent que ces produits ont connu une très large diffusion, principalement dans le secteur de la mer Tyrrhénienne mais aussi bien au-delà, jusqu'en Provence et en Languedoc. Néanmoins, contrairement à la Corse et peut-être à la Sardaigne, ces régions, beaucoup plus ouvertes sur l'Espagne et principalement sur la

Catalogne, ne sont pas marquées par ce monopole pisan (Démians d'Archimbaud, Vallauri 1998 : 86-89).

Ni les conditions d'accès, particulièrement difficiles, ni le statut social des habitants de ces *castra*, plutôt modeste, ne sont en mesure d'expliquer cette situation originale de l'île qui ne peut être liée qu'à son intégration dans le dynamique réseau commercial pisan.

On peut alors se demander si la diffusion de ces céramiques s'est accompagnée d'un transfert des techniques et des savoir-faire, susceptible d'avoir transformé la production régionale, aussi bien dans la typologie des ustensiles que dans l'organisation du travail. Contrairement à toute attente, l'élément le plus frappant de cet artisanat local n'est pas l'imitation des objets importés, mais bien la non-acquisition des nouvelles techniques. Jusqu'à la fin de l'époque moderne, les potiers corses ne fabriquent que de la céramique de cuisine, de facture très grossière et n'utilisent ni le tour ni la glaçure. Ils ne produisent que des vases modelés sans aucun revêtement et sans décor. Pourtant, ce secteur d'activité ne semble pas avoir joué un rôle marginal dans le cadre de l'économie insulaire. Certains centres producteurs, comme celui de Castagniccia (nord-est de l'île) qui a largement diffusé, ont su s'adapter très vite aux nouvelles exigences en faisant rapidement évoluer les formes et en adaptant ces marchandises aux contraintes imposées par le transport terrestre sur de longues distances et dans des conditions difficiles. L'abandon de la marmite à bord déversé et l'adoption du *paiolo*, une marmite à une seule anse médiane et verticale, réalisée à l'aide d'argile dans laquelle sont intégrées de longues fibres d'amiante, en est l'un des exemples les plus significatifs[4]. De fait, ce caractère « archaïque » de l'artisanat ne pourrait-il pas être la conséquence de l'absence de besoins spécifiques, dans la mesure où les importations pouvaient satisfaire très largement la demande en vaisselle de table, émaillée et décorée ?

Les ossements d'animaux

L'étude des ossements d'animaux se base sur un ensemble de près 20 000 fragments dont environ 15000 ont été découverts sur le site de Rostino et 5000 sur celui de la Mugliunaccia. Il s'agit de déchets culinaires qui proviennent soit de dépotoirs soit des sols des maisons. Dans tous les cas, ces contextes sont apparus comme très stables et parfaitement adaptés à une excellente conservation des vestiges osseux[5].

L'étude de cet ensemble, réalisée par Thomas Cucchi (2000) et Marie Balasse (rapport inédit), a montré que l'élevage des caprinés (chèvres et moutons), occupait une place prépondérante dans l'économie du village. À Rostino, la part de ces deux espèces passe de 43 % au XIIIe siècle à 75 % durant la première moitié du XIVe. À la Mugliunaccia, les contextes de la première moitié du XIVe siècle ont fourni des taux d'ossements de ces deux espèces exceptionnellement élevés : entre 69 % et 96 % des restes suivant les structures. Les ossements de suidés et de bovidés n'occupent donc qu'une place très marginale sur ces deux sites. Quant au gibier et aux animaux de basse-cour, ils ne sont représentés que par moins de 2 % des restes (Fig. 2).

Les courbes d'abattage des caprinés permettent de constater la mise en place d'une gestion différenciée des troupeaux de moutons, destinés essentiellement à la production de viande et des troupeaux de chèvres, dont l'élevage est principalement orienté vers la production de lait et de poils.

Enfin, il faut souligner l'absence d'agneaux et de cabris de lait (0-2 mois) dans les niveaux de la première moitié du XIVe siècle alors que ces animaux, appréciés pour la qualité de leur viande et pour leur cuire, sont bien représentés dans les contextes des XIIe et XIIIe siècles.

Cette gestion particulière des caprinés se fait au détriment du porc dont les restes osseux – par ailleurs encore impossibles à distinguer de ceux du sanglier - deviennent plus rares durant la première moitié du XIVe siècle. Son élevage est désormais, et contrairement aux siècles précédents, dirigé vers une production carnée de complément. Pourtant, l'étude a pu mettre en évidence l'absence des fémurs et des proximaux de tibias, c'est-à-dire des os du jambon.

S'agissant d'os importants et résistants, ces deux situations ne peuvent être que le résultat d'une sélection anthropique, c'est-à-dire d'une non-consommation sur le site même.

L'analyse de ces vestiges fait donc apparaître une forte spécialisation de l'élevage durant la première moitié du XIVe siècle avec la mise en place d'une gestion différenciée des troupeaux de chèvres et de moutons. D'autre part, l'absence d'ossements de très jeunes caprinés et des jambons de porcs, semblant découler d'un choix humain et non de problèmes de conservation différentielle, indique que ces pièces de qualité n'étaient pas, ou plus exactement n'étaient plus, consommées sur le site durant la première moitié du XIVe siècle mais, exportées pour être consommées ailleurs.

Ces données suggèrent l'existence, durant la première moitié du XIVe siècle, d'un commerce de la viande des jeunes caprinés et des porcs élevés dans ces sites de montagne. Partant de ces données, Thomas Cucchi (2000) propose d'opposer ces sites aux colonies génoises installées sur le littoral et particulièrement à Bonifacio, où les ossements de jeunes caprinés, retrouvés dans les contextes du XIVe siècle, sont largement majoritaires. Mais, c'est aussi à ce moment qu'est documentée l'exportation d'ovi-caprins vers la Toscane. Ainsi, en

1358, une autorisation est délivrée pour transporter des moutons corses de Pise jusqu'à Lucques[6] et, en 1389 et 1390, ce sont respectivement 700 et plus de plus 1000 agneaux qui sont embarqués à Brando, dans le Cap, pour être transportés jusqu'à Pise (Chatel 1970).

CONCLUSION

Alors que la documentation écrite nous informe sur l'exportation de denrées alimentaires vers l'Italie septentrionale, l'archéologie permet, elle, de mettre en exergue deux phénomènes importants qui marquent la première moitié du XIVe siècle. Tout d'abord on constate une importation massive d'objets qui ont envahi la demeure seigneuriale comme la maison paysanne et qui ont probablement été un frein à l'acquisition de nouvelles techniques dans divers domaines de la production artisanale. D'autre part on assiste, au moment même où le marché du vin et des céréales est en pleine expansion, à une très forte spécialisation de l'élevage, à la mise en place d'une gestion différenciée des troupeaux de moutons et de chèvres ainsi qu'à l'apparition d'un commerce de la laine, de la viande et des animaux de boucherie.
Ces mutations n'ont pourtant que peu d'incidences directes dans l'île : elles n'induisent pas la naissance d'un urbanisme (jusqu'au XVe siècle les seules villes sont les colonies génoises de Bonifacio et Calvi) et elles n'entraînent pas la création de marchés ou de foires. En revanche, on assiste à la multiplication des zones de mouillage qui sont désormais contrôlées, tout comme les voies de circulation importantes par où transitaient les marchandises, au moyen de forteresses construites par les grandes familles seigneuriales insulaires (Istria 2002).

Ces données doivent être interprétées dans le cadre du contexte historique particulier d'une île qui est encore aux XIII-XIVe siècles largement sous-peuplée mais qui s'inscrit, plus que jamais, dans les aires d'influences des deux grandes cités maritimes dont les besoins en denrées alimentaires ne sont plus à démontrer. Avec, d'un côté Pise qui au XIVe siècle est rabaissée du rang de puissance méditerranéenne à celui de puissance tyrrhénienne et qui, pour compenser cette perte de vitesse, semble vouloir dynamiser son activité commerciale dans le nord de l'île ; et de l'autre Gênes, qui installe des *castra* de colonisation, dont la place forte côtière de Calvi (vers 1260) qui apparaît comme le pendant de Bonifacio dans le nord de l'île.

Le croisement des informations archéologiques et de celles qui sont fournies par les textes, permet de supposer que la transformation du cheptel et de son mode de gestion peut traduire, non seulement un développement de l'économie insulaire – cela est incontestable - mais aussi la mise en place d'un marché, non plus local mais trans-tyrrhénien, reposant sur l'importation de produits manufacturés et l'exportation de denrées alimentaires de qualité (orge et froment, agneaux de lait, jambons, vin muscat...) destinées à alimenter les centres urbains. La Corse apparaîtrait ainsi comme un prolongement des *contadi* dont le développement est maîtrisé, même indirectement, par les puissances étrangères selon un processus en tout point identique à celui reconnu dans la Maremme toscane par Ch. Wickham et défini par lui comme un système d'économie coloniale (Wickham 2002).

Si cette brève présentation permet d'insister, une fois de plus, sur le caractère indispensable d'une confrontation systématique des sources écrites et archéologiques, elle montre aussi que l'étude des restes osseux des animaux du cheptel, particulièrement de l'assemblage caprinés/suidés/bovidés, apparaît, au même titre que celle des produits manufacturés comme la céramique, un moyen d'approche non négligeable, sinon essentiel, de l'histoire de l'économie médiévale.

NOTES :

1 Sur les expériences d'interdisciplinarité et de croisement des sources écrites et archéologiques dans le cadre d'études d'écologie historique, voir par exemple les recherches conduites depuis les années 80 dans les Pyrénées : Davasse et *al.* 1997.
2 Cet article a été en grande partie élaboré à partir des rapports inédits rédigés par Marie-Pierre Ruas (U.R.A 247 du C.N.R.S., Laboratoire d'Etudes Méridionales, U.T.M., Maison de la recherche, Toulouse : étude carpologique) et Thomas Cucchi (Université Paris I, Panthéon Sorbonne : étude archéozoologique).
3 En Sardaigne, la majolique archaïque pisane est aussi quantitativement la plus importante dans les contextes urbains et ruraux du XIVe siècle. Cependant, la céramique de cuisine glaçurée, produite en Ligurie et en Provence, semble totalement absente (Milanese et *al.* 2000).
4 Le modèle de cette marmite, dite aussi « à anse de panier » est à rechercher en Toscane. L'abandon de la marmite à bord déversé et l'adoption de cette nouvelle forme peut être située vers le milieu du XIVe siècle. C'est aussi à ce moment que la production du *testu* - plat destiné à la cuisson des galettes – est abandonnée. Ces changements semblent liés à une évolution des modes alimentaires.
5 Cette caractéristique, liée à la nature du substratum – calcaire à la Mugliunaccia – à la composition des sédiments, très riches en cendre et – à Rostino – à la présence de structures maçonnées à la chaux, permet d'écarter d'éventuels

problèmes de conservation différentielle qui pourraient fausser l'interprétation des données ; c'est-à-dire que tous les os, même les plus petits et les plus fragiles, y compris ceux des fœtus, sont bien représentés dans tous les espaces fouillés.
6 Archivio di Stato di Pisa, Comune A, n°128, p.86r., 1358.

BIBLIOGRAPHIE

Berti, G., 1997a, Pisa: ceramiche e commerci (2° metà X-1° metà XIV s.), *I congresso nazionale di archeologia medievale, Pise, 29-31 mai 1997*, Florence, 346-351.

Berti, G., 1997b, Pisa. *Le "maioliche arcaiche". Secc. XIII-XV, (Museo Nazionale du S. Matteo). Appendice du Renzi Rizzo C., "Nomina Vasorum"*, Florence.

Berti, G., Cappelli, L., Francovich, R., 1986, La maiolica arcaica in Toscana, in *La ceramica medievale nel Mediterraneo occidentale. IIIe colloquio, Siena-Faenza, 1984,* Siena, 483-510.

Boldrini, E., Roncaglia G., 1984, Prime osservazioni sul materiale ceramico del castrum di Montarrenti, *Archeologia Medievale*, XI, 268-274.

Cancellieri, J.-A., 1984, Directions de recherche sur la démographie de la Corse médiévale (XIIIe-XVe siècles), Actes du colloque *Strutture familiari, epidemia, migrazioni nell'Italia medievale*, Naples.

Chatel, B., 1970, *Le commerce entre la Corse et Pise du XIIe au milieu du XVe siècle*, mémoire de maîtrise dactylographié, Université d'Aix-en-Provence.

Colin, M.G., Darnas I., Pousthomis N., Schneider L., 1996, La maison du *castrum* de la bordure méridionale du massif central, *Archéologie du Midi Médiéval*, supplément n°1.

Comet, G., 1992, *Le paysan et son outil, essai d'histoire technique des céréales (France VIIIe-XVe siècle)*, Collection de l'Ecole Française de Rome, 165.

Cucchi, Th., 2000, *Le castellu de Rostino (XIIIe-XIVe siècle), étude archéozoologique*, mémoire de maîtrise, université Paris I, Panthéon Sorbonne.

Davasse, B., Galop, D., Rendu, Ch., 1997, Paysages du Néolithique à nos jours dans les Pyrénées de l'Est d'après l'écologie historique et l'archéologie pastorale, Actes des XVIIe rencontres Internationales d'Archéologie et d'Histoire d'Antibes, *La dynamique des paysages protohistoriques, antiques, médiévaux et modernes*, Sophia Antipolis, 577-599.

Day, J., 1987, *La Sardegna sotto la dominazione pisano-genovesa*, Torino.

Démians d'Archimbaud, G., Vallauri, L., 1998, Productions et importations de céramiques médiévales dans le midi méditerranéen français, *Monografies d'arqueologia medieval i postmedieval*, 4, Barcelone, 73-110.

Gambaro, L., 1987, Monte Zignago, *Archeologia in Liguria III. 2. Scavi e scoperte 1982-86*, Genova, 279-286.

Istria, D., 2000, Les marquis Obertenghi dans le nord de la Corse (fin XIe-milieu du XIVe siècle). La mise en place d'un réseau de fortifications, *Mélanges de l'Ecole Française de Rome, Moyen Age*, 112, 1, 225-258.

Istria, D., 2002, Le château, l'habitat et l'église dans le nord de la Corse aux XIIe et XIIIe siècles, *Mélanges de l'Ecole Française de Rome, Moyen Age*, 114, 1, 227-301.

Istria, D., Comiti, P., 2000, La Corsica e il Mediterraneo nella prima metà del XIV secolo: le testimonianze dello scavo del villaggio di La Mugliunaccia, *Medioevo, saggi e rassegne*, 24, 27-46.

Milanese, M., Biccone, L., Fiori, M., 2000, Produzione, commercio e consumo di manufatti ceramici nella Sardegna nord-occidentale tra XI e XV secolo, *II congrsso nazionale di archeologia medievale, Brescia 28 settembre-1 ottobre 2000, Firenze*, 435-443.

Molard, M., 1875, Rapport sur les archives provinciales de Pise et sur les collections Roncioni et Agostini della Seta, *Archives des missions scientifiques et littéraires,* serie terza, II.

Origone, S., 1979, *Notai genovesi in Corsica, Calvi 1370, Bonifacio 1385-86*, Genova.

Pistarino, G., 1944, Le carte del monastero di San Venerio del Tino relative alla Corsica (1080-1500), *Deputazione subalpina di Storia Patria*, CLXX.

Ribot, H., 1985, Les fouilles du *castrum* de Sainte-Madeleine (La Môle, Var), *Archéologie Médiévale*, XV, 103-156.

Ruas, M.-P., 1998, Les plantes consommées au Moyen Age en France méridionale d'après les semences archéologiques, *Archéologie du Midi Médiéval*, 15-16, 197-204.

Vigne, J.-D., Ruas, M.-P., 1995, Perspectives archéobotaniques et archéozoologiques pour les périodes historiques en Corse, *Patrimoine d'une île. Recherches récentes d'archéologie médiévale en Corse,* Ajaccio, 113-126.

Wickham, C., 2002, Paludi e miniere nella Maremma toscana, XI-XIII secoli, *Actes du colloque Castrum VII, Zones côtières littorales dans le monde méditerranéen au Moyen Age : défense, peuplement, mise en valeur, Rome 23-26 octobre 1996*, Rome-Madrid, 451-466.

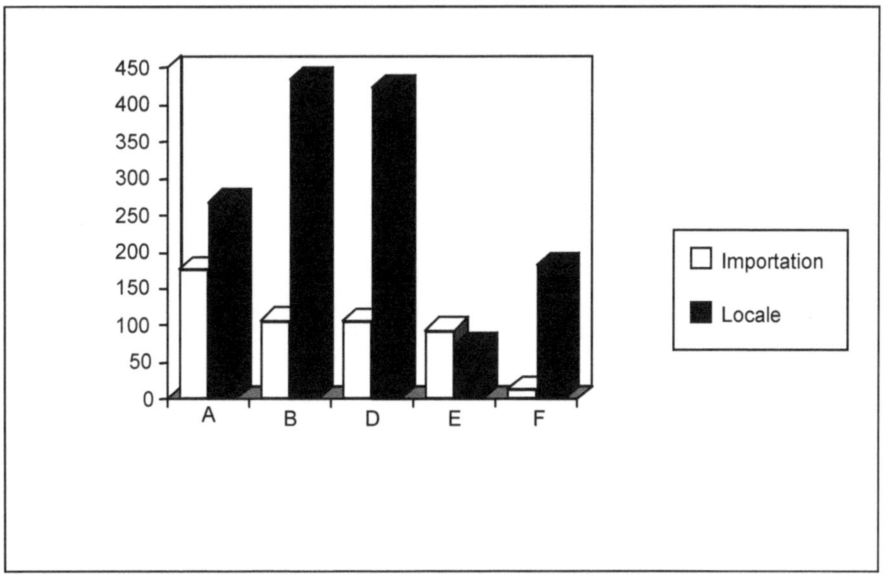

Fig. 1. Proportions des céramiques dans les maisons de la Mugliunaccia (en nombre de tessons).

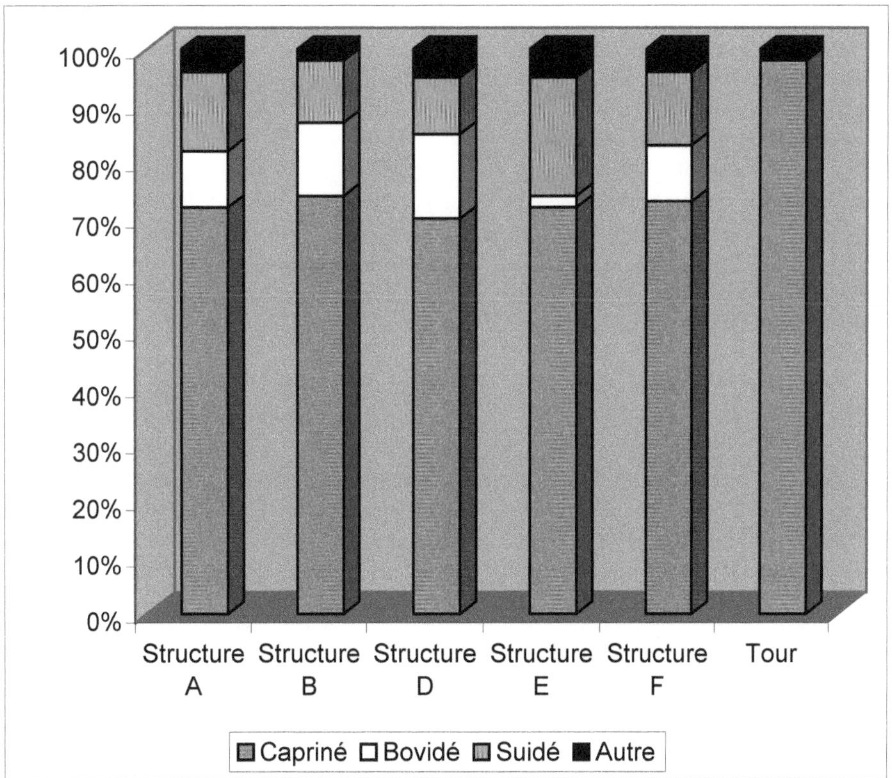

Fig. 2. Proportions des ossements d'animaux dans les maisons de la Mugliunaccia.

I PITHOI DI ISPIRAZIONE EGEA DEL TARDO BRONZO NELL'ITALIA MERIDIONALE: TECNOLOGIA, CONTENUTO, IMMAGAZZINAMENTO, CIRCOLAZIONE

SARA TIZIANA LEVI (Universty of Glasgow)
ANDREA SCHIAPPELLI (Università di Roma "La Sapienza")

Abstract: In the course of the late Bronze Age (ca. 13th century BC), a class of pottery that had until this time only been manufactured in the Aegean and central Mediterranean Seas made its first appearance in South Italy and would endure until the early Iron Age. Dolia manufactured in both a fine-bodied clay and in "Impasto" were partially formed on a potter's wheel and often decorated with "cordoni", relief decoration or impressed motifs. In the present contribution, the authors delineate the state of research, issues connected to production and circulation, tecnological characteristics, a typology of the most common decorative motifs, the socio-economic implications of the existence of specialized storerooms for the conservation of foodstuffs as well as the evidence for an Aegean-Oriental progenitura of *pithoi* found in Italy.

PREMESSA METODOLOGICA

Dal 1990, alle tradizionali indagini tipologiche delle classi ceramiche presenti nel sito protostorico di Broglio di Trebisacce (Sibaritide, Calabria ionica settentrionale) è stato affiancato, nell'ambito delle ricerche condotte dall'équipe che effettua da anni gli scavi, lo studio tecnologico, curato da S. T. Levi. Per quanto riguarda i dolii, proprio partendo dal vasto campione (per varietà di forme e d'impasti) disponibile per Broglio, in questi ultimi anni la ricerca, condotta da Andrea Schiappelli e orientata alla definizione degli aspetti sia crono-tipologici che socio-economici, è stata estesa in primo luogo all'intera Italia meridionale, comprendendo materiali editi e inediti, quindi al mondo egeo-mediterraneo, dove sono documentati i "prototipi" della classe in discorso.

Più in particolare, lo studio tecnologico si pone come finalità l'individuazione del luogo di produzione (approvvigionamento delle materie prime, aree di attività) e la comprensione dei processi di manifattura (caratteristiche delle materie prime, preparazione degli impasti, metodi di foggiatura, rifinitura, decorazione e cottura). Questo fine viene perseguito, oltre che con osservazioni dirette dei materiali, attraverso l'impiego di metodi analitici scientifici, dunque archeometrici: analisi petrografica al microscopio polarizzatore (sezioni sottili), diffrazione a raggi X e analisi chimica "in massa" (attivazione neutronica strumentale o spettrometria di assorbimento atomico), utile quest'ultima alla determinazione della provenienza (a scala regionale) della ceramica (Levi 1999, pp. 17-27).

1. DEFINIZIONE DELLA CLASSE CERAMICA

Nel corso del Bronzo recente (XIII sec. a.C. circa) in Italia meridionale fa la sua comparsa una classe di vasi fino a quel momento prodotta esclusivamente nel mondo egeo-orientale: i dolii di argilla "depurata" (c.d. ceramica figulina) e d'impasto più o meno fine, in entrambi i casi almeno parzialmente lavorati al tornio e il più delle volte decorati con cordoni, fasce in rilievo o fasci di scanalature impresse.

Si tratta di contenitori di grandi dimensioni, di forma da ovoide a globulare, dotati di norma di anse verticali impostate sull'orlo o di maniglie sulla spalla, alti, in alcuni casi, oltre un metro e trenta, con orli fino a 50 cm di diametro e massima espansione di 1,20 m, con una capacità che può raggiungere i mille litri. Vasi dunque adatti a contenere grandi quantità di derrate alimentari, sia solide, come ad esempio grano ed olive, sia liquide, come acqua, vino (perlomeno in ambiente minoico-miceneo) e soprattutto olio, come si è potuto constatare grazie all'analisi chimica delle impregnazioni residue sul fondo o sulle pareti di alcuni esemplari rinvenuti in Puglia e in Calabria. Del resto, tale dato appare funzionalmente coerente con la prevalente notevole larghezza dell'imboccatura, adatta alla conservazione dell'olio piuttosto che del vino, il quale, per sua natura, necessita preferibilmente di imboccature più strette e quindi più agevolmente sigillabili.

La definizione della classe in esame, tuttavia, non si basa esclusivamente sull'aspetto dimensionale, né tanto meno su quello funzionale: in effetti contenitori di grandi dimensioni e di forma "panciuta" sono documentati in Italia centro meridionale ben prima del Bronzo recente: basti qui citare, tra le località più note, quelli rinvenuti nei villaggi della cultura di Capo Graziano (2300-1500 a.C.) nelle Isole Eolie (Bernabò Brea and Cavalier 1980 e 1991) e nella vicina Milazzo (Tigano et al. 1994, tav. IX). Ma si tratta, in questi casi, di vasi d'impasto realizzati a mano e privi delle decorazioni che caratterizzano le produzioni più recenti.

2. Distribuzione in Italia

In questi ultimi anni di ricerche archeologiche in Italia meridionale, la documentazione relativa ai grandi *pithoi* cordonati di argilla depurata ha subito notevoli progressi, da quando, a Broglio di Trebisacce, alla fine degli anni '70 i dolii sono stati riconosciuti per la prima volta in Italia come classe ceramica databile già nella tarda età del Bronzo (Levi 1999, con bibliografia precedente). Attualmente la presenza di questa produzione specializzata è stata riscontrata in numerosi centri (fig. 1) riferibili alla tarda età del bronzo e alla prima età del ferro (Levi 1999, pp. 108-109 e fig. 66, con bibliografia relativa ai siti citati in questa sede, vd. *infra*), con una particolare incidenza sulla costa adriatica e lungo l'arco ionico: a partire dalla Puglia settentrionale, si vogliono qui ricordare, tra i principali, i siti di Manaccora, dove ai pochi frammenti raccolti all'interno della grotta vanno ad aggiungersi i numerosi esemplari di recente raccolti sul soprastante promontorio; di Santa Maria di Ripalta, il più "interno" degli abitati della regione; di Roca Vecchia, villaggio su penisola dotato di imponenti strutture difensive, all'interno del quale sono stati rinvenuti centinaia di frammenti di dolii in figulina; di Otranto, per il quale sono documentati anche dolii con decorazione dipinta; di Punta Meliso presso Santa Maria di Leuca, all'estremità della penisola salentina; e infine di Torre Castelluccia e Porto Perone sul golfo di Taranto.

A differenza delle altre regioni, la presenza di *pithoi* in Basilicata è attestata in località piuttosto distanti dalla costa, come nel caso di Timmari, Matera e Tursi, mentre una diffusione territorialmente più articolata si riscontra nella Sibaritide (fig. 2), dove nel corso dell'età del bronzo e della prima età del ferro le comunità sono insediate principalmente sui bassi rilievi disposti ad arco intorno alla valle del Crati. Oltre che a Broglio di Trebisacce, per limitarsi ai centri maggiori, dolii della tarda età del Bronzo sono noti a Torre Mordillo, *central place* del comprensorio sibarita e al Timpone Motta di Francavilla Marittima, centro che manterrà la sua importanza anche in seguito, quando diverrà sede di un complesso templare greco.

Sempre nella Calabria ionica, ricerche di superficie effettuate in questi ultimi anni hanno consentito l'individuazione di una seconda area di diffusione di dolii cordonati, costituita da Crotone e dal suo *hinterland* (Marino 1998).

In Sicilia e in Sardegna i dolii documentati sono esclusivamente del tipo d'impasto, e le attestazioni riguardano principalmente la provincia di Messina, con i siti di Lipari, Monte di Giove e Monte Belvedere; inoltre, in almeno due casi, Cannatello sulla costa agrigentina e Antigori sul golfo di Cagliari, oltre a *pithoi* di produzione locale, sembra sicura la presenza di vere e proprie importazioni da Cipro, aspetto sul quale si tornerà tra breve.

3. Produzione e circolazione

Circa duecento analisi archeometriche petrografiche e chimiche, effettuate in collaborazione con M. Sonnino e R. E. Jones, hanno permesso di individuare i principali centri produttivi, i circuiti di circolazione e le caratteristiche tecnologiche (Levi 1999).

Alcuni esemplari rinvenuti in Sicilia e in Sardegna risultano importati da Cipro e da Creta, ma la grande maggioranza è prodotta in Italia in diversi centri (almeno dieci) ad opera di artigiani verosimilmente formatisi in ambiente egeo (fig. 3).

Questo modello è gia stato proposto per la ceramica micenea (TE IIIB e IIIC), per la quale, in numerosi siti dell'Italia meridionale, la compresenza di vasellame di importazione e di riproduzioni locali di modelli egei è ormai ben attestata (Bettelli 2002). A questo proposito, è opportuno sottolineare come i dolii cordonati nel Bronzo recente si rinvengano pressoché esclusivamente nell'ambito dell'area caratterizzata dalle attestazioni di ceramica micenea, in parziale coincidenza con la produzione pseudominia (detta anche ceramica "grigia"), mentre nel Bronzo finale la distribuzione dei dolii in figulina coincide con quella della ceramica protogeometrica, testimoniando la prosecuzione e il rinnovamento dell'artigianato specializzato che era fiorito in Italia dal contatto con il mondo egeo (fig. 4).

Ma la circolazione dei dolii, una volta avviata la produzione locale, e del loro contenuto avveniva senza dubbio anche tra i villaggi dell'Italia meridionale: ad esempio a Broglio di Trebisacce è stato possibile, grazie alle analisi archeometriche, constatare come tra la tarda età del Bronzo e il primo Ferro circa un quarto dei *pithoi* rinvenuti venisse importato dalla Sibaritide meridionale, ovvero da una distanza di almeno 20 km (fig. 5). Ma i traffici di dolii non sembrerebbero limitarsi ad aree geograficamente contigue: è quanto risulta dalle analisi petrografiche di alcuni campioni di *pithoi* da Otranto, le quali documentano un'importazione degli stessi da un'area compresa tra la Sibaritide meridionale e la costa messinese (Levi 1999, pp. 112-113).

4. Tecnologia

Si è più volte definita la produzione di questa classe come specializzata, come ricorda anche l'antico proverbio greco "imparare l'arte ceramica iniziando dal *pithos*" (Guglielmino 2002, p. 183); circa le forme di produzione, è possibile definire la relativa organizzazione come a livello di bottega artigianale, sulla base delle seguenti caratteristiche tecniche:

1) la materia prima è molto fine, solitamente argilla figulina molto depurata (gli esemplari in impasto sono concentrati al di fuori dell'area principale di produzione: la Puglia e l'arco Jonico, vedi fig. 4);

2) i correttivi, quando presenti, sono ben selezionati tra una varietà più ristretta rispetto a quella impiegata per la ceramica d'impasto comune. Ad esempio, a Broglio si usano materiali ricorrenti: nel Bronzo recente la siltite e

la calcite; nel Bronzo finale la siltite e la siltite fossilifera (fig. 6).

La tecnica di foggiatura è molto complessa e richiede notevole esperienza: si tratta di una lavorazione che doveva prevedere il montaggio progressivo di grossi cercini (circa 4-5 cm di diametro) uno sull'altro, con pause finalizzate a un parziale essiccamento che garantiva un preliminare consolidamento degli anelloni ottenuti, a loro volta assemblati, con l'ausilio del tornio e mediante la preparazione di immorsature lungo la circonferenza. Nel Bronzo recente i punti di giunzione vengono rinforzati con l'applicazione di argilla stesa in fasce lisce (talvolta recanti una decorazione incisa), secondo un principio che potrebbe ricordare in qualche modo quello impiegato in seguito per le botti di legno. A rivelare inequivocabilmente la tecnica di montaggio degli "anelloni" di cercini in questa fase sono peraltro le modalità di rottura del vaso stesso: in questo caso, appaiono difatti numerose le fratture con andamento orizzontale, mentre le fratture ad andamento curvilineo, tipiche del periodo successivo, testimoniano una lavorazione più sequenziale nell'assemblaggio dei cercini (fig. 7).

In effetti, nel corso del Bronzo finale si riscontra un migliore sfruttamento delle potenzialità del tornio, con la conseguente perdita della funzione "statica" delle fasce applicate, che d'ora in poi avranno un ruolo esclusivamente decorativo; si tratta in realtà di un fenomeno in controtendenza, considerato lo scadimento tecnico che si osserva nella manifattura della figulina protogeometrica, che evidenzia la particolarità della produzione dei dolii, apparentemente insensibile al venir meno dei rapporti con il mondo egeo, alle prese in questo periodo con i suoi "secoli bui".

Tornando agli aspetti tecnici, va ricordato come una grande attenzione dovesse essere prestata alla cottura, che avveniva in veri e propri forni con buona ossigenazione e ad alta temperatura (intorno ai 900°): una temperatura alla quale la materia prima, calcarea, diveniva particolarmente resistente agli shock meccanici, rendendo pertanto i dolii adatti sia all'immagazzinamento che al trasporto (fig. 8).

5. Tipi principali di dolio e di decorazioni

In termini di quantità complessiva dei frammenti significativi di dolii disponibili per i quasi cinquanta centri in discorso (fig. 9), i numeri risultano piuttosto bassi: la maggior parte dei contesti non offre che poche unità o al massimo qualche decina di reperti diagnostici, fatta eccezione per Roca Vecchia e soprattutto per Broglio di Trebisacce, dove il numero delle varietà supera di gran lunga quello degli abitati coevi.

E' stato così possibile isolare alcuni tipi con valore cronologico (fig. 10), come ad esempio, tra quelli maggiormente diffusi, i dolii di forma ovoide rastremata, a "botte", decorati con alte fasce lisce applicate in diversi punti del corpo, caratteristici del Bronzo recente, cui fanno seguito i *pithoi* di forma panciuta con fasci orizzontali di scanalature multiple; lo stesso elemento decorativo si protrae fin nella prima età del ferro, associato, in un tipo di dolio abbondantemente diffuso nella Sibaritide, con prese a lingua eretta applicate su una spalla molto pronunciata.

Per maggior chiarezza sembra a questo punto opportuno illustrare, anche se solo in rapida rassegna, i principali elementi decorativi con significato cronologico, anche al fine di richiamare l'attenzione su una classe ceramica nel passato spesso trascurata e non di rado erroneamente riferita ad epoca arcaica o classica.

Si è già detto della alta fascia liscia (figg. 10, 11:1 e 12:A) tipica del Bronzo recente e documentata, oltre che a Broglio e in Sibaritide, nei siti della Puglia ionica e a Monte di Giove in Sicilia.

Ancora più diffusa è la variante con decorazione incisa della stessa alta fascia (figg. 12:B e 13) nell'ambito della quale è possibile riconoscere motivi ricorrenti, quali lo *chevron* e lo zig zag associato a punti; per ciò che concerne la cronologia, recenti rinvenimenti hanno portato a riconsiderare la datazione al Bronzo recente finora invalsa, prolungandone l'orizzonte fino alle fasi non avanzate del Bronzo finale.

Prevalentemente riferibile al Bronzo finale, e in misura minore al primo Ferro, è la fascia con costolature orizzontali, di norma tre (fig. 11:4-5), in alcuni casi due o quattro (fig. 11:6-7); per quanto abbondantemente presente a Broglio (fig. 12:C), altrove la sua distribuzione è limitata a pochi altri centri in Calabria e in Puglia.

Pur essendo riferibili allo stesso lungo periodo, i fasci orizzontali di scanalature multiple (fig. 11:8) vantano una diffusione decisamente maggiore (fig. 12:D), anche per via della semplicità del motivo decorativo e della sua esecuzione.

6. I magazzini

Proprio di quest'ultimo tipo sono i dolii rinvenuti sull'acropoli di Broglio, coricati su di un fianco e schiacciati in frammenti, all'interno di due strutture destinate esclusivamente allo stoccaggio di tali grandi contenitori per derrate: veri e propri magazzini dell'inizio del Bronzo finale, dunque, posti in prossimità di una grande abitazione. Nel primo caso, come si vede nella ricostruzione (fig. 14), si tratta di un ambiente a pianta rettangolare (circa 7 x 3,5 m), con il pavimento piuttosto infossato rispetto al piano esterno, e con un ingresso a rampa; sul lato opposto all'entrata, disposti a ferro di cavallo, erano collocati cinque grandi dolii. Anche all'interno della seconda struttura, in origine un'abitazione poi adattata a magazzino, si rinvennero numerosi frammenti di *pithoi* e, a breve distanza, la medesima funzione ebbe anche un terzo ambiente, riferibile in quest'ultimo caso al primo Ferro.

Ma di certo il sito enotrio non sarà stato l'unico in cui la conservazione delle risorse era concentrata in strutture specificamente attrezzate: in effetti, per quanto meno evidenti, indizi della probabile esistenza di analoghi magazzini di dolii sono stati rilevati ad esempio a Roca Vecchia (Guglielmino 2002) e a Santa Maria di Ripalta in Puglia e, forse, a Bisignano nella Sibaritide meridionale (Schiappelli 1999).

Le implicazioni socio-economiche della presenza di una forma di immagazzinamento, in qualche modo centralizzato, in questi siti della tarda età del bronzo appaiono tutt'altro che trascurabili: trattandosi di quantità di derrate sovradimensionate rispetto al fabbisogno di un singolo gruppo famigliare, per il primo magazzino è stata calcolata una capacità complessiva di poco meno di 5000 litri, sembrerebbe lecito postulare una facoltà redistributiva delle risorse alimentari, esercitata nella comunità da parte di gruppi socialmente rilevanti, come peraltro le notevoli dimensioni della capanna sull'acropoli di Broglio, cui vanno riferiti i due magazzini, sembrerebbero attestare.

7. L'ispirazione egeo-orientale

L'idea di magazzino, associata a figure eminenti che ne controllano la gestione, avrà probabilmente proiettato l'immaginario del lettore, e non a sproposito, nel mondo minoico-miceneo, ad esempio a Knosso, Mallia o Monastiraki, dove, a partire dall'Antico Minoico, ovvero diversi secoli prima della comparsa dei dolii cordonati in Italia, la centralizzata gestione delle risorse del territorio prevedeva la loro conservazione in grandi *pithoi*, talvolta recanti segni incisi, stoccati in ampi ambienti ubicati in apposite ali dei palazzi (Panagiotaki 1999). Per inciso, in questi ultimi anni il recupero di alcuni carichi di navi naufragate nelle acque dell'Egeo e del Mediterraneo nell'età del Bronzo (Vagnetti 1999, con bibliografia precedente), ha consentito, oltre ad estendere la gamma funzionale da vaso per immagazzinamento "statico" a contenitore da trasporto, di verificare come la natura del contenuto dei dolii nelle stive non si limitasse alle derrate alimentari, bensì prevedesse lo stipaggio di altri manufatti, ad esempio vasellame ceramico, come nel caso del relitto di Ulu Burun, a largo della costa meridionale della Turchia (Bass 1986).

Tornando al problema dell' "albero genealogico" dei dolii, la "progenitura" egeo-orientale della classe in esame appare certa, suffragata da un crescente numero di confronti tipologici tra i *pithoi* "italiani" con esemplari esotici: oltre alle già citate importazioni da Cipro a Cannatello e ad Antigori, fossile guida, in questa direzione di ricerca, sono i dolii con le alte fasce decorate, come ha messo opportunamente a fuoco Marco Bettelli nella sua recente pubblicazione (2002, pp. 106-113).

Nella figura 15 rielaborata, con integrazioni, da una tavola del succitato lavoro, si offre infine un quadro sinottico della distribuzione, e quindi delle direttrici finora riconosciute, delle importazioni in Italia di dolii *in re*, intendendo con tale termine l'adozione da ambiente "extra-italico", nell'ambito delle produzioni locali, di soli motivi decorativi, e delle importazioni *in se*, ovvero dei *pithoi* veri e propri.

I punti di origine della prima di queste categorie, limitata alla circolazione degli elementi stilistici, sono localizzati in Grecia e a Creta, e si collocano di fatti nel periodo di intensa frequentazione delle coste dell'Italia meridionale e insulare da parte dei navigatori micenei. Tra i motivi decorativi più diffusi si distingue lo *chevron*, o spina di pesce, seguito, per "popolarità", dalle assortite combinazioni di zig-zag con punti e dalle fasce con punti liberi, quest'ultimo forse di più lunga durata rispetto agli altri.

Alla rarefazione dei contatti con il mondo miceneo, in seguito al crollo dei palazzi avvenuto alle soglie del nostro Bronzo finale, segue un'intensificazione dei rapporti con Cipro, comunque avviati da tempo, come provano le esportazioni *in se* in Sardegna e in Sicilia risalenti al Bronzo recente; tale dato troverebbe conferma, oltre che dalla grande diffusione in Italia dei fasci di scanalature comuni nei siti dell'isola del Vicino Oriente, anche dalla presenza in diversi insediamenti "italiani" di altri manufatti di natura cipriota (Ferrarese Ceruti et al. 1987) e ancora, nel caso di Broglio, dalle tracce di una precoce metallurgia del ferro.

BIBLIOGRAFIA

Archeo 2000: In Calabria prima dei Greci. Vent'anni di scavi a Broglio di Trebisacce, a cura di R. Peroni, Dossier in Archeo nr. 8 (186), agosto 2000.

Bernabò Brea and Cavalier 1980: L. Bernabò Brea, M. Cavalier, *Meligunìs Lipàra IV*, Palermo 1980.

Bernabò Brea and Cavalier 1991: L. Bernabò Brea, M. Cavalier, *Meligunìs Lipàra VI*, Palermo 1991.

Bettelli 2002: M. Bettelli, *Italia meridionale e mondo miceneo*, Firenze 2002.

Ferrarese Ceruti et Al.: M.L. Ferrarese Ceruti, L. Vagnetti, F. Lo Schiavo, Minoici, Micenei e Ciprioti in Sardegna alla luce delle più recenti scoperte, in *Studies in Sardinian Archeology, III. Nuragic Sardinia and the Mycenean World*, di M.S. Balmuth, BAR Int. Series 387, Oxford.

Guglielmino 2002: Guglielmino R., *Ceramiche egee ed egeizzanti da Roca Vecchia (Melendugno, Lecce)*, in *Strutture e modelli di abitati del Bronzo tardo da Torre Castelluccia a Roca Vecchia*, a cura di M. Gorgoglione, Atti del Convegno di Studio 28-29 novembre 1996, Pulsano (TA)-Castello De Falconibus, Manduria 2002, pp. 171-192.

Levi 1999: S. T. Levi ed altri autori, *Produzione e circolazione della ceramica nella Sibaritide protostorica. I – Impasto e dolii*, Firenze 1999.

Marino 1998: D. Marino, Settlement and economy in Eastern Central Calabria, Southern Italy, in *Proceedings of the XIII UISPP Congress 1996*, vol. 4, Sections 10-12, ed. R. De Marinis, A.M. Bietti Sestieri, R. Peroni, C. Peretto, Firenze 1998, pp. 271-276.

Panagiotaki 1999: M. Panagiotaki, *The Central Palace Sanctuary at Knossos*, Supplementary Volume n. 31, The British School at Athens, London 1999.

Schiappelli 1999: A. Schiappelli, Bisignano, in LEVI 1999, pp. 51-54.

Tigano et Al. 1994: G. Tigano, S.T. Levi, C. Moffa, A. Vanzetti, Milazzo. Resti di abitato preistorico nella zona del Borgo. Relazione preliminare (campagna di scavo 1995-96), in *Quaderni dell'Istituto di Archeologia della Facoltà di Lettere e Filosofia della Università di Messina*, 9, 1994, pp. 5-15.

Vagnetti 1999: L. Vagnetti, Myceneans and Cypriots in the Central Mediterranean before and after 1200 bC, in *The Point Iria Wreck: Interconnections in the Mediterranean ca. 1200 b.C.. Proceedings of the International Conference. Island of Spetses, 19 September 1998*. Ed. William Phelps, Yannos Lolos, Yannis Vichos. Athens 1999.

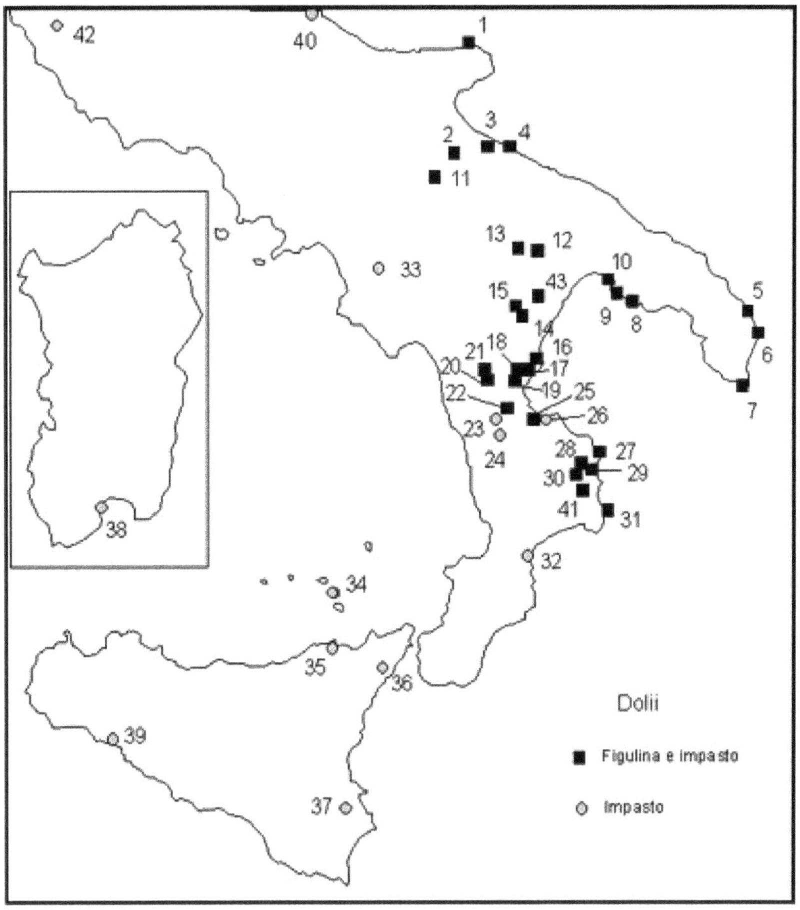

Fig. 1. Carta di distribuzione dei dolii di impasto e figulina tra tarda età del bronzo e prima età del ferro in Italia centro-meridionale e insulare; 1: Manaccora (FG), 2: S. Maria di Ripalta (FG), 3: Madonna del Petto (BA), 4: Capo Colonna (BA), 5: Roca Vecchia (LE), 6: Otranto (LE), 7: Leuca-Punta Meliso, 8: Torre Castelluccia (TA), 9: Porto Perone (TA), 10: Taranto-S. Domenico, 11: Toppo Daguzzo (PZ), 12: Timmari (MT), 13: Matera, 14: Tursi-Castello (MT), 15: Tursi-S. Martino (MT), 16: Amendolara (CS), 17: Broglio di Trebisacce (CS), 18: Timpone Motta di Cerchiata (CS), 19: Timpone Motta di Francavilla Marittima (CS), 20: Belloluco (CS), 21: S. Maria di Castello-Castrovillari, 22: Torre Mordillo (CS), 23: la Prunetta-Roggiano Gravina (CS), 24: Bisignano (CS), 25: Basili di Rossano (CS), 26: Bucita (CS), 27: Cirò (KR), 28: Serre d'Altilia (KR), 29: Serra dell'Aranco (KR), 30: Monte Fuscaldo (KR), 31: Crotone (KR), 32: Vucia e Mango (Soverato, CZ), 33: Grotta dello Zachito (SA), 34: Lipari (ME), 35: Monte di Giove (ME), 36: Monte Belvedere (ME), 37: Pantalica (SR), 38: Antigori (CA), 39: Cannatello (AG), 40: Fonte Tasca-Archi (CH), 41: Timpa della Zita (KR), 42: Veio (RM), 43: Serre di Pisticci (MT). (Elaborazione di A. Schiappelli).

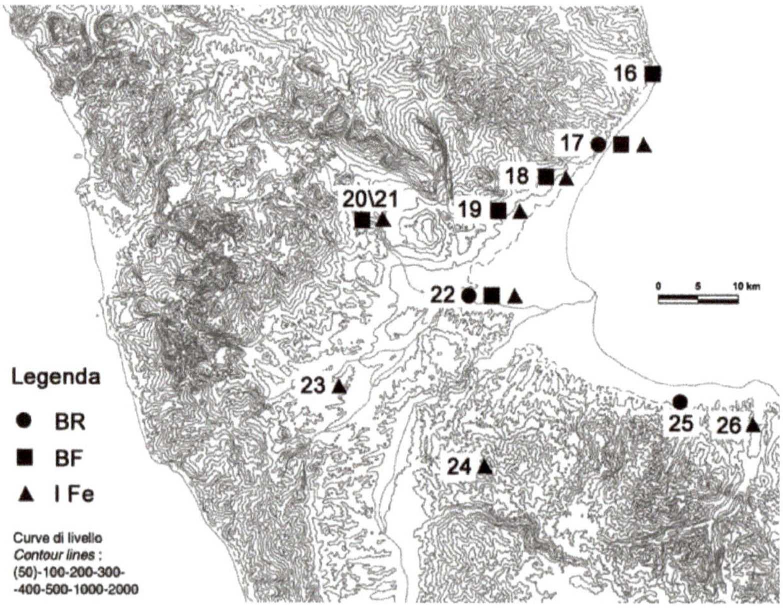

Fig. 2. I siti con dolii nella Sibaritide (si mantiene la medesima numerazione della figura precedente): 16: Amendolara (CS), 17: Broglio di Trebisacce (CS), 18: Timpone Motta di Cerchiata (CS), 19: Timpone Motta di Francavilla Marittima (CS), 20: Belloluco (CS), 21: S. Maria di Castello-Castrovillari, 22: Torre Mordillo (CS), 23: la Prunetta-Roggiano Gravina (CS), 24: Bisignano (CS), 25: Basili di Rossano (CS), 26: Bucita (CS); BR: età del Bronzo recente, BF: Bronzo finale, I Fe: prima età del Ferro. (Elaborazione di A. Schiappelli).

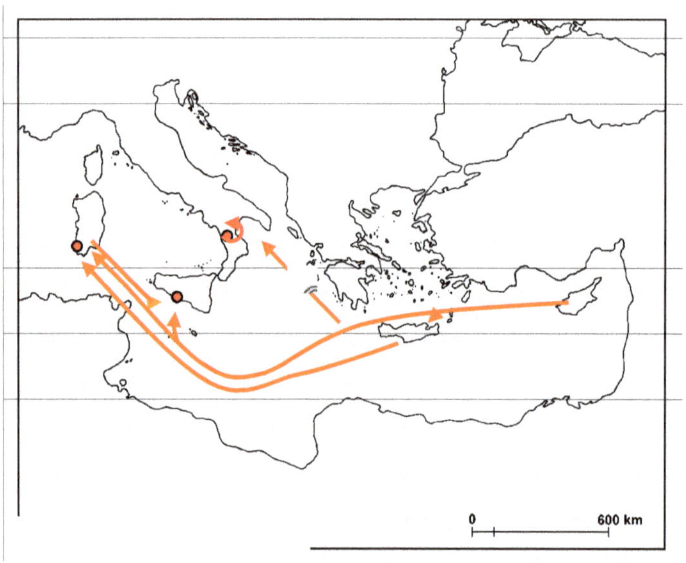

Fig. 3. Centri di produzione e circuiti di circolazione dei dolii nel Bronzo recente (elaborazione di S. T. Levi, realizzazione grafica di Daniele Pantano).

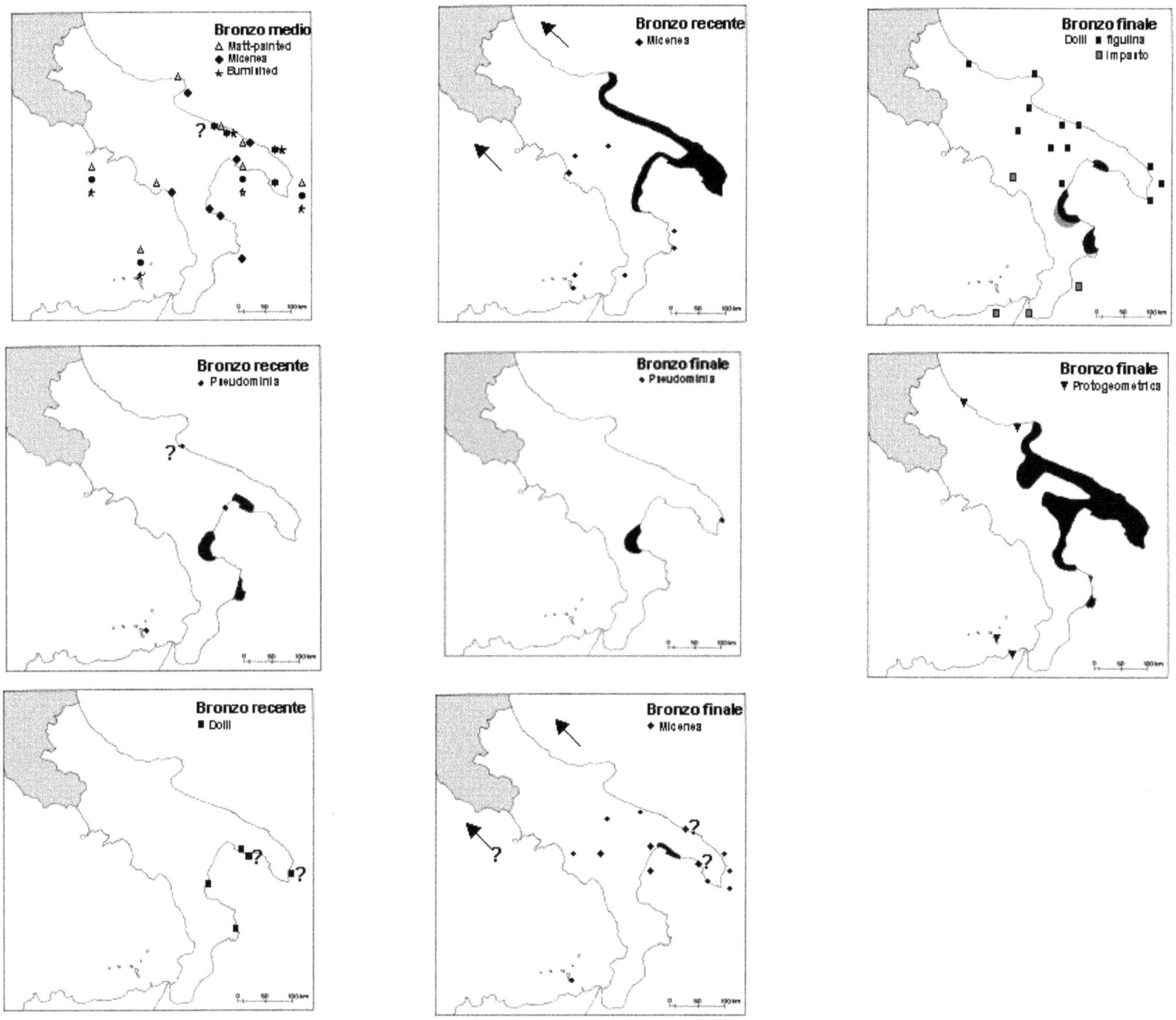

Fig. 4. Distribuzione delle classi ceramiche specializzate in figulina nelle varie fasi (da Battelli 2002, realizzazione grafica Daniele Pantano).

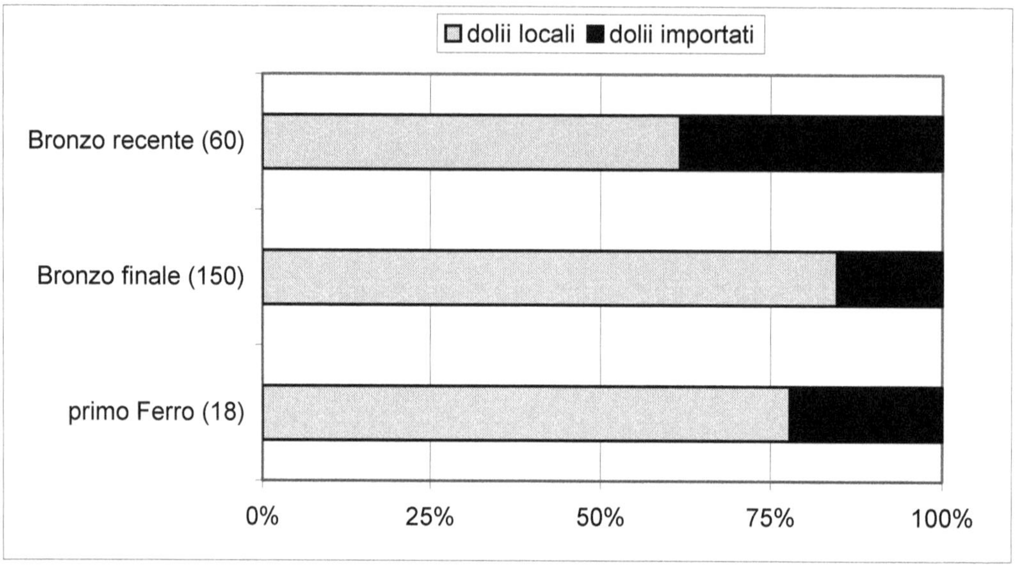

Fig. 5. Diagramma a barre con la percentuale di dolii importati a Broglio di Trebisacce dalla Sibaritide meridionale, distinto per fasi (rielaborazione da Levi 1999).

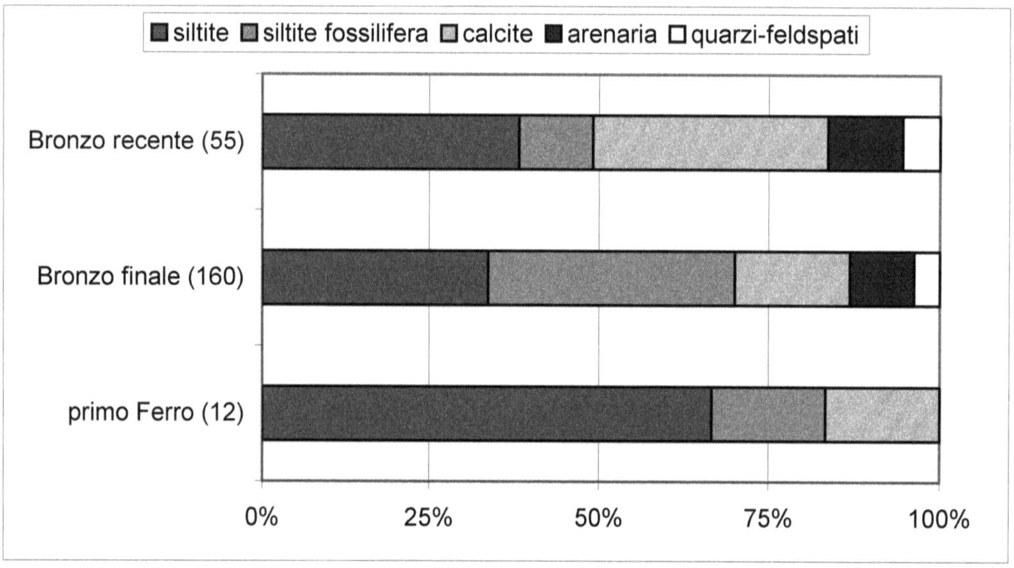

Fig. 6. Percentuali dei correttivi impiegati nella produzione dei dolii a Broglio nelle diverse fasi (elaborazione di S. T. Levi).

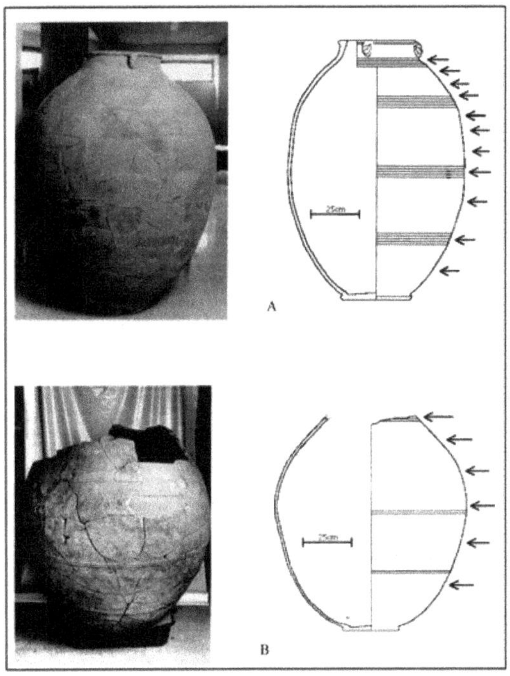

Fig. 7. Due dei cinque grandi dolii del "magazzino 1" sull'acropoli di Broglio di Trebisacce, con le frecce sono indicate le giunture tra i cercini (da Levi 1999, fig. 200).

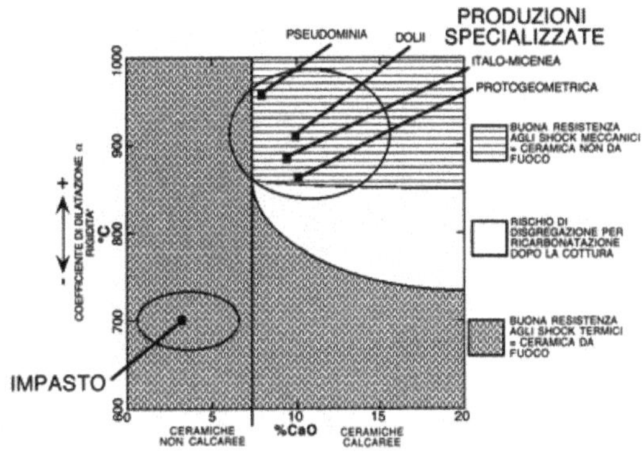

Fig. 8. Schema della temperatura di cottura (basato sull'analisi diffrattometrica), della quantità di calcio (sulla base dell'analisi chimica per spettrometria di assorbimento atomico) e della potenziale funzione per le diverse classi ceramiche (da Levi 1999, fig. 238).

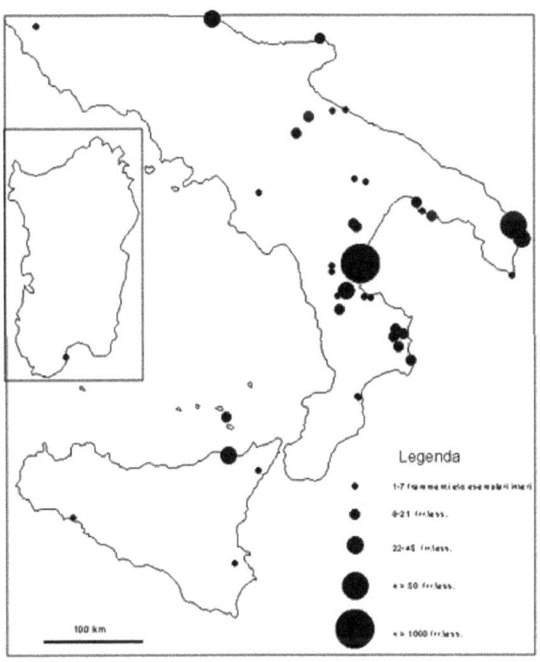

Fig. 9. Carta esemplificativa del numero di frammenti di dolii cordonati rinvenuti e documentati in Italia centro meridionale e insulare; cerchio piccolo: 1-2 frammenti diagnostici, cerchi intermedi: tra i 3 e i 50 frammenti, cerchio grande: oltre 1000 frammenti (elaborazione di A. Schiappelli).

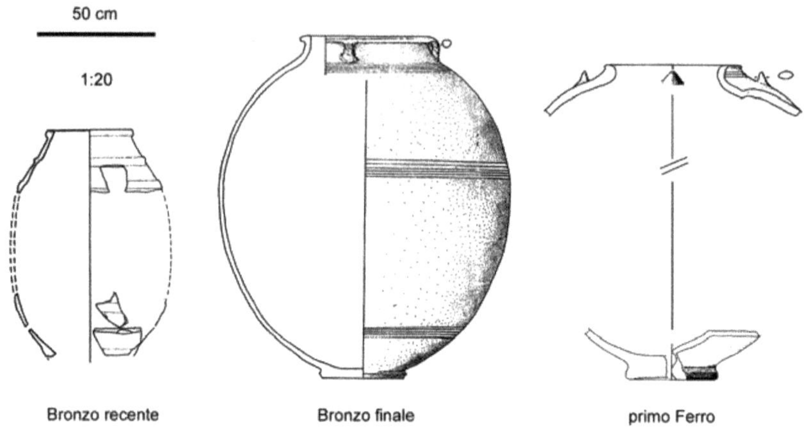

Fig. 10. Dolii caratteristici delle fasi considerate (da Broglio di Trebisacce i primi due, da la Prunetta di Roggiano Gravina il terzo, da sinistra).

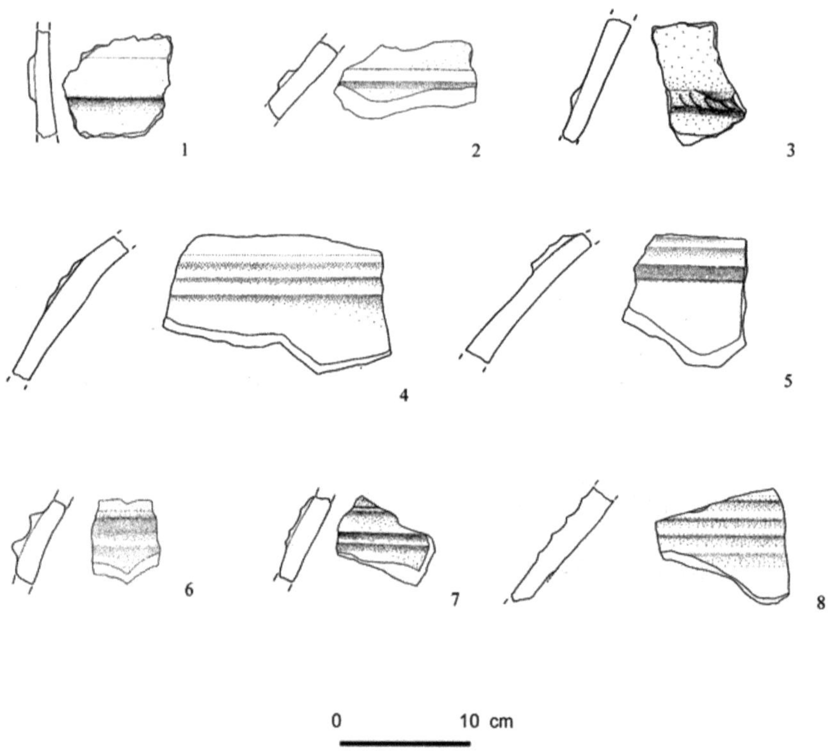

Fig. 11. Principali tipi di fasce cordonate (nr. 1: da Porto Perone, nrr. 2-8 da Broglio di Trebisacce; scala 1:4).

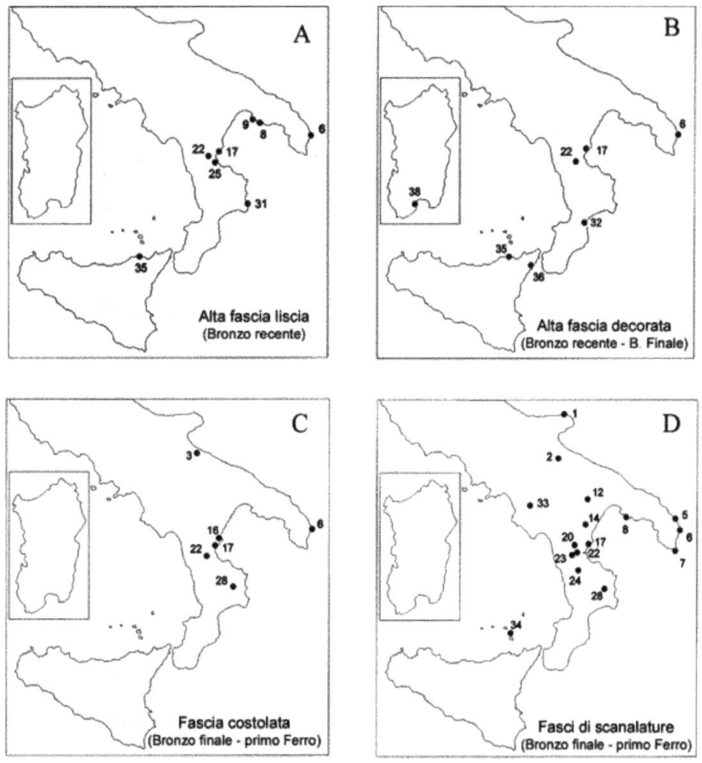

Fig. 12. Carte di distribuzione dei principali tipi di fasce cordonate (elaborazione di A. Schiappelli).

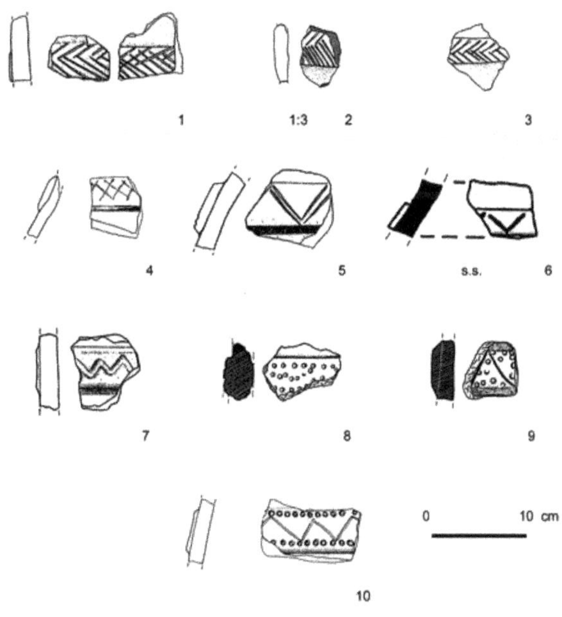

Fig. 13. Esempi di alte fasce lisce con decorazione incisa (nrr. 1, 4, 5 e 10 da Broglio di Trebisacce, nr. 2 da Antigori, nrr. 3 e 7 da Torre Mordillo, nr. 6 da Monte di Giove, nrr. 8 e 9 da Otranto; scala 1:4, eccetto nr. 2, 1:3 e nr. 6, senza scala).

Fig. 14. Il "magazzino 1" dei dolii (Bronzo finale, orizzonte non avanzato) di Broglio di Trebisacce (rielaborazione grafica di Fiammetta Sforza di figura in Archeo 2000, p. 77).

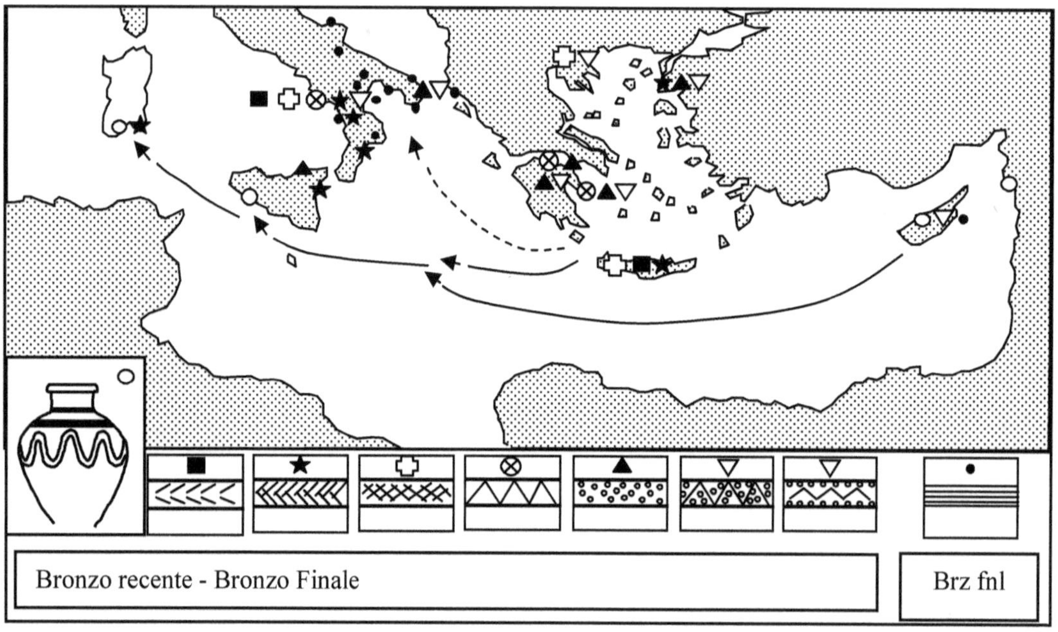

Fig. 15. Bacino del Mediterraneo: carta schematica della distribuzione e delle direttrici di esportazione di dolii con alte fasce incise e fasci di scanalature (elaborazione di A. Schiappelli).

EVIDENZE RELATIVE ALLA PRODUZIONE CERAMICA A FIDENE NELLA PRIMA ETÀ DEL FERRO

FRANCESCO DI GENNARO (Sopraintendenza per i Beni Archeologici di Roma)
CRISTIANO IAIA (collaboratore della S.B.A.R)

ABSTRACT: This paper summarizes the results of recent excavations conducted in the ancient city of Fidene where Iron Age pottery kilns have been identified. Two kilns with horizontally-linked combustion and firing chambers were discovered in association with a broad repertoire of Impasto pottery dated between Iron Age phases IIA and III.

Ricostruire l'aspetto e le vicende di una città millenaria cancellata dapprima dalla secolare incuria e poi dal più colpevole sviluppo urbano contemporaneo, nella cui pianificazione - ove essa esista - non c'è riguardo per le testimonianze della Storia; questo è l'intento, di facile definizione ma di assai gravosa e difficile attuazione, che la Soprintendenza Archeologica di Roma persegue nell'area di Fidene, ormai inglobata nella città di Roma. La strategia posta in essere è la sola possibile in assenza di finanziamenti per la ricerca e per lo studio dei ritrovamenti: controllo di tutti i progetti di attività di trasformazione che interessano il sottosuolo e il suolo[1], imposizione dell'assistenza costante dell'archeologo in fase di esecuzione delle opere, attribuzione del lavoro di analisi agli studiosi interessati, in particolare attraverso progetti di collaborazione con le Università, articolati in più tesi di laurea.

L'antica *Fidenae* è situata sulle alture in prima fila sul Tevere a circa 7 km dalle mura di Roma e a poco più di 3 km dalla foce dell'Aniene, il fiume che prima della conquista romana marcava il confine tra i due centri del Lazio antico.

Per quanto riguarda l'abitato di età protostorica, occorre anzitutto fissare l'attenzione su alcuni argomenti di carattere generale.

Il primo aspetto da considerare è l'assenza di documenti del Bronzo Recente e Finale, non soltanto nell'area della città antica ma anche nel territorio; la disconoscenza di resti della Tarda età del Bronzo è condivisa dalla contigua città latina di *Crustumerium*, distante solo 4 km e mezzo da *Fidenae*. E' per il momento consigliabile sospendere il giudizio su questa lacuna delle conoscenze, come non può considerarsi un dato definitivo la scarsità delle testimonianze riguardanti le fasi non avanzate del periodo IIA della sequenza laziale. Comunque in ambedue gli abitati, materiali della prima età del ferro, databili a partire dall'incipiente periodo IIB sono stati rinvenuti all'interno del perimetro urbano - che corrisponde a quello del centro della fase protourbana - dovunque si siano potute condurre indagini di una certa estensione.

In secondo luogo, prendendo in considerazione i dati topografici, occorre osservare che la borgata moderna occupa la maggior parte del rilievo articolato su cui si è sviluppata la città antica, di cui ha notevolmente alterato la morfologia originaria; la viabilità del nucleo edificato abusivo sottolinea, tuttavia, in particolare sul versante meridionale, l'antico limite naturale. La ricostruzione di Lorenzo e Stefania Quilici (Quilici, Quilici Gigli 1986, tavv. XX e XXI) restituisce una planimetria del centro urbano che ingloba in parte le incisure vallive che separavano le membra del sistema collinare, marcatamente digitato; tale articolazione del c.d. pianoro risulta in modo più netto dalla velina disegnata nella seconda metà dell'800 da Pietro Rosa per la sua grande carta incompiuta di Roma e dell'agro viciniore, sulla quale del resto si sono basati i Quilici. Se una rettifica della tormentata linea perimetrale naturale, per quanto non documentata archeologicamente, è ammissibile con riferimento alla città di epoca storica anche per analogia con le strutture di fortificazione note altrove, per la fase protostorica si può ritenere che la rottura di pendio costituita dal ciglio naturale del "pianoro" rappresentasse il limite dell'area abitata; e che le vallecole radiali, non per questo precluse all'impianto di strutture connesse all'insediamento, restassero di fatto "esterne" rispetto al ciglio, eventualmente valorizzato quale limite fisico, con strutture difensive artificiali.

Venendo infine ai dati archeologici disponibili sull'abitato del Primo Ferro, si può notare che le evidenze protostoriche fidenati, che restano numericamente ridotte per l'impossibilità di condurre ricerche nel moderno abitato consolidato, sembrano riassumere i termini dell'annoso dibattito tra la posizione dei sostenitori del prevalente carattere non unitario ma composito degli abitati della prima età del ferro da una parte, e di chi ritiene storicamente più significativo il fenomeno della concentrazione delle comunità in un luogo circoscritto e unitario, distinto dal territorio circostante, dall'altra[2]; infatti i dati disponibili ripropongono in particolare gli elementi che non hanno finora consentito per la prima Fidene una condivisibile opzione tra le due diverse ricostruzioni: indizi sicuri, ma non regolarmente diffusi, di concentrazione insediativa sull'unità orografica; "assenza", che non può assumersi come definitivamente provata, di abitati sparsi nel territorio circostante; di contro, si hanno attestazioni di sepolture non solo sulle pendici ma anche all'interno del perimetro dell'unità orografica dell'abitato, sia pure in posizione marginale.

Quanto sopra può essere colto osservando la carta archeologica dell'unità orografica fidenate[3] (fig. 1, A) da cui risalta la linea perimetrale, definita dalle rotture di pendio naturali(linea interrotta), all'interno della quale si pongono i ritrovamenti della prima età del ferro (cerchielli). Da sottolineare che l'apparente vuoto di testimonianze nella zona centrale è reso particolarmente evidente dalla presenza della grande trincea artificiale in cui corre la ferrovia; si deve pertanto considerare che i due settori campiti a tratteggio obliquo, sbancati nella pima metà del '900, non hanno potuto e non potranno restituire alcun dato.

Nel settore orientale sono indicati i due contesti che andiamo ad illustrare: le tombe di via San Gennaro meridionale (n. 2) e le fornaci di via Sovicille (n. 1).

I frammenti di ceramiche della prima età del ferro di *Fidenae* sono spesso decorati (se ne veda una esemplificazione alla fig. 2)[4] con incisioni di stile lineare, tracciate anche con uno strumento a due denti, mentre è raro l'uso del pettine che traccia un fascio di più linee, e con impressioni a rotella e cordicella. Si è già notata altrove (di Gennaro, Iaia 2000), tra il periodo IIB e gli inizi del III, l'affermazione in questa area dello stile decorativo ad incisione lineare, la cui massima densità di attestazioni si riscontra nel poligono ideale fra Veio, *Crustumerium*, *Gabii* e Roma, e di cui *Fidenae* e *Crustumerium*, con il suo possibile avamposto di Colle Lupo[5], costituiscono le estreme testimonianze in direzione della Sabina tiberina, dove esso allo stato attuale delle conoscenze non è documentato.

Le tombe a fossa di via San Gennaro, la cui disposizione non permette comunque di parallelizzarle a *suggrundaria*, sono certamente in parte di adulti e si trovano (n. 2 nella fig. 1) in prossimità del ciglio perimetrale, e in particolare presso uno degli accessi del suo lato orientale, ma molto vicine a strutture abitative coeve. I materiali ceramici, che, come i resti umani non sono stati ancora restaurati e studiati, si inquadrano tra la fine del periodo IIA e il IIB.

Tra gli oggetti deposti in queste sepolture spicca per caratteri qualitativi un orciolo biconico con decorazione geometrica tracciata con rotella dentata (fig. 3); i materiali decorati, che naturalmente non forniscono precise e dirette indicazioni sull'organizzazione della produzione - ma insieme a quelli provenienti dall'abitato costituiscono le premesse su cui si potrà pervenire alla definizione del gusto stilistico delle produzioni fidenati - nelle tombe sono, come di consueto, associati a fittili privi di incisioni. Già attraverso un confronto istituibile tra due orcioli indecorati (fig. 4) ed esemplari ritrovati nelle due fornaci per ceramica scoperte poche decine di metri più a nord, in un lotto affacciato su Via Sovicille, restato inedificato fino a una dozzina di anni fa[6], è possibile stabilire un parallelo cronologico, anche se non desumere una puntuale contemporaneità, tra questi due contesti di carattere funzionale del tutto diverso.

Le due fornaci sono state rinvenute in un'area su cui, dopo che si sono succeduti impianti urbani della prima età del ferro ed arcaica, venne costruita una villa; il forte processo di erosione ha risparmiato, per le fasi preromane, soltanto le cavità.

A tale proposito deve ricordarsi che anche l'ormai celebre fondo di capanna di via Quarrata[7] si è salvato in quanto risultava protetto dal riempimento di una depressione del versante collinare; il punto in cui gli scavi hanno restituito la struttura abitativa era stato infatti identificato da chi scrive attraverso una trincea di saggio, e distinto sui giornali di scavo come "all'imbocco della vallecola", in quanto alloggiato nel tratto più elevato di un'incisura trasversale del fianco del "pianoro", il cui riempimento fortunatamente era stato solo in parte intaccato dai lavori agricoli.

(F.d.G.)

Le fornaci (Iaia 1996), che denomineremo 1 (a nord) e 2 (a sud), consistono in due depressioni di modesta profondità, scavate nel terreno argilloso di base, e poste ad una distanza reciproca di circa 8 metri.

La cavità della fornace 1 (fig. 5A, n. 1), come del resto quella della 2, era costituita da due settori in origine collegati: una fossa a pianta sub-ellittica, con pareti convergenti verso il basso in sezione, separata per mezzo di un sottile diaframma argilloso da una cavità molto più piccola, di forma tendente al rettangolo; la profondità di entrambi i settori è di circa 45 cm, le dimensioni sono rispettivamente di metri 3 x 1,90 per il settore grande, 2 x 1 per il settore piccolo. Dalla cavità minore alla maggiore la struttura si dispone lungo una pendenza in senso sudovest-nordest. Gran parte del settore più grande era occupato da una concentrazione di concotto disgregato di forma grosso modo circolare, certamente riconducibile ad un forno fisso in argilla refrattaria dalla forma a cupola, che copriva uno strato nerastro con grossi frammenti ceramici e ossa annerite, ed era a sua volta circondato da uno strato grigio cineroso direttamente a contatto con le pareti della cavità. Alcuni frammenti fittili qui rinvenuti presentano chiare tracce di ricottura secondaria, dovuta probabilmente ad un incendio successivo alla fase di utilizzazione. Del forno restano parti della base, con parete curva (fig. 5A, n. 2), dello spessore di circa 8,5 cm, accuratamente lisciata all'interno; vi sono poi altri frammenti, dello spessore di circa 8-11 cm, anch'essi con accentuata curvatura, di cui uno presenta ancora il foro di sfiato della sommità.

La cavità 2 (fig. 5B, n. 1) presentava pianta e riempimento quasi identici alla precedente: si tratta anche in questo caso di una depressione scavata nell'argilla, di forma sub-quadrata ad angoli tondeggianti, separata per mezzo di una sorta di diaframma o gradino da una cavità minore quasi rettangolare. La profondità del settore maggiore era di 40 cm, dell'altro di 50 cm; le dimensioni erano rispettivamente di metri 3,20 x 3, e di 1,60 x 1,20. Presso l'angolo occidentale della depressione maggiore restavano tracce disgregate di un forno fisso a cupola in argilla refrattaria, sovrapposto a terra nerastra, ossa bruciate e vasellame d'impasto, talvolta in parte ricomponibile e con evidenti tracce di esposizione al fuoco, ma in quantità minore che nella cavità 1. Del forno, in peggiore stato di conservazione dell'altro, si conserva in particolare una porzione di parete curva con foro di sfiato (fig. 5B, n. 2); non è chiaro quanta parte occupasse della cavità.

Le caratteristiche strutturali dei due complessi ora descritti rendono plausibile l'interpretazione come fornaci per ceramica[8]. Elemento peculiare è che la struttura a cupola in concotto era infossata in una cavità al fine di evitare dispersione del calore, e si disponeva lungo una pendenza, in maniera da convogliare l'energia termica dalla cavità minore alla maggiore, o per usare la terminologia invalsa per le fornaci di età classica, dal "prefurnio" al forno vero e proprio; in altri termini, la "camera di combustione", cioè lo spazio dove si poneva il combustibile per il tiraggio, e la "camera di cottura", contenente il forno in argilla con i vasi, sono disposte in orizzontale, per cui si parla di "fornaci a tiraggio orizzontale". Il procedimento è abbastanza primitivo, ma certo - rispetto alle fosse e ai focolari all'aperto usati tradizionalmente nella preistoria per la cottura di ceramiche- consente di controllare assai meglio il calore e l'areazione, evitando l'effetto diretto del fuoco, così come improvvise immissioni di aria e sbalzi termici. In Italia, sebbene possibili esempi di forni con tiraggio orizzontale si conoscano fin dal Neolitico, ad esempio nell'insediamento dell'Olivento in Basilicata (Cassano et Al. 1995, p. 49), quelli meglio noti sono di età protostorica

I confronti più stretti per le due fornaci di Fidene si hanno rispettivamente nell'insediamento terramari-colo di Basilicanova, presso Parma (fig. 11A,B), dove è stata rinvenuta una struttura analoga, anche se non identica databile al Bronzo Recente (Cattani 1997), e nel sito calabrese di Torre Galli, dove si conosce, grazie all'accurata relazione di scavo di Paolo Orsi, una fornace molto simile a quelle laziali (fig. 11C), databile in base al riempimento ad un orizzonte evoluto della prima età del Ferro (Orsi 1926, coll. 85 ss., fig. 72; Pacciarelli 1999, p. 204, tav. 180). Pianta non dissimile dalle fornaci di *Fidenae* sembrerebbe presentare anche la fornace ceramica di *Lavinium*, datata dagli autori dello scavo all'VIII secolo a.C. (Fenelli 1984, p. 341, fig. 15). Dato il cattivo stato di conservazione dei complessi, non è sicuro se allo stesso tipo appartengano inoltre alcune fornaci, di cui si è ipotizzata la destinazione alla produzione ceramica, rispettivamente rinvenute a *Cures* (Guidi 1988, p. 46, fig. 6), e nel quadrato C27 di *Satricum*, quest'ultima contenente frammenti ceramici ipercotti (Nijboer 1995, p. 532, fig. 2).

Un altro aspetto che avvalorerebbe l'interpretazione qui proposta è la presenza, all'interno delle cavità contenenti le due fornaci fidenati, di grandi quantità di ceramica, ma soprattutto di forme vascolari ripetute in numerosi esemplari, tanto da far pensare a veri e propri "lotti". Al contrario, non costituisce un problema l'assenza, nell'ambito dei riempimenti, dei cosiddetti "scarti di fornace", cioè di frammenti o forme intere con difetti di cottura (deformazioni, vetrificazione delle superfici, formazione di bolle ecc), che generalmente venivano scaricati in fosse adiacenti le fornaci. Del resto, è noto che tali fenomeni di trasformazione chimico-fisica si verificano per lo più a temperature superiori ai 1000° gradi centigradi (Rice 1987, p. 86), le quali invece generalmente non sono raggiunte in forni tecnologicamente modesti come quelli in questione[9], dove, date le basse temperature, si verifica piuttosto la rottura del vaso.

Per la fornace 1, in base alla distribuzione delle ceramiche, si potrebbe pensare a due lotti di materiale ben distinti, di cui uno interno al forno, comprendente boccali, olle e orcioli ed un altro posto al di fuori, fra il forno e le pareti della fossa, comprendente soprattutto ceramica fine da mensa come tazze e scodelle. Un'ipotesi possibile è che nel momento in cui si verificava l'incendio che ha cotto il forno (evidenziato dalle ceneri e carboni che caratterizzano tutto il riempimento), si stessero cuocendo alcuni vasi (che dunque sono stati rinvenuti nel riempimento nerastro sottostante all'ammasso di concotto), mentre altri, frutto di una precedente cottura difettosa, si trovassero accatastati al di fuori: ciò potrebbe peraltro spiegare l'assenza dell'ansa in alcuni di questi stessi vasi. Nel caso della cavità 2, al contrario, i resti più limitati del forno, così come la frammentarietà assai più spiccata del materiale ceramico e la sua minore presenza, potrebbe far pensare ad una struttura in abbandono, in cui forse il vasellame intero era già stato recuperato.

Questi dati sembrano documentare per l'Italia centro-settentrionale della tarda protostoria l'impiego di strutture per la cottura della ceramica più complesse del semplice focolare all'aperto; pur essendo quest'ultimo uso ampiamente documentato in contesti etnografici attuali, in quanto dotato di una sua indubbia economicità ed efficienza, esso dovette ben presto essere abbandonato, o almeno trascurato, a favore di strutture fisse come quelle documentate, che consentivano di ottenere prodotti dall'aspetto finale meglio controllato e più omogeneo, evitando i rischi connessi con il sistema più primitivo: colore a chiazze delle superfici, rottura del vaso, ecc. Ciò non esclude, comunque, che la cottura all'aperto potesse talvolta venire ancora praticata, ad esempio nel caso di produzioni meno curate[10].

Per comprendere il significato del tipo di fornace adottato è necessario tenere presente che esso era in uso, in alcune zone d'Italia, almeno fin dagli inizi della tarda età del Bronzo (ma con tracce di impiego già nel Neolitico dell'Italia meridionale). Alcuni indizi indiretti condurrebbero a ritenere che un primo cambiamento nei sistemi di cottura della ceramica d'impasto di tradizione locale (prescindendo cioè dalle produzioni di modello egeo) si sia verificato nella Penisola tra Bronzo Recente e Finale: è in questo periodo che si diffondono infatti in buona parte d'Italia ceramiche d'impasto di colore omogeneamente nero (Levi 1999, p. 220), che attestano un notevole controllo dell'atmosfera all'interno delle fornaci (sia pure in senso "riducente"), forse già con l'uso di sistemi indiretti di esposizione al calore, come sembrerebbe indicato dalla fornace terramaricola di Basilicanova. Le ceramiche restituite dalle strutture fidenati 1 e 2, dai colori compattamente grigio-neri soprattutto nell'ambito delle tazze, sembrano un frutto ormai maturo della stessa tradizione produttiva, che avvalora l'idea di un certo conservatorismo nella produzione ceramica dell'area medio-tirrenica del Primo Ferro iniziale. In parte differente, ma soprattutto più articolato, è il quadro di alcune aree "miceneizzate" del Meridione, dove fornaci con diaframmi forati, che consentivano una buona areazione e il raggiungimento di temperature molto elevate, devono essere state utilizzate almeno dalla tarda età del Bronzo[11].

Per l'area medio-tirrenica si potrebbe pertanto ritenere che fornaci fisse del tipo di *Fidenae* abbiano costituito il precedente concettuale diretto delle strutture con distinzione verticale fra camera di combustione e camera di cottura, e dunque basate sull'uso di diaframmi forati, la cui introduzione in questa zona - non documentata direttamente, ma desumibile dai caratteri tecnologici delle produzioni - non sembra anteriore alla diffusione di ceramiche a copertura rossa e di figuline dipinte nel tardo VIII secolo a.C.

Venendo ad un breve esame dei reperti vascolari, pur alla luce del carente stato di conoscenza delle ceramiche d'impasto di ambito domestico dell'età del ferro laziale, e trattandosi per lo più di forme di uso corrente, spesso generiche e di lunga durata, i confronti rintracciabili per esse consentono di attribuire le due fornaci ad un orizzonte pieno della fase iniziale della prima età del ferro, IX secolo a.C. secondo le posizioni di cronologia assoluta oggi prevalenti. Nei termini della cronologia relativa locale, ci troveremmo probabilmente nel IIB iniziale, sebbene alcuni elementi tipologici si richiamino già all'orizzonte immediatamente precedente (IIA2).

Nell'ambito dell'ingente complesso ceramico restituito dalle fornaci, si segnalano in particolare le numerose tazze riferibili ad tipo con *ansa bifora, collo da cilindrico a troncoconico con accenno di labbro, e corpo globulare schiacciato* (fig. 6; fig. 6, n. 5), generalmente ornate sul corpo a larghe scanalature verticali e bugnette, che trovano numerosi confronti in contesti tombali di Osteria dell'Osa e di Roma-Esquilino di momenti centrali della fase II[12]. Come a Osteria dell'Osa esse sono articolate in almeno 3 varietà dimensionali: una versione piccola, che annovera il numero maggiore di esemplari, una media, e una molto grande, attestata da un unico esemplare dalla fornace 2 (fig. 10, n. 7), quasi un 'antenata delle "tazze cratere" di epoca orientalizzante.

Nel caso di questa classe vascolare, molto più che nelle altre attestate nelle due cavità fidenati, l'omogeneità complessiva del colore dell' impasto - così come nelle scodelle ad orlo rientrante - fa pensare ad una intenzionale cottura in atmosfera ossido-riducente, mentre molto accurata è la lisciatura e lucidatura delle superfici. La scarsa variabilità formale (ed in parte dimensionale) di queste tazze, suggerisce inoltre una moderata tendenza alla serializzazione della produzione ceramica: molto forte è in ogni caso l'impressione che gran parte degli esemplari sia stata realizzata da un'unica mano.

Fra le altre forme presenti in numerosi esemplari, più o meno frammentari, ma meno significative per un inquadramento cronologico e culturale sono: scodelle troncoconiche con presa trapezoidale (fig. 7, n. 2; fig. 10, n. 2), tipo risalente al Bronzo finale[13]; scodelle ad orlo rientrante con bugnette coniche (fig. 7, nn. 3-8; fig. 10, nn. 3,4); boccali ovoidi (fig. 8, nn. 1-7; fig. 10, nn. 8-11), questi ultimi spesso quasi integralmente ricostruibili nella fornace 1; alcuni orcioli (fig. 8, nn. 8,9); olle globulari e cilindro ovoidi (fig. 9, nn. 1-6), forse associate con i numerosi coperchi troncoconici (fig. 9, nn. 7, 8). Non mancano, anche se in misura assai minore, frammenti di fornelli, fuseruole e rocchetti.

Si tratta in sostanza di un complesso che copre quasi integralmente il repertorio delle forme vascolari di uso domestico, ma certo non l'intera gamma delle classi di produzione. Per una caratterizzazione ulteriore deve essere segnalata l'assenza totale, in entrambe le cavità, ad eccezione di due minuscoli frammenti in giacitura secondaria (ad es. fig. 9, n. 11), di materiali d'impasto con ornati geometrici a incisione, e a impressione a cordicella e rotella, di contro al ricorrere costante, nell'ambito di varie classi vascolari, di ornati a larghe scanalature verticali; questo fatto, appare singolare in confronto a quanto generalmente attestato a *Fidenae* nei livelli abitativi della prima età del Ferro (cfr. di Gennaro, Iaia 2000) e potrebbe essere per l'appunto spiegato con il fatto che, a parità di livello tecnologico, esistessero produzioni distinte per tipo di gusto e tecniche impiegate, eventualmente dovute ad individui o gruppi differenti. Tali fornaci sarebbero pertanto riferibili a produzioni di livello qualitativo "medio", che non comprendevano ornati di natura disegnativa.

A tale proposito, sembra prematuro, dato lo stato attuale della conoscenza delle ceramiche d'impasto del primo ferro di area medio-tirrenica, prendere posizione su una loro eventuale caratterizzazione come produzioni "domestiche" o di tipo "specialistico": è questa una dicotomia evoluzionista insoddisfacente e schematica, che non tiene conto dell'esistenza di possibili livelli intermedi di articolazione delle attività manifatturiere, indiziati dalla complessità del quadro socio-economico generale dell'epoca. Da evitare sembrano anche ricostruzioni rigidamente evolutive in senso unilineare dei procedimenti tecnologici impiegati: come appare dalla frammentaria, ma pur vasta, documentazione sulle fornaci della pre-protostoria italiana, sistemi di cottura diversi, più o meno efficaci e sofisticati, possono essere convissuti per secoli in uno stesso territorio, prima che le fornaci a tiraggio verticale si affermassero definitivamente.

(C.I.)

NOTE

[1] Frequenti ispezioni del territorio si impongono tuttavia per l'esistenza di lavori che, sia perché abusivi, sia per inadeguatezza delle procedure previste dagli enti locali, vengono avviati senza alcuna fase progettuale.
[2] Se nella prima delle due accezioni i vasti abitati medio-tirrenici della prima età del ferro possono essere classificati semplicemente come pre-urbani, la seconda ne giustifica e sostanzia lo specifico attributo di "protourbani".
3 Redatta con la collaborazione di Manuela Merlo, Luca Giovannetti e Elena Foddai
4 I disegni sono stati realizzati per le tesi di laurea di Federica Bartoli, Silvia ten Kortenaar, Manuela Merlo e Beatrice Giorgetta e per la tesi di specializzazione di Cristiano Iaia.
5 Per Colle Lupo si veda il frammento illustrato in Monterotondo 1995, fig. 26 a pag. 55, n. 15. L'insediamento, ivi presentato con una segnalazione di carattere decisamente preliminare, si poneva a contatto dell'importante frontiera che dalla prima età del ferro divideva Latini e Sabini; l'ipotetica attribuzione al territorio dipendente da *Crustumerium* (la cui presenza è omessa nelle carte topografiche che corredano il volume citato) tiene conto delle piccole dimensioni di *Nomentum* e dell'abitato di Cretone, nell'area di pertinenza del quale, a rigore, dovrebbe ricadere Colle Lupo (si veda la ricostruzione di Angelo Amoroso: di Gennaro, Schiappelli, Amoroso cs; Amoroso, Barbina cs).
6 La denominazione convenzionale del terreno fa riferimento ai titolari della proprietà al momento delle indagini, sigg. Brusco e Berardi; i dati di scavo sono illustrati da E. Foddai e L. Giovanetti in DI GENNARO et al. 2003, pp. 220-223.
7 BIETTI SESTIERI et al. 1998.
8 Una rassegna parziale (e comunque da aggiornare) di rinvenimenti italiani riguardanti forni per cibo e fornaci pre-protostoriche e storiche è stata redatta da M. Miari, in Negroni Catacchio 1995, pp. 276 ss., dove la distinzione fra forni fissi, forni in fossa e fornaci vale più in un senso tipologico che funzionale (cfr. Cassano et al. 1995). Manca comunque uno studio che analizzi approfonditamente i caratteri tecnologici delle fornaci di tipo meno evoluto: utile solo per la classificazione di fornaci molto complesse, con disposizione verticale delle camere di combustione e di cottura, è Cuomo di Caprio 1971.
9 Ad esempio, in un contesto quale quello della Sibaritide nell'età del Bronzo-Prima età del Ferro le temperature di cottura dell'impasto non superano in media gli 850°C: Levi 1999, p. 221.
10 Uno studio sperimentale, accompagnato da analisi archeometriche, sui materiali della necropoli di Osteria dell'Osa ha condotto ad ipotizzare, per la fase laziale II, il prevalente uso di cuocere la ceramica all'aperto, senza strutture fisse di copertura: Cuomo di Caprio 1992, pp. 439 ss. Ritengo tuttavia che la documentazione qui raccolta induca a rivedere almeno in parte il quadro della produzione ceramica del Lazio offerto dall'Autrice, condizionato da un pregiudizio "primitivista" di fondo.
11 Fra le più antiche fornaci con possibile uso di diaframmi forati è quella documentata nel sito pugliese di Salapia, databile al Bronzo Finale: Alberti et Al. 1981, p. 162.
12 Bietti Sestieri 1992, fig. 3a.5, t. 104, n. 5 (fase IIA); fig. 3a.12, t. 132, n. 1 (fasi IIA2-IIB1); fig. 3a.57, t. 160, n. 5bis (fasi IIA2-IIB1); fig. 3a.132, t. 180, n. 3 (IIA2-IIB1); fig. 3a. 139, t. 182, n. 2 (IIA2); fig. 3a. 324, t. 203, n. 2 (IIA2-IIB). A Roma-Esquilino è documentata la versione media: cfr. Müller-Karpe 1962, tav. 7A, n. 5 (t. 11: fase IIB1); tav. 8A, n. 5 (t. 90: fase IIB1); tav. 10C, n. 4 (t. 40: IIB1).
13 Esemplari dai Colli Albani: Gierow 1966, vol. I, p. 103, fig. 19, nn. 9-17. Osteria dell'Osa: Bietti Sestieri 1992, fig. 3a. 425, n. 1. Il tipo è caratteristico della fase IIB1 nella necropoli di *Gabii*-Castiglione: Bietti Sestieri, De Santis 2000, p. 81, fig. 94.

BIBLIOGRAFIA

Amoroso A., Barbina P. (c.s.), *L'istituzione delle tribu Claudia e Clustumina nel Latium Vetus. Un esempio di gestione del territorio da parte di Roma nel V secolo a.C.* in corso di stampa su Bull.Comm. Roma.

Alberti M. A., Bettini A., Lorenzi S. (1981), *Salapia (Foggia) – Notizia preliminare sugli scavi nella città dauna di Salapia. Campagna 1978-1979*, in <<NSc>>, XXXV: 159-182.

Bietti Sestieri A.M. (a cura di) (1992), *La necropoli laziale di Osteria dell'Osa*, Roma.

Bietti Sestieri A.M., De Santis A. (2000), *Protostoria dei Popoli Latini*, Guida del Museo Nazionale Romano, Terme di Diocleziano, Milano.

Bietti Sestieri A. M., Damiani I., De Grossi Mazzorin J., De Santis A., Recchia G., Remotti E. (1998), *Un edificio della prima età del ferro nell'abitato di Fidene (Roma): posizione stratigrafica, caratteristiche strutturali*, materiali, in Atti XIII Congresso U.I.S.P.P. (Forlì 1996), vol. 4, pp. 595-604.

Cassano S. M., Muntoni I., Conati Barbaro C. (a cura di) (1995), *Dall'argilla al vaso. Fabbricazione della ceramica in una comunità neolitica di 7000 anni fa*, Museo delle Origini, Roma.

Cattani M. (1997), *Una fornace per ceramica delle terramare*, in Bernabò Brea M., Cardarelli A., Cremaschi M. (a cura di), *Le Terramare – La più antica civiltà padana*, Catalogo della Mostra (Modena 1997), Milano, pp. 507-511.

Cuomo di Caprio N. (1971), *Proposta di classificazione delle fornaci per ceramica e laterizi dell'area italiana*, in <<Sibrium>>, XI, 1971-72, pp. 371-461.

Cuomo di Caprio N. (1992), *Studio tecnologico e analisi di microscopia ottica di 63 campioni ceramici dalla necropoli di Osteria dell'Osa*, in Bietti Sestieri 1992, pp. 449-478.

di Gennaro F., Schiappelli A., Amoroso A. (c.s.), *Un confronto tra gli organismi protostatali delle due sponde del Tevere. Le prime fasi di Veio e di Crustumerio*, in corso di stampa da parte della British School at Rome.

di Gennaro F., Belelli Marchesini B. (1993), *Fidenae (com. di Roma)*, in <<StEtr>>, 58: 515- 522.

di Gennaro F., Iaia C. (2000), *Elementi culturali della prima età del ferro nell'area di cerniera fra Sabina, Etruria e Latium vetus*, in Atti IV Incontro di Studi "Preistoria e Protostoria in Etruria" (Manciano-Montalto di Castro-Valentano 1997), Milano, pp. 245-253.

F. di Gennaro e altri (2003), "*Fidenae. Contributi per la ricostruzione topografica del centro antico. Ritrovamenti 1986-1992*", *Bullettino della Commissione Archeologica Comunale di Roma*, CII: 204-256.

Fenelli M. (1984), *Lavinium*, in QuadAEI, 8 (Archeologia Laziale VI), pp. 325-344.

Gierow P. G. (1966), *The Iron Age culture of Latium. I. Classification and analysis*, Lund.

Guidi A. (1988), *Cures Sabini*, in <<Quaderni della Soprintendenza Archeologica del Lazio>>, 1, Roma, pp. 41-50.

Iaia C. (1996), *Materiali dell'età del ferro dall'abitato laziale di Fidenae*, Tesi di Perfezionamento in Archeologia, Roma.

Levi S.T. (con contributi di altri Autori) (1999), *Produzione e circolazione della ceramica nella Sibaritide protostorica. I. Impasto e dolii*, <<Grandi Contesti e Problemi della Protostoria Italiana>>, 1, Firenze.

Monterotondo (AA.VV.) (1995), *Monterotondo e il suo territorio*, a cura del Centro regionale per la documentazione dei beni culturali e ambientali della Regione Lazio, Bari, Dedalo.

Müller-Karpe H. (1962), *Zur Stadtwerdung Roms*, Heidelberg.

Negroni Catacchio N. (a cura di) (1995), *Sorgenti della Nova. L'abitato del Bronzo Finale. L'insediamento e le sue strutture*, Istituto Italiano di Preistoria e Protostoria, Firenze.

Nijboer A. J. (1995), *Industry and Technology at Borgo Le Ferriere-Satricum, 700-300 BC*, in N. Christie (ed.), *Settlement and Economy in Italy 1500 BC – AD 1500*, <<Papers of the Fifth Conference of Italian Archaeology>>, Oxbow Monograph 41, pp. 531-539.

Orsi P. (1926), *Le necropoli preelleniche di Torre Galli e di Canale, Ianchina, Patariti*, in <<M.A.L.>>, XXXI, coll. 1-376.

Pacciarelli M. (1999), *Torre Galli. La necropoli della prima età del ferro (scavi Paolo Orsi 1922-23),* Soveria Mannelli (Catanzaro).

Quilici L., Quilici Gigli S. (1986), *Fidenae (Latium vetus V),* CNR, Roma.

Rice P. M. (1987), *Pottery Analysis. A sourcebook*, Chicago.

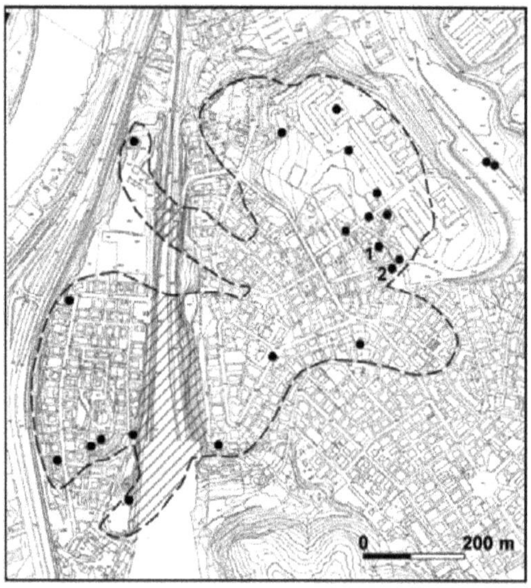

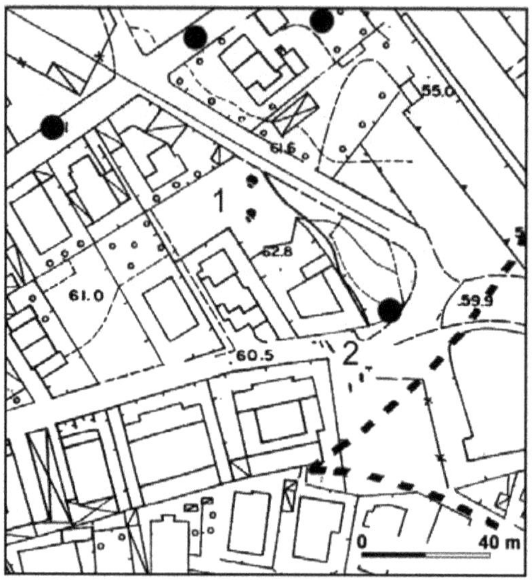

Fig. 1. *Fidenae*. A. Ritrovamenti del Primo Ferro nell'area urbana. B. Particolare: n. 1, fornaci; n. 2 tombe protostoriche di Via San Gennaro merid. I settori a tratteggio obliquo sono stati demoliti prima della lettura dei dati archeologici.

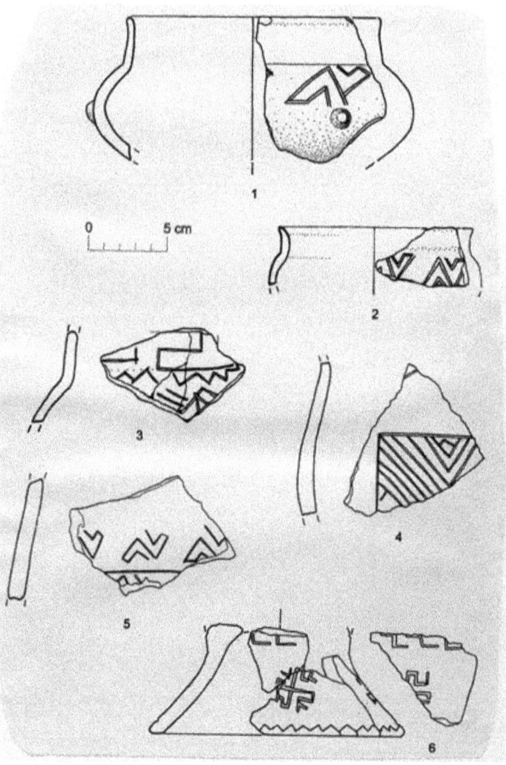

Fig. 2. *Fidenae*. Frammenti vascolari della prima età del ferro con ornati ad incisione lineare, da diverse aree dell'abitato (da originali F. Bartoli, S. ten Kortenaar e C. Iaia).

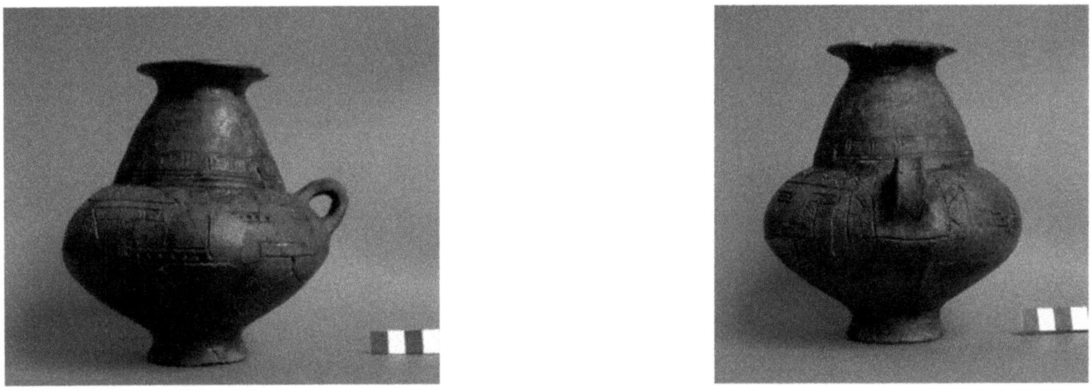

Fig. 3. *Fidenae.* Orciolo da una tomba di Via San Gennaro meridionale.

Fig. 4. *Fidenae.* Orcioli da tombe di Via San Gennaro meridionale.

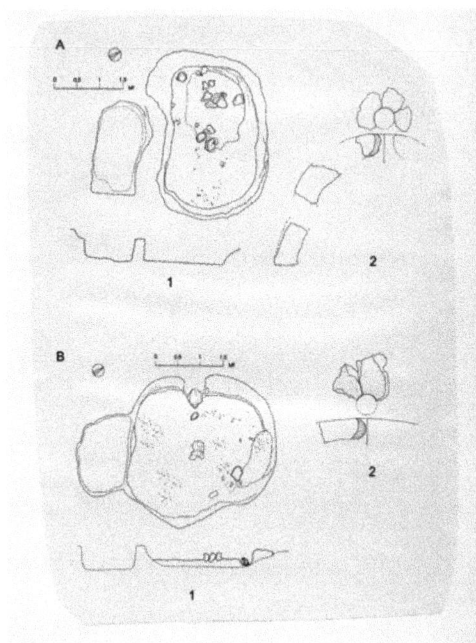

Fig. 5. *Fidenae.* Via Sovicille, lotto Brusco e Berardi: A: Fornace n. 1; B: Fornace n. 2.

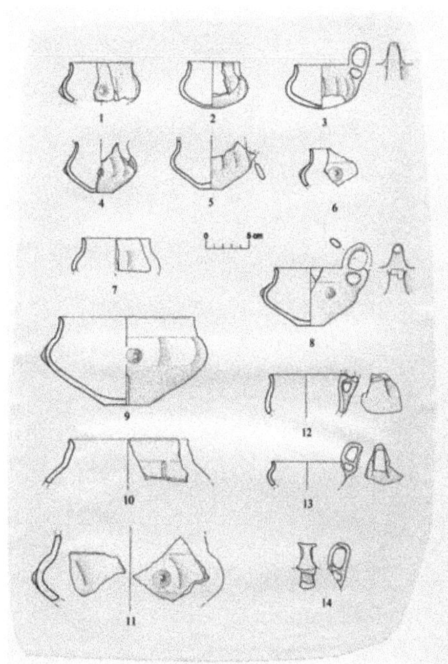

Fig. 6. *Fidenae.* Frammenti fittili dalla Fornace 1.

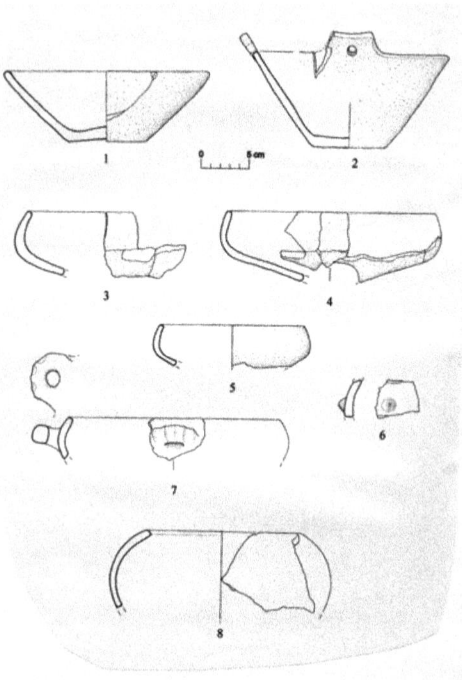

Fig. 7. *Fidenae.* Frammenti fittili dalla Fornace 1.

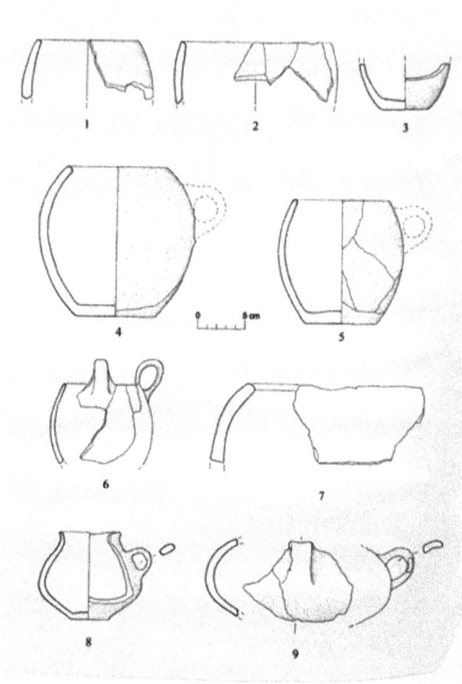

Fig. 8. *Fidenae.* Frammenti fittili dalla Fornace 1.

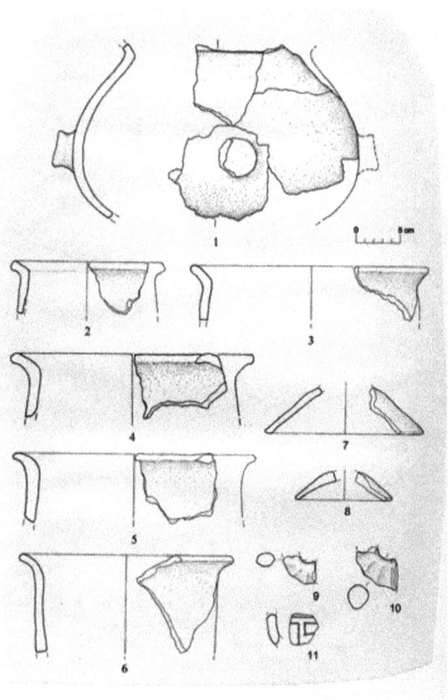

Fig. 9. *Fidenae.* Frammenti fittili dalla Fornace 1.

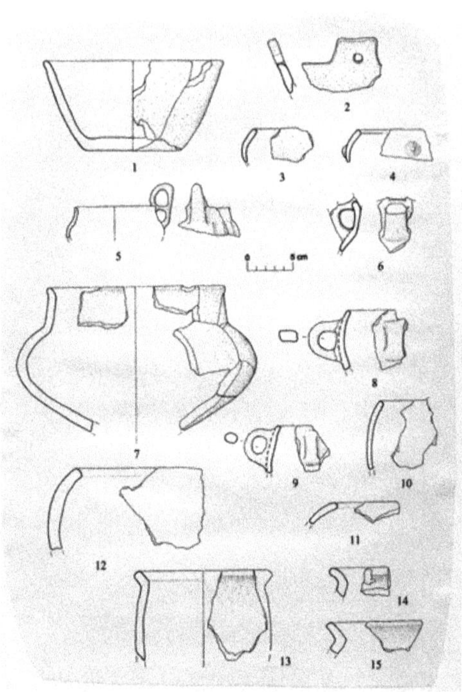

Fig. 10. *Fidenae.* Frammenti fittili dalla Fornace 2.

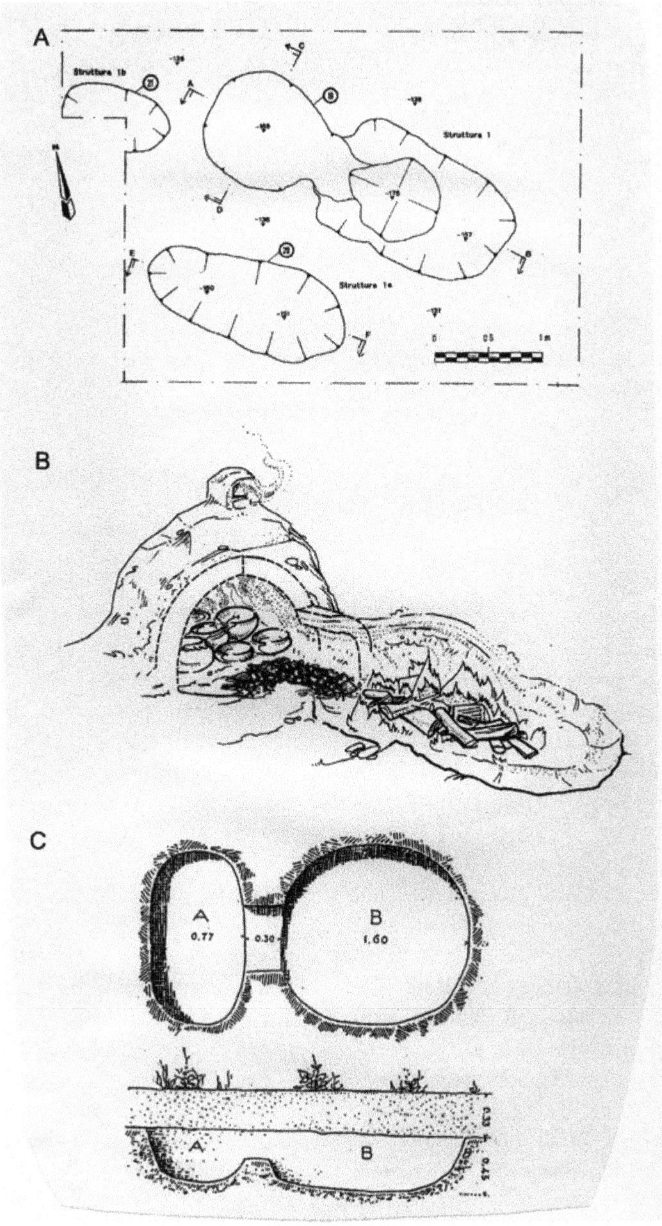

Fig. 11. Esempi di probabili fornaci ceramiche di età protostorica confrontabili con quelle di *Fidenae*. A-B: Basilicanova (Parma), planimetria e ricostruzione assonometrica (da Cattani 1997); C: Torre Galli (Drapia, CZ), pianta e sezione (da Orsi 1926).

Lo sviluppo e la circolazione della ceramica di impasto rosso in Etruria meridionale e nel Lazio

Alessandra PIERGROSSI - Silvia TEN KORTENAAR – Valeria ACCONCIA
(Università di Roma "La Sapienza")

Abstract: This paper addresses the question of the excahnge of Red Impasto pottery in southern Etruria and Latium during the archaic period. The authors consider attributes such as morphology and technology in order to distinguish between various local production groups. The Impasto from Caere, Veii and Latium are examined.

Introduzione

Per *impasto rosso* si intende attualmente una classe ceramica diffusa tra l'orientalizzante antico e parte dell'età arcaica nei territori dell'Etruria meridionale e del Lazio, caratterizzata dalla presenza di un ingobbio, ovvero un rivestimento argilloso che in cottura assume appunto una colorazione rossa (Gjerstad 1966: 117; Gierow 1966: 276-283; Colonna 1988: 303-304; Cuomo Di Caprio 1985: 98-100).

Si tratta di una tra le classi meglio attestate non solo in contesti funerari, ma anche abitativi nei siti dell'Italia centro tirrenica, di cui però non sono stati individuati con sufficiente chiarezza i centri di produzioni e le diverse fabbriche, che pure dovevano essere numerosi. Data l'importanza della classe, con questo contributo si intende stabilire lo stato attuale delle conoscenze affrontando la documentazione relativa a tre diversi centri produttivi.

Se già dalla prima età del ferro in ambito tirrenico sono comunque attestate ceramiche d'impasto a superficie lisciata o steccata rossiccia, la presenza dell'ingobbio segnala un'innovazione nelle pratiche artigianali locali, attribuita nella storia degli studi a un fenomeno di imitazione della ceramica *red slip* fenicia.

Secondo l'interpretazione tradizionale, infatti, la classe si sarebbe sviluppata in Etruria, soprattutto nel centro di Cerveteri, con la mediazione di Pithecusa (Buchner 1982b: 106; Rathje 1983: 26, nota 3; Delpino 2001: 195) dove, in contesti datati da Giorgio Buchner al TGII, sono presenti piatti d'importazione orientale ingubbiati in rosso, e una loro pressoché coeva imitazione locale (Buchner 1982a).

Il quadro così delineato, chiaro dal punto di vista delle analogie tecniche ma solo in parte morfologiche, non spiega alcune incongruenze che probabilmente devono essere lette alla luce delle recenti acquisizioni circa i fenomeni di precolonizzazione (Martelli 1991: 1059; Bartoloni 1988: 492; Botto 1995).

Se pure la presenza fenicia nel Mediterraneo occidentale è attestata anche da fasi precedenti, è soprattutto dall'orientalizzante antico che in Etruria sembrano diffondersi prodotti dell'artigianato levantino, e prevalentemente oggetti di oreficeria, *tripod bowls* di impasto e rare anfore da trasporto. Eccezionale in questo senso sembra essere la nota brocchetta tarquiniese conservata al Museo di Firenze, databile già alla fine del IX sec. a.C. (Esposito 1986: 78, n. 123; Martelli 1991: 1056, fig. 4c)

Per quanto riguarda la *red slip ware*, i primi esemplari di importazione noti in Etruria sembrano invece risalire alla metà del VII sec. a.C.[1]

Tale panorama, che ancora necessita di approfondimenti e probabilmente attende nuovi apporti dalla ricerca archeologica, non consente quindi di definire un processo di trasmissione lineare dall'area del Mediterraneo orientale verso le coste etrusco-laziali.

A tali considerazioni si aggiunge la tendenziale estraneità rispetto a quello fenicio del repertorio morfologico dell'impasto rosso, il quale sembra sviluppare, a fianco di suggestioni levantine (*infra*), un percorso già segnato dalle esperienze d'età protostorica.

Se pure non si vuole considerare un'olletta a rete in un corredo vulcente esposta al Museo Nazionale di Villa Giulia (I sala) e datata tra la fine del IX e l'inizio dell'VIII sec. a.C., apparentemente ingubbiata in rosso, come testimonianza di una ancor più antica conoscenza di tale trattamento delle superfici, vi sono indizi per ipotizzare una sua trasmissione di qualche decennio più antica rispetto a quanto normalmente prospettato. Nel Lazio o anche a *Cures Sabini*, infatti, in contesti della fine della prima età del ferro, sono attestati materiali ingubbiati in rosso estranei al repertorio della *red slip* orientale, così a Tarquinia a Poggio Cretoncini, sono stati rinvenuti frammenti di olle di impasto a copertura rossa, datati già alla fine del IX-inizi dell'VIII sec. a.C., considerati dagli autori dello scavo capostipiti della successiva produzione di età orientalizzante (Iaia *et alii* 2001:10, fig. 6).

Pur essendo la classe abbondantemente diffusa sia nelle necropoli che in abitato, essa sembra scarsamente analizzata nella letteratura archeologica. Tale carenza si riscontra soprattutto per l'Etruria dove sono stati considerati solo alcuni aspetti (ad esempio i bracieri decorati a cilindretto e i *pithoi* dell'orientalizzante recente cerite (Coen 1991: 67).

Lo stato carente della documentazione è probabilmente da attribuirsi al fatto che l'impasto rosso non è considerato né un elemento particolarmente adatto ad elaborare datazioni, né vi si riscontrano puntuali influenze dalle classi di pregio importate.

Pur non potendo negare l'effettiva difficoltà di utilizzarlo come *marker* cronologico e la tendenziale stabilità del suo repertorio morfo-tipologico, anche ad un primo esame è evidente come la classe possa essere analizzata per verificare dati di altra natura, come, ad esempio, le dinamiche legate alla sua nascita e al suo sviluppo, anche in relazione alle produzioni regionali; l'elaborazione di una sequenza tipologica e cronologica articolata per siti; gli aspetti tecnici e produttivi e la funzionalità delle principali forme attestate.

A tale proposito dall'analisi condotta su corredi funerari e contesti insediativi, laddove la classe sembra attestata in percentuali nettamente inferiori rispetto alle altre ceramiche d'impasto, emerge una sua possibile connotazione come indicatore di status.

Per porre dei limiti ad un argomento oltremodo vasto, si è qui limitata l'analisi al problema della ricezione e delle prime esperienze all'interno di un'area geograficamente coerente rappresentata dai comprensori di Cerveteri, Veio e il *Latium vetus*, per tentare una lettura dei processi diffusionali.

Saranno inoltre presi in considerazione solo contesti databili omogeneamente all'orientalizzante antico e alla prima parte della fase successiva (730-650 a.C.), escludendo nelle necropoli i corredi che, pur con una deposizione attribuita a tale periodo, ne presentano una o più recenziori alle quali non siano riferibili puntualmente i materiali di impasto rosso.

Nel corso dell'indagine, infine, è emersa la necessità di considerare solo esemplari per i quali fosse specificata la presenza di un ingobbio o di un rivestimento rosso/rossiccio, supportando tale scelta anche - laddove possibile - con un esame autoptico degli esemplari. Sono stati invece esclusi quelli per i quali il riferimento cromatico fosse limitato a più generiche definizioni, come ad esempio '*rossiccio*', '*color rame*', o anche '*rosso*' senza ulteriori specificazioni, che sembrano spesso riferirsi più all'impasto bruno tornito e lucidato che in fase di cottura abbia assunto delle sfumature rossastre.

S. K.

L'elaborazione delle forme ricorrenti e lo sviluppo in area cerite

In coincidenza con la fine dell'età del ferro, quando proprio la documentazione relativa a Cerveteri – tradizionalmente identificato come luogo di elaborazione della classe - risulta lacunosa, l'impasto rosso sembra omogeneamente presente nell'area considerata, con un repertorio morfologico tendenzialmente autonomo rispetto alle suggestioni orientali[2].

A fianco di modelli ricorrenti e di lunga durata, la cui standardizzazione potrebbe essere legata anche a motivi rituali (*infra*), sembra di riscontrare nei contesti esaminati tratti peculiari che farebbero pensare a tradizioni artigianali sviluppate localmente, escludendo così la priorità di un centro rispetto agli altri.

Per quanto riguarda le forme comuni riconosciute nell'area campione, molto diffusa nel periodo considerato e anche per fasi più avanzate è probabilmente l'olla globulare biansata con solcature parallele sull'orlo (figg. 1, A; fig. 3, B), attestata con regolarità e in più di un esemplare nei corredi ceriti e veienti[3].

La tendenziale stabilità morfologica di quest'ultima, potrebbe essere legata alla sua originaria funzione, attestata anche da fonti letterarie. Il passo di Varrone (*de vita populi Romani, I, fr. 57 Riposati*) sui modi del bere, infatti, riferisce di un uso delle '*tinas aut cupas*' per contenere il vino. Le *tinae* sono state identificate, grazie al riscontro con iscrizioni etrusche di possesso, proprio nelle olle biansate lisce, suggerendo così un legame con le pratiche rituali del simposio, che, soprattutto in Etruria, potrebbe avere determinato la necessità di conservarne la forma[4].

Un recente rinvenimento da Piazza d'Armi a Veio, composto da un'olla di questo tipo alloggiata in un taglio nel banco geologico, all'interno della quale era deposto un calice in impasto bruno in frammenti, sembra confermare anche l'ipotesi, già avanzata da M. Martelli, di un'associazione cerimoniale delle due forme (Martelli 1984 ; Acconcia 2001).

L'olla globulare ricorre nei corredi ceriti in associazione con olle a profilo troncoconico prive delle anse, di varie dimensioni (fig. 1, B) (Tipi Ricci 1955, 4 e 8).

Un'altra forma molto diffusa, probabilmente di diretta ispirazione orientale, è il piatto, che nella redazione a vasca aperta e basso piede è identificato dalle iscrizioni come *spanti* (fig. 1, C) (Ricci 1955, 183. Bosio-Pugnetti 1986: 92-93; Micozzi 1994: 56-58).

L'area cerite, a fianco delle forme elencate, che ne caratterizzano ampiamente la cultura materiale, presenta in impasto rosso *oinochoai* di ispirazione levantina (fig. 1, E) (Culican 1968: 277, tav. 20. 1 ; Bruni 2001), calici globulari (fig. 1, F) (Ricci 1955, 168), piattelli su tre piedi (fig. 1, G) presenti anche a Veio, rari calici carenati e scodelloni inornati a vasca ampia (fig. 1, D).

Per i motivi decorativi, le scanalature, frequenti dall'orientalizzante recente su *pithoi* decorati a cilindretto, sono presenti già dalla fase antica dello stesso periodo su olle ingobbiate in nero e, per la fase media, sull'olla di impasto rosso utilizzata come cinerario dalla camera destra della tomba Regolini-Galassi (fig. 1, I).

Sono attestate anche olle biansate con scanalature a ferro di cavallo, associate a *holmoi*, realizzate però in un impasto di colore bruno-rossiccio (Olle tipo Ricci 1955, 5 ; Micozzi 1994: 137).

Rarissimi sembrano per le fasi in esame i motivi stampigliati, che invece sembrano ricorrere più frequentemente nelle altre aree esaminate in questo contributo (*infra*) (Bosio-Pugnetti 1986, n. 1).

Fin dall'orientalizzante antico, inoltre, si registra l'avvio della produzione dell'impasto rosso sovradipinto, cd. '*white on red*' (Micozzi 1994) che, rispetto ad altri comprensori (come quello veiente o falisco-capenate), sembra rispondere ad una richiesta maggiore da parte della committenza aristocratica (Dik 1981: 48; Nardi 1993: 237).

Per quanto riguarda i contesti insediativi, a Cerveteri l'area della Vigna Parrocchiale ha restituito una discreta quantità di materiali pertinenti alla classe, ma non attribuibili puntualmente a fasi particolarmente antiche (Rendeli 1993).

Nel cd. *Semi-subterranean Building* nell'Area B di San Giovenale (databile al periodo qui esaminato e identificato come luogo sacro o scarico domestico, i cui caratteri fanno comunque propendere verso un'attribuzione a segmenti elevati della società), invece, sono attestati frammenti di olle globulari biansate (Olinder-Pohl 1981: 37-40)[5].

V.A.

Veio e il territorio veiente

A Veio, pur essendo il numero dei contesti editi limitato, la classe sembra piuttosto diffusa, con l'attestazione di una notevole varietà di forme e tipi. Soprattutto nelle fasi più antiche dell'orientalizzante, la produzione veiente, anche per quanto riguarda le forme comuni, sembra distinguersi da quelle degli altri comprensori presi in considerazione (De Santis in Bartoloni et alii 1994: 29 ss.; De Santis 1997: 101 ss).

Per le olle, parallelamente al tipo biansato e a quello liscio privo di anse, sono presenti esemplari costolati e stampigliati. Anche i piatti sono attestati in esemplari tipologicamente diversificati.

A fianco delle forme ricorrenti, tra le quali vanno annoverati anche i piatti su piede, in alcuni casi forniti di prese a rocchetto o rettangolari (tipo 47 Guidi 1993), gli scodelloni inornati e piccoli *holmoi* con base traforata, è possibile riconoscere una produzione, probabilmente di breve durata, di oggetti che, allo stato attuale delle conoscenze, risultano abbastanza isolati. Tra questi, particolari risultano alcuni materiali provenienti dalla tomba 1 di Macchia della Comunità, e soprattutto l'olla globulare decorata da grosse costolature distanziate; altrettanto caratteristica appare la scodella biansata su alto piede, decorata da bugne.

Si discosta da quelli più diffusi anche un tipo di olla globulare con collo cilindrico e listello rilevato sulla spalla, conosciuto attualmente in due esemplari (di cui uno decorato in *white on red*) da due tombe della necropoli della Vaccareccia (Micozzi 1994: 46).

Inoltre i piedini configurati a gamba umana che, come visto, si trovano a Cerveteri a sostegno di piatti, a Veio sono presenti anche su forme diverse, come la ciotola attribuita dubitativamente alla tomba B di Monte Michele.

Si riscontra, inoltre, almeno per questa fase iniziale, una propensione a imitare forme dell'artigianato metallico (Buranelli et alii 1997: 82). Sembra infatti molto diffuso il motivo della baccellatura su olle, coppe su piede, patere che, come le coppe emisferiche, imitano esemplari realizzati prevalentemente in metallo pregiato e di produzione orientale (Botto 1995: 52 ; Botto 2000: 79).

Meno direttamente utilizzabile appare la documentazione dall'area urbana. Nel sito di Piazza d'Armi, infatti, frequentato tra la fine dell'età del ferro e l'età arcaica e caratterizzato da un impianto monumentale, probabilmente dalla prima metà del VI sec. a.C., che oblitera le strutture precedenti, l'impasto rosso non si trova quasi mai in giacitura primaria e va prevalentemente attribuito alla categoria dei residui.

Una stima quantitativa realizzata sui materiali rinvenuti all'interno di uno dei contesti indagati[6] (fig. 2.1) evidenzia che, tra le classi di impasto, quella in esame è sicuramente la meno attestata, confermando una sua specifica destinazione come classe di pregio.

Il panorama complessivo restituito vede comunque, a fianco di una ricorrenza di forme tipiche quali le olle (vedi *supra*), biansate o meno, i *pithoi* e i piatti di varie dimensioni e tipi (figg. 1, 6-10), anche oggetti particolari, quali: piatti con prese a rocchetto (fig. 2, 9); un frammento di olla scanalata con prese sempre a rocchetto (fig. 2, 4); un coperchio con ricca decorazione impressa e plastica (fig. 2, 2), forse relativo a un'olla frammentaria con scanalature e impressioni circolari (fig. 2, 3); oltre a un *unicum* nella documentazione degli stampigli, con motivo ornitomorfo rinvenuto nel corso degli scavi S.A.E.M. 1968-1970, che potrebbe essere avvicinato a quello attestato sull'olla di Monte Michele[7].
S. K.

Le caratteristiche e lo sviluppo della produzione di impasto rosso laziale

L'inizio della produzione di ceramica d'impasto rosso in ambito laziale può essere collocato nella tarda età del ferro, confermando l'impressione che l'acquisizione di tale innovazione tecnica nel trattamento delle superfici e dell'adozione del repertorio morfologico tipico di questa classe sia avvenuto contemporaneamente all'ambiente etrusco[8].

Recentemente la quantità di materiale pertinente a questa classe è significativamente aumentato nel Lazio, ma i contesti di cronologia affidabile sono rappresentati quasi esclusivamente da necropoli, come riscontrabile nelle sintesi finora edite[9]. Allo stato attuale delle conoscenze l'ordinamento tipologico e l'elaborazione di una dettagliata sequenza cronologica valida ed applicabile a tutti i siti laziali risulta ancora piuttosto carente, come anche la documentazione grafica e la notazione esatta delle caratteristiche tecniche[10].

L'area presa in esame in questo lavoro comprende Roma ed i principali siti del territorio circostante, includendo le regioni alla foce e lungo il corso superiore del Tevere. In queste aree ricadono alcuni dei principali centri latini (Ficana, Castel di Decima-*Politorium* (?), *Lavinium, Fidenae, Crustumerium, Gabii*) e siti di minore portata, identificati presso Laurentina Acqua Acetosa, Tor de' Cenci, Torrino, La Rustica, che rappresentarono probabilmente avamposti di Roma sin dalla prima età regia[11].

La classe presenta un'ampia diffusione ed un progressivo aumento della varietà di forme realizzate. Nella fase più antica, tra l'ultimo ventennio dell'VIII ed i primi decenni del VII sec. a.C., ove la sua presenza sembra limitata a Roma, Castel di Decima e Gabii-Osteria dell'Osa le forme peculiari, condivise con le altre aree in esame sono quelle dell'olla globulare e del piatto, seppure alcune fogge sembrano ricorrere in quantità inversamente proporzionale rispetto all'Etruria.

L'olla di forma globulare, contenitore di uso collettivo, si presenta soprattutto nella versione inornata, fatta eccezione per le solcature sull'orlo (fig. 3, A)[12], e solo in un caso è attestata la presenza delle anse (fig. 3, B.12)[13]. Tale fenomeno caratterizza anche nella fase successiva quasi tutti i contesti funerari[14].

Sia a Roma che a Castel di Decima[15] si trovano accoppiate un'olla biansata ed una o due senza anse, l'una deputata a versare e l'altra a mescere, o forse destinate a contenere acqua e vino separatamente. Limitate le versioni con la decorazione a scanalature verticali, che troveranno più ampia diffusione dalla seconda metà del VII sec. a.C. accompagnate da stampigli (Bartoloni 1980).

A questo proposito all'orientalizzante antico risale un solo esemplare con costolature rade dalla t. 15 di Castel di Decima (fig. 3, C.17) (N. 27), mentre nella fase successiva solcature verticali sotto un listello si trovano su olle da Roma (fig. 3, C.18)[16], *Lavinium*[17] e Ficana[18]. Decorazione e forma insolite si riscontrano su un'olla globulare dall'Esquilino con labbro verticale: sul collo, subito sotto l'orlo, sono incise tre solcature orizzontali e sulla massima espansione sono presenti quattro bugne racchiuse da costolature sovrastanti a semicerchio (fig. 3, C.20) (T. 82, n. 1). Tre bugne triangolari sono presenti anche su un'olla da Tor de' Cenci (fig. 3, C. 21) (T. 4). Si tratta di motivi decorativi tipici dell'espressione del gusto locale di ascendenza protostorica.

Singolare risulta l'olla-*kernos* a pareti costolate con quattro prese figurate a piattello montate sulla spalla e presente a *Lavinium* e *Crustumerium* (fig. 3, C.19)[19], sicuramente attribuibile ad una produzione laziale e dalla chiara connotazione rituale. I piattelli potevano contenere spezie da aggiungere alla bevanda o il formaggio grattugiato per la confezione del *kukeon*, bevanda a base di vino e formaggio di capra, evocato nell'Iliade (XI, 628-643), come suggerito dal ritrovamento di grattugie (Ridgway 1997; Gras 2001: 17).

A Roma è presente sin dall'orientalizzante antico anche l'olla cilindro-ovoide[20], attestata in un numero maggiore di esemplari nella fase media (fig. 3, D.22-25)[21] e successivamente in impasto rosso-bruno[22]. Legati all'ambito domestico sono anche ciotole e coperchi di varie forme (Carafa 1995, tipi 237, 238, 240, 241: 108-109): unica eccezione la ciotola a corpo globulare dalla t. 4 di Castel di Decima (fig. 3, D.27-31) (N. 31).

Per le forme aperte, il piatto, raro nel tipo a vasca aperta e basso piede, è attestato inizialmente su alto piede con vasca carenata schiacciata[23] e, dai primi decenni del VII sec. a.C., con vasca profonda[24] anche su basso piede[25], che gradualmente prevale sui primi (fig. 3, E. 32-36).

Da rilevare la presenza a Ficana[26] anche di un piattello su alto piede con prese a rocchetto, del tutto simile agli esemplari veienti, spiegabile con gli stretti rapporti tra i due centri facilitati dal contatto con il Tevere (Zevi 1997; Bartoloni 1986; Algreen-Ussing, Fischer Hansen 1985).

Un esemplare isolato sembra essere la coppa quadriansata dall'Esquilino (fig. 3, E.37).

Un'altra forma ampiamente diffusa nella fase piena dell'orientalizzante e meno frequente in Etruria, è rappresentata dal calice carenato su piede (fig. 3, E.38-44)[27], realizzato anche in impasto bruno.

Come negli altri comprensori, anche in quest'area sono stati riscontrati tentativi di imitare forme metalliche. Esclusivi dell'area laziale e delle deposizioni femminili sono i calderoni con protomi di grifo sull'orlo[28] – traduzione locale degli esemplari bronzei d'importazione orientale (Botto 1995: 52) – e le tazze-cratere il cui tipo più antico sembra essere attestato a Ficana (fig. 3, F.45)[29] e che compare nel corso della prima metà del VII sec. a.C. a Tor de' Cenci (fig. 3, F.46)[30], ispirate alle grandi tazze di bronzo da alcuni contesti laziali del periodo di passaggio tra la III e la IV fase locale e poi nel VII sec. a.C.[31]. Questi recipienti erano alloggiati, come le olle globulari biansate in ambito etrusco, sugli *holmoi* (fig. 3, F.47)[32].

Chiara imitazione delle versioni in bronzo sono anche i bacili ad orlo perlato da *Crustumerium* (di Gennaro 1999: 29) e da *Fidenae* (ten Kortenaar 2001: 18, fig. 28, 9).

Per gli abitati sono note evidenze chiaramente connotate in senso elitario. Tra i casi relativi al periodo in esame, la struttura residenziale di Ficana, indagata da A. Rathje (1983), ha restituito un servizio da banchetto composto prevalentemente da forme realizzate in impasto rosso, databile alla prima fase dell'orientalizzante medio.

A. Beijer (1991) ha rilevato anche per un edificio del secondo quarto del VII sec. a.C. di *Satricum*, attribuito ad un gruppo familiare particolarmente elevato, la presenza di un *holmos* di impasto rosso, forma che ricorre anche in alcune tombe di particolare rilievo dallo stesso sito.
A. P.

Conclusioni

Pur ribadendo l'impossibilità di sviluppare in questa sede tutte le problematiche prospettate all'inizio di questo contributo, e soprattutto quella relativa all'origine della classe, dall'analisi dei contesti ceriti, veienti e laziali, emerge come, oltre alla chiara pertinenza della classe all'ambito gentilizio, le dinamiche di formazione e diffusione sembrino divergere dal quadro tradizionalmente proposto. L'impasto rosso, infatti, soprattutto sulla base di recenti acquisizioni di scavo, sembra adottato in ambito medio-tirrenico almeno alla piena prima età del ferro. Nel periodo successivo, inoltre, non si è riconosciuto un vero e proprio fenomeno di trasmissione lineare da un centro verso gli altri, bensì, con una costante circolazione di forme comunque ricorrenti, una tendenza dei vari comprensori a elaborare forme e repertori indipendenti
V. A., A. P., S. K.

NOTE

1 Cerveteri: *oinochoai* da tomba recuperata nel 1971 (primo esempio attestato sulle coste tirreniche in area non fenicia secondo M. A. Rizzo) e Tumuletto III bis (Rizzo 1991). Per un quadro generale sulle interrelazioni fra le produzioni fenicia ed etrusca (in un periodo successivo), v. anche Gran Aymerich 1983.
2 Non si esclude però che per l'area cerite l'edizione di contesti databili alla fase precedente possa mutare sostanzialmente tale quadro.
3 Corrispondente al tipo Ricci 1955, 42; Bosio-Pugnetti 1986: 91-92. M. Micozzi ipotizza che la forma sia stata elaborata proprio a Cerveteri (1994: 43-44).
4 Per le iscrizioni recanti il vocabolo *θina*, Colonna 1973-1974: 145-146. Per l'identificazione delle *cupae* con le tazze-cratere laziali, Zevi 1977: 267.
5 L'esemplare n. 251 è strigilato, ed è identificato come un oggetto di importazione.
6 Si tratta della cd. *struttura B* (databile alla fine del VI sec. a.C.).
7 Frammento inedito, (M. Milletti, *Lo scavo della Piazza degli anni 1968-1969. I materiali: l'impasto rosso e l'impasto rosso-bruno,* tesi di laurea, A.A. 2000-01)
8 La forma dell'olla globulare con orlo decorato a solcature appare alla fine del III periodo laziale in alcune tombe a Castel di Decima, a Roma e al Torrino (AA.VV. 1980, tav. 14.11; Bedini 1985: 57, fig. 11.18). Inoltre a tale proposito, è necessario ricordare la presenza in ambiente sabino, culturalmente vicino a quello laziale, di un'olla globulare priva di

anse con ampio labbro decorato a scanalature e listello sulla spalla, proveniente da un contesto abitativo da *Cures* (Colazingari, Fulgenzi 1996: 173, fig. 19.5) e datato agli inizi dell'ultimo quarto dell'VIII secolo a.C., in un momento finale della fase avanzata della prima età del ferro.
9 AA.VV. 1980; Anzidei ed Alii 1985: 195 ss. Da ultimo il lavoro di P. Carafa, che segna attualmente il punto di arrivo delle analisi sulla classe (Carafa 1995: 91 ss.).
10 Soprattutto nel Lazio si è incerti per alcuni esemplari, se la definizione d'impasto rosso implichi la presenza dell'ingobbio o la semplice colorazione rossa dell'argilla, dovuta dalle modalità di cottura (*supra*: 00). Nel catalogo che segue si sono considerati solo i casi in cui viene specificato il particolare trattamento delle superfici, anche se permangono alcuni dubbi, non essendo stata possibile, nella maggior parte dei casi, una revisione autoptica del materiale.
11 Databili all'orientalizzante antico sono i seguenti contesti: Roma: Via Nova-via Sacra, att. 1, 6, 7, (Carafa 1995: 94 ss.); Foro, t. M, (Gjerstad 1956: 88-96); Esquilino, t. 127, (Gjerstad 1956: 257, fig. 227; AA.VV. 1976: cat. 43, tav. XXI, D-E-F); Castel di Decima: t. 15, (AA.VV. 1975: 251-294); t. 152, (Ibidem: 294-322); nell'orientalizzante medio: Roma: Via Nova-via Sacra, att. 10, 11, 14, 15, (Carafa 1995: 94 ss.); Deposito *Equus Domitiani*, (Gjerstad 1966, fig. 79.7); *Equus Domitiani*, strato 25, (Carafa 1995: 109); Divo Giulio, strato A10, (Gjerstad 1960: 274); Divo Giulio, strato B10, (Carafa 1995: 109); Foro, t. D, (Gjerstad 1956: 117-120, figg. 114-116): Foro, t. I, (Gjerstad 1956: 125-133, figg. 126-127); t. K, (Gjerstad 1956: 133-138, fig. 132); Foro, t. AA, (Gjerstad 1956: 141-144, figg. 76, 138, 139); Esquilino, t. 82, (Gjerstad 1956: 250, fig. 222); Crustumerium: Monte Del Bufalo, t. 5 (di Gennaro 1988) e t. 9, (di Gennaro 1990: 70, cat. 31); Pratica di Mare (Lavinium): tomba a cassone sotto l'heroon di Enea, (AA.VV. 1976: cat. 102.23); Tor de' Cenci: tt. 4, (Bedini 1988-89: 241-254) e t. 1, (Ibidem: 260-263); Laurentina Acqua Acetosa: t. 70, (Bedini 1990: 52-60); Ficana: area 5a, pozzo I, (AA.VV. 1981: 82-85; Rathje 1983); Castel di Decima: t. 7, (AA.VV. 1975: 322-333); t. 4, (Ibidem: 333-344); t. 3, (Bedini, Zevi 1973); Vengono incluse in questo censimento alcune tombe dalla necropoli di Osteria dell'Osa della fase IVA1 (730/720-660/650 a.C.): t. 116, (Bietti Sestieri 1992: 835-6, figg. 3c.34-37); t. 204, (Ibidem: 834-5, figg. 3c.32-33); t. 233, (Ibidem: 802, figg. 3b. 35-36); t. 549, (Ibidem: 837, figg. 3c. 39-40); t. 120, (Ibidem: 849-850, figg. 3c.66-67); t. 573, (Ibidem: 836-7, fig. 3c.38).
12 Roma: Foro, t. D, n.3; t. I, n. 5-6; t. K, n. 3; Carafa 1995, tipi 197, 198, 199, 200, 206, 217: 94 ss.; Castel di Decima: t. 15, n. 26-27; t. 152, n. 24; Tor de' Cenci, t. 4, nn. 16, 17,18. Ad Osteria dell'Osa sono presenti solo versioni senza anse: tipi 92e, con corpo liscio, e 92f con listello sulla spalla. I tipi con scanalature e stampigli appaiono solo nella fase IVA2, posteriore al 660/650 a.C., in coincidenza con l'orientalizzante recente.
13 Carafa 1995, tipo 193: 94 ss., da uno strato dello scavo Via Nova-via Sacra, ritenuto simile al l'esemplare dalla t. 128 dell'Esquilino dell'orientalizzante recente.
14 Le anse si ritrovano su due olle dalla necropoli del Foro, (t. AA, n. 8; t. I, n. 4) e a Castel di Decima, (t. 7, n. 19; t. 4, n. 26).
15 Tomba I del Foro (nn. 4, 5 e 6); a Decima: t. 4 (nn. 24, 25 e 26) e t. 7 (nn. 18-19).
16 Deposito Equus Domitiani, tipo 201 Carafa.
17 Tomba sotto l'heroon di Enea, n. 23. Sotto il listello triangolare da cui partono le solcature trovano spazio anche dei motivi impressi a doppia S coricata
18 Pozzo 1, zona 5a, nn. 34a-d, (AA.VV. 1981).
19 La forma è presente anche a Roma nella tomba 128 dell'Esquilino datata alla seconda metà del VII sec. a.C. (AA.VV. 1976: 141, cat. n. 43.1, tav. XXI.f)
20 Via Nova-via Sacra, att. 7, (730/720-700 a.C.), (Carafa 1995, tipo 225: 104.).
21 Via Nova-via Sacra, att. 10, 14 e 11, (700-675 a.C.), (Carafa 1995, tipi 227, 230, 234: 104 ss.)
22 L'utilizzo dell'impasto rosso ingubbiato per forme quali l'olla cilindro-ovoide tradizionalmente legate alla produzione del cd. impasto rosso-bruno o coarse ware di epoca arcaica, è attestata a Ficana, negli strati relativi all'abitazione della zona 6a, (A. Piergrossi, *Ficana. Monte Cugno, pendici occidentali. I materiali arcaici*, tesi di laurea, 1993-94). Un fenomeno similare è stato accertato da S. Falzone per gli impasti rossi dallo scavo della struttura ipogea sotto la cella del tempio della Vittoria a Roma (Falzone 2002: 185 ss.).
23 Orientalizzante antico: Foro, t. M, n. 1; Castel di Decima, t. 15, n. 25; orientalizzante medio: *Crustumerium,* Monte del Bufalo, t. 5, n. 8; Ficana, zona 5a, pozzo I , (AA.VV. 1981, nn. 30.e,g).
24 Carafa, tipo 267: 118; Castel di Decima, t. 7, n. 26.
25 Castel di Decima, t. 4, nn. 29-30; Ficana, zona 5a, pozzo I, (Rathjie 1983, figg. 5 e 12).
26 Zona 5a, pozzo I, (AA.VV. 1981, n. 30.a).
27 Tor de' Cenci, t. 4, n. 24; Castel di Decima, t. 7, n. 21, 22, 23, 24, 25; t. 4, nn. 27-28; Ficana, zona 5a, pozzo I, (AA.VV. 1981, n. 31 a-h)
28 Ficana, zona 5a, pozzo I, (AA.VV. 1981, n. 29).
29 Zona 5a, pozzo I, n. 33b. Cfr. anche Bartoloni 1985: 19 e nota 69.
30 T. 4, n. 15. A Castel di Decima nell'orientalizzante pieno e recente l'associazione di holmos e tazza-cratere ricorre in quasi tutti i corredi più importanti (t. 3 e varie tombe inedite, (Bedini, Zevi 1973: 41, tav. VIII.e; Zevi 1977: 265,

tabella; Bedini 1990: 59). Al 630-625 a.C. risale il corredo della t,. 33 de La Rustica che conserva il medesimo accostamento.
31 Ardea, t. 2, (AA.VV. 1983: cat. 24.15); *Lavinium*, t. L, (AA.VV. 1976: cat. 99.30); Laurentina, t. 70 (Bedini 1990: 59, n. 24).
32 Puntualmente ritrovati nei medesimi contesti delle tazze-cratere e dei calderoni con protomi di grifo.

BIBLIOGRAFIA

AA.VV., 1975, Castel di Decima (Roma). La necropoli arcaica, in NSc, 233-.408

AA.VV., 1976, Civiltà del Lazio Primitivo, catalogo della mostra di Roma, a cura di G. Colonna, Roma.

AA.VV., 1980, La formazione della città nel Lazio, Atti del seminario, Roma, 24-26 giugno 1977, DdA II, 1-2, Roma.

AA.VV., 1981, Ficana. Una pietra miliare sulla strada per Roma, catalogo della mostra di Roma, Roma.

AA.VV., 1982, La Céramique grecque ou de la tradition grecque au VIII siécle en Italie centrale et méridionale, Cahier du Centre J. Bérard Naples.

AA.VV., 1983, Ardea. Immagini di una ricerca, catalogo della mostra di Roma, Roma.

Acconcia, V., 2001, Schede I. E. 2-3, in AA.VV. 2001b, 31-32.

AA.VV., 1990, Archeologia a Roma. La materia e la tecnica nell'arte antica, catalogo della mostra di Roma, Roma.

AA.VV., 2001a , Principi etruschi tra Mediterraneo ed Europa, Catalogo della mostra di Bologna, Venezia.

AA.VV. 2001b, Veio, Cerveteri, Vulci. Città d'Etruria a confronto, catalogo della mostra di Roma, a cura di A.M. Sgubini Moretti, Roma.

Adriani, A., 1930, Veio. Macchia della Comunità, NSc, 46-56.

Algreen-Ussing, G., e Fischer Hansen, T., 1985, Ficana, le saline e le vie della regione bassa del Tevere, in ArchLaz VII, (QuadAEI 11), 65-71.

Anzidei, A.P., Bietti Sestieri, A. M. e De Santis, A., 1985, Roma ed il Lazio dall'età della Pietra alla formazione della città, Roma.

Bagnasco Gianni, G., 1994, Circolazioni culturali nel mondo antico. Un esempio in Etruria: il piatto spanti, SE LIX, 3-27.

Bartoloni, G., (a cura di), 1997, Le necropoli arcaiche di Veio. Giornata di studio in memoria di M. Pallottino (Roma 1995), Roma.

Bartoloni, G., 1980, Il corredo della tomba 115 dell'Osteria dell'Osa, in ArchLaz III, (QuadAEI 4), 43-50.

Bartoloni, G., 1985, L'urna a capanna dell'Esquilino: una nuova lettura, AC XXXVII, 1-26.

Bartoloni, G., 1986, I Latini e il Tevere e le altre vie d'acqua del Lazio Antico, in QuadAEI 12, 98-110.

Bartoloni, G., Berardinetti, A. e Drago, L., Le comunità della bassa valle tiberina e il Mediterraneo orientale prima della colonizzazione greca, Atti del Convegno Die Ägäis und das Westliche Mittelmeer, Vienna, marzo 1999, in stampa.

Bartoloni, G., Berardinetti, A., De Santis, A. e Drago, L., 1994, Veio tra IX e VI secolo a C.: primi risultati sull'analisi comparata delle necropoli veienti, AC XLVI, 1-46.

Bartoloni, P., 1988, La ceramica, in Moscati, S. (a cura di), I Fenici, Catalogo della mostra di Venezia, Venezia, 492-510.

Bedini, A. e Zevi, F., 1973, La necropoli arcaica di Castel di Decima, SE 41, 27-40.

Bedini, A., 1985, Tre corredi protostorici dal Torrino. Osservazioni sull'affermarsi e la funzione delle aristocrazie terriere nell'VIII sec. a.C. nel Lazio, Archeologia Laziale VII, QuadAEI 11, 44-64.

Bedini, A., 1988-89, Tor de' Cenci (Roma) – Tombe protostoriche, NS 1988-1989 (1992), 221-279.

Bedini, A., 1990, Abitato protostorico in località Acqua Acetosa Laurentina, in AA. VV. 1990, 48-64.

Bejer, A. J., 1991, Impasto pottery and social status in Latium Vetus in the Orientalising period (725-575 BC): an example from Borgo Le Ferriere ("Satricum"), in Papers of the fourth Conference of Italian Archaeology. The Archaeology of Power, London 1990, 21-39.

Bietti Sestieri, A.M., 1992, (a cura di), La necropoli laziale di Osteria dell'Osa, Roma.

Boitani, F., 1983, Veio, la tomba "principesca" della necropoli di Monte Michele, in SE LI, 536-56.

Bosio, B. e Pugnetti, A., 1986, Gli Etruschi di Cerveteri, catalogo della mostra di Milano, Milano.

Botto, M., 1995, I commerci fenici nel Tirreno centrale: conoscenze, problemi e prospettive, in I Fenici: ieri oggi e domani, ricerche, scoperte, progetti, Convegno di Roma 1994, Roma, 43-53.

Botto, M., 2000, Tripodi siriani e tripodi fenici dal Latium Vetus e dall'Etruria meridionale, in La ceramica fenicia di Sardegna. Dati, problematiche, confronti (Atti del I congresso internazionale sulcitano, Sant'Antioco 1997), Roma, 63-98.

Brocato P., 2000, La necropoli etrusca della Riserva del Ferrone, Roma

Bruni, S., 2001, Scheda 239. Brocca con becco a filtro, in AA.VV. 2001a, 215.

Buchner, G., 1982a, Die Beziehungen zwischen der euböischen Kolonie Pithekoussai auf der Insel Ischia und dem nordwestsemitischen Mittelmeerraum in der zweiten Hëlfte des 8.Jhs., in Phönizier im Westen. Die Beiträge des Internationalen Symposions über die phönizische Expansion im westlichen Mittelmeerraum in Köln vom 24-27 April 1979, a cura di H. Niemeyer, MadB VIII, 283-85.

Buchner. G., 1982b, Pithekussai (Ischia), in AA.VV. 1982.

Buranelli, F., Drago, L., e Paolini, L., La necropoli di Casal del Fosso, in Bartoloni, G., (a cura di), 1997,63-83.

Canciani, F., 1987, Scheda 28.3. Piatto, in M. Martelli, La ceramica degli Etruschi, Novara, 256.

Carafa, P., 1995, Officine ceramiche di età regia, Roma.

Cavagnaro Vanoni, L., 1966, Concessioni alla Fondazione Lerici. Cerveteri. Materiali di Antichità Varia V, Roma

Coen, A., 1991, Complessi tombali di Cerveteri con urne cinerarie tardo-orientalizzanti, Firenze.

Colazingari, O. e Fulgenzi, M.T., 1996, in Guidi, A. et Alii, Cures Sabini: Lo scavo, le strutture, la cultura materiale, le attività economiche, Identità e Civiltà dei Sabini, Atti del XVIII Convegno di Studi Etruschi ed Italici, Rieti – Magliano Sabina, 30 maggio- 3 giugno 1993, Firenze.

Colonna, G. e Di Paolo Colonna, E., 1997, Il letto vuoto, la distribuzione del corredo e la 'finestra' della Tomba Regolini-Galassi, in Etrusca et Italica. Scritti in ricordo di Massimo Pallottino, Roma, 131-172.

Colonna, G., 1970, Una nuova iscrizione etrusca del VII secolo e appunti sull'epigrafia ceretana dell'epoca, in MEFRA 82, 637-672.

Colonna, G., 1973-1974, Nomi etruschi di vasi, in AC 25-26, 132-150.

Colonna, G., 1988, La produzione artigianale, Storia di Roma, 1, Torino, 291-316.

Colonna, G., e von Hase, F.W., 1986, Alle origini della statuaria etrusca: la tomba delle Statue presso Ceri, SE LII, 13-59.

Cristofani, M. e Rizzo, M.A., 1987, Iscrizioni vascolari dal tumulo III d Cerveteri, SE LIII, 150-159.

Cristofani, M., (a cura di), 1993, Caere 3. Lo scarico arcaico della Vigna Parrocchiale, Roma.

Cristofani, M., 1969, Le tombe di Monte Michele nel museo archeologico di Firenze, Firenze.

Cristofani, M., 1982, Intervento nel dibattito, in AA.VV. 1982, 202.

Culican, W., 1968, Quelques aperçus sur le ateliers phéniciens, Syria 45, 275.

Cuomo di Caprio, N., 1985, La ceramica in archeologia, Milano.

De Santis, A., 1997, Alcune considerazioni sul territorio veiente in età orientalizzante e arcaica, in Bartoloni, G., (a cura di), 1997, 101-143.

Delpino, F., 2001, Il principe e la cerimonia del banchetto, in AA.VV. 2001a, 193-195.

di Gennaro, F., 1988, Primi risultati degli scavi nella necropoli di Crustumerium: tre complessi funerari della fase IVA, in ArchLaz IX, QuadAEI 16, Roma, 113-123.

di Gennaro, F., 1990, Crustumerium. Il centro protostorico e arcaico e la sua necropoli, in AA.VV 1990, 68-72.

di Gennaro, F., 1999, Itinerario di visita a Crustumerium, Roma.

Dik, R., 1981, Un'anfora orientalizzante etrusca nel Museo Allard Pierson, Babesch 56, 45-74.

Esposito, A.M., 1986, Scheda C, in M. Bonghi Jovino (a cura di), Gli Etruschi di Tarquinia, catalogo della mostra, 78.

Falzone, S., 2001, Ceramica di impasto rosso di epoca orientalizzante, in P. Pensabene (a cura di), Scavi del Palatino I. L'area sud-occidentale del Palatino tra l'età protostorica e il IV sec. a.C: scavi e materiali della struttura ipogea sotto la cella del tempio della Vittoria, Roma, 185-196.

Gierow, P. G., 1966, The Iron Age Culture of Latium. I. Classification and Analysis, Lund.

Gjerstad, E., 1956, Early Rome II. The Tombs, Lund.

Gjerstad, E., 1960, Early Rome III. Fortifications, Domestic Architecture, Sanctuaries, Stratigraphic Excavations, Lund.

Gjerstad, E., 1966, Early Rome IV, 1-2. Synthesis of Archeological Evidence, Lund .

Gran Aymerich, J. M. J., 1983, Les Céramiques Phénico-Puniques et le bucchero Etrusque: cas concrets et considerations générales, in Atti del I Congresso di Studi Fenici e Punici, I, Roma 5-10 novembre 1979, 77-87.

Gras, M., 2001, Il Mediterraneo in età orientalizzante. Merci, approdi, circolazione, in AA.VV 2001a, 15-26.

Guidi, A., 1993, La necropoli veiente dei Quattro Fontanili nel quadro della della fase recente della prima età del Ferro italiana, Firenze.

Iaia, A., Mandolesi, A. e Pacciarelli, M., 2001, Cretoncini: un'indagine nell'area settentrionale dell'abitato, in Tarquinia etrusca. Una nuova storia, catalogo della mostra di Tarquinia, a cura di A.M. Moretti Sgubini, Roma, 7-10.

Martelli, M., 1984, Per il dossier dei nomi etruschi di vasi: una nuova iscrizione ceretana del VII sec. a.C., Bollettino d'Arte 27, 49-54.

Martelli, M., 1991, i Fenici e la questione orientalizzante in Italia, in Atti del II Congresso Internazionale di Studi Fenici e Punici (Roma 1987), Roma, 1049-1072.

Micozzi, M., 1994, 'White-on red'. Una produzione vascolare dell'orientalizzante etrusco, Roma.

Moretti Sgubini, A.M. e Ricciardi, L., 2001, Vulci. III.B.2. Necropoli settentrionale, loc. Marrucatello. Tomba G, in AA. VV. 2001b, 200-201.

Moretti, M., 1970, Trevignano Romano, tomba dei Flabelli, in Nuovi tesori dell'antica Tuscia, Catalogo della Mostra di Viterbo, 23-31.

Nardi, G., 1993, Impasti orientalizzanti, in Cristofani, M., (a cura di), 1993, 237-253.

Olinder, B., e Pohl, I., 1981, San Giovenale II: 4. The Semi-subterranean Building in Area B, Stockholm.

Palm, J., 1952, Veian tomb groups in the Museo Preistorico Rome, OpArch 7, 50-86.

Pareti, L., 1948, La tomba Regolini Galassi del Museo Gregoriano Etrusco e la civiltà dell'Italia centrale nel sec. VII a.C., Città del Vaticano.

Pohl, I., 1972, The Iron Age Necropolis of Sorbo at Cerveteri, Rome.

Rathje, A., 1983, A Banquet Service from the Latin City of Ficana, AnalRom 12, 7-29.

Rathje, A., 1997, Gli Etruschi e gli altri: il caso di Veio, in Bartoloni 1997, 201-205.

Rendeli, M., 1993, Impasti rossi non decorati, in Cristofani, M., (a cura di), 1993, 261-271.

Ricci, G., 1955, Necropoli della Banditaccia. Zona 'A' del 'Recinto', in Caere. Scavi di Raniero Mengarelli, MonAnt XLII, coll. 201- 1048.

Ridgway, D., 1997, Nestor's Cup and the Etruscans, OJA 16, 3, 325-344.

Rizzo, M.A., 1989, Ceramica etrusco-geometrica da Caere, in Miscellanea Ceretana, Roma, 9-39.

Rizzo, M.A., 1991, Alcune importazioni fenicie da Cerveteri, in Atti del II Congresso Internazionale di Studi Fenici e Punici (Roma 1987), Roma, 1169-1181.

Scotti, C. e Tarella, A., 1980, Tomba 65, in Bosio, B. e Pugnetti, A. 1986, 257-259.

ten Kortenaar, S., 2001, Settore 6. Via San Gimignano. Probabile capanna di età orientalizzante (1989) (n. 17), in di Gennaro et alii, Fidenae. Contributi per la ricostruzione topografica del centro antico. Ritrovamenti 1986-1992, Bullettino Comunale di Roma, 18.

Vighi, R., 1935, Veio. Scavi nella necropoli degli alunni dell'anno 1927-28 del corso di Topografia dell'Italia Antica della R. Università di Roma, NSc, 39-68.

Zevi, F., 1977, Alcuni aspetti della necropoli di Castel di Decima, in PP XXXII, 241-273.

Zevi, F., 1982, Intervento nel dibattito, in AA.VV. 1982, 201-202.

Zevi, F., 1997, Una nota su Pitecusa, Veio e il Lazio, in Bartoloni, G., (a cura di) 1997, 179-184.

Zifferero, A., 2000, Architettura costruita e paesaggio rurale in Etruria meridionale: un contributo dal territorio cerite, in Idem (a cura di), L'architettura funeraria a Populonia tra IX e VI secolo a.C., Atti del Convegno Castello di Populonia 1997, Firenze, 193-250.

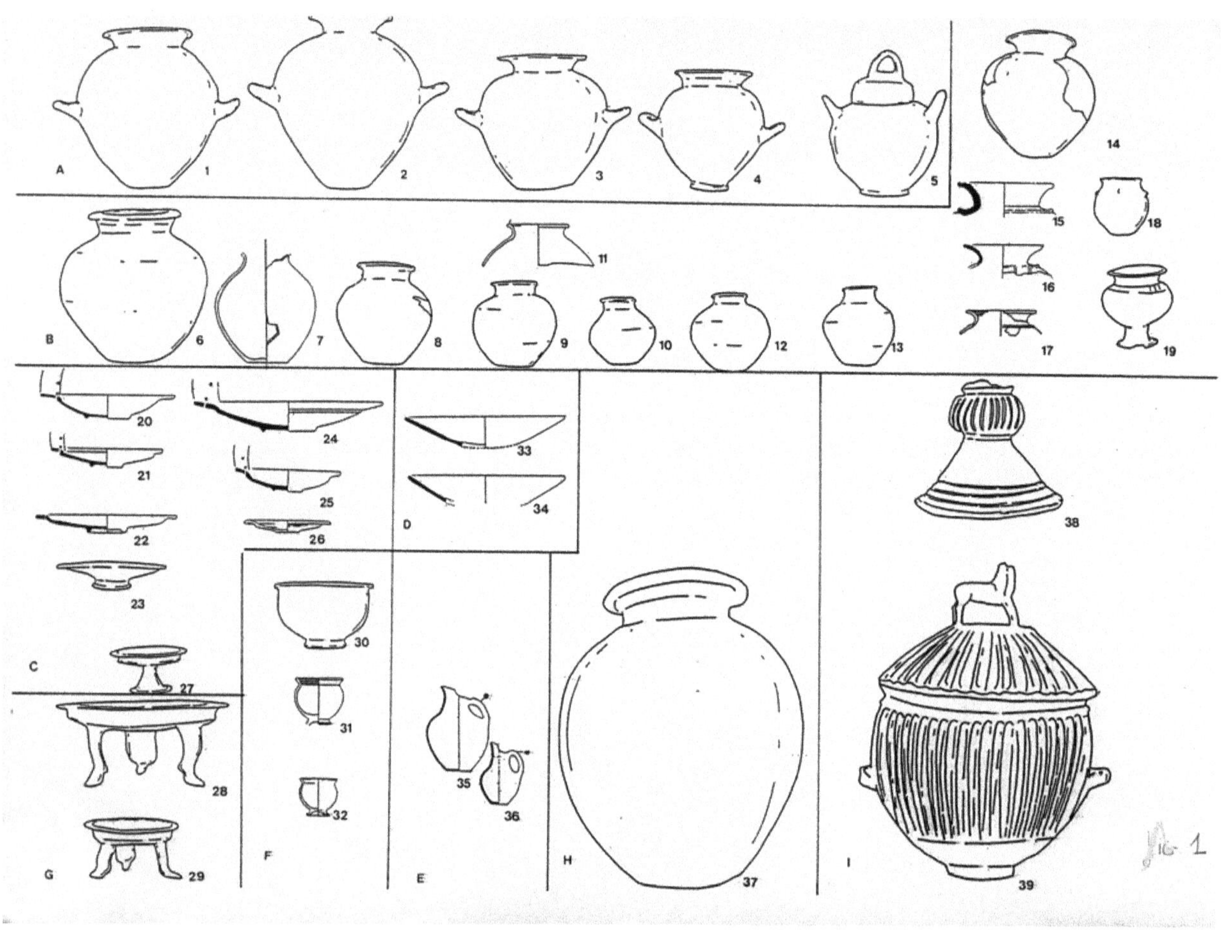

Fig. 1. Tavola riassuntiva delle principali attestazioni di materiali di impasto rosso da Cerveteri e dal territorio cerite (contesti funerari citati al par. 2). Rielaborazione grafica proposta da V. Acconcia., con un tentativo di riportare a una scala uniforme i vari esemplari.

1: tum. della Speranza, Inv. 108397; 2: Laghetto I, t. 65, n. 6; 3: Laghetto I, t. 153, n. 1; 4: t. Giulimondi, n. 486a; 5: Laghetto I, t. 64, n. 32; 6: Banditaccia, t. 81, n. 1; 7: Ferrone, t. 33, n. 8; 8: Banditaccia, t. 78, Inv. 44831; 9-10: Laghetto II, t. 274, nn. 5-6; 11: tum. Bandita Grande 1, n. 43; 12: Laghetto I, t. 150, n. 3; 13: Laghetto I, t. 155, n. 4; 14-16: Monte Abatone, t. 76, nn. 4, 6, 3; 17: tum. Monte Seccareccio, n. 26; 19: t. Giulimondi, n. 487; 20: Banditaccia, t. 81, n. 2; 20-22, 24-25: Monte Abatone, t., nn. 41-42, 44, 6, 43; 23: Banditaccia, tum. XXIV, Inv. 106992; 26: tum. Bandita Grande 1, n. 52; 27-29: Banditaccia, t. Capanna, nn. 7, 26-27; 30: Laghetto, t. 71, n. 11; 31: Ferrone, t. 33, n. 7; 32: tum. Bandita Grande, n, 49; 33-34: Monte Abatone, t. 76, nn. 39-40; 35-36: Monte Abatone, t. 89, nn. 10-11; 37: t. Capanna n. 25; 38: Monte Abatone, t. 76, n. 2; 39: t. Regolini-Galassi, n. 232.

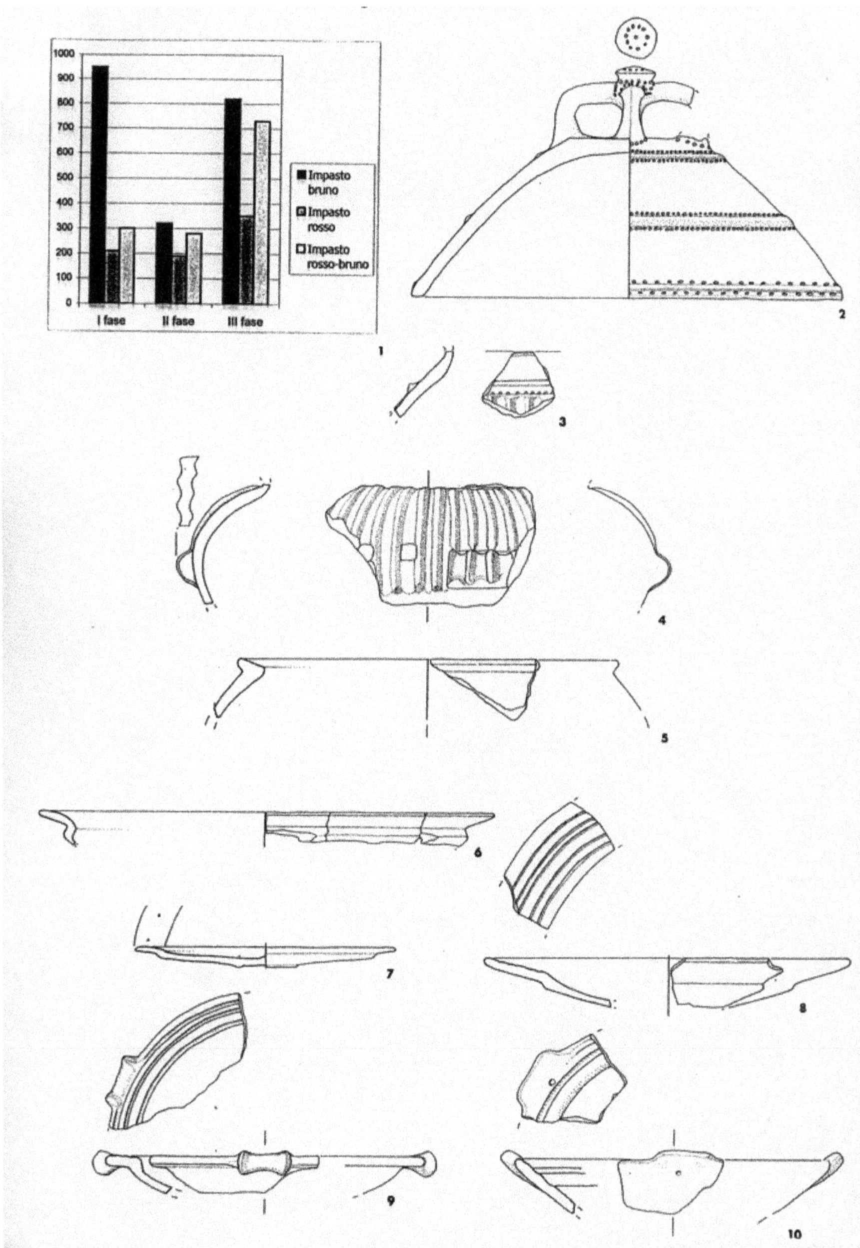

Fig. 2. Veio – Piazza d'Armi: materiali di impasto rosso (citati al par. 3). (Dis. S. ten Kortenaar).
Veio Piazza d'Armi: materiali residui dalla c.d. struttura B; Coperchio con presa quadriansata, decorato da tre listelli lisci e impressioni circolari (frammentario); Frammento di olla decorata da costolature verticali, delimitate in alto da un listello liscio, e da impressioni circolari; Frammento di pisside globulare costolata con presa a rocchetto e probabile ansa orizzontale; Frammento di coppa emisferica; Piatto con orlo a tesa e vasca profonda (frammentario); Piatto con orlo a tesa fornito di due fori, vasca bassa e fondo ombelicato (ricomposto da vari frammenti); Frammento di piatto con orlo a tesa decorato da cinque solcature concentriche e fornito di due fori; Frammento di piatto con prese a rocchetto, orlo a tesa decorato da tre solcature concentriche; Frammento di piatto con prese quadrangolari a vasca profonda, decorato da due solcature.

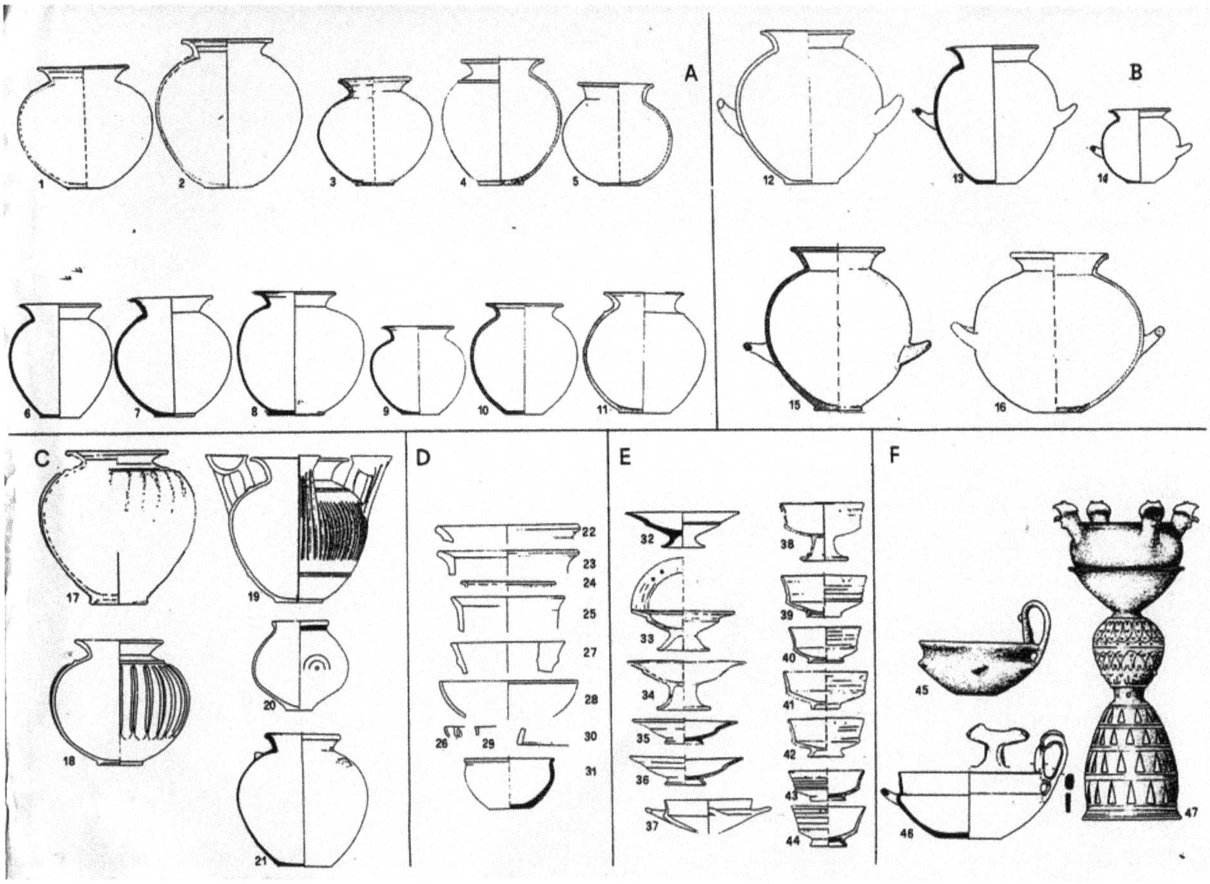

Fig. 3. Tavola riassuntiva delle attestazioni di ceramica di impasto rosso da Roma ed il Latium Vetus (contesti citati al par. 4). Rielaborazione grafica di A. Piergrossi (gli esemplari presentati sono a scala uniforme, fatta eccezione per il n. 49). 1: Castel di Decima, t. 15 n. 26; 2: Castel di Decima, t. 152, n. 24; 3: Castel di Decima, t. 7, n. 18; 4-5: Castel di Decima, t. 4, nn. 24-25; 6-7: Foro, t. I, nn. 5-6; 8-9: Tor de' Cenci, t. 4, nn. 16-17; 10-11: Osteria dell'Osa, tipi 92 e, 92f; 12: Esquilino, t. 128, n. 1; 13: Foro, t. I, n. 4; 14: Foro, t. AA, n. 8; 15: Castel di Decima, t. 7, n. 19; 16: Castel di Decima, t. 4, n. 26; 17: Castel di Decima, t. 15, n. 27; 18: Roma, Equus Domitiani, Carafa tipo 201; 19: Esquilino, t. 128, Carafa tipo 220; 20: Esquilino, t. 82, n. 1; 21: Tor de' Cenci, t. 4, n. 18; 22-30: Roma, Via Sacra-via Nova, Carafa tipi 225, 227, 230, 234, 237, 238, 240, 241, 248; 31: Castel di Decima, t. 4, n. 31; 32: Foro, t. M, n. 6; 33: Castel di Decima, t. 15, n. 25; 34: Castel di Decima, t. 7, n. 26; 35-36: Castel di Decima, t. 4, nn. 29-30; 37: Esquilino, t. 127, n.1; 38-42: Castel di Decima, t. 7, nn. 25, 21, 23, 22, 24; 43-44: Castel di Decima, t. 4, nn. 27-28; 45: Ficana, zona 5a, pozzo I, n. 32b; 46: Tor de'Cenci, t. 4, n. 15; 47: Ficana, zona 5a, pozzo I.

LA TECNOLOGIA DEL BUCCHERO: ALCUNE CONSIDERAZIONI SULLE PRODUZIONI DELL'ETRURIA MERIDIONALE E SETTENTRIONALE

VALERIA ACCONCIA
(Università di Roma "la Sapienza")

ABSTRACT: The class of pottery known as bucchero presents a broad range of morphological/stylistic and technological variability across space and over time. This situation appears to correspond to stylistic and functional decisions as well as in differences in production processes. But while it is possible to define the technological characteristics of other pre-Roman pottery based in part upon evidence of kilns, there is a paucity of evidence for production centers of bucchero. There is also the difficulty of arriving to general conclusions through archaeometric or experimental investigations. This paper presents a summary of the state of the question and suggests possible directions for research based upon recent discoveries.*

Introduzione

Il bucchero è una delle produzioni più caratteristiche dell'area etrusca dalla prima metà del VII fino agli inizi del V secolo a.C., ed è anche attestato in altri comprensori culturali della penisola italiana come importazione, che stimola a sua volta imitazioni locali (Bonghi Jovino 1993; Acconcia *c.s.*).

Per una sintesi pressoché completa delle problematiche legate alla classe (tipologia, cronologia, diffusione regionale, tecnologia, funzionalità), si rimanda al contributo di J.M.J. Gran Aymerich (Gran Aymerich 1993.). In tale sede sono esposti sinteticamente gli approcci metodologici di lavori precedenti (che tradizionalmente sviluppano aspetti morfologici e stilistici), facendo emergere la variabilità non soltanto tipologica ma anche tecnica del bucchero correlandola alle aree di produzione e agli aspetti cronologici[1].Questo lavoro vuole delineare alcune problematiche relative alla manifattura di tale ceramica, puntualizzandone gli sviluppi nei territori dell'Etruria propria.

Malgrado vi sia una tendenza a considerare il bucchero una sorta di *marker* della cultura materiale etrusca, esso offre nel suo complesso caratteri molto eterogenei. Fin dai primi tentativi di inquadramento, quindi, si è dovuta ipotizzare una sorta di 'evoluzione' interna, con la nota successione: 'bucchero sottile, di transizione, pesante' (Gran Aymerich 1993: 20; Mannoni 1993). Questa articolazione, pur non corrispondendo all'effettivo sviluppo della classe, soltanto per il fatto di associare un ampio arco cronologico a uno spazio geografico molto esteso (dalle prime produzioni etrusco-meridionali a quelle dell'Etruria centrale nel VI secolo a.C.), per quanto superata nelle ricerche successive, fa emergere la difficoltà di ricondurre all'unità un insieme decisamente vario anche da un punto di vista tecnologico.

Come infatti lo stesso Gran Aymerich ha formulato in vari contributi, un solo esame autoptico è in grado di riconoscere un alto grado di variabilità nel complesso delle attestazioni.Tale concetto è stato puntualizzato da M. Bonamici e P. Tamburini in una analisi del bucchero orvietano, che intorno alla metà del VI secolo a.C. sarebbe segnato da una '*rottura tecnologica nella continuità della produzione*', ovvero da un fenomeno di normalizzazione, da manifattura pregiata con precisi standard qualitativi (il colore nero e la compattezza delle paste, la resa metallica delle superfici), a una produzione caratterizzata da un colore tendenzialmente grigio, con superfici scarsamente trattate e porose. A tale impoverimento si accompagnerebbe anche un mutamento di destinazione: da vasellame da mensa attestato in numerose forme e utilizzato prevalentemente dai segmenti elevati della società, si passerebbe a un uso più esteso, ma limitato a un numero ristretto di forme (coppe, scodelle, brocche etc.) (Gran Aymerich 1981, 1993: 23; Tamburini 1985: 96-98; Bonamici 1985: 106). Questi sviluppi si riscontrano anche per altre aree e vanno letti come uno scadimento nella pratica artigianale (a fronte di un incremento della domanda da parte di più ampie fasce sociali): essi sono però da ritenere la spia di un cambiamento nel gusto, che in alcune aree avrà come esito la produzione di ceramiche 'grigie'[2]. Una difformità tecnologica si registra, come già accennato, non solo in senso diacronico nelle singole cerchie artigianali, ma anche attraverso il confronto di vari comprensori per periodi coerenti.

Il bucchero dei principali centri dell'Etruria meridionale, infatti, fino alla prima metà del VI sec. a.C. tende a conservare il colore nero delle superfici e del corpo ceramico, la lucentezza, la compattezza, lo spessore non troppo elevato delle pareti e un notevole grado di depurazione delle paste.All'esterno di quest'area, invece, la stessa classe sembra non rispettare tali standard, caratterizzandosi per un'incostante colorazione delle superfici, che può differire in tipi ricorrenti all'interno di uno stesso sito, rispetto a corpi ceramici non completamente depurati, ricchi di inclusi e vacuoli. Tale fenomeno, riscontrabile spesso nell'Etruria settentrionale, sia interna che marittima, induce in alcuni casi a formulare definizioni tecniche quali 'impasto buccheroide'[3]. Sembra inoltre necessario puntualizzare come la diffusione e la circolazione della classe possano essere lette anche in rapporto alla sua destinazione: inizialmente come bene di pregio riservato ai ceti emergenti, poi diffusa anche tra quelli medi o inferiori, a sostituire o integrare i servizi da mensa in impasto o in semplice ceramica depurata.

La produzione del bucchero: aspetti tecnici, archeometrici e sperimentali

Tale complessità dovrebbe quindi corrispondere a una varietà tecnologica e produttiva, che però non trova ancora un inquadramento preciso nella storia degli studi. Oltre all'assenza di specifici riferimenti letterari, epigrafici o iconografici (come per gran parte della ceramica etrusca, ma a differenza di quella greca dello stesso periodo) (Richter 1923), per il bucchero sono estremamente rari i rinvenimenti in contesti di manifattura. Tale situazione, quindi, ha indotto a procedere nella ricerca soprattutto con prove sperimentali e archeometriche che, dopo le prime ipotesi non supportate scientificamente, hanno consentito di attribuire i caratteri peculiari della classe all'esito di processi di cottura diversi da quelli impiegati per altre ceramiche coeve, ovvero alla creazione all'interno della fornace di un'atmosfera essenzialmente riducente, in grado di trasformare uniformemente gli idrossidi e ossidi di ferro presenti nell'argilla in ossidi ferrosi e ferroso-ferrici[4].

Con tali presupposti, il processo di cottura del bucchero è attualmente riconducibile a due ipotesi. La prima prevede l'uso di strutture del tipo del 'focolare all'aperto'/'fornace a catasta', simili alle carbonaie (Fig. 1), in atmosfera fortemente riducente e con temperature non elevate (intorno ai 600-700 °C), nelle quali la combustione lenta in assenza di ossigeno avrebbe favorito un processo omogeneo di colorazione (Flamini *et al.* 1979).

L'ipotesi alternativa, con l'impiego di fornaci a camera verticale, completamente chiuse per evitare l'afflusso di ossigeno e ottenere quindi un'atmosfera riducente, è stata corretta da N. Cuomo di Caprio in relazione al fatto che l'assenza di aria determinerebbe lo spegnimento del combustibile e quindi l'interruzione del processo (Cuomo di Caprio 1993). Prove sperimentali supportate dalle conoscenze di artigiani moderni e condotte su vasi imitanti le originarie forme del bucchero, rendono verosimile una cottura dei manufatti in fornaci sostanzialmente tradizionali, con i vasi impilati all'interno di contenitori in argilla refrattaria chiusi accuratamente e riempiti di sostanze riducenti (Fig. 2)[5]. La riuscita di tali esperimenti sembra inoltre più convincente di quelli effettuati con il sistema di cottura a catasta, sostituendo barrette di argilla al vasellame. Allo stato attuale della ricerca, però, l'approccio sperimentale e quello archeometrico non sembrano fornire indicazioni univoche.

Per quanto riguarda almeno le sperimentazioni edite, esse sembrano condurre a soluzioni diametralmente opposte. I risultati delle analisi condotte da Francaviglia, Minardi e Palmieri, ad esempio, escludono l'apporto decisivo dei processi di riduzione degli idrossidi e ossidi di ferro delle argille, suggerendo invece che la colorazione nera potesse essere ottenuta con l'aggiunta alle paste di materiali carboniosi e con una cottura per fumigazione (Francaviglia *et al.* 1975). Questi dati si pongono in contrasto con quelli presentati al Convegno di Aix-en-Provence del 1975 o con quelli ottenuti più recentemente su campioni dal sito di San Piero a Sieve (*infra*), che sembrano invece confermare il ruolo degli stessi processi di riduzione (Flamini *et al.* 1979; Maglietta *et al.* 1999).

Nella prospettiva dell'archeologia sperimentale, però, se l'effettiva efficienza del sistema proposto da N. Cuomo di Caprio è stata verificata con numerose prove condotte indipendentemente l'una dall'altra, si deve comunque segnalare quanto nel 1965 registrava J.V. Noble circa l'avvio da parte dei Pueblos di Santa Clara di una produzione di ceramica ottenuta con argilla ricca di ferro, cotta nel sistema 'a catasta', con l'aggiunta di combustibile animale e che, a detta dello stesso Noble, era molto simile al bucchero etrusco (Noble 1965: 43).

Per verificarne l'identità tecnologica sarebbe di certo necessario ricorrere ad analisi archeometriche incrociate, ma sembra evidente che, in assenza di dati certificati da una sufficiente quantità di contesti produttivi, sia ancora difficile proporre una soluzione univoca per definire i processi di realizzazione del bucchero.

La produzione del bucchero alla luce dei rinvenimenti archeologici

Si sottolineano a tale proposito i due aggettivi 'sufficiente' e 'univoca' per evidenziare un'ulteriore anomalia, relativa al carattere e alla consistenza delle aree artigianali destinate alla produzione del bucchero note alla ricerca archeologica. Pur essendo il loro numero discretamente incrementato nel corso degli ultimi anni (Nijboer 1998), esse presentano comunque difficoltà di interpretazione e, soprattutto, si collocano all'esterno dell'area e dei limiti cronologici che inquadrano i primi sviluppi della classe: ovvero mancano finora dati certi dall'Etruria meridionale tirrenica, ascrivibili ai decenni centrali del VII secolo a.C.

I casi noti (Fig. 7), infatti, sono prevalentemente localizzati in area etrusco-settentrionale, laddove, come già accennato, le produzioni di bucchero sembrano in qualche modo discostarsi nei caratteri tecnologici dalla 'tradizione' dei centri meridionali, elaborando repertori morfologici e decorativi autonomi. La stessa tipologia delle strutture produttive rinvenute, inoltre, sembra variare notevolmente.

Aree artigianali probabilmente connesse alla manifattura del bucchero sono:

1) Località *I Monti*, a S. Piero a Sieve (FI): due fornaci allestite nei pressi di un pozzo. Secondo gli autori dello scavo, le due strutture erano prive di divisioni interne, e quindi sarebbero attribuibili al tipo 'a catasta'. Ambedue hanno restituito scarti di lavorazione relativi a forme in bucchero e impasto, con tipi corrispondenti. Insieme sono stati rinvenuti anche distanziatori, tappi degli sfiatatoi ecc. Il complesso è databile alla seconda metà del VII-primo quarto del VI sec. a.C. (Salvini 1994; De Marinis *et al.* 1994).
2) Località *Quartaia*, Colle Val d'Elsa (SI): area artigianale di ampie dimensioni con cinque fornaci a camera verticale (circolare e rettangolare). Associati a tali strutture sono stati rinvenuti numerosi scarti di lavorazione e aree di approvvigionamento e di conserva delle materie prime. La presenza degli scarti testimonia una probabile produzione di buccheri, ceramiche comuni e rivestimenti architettonici tra la fine del VII e il V secolo a.C. (Acconcia, Bandinelli and Zinelli 2002).
3) In località *Montecastello*, Pontelatone (CE), è stata rinvenuta una fornace del tipo verticale a pianta circolare, attiva tra la fine del VI e il V sec. a.C. nella produzione di ceramica domestica, bucchero nero e 'bucchero rosso'[6].
4) Più promettente sembra invece il caso di *via T. Vanni* a Pisa, dove è stata indagata una struttura realizzata, a quanto riferito dall'autore dello scavo, da una copertura in terracotta fornita di sfiatatoi, con l'ultima infornata di coppe in bucchero e/o impasto posta a diretto contatto con il combustibile, obliterata dal crollo della copertura, databile tra la fine del VII e il VI secolo a.C.[7]

Come sopra accennato, questi casi non sono decisivi per definire i caratteri pratici delle prime produzioni di bucchero, e sembrano invece restituire dati contraddittori.

A S. Piero a Sieve, infatti, le fornaci sembrano assimilabili al tipo del cosiddetto 'focolare all'aperto', anche se la presenza di sfiatatoi e distanziatori, funzionali al tiraggio dell'aria e alla disposizione del vasellame, indizia una struttura a doppia camera. Le griglie delle fornaci, non rinvenute nello scavo, potrebbero essere state asportate a cottura ultimata e riutilizzate o scaricate altrove. Anche se dall'edizione dello scavo non risultano frammenti di griglia, il rinvenimento di utensili funzionali al tiraggio e alla disposizione del vasellame all'interno delle camere di cottura suggerisce comunque l'esistenza di un setto.

L'impianto di via T. Vanni a Pisa sembra, in attesa dell'edizione dei dati di scavo, mentre a Quartaia e a Pontelatone le fornaci sarebbero del tipo verticale con setto divisorio tra camera di combustione e camera di cottura (Cuomo di Caprio 1985: 136-143).

Possibili indizi della tecnologia del bucchero dal sito di Veio-Piazza d'Armi

Un recente e inedito ritrovamento fornisce un'ulteriore prova della complessità del problema. Si tratta di un calice di bucchero lacunoso di parte della vasca e dell'orlo, rinvenuto nel corso della campagna di scavo 1999 dell'Università di Roma 'La Sapienza' nel sito di Piazza d'Armi a Veio (RM). Il frammento proviene dal riempimento di una cavità di forma rettangolare realizzata nel banco tufaceo, localizzata a sud-ovest dell'accesso settentrionale del sito. Tale cavità, probabilmente in origine una cisterna per la raccolta delle acque, era stata riempita alla metà del VI sec. a.C. con scarichi consistenti di materiali ceramici, e resti ossei, al fine di bonificare l'area circostante[8].

Il calice, con basso piede ad anello, vasca profonda e tre solcature a incisione sulla vasca, è attribuibile al tipo 4b della classificazione del Rasmussen (1979: 100-101, n. 152), diffuso tra il VI e gli inizi del V sec. a.C. (Figg. 3-5). Il carattere peculiare dell'esemplare risiede però nella presenza sul fondo di un foro circolare di circa 3 cm di diametro, realizzato prima della cottura, e nel trattamento o nell'esito finale delle superfici conservate. L'interno del vaso, infatti, è lucidato, con resa quasi metallica, mentre l'esterno è ruvido al tatto, come se avesse perduto il rivestimento. Il corpo ceramico, infine, presenta una durezza superiore a quella solitamente attestata per il bucchero locale.

L'insieme delle caratteristiche del calice, quindi, ha indotto chi scrive a ritenere che ad esso potessero essere attribuite funzionalità peculiari, da individuare probabilmente nell'ambito dei processi di manifattura e cottura della ceramica.

Sarei a tale proposito dell'opinione di escludere un rapporto con altri materiali noti da bibliografia che presentano fori sul fondo. Si tratta di vasi (di solito integri e probabilmente provenienti da corredi funerari) privi di tracce evidenti di cottura anomala, con più fori (molto piccoli) sul fondo. Tali esemplari dovevano essere probabilmente utilizzati a fini rituali nel cerimoniale del banchetto. Si tratta di due orcioli biconici di impasto databili all'età del ferro nella Collezione Massimo al Museo di Villa Giulia (Falconi Amorelli 1969, nn. 4-5); una *oinochoe* di impasto bruno iscritta, con venti fori, da Veio (Colonna 1981; Biondi 1997: 4,e); una boccetta in impasto nella Collezione C.A., anch'essa iscritta, con numerosi fori sul fondo (Camporeale 1991: 22-25, n. 22); una *oinochoe* di impasto ad Heidelberg, con un foro sul fondo e altri tre sul becco (Prückner 1970); una *oinochoe* EPC al British Museum (Williams 1986: 296).

Le ipotesi percorribili, che dovranno comunque essere verificate al termine delle analisi archeometriche ancora in corso[9], sembrano sostanzialmente due:
- la prima si sviluppa dal confronto con materiali simili rinvenuti in contesti artigianali della Grecia e dell'area coloniale, identificati tradizionalmente come 'provini'. Con questo termine si identificano vasi integri o frammenti (di solito trattati con la tecnica delle figure nere o rosse), probabilmente mal riusciti e forati prima della cottura, che potevano essere periodicamente estratti dalla camera superiore della fornace tramite un'asta metallica al fine di controllare lo stadio di pigmentazione delle superfici e verificare il grado di avanzamento della cottura dell'intera infornata[10].

Il loro utilizzo sembra testimoniato anche iconograficamente da una delle lastre corinzie del 'ciclo dei ceramisti', che rappresenta l'interno di una fornace arcaica, nella quale sono visibili alcuni frammenti forati nei pressi dello sfiatatoio superiore (Fig. 6, a) (Cuomo di Caprio 1984). Le condizioni di rinvenimento degli impianti di età preromana rende almeno fino ad ora impossibile verificare l'applicazione di tale tecnica, dato che di essi si conserva soprattutto la parte inferiore (corrispondente alla camera di combustione) realizzata in murature a secco o interrata, mentre la camera superiore era approntata con un'impalcatura in materiale deperibile rivestito di argilla refrattaria (Fig. 6, b) (Schleiber 1983, fig. 91, n. 19).

Volendo applicare l'uso di provini anche alla catena operativa del bucchero, però, il momento della verifica avrebbe reso comunque necessaria l'apertura della camera di cottura o del/dei contenitori del vasellame di bucchero posti al suo interno (come proposto dalla Cuomo di Caprio), con il conseguente afflusso di ossigeno e quindi con l'annullamento o la riduzione delle condizioni atmosferiche utili alla riuscita del processo. A tale difficoltà, del resto, si potrebbe ovviare ipotizzando la presenza di più contenitori isolanti nella camera di cottura, uno solo dei quali avrebbe potuto essere predisposto per la verifica.

Un'altra possibilità potrebbe indurre a considerare l'esemplare non ultimato per ragioni attualmente non comprensibili. Esso potrebbe quindi essere stato forato intenzionalmente prima della cottura e utilizzato come una sorta di distanziatore funzionale al passaggio uniforme del calore. Tale utilizzo[11] risponderebbe alla pratica artigianale di ricorrere a strumenti realizzati con i materiali reperibili sul momento, verificabile ancora in manifatture non industrializzate[12].

In ambedue i casi, un reperto come quello appena presentato consente alcune considerazioni circa le tecniche di cottura del bucchero, almeno per Veio, che in ultima analisi potranno essere verificate solo con il rinvenimento della fornace stessa.

Sia un'interpretazione come provino, sia come distanziatore, suggerisce un suo utilizzo in una fornace a camera verticale, e non in una struttura a catasta. Ci sentiremmo in ogni caso di escludere il sistema del semplice 'focolare all'aperto', utilizzato di solito per gli impasti, che consente di raggiungere in maniera incontrollata temperature molto elevate in poco tempo, con una resa dei materiali estremamente eterogenea, che difficilmente sembra conciliarsi con i caratteri uniformi dei bucchero meridionale. Questa struttura, infatti, pur consentendo una cottura prolungata e omogenea, è sostanzialmente incontrollabile: almeno nella pratica carbonara verificata in tempi recenti, infatti, la catasta è 'lasciata' produrre, senza possibilità di essere regolata. In questo senso, l'uso di un provino sarebbe pressoché inutile (Cuomo di Caprio 1985: 136; Rye 1981: 25 ; Lugli and Pracchia 1994). Allo stesso modo, anche un utilizzo come distanziatore per facilitare il passaggio del calore non coinciderebbe con il metodo della catasta, nella quale il combustibile è necessariamente a contatto diretto con il vasellame.

Conclusione

A fronte di un quadro così eterogeneo della documentazione archeologica, nonché delle analisi sperimentali e archeometriche, sembra difficile delineare un modello univoco per gli aspetti legati alla tecnologia del bucchero. Questo dato, in attesa che il prosieguo delle ricerche non porti a una maggiore chiarezza, potrebbe in realtà fornire la chiave di interpretazione della varietà e degli sviluppi dei caratteri morfo-tipologici e produttivi, rispondendo al principio delle 'scelte tecnologiche', così come formulato recentemente da B. Sillar e M.S. Tite (2000: 3; Mannoni e Giannichedda 1996: 8-18, 25-29), ovvero all'assunto che nella pratica artigianale svolgano una funzione determinante una serie di fattori, quali la *disponibilità di materie prime*, gli *utensili*, le *fonti energetiche*, le *tecniche* e le *sequenze produttive*, i *modi di produzione*, che a seconda della loro reciproca integrazione determinano risultati più o meno simili.

In questo senso, quindi, l'elaborazione della classe in esame, che presenta a parere di chi scrive forti connotati innovativi rispetto alle precedenti e coeve ceramiche di impasto (Mannoni 1993: 226), oltre che a quelle depurate, sembra essersi articolata sulla base di scelte tecnologiche originariamente realizzate in un'area abbastanza definita, corrispondente ai territori etrusco-meridionali. Tali dinamiche sembrano privilegiare essenzialmente centri connotati da caratteri proto- o pienamente urbani e non sembrano penetrare nel loro complesso nelle aree settentrionali dell'Etruria. Qui, dove il bucchero non presenta standard qualitativi paragonabili, la trasmissione della catena operativa potrebbe essere stata parziale, veicolando solo la suggestione di una ceramica caratterizzata dal colore nero, il cui aspetto poteva anche essere replicato con procedimenti meno elaborati, già sperimentati per l'impasto, ma per questo meno efficaci.

NOTE

* Ringrazio per i consigli e la disponibilità fornitami per questo lavoro i professori Gilda Bartoloni e Stefano Bruni; inoltre Enrico Giannichedda, Federica M. Rossi, Iefke van Kampen, Giuseppe Pulitani e Andrea Zifferero.

1 I lavori di N. Hirschland Ramage (1970) e di T.B. Rasmussen (1979) per il bucchero etrusco-meridionale, o quelli dedicati ai buccheri decorati a cilindretto e ad applicazioni plastiche dell'are vulcente, chiusina e orvietana, cui si aggiungono progressivamente altri contributi relativi a centri o a comprensori regionali (v. nota 8).Recentemente sul bucchero in generale, v. Camporeale 2000.

2 Per la ceramica grigia dell'Etruria settentrionale: De Tommaso 1987; Maggiani 1990; per un esempio dello scadimento della qualità del bucchero più tardo, ad es. a Casale Pian Roseto: Murray-Threipland and Torelli 1970: 72.

3 Per l'agro chiusino e senese: Monaci 1965; Pecchiai 1967; Scalia 1968; Donati 1968, 1977. Per Orvieto: Donati 1969; Camporeale 1972. Per Volterra: Cateni and Maggiani 1997: 78-79, 83. Per l'agro fiorentino: Nicosia 1972, 1974. Per l'area costiera: Donati 1984-1985; Gregori 1991. Per l'impasto 'buccheroide', v. Mannoni 1993: 225-226.

4 Gran Aymerich *et al.* 1985: 613, nota 7; Cuomo di Caprio 1993. Si rimanda a tale lavoro per la disamina delle ipotesi, ormai abbandonate, circa l'applicazione di sostanze coloranti (ocra, resine, cera) o di particolari tecniche di levigatura, o di minerali all'argilla (manganese, polvere di carbone): Del Vita 1927; Mazzoni 1934; Richter 1936; Leoni and Trabucchi 1962. Per i primi esperimenti, condotti nel XIX secolo da A. Klitsche de La Grange e A. Brogniart: Gran Aymerich *et al.* 1985: 612.

5 Wadsworth 1983; v. anche gli esperimenti proposti da M. Vallesi e G. Pulitani nel corso dei seminari sul bucchero etrusco di Blera del novembre 1999 e 2000.

6 Si inserisce questo sito, pur all'esterno dell'area considerata per il presente lavoro, proprio per la generale scarsità di dati sulle aree produttive del bucchero. Albore Livadie 1991.

7 Notizia preliminare in, Bruni 1998: 21. Si ringrazia il prof. S. Bruni per la disponibilità a discutere del rinvenimento.

8 Si ringraziano Iefke Van Kampen e Federica M. Rossi, che hanno realizzato lo scavo della cisterna ; Federica Rossi, M. Helena Marchetti e Ferdinando Sciacca si occupano dello studio del bucchero rinvenuto nello scavo di Piazza d'Armi ; lo scavo del sito, realizzato dall'Università di Roma 'La Sapienza', in collaborazione con la Soprintendenza Archeologica dell'Etruria Meridionale, è diretto dalla prof.ssa Gilda Bartoloni ; si segnalano dallo stesso contesto altri frammenti di bucchero con tracce evidenti di cottura anomala.

9 Le analisi del campione di bucchero sono ancora in corso da parte del dott. Giannichedda e del dott. C. Cappelli.

10 Per una sintesi dei ritrovamenti in Atene e in Attica: Monaco 2000. In questo puntuale lavoro sono spesso citati questi materiali, e si rimanda a una sua lettura completa, i frammenti editi sono pareti e fondi forati di forme aperte (*skyphoi*?) decorati a fasce e a denti di lupo, databili alla seconda metà del VII sec. a.C., rinvenuti nel deposito S 17:2 dell'Agorà (Monaco 2000: 101-102, A XIV/6-9, tav. 10,b-11); parete con traccia di foro intenzionalmente realizzato prima della cottura, probabilmente pertinente a un vaso di grandi dimensioni databile all'età ellenistica, dal riempimento del Monumento al 3. *Horos (*209, C IV/VI, 3, tav. 29,c). V. anche Monaco 1999: 112-113. Sui provini in generale: Farnsworth 1960; Rye 1981: 105; Fillieres *et al.* 1983: 57; Monaco 2000: 17-18. Per i rinvenimenti nel *Vrysoula Deposit* a Corinto: Pemberton 1970: 302-303, nn. 146-150. Per il *Kerameikos* di Metaponto: D'Andria 1975: 376, figg. 45-46.

11 Suggeritomi da Giuseppe Pulitani.

12 V. *Appendice.*

BIBLIOGRAFIA

Acconcia, V., *c.s.*, Note sulla produzione e tecnologia del bucchero etrusco, in *Il Bucchero etrusco, Atti delle Giornate di Studio 1999-2000, Blera* (ed. A. Naso), corso di stampa.

Acconcia, V., Bandinelli, G.and Zinelli D., c.s., Località Quartaia (Colle Val d'Elsa; SI): le prime campagne di scavo, in *Città e territorio nell'Etruria settentrionale, Atti del Seminario di Colle Val d'Elsa 1998, Atti delle Giornate di studio, Colle di Val d'Elsa 1998*, Colle di Val d'Elsa 2002, pp. 149-160.

Albore Livadie, C., 1991, Fornace tardo arcaica, *BA*, 11/12, 149-151.

Amyx, D.A., 1988, *Corinthian Vase-Painting of the Archaic Period*, Oxford.

Arafat, K. and Morgan C., 1991, Pots and Potters in Athens and Corinth: a Review, *OxfJA*, 8 (3), 311-347.

Biondi, L., 1997, ΚΩΘΟΝ nell'Italia medio-tirrenica, *Acme*, 50, 5-31.

Binns, C.F. and Fraser, A.D., 1929, The Genesis of the Greek Balck Glaze, *AJA*, 33, 1-9.

Bonamici, M., 1985, Necropoli della Cannicella. Le ceramiche di importazione e il bucchero, *AnnFaina*, 3, 99-110.

Bonghi Jovino, M. (ed.), 1993, *Produzione artigianale ed esportazione nel mondo antico. Il bucchero etrusco, Atti del Colloquio Internazionale, Milano 1990*, Milano.

Brijder, H.A.G., 1984 (ed.), *Ancient Greek and Related Pottery, Proceedings of the International Vase Symposium, Amsterdam 1984*, Amsterdam.

Bruni, S., 1998, *Pisa etrusca. Anatomia di una città scomparsa*, Milano.

Camporeale, G., 1972, *I buccheri a cilindretto di produzione orvietana*, Firenze,

Camporeale, G., 1991, *La Collezione C.A. Impasti e buccheri*, Roma.

Camporeale, G., 2000, La ceramica arcaica: impasti e buccheri, in *Gli Etruschi, Catalogo della Mostra di Venezia, Venezia 2000* (ed. M. Torelli), 405-419.

Cateni, G. and Maggiani, A., 1997, Volterra dalla prima età del ferro al V secolo a.C. Appunti di topografia urbana, in *Aspetti della cultura di Volterra etrusca fra l'età del ferro e l'età ellenistica e contributi alla ricerca antropologica alla conoscenza del popolo etrusco, Atti del XIX Convegno Studi Etruschi ed Italici, Volterra 1995*, Firenze, 43-92

Colonna, G., 1981, *Veii*, in *REE*, 258-259, n. 30.

Cuomo di Caprio, N., 1985, *La ceramica in Archeologia*, Milano.

Cuomo di Caprio, N., 1993, *Annotazioni tecniche circa la cottura del bucchero*, in *Produzione artigianale ed esportazione nel mondo antico. Il bucchero etrusco, Atti del Colloquio Internazionale, Milano 1990* (ed. M. Bonghi Jovino), Milano, 217-221.

D'Andria, F., 1975, Scavi nella zona del Kerameikos, in *Metaponto I* (eds. D. Adamesteanu, D. Mertens, F. D'Andria), *NSc Suppl.*, 355-452.

Del Vita, A., 1927, Osservazioni sulla tecnologia del bucchero, *StEtr*, 1, 187-194.

De Marinis, G., Franchi, R., Pallecchi, P. and Salvini, M., 1994, Fornaci e manufatti etruschi a S. Piero a Sieve, in *Archeologia in Alto Mugello – Val di Sieve e il Caso di S. Piero a Sieve, Atti della Giornata di Studio, S. Piero a Sieve 1994*, Firenze, 103-108

De Tommaso, G., 1987, Ceramica grigia, in *Artimino (Firenze). Scavi 1974. L'area della Piaggeria medicea: relazione preliminare* (ed. G. Capecchi), Firenze, 118-121.

Donati, L., 1967, Vasi di bucchero decorati con teste plastiche umane. Zona di Vulci, *StEtr*, 35, 619-632.

Donati, L., 1968, Vasi di bucchero decorati con teste plastiche umane. Zona di Chiusi, *StEtr*, 36, 319-355.

Donati, L., 1969, Vasi di bucchero decorati con teste plastiche umane. Zona di Orvieto, *StEtr*, 37, 443-462.

Donati, L., 1984-1985, Roselle. Le ceramiche di due pozzetti in roccia sulla collina settentrionale, *NSc*, pp. 69-94.

Falconi Amorelli, M.T., 1969, *La Collezione Massimo. Quaderni di Villa Giulia*, **2**, Roma.

Farnsworth, M., 1960, Draw pieces as aids to correct firing, *AJA*, 64, 72-75.

Fillieres, D., Harbottle, G. and Sayre, E.V., 1983, Neutron-Activation Study of Figurines, Pottery and Workshop Materials from the Athenian Agora, Greece, *JFieldA*, **10**, 55-69.

Flamini, A., Graziani, G., Gubressi, O. and De Lorenzo, P., 1979, La technique de préparation di bucchero étrusque, in *Le bucchero nero étrusque et sa diffusion en Gaule Méridionale, Actes de la Table-Ronde, Aix en Provence 1975*, 72-81, Coll. Latomus, **160**, Bruxelles.

Francaviglia, V, Minardi, M.E. and Palmieri A., 1975, Comparative Study of various Samples of Etruscan Bucchero by X-Ray Diffraction, X-Ray Spectrometry and Thermoanalysis, *Archaeometry*, **17**, 223-231.

Gran Aymerich, J.M.J., 1981, Le bucchero étrusque. Rupture et continuité, *CuadRom*, **15**, 1-18.

Gran Aymerich, J.M.J., 1993, Observations generales sur l'evolution et la diffusion du bucchero, in *Produzione artigianale ed esportazione nel mondo antico. Il bucchero etrusco, Atti del Colloquio Internazionale, Milano 1990* (ed. M. Bonghi Jovino), Milano, 19-41

Gran Aymerich, J.M.J., Lahanier, Chr., Gautier, J., Duval, A., Malfoy, J.M. and Boyer, C., 1985, Sur deux groupes de bucchero examinés au Louvre, *MEFRA*, 97, 611-638.

Gregori, D.,1991, Una bottega vetuloniese di buccheri ed impasti orientalizzanti, *Studi e Materiali*, 6, 64-81.

Hirschland Ramage, N., 1970, Studies in Early Etruscan Bucchero, *BSR*, 38, 1-61.

Leoni, M., and Trabucchi, C., 1962, Alcuni dati tecnici sulla colorazione nera dei buccheri etruschi, *StEtr*, 30, 257-266.

Lugli, F. and Pracchia, S., 1994, Modelli e finalità nello studio della produzione di carbone di legna in archeologia, *Origini*, 18, 425-479.

Maggiani, A., 1990, Pozzi, Casa Baldi (Seravezza). I materiali, in *"Etruscorum ante quam Ligurum". La Versilia tra VII e III secolo a.C., Catalogo della Mostra di Pietrasanta* (ed. E. Paribeni), Pontedera, 138-146.

Maglietta, M., Pallecchi, P. and Spina, G., 1999, Mössbauer and XPS Investigation of Etruscan Ceramics, *Science and Technology for Cultural Heritage*, 8 (1-2), 7-10.

Mannoni, T., 1993, Il termine "bucchero" visto alla luce delle analisi microscopiche in sezione sottile, in *Produzione artigianale ed esportazione nel mondo antico. Il bucchero etrusco, Atti del Colloquio Internazionale, Milano 1990* (ed. M. Bonghi Jovino), Milano, 224-227.

Mannoni, T. and Giannichedda E., 1996: *Archeologia della produzione*, Torino.

Monaci, M., 1965, Catalogo del Museo Archeologico Vescovile di Pienza, *StEtr*, 33, 425-468.

Monaco, M.C., 1999, Fornaci da ceramica e scarti di produzione di età classica e tardo-classica, *AM*, 114, 105-116.

Monaco, M.C., 2000, *Ergasteria. Impianti artigianali ceramici ad Atene e in Attica*, Roma.

Murray Threipland, L. and Torelli, M., 1970, A Semi-Subterranean Etruscan Building in the Casale Pian Roseto (Veii) Area, in *BSR*, 38, 62-121.

Nicosia, F., 1972, Un bucchero di Artimino, *StEtr*, 40, 375-390.

Nicosia, F., 1974, Orientalizzante nella media valle dell'Arno: aspetti dell'artigianato artistico. Prima messa a punto sulla produzione del bucchero, in *Aspetti e problemi dell'Etruria Interna, Atti dell'VIII Convegno di Studi Etruschi e Italici, Orvieto 1972*, 55-66.

Nijboer, A.J., 1998, *From Household Production to Workshops. Archaeological Evidence for Economic Transformation, pre-monetary Exchange and Urbanisation in Central Italy from 800 to 400 BC*, Gröningen.

Noble, J.V., 1965, *The Techniques of Painted Attic Pottery*, New York.

Noble, J.V., 1984, An Overview of the technology of Greek and Related Pottery, in *Ancient Greek and Related Pottery, Proceedings of the International Vase Symposium, Amsterdam 1984* (ed. H.A.G. Brijder), Amsterdam, 31-40.

Pecchiai, I., 1967, Catalogo dei buccheri del Museo Civico di Fiesole, *StEtr*, 35, 487-514.

Pemberton, E.G.,1970, The Vrysoula Classical Deposit from Ancient Corinth, in *Hesperia*, 29, 265-307.

Prückner, H., 1971, scheda n. 60, in *Katalog der Sammlung Antiker Kleinkunst des Archäologischen Instituts der Universität Heidelberg. Neuerwerbungen 1957-1970* (ed. R. Hampe), Mainz am Rein, 35-36.

Rasmussen, T.B.,1979, *Bucchero Pottery from Southern Etruria*, Cambridge.

Richter, G.M.A., 1923, *The Craft of the Athenian Pottery*, New Haven.

Richter, G.M.A., 1936, The technique of Bucchero Ware, *StEtr*, **10**, 61-65.

Rye, O.S., 1981, *Pottery Technology. Principles and Reconstruction*, Washington .

Salvini, M., 1994, L'intervento archeologico in loc. I Monti a S. Piero a Sieve: lo scavo, in *Archeologia in Alto Mugello – Val di Sieve e il Caso di S. Piero a Sieve. Atti della Giornata di Studio. S. Piero a Sieve 1994*, Firenze, 25-37.

Scalia, F., 1968, I cilindretti di tipo chiusino con figure umane, *StEtr*, **36**, 358-379.

Schleiber, I., 1983, *Griechische Töpferkunst. Herstellung, Handel und Gebrauch der antike Tongfässe*, München.

Sillar, B. and Tite, M.S. Tite, 2000, The Challenge of 'Technological Choices' for Material Science Approaches in Archaeology, *Archaeometry*, 42, 1, 2-20.

Tamburini, P., 1985, Contributo preliminare alla definizione della ceramica di impasto volsiniese e qualche nota sul bucchero mal cotto di produzione locale, *AnnFaina*, **3**, 83-98.

Wadsworth, M.,1983, A Potter's Experience with the Method of Firing Bucchero, *OpRom*, 14, 65-68.Williams, D, 1986, Greek Potters and their Descendants in Campania and Southern Etruria, c. 720-630, in *Italian Iron Age Artifacts in the British Museum, Papers of the VI British Museum Classical Colloquium, 1982* (ed. J. Swaddling), London, 295-304.

Fig. 1. Realizzazione di una carbonaia moderna nel territorio di Allumiere, RM (foto: A. Zifferero)

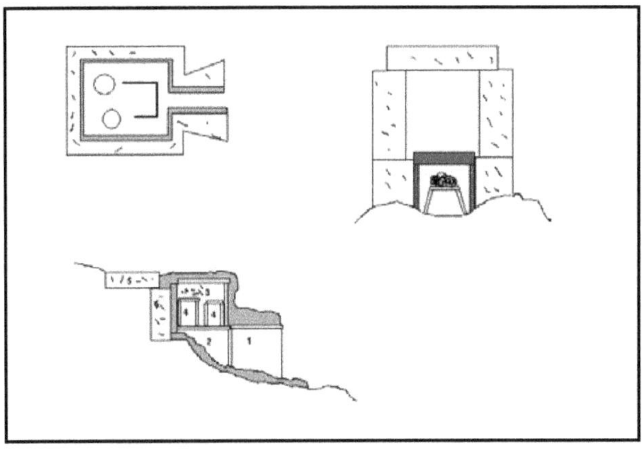

Fig. 2. Ipotesi ricostruttiva di una fornace da bucchero (da, Wadsworth 1983): 1: prefurnio; 2: camera di combustione; 3: camera di cottura; 4: contenitori per il vasellame di bucchero; 5: blocchi in tufo; 6: rivestimento in argilla refrattaria.

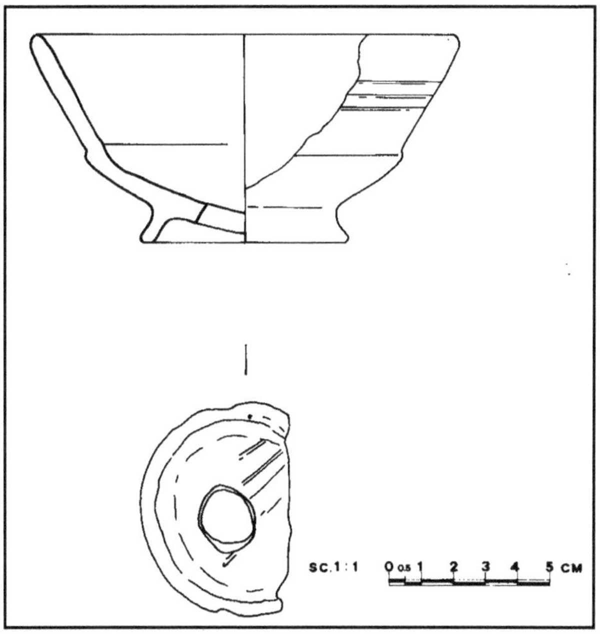

Fig. 3. Veio, località Piazza d'Armi (RM): calice di bucchero dalla cisterna nell'Area V (disegno V. Acconcia)

Fig. 4. Veio, località Piazza d'Armi (RM): calice di bucchero dalla cisterna nell'Area V, superficie esterna (foto: A. Zifferero)

Fig. 5. Veio, località Piazza d'Armi (RM): calice di bucchero dalla cisterna nell'Area V, superficie interna (foto: A. Zifferero)

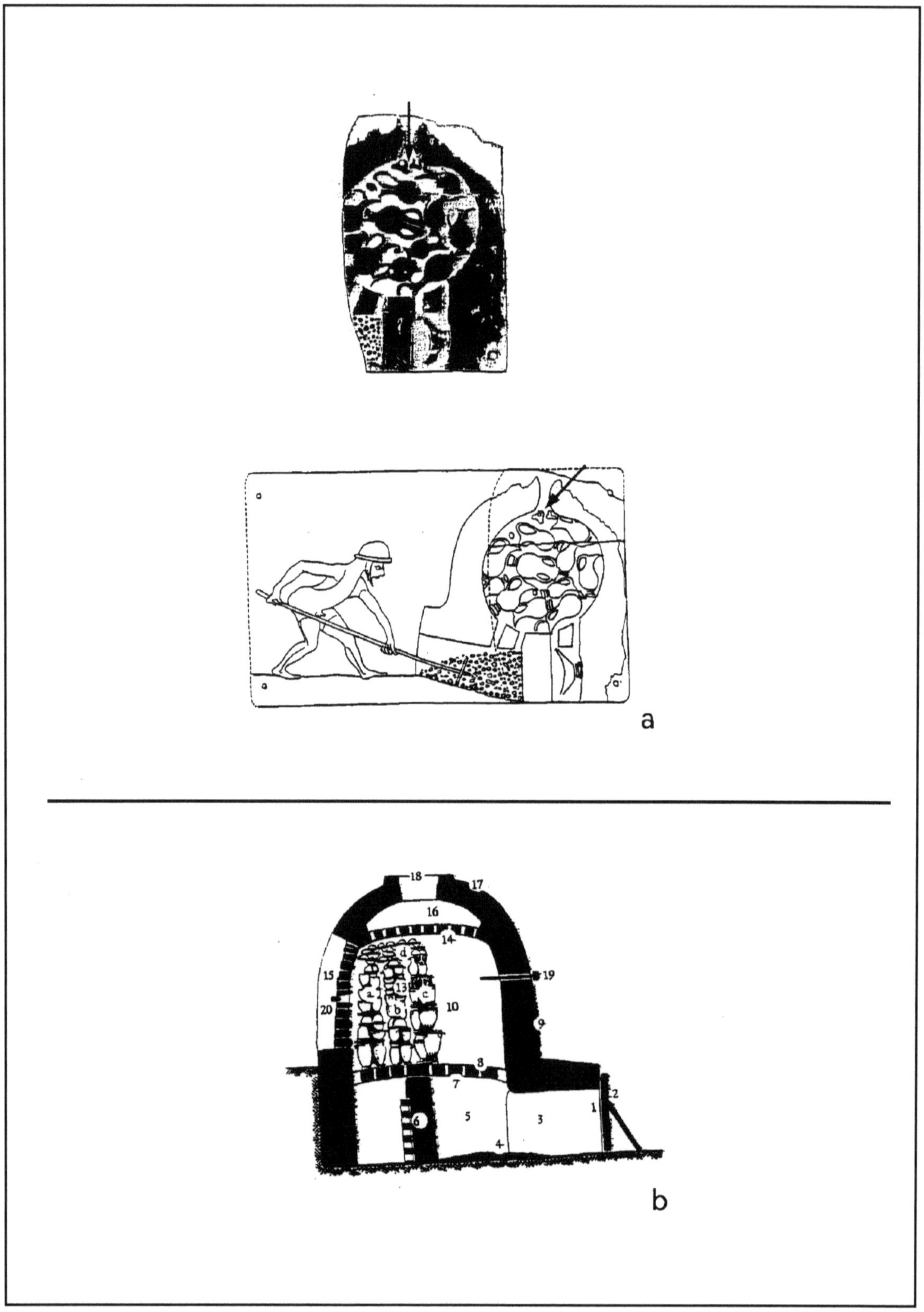

Fig. 6. a) framm. di placchetta corinzia in terracotta rappresentante l'interno di una fornace arcaica, con presenza di provini presso uno degli sfiatatoi, e ricostruzione dello stesso esemplare (da, Noble 1965); b) ricostruzione di una fornace di età classica (da, Schleiber 1983).

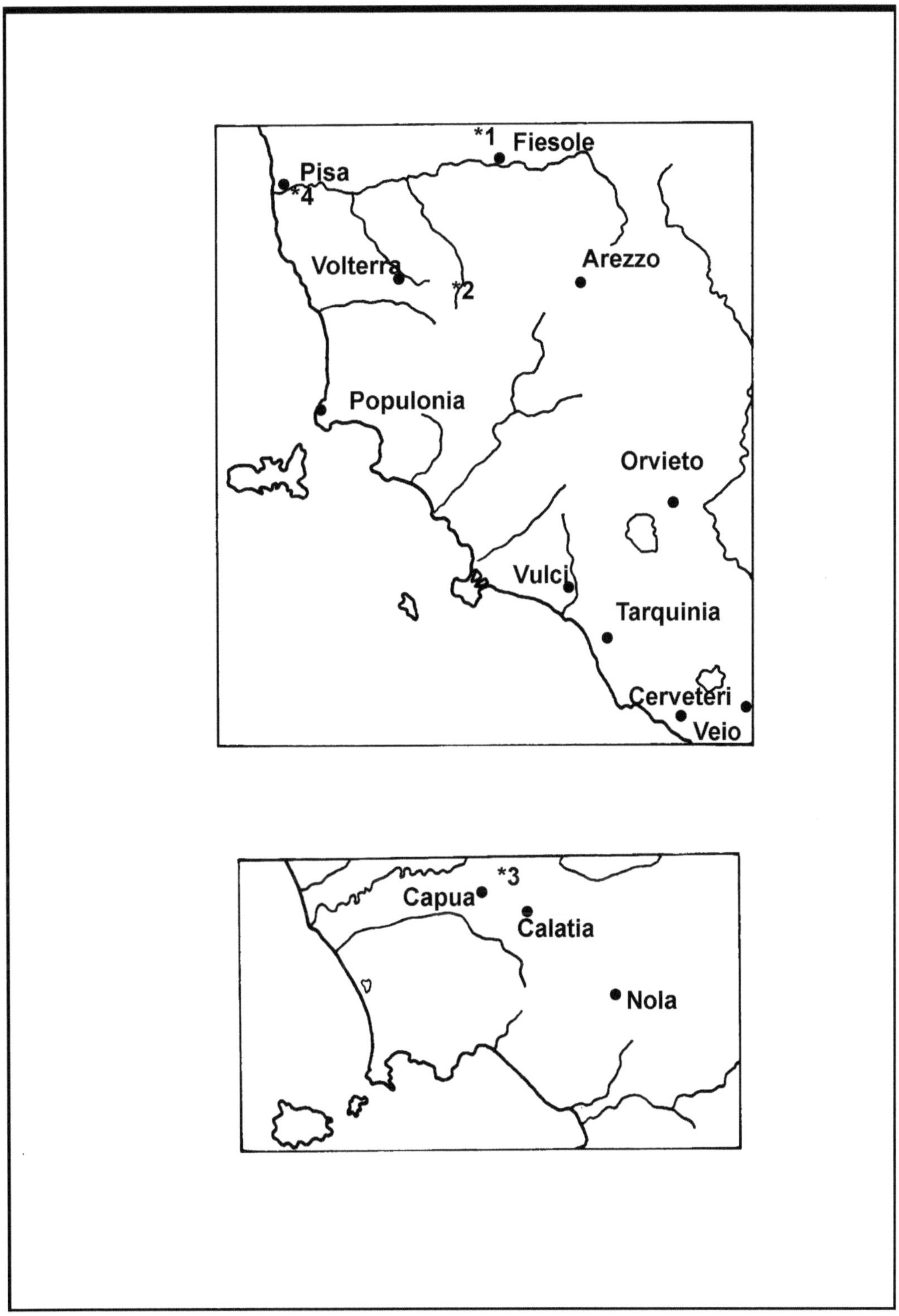

Fig. 7. posizionamento generale dei rinvenimenti di aree industriali legate alla produzione del bucchero. 1) loc. I Monti (San Piero a Sieve; FI); 2) loc. Quartana (Colle Vald'Elsa; SI); 3) loc. Montecastello (Pontelatone; CE); 4: via Tommaso Vanni (Pisa)

NUOVI DATI SULLA PRODUZIONE E SULLA CIRCOLAZIONE DELLA CERAMICA ITALIOTA A FIGURE ROSSE NEL IV SECOLO A.C. A LOCRI EPIZEFIRI

Diego ELIA
(Università di Torino)

ABSTRACT: Locri Epizefiri, a *polis* founded by Greek colonists on the Ionian coast of Calabria, has yielded abundant evidence for the manufacture and circulation of figured pottery during the 4th century BC. This paper proposes an approach to this material in a way that links traditional stylistic analysis, the study of distributional patterns and workshop organization, as well as archaeometric analysis. This research suggests that Locri was an important and original center of production and allows us to deepen our knowledge of the historical, cultural and economic context in which the ceramic *ateliers* operated.*

L'identificazione e la localizzazione dei centri di produzione rappresentano evidentemente un problema centrale nella ricerca archeologica in quanto la determinazione 'topografica' di una produzione permette di attribuire coordinate spaziali ad una complessa ed articolata serie di fenomeni storici, quali ad esempio la fisionomia di un centro produttivo, la sua capacità di diffusione dei manufatti, la direzionalità dei contatti commerciali (Blondé e Perreault 1992; Blondé e Muller 1998; Villanueva Puig *et al.* 1999).

Nel caso della ceramica figurata, in particolare, la localizzazione di singoli *ateliers* consente di definire spazialmente un numero elevato di fattori connessi a questo artigianato di pregio, permettendo innanzi tutto di delineare i tratti originali dell'*imagerie* propria del centro produttore rispetto alle realizzazioni coeve, ma anche di contestualizzare più puntualmente i caratteri della produzione delle singole botteghe, il loro sviluppo e la diffusione del patrimonio figurativo, i modi di contatto e di trasmissione degli schemi iconografici, i criteri della selezione di determinate forme vascolari in rapporto alla funzione ed al ruolo rivestito sia nelle pratiche della vita quotidiana, sia nell'ambito dei riti funerari.

Nonostante queste premesse, nello studio della ceramica figurata di produzione occidentale, a partire dalla fine degli anni '30 del secolo scorso, è prevalsa l'impostazione classificatoria elaborata da Arthur Dale Trendall (1967, 1983, 1989), che costituisce una sistematizzazione stilistica del materiale figurato basata su criteri attribuzionistici; tale prospettiva ha posto per molti decenni ai margini della ricerca la localizzazione dei centri di produzione, nonché le problematiche connesse alla fabbricazione ed al commercio di questa peculiare classe ceramica (Lippolis 1996).

Solo negli ultimi anni si è andata affermando una nuova sensibilità, rivolta principalmente alla dimensione storica delle problematiche connesse alla ceramica figurata e caratterizzata da una particolare attenzione ai contesti di rinvenimento (Pontrandolfo 1991; Denoyelle *et al.* 2000); questa impostazione ha evidenziato come la definizione dei luoghi e dei modi di produzione, nonché l'analisi della diffusione e della circolazione dei prodotti dei singoli *ateliers* di questa prestigiosa classe ceramica, costituiscano un significativo osservatorio per indagare la realtà artigianale e le forme di contatto e di commercio nell'Occidente greco tra gli ultimi decenni del V ed il secolo successivo.

In questo senso la *polis* magnogreca di Locri Epizefiri rappresenta un caso sintomatico e di particolare interesse per quanto riguarda i problemi inerenti la produzione e la circolazione della ceramica figurata occidentale nel corso del IV secolo. In particolare le caratteristiche della documentazione locrese consentono di verificare l'ipotesi che la ricchezza dei rinvenimenti sia riconducibile a prevalenti ed iterati contatti commerciali con aree esterne -in particolare la Sicilia, come è stato proposto (Spigo 1987: 3; Spigo 2000: 32)- o se piuttosto essa non si debba attribuire ad un'articolata produzione locale, con il concorso di artigiani di formazione differenziata.

Ricordo brevemente che la prima ipotesi è stata sostenuta sulla base della presenza in Sicilia di alcuni vasi di particolare impegno attribuiti al Gruppo di Locri, i cui prodotti sono altrimenti ampiamente attestati a Locri, nonché sulla base delle accentuate affinità stilistiche e formali di questa bottega con produzioni coeve localizzate nell'isola, quali il Gruppo della Scacchiera ed i Pittori di Himera e Santapaola (Trendall 1983: 30; Spigo 1987: 3; Spigo 2000: 34).

Tuttavia se considerazioni di ordine stilistico e inerenti la distribuzione dei prodotti di un'officina costituiscono importanti elementi di valutazione, a mio avviso queste devono essere confrontate con una serie più ampia di informazioni al fine di definire con sufficiente attendibilità l'identità del luogo di fabbricazione.

A questo proposito ricordo che Villard e Blondé (1992; 1999) hanno efficacemente delineato alcuni elementi discriminanti per la verifica dell'esistenza di una produzione ceramica locale, che possono essere applicati al caso in esame:
a) disponibilità di un significativo lotto di reperti rinvenuti nell'area produttiva indiziata, con caratteristiche nettamente distinguibili dalle produzioni importate;
b) possibilità di riconoscere nelle forme e nella decorazione una creazione originale ad opera di artigiani locali, pur sotto l'influenza esercitata da prodotti importati;
c) ritrovamento di specifiche installazioni produttive oppure, in mancanza di queste, analisi chimico-fisiche sul corpo ceramico finalizzate ad evidenziarne i caratteri peculiari e le differenze rispetto ad altre produzioni.

La documentazione a Locri Epizefiri
A Locri Epizefiri, fin dalle prime decadi del secolo scorso, le esplorazioni condotte da Paolo Orsi nelle aree funerarie portarono alla luce una ricca documentazione di vasi deposti nei corredi e un'abbondante messe di frammenti rinvenuti nel cosiddetto "soprassuolo della necropoli" (Orsi 1911, 1912, 1913, 1917; Spigo 1980; Elia 2001; Elia, *Nelle case di Ade*).

Gli scavi effettuati a partire dagli anni '50 nell'area dell'abitato hanno ulteriormente confermato l'ampia diffusione di questa classe ceramica a Locri (Spigo 1977; Sguaitamatti 1992), arricchendo significativamente la documentazione disponibile che raggiunge ormai le 150 attestazioni (forme intere e frammenti), quantità che si rivela in continuo incremento.

A fronte di questa documentazione cospicua dal punto di vista quantitativo, un motivo di interesse è rappresentato dal fatto che il panorama delle presenze evidenzia la ricorrente attestazione di un numero limitato di ceramografi (Sguaitamatti 1992: 173; Elia 2000) che rivelano accentuate affinità di tipo stilistico e compositivo. Tra questi sono stati da tempo segnalati gli artigiani raccolti nel Gruppo di Locri e -in misura sensibilmente inferiore sotto l'aspetto quantitativo- il Pittore dell'Erote inginocchiato e il Pittore della Pisside RC 5089 (Elia 2000: Fig. 1). Un computo parziale sulla base dei dati editi e di alcuni rinvenimenti ancora inediti (Elia, *Nelle case di Ade*: Appendici I-III) evidenzia infatti come queste produzioni corrispondano ad oltre il 75% delle presenze registrate nei primi due terzi del IV secolo, periodo in cui si concentra la diffusione di questa classe ceramica a Locri.

La già ricordata diffusione in area siciliana di vasi del Gruppo di Locri è stata origine in passato di molteplici valutazioni che hanno portato ad ipotizzare uno sviluppo prevalente di questa bottega in Sicilia, tuttavia le caratteristiche della distribuzione della ceramica figurata a Locri hanno permesso di proporre l'ipotesi che tale quadro rifletta piuttosto la presenza in questo centro di un'articolata produzione locale, confermata dall'analisi stilistica e formale delle opere di questi *ateliers* (Elia, *Nelle case di Ade*), nonché dagli areali di distribuzione delle singole produzioni (Fig. 1; Elia 2000). Tale proposta sembrerebbe trovare conferma anche dall'analisi della sequenza produttiva del Gruppo di Locri, che evidenzia come la documentazione dall'area calabrese corrisponda ad una fase successiva rispetto alle opere iniziali (Spigo 2000; Elia 2000). Rimando per gli aspetti stilistici e distributivi ai relativi contributi editi[1], mentre mi pare opportuno presentare a conferma dell'ipotesi avanzata alcuni nuovi elementi di valutazione.

Le forme vascolari
Un elemento di analisi ancora poco utilizzato negli studi dedicati alla produzione figurata occidentale è rappresentato dal panorama delle forme vascolari adottate dalle singole botteghe, che consente di formulare significative osservazioni di carattere produttivo.

In questo senso la distribuzione delle realizzazioni riconducibili al Gruppo di Locri appare particolarmente indicativa, in quanto le presenze in Sicilia e a Locri divergono in modo evidente (Fig. 2)[2]. Se si escludono infatti i crateri, che costituiscono circa la metà dei vasi ricondotti a questa bottega, in Sicilia si registra la peculiare presenza di forme chiuse di grandi o medie dimensioni, come l'*hydria* di Siracusa e la *pelike* di Vassallaggi, con soluzioni talvolta piuttosto ricercate ed insolite, come il *deinos* di Selinunte o l'anfora di Agrigento; l'unica forma di ridotte proporzioni attestata nell'area insulare è rappresentata dallo *skyphos* (5 esemplari)[3].

Le forme chiuse appaiono invece assenti a Locri, dove anche le attestazioni degli *skyphoi* sono episodiche (3 frammenti). Al contrario sono presenti, accanto ai già citati crateri, numerosi vasi di medie e soprattutto piccole dimensioni, tra i quali prevalente risulta senza dubbio la *lekane* (pari a ca. il 20% delle attestazioni), predominante anche nelle produzioni dei Pittori dell'Erote inginocchiato e della Pisside RC 5089. Tale forma, per lo più adottata dai ceramografi ricondotti al Gruppo di Locri piuttosto che dal Pittore omonimo[4], risulta del tutto assente al di fuori del sito calabrese, dove invece negli stessi decenni essa è ampiamente attestata anche da una eterogenea serie di esemplari decorati esclusivamente con motivi geometrici o fitomorfi (Fig. 3,f-i)[5]. Si tratta di vasi che presentano dimensioni e profili pressoché identici alle *lekanai* figurate (Fig. 3,l-m) e che appaiono verosimilmente riconducibili alle stesse officine: i motivi decorativi risultano infatti tratti dalla decorazione accessoria di queste ultime, con cui condividono anche un *miltos* di colore rosso, caratteristico delle produzioni figurate rinvenute a Locri (Trendall 1967: 74). Gli esemplari alla Fig. 3 costituiscono una significativa esemplificazione di questa produzione, che fra i tratti comuni annovera il largo e basso piede ad anello, la vasca ampia e poco profonda con fascia ad aggetto al di sotto della battuta, nonché il coperchio con tesa quasi orizzontale, tozzo stelo e largo pomello a disco. Queste *lekanai* possono presentare una decorazione realizzata nella tecnica delle figure rosse, oppure a vernice sul fondo risparmiato, con motivi che trovano confronto in area siciliana[6].

Del tutto caratteristici nell'ambito dei ritrovamenti figurati operati a Locri risultano invece gli esemplari sovraddimensionati di *lekane*, produzione 'monumentale' estremamente peculiare, recentemente segnalata a proposito di un frammento di coperchio dalla necropoli (Elia, *Nelle case di Ade*: n. LF13; v. anche Elia 2000).

Una conferma della fortuna nel centro locrese di questa forma, per la quale i confronti in Occidente sono estremamente rari, è rappresentata dal recente riconoscimento di due ulteriori frammenti di coperchio, uno dal sep. 749 (Appendice n. 1; Fig. 4,a), con diametro dell'orlo pari a 46 cm, ed uno da contesto ignoto (Appendice n. 2; Fig. 4,d).

Ad ulteriore testimonianza di questa diffusione, il riordino dei materiali scavati dall'Orsi (Elia 2001) ha permesso di identificare il colossale esemplare rinvenuto nel sep. 1502 (Appendice n. 3; Fig. 4,b-c) -purtroppo anch'esso assai lacunoso- alto oltre 34 cm (privo del piede), con diametro del coperchio pari a 49 cm e diametro del pomello di 18,8 cm (Fig. 3,a): si tratta di un rinvenimento già segnalato dallo scavatore (Orsi 1917: 135, fig. 40), ma rimasto fino ad ora irreperibile.

In tutti i casi citati comunque, nonostante lo stato frammentario dei reperti, l'attribuzione al Gruppo di Locri risulta ben documentabile (v. Appendice).

La frequente ricorrenza della *lekane* sovraddimensionata a Locri, in particolare nei contesti funerari, è ulteriormente confermata da una vasca lacunosa dal sep. 1210 (diametro max di 32 cm) (Elia 2001: 214, Fig. 32) e da un gruppo di 4 pomelli sporadici dalla necropoli (diametro compreso tra 11 e 17 cm), sicuramente pertinenti ad esemplari di grandi dimensioni; questi ultimi possono recare una decorazione fitomorfa (Fig. 3,b), oppure risultano completamente verniciati (Fig. 3,c-e); non esistono evidentemente elementi sufficienti per un inquadramento stilistico, ma le dimensioni sembrano comprovarne la pertinenza allo stesso ambito produttivo dei precedenti.

Ritornando al confronto tra le forme vascolari del Gruppo di Locri diffuse in Sicilia e quelle rinvenute nel centro calabrese, emerge con evidenza la presenza a Locri di numerose forme, per lo più di piccole dimensioni, altrove assenti e stilisticamente affini alle *lekanai* (Fig. 2). Queste realizzazioni rappresentano veri e propri *unica* nella produzione di questa officina e sono spesso prive di confronto nella coeva produzione figurata occidentale. Significativo a questo proposito risulta il noto bariletto dal sep. 884 (Fig. 5,a), la cui forma sembra costituire un'elaborazione originale di questo *atelier*[7]; questa sorta di *askos* cilindrico appare infatti ulteriormente attestato da due frammenti: il primo (Appendice n. 4; Fig. 5,b), con versatoio configurato a protome leonina, rappresenta un ritrovamento sporadico dalla necropoli in contrada Lucifero, mentre il secondo è stato recentemente rinvenuto nell'area dell'abitato[8].

Particolarmente indicativa risulta anche l'originale scelta operata a Locri da questa bottega a proposito delle coppe, come testimoniano una coppia di *kylikes* su stelo (tomba 7 dello scavo del 1956; Elia, *Nelle case di Ade*: FR15-16), forma ben attestata nella coeva produzione attica (Campenon 1994: 64-68) ma altrimenti assai rara in Occidente soprattutto nell'area più meridionale, e l'inedita versione figurata di una coppa a pareti sottili rinvenuta nella zona dell'abitato[9].

Tra le realizzazioni più curiose rientrano anche le riproduzioni miniaturistiche di cratere; all'esemplare integro del sep. 162, riconosciuto da U. Spigo (1980: 584, n. 9; 2000: 44), si può ora avvicinare un frammento sporadico dalla necropoli (Appendice n. 5; Fig. 4,f).

La varietà dei supporti vascolari utilizzati è infine ribadita dall'*askos* lenticolare dal sep. 83 (Spigo 1991: 56, Fig. 9), forma attestata anche da un frammento inedito dall'abitato[10], e da una rara (a Locri) *lekythos* ariballica (Appendice n. 6; Fig. 5,c), sporadica dalla necropoli di Lucifero.

Considerate le accentuate peculiarità del repertorio vascolare del gruppo di Locri attestate nel centro locrese rispetto alla coeva produzione figurata occidentale, appare verosimile mettere in rapporto le scelte operate nella produzione di questa bottega con le richieste del mercato locale: l'analisi della necropoli evidenzia ad esempio come la deposizione delle originali forme con versatoio (bariletto, *askos*) o miniaturistiche (cratere) ricorra costantemente in contesti pertinenti ad individui defunti prima dell'età adulta, mentre la presenza di *lekanai* monumentali corrisponda a particolari forme del rito funerario che coinvolgono anche i crateri (Elia, *Nelle case di Ade*).

Una conferma indiretta di questa ricercatezza nella selezione e nella creazione delle forme vascolari è rappresentata dalle attestazioni ricondotte al Gruppo dell'Erote inginocchiato -tra le quali la *lekane* appare assolutamente predominante- e soprattutto al Pittore RC 5089, tra le cui attribuzioni, oltre alle immancabili *lekanai*, compaiono due insoliti prodotti. Il primo è rappresentato da un frammento di situla a beccuccio (Elia, *Nelle case di Ade*: n. FR39), originale forma munita di versatoio, altrimenti attestata a Locri da un esemplare integro (Orsi 1913: 42-44) -ricondotto dallo Spigo allo stile del Pittore di Maron (Spigo 1977: 146; Spigo: 1980: 385-386; Bernabò Brea e Cavalier 1997: 69)- e da un frammento decorato con protome plastica (Elia, *Nelle case di Ade*: n. C76); nel secondo caso, inedito, si tratta invece della spalla (?) di una forma chiusa (Appendice n. 7; Fig. 6,c) dal profilo del tutto insolito, forse identificabile come un sostegno.

Le caratteristiche di questo gruppo di reperti evidenziano la specificità delle forme vascolari del Gruppo rinvenute a Locri rispetto alla Sicilia, nonché l'omogeneità con la produzione dei Pittori dell'Erote inginocchiato e della Pisside RC 5089, confermando l'ipotesi di una produzione locale che presenta carattere innovativo e sperimentale in merito alle forme vascolari: in questo senso sembra infatti interpretabile l'adozione di vasi altrimenti rari o inutilizzati nella produzione figurata occidentale (*lekane* 'monumentale', bariletto, *kylix* su stelo, cratere miniaturistico) oppure il ricorso a forme di norma realizzate solo nella versione a vernice nera (*askos* lenticolare, coppa a pareti sottili).

Considerazioni di ordine cronologico

L'analisi dei corredi rinvenuti da Paolo Orsi consente di individuare alcuni elementi utili a definire più puntualmente la cronologia delle produzioni attestate a Locri.

La novità di maggiore interesse è rappresentata dalla ricostruzione originaria del corredo del noto sepolcro 1119, da cui provengono tre crateri attribuiti al Pittore di Locri (Trendall 1983: 30, nn. 374-375; Spigo 2000: 47, nota 2). Rispetto alla situazione descritta dall'Orsi (1917: 106-111), la documentazione di scavo permette infatti di individuare la presenza originaria di un ulteriore vaso, una *lekane* rinvenuta deposta all'interno del cratere a campana[11]. L'analisi stilistica del vaso, solo recentemente isolato tra i materiali della necropoli, permette un'attribuzione al Pittore della Pisside RC 5089, nonostante la ridotta porzione di coperchio conservato (Appendice n. 8; Fig. 6,b). Tale riconoscimento risulta assai pregnante in quanto, per la prima volta, si individua a Locri l'associazione all'interno della stessa tomba di opere attribuibili a botteghe 'locresi' distinte.

La presenza del Pittore RC 5089 nella tomba 1119 permette di proporre per questo contesto una datazione non anteriore al secondo quarto del IV secolo. Si tratta infatti di un ceramografo inizialmente ricondotto dal Trendall alla produzione protosiceliota e protocampana (Trendall 1967: 220, n. 113) e successivamente avvicinato al Pittore di Lentini (Trendall 1989: 113), per il quale lo Spigo ha evidenziato affinità con la produzione del Gruppo Nyn e con altri rinvenimenti eoliani (Spigo 2000: 40-41); recentemente ne sono state riconosciute alcune nuove attestazioni a Locri (Elia 2001; Elia, *Nelle case di Ade*, Appendice III). Per questa produzione è stata proposta una cronologia tra il secondo quarto del IV e il primo decennio della seconda metà dello stesso secolo (Spigo 1987: 5), ipotesi che appare sostanzialmente confermata dal sep. 1119. Questo corredo sembra infatti restituire il più antico termine cronologico noto per questo ceramografo[12], mentre un momento più avanzato, caratterizzato dal modo disegnativo meno accurato e dall'uso più spregiudicato del colore sovraddipinto, è rappresentato dalla pisside eponima, proveniente da un contesto con ceramica riconducibile alla fase iniziale della produzione sovraddipinta (sep. 1264), databile al decennio 350-340 a.C.[13] Al tempo stesso il corredo del sep. 1119 rappresenta un fondamentale indicatore cronologico per la diffusione a Locri del Gruppo omonimo -e in particolare del Pittore- nel corso del secondo quarto del IV secolo.

Una conferma della diffusione dei prodotti del Gruppo di Locri in un momento avanzato della prima metà del IV è rappresentata per altro dal corredo del sep. 749 (Orsi 1913: 30-32), sulla cui originaria composizione sono state avanzate riserve. Tuttavia il riesame della documentazione d'archivio ha confermato che la tomba ad arconi fittili semicilindrici fu rinvenuta ben conservata, con le ossa dello scheletro ancora in connessione anatomica e lo spazio interno quasi completamente libero da terriccio; all'interno erano deposti, tra gli altri oggetti, il già ricordato frammento di coperchio pertinente ad una *lekane* monumentale[14] ed una *lekythos* Pagenstecher (Fig. 6,d; Orsi 1913: Fig. 36). Quest'ultima reca l'immagine di un cinghiale in corsa, al di sopra di un basso pilastrino (o un altare?) su cui sono deposte 5 piccole sfere di colore bianco (uova?); in alto, appesa, è una palla quadripartita. Lo stile accurato del disegno, il sobrio utilizzo del colore sovraddipinto, il profilo del vaso e il motivo decorativo accessorio del largo fiore campanato con pistillo allungato sembrano suggerire una cronologia nella prima metà del IV secolo, verosimilmente al secondo quarto[15].

Nella necropoli di Lucifero questo orizzonte avanzato per il Gruppo di Locri presenta come termine inferiore il corredo del sep. 884, databile alla metà del secolo, dove il già citato bariletto risulta associato ad una situla a beccuccio attribuita al Pittore di Maron (Spigo 1987: 4-5); tale datazione è per altro confermata dalla tomba liparota 1155, dove un cratere del Gruppo di Locri è in associazione con il vaso eponimo del Pittore di Adrasto (Spigo 2000).

Una cronologia ai decenni 380-350 a.C. per la presenza di questa officina a Locri risulta ulteriormente attestata dalle forme a vernice nera associate nei sepp. 83, 1242, ed in particolare dalle varianti di coppa a pareti sottili (4200 A3; Buzzi Auxilia 1989: 124) e di bolsal (4100 A4; Buzzi Auxila 1989: 113-114) presenti nel sep. 975 (Elia 2001). Questa datazione è inoltre confermata dalle già ricordate *lekanai* con decorazione floreale o geometrica, alcune delle quali associate ad esemplari figurati (sepp. 162, 892, 1242, 1219).

Il quadro cronologico che si viene a delineare, dunque, evidenzia ulteriormente la coerenza e l'omogeneità della documentazione locrese, fornendo ulteriore sostegno all'ipotesi di una produzione locale. Rispetto ai contesti siciliani che hanno restituito vasi del Gruppo di Locri, infatti, emerge qui un orizzonte più avanzato, dal momento che i corredi della *pelike* di Vassallaggi e del *deinos* di Selinunte sono accomunati da una datazione compresa tra la fine del V e i primi decenni del secolo successivo (Spigo 2000: 33-34).

Analisi archeometriche

Gli elementi finora analizzati, sia di ordine stilistico e distributivo (in dettaglio in Elia 2000), che di carattere produttivo e cronologico, sembrano dunque confermare l'ipotesi che, a partire dagli anni centrali della prima metà del IV fino al primo decennio della seconda metà, si sia sviluppata a Locri Epizefiri un'intensa esperienza produttiva nell'ambito della ceramica figurata, parallela a quella più seriale e corrente della ceramica a vernice nera, con il concorso di numerosi artigiani organizzati in una o più botteghe strettamente collegate e stilisticamente influenzati dallo sviluppo delle officine tradizionalmente collocate in area siciliana e tirrenica[16]. L'attività di questi ceramografi corrisponderebbe dunque ad un importante segmento della sequenza produttiva dell'*atelier* del Gruppo di Locri, nonché a quella delle botteghe dei Pittori dell'Erote inginocchiato e della Pisside RC 5089.

Assai più limitata parrebbe invece l'incidenza di reperti importati: rispetto al ridotto quadro delle presunte importazioni dall'area siciliana delineato dallo Spigo (1987: 17, nota 21), per le quali è stata proposta una relazione con una via commerciale intermedia dalla Sicilia alla Campania (Giudice 1985: 256), scarse sono infatti le attestazioni aggiuntesi negli ultimi anni[17].

Un tassello fondamentale al quadro sin qui delineato è stato restituito dai risultati di un ampio progetto di analisi archeometriche applicate alle ceramiche figurate, la cui prima fase, rivolta ad una selezione di reperti rinvenuti a Locri, è stata recentemente portata a termine[18].

Tale progetto, condotto in collaborazione con il prof. Piero Mirti ed i dott. Monica Gulmini e Marco Pace, membri del suo gruppo di ricerca nell'ambito del Dipartimento di Chimica Analitica dell'Università di Torino, si è avvalso della spettroscopia di emissione con eccitazione mediante plasma ad accoppiamento induttivo, consolidato metodo di analisi che permette l'individuazione di 18 elementi chimici, dai componenti maggiori a quelli in traccia, e consente la raccolta di un ampio spettro di dati sulla composizione, finalizzata a studi di provenienza. Tale progetto si è innestato su una prima fase di analisi dedicata alle produzioni di ceramica fine a vernice nera in cui erano stati analizzati 55 campioni; tra questi era un cospicuo lotto di frammenti ricondotto a botteghe locali sulla base dell'esame autottico delle argille, dei rivestimenti e del profilo delle forme; alcuni frammenti presentavano inoltre evidenti tracce di cottura irregolare (Mirti *et al.* 1995). Queste analisi hanno permesso di evidenziare l'omogeneità della composizione chimica di questo gruppo di campioni compresi tra la fine del V e il III secolo, nettamente distinguibile da quelle dei materiali importati.

Utilizzando questo insieme come gruppo di controllo, si è dunque proceduto alla campionatura di un ampio lotto di ceramiche figurate. I prelievi hanno riguardato un totale di 39 reperti (vasi interi e frammenti), di cui 11 attici e 28 di produzione occidentale; di questi ultimi 16 sono attribuibili al Gruppo di Locri -tra cui alcuni riconducibili al Pittore omonimo, come il coperchio della *lekane* del sep. 749- e 4 ai Pittori dell'Erote inginocchiato e della Pisside RC 5089; inoltre è stato inserito un frammento di coperchio con decorazione geometrica su fondo risparmiato, pertinente all'eterogeneo gruppo di *lekanai* già descritto (Elia, *Nelle case di Ade*: n. FR50).

Le analisi hanno confermato la netta distinzione tra la composizione della ceramica attica e quella delle produzioni occidentali, ma hanno altresì evidenziato un'accentuata similarità tra le ceramiche fini locresi a vernice nera e quelle figurate; queste ultime non appaiono infatti distinguibili sulla base della composizione chimica, riflettendo un'omogeneità che costituisce un'importante conferma della produzione locale a figure rosse.

Un ulteriore aspetto, tuttavia, deve essere preso in considerazione, in quanto tra i reperti selezionati per l'indagine archeometrica è stato scelto anche un limitato gruppo di 6 campioni di ceramiche figurate attribuite ad officine siceliote. Oltre a 2 frammenti che conservano solo parti molto ridotte della decorazione, confrontabili con prodotti del Gruppo Prado-Fienga (Elia, *Nelle case di Ade*, nn. FR41-42), il lotto comprende i frammenti di un cratere dall'abitato attribuiti dal Trendall al Pittore Prado-Fienga (Trendall 1983: 109, n. 136) e dallo Spigo al Gruppo di Dirce (Spigo 1977: 137-139, n. C59), nonché un coperchio lacunoso di *lekane* riferito genericamente ad un "ceramografo siceliota di età dionigiana" (Spigo 1977: 129-130, n. C51; Spigo 1987: 17, nota 21). A questi è stato associato un frammento inedito pertinente ad una pisside skyphoide di dimensioni colossali dall'area funeraria di contrada Parapezza, che trova puntuali confronti nella produzione del Pittore di Dirce[19] (Appendice n. 9; Fig. 5,d).

Completa il quadro dei campioni "sicelioti" un pomello di *lekane* dalla necropoli in contrada Monaci (Appendice n. 10; Fig. 6,e), che presenta uno schema decorativo ampiamente diffuso nella produzione siceliota a partire dai decenni centrali del IV secolo e di norma assente sulle *lekanai* delle botteghe locresi[20].

Rispetto alle valutazioni emerse sulla base dell'esame stilistico, i risultati delle analisi archeometriche hanno evidenziato una composizione chimica del corpo ceramico in tutto simile al 'gruppo locrese' descritto in precedenza, comprendente produzioni figurate e a vernice nera, suggerendo una comune provenienza per tutti i campioni.

Tale dato delinea evidentemente uno scenario inedito, in cui l'attività di ceramografi tradizionalmente ricondotti all'area siciliana e campana potrebbe avere conosciuto una fase produttiva a Locri. Si tratta di un risultato di particolare suggestione che sembra offrire un rilevante elemento di valutazione per la comprensione storica della diffusione dei prodotti di queste botteghe ed un importante tassello per lo studio della circolazione della ceramica figurata nella prima metà del IV secolo. Il campione analizzato è tuttavia eccessivamente ridotto per consentire di trarre conclusioni definitive, per cui appare necessario il prosieguo della ricerca; questa, avvalendosi delle previste nuove fasi di campionamento, potrà offrire un quadro più ampio e completo per ponderare i dati sinora emersi[21].

Appendice

1) Frammento di coperchio di *lekane* sovraddimensionata (Fig. 4,a); da Locri, necropoli in contrada Lucifero, sep. 749 (n. inv. 4633; Museo Archeologico Nazionale di Reggio Calabria, in esposizione; Elia 2001: 213-214, n. 749/7, Fig. 14).

Descrizione: la porzione di tesa conserva la parte inferiore di tre figure femminili volte verso destra; il personaggio più arretrato, separato dagli altri due da un elemento vegetale con boccioli triangolari, sembra essere raffigurato in corsa. Sull'orlo si sviluppa una decorazione a gruppi di tre meandri intervallati da riquadri con motivo a scacchiera.

Nonostante la limitatezza della porzione conservata è possibile riconoscere nella *lekane* un prodotto del Gruppo di Locri: in particolare i panneggi trovano strettissime affinità con il noto cratere della follia di Licurgo dal sep. 1119, attribuito al Pittore omonimo (Trendall 1967: 74, n. 374); le similitudini formali e disegnative risultano tanto strette da indurre a pensare ad un'unica mano, come suggeriscono lo schema delle pieghe dell'*himation* e del chitone sottostante, il disegno degli orli con una spessa linea a vernice, il caratteristico motivo ad archetti sulle stoffe (cfr. ad es. Fig. 4,e); anche il disegno vivace della veste del primo personaggio a sinistra, forse rappresentato in corsa, trova puntuale confronto nel mosso panneggio della donna in fuga da Licurgo sul medesimo cratere.

2) Frammento di coperchio di *lekane* sovraddimensionata (Fig. 4,d); da Locri, contesto ignoto (non inv.; Museo Archeologico Nazionale di Reggio Calabria, non esposto; inedito).

Descrizione: il lacerto di tesa conserva la parte superiore di due personaggi femminili volti verso sinistra; quello sulla sinistra ha i capelli raccolti in un gonfio *sakkos*, quello a destra reca una cassettina decorata nella mano sinistra, mentre porta in alto il braccio destro teso.

Il frammento risulta genericamente riconducibile al Gruppo di Locri sulla base dell'approssimativo disegno della mano e della bocca resa con un archetto volto verso il basso; ricorrente risulta anche il disegno della bandoliera a X incrociata sul petto (cfr. Elia, *Nelle case di Ade*, n. FR13). In questo caso la resa appare particolarmente sommaria e poco curata, con un'accentuata rigidità nei panneggi, quale si registra ad esempio sul cratere da Lipari, datato alla metà del IV secolo a.C. (Spigo 2000: Figg. 6-10).

3) *Lekane* sovraddimensionata, frammentaria e lacunosa (Figg. 3,b-c); da Locri, necropoli in contrada Lucifero, sep. 1502 (nn. inv. 113338, 113344, 113349; Museo Archeologico Nazionale di Reggio Calabria, non esposta; Elia 2001: 214-215, Figg. 15, 32).

Descrizione: mentre la vasca si conserva in gran parte, del coperchio restano solamente due ampi frammenti; nel primo è la parte superiore di due figure femminili volte verso destra, precedute da un mostro marino di cui si riconosce un tratto di una spira crestata; nel secondo si conservano in parte tre figure femminili panneggiate.

Le teste dei personaggi femminili con i lunghi capelli sciolti sul collo e sulle spalle (Fig. 4,b) mostrano evidenti analogie con vasi attribuiti al Pittore di Locri, quali il cratere da Gela (Spigo 1987: Fig. 1) e quello recentemente riconosciuto a Locri nella tomba 13 (scavo 1956; Elia, *Nelle case di Ade*, n. FR1). Analogamente la posa degli *himatia* (Fig. 4,c), ripropone lo schema caratteristico di questa produzione: la veste scende dalla spalla sinistra ed avvolge strettamente il braccio corrispondente, cingendo la vita e lasciando scoperto il lato destro; in questo caso il disegno appare poco accurato, come in alcune realizzazioni che sembrano collocarsi in un momento avanzato della produzione di questo ceramografo. Anche la decorazione accessoria conferma l'attribuzione a questo ambito stilistico; in particolare le coppie di palmette affrontate e disposte in diagonale sulla fascia sottostante la battuta (Orsi 1917: 135, Fig. 40) trovano puntuale confronto in un cratere a calice dalla tomba 1119 (Trendall 1967: 76, n. 386), anch'esso recentemente ricondotto alla mano del Pittore di Locri (Spigo 2000: 47, nota 2).

4) Frammento di bariletto (Fig. 5,b); da Locri, necropoli in contrada Lucifero, rinvenimento sporadico (n. inv. MAC 466; Museo Archeologico Nazionale di Locri, in esposizione; inedito).

Descrizione: si conserva l'estremità superiore del bariletto sormontata da una presa forata a sviluppo verticale; applicato alla sommità della parete laterale, è un versatoio plastico a protome leonina. Resta solo un limitatissimo lacerto della scena figurata, delimitata superiormente da una cornice ad ovuli, analoga a quella attestata sul bariletto dal sep. 884 (Fig. 5,a; Orsi 1913: 41-42, Figg. 53-54); si riconosce una testa maschile dai corti riccioli, volta verso destra.

Le caratteristiche dei rivestimenti (vernice nera, *miltos*) sostengono l'attribuzione ad una produzione locale; inoltre la decorazione accessoria e l'uso di vernice diluita per rendere la mossa chioma del personaggio maschile coincidono con le cifre disegnative diffuse tra i ceramografi minori del Gruppo di Locri.

5) Frammento di cratere miniaturistico (Fig. 4,f); da Locri, necropoli in contrada Lucifero, rinvenimento sporadico (non inv.; Museo Archeologico Nazionale di Reggio Calabria, non esposto; inedito).

Descrizione: si conserva parte di un personaggio maschile barbato, forse un satiro; è ritratto in un'insolita posa: porta le braccia in avanti e solleva una gamba flessa; la falda di un mantello (?) ne ricopre il braccio sinistro. In alto resta un breve tratto dell'orlo con un motivo ad onda ricorrente verso destra.

L'attribuzione alla produzione di un ceramografo minore del Gruppo di Locri è confermata dal profilo del volto, dalla resa della barba e dal disegno delle mani, con l'indice ad uncino, sproporzionatamente allungato. Il curioso schema della figura richiama quello di alcuni satiri sul coperchio di una *lekane* dalla tomba 1242 (Orsi 1917: 116, Fig. 20; Spigo 1976: 583, n. 2; Elia 2001: 217, n. 1242/21, Fig. 19) e su una *kylix* dalla tomba 6 (scavo 1956; Elia, *Nelle case di Ade*: n. FR15). Inoltre, per i particolari del volto e delle braccia, accentuate affinità sono riconoscibili con personaggi maschili raffigurati sulla già citata *lekane* dal sep. 1242, su un esemplare dalla necropoli in contrada Monaci con la figura di un tritone (Spigo 1976: 584, n. 7; Elia, *Nelle case di Ade*) e su una seconda *kylix* dalla tomba 6 di contrada Lucifero (scavo 1956; Elia, *Nelle case di Ade*: n. FR16).

6) *Lekythos* ariballica (Fig. 5,c); da Locri, necropoli in contrada Lucifero, rinvenimento sporadico (n. inv. MAC 52; Museo Archeologico Nazionale di Locri, in esposizione; inedita).

Descrizione: si conserva il corpo globulare su basso piede ad anello; la superficie si presenta fortemente corrosa e scrostata.

Sul lato destro si riconosce la sagoma di una figura femminile seduta su una sedia con gambe accentuatamente ricurve e largo schienale, cui si appoggia con il gomito sinistro; verso questa cammina un Erote, con le braccia distese in avanti.

La decorazione accessoria presenta una cornice di sottili tralci d'edera resi a vernice, rettilinei e verticali, che delimita la scena lateralmente Al di sotto dell'ansa (perduta) è un'alta palmetta inquadrata da sottili viticci con girali spiraliformi, lunghe foglie e boccioli triangolari.

La scena presenta uno schema ed una composizione assai simili a quelli raffigurati su uno dei lati del bariletto del sep. 884 (Fig. 5,a), sebbene in questo caso l'Erote sia in volo. Anche lo sviluppo della decorazione accessoria mostra evidenti similitudini e consente di proporre, nonostante il cattivo stato di conservazione, l'attribuzione ad un ceramografo minore del Gruppo di Locri.

7) Frammento di forma chiusa (sostegno?) (Fig. 6,c); da Locri, necropoli in contrada Lucifero, rinvenimento sporadico (n. inv. 55941; Museo Archeologico Nazionale di Locri, in esposizione; inedito).

Descrizione: al di sotto di una massiccia cornice aggettante, si conserva la parte superiore di un Erote volto verso destra, forse inginocchiato a giudicare dalla curvatura delle spalle. Di fronte resta un limitato lacerto di un oggetto appeso, forse una benda decorata a piccoli cerchi.

La testa dell'Erote risulta essere una replica quasi identica di quella dello stesso personaggio su un coperchio di *lekane* dalla "Casa dei leoni" (Fig. 6,a; Sguaitamatti 1992: 178-179, 185, n. 135), consentendo un'attribuzione al Pittore della pisside RC 5089; in particolare appaiono caratteristici il disegno peculiare dell'occhio, della bocca, della massa dei corti riccioli, nonché la resa delle ali: quella in primo piano ha la parte superiore campita in nero, mentre l'altra, appena discosta e risparmiata, presenta un profilo spigoloso.

8) *Lekane* lacunosa e frammentaria (Fig. 6,b); da Locri, necropoli in contrada Lucifero, sep. 1119 (non inv.; Museo Archeologico Nazionale di Reggio Calabria, non esposta; Elia 2001: 220-221, n. 1119/5, Figg. 20, 31).

Descrizione: oltre alla vasca, si conserva un solo frammento del coperchio con il corpo di un Erote inginocchiato privo della testa. È rivolto verso destra e sembra tendere il braccio destro in gesto di offerta. Alle sue spalle è un elemento vegetale composto da due foglie venate da cui scaturisce un bocciolo triangolare. Vi è traccia di un diffuso utilizzo del colore bianco sovraddipinto per decorare le punte delle penne delle ali, nonché una bandoliera ed un monile sulla coscia destra, entrambi resi con puntini ravvicinati.

Il frammento trova un confronto puntuale con la figura dell'Erote rappresentato sul coperchio di *lekane* dalla "Casa dei leoni", attribuito al Pittore della pisside RC 5089 (Fig. 6,a); identici appaiono infatti lo schema della figura, le notazioni anatomiche del petto, del ventre e del sesso, l'uso dei fitti puntini di colore bianco per rendere i monili e decorare le ali, nonché il motivo vegetale che scaturisce da terra.

9) Frammento di pisside sovraddimensionata (Fig. 5,d); da Locri, necropoli in contrada Parapezza, ritrovamento sporadico (non inv.; Museo Archeologico Nazionale di Locri, non esposto; inedito).

Descrizione: parete leggermente curvilinea con orlo superiormente appiattito e battuta interna. Si conserva la parte superiore di una figura maschile di profilo verso destra. Il personaggio indossa un mantello fittamente pieghettato e decorato da crocette, fermato al petto da una fibula circolare; dietro la nuca è un *petasos* rovesciato, fermato da una coppia di sottili laccetti, resi a colore sovraddipinto. Dietro al capo è un tratto superstite della decorazione accessoria, tra cui si riconosce un fiore 'a patera' con pistillo centrale globulare.

I capelli ricci, resi con un fitto motivo ad archetti ravvicinati, rientrano nella tradizione del Gruppo della Scacchiera, trovando puntuali confronti nella produzione del Pittore di Dirce. In particolare, oltre alla peculiare capigliatura ed alla foggia dell'abito, risultano caratteristici il profilo rettilineo fronte-naso ed il tracciato sinuoso della linea della bocca ravvisabili in alcuni vasi attribuiti a questo ceramografo, come il cratere omonimo con il supplizio di Dirce e l'esemplare siracusano con la scena dell'incontro tra Elettra ed Oreste (Trendall 1989: Figg. 60-61). La decorazione secondaria, in particolare la peculiare foggia del fiore, trova inoltre confronto con alcuni frammenti da Locri, ricondotti all'ambito del Gruppo Prado-Fienga (Elia, *Nelle case di Ade*, n. FR41).

10) Pomello di *lekane* (Fig. 6,e); da Locri, necropoli in contrada Monaci, rinvenimento sporadico (non inv.; Museo Archeologico Nazionale di Reggio Calabria, non esposto; inedito).

Descrizione: presa a disco con profilo modanato; sulla faccia superiore si sviluppa la decorazione costituita da una coppia di palmette a 7 petali, affrontate ed associate a rosette realizzate con puntini.

Lo schema decorativo risulta attestato nella produzione siceliota a partire dalla produzione del Gruppo di Lentini (cfr. Giudice 1985: Figg. 288-290), mentre costituisce finora un'eccezione sulle *lekanai* attribuibili all'attività di botteghe locresi.

* Questo contributo integra ed approfondisce alcune tematiche affrontate nell'intervento presentato a Napoli nel dicembre 2000 in occasione della Tavola Rotonda *La ceramica apula: bilanci e prospettive* (Elia 2000). Nel presente saggio vengono presentati alcuni reperti inediti: uno studio analitico dei singoli reperti citati sarà inserito nella pubblicazione della Tesi di Dottorato (Elia 2001), attualmente in corso di preparazione.

1 Ricordo brevemente che rispetto alla Sicilia, dove prevalgono nettamente le opere ricondotte al Pittore di Locri, a Locri insieme alle realizzazioni attribuibili a questo ceramografo risultano particolarmente diffuse le attestazioni di altri artigiani del Gruppo omonimo (Elia 2000); queste ultime presentano inoltre evidenti affinità compositive, stilistiche e disegnative con le opere di ceramografi presenti quasi esclusivamente a Locri, quali il Gruppo dell'Erote inginocchiato e il Pittore della Pisside RC 5089 (Elia, *Nelle case di Ade*).

2 Rispetto ai dati quantitativi riassunti nella Fig. 1, la Fig. 2 rappresenta un recente aggiornamento, frutto di ulteriori riconoscimenti tra i materiali inediti; tali scoperte hanno portato ad arricchire le attestazioni a Locri del Gruppo dell'Erote inginocchiato e del Pittore della Pisside RC 5089. Per i ritrovamenti siciliani del Gruppo di Locri si è invece aggiunto un cratere a calice da Monte Adranone, ancora inedito (necropoli meridionale, tomba 35, in mostra al Museo Archeologico di Agrigento in occasione del Congresso Internazionale "La Sicilia dei due Dionisî", Agrigento, 24-28 febbraio 1999).

3 Per la bibliografia completa dei rinvenimenti in Sicilia: Elia 2000: nota 9.

4 L'unico esemplare riconducibile al Pittore di Locri sembra da riconoscere nella *lekane* dal sep. 1247 (Spigo 1980: 583, n. 1; Spigo 2000: 47, nota 2), che presenta strettissime affinità stilistiche e disegnative con un cratere a calice dal sep. 1119 (Elia 2001: 215-216).

5 Si tratta di una forma particolarmente diffusa in ambito funerario: il riesame dei corredi scavati nella necropoli di Lucifero tra il 1913 e il 1914 ha permesso il riconoscimento di 15 esemplari (Elia 2001: 232); un ulteriore frammento di coperchio è tra i materiali raccolti nel 1956 (Elia, *Nelle case di Ade*: n. FR50). Nei contesti esaminati la cronologia ai decenni 380-350 a.C. risulta omogenea.

6 Più rari appaiono gli esemplari nella tecnica a figure rosse (Lentini: Montironi 1992: Fig. 2), mentre assai diffusi risultano quelli con decorazione su fondo risparmiato (Vassallaggi: Orlandini 1971: 147, Fig. 115; Lipari: Bernabò Brea e Cavalier 1997: 91, Fig. 100; Lentini: Montironi 2000: 118, n. 1, Fig. 73; Gela: n. inv. 35956, esemplare inedito dall'acropoli esposto nel Museo Archeologico).

7 Sono infatti rimaste isolate le attestazioni di questa forma segnalate dall'Orsi dall'area campana (1913: 42).

8 Il frammento proviene da uno strato ricchissimo di materiali ceramici in c.da Centocamere, interpretato come il "riutilizzo di un grande scarico" (Barra Bagnasco 2000: nota 69). Ringrazio Marcella Barra Bagnasco per avermi gentilmente concesso di segnalare alcuni dei reperti rinvenuti.
9 N. inv. C98/VN968: resta solo parte del fondo con tondo interno figurato; sebbene l'attribuzione sia dubbia a causa della limitatezza della porzione figurata conservata, il profilo del vaso e l'utilizzo di un *miltos* particolarmente spesso e di tonalità accesa ne confermano comunque la pertinenza ad una bottega locale. Per il contesto di rinvenimento. v. nota precedente.
10 N. inv. C98/VN1020; v. nota 8.
11 "Dentro il cratere a campana che è quello laterale all'arcone v'era una lekane nera frammentata" (taccuino Orsi Sic. 103: 4). La pertinenza dell'esemplare figurato al contesto è accertata sulla base delle indicazioni allegate; nella documentazione manoscritta la confusione nella descrizione con una *lekane* interamente a vernice deve essere verosimilmente imputata al fatto che mentre si conserva gran parte della vasca, si raccolse solo un frammento del coperchio figurato, con tutta probabilità confuso tra i frammenti del cratere. Per altro la documentazione d'archivio relativa a questo eccezionale contesto reca ulteriori 'sviste', come l'inversione della descrizione delle scene sul cratere a campana con quelle di uno degli esemplari a calice. Non appare invece spiegabile il silenzio di Orsi nell'edito, dove lo scavatore dedicò al cratere a campana solo poche righe; a questo proposito, tuttavia, appare opportuno ricordare che nei rapporti preliminari editi non sono assenti dimenticanze o confusioni rispetto alla documentazione redatta durante lo scavo (Elia 2001: Catalogo dei sepolcri).
12 Già lo Sguaitamatti (1992: 185) indicava per il coperchio dalla "Casa dei leoni" una datazione al secondo quarto del secolo.
13 Una datazione leggermente posteriore è stata proposta dalla Montironi, mentre lo Spigo accetta una cronologia intorno al 340 (Spigo 2000: 40, nota 39). Per la cronologia della prima produzione con decorazione sovraddipinta in area siciliana, particolarmente significativi appaiono alcuni sepolcri liparoti che ne presentano l'associazione con opere attribuite al pittore di Maron (t. 402) e al Pittore Nyn (tt. 2127, 2287) (Bernabò Brea e Cavalier 1997: 72, 140).
14 La pertinenza del grosso frammento al corredo, oltre che dall'integrità del contesto al momento dello scavo, appare confermata dalla frequenza dei casi in cui solo parti di grandi forme decorate sono state deposte all'interno di sepolcri locresi (Elia, *Nelle case di Ade*): una situazione analoga è testimoniata, ad esempio, per la *lekane* del sep. 1502, rinvenuta in frammenti e deposta solo parzialmente all'interno di un sepolcro con copertura conservata (Orsi 1917: 135).
15 Sul rialzamento della tradizionale cronologia iniziale delle *lekythoi* Pagenstecher: Sguaitamatti 1992: 181-182; Montironi 1992: 63-66; Montironi 2000: 127. Per l'esemplare locrese la decorazione accessoria richiama quella di alcune *lekythoi* dall'area siciliana: cfr. Bernabò Brea e Cavalier 1997: 95, n. 3, Figg. 108a-109; 97, n. 6, Figg. 110b-111b; Montironi 1992: Fig. 4.
16 Per un quadro articolato delle molteplici connessioni di carattere stilistico, compositivo e formale: Spigo 1987, 1991, 2000.
17 Si può annoverare ad esempio la piccola *lekythos* ariballica del sep. 528, attribuita alla cerchia del Pittore di Nyn (Spigo 2000: 38-39, figg, 24-25). V. anche *infra*.
18 Propongo in questa sede un breve riassunto dei risultati presentati dal nostro gruppo di ricerca in occasione del 6th European Meeting on Ancient Ceramics "Ceramic in Society", tenutosi a Friburgo (CH) nei giorni 3-6/10/2001. Il contributo definitivo è in corso di stampa sulla rivista *Archaeometry* (Mirti *et alii*, c.s.).
19 Sulla produzione di questo ceramografo: Trendall 1967: 202-204; Trendall 1983: 99-100; Trendall 1989: 30-31; Spigo 1987: 5; Bernabò Brea e Cavalier 1997: 18-19.
20 Un'eccezione è rappresentata dalla *lekane* del Pittore dell'Erote inginocchiato conservata ad Amburgo (Trendall 1967: 219, n. 108, tav. 87.2).
21 La seconda fase ha avuto avvio nei primi mesi del 2003.

BIBLIOGRAFIA

Barra Bagnasco, M., 2000, Spazi interni ed esterni alle mura nella zona costiera di Locri Epizefiri: un esempio di pianificazione integrata, *Orizzonti. Rassegna di archeologia*, I, 11-33.

Bernabò Brea, L. e Cavalier, M., 1997, *La ceramica figurata della Sicilia e della Magna Grecia nella Lipàra del IV sec. a.C.*, Milano.

Blondé, F. e Perreault, J.Y. (a cura di), 1992, *Les ateliers de potiers dans le monde grec aux époques géométrique, archaïque et classique, Actes de la Table Ronde (Athènes 1987), BCH, Supplement*, XXIII.

Blondé, F. e Muller, A. (a cura di), 1998, *L'artisanat en Grèce ancienne: les artisans, les ateliers, Actes du XXe Colloque international de HALMA Lille 3 (Lille 1997), Topoi*, 8,2.

Buzzi Auxilia, M.C., 1989, Il vasellame del II strato. Vasi per bere, in *Locri Epizefiri II. Gli isolati I2 e I3 dell'area di Centocamere* (a cura di M. Barra Bagnasco), 107-141, Firenze.

Campenon, Ch., 1994, *La céramique attique à figures rouges autour de 400 avant J.-C.*, Paris.

Denoyelle, M., Lippolis, E., Mazzei, M. e Pouzadoux, C. (a cura di), *La céramique apulienne. Bilan et perspectives, Actes de la Table Ronde (Napoli 2000)*, Cahiers du Centre Jean Bérard, Napoli, in corso di stampa.

Elia, D., 2000, La diffusione della ceramica figurata a Locri Epizefiri nella prima metà del IV secolo: problemi di stile, produzione e cronologia, in Denoyelle *et al.* 2000.

Elia, D., 2001, *La necropoli in contrada Lucifero: nuove ricerche sulle aree funerarie di Locri Epizefiri tra V e IV secolo a.C. (Campagne di scavo degli anni 1913-1914)*, Tesi di Dottorato, XII ciclo, Università di Messina.

Elia, D., *Nelle case di Ade. Rito, morte e società a Locri Epizefiri*, Firenze, in corso di stampa.

Giudice, F., 1985, I ceramografi del IV secolo a.C., in *Sikanie. Storia e civiltà della Sicilia greca* (a cura di G. Pugliese Carratelli), 243-260, Milano.

Lippolis, E., 1996, La ceramica a figure rosse italiota, in *I Greci in Occidente. Arte e artigianato in Magna Grecia* (a cura di E. Lippolis), 357-361, Napoli.

Mirti, P., Casoli, A., Barra Bagnasco, M. e Preacco Ancona, M.C., 1995, Fine ware from Locri Epizephiri: a provenance study by ICP emission spectroscopy, *Archaeometry*, 37, 41-51.

Mirti, P., Gulmini, M., Pace, M. e Elia, D., *The provenance of red figure vases from Locri Epizephiri. New evidence by chemical analysis*, *Archaeometry*, in corso di stampa.

Montironi, A., 1992, Una tomba da Leontini e la cronologia delle lekythoi Pagenstecher, *Cronache di Archeologia*, 31, 61-66.

Montironi, A., 2000, Cronologia delle tombe nell'area antistante la porta sud di Leontini, in S. Rizza, *Studi sulle fortificazioni greche di Leontini*, 113-128, Catania.

Orlandini, P., 1971, Vassallaggi (S. Cataldo). Scavi 1961: I. La necropoli meridionale, *NSc*, *Supplemento*.

Orsi, P., 1911, Rapporto preliminare sulla quinta campagna di scavi nelle Calabrie durante l'anno 1910, *NSc*, *Supplemento*, 3-76.

Orsi, P., 1912, Scavi di Calabria nel 1911 (relazione provvisoria), *NSc*, *Supplemento*, 3-18.

Orsi, P., 1913, Scavi di Calabria nel 1913 (relazione preliminare), *NSc*, *Supplemento*, 3-54.

Orsi, P., 1917, Locri Epiz. Campagne di scavo nella necropoli Lucifero negli anni 1914 e 1915, *NSc*, 101-167.

Pontrandolfo, A., 1991, Le prime esperienze dei ceramografi sicelioti e le altre officine tirreniche, in *I vasi attici ed altre ceramiche coeve in Sicilia, Atti del Convegno Internazionale (Catania-Camarina-Gela-Vittoria 1990)*, *Cronache di Archeologia*, 30, 35-49.

Sguaitamatti, M., 1992, I frammenti di ceramica italiota a figure rosse, in *Locri Epizefiri IV. Lo scavo di Marasà Sud. Il sacello tardo arcaico e la "Casa dei Leoni"* (a cura di M. Barra Bagnasco), 173-186, Firenze.

Spigo, U., 1977, La ceramica italiota, in *Locri Epizefiri I. Ricerche nella zona di Centocamere*, 128-146, Firenze.

Spigo, U., 1980, intervento in *Atti del 16° Convegno Internazionale di Studi sulla Magna Grecia (Taranto 1976)*, 583-586, Napoli.

Spigo, U., 1987, La ceramica siceliota a figure rosse: variazioni sul tema, *BdA*, LXXII, 1-24.

Spigo, U., 1991, Il problema degli influssi della pittura vascolare attica nella ceramica a figure rosse siceliota, in *I vasi attici ed altre ceramiche coeve in Sicilia, Atti del Convegno Internazionale (Catania-Camarina-Gela-Vittoria 1990)*, *Cronache di Archeologia*, 30, 51-65.

Spigo, U., 2000, Fra Lipára e Lokroi Epizephýrioi. Il cratere a campana del Gruppo di Locri nella tomba 1155 di c/da Diana e alcune considerazioni sui rapporti fra ceramografi presenti a Lipari e nella Calabria meridionale nel secondo e terzo venticinquennio del IV secolo a.C., *Quaderni del Museo Archeologico Regionale Eoliano "L. Bernabò Brea"*, 3, 29-54.

Trendall, A.D., 1967, *The Red-figured Vases of Lucania, Campania and Sicily*, Oxford.

Trendall, A.D., 1983, *The Red-figured Vases of Lucania, Campania and Sicily. Third Supplement*, BICS, 41, University of London, London.

Trendall, A.D., 1989, *Red Figure Vases of South Italy and Sicily*, London.

Villanueva Puig, M.-Ch., Lissarague, F., Rouillard, P. e Rouveret, A. (a cura di), 1999, *Céramique et peinture grecques. Modes d'emploi, Actes du colloque international École du Louvre (Paris 1995)*, Paris.

Villard, F., 1992, Les céramiques locales: problèmes généraux, in Blondé e Perreault 1992, 3-9.

Villard, F. e Blondé, F., 1999, La localisation des ateliers, in Villanueva Puig *et al.* 1999, 107-120.

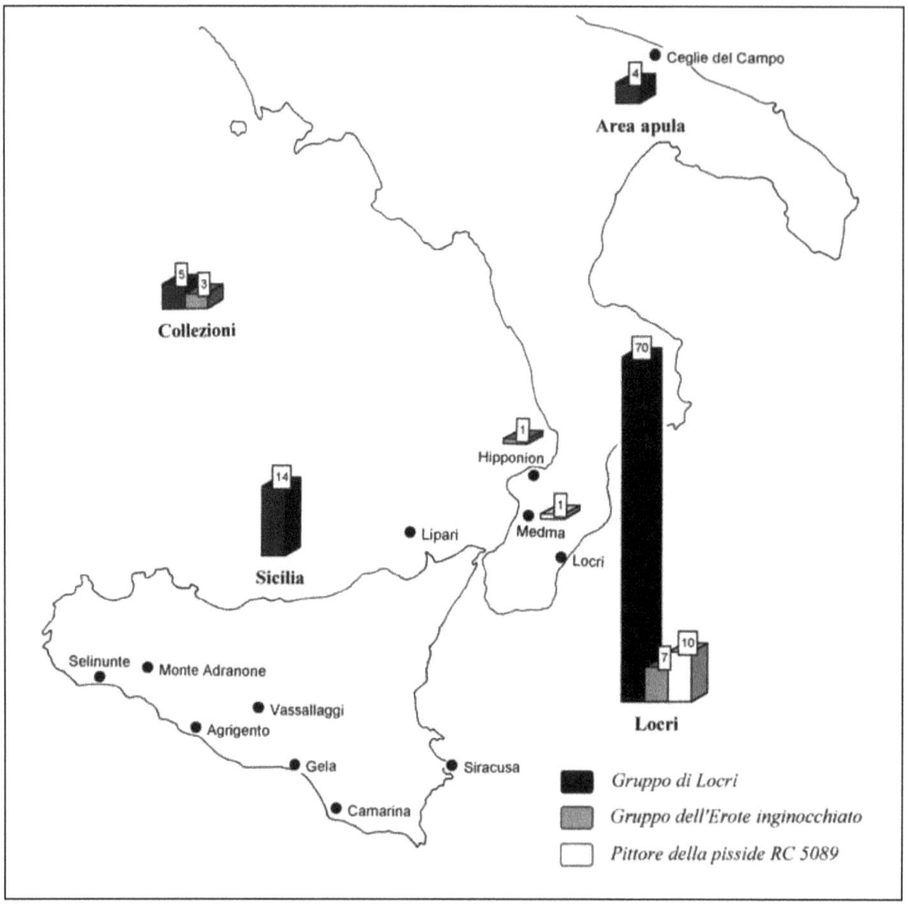

Fig. 1. Localizzazione dei rinvenimenti attribuiti al Gruppo di Locri, al Gruppo dell'Erote inginocchiato e al Pittore della Pisside RC 5089; dati aggiornati al 2000 (da Elia 2000: Fig. 2).

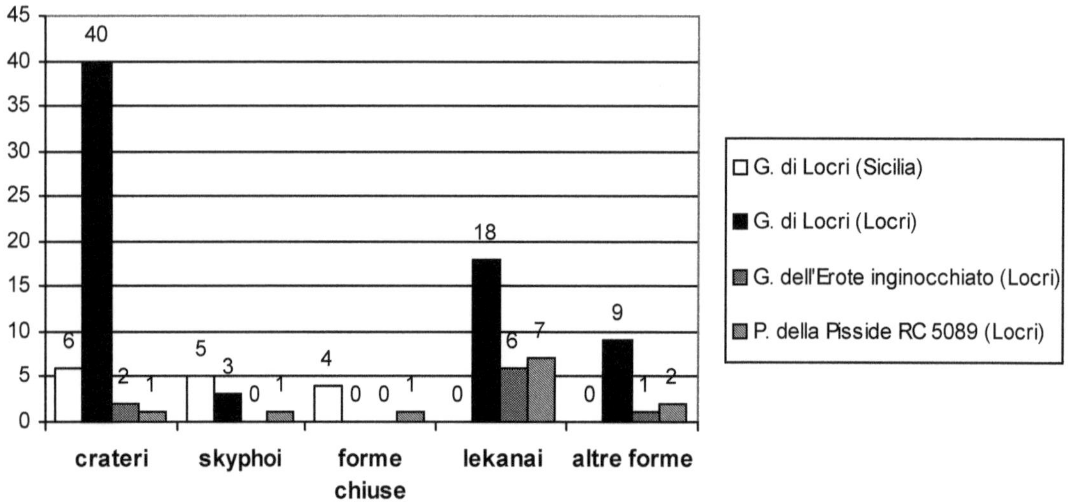

Fig. 2. Grafico della distribuzione delle forme attribuite al Gruppo di Locri, al Gruppo dell'Erote inginocchiato e al Pittore della Pisside RC 5089; dati aggiornati alla primavera 2003.

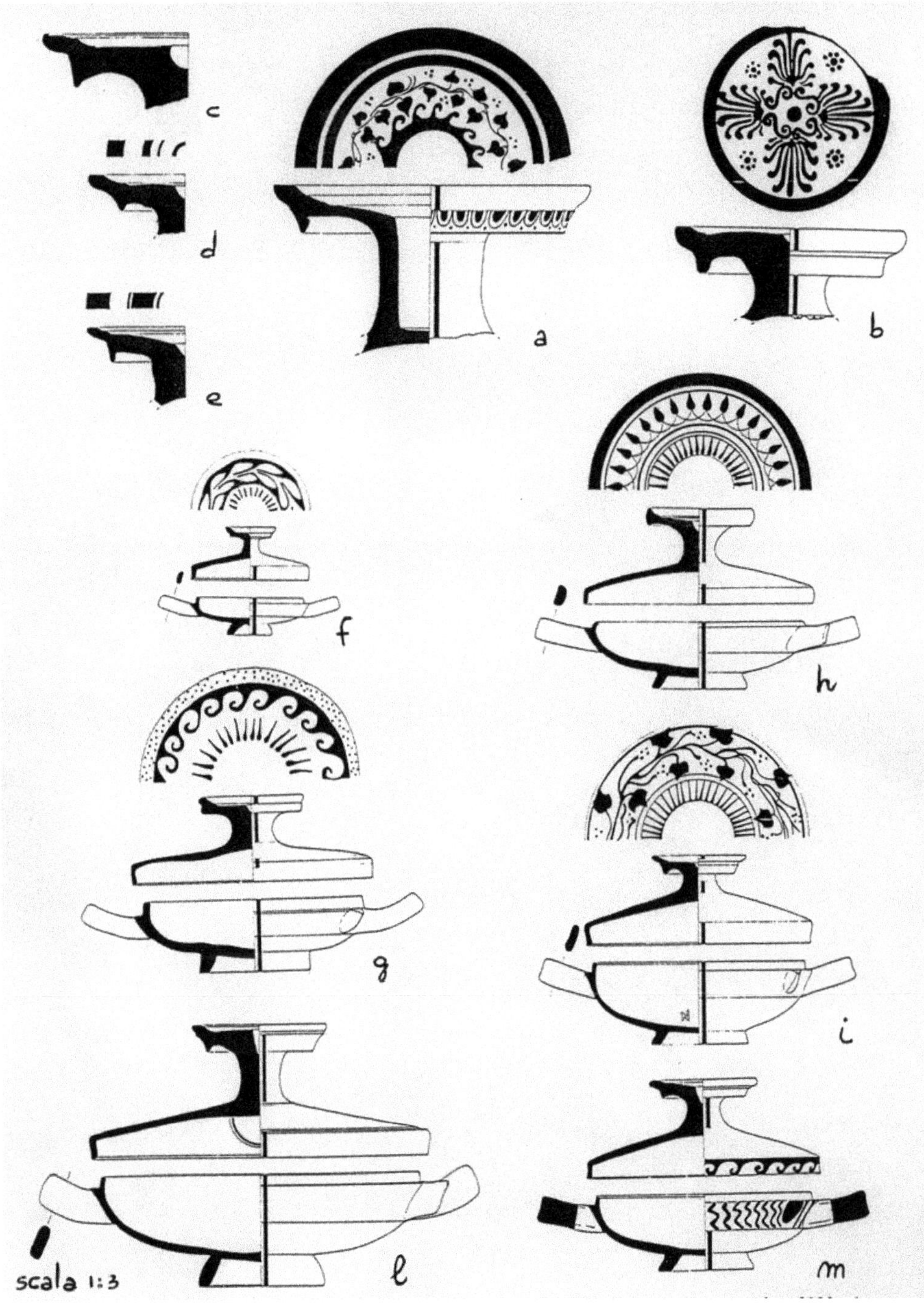

Fig. 3. Pomelli di lekane: a) Gruppo di Locri, sep. 1502, n. inv. 113338; b) sporadico, n. inv. 9233; c) sporadico, n. inv. MAC506; d) sep. 1603, non inv.; e) sporadico, non inv. Lekanai decorate: f) sep. 945, n. inv. 4840; g) sep. 892, n. inv. 4799; h) sep. 1219, n. inv. 5045; i) sep. 868, n. inv. 4789. Lekane a figure rosse, Gruppo di Locri: sep. 1247, n. inv. MAC35. m) lekane a figure rosse, Pittore dell'Erote inginocchiato: sep. 1088, n. inv. 4897.

Fig. 4. a-d) frammenti di coperchio di lekane, Gruppo di Locri: a) sep. 749, n. inv. 4633; b-c) sep. 1502, n. inv. 113338; d) contesto ignoto, n. inv. C735; e) riproduzione grafica di particolari: dal cratere del sep. 1119, n. inv. 5013, e dal frammento del sep. 749; f) frammento di cratere miniaturistico, Gruppo di Locri : sporadico, non inv.

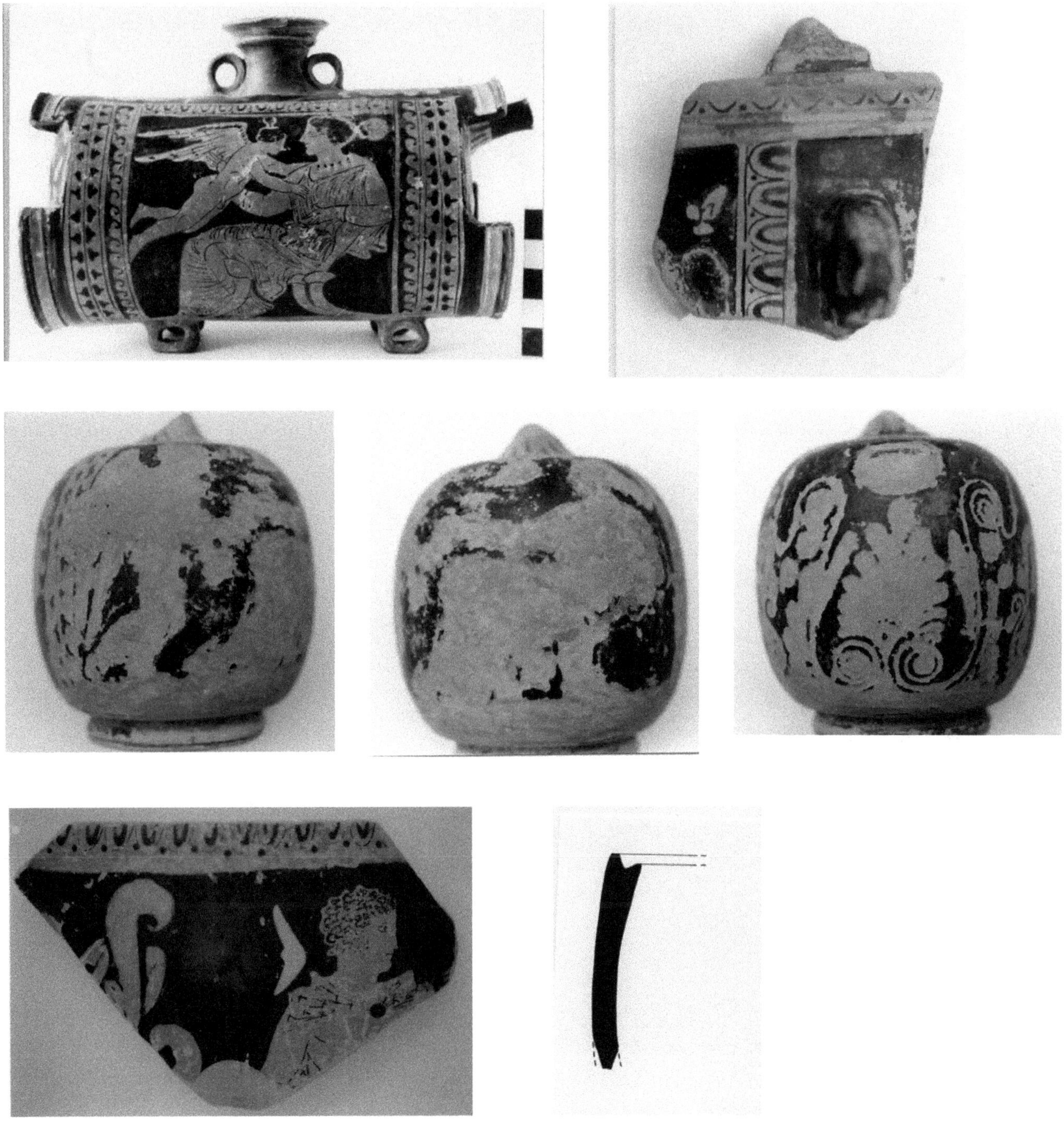

Fig. 5. a) bariletto, Gruppo di Locri: sep. 884, n. inv. 4794; b) frammento di bariletto, Gruppo di Locri: sporadico, n. inv. MAC466; c) lekythos ariballica, Gruppo di Locri: sporadica, n. inv. MAC52; d) frammento di pisside skyphoide, Pittore di Dirce: sporadico, non inv.

Fig. 6. a) coperchio di lekane, Pittore della Pisside RC 5089: "Casa dei leoni", n. inv. M89/VN858; b) frammento di coperchio di lekane, Pittore della Pisside RC 5089: sep. 1119, non inv.; c) frammento, Pittore della Pisside RC 5089: n. inv. 1950/161A; d) lekythos Pagenstecher: sep. 749, n. inv. 4630; e) pomello di lekane: sporadico, non inv.

PER CHI SUONA LA CAMPANA B?

FRANCA CIBECCHINI (Università degli Studi di Pisa)
JORDI PRINCIPAL (Institut Català d'Arqueologia Clàssica)

ABSTRACT: This paper reviews the problems as to how Campana B pottery should be defined. Traditionally, Campana B refers strictly to black gloss pottery manufactured in Etruria, yet there were many contemporaneous production groups throughout Italy and the western Mediterranean. The authors present suggestions as to how to address this complex group of ceramic material.

INTRODUZIONE

Questo lavoro intende ricostruire una cronistoria degli studi che hanno portato alla definizione di una delle produzioni più problematiche e dibattute tra i ceramologi, la campana B, con l'intento di dipanare il groviglio di denominazioni e produzioni che si è creato dalla coniazione del termine nel 1952 ad oggi. Si cercherà di illustrare quali siano stati i punti cruciali che hanno portato alla definizione di queste produzioni di ceramica a vernice nera e pasta chiara che hanno marcato i grandi cambiamenti socio-economici del II sec. a.C. La confusione terminologica connessa a queste ceramiche non appare fine a se stessa ma riflette problematiche legate all'individuazione dei centri produttivi: chiarire quali siano e quali tipi ceramici abbiano prodotto tali centri, nonché affinare la terminologia legata alla "cerchia della B" è un'operazione per strumento l'analisi e la comunicazione di dati corretti e comprensibili in maniera univoca all'interno della comunità scientifica.

1. STORIOGRAFIA DELLA RICERCA SULLA CAMPANA B

1.1. La nascita di una definizione (Fig. 1)

Nella sua "Classificazione Preliminare" Lamboglia (1952) definisce la campana B a diffusione universale come una ceramica d'ispirazione toreutica a pasta chiara, depurata, vernice nera o bluastra di buona qualità, d'origine etrusca. Nella postilla, tuttavia, già osserva che esistono due tipi simili ma chiaramente distinti di campana B, uno presente ad Arezzo e Firenze ed uno a diffusione mediterranea (Lamboglia 1952: 206). Nel 1957 la Taylor distingue per la ceramica a vernice nera di Cosa un tipo II assimilato alla campana B di Lamboglia, rafforzando così l'idea di un'origine etrusca costiera di questa ceramica (Taylor 1957: 71 e 191). Lo stesso Lamboglia invece, pochi anni dopo, individua nella Campania settentrionale, e più precisamente a Cales, l'area di produzione della campana B a diffusione mediterranea (Lamboglia 1960: 294; 1961: 150).

L'idea di un'origine etrusca della campana B viene ripresa da Morel (1963: 16-17 e 35) e mantenuta energicamente (Morel 1965b: 235; 1968: 60-61; 1978: 160), con una netta distinzione tra "vera campana B etrusca" e ceramica "Bioide", entrambe oggetto di ampia diffusione mediterranea anche se con aree preferenziali diverse. La prima viene associata al tipo II di Cosa (nota soprattutto ad Ampurias, Cartagena e Alicante) dal carattere non unitario (e.g. la "*B lourde*" -Morel 1965a: 81) e probabilmente frutto di un gruppo di officine strettamente apparentate; la seconda viene prodotta per imitazione al di fuori dell'Etruria, prevalentemente in Campania settentrionale, ed è ben nota in Gallia nel I sec. a.C. Come vedremo, questa terminologia, divenuta tradizionale e canonica condizionerà il successivo sviluppo della problematica.

Contemporaneamente le ricerche svolte nell'Etruria propria e/o in altre aree di diffusione della "vera campana B" hanno contribuito a mettere in luce la complessità delle produzioni etrusche di qualità. Dopo la fondamentale classificazione delle ceramiche volterrane di M. Pasquinucci (1972) e l'individuazione di una ceramica aretina a vernice nera (Morel 1980: 103-104; 1981: 46), vengono distinte diverse varianti all'interno delle produzioni dell'Etruria settentrionale, tra cui alcune di alta qualità tecnica con pasta camoscio o beige, depurata e vernice per lo più bluastra (la volterrana D) o decisamente nera (sopratutto l'aretina), più o meno brillante. Entrambe le produzioni affondano le loro radici nelle varietà etrusche a vernice nera di qualità e di tradizione toreutica del IV-III sec., notamente Malacena e *anses en oreilles* (Balland 1969: 151-162), ma verso la fine del III-inizio del II sec. a.C. sembrano sviluppare un repertorio formale che si cristallizerà nella cosidetta campana B.

La pubblicazione delle ceramiche di Luni (Cavalieri Manasse 1977: 80-81) è forse la prima a mettere in evidenza proprio in Etruria la non omogeneità del blocco etrusco della campana B, riscontrata anche a Cosa (Cavalieri Manasse 1977: 81, nota 13); si distinguono due tipi, B e B1, sulla base delle caratteristiche tecniche e del repertorio formale. Le analisi minero-petrografiche eseguite su un campione del tipo B indicavano un'origine campano-laziale, portando ad una prima proposta d'identificazione di queste ceramiche con la "pseudo B" di Morel (1965c: 81).

D'altra parte, diversi studi che partono dai dati di scavo in alcuni dei siti recettori di tali ceramiche (Penisola Iberica e Africa settentrionale), ipotizzano la possibile presenza d'imitazioni locali della campana B, come i tipi E d'Ippona (Morel 1962-65: 120-122) e D-E di Thamusida (Morel 1965a: 82), o i tipi ampuritani F, G e H (Sanmartí Grego 1978: 25). In Gallia Arcelin, e Chabot (1980: 187) dimostrano chiaramente che nel Languedoc orientale e in Provenza la maggior parte delle forme *de type B* si possono ricollegare ad *ateliers* campani, e più precisamente a quelli della regione di Cales. Nell'area campana, la pubblicazione del primo volume sullo studio della ceramica a vernice nera da Cales (Pedroni 1986) offre, per la prima volta, un tentativo di sistemazione dell'insieme della produzione calena dal IV al I sec. aC.

1.2. Le prime reazioni critiche

Con il secondo volume dedicato alla ceramica di Cales, Pedroni (1990), riconoscendo l'equivalenza tra il gruppo caleno degli stampigli a cuoricino e la classe definita da Morel "Byrsa 661" (Morel 1986: 31-34), completa la sequenza evolutiva e cronologica della produzione calena dalle origini, con la ceramica a rilievo, fino alle più tarde serie definite Bioidi e diffuse soprattutto in Gallia e Penisola Iberica (III-I sec. a.C.). Si stabilisce inoltre un'unica origine calena per la decorazione a losanga, con l'eccezione del gruppo "marocchino D" a pasta grigia (Morel 1968: 65), e si critica per la prima volta la terminologia ormai canonizzata per il tipo B. Pedroni ritiene metodologicamente scorretta la distinzione, anche qualitativa, tra una ceramica Bioide e una vera B, poiché interpreta l'assunzione del repertorio formale della B (toreutico) come un'evoluzione coerente e propria delle officine di Cales, autonoma dalle officine etrusche (Pedroni 1990: 185-187). Nei primi anni novanta le osservazioni incrociate tra Valencia e Cales portano Escrivà, Marín e Ribera (1992) ad identificare per la prima volta nella Penisola Iberica, in contesti ascrivibili agli anni centrali del II sec. a.C, una ceramica di buona qualità a pasta chiara e vernice nera non come "Byrsa 661" né come campana B etrusca, ma come calena liscia. Tra le forme indicative analizzate a Valencia spicca il cratere F 4753, ritenuto tradizionalmente etrusco; lo studio della diffusione di questa forma nel bacino Mediterraneo, a cura di Pérez Ballester (1992), sembra eliminare ogni dubbio sulla sua origine calena (poiché a Cales la forma è attestata in quantità rilevanti) e ne mette in evidenza la diffusione marittima.

Morel e Picon (1994) tentano un approccio archeometrico per cercare di chiarire la provenienza delle ceramiche della "cerchia della B", con particolare riferimento alle attestazioni in Gallia e Penisola Iberica. Le conclusioni portano a tre gruppi differenziati in maniera piuttosto netta: una conferma della provenienza calena per le ceramiche Bioidi della Gallia; una produzione sicuramente etrusca per la B di Cosa e assimilate; una provenienza dalla Campania settentrionale, circoscrivibile all'area di Cales-Teano, per molte delle ceramiche definite Bioidi della Penisola Iberica, mentre una parte non ben chiarita apparterrebbe alla produzione etrusca. Si continua, tuttavia, a mantenere una terminologia che distingue tra vera campana B etrusca e ceramiche Bioidi, quali produzioni d'imitazione esterne all'Etruria. Nella stessa linea si inserisce il contributo di Morel (1998) al convegno su Archeometria di Milano (Milano 1998), in cui si riprende la distinzione tra una campana B etrusca, vera, definita ora B "antica" fino alla metà del II sec., e una ceramica Bioide diversificata, vista come una nebulosa di produzioni (nate per imitazione e contraffazione della B etrusca, e distinte essenzialmente per la mediocre qualità) solo in parte riferibile all'area compresa tra Cales, Teano e Capua. Come continuazione della B antica si individua una "bella B etrusca" e una "campana B" di qualità inferiore alla "bella B etrusca" ma superiore alla Bioide, presente in tutto il mediterraneo (Penisola Iberica, Gallia, Marocco e Delo), per la quale si suggerisce velatamente un'origine in Etruria settentrionale. All'interno di questa "cerchia della B" si prendono in esame alcuni casi particolari, tra i quali quello del cratere F 4753a (cf. *supra*), analizzato però non come singola forma-tipo ma come serie F 4750, attribuita all'Etruria sulla base delle attestazioni di alcune forme di tale serie. Infine, a seguito delle analisi archeometriche svolte da Picon, si stabilisce definitivamente l'origine calena e non cartaginese per la produzione "Byrsa 661".

Nello stesso convegno, le ricerche sulla fascia costiera dell'Etruria settentrionale (*agri Pisanus* e *Volaterranus*) presentate dall'*équipe* di M. Pasquinucci e da C. Capelli hanno portato alla distinzione su base archeometrica di un gruppo di produzione Bioide (campano-laziale), nel quale sono presenti le forme più peculiari del tipo B (Pasquinucci *et al.* 1998). Sempre partendo da studi in Etruria, L. Palermo (1998) indica la forte similitudine, difficilmente casuale, riscontrabile tra campana B, produzione aretina e la migliore produzione volterrana (la D) a partire dal II sec. a.C., momento in cui le ultime due produzioni rinnovano il repertorio morfologico.

Si deve infine citare la proposta di Stanco (1994: 31-34; 1999: 15) che ritiene la vera campana B prodotta a Roma, direttamente derivata dall'*atelier des petites estampilles*, e considera la B etrusca una produzione parallela di Volterra, Arezzo e Bolsena. La ceramica Bioide viene vista in un primo momento (Stanco 1994: 32-34) come un insieme di produzioni locali affini alla B ma scadenti, tipiche di diverse regioni del Mediterraneo, in particolare della Campania settentrionale (Cales?), Etruria e Lazio; in seguito distingue più precisamente alcune "Bioidi romane", ovvero produzioni affini alla campana B romana ma di peggiore qualità, frutto di una tardiva interpretazione del repertorio "toreutico" della B da parte di officine minori (Stanco 1999: 15-22).

Molte di queste problematiche legate alla campana B confluiscono nella tavola rotonda di Ampurias (Ampurias 2000), che ha visto riunite, dopo 46 anni di studi, ricerche svolte sia nei centri produttori (Etruria settentrionale e Campania) sia nei centri recettori (Liguria, Gallia meridionale, Penisola Iberica). Per l'Etruria, lo studio della fascia settentrionale marittima ha confermato la presenza di due gruppi ceramici di qualità nel II sec. a.C: da un lato le produzioni etrusche (volterrana D e aretina a vernice nera), dall'altro una produzione a pasta chiara e vernice nera, distinguibile anche autopticamente, d'origine campano-laziale per le analisi mineropetro-grafiche, che copre le principali forme del repertorio del tipo B ed in particolare la forma Lamb. 1, presente solo in questo secondo gruppo (Bianchini *et al.* 2000). Per la Campania settentrionale, viene rivalutato il centro di Cales quale produttore per eccellenza delle ceramiche a larga diffusione, con una sistemazione crono-tipologica che copre l'intero arco di attività degli *ateliers* caleni (Pedroni 2000). Le conclusioni scaturite dall'analisi incrociata dei dati emersi dai centri produttori e recettori portano da un lato al ridimensionamento del termine "universale" per la campana B etrusca, data la scarsa incidenza nei contesti mediterranei occidentali, dall'altro ad un'assimilazione di tutte le ceramiche "Bioidi" presenti nei siti recettori con la produzione calena. Viene accettata un'evoluzione diacronica in 6 fasi (come da tempo assunto per la campana A) della ceramica calena: 1) Primitiva IV sec.; 2) Arcaica III-inizi II sec. a.C.; 3) Antica 200-130/120 a.C.; 4) Media 130/120-90/80 a.C.; 5) Tarda 90/80-40/20 a.C.; 6) Terminale o Finale 40 a.C.-20 d.C., con l'elaborazione di un repertorio formale per le fasi centrali, ovvero quelle maggiormente coinvolte nell'esportazione transmarina (Figg. 2-4). Si stabilisce poi in maniera netta l'appartenenza alla calena antica e media di quelle ceramiche di migliore qualità attestate soprattutto nella Penisola Iberica, definite genericamente pertinenti alla "campana B" da Morel e ricollegate preferibilmente all'area etrusca (in particolare per le forme Lamb. 6, Pasq. 127 e F 4753). Viene infine decretata la fine del termine "Bioide", ormai esautorato e implicitamente connesso ad un'idea di subordinazione qualitativa, estetica e quantitativa che ha perso la sua ragion d'essere.

Queste conclusioni sono state completamente ribadite e assimilate nell'ultima monografia sulla ceramica calena, a cura di Pedroni (2001).

1.3. Lo stato attuale degli studi: è necessaria una nuova terminologia?

A quattro anni dal convegno di Ampurias, il tentativo di risistemazione del "mondo della B" ha provocato reazioni diverse nelle varie aree interessate da queste ceramiche. Nella penisola Iberica, dove questa ceramica è presente a partire dalla seconda metà del II sec. a.C. e prevalente sulla campana A già all'inizio del I sec. a.C., la proposta emersa dal convegno è stata assunta in maniera quasi integrale, in alcuni casi anche acriticamente, con una volontà di semplificazione che non sempre trova riscontro nei dati archeologici. Si deve tuttavia riconoscere che la maggior parte delle importazioni ceramiche a vernice nera ascrivibili al tipo B appartengono *in primis* a Cales. In Gallia meridionale la questione è realmente più semplice, dato che la recezione di queste ceramiche è più tarda, sempre minoritaria e molto omogenea. Sebbene la terminologia sia rimasta confusa e spesso ancorata alla distinzione tra vera campana B e Bioide (nonostante il lavoro di mediazione di P. Arcelin), è opinione comune che la ceramica attestata in quantità rilevanti e definita Bioide sia di produzione calena (Py *et al.* 2001: 557-558). Ben diverso appare invece il quadro in Italia, dove peraltro le riflessioni emerse dalla tavola rotonda d'Ampurias hanno avuto scarsissima diffusione. La realtà archeologica nelle principali aree produttrici/esportatrici e non presenta qui molteplici sfaccettature e una pluralità di produzioni, con vari livelli qualitativi, difficilmente riconducibili soltanto ai tradizionali *ateliers* conosciuti. Appare qui evidente come l'assioma campana B di qualità = Etruria e ceramica Bioide = Cales non sia applicabile. In aerea etrusca, come si è visto, si riconoscono almeno tre produzioni di qualità per il II sec.: la ceramica aretina a vernice nera, la volterrana D e verosimilmente il tipo II di Cosa, sebbene per questi ultimi due centri non siano mai state documentate fornaci e si attende ancora una revisione della ceramica di Cosa, ferma allo studio della Taylor del 1957. Queste produzioni condividono tra di loro un repertorio morfologico (Figg. 5-6) proprio della "campana B" tradizionale (Lamb. 2, 3, 4 5, 6, 8 e 10) ed appare quindi verosimile che il concetto di "vera B" etrusca coincida almeno con tutte e tre le produzioni. D'altra parte, una delle forme più tipiche del tipo B, la Lamb. 1, non appare nè nella volterrana D né nella ceramica aretina e, malgrado a Cosa sia inserita nel tipo II, i recenti studi negli *agri* pisano e volterrano, citati sopra, hanno dimostrato archeometricamente l'origine campano-laziale di tutti gli esemplari rinvenuti.

Passando all'area campana, sembra ormai incontestabile l'importanza di Cales quale centro produttore/esportatore almeno fin dalla metà del II sec. a.C., così come hanno dimostrato gli studi di sistemazione crono-tipologica e archeometrica nonché gli scavi effettuati nel giacimento (Johanowsky 1961; Morel 1998). Senza dubbio, all'interno della produzione calena si registra una notevole variabilità qualitativa, dal momento che si ascrivono a questa produzione tanto pezzi dalla qualità eccellente quanto altri molto mediocri; queste differenze sembrano legate al progressivo scadimento tecnico e alla presenza di numerosi *ateliers* ubicati nella colonia stessa o nelle immediate vicinanze. In effetti anche le analisi archeometriche (Morel, Picon 1994) indicano un'area "d'incertezza" produttiva localizzabile tra Cales-Teano e forse Capua. Si ricorda infine che alcune delle forme tipiche del repertorio del tipo B si trovano già nella variante antica della produzione (Lamb. 3 e 6) e che già nella calena media tale repertorio risulta pienamente adottato, con l'aggiunta di alcune forme propriamente calene, tra cui significativamente la Lamb. 1 e il cratere F 4753 (Fig. 3).

L'area laziale rappresenta una realtà altrettanto complessa. Secondo gli ultimi lavori di Stanco vi sarebbe stata a Roma una produzione di "vera campana B" di alta qualità, derivata direttamente dalle migliori produzioni laziali di IV-III sec. a.C e con le stesse caratteristiche tecniche, accanto a produzioni minori, sempre comprese nel gruppo della B e identificate come Bioidi. Non è chiaro tuttavia come sia stato elaborato il repertorio morfologico di questa presunta campana B romana (Stanco 1994: 31-32), né quali siano i rapporti tra questa e le coeve produzioni etrusche, con le quali, in particolare l'aretina, esistono forti similitudini per ammissione dello stesso autore (Stanco 1999: 22).

Infine, si deve citare per la fascia centro-adriatica il caso di *Aesis* (Jesi), dove è nota almeno un'officina attiva tra la metà del III sec. a.C. e l'età augustea (Brecciaroli Taborelli 1998a; 1998b; Predieri e Sfrecola 1998) che, dalla metà del II sec. fino al 40/30 a.C., mostra un rinnovato repertorio formale, assumendo a modello alcuni tipi della campana B (Lamb.1, 2, 3, 4, 5 e 6) oltre alla F 2653 dal repertorio nord-etrusco (Fig. 7). La pasta è di norma chiara, dal beige nelle migliori produzioni al grigio-marrone nelle peggiori (classe locale I e II), e la vernice di migliore qualità è nero-marronosa, prevalentemente opaca.

2. Proposta terminologica

Alla luce dei dati archeologici emersi negli ultimi anni appare dunque accertata da un lato l'inadeguatezza della terminologia tradizionale, dall'altro la necessità di adottarne una nuova che rispecchi l'attuale panorama delle conoscenze. Altrettanto forte ci sembra l'esigenza di non produrre fratture traumatiche con una tradizione lunga e radicata, ormai pienamente assimilata e codificata dalla comunità scientifica internazionale, in modo da non creare nomenclature obsolete destinate soltanto ad accrescere la confusione. D'altro canto, anche la proposta avanzata ad Ampurias sembra peccare di eccessiva semplicazione e non rispecchiare pienamente il complesso panorama delle produzioni di tipo B, soprattutto in Italia. Un'ultima necessità, ma non meno importante, è quella di possedere una nomenclatura gerarchizzata e "aperta", seguendo in questo la fondamentale lezione di Morel.

Si propone dunque di utilizzare il termine, già coniato da Morel, di **Cerchia della campana B** quale contenitore globale per tutte le ceramiche a pasta chiara che presentino essenzialmente il repertorio morfologico tracciato da Lamboglia (forme Lamb. B 1-10) con l'aggiunta di alcune forme (Pasq. 127, F 4753a, San. 166, ecc.) che riflettono l'orizzonte culturale creatosi con le profonde modificazioni socio-economiche del II sec. a.C.

All'interno di questo gruppo si propone di distinguere i principali sotto-gruppi regionali finora individuati: **Tipo B campano**; **Tipo B etrusco**; **Tipo B laziale**; **Tipo B adriatico** e così via. Per ognuno poi di questi sotto-gruppi regionali si distingueranno i singoli *ateliers*, ma solo quando questi siano individuabili con un buon margine di sicurezza, grazie a caratteristiche tecniche e morfologiche fortemente distintive, decorazioni peculiari, presenza di bolli o, quando possibile, con analisi archeometriche (Fig. 8).

Il complesso "nodo gordiano" quale è oggi la campana B non richiede soluzioni radicali bensì soluzioni che riscontrino un vasto consenso e che tendano a chiarire, con la massima logica e semplicità, una realtà aperta e in continua evoluzione. La nostra proposta non vuol essere nient'altro che questo, una proposta che nasce dalla stessa storia e dinamica della ricerca ceramologica. Si dovrebbe ora confrontarla e comprovare la sua validità quale strumento utile all'indagine archeologica.

BIBLIOGRAFIA

Ampurias 2000 = Aquilué, X., Garcia Roselló, J. e Guitart, J. (a cura di), *La ceràmica de vernís negre dels segles II i I aC: Centres productors mediterranis i comercialització a la Pení nsula Ibérica*, Mataró.

Arcelin, P. e Chabot, L., 1980, Les céramiques à vernis noir du village préromain de La Cloche, commune des Pennes-Mirabeau (B.-du-Rh., France) (fouilles 1967-1979), *MEFRA*, XCII, 1, 109-197.

Balland, A., 1969, *Bolsena III.1. Céramique étrusco-campanienne à vernis noir*, MEFRA, supp. 6, Roma.

Bianchini, S., Cibecchini, F. e Pasquinucci, M., 2000, Aspetti e problemi della ceramica a vernice nera del II-I sec. a.c. nell'Etruria nord-occidentale, in *La ceràmica de vernís negre dels segles II i I aC: Centres productors mediterranis i comercialització a la Península Ibérica* (a cura di X. Aquilué, J. Garcia Roselló e J. Guitart), 7-17, Mataró.

Brecciaroli Tarborelli, L., 1998a, La ceramica a vernice nera di Aesis, in *Indagini archeometriche relative alla ceramica a vernice nera: nuovi dati sulla provenienza e la diffusione* (a cura di P. Frontini e M.T. Grassi), 153-169, Como.

Brecciaroli Tarborelli, L., 1998b, Jesi (Ancona). L'officina ceramica di Aesi (III sec. aC-I sec. dC), *NSA*, 5-250.

Cavalieri Manasse, G., 1977, Zona sud del foro (CM). Ceramica a vernice nera, in *Scavi di Luni II. Relazione delle campagne di scavo 1972-1974* (a cura di A. Frova), 78-114, Roma.

Goudineau, C., 1968, *Bolsena IV. La céramique aretine lisse*, MEFRA supp. 6, Roma.

Escrivà, V., Marín, C. e Ribera, A., 1992, Unas producciones minoritarias de barniz negro en Valentia durante el s. II a. J.C., in *Estudios de arqueología ibérica y romana. Homenaje a Enrique Pla Ballester*, 443-468, Trabajos Varios, 89, Valencia.

Johannowsky, W., 1961, Relazione preliminare sugli scavi di Cales, *BA*, XLVI, 3, 259-268.

Lamboglia, N., 1952, Per una classifiaczione preliminare della ceramica campana, *Atti del I Congresso Internazionale di Studi Liguri, Bordighera, 1950*, 139-206, Bordighera.

Lamboglia, N., 1960, Polemiche campane, *RSL*, XXVI, 292-304.

Lamboglia, N., 1961, Problemi tecnici e cronologici dello scavo sottomarino al Grand Congloué, *RSL*, XXVII, 138-154.

Milano 1998 = Frontini, P. e Grassi, M.T. (a cura di), *Indagini archeometriche relative alla ceramica a vernice nera: nuovi dati sulla provenienza e la diffusione*, Como.

Morel, J.-P., 1962-65, Céramiques d'Hippone, *Bulletin d'Archéologie Algérienne*, I, 107-137.

Morel, J.-P., 1963, Notes sur la céramique étrusco-campanienne: vases à vernis noir de Sardaigne et d'Arezzo, *MEFRA*, LXXV, 1, 7-58.

Morel, J.-P., 1965a, Les niveux préromains, in *Thamusida, 1. Fouilles du Service des antiquités du Maroc* (a cura di J.-P. Callu, J.-P. Morel, R. Rebuffat e G. Hallier), 61-111, MEFRA, supp. 2, Roma.

Morel, J.-P., 1965b, *Céramique à vernis noir du Forum Romain et du Palatin*, MEFRA, supp. 3, Roma.

Morel, J.-P., 1965c, Céramiques à vernis noir de Pompéi, *RCFA*, VII, 81-103.

Morel, J.-P., 1968, Céramique à vernis noir du Maroc, *AA*, 2, 55-76.

Morel, J.-P., 1978, À propos des céramiques campaniennes de France et d'Espagne, *Archéologie en Languedoc*, 1, 149-168.

Morel, J.-P., 1980, La céramique campanienne: acquis et problèmes, *Céramiques hellénistiques et romaines*, 85-122, ALUB, 242, Parigi.

Morel, J.-P., 1981, *Céramique campanienne: les formes*, CEFR, 244, Roma.

Morel, J.-P., 1986, La céramique à vernis noir de Carthage, sa diffusion, son influence, *CEA*, XVIII, 25-68.

Morel, J.-P., 1992, La céramique à vernis noir du Maroc: une révision, *Lixus*, 217-233, CEFR, 166, Roma.

Morel, J.-P., 1998, L'étude des céramiques à vernis noire, entre archéologie et archéometrie, in *Indagini archeometriche relative alla ceramica a vernice nera: nuovi dati sulla provenienza e la diffusione* (a cura di P. Frontini e M.T. Grassi), 9-22, Como.

Morel, J.-P. e Picon, M., 1994, Les céramiques étrusco-campaniennes: recherches en laboratoire, in *Ceramica romana e archeometria: lo stato degli studi* (a cura di G. Olcese), 23-46, Firenze.

Palermo, L. 1998, Contributo alla conoscenza della ceramica aretina a vernice nera: i materiali dello scavo di Chiusi, Orto del Vescovo, in *Indagini archeometriche relative alla ceramica a vernice nera: nuovi dati sulla provenienza e la diffusione* (a cura di P. Frontini e M.T. Grassi), 119-130, Como.

Pasquinucci, M., 1972, La ceramica a vernice nera del Museo Guarnacci di Volterra, *MEFRA*, LXXXIV, 269-489.

Pasquinucci, M., Alessi, D., Bianchini, S., Cibecchini, F., Cherubini, L., Del Rio, A., Menchelli, S., Spinesi, P., Vallebona, M. e Capelli, C., 1998, Ceramica a vernice nera dall'Etruria settentrionale costiera. Primo contributo alla caratterizzazione delle produzioni locali e delle importazioni, in *Indagini archeometriche relative alla ceramica a vernice nera: nuovi dati sulla provenienza e la diffusione* (a cura di P. Frontini e M.T. Grassi), 101-118, Como.

Pedroni, L., 1986, *La ceramica a vernice nera da Cales 1*, Napoli.

Pedroni, L., 1990, *La ceramica a vernice nera da Cales 2*, Napoli.

Pedroni, L., 2000, Produzione e diffusione della ceramica calena "media": problemi e ipotesi di lavoro, in *La ceràmica de vernís negre dels segles II i I aC:Centres productors mediterranis i comercialització a la Península Ibérica* (a cura di X. Aquilué, J. Garcia Roselló e J. Guitart), 345-361, Mataró.

Pedroni, L. (a cura di), 2001, *Ceramica calena a vernice nera. Produzione e diffusione*, Napoli.

Pérez Ballester, J., 1992, El vaso crateroide de barniz negro decorado con ovas F 4753, una probable producción calena, *Saguntum*, 25, 119-131.

Predieri, G. e Sfrecola, S., 1998, Analisi archeometriche su materiali ceramici provenienti dall'officina di Aesis (Jesi, AN), *NSA*, 265-267.

Py, M., Adroher, A.M. e Sanchez, C., 2001, Céramique campanienne B, *Lattara*, 14, 1, 557-576.

Sanmartí Grego, E., 1978, *La cerámica campaniense de Emporion y Rhode*, Monografies Emporitanes, IV, Barcelona.

Stanco, E.A., 1994, Ceramica a vernice nera, in *Ceramica Romana. Guida allo Studio*, I (a cura di M. Balzano e A. Camilli), 19-90, Roma.

Stanco, E.A., 1999, La ceramica a vernice nera dello scavo di Lungotevere Testaccio, *BCAR*, C, 7-36.

Taylor, D.M., 1957, Cosa: black-glaze pottery, *MAAR*, XXV, 68-193.

ANNO	AUTORE	DEFINIZIONE	ALTRI APPORTI
1952	LAMBOGLIA	Campana B = ceramica etrusca universale	
1957	TAYLOR	Cosa II = prod. etrusca	
1960	LAMBOGLIA	Camp. B = prod. soprattutto campana (Cales)	
1965-78	MOREL	Camp. B "vera" = etrusca; Bioide = altre prod. extra Etruria tra cui Cales	1972: Pasquinucci: volterrana D; 1977: Luni II: camp. B = B e B1
1980	ARCELIN, CHABOT	Bioide attestata in Gallia = Calena	
1986	PEDRONI	Prima sistemazione ceramica di Cales	
1990	PEDRONI	Ceramica calena = prod. autonoma che copre tutto il repertorio camp. B	

1992	ESCRIVÁ, MARÍN, RIBERA	Byrsa 661 = calena (dec. a cuoricini); F 4753a = prob. calena	1992: Pérez Ballester: F4753a = calena
1994	MOREL, PICON	Bioide = prod. da area "d'incertezza" Teano-Cales-Capua; Cosa II = prod. etrusca = in parte vera camp. B	
1998	MOREL	Byrsa 661 = calena; B etrusca "antica" – bella B etrusca; Bioide = nebulosa di prod. fuori Etruria; serie F4750 = etrusca = F4753a etrusca	1998: équipe Pisa: prod. qualità dell'Etruria sett. = volterrana D, aretina e prod. campano-laziale (e.g. forma Lamb. 1); Palermo: aretina, volterrana D sono in parte = Camp. B
1999	STANCO	Vera camp. B = prod. romana di qualità; Bioide = prod. romane minori, stesso repertorio	
2000	ATTI AMPURIAS	Camp. B etrusca = prod. Volterra, Arezzo, Cosa (?); Biode = calena; sistemazione cronotipologica prod. calena	

Fig. 1. Cronogramma degli studi sulla campana B con i contributi più importanti.

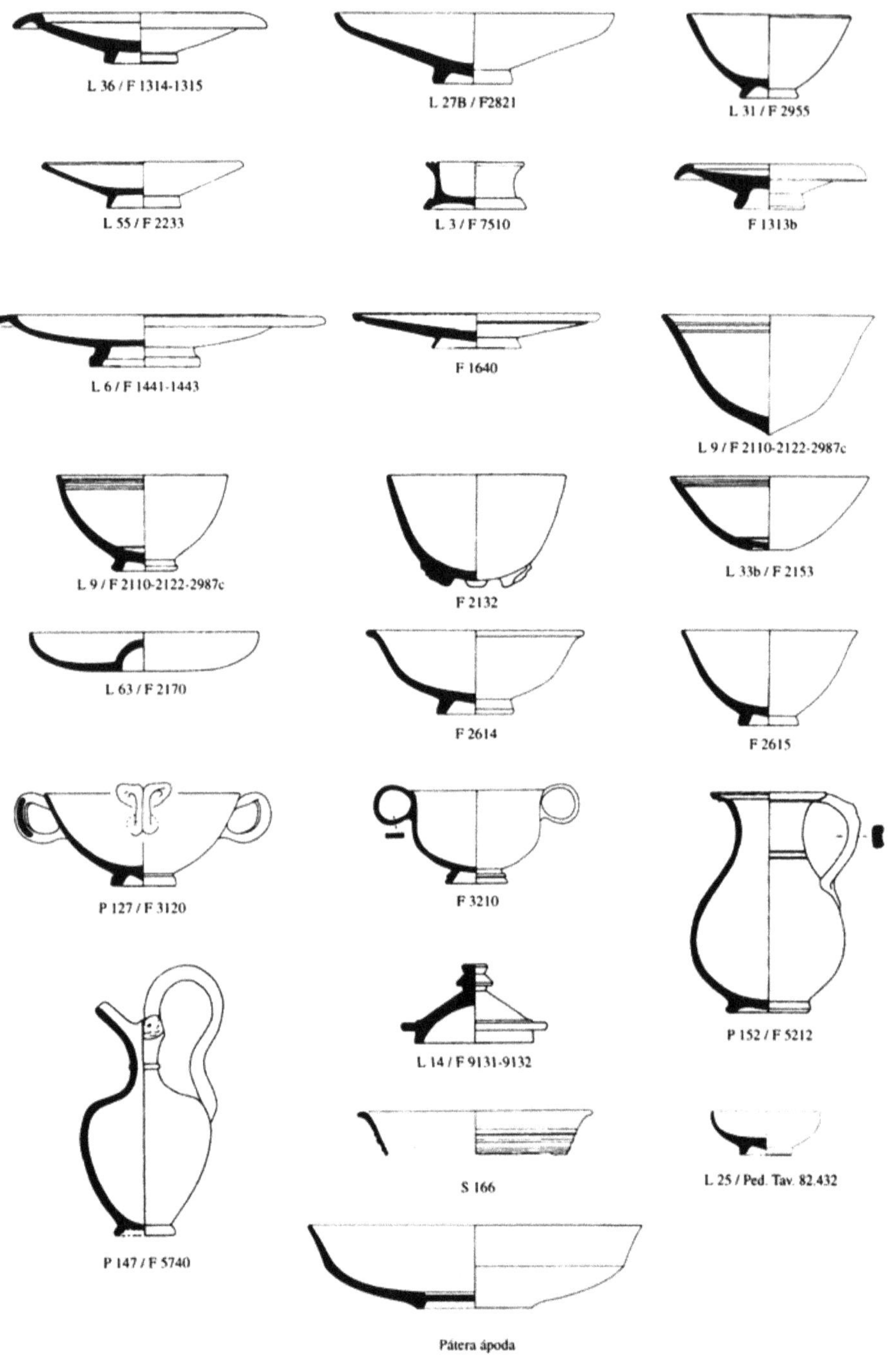

Fig. 2. Forme pertinenti alla variante calena antica (secondo Ampurias 2000).

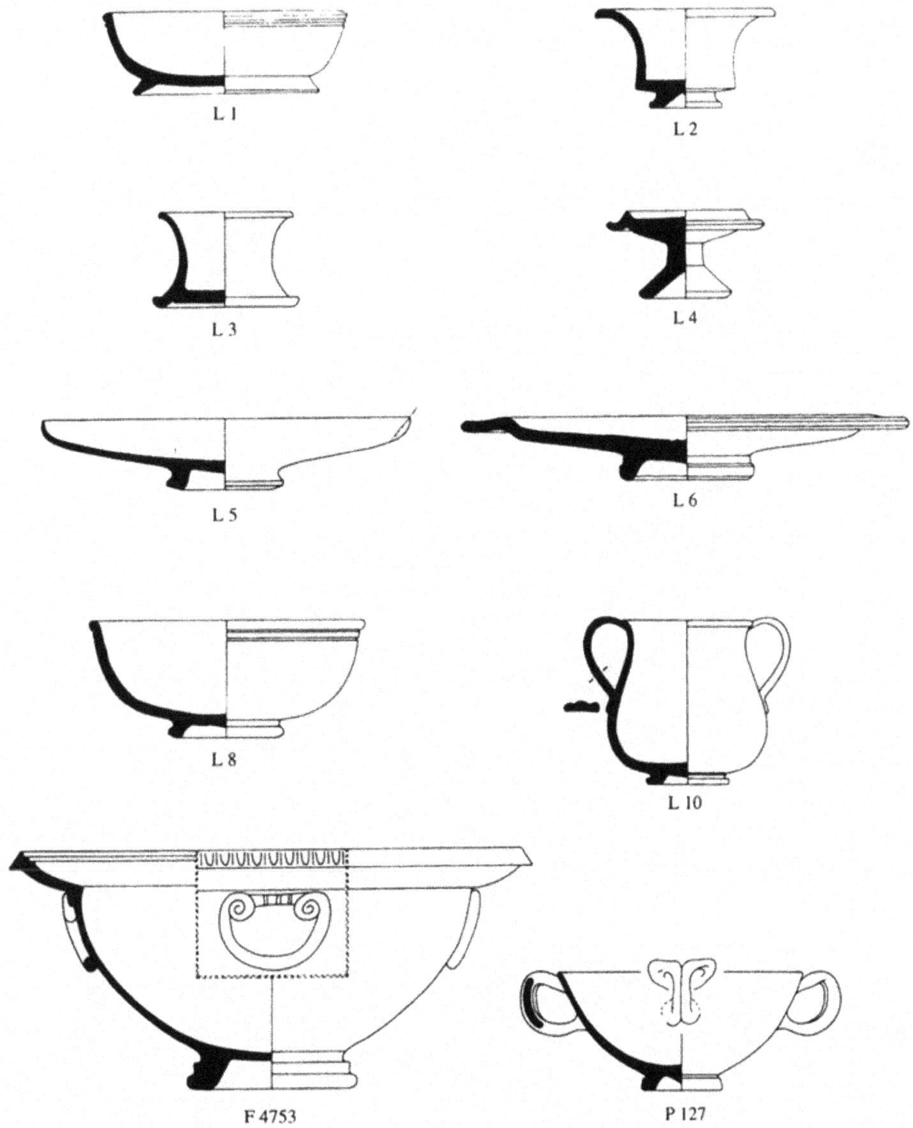

Fig. 3. Forme pertinenti al Tipo B di Cales, calena media (secondo Ampurias 2000).

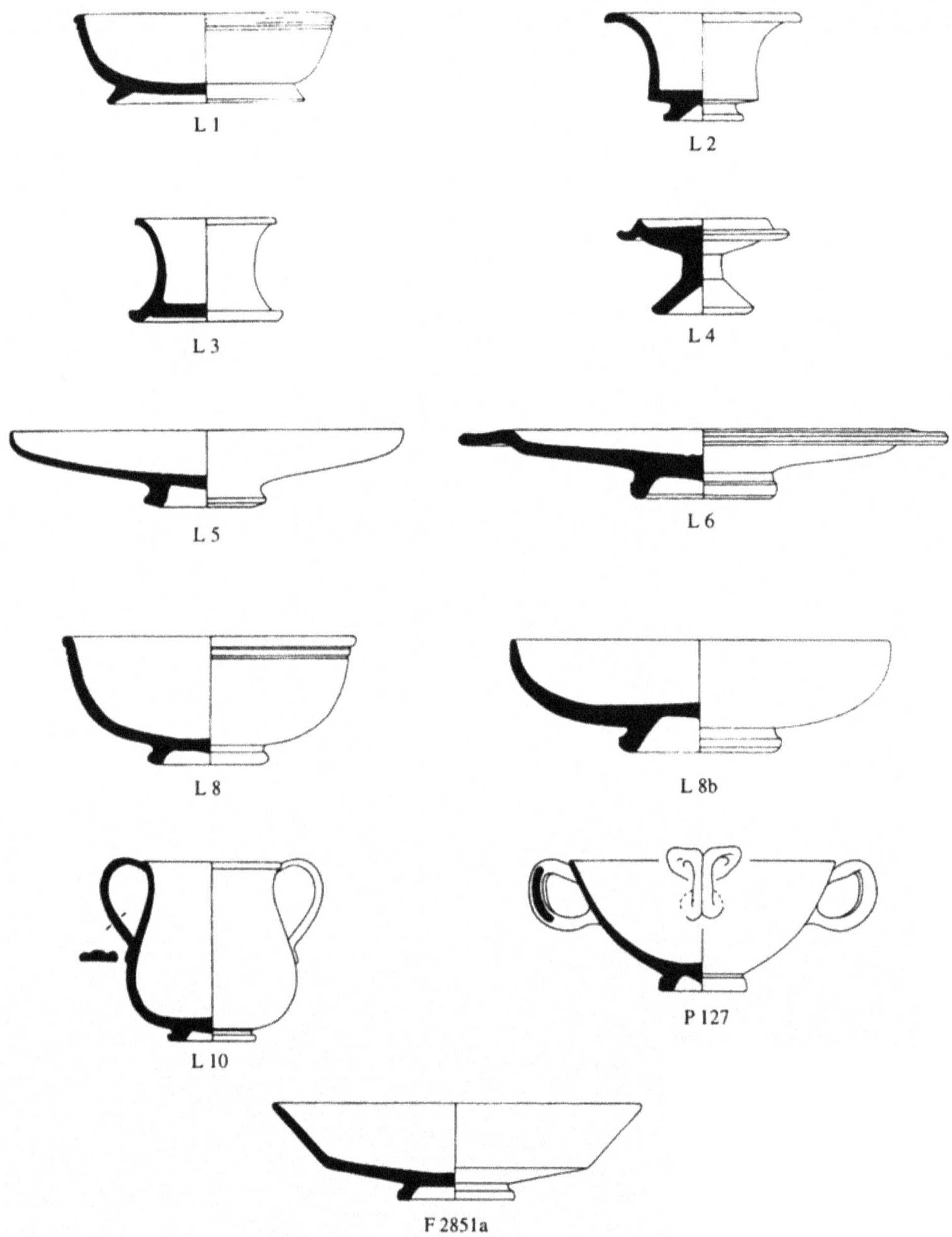

Fig. 4. Forme pertinenti al Tipo B di Cales, calena tarda (secondo Ampurias 2000).

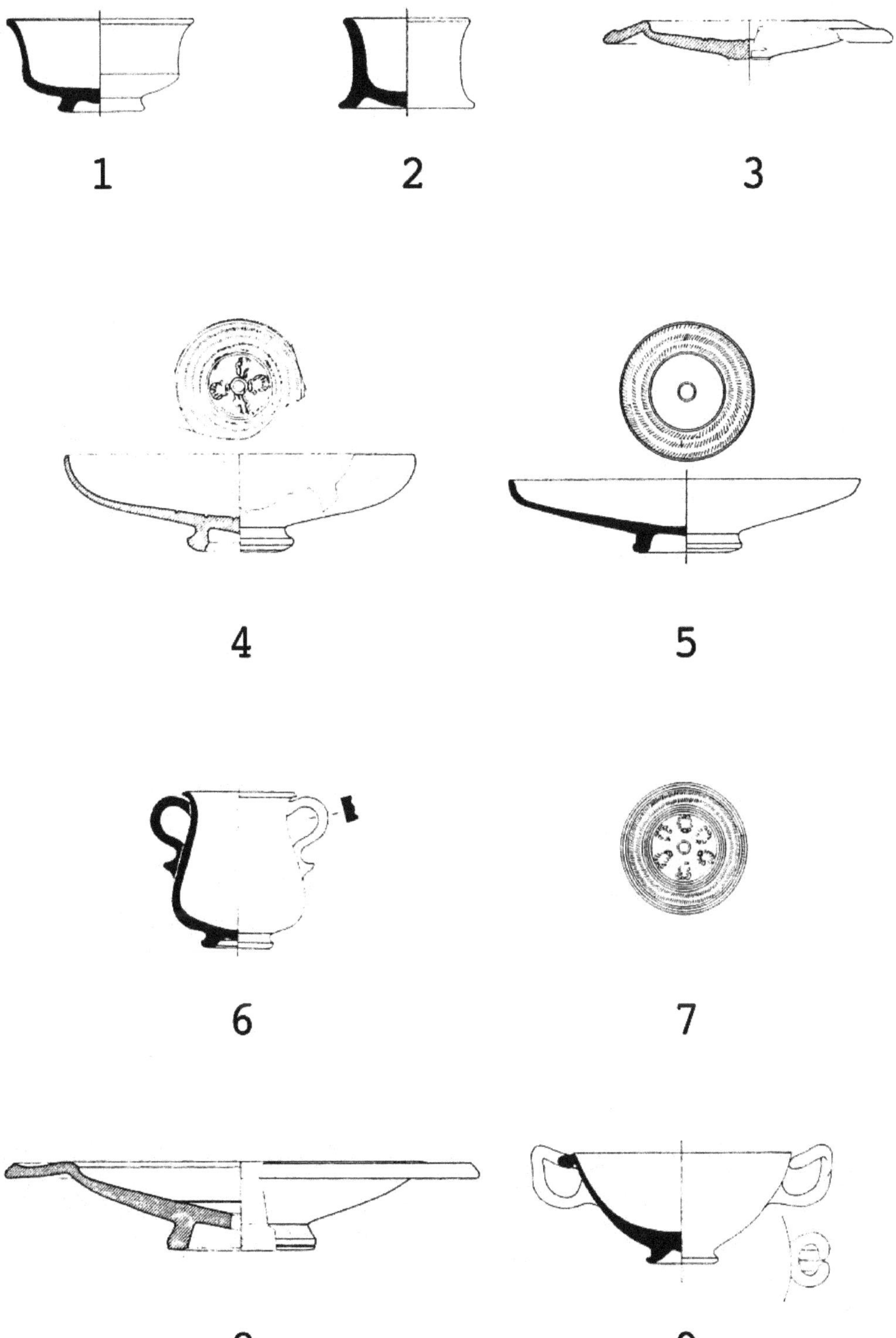

Fig. 5. Frome pertinenti al Tipo B volterrano. 1. Lamb. 2/F 1220 (1:4, da Pasquinucci 1972); 2. Lamb. 2/F 7540 (1:4, da Pasquinucci 1972); 3. Lamb. 4/F 1410 (1:2, da Cavalieri Manasse 1977); 4. Lamb. 8b/F 2961 (1:2, da Cavalieri Manasse 1977); 5. Lamb. 5/F 2250 (1:4, da Pasquinucci 1972); 6. Lamb. 10/F 3451 (1:4, da Pasquinucci 1972); 7. Decorazione caratteristica Tipo B Volterrano (1:4, da Pasquinucci 1972); 8. Lamb. 6/F 1441 (1:2, da Cavalieri Manasse 1977); 9. Pasq. 127/F 3121 (1:4, da Pasquinucci 1972).

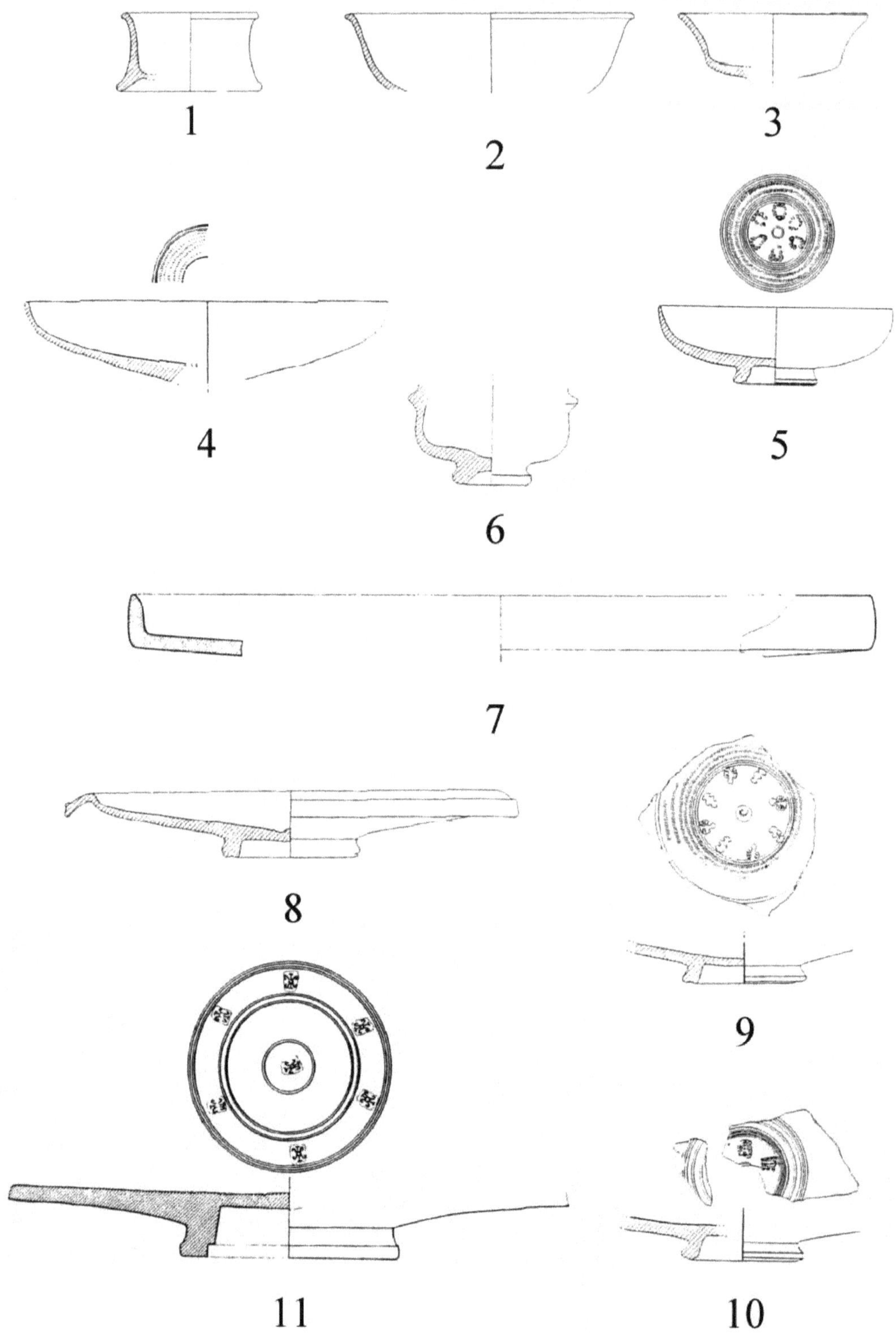

Fig. 6. Forme pertinenti al Tipo B aretino. 1. Lamb. 3/F 7544 (1:4); 2. F 2653 (1:4, da Palermo 1984); 3. Lamb. 28ab/F 2642 (1:4, da Palermo 1984); 4. Lamb. L27B/F 2823 (1:4, da Palermo 1984); 5. Lamb. 8b/F 2961, 2964 (1:4, da Palermo 1984); 6. Lamb. 10/F 3450 (1:4, da Palermo 1984); 7. Lamb. 7/F 2284 (1:2, da Cavalieri Manasse 1977); 8. Lamb. 6/F 1441-1443 (1:4, da Palermo 1984); 9-10. Decorazini caratteristiche ceramica aretina a vernice nera (1:4, da Palermo 1984); 11. Decorazione caratteristica ceramica aretina a vernice nera (1:2, da Cavalieri Manasse 1977).

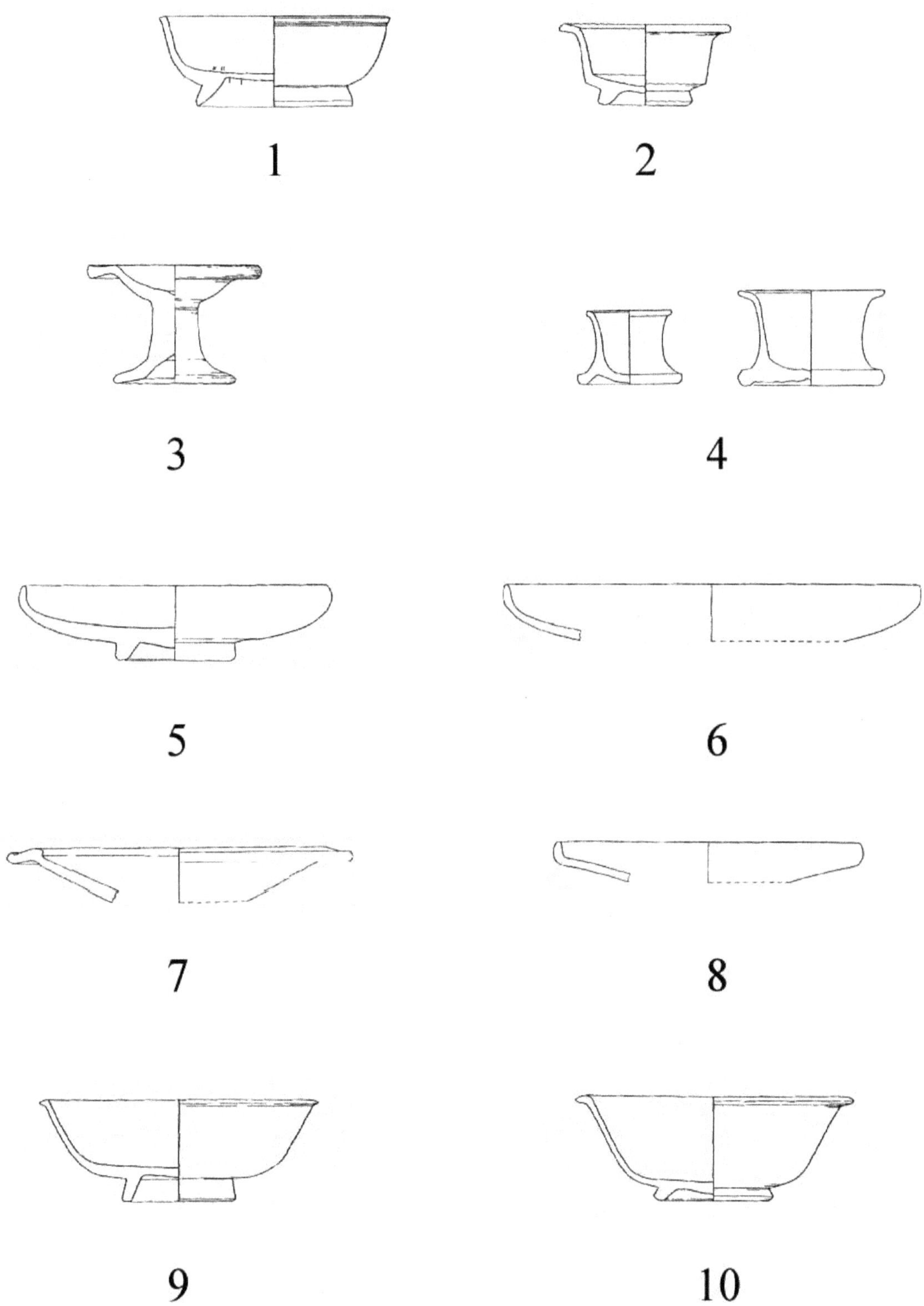

Fig. 7. Forme pertinenti al Tipo B di Jesi (1:4, da Brecciaroli Taborelli 1984). 1. Lamb. 1/F 2323; 2. Lamb. 2/F 1220-1230; 3. Lamb. 4/F 1410; 4. Lamb. 3/F 7530-7550; 5. Lamb. 5/F 2254; 6. Lamb. 5/F 2250; 7. Lamb. 6/F 1443; 8. Lamb. 5-7/F 2283; 9-10. F 2653.

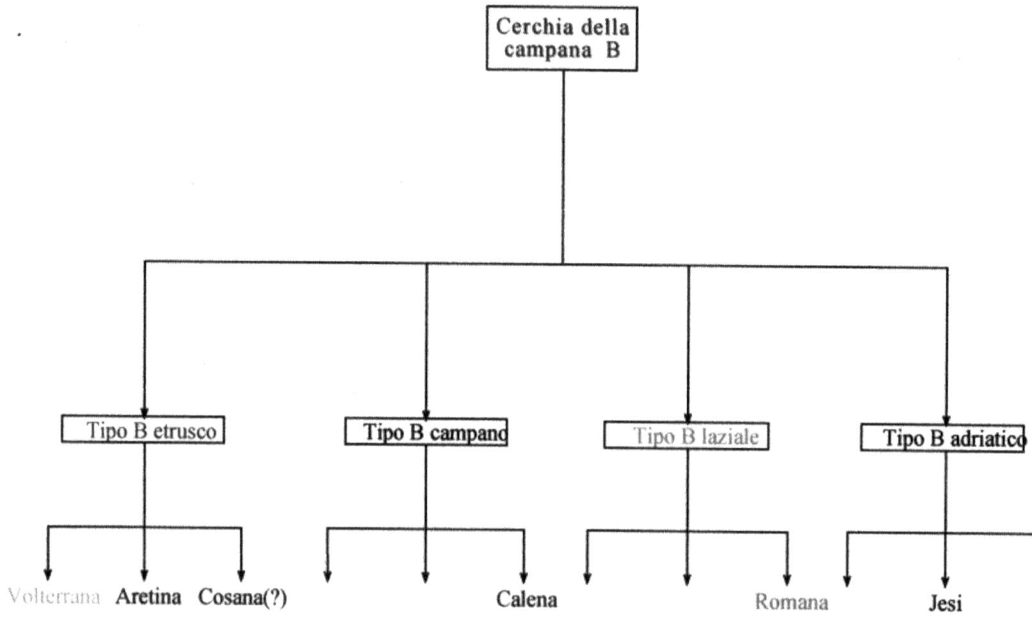

Fig. 8. Schema-proposta terminologica e di nomenclatura.

ANFORE GRECO-ITALICHE ANTICHE: ALCUNE OSSERVAZIONI SULL'ORIGINE E SULLA CIRCOLAZIONE ALLA LUCE DI RECENTI RICERCHE ARCHEOLOGICHE ED ARCHEOMETRICHE.

Gloria OLCESE
(Università La Sapienza, Roma)

ABSTRACT: Research conducted on the island of Ischia have allowed us to establish that many Greco-Italic amphorae recovered during the excavations at Santa Restituta (Lacco Ameno) (MGS III, IV, V ?) were manufactured locally (4th-3rd centuries B.C.). These containers have a characteristic type of "fabric" whose distinctive morphologic features make them unmistakable. Moreover, other greco-Italic amphorae (MGS IV to small degree, but mostly MGS V, V/VI) with similar characteristics have been found at many sites throughout the western Mediteranean (Ischia, Lipari, Pech Maho, Ensèrune), and sometimes with the same maker's stamps, in contexts dating to the mid/late 4th to 3rd centuries BC. The origin of this group of amphorae, probably a common source, cannot be confirmed at this time even though laboratory analyses suggest that their provenience was perhaps Campania (Bay of Naples?).
The cross-examination of data produced earlier suggests that the exportation of Campanian wine in the western Mediterranean, generally thought to have been traded after the 2nd Punic War, was probably marketed at an earlier date.

1. Le anfore greco-italiche: un argomento complesso che necessita di approcci di studio diversi

In questo articolo[1] viene affrontato il problema dell'origine e della diffusione di alcune anfore greco-italiche antiche, tipi Will A1 e A2 (Will 1882), MGSV e MGSIV (Van der Mersch 1994)[2], prodotte dalla metà/fine del IV e nel III secolo a.C. Si tratta di recipienti destinati probabilmente al contenimento del vino, ampiamente diffusi nel Mediterraneo occidentale e di cui non si conoscono i centri produttori, anche se è accettata l'ipotesi che alcuni di essi fossero situati in Italia centro-meridionale.

Le principali difficoltà nello studio delle anfore greco-italiche sono dovute alla esistenza di centri di produzione diversi anche molto lontani fra loro, con una cronologia ampia (dal IV al II secolo a.C.). L'approccio di studio alle anfore greco-italiche, inoltre, è incentrato di solito sulle caratteristiche morfo-tipologiche dei recipienti, oppure sui dati epigrafici, se i contenitori sono bollati. L'approccio tipologico e quello epigrafico, però, se vengono utilizzati da soli, non sempre consentono di arrivare a determinare con certezza l'area di origine del contenitore. Mancano invece dati sugli impasti e ancor di più scarseggiano studi di laboratorio tesi ad accertare e a caratterizzare l'esistenza di produzioni locali[3], nonostante sia ormai chiaro che è quasi impossibile affrontare il tema delle produzione e della circolazione di contenitori ceramici senza tener conto anche dei dati relativi agli impasti. Lo studio delle anfore greco-italiche, utilizzate per interpretare l'economia dell'età ellenistica e repubblicana, dovrebbe basarsi quindi di più su dati tipologici e macroscopici verificati direttamente, mentre spesso la tendenza è quella di interpretare in chiave storico-economica dati bibliografici lacunosi. Per ricostruire correttamente dinamiche di circolazione e proporre una lettura dei dati archeologici in chiave economica, è indispensabile portare nuovamente l'attenzione sulle aree e i centri di produzione, con l'elaborazione di tipologie "locali".

In questo contributo prenderò in considerazione soprattutto le anfore greco-italiche di tipo più antico[4], pur essendo evidenti i rapporti tra questi contenitori e le greco-italiche più recenti.[5] Il punto di partenza è costituito dai dati ottenuti grazie allo studio archeologico e archeometrico di un quartiere artigianale ad Ischia - Lacco Ameno[6], attivo per un lungo periodo di tempo e con una importante fase produttiva in età ellenistica. Tale studio ha permesso di stabilire che in alcune delle fornaci, parzialmente conservate insieme a spazi destinati alla lavorazione, venivano prodotte anfore tra il IV e il III secolo a.C.[7] Una buona parte delle anfore è bollata con nomi greci o oschi, scritti in greco. Si tratta di uno dei pochi quartieri artigianali conosciuti che ha prodotto anfore greco-italiche, bollate con una grande varietà di bolli (alcune decine di nomi) ed è quindi un importante punto di riferimento per riconsiderare, alla luce di nuovi dati - archeologici, epigrafici ed archeometrici - la produzione di anfore di un'area chiave dell'Italia meridionale tirrenica, il Golfo di Napoli.

Ai dati di Ischia si aggiungono, poi, osservazioni desunte dall'esame diretto di anfore greco-italiche recuperate in alcuni siti e relitti del Mediterraneo occidentale (si veda *infra* l'elenco dei siti considerati)[8]. Da questa indagine preliminare è emersa l'esistenza di un gruppo di anfore greco-italiche antiche dalle caratteristiche tipologiche, di impasto e di lavorazione molto simili tra loro, in qualche caso con gli stessi bolli, la cui origine è con tutta probabilità da ricondurre alla stessa area geografica, forse alla Campania. Contemporaneamente si è registrata la presenza di anfore greco-italiche antiche con impasti diversi, distinguibili da quelli di area campana (come nel caso delle anfore greco-italiche antiche di Camarina e di Adria). L'indagine macroscopica e l'osservazione delle modalità di lavorazione si sono rivelate criteri importanti per l'accorpamento di esemplari simili e per la separazione di recipienti di forma analoga, ma prodotti in aree diverse.

Un contributo fondamentale alla ricerca archeologica, infine, hanno apportato le analisi di laboratorio, che hanno permesso la caratterizzazione chimica e mineralogica delle anfore.

2. L'origine delle anfore greco-italiche : le ipotesi

L'anfora greco-italica nasce secondo alcuni studiosi come imitazione di contenitori prodotti nel bacino orientale del Mediterraneo: la Will ritiene che le prime greco-italiche - in particolare il tipo A - siano state prodotte in Grecia e che in seguito la forma sia stata adottata in officine della Sicilia e del Mediterraneo occidentale; le anfore corinzie B, in modo particolare, sono state viste come i prototipi dell'anfora greco-italica (Will 1982, p.341 nota 4). Altri autori considerano le anfore greco-italiche recipienti nati dall'evoluzione di anfore prodotte in area magno greca e siceliota (Empereur, Hesnard 1987, p.26-28; van der Mersch 1994, p.78). Il problema più spinoso concerne però l'individuazione dell'area o delle aree di origine delle produzioni che hanno circolato, anche a causa della mancanza di dati su siti produttori. Sono state formulate diverse ipotesi relative alle aree di origine delle anfore greco-italiche e lo *status questionis* è desumibile da diversi lavori (Manacorda 1981 e 1986; Empereur, Hesnard 1987; van der Mersch 1994).

Le anfore greco-italiche antiche bollate in greco sono state attribuite preferibilmente alla Sicilia e alla Magna Grecia, senza che tuttavia venissero escluse aree di produzione in Campania, soprattutto là dove si riscontrano impasti tipici della zona vesuviana (Empereur, Hesnard 1987, p.26; van der Mersch 1986, p.79; Id. 1994, p.131); le anfore bollate in latino sono state collegate all'Italia centrale tirrenica.

Il carico di anfore del relitto della Secca di Capistello, ad esempio, - costituito da anfore MGS V bollate in greco - è stato attribuito da alcuni studiosi alla Campania (C. Albore Livadie in AA.VV. 1985, p. 61), da altri alla Sicilia (Blanck 1978 e, sulla scorta delle sue osservazioni, Empereur, Hesnard 1987, p.26). Alla Sicilia orientale rimanderebbe la maggior parte dei bolli sulle anfore (van der Mersch 1994, p.79).

Oggetto di discussione è anche l'attribuzione dei più antichi bolli latini, documentati sulle anfore greco-italiche più recenti. Ancora incerta è, ad esempio, l'origine del bollo di *Tr. Loisio* su anfore MGS VI, collegato da alcuni studiosi alla Campania e in particolare alla zona di Napoli, (Buchner, Rittman 1948, p.58; Lepore 1952, p. 313; Id. 1967 p.248-252; Manacorda 1986, p. 582-583), da altri invece alla Sicilia - la "piste sicilienne" di cui parla Tchernia (Tchernia 1985, p.49; Empereur, Hesnard 1987, p.26; Hesnard et Al. 1989 p.31). Analisi di laboratorio su bolli di *Tr. Loisio* sono state effettuate nell'ambito di questo lavoro (paragrafo 6, *infra*).

Alle diverse prese di posizione non sempre corrisponde un controllo diretto sui materiali, un censimento dei dati tipologici, epigrafici e di impasto delle anfore greco-italiche nelle due zone considerate "chiave" per la produzione, la Campania e la Sicilia. Una ricognizione preliminare effettuata da chi scrive in alcuni musei della Sicilia ha permesso di ridimensionare il problema della distinzione delle produzioni delle due aree, dal momento che anche solo a livello macroscopico, almeno una parte delle anfore greco-italiche siciliane (ad esempio quelle di Camarina) presenta impasti che si distinguono piuttosto agevolmente da quelli campani. Se anche lo *screening* su tipi e impasti non scioglie tutti i dubbi, le analisi di laboratorio hanno recentemente dimostrato la diversità di composizione dei materiali delle due aree e la possibilità di una loro distinzione (si veda *infra).*

3. La tipologia delle anfore greco-italiche antiche

La prima tipologia delle anfore greco-italiche è stata realizzata dalla Will che ha individuato 5 tipi (denominati con le lettere *a-e*) (Will 1982). Tale classificazione, anche se datata, consente di definire a grandi linee i gruppi principali delle anfore greco-italiche.

Il lavoro del van der Mersch (van der Mersch 1994) contempla tipi differenti di anfore, per cui si presuppone una produzione in area magno-greca e in Sicilia (MGS III – VI) e la cui datazione copre un periodo ampio, dal V secolo a.C. al II a.C. Per ammissione dello stesso Autore lo scopo dello studio non è quello di fornire una classificazione delle anfore greco-italiche. Data la mancanza di tipologie, il bel volume del van der Mersch viene ormai usato anche come strumento classificatorio, pur presentando proprio in questo ambito alcuni problemi. Uno di essi riguarda l'accorpamento all'interno di uno stesso gruppo di più tipi di anfore che dovrebbero invece, in base alla morfologia, essere separati[9]. Inoltre, proprio per l'ottica generale del lavoro, che è quella di studiare "au sens large" il vino e le anfore da trasporto prodotte nel IV-III secolo a.C. in Italia del sud, non vengono presi in considerazione dati tecnici, ad esempio quelli relativi agli impasti dei contenitori, che contribuiscono però in modo determinante alla distinzione delle anfore prodotte in aree diverse.

Poiché lo scopo di questo articolo non è la redazione di una tipologia delle anfore greco-italiche, si è utilizzata la terminologia già in adozione, per evitare di complicare ulteriormente la situazione. Risulta però evidente che la tipologia delle greco-italiche dovrà essere rivista e riproposta sulla base di un esame diretto dei materiali, che tenga conto dei dati tipologici, tecnologici e di impasto.

4. Le analisi di laboratorio sulle anfore greco-italiche: i dati della bibliografia

Le analisi di laboratorio possono dare un contributo determinante alla individuazione delle aree di origine dei recipienti ceramici.

Riferimenti ad analisi di laboratorio (chimiche e mineralogiche) su anfore greco-italiche si trovano in alcuni lavori relativi al materiale di Velia (Lyko 2000), Pompei (Mannoni 1984), di Ugento (Desy, De Paepe 1990), di Locri (Barra Bagnasco 1995), della Sicilia (Alaimo et Al. 1997, p.62), di Berenice (Riley 1985, p.131) e di alcuni relitti (Mannoni, a proposito delle sezioni effettuate sulle anfore greco-italiche del relitto della Meloria, citato in Bargagliotti et Al. 1996, p. 48 nota 19). Qualche dato mineralogico si ricava anche dal volume di Peacock e Williams (Peacock, Williams 1986, p.85). Da questi studi emerge l'esistenza di produzioni attribuite alla Campania ma anche ad altre aree, in Magna Grecia e in Sicilia.

Metodi chimici e mineropetrografici sono stati utilizzati per determinare l'origine di anfore greco-italiche e Dressel 1 rinvenute in Francia; oggetto di studio è stato il cospicuo gruppo di anfore greco-italiche rinvenute nell'*oppidum* di Pech Maho, nell'Aude (Hesnard et Al. 1989; Thierrin Michael 2000), con lo scopo di individuare le aree di approvvigionamento del vino italico esportato verso la Francia. L'articolo di Hesnard et Al. pubblicato nel 1989, pionieristico nel suo campo, insieme ad un altro (Ricq de Bouard et Al. 1989), è a tutt'oggi imprescindibile per chi voglia occuparsi delle aree di produzione delle anfore in Italia centro-meridionale.

I dati di laboratorio (chimici) editi in tale lavoro si riferiscono principalmente ad anfore Dressel 1 e alle anfore greco-italiche di tipo più recente, rinvenute in zone di produzione (officine individuate in Etruria, Lazio e Campania) e in alcuni siti della Francia (La Lagaste, Lastours, Lyon) o in Spagna (Ampurias, Numantia), in contesti principalmente di II e I secolo a.C. In un caso, quello dell'*oppidum* di Pech Maho (Sigean, Aude), si tratta di materiali dell'ultimo quarto del III secolo a.C.

Esistono però alcuni problemi legati alla tipologia delle anfore: non vengono infatti indicati dati di collegamento con le anfore analizzate (nel sito di Pech Maho sono presenti tipi diversi di greco-italiche). Inoltre le anfore greco-italiche e le Dressel 1 vengono trattate "in blocco", senza distinzione e non è possibile distinguere i risultati ottenuti in laboratorio per le Dressel 1 da quelli delle greco-italiche.

Un articolo recentemente pubblicato ha come oggetto lo studio mineralogico sempre delle anfore greco-italiche del sito di Pech Maho (Thierrin Michael 2000). La pubblicazione si propone di stabilire se le anfore greco-italiche dell'*oppidum* della Gallia meridionale, rinvenute in un contesto datato al terzo quarto del III secolo a.C., siano originarie dell'Italia peninsulare o della Sicilia. L'Autrice, dopo aver presentato i dati mineralogici e averli confrontati con i dati chimici ottenuti da M. Picon per la pubblicazione precedentemente ricordata (Hesnard et Al. 1989), individua più gruppi di anfore corrispondenti a diverse officine. Tali officine sarebbero nella maggior parte dei casi da collocare in area italica peninsulare (tra Cosa e Sorrento), per la presenza nella maggior parte delle anfore di inclusioni vulcaniche predominanti tipiche del vulcanismo dell'Italia centrale e per l'associazione di alcuni minerali. I dati sono di grande interesse anche se, essendo la campionatura di base per le analisi di laboratorio la stessa utilizzata per l'articolo di Hesnard et Al. del 1989, valgono le osservazioni precedentemente formulate.[10] L'impiego di criteri tipologici, macroscopici ed epigrafici, inoltre, consente proprio nel caso di Pech Maho di restringere ulteriormente l'area di possibile origine di una parte delle anfore greco-italiche antiche alla Campania, rispetto allo spettro molto ampio - da Cosa a Sorrento - proposto sulla base delle sole analisi di laboratorio.[11]

5. Un centro di produzione di anfore greco-italiche: Ischia

La produzione di anfore greco-italiche ad Ischia era stata ipotizzata da molto tempo, anche se la questione è rimasta aperta fino ad ora, in mancanza di dati conclusivi. L'isola è conosciuta per la produzione di ceramica già dall'epoca della colonizzazione e anfore vi sono state fabbricate nel VII/VI secolo a.C. (Di Sandro 1986).

Il riesame di tutti i reperti rinvenuti nell'area di Santa Restituta, effettuato nell'ambito di un progetto di edizione delle fornaci ceramiche (Olcese et al. 1996), ha consentito di riprendere in considerazione alcune centinaia di frammenti di anfore di tipo greco-italico, in modo particolare anse bollate, alcuni orli e puntali (Figg. 1 e 3.3). I reperti sono stati considerati e studiati con le strutture. Scarti di fornace di anfore greco-italiche provengono dall'interno delle fornaci (3 e 5) o dall'area immediatamente circostante (Fig. 3.4).

Il problema principale del sito è costituito dalla mancanza di dati stratigrafici che avrebbero permesso di stabilire la successione cronologica delle anfore e una migliore ricostruzione delle fasi di vita di questo interessantissimo quartiere artigianale. In ogni caso, una fase della produzione è databile, in base ai confronti tipologici, alle osservazioni sull'epigrafia dei bolli, alle datazioni con termoluminescenza delle strutture, ad un periodo compreso tra la metà/fine del IV secolo a.C. e la prima metà del III secolo a.C.

Per delimitare la produzione locale è stata effettuata l'analisi tipologica e macroscopica degli impasti delle ceramiche di diverse epoche, infine una serie di analisi chimiche di laboratorio la cui elaborazione definitiva è ancora in corso con V. Thirion Merle e con M. Picon.

5.1. I tipi documentati

La produzione di anfore greco-italiche antiche ad Ischia doveva essere sicuramente ampia e articolata, come conferma l'abbondanza dei reperti e la varietà dei bolli rinvenuti. Alcune anfore appartengono al tipo MGS III del van der Mersch, classificate abitualmente nel gruppo delle "magno greche" e considerate come una sorta di contenitore di passaggio tra le anfore prodotte in età classica e i primi tipi di greco-italiche vere e proprie (Empereur, Hesnard 1987, p.26). Inoltre, sono ben documentati i tipi MGS IV e V (van der Mersch 1994, Will A2 e A1).

Purtroppo la maggior parte delle anfore di Santa Restituta è costituita da frammenti, per lo più anse, alcuni orli, pochi frammenti di spalla e alcuni puntali (Fig. 3.3). Contando solo su frammenti di orlo non sempre è possibile risalire al tipo; in alcuni casi rimane infatti incerta la pertinenza ad un tipo piuttosto che ad un altro. Ulteriori accertamenti sono in corso per stabilire con certezza se a Ischia si producessero anche i tipi più recenti delle greco-italiche (MGS VI), presenti tra i materiali dello scarico Gosetti e in alcune tombe della necropoli di S. Montano, ma documentati nell'area di Santa Restituta in percentuale inferiore rispetto agli altri tipi (Fig. 3.5).[12]

La maggior parte delle anse sono bollate con nomi greci o oschi, scritti in greco, che spesso riportano all'onomastica di area campana e che si ritrovano anche su laterizi rinvenuti nella zona di scavo[13]. Per uno stesso nominativo sono documentati più bolli (alcune decine) talora ricavati da una stessa matrice, fatto che è un'ulteriore conferma della produzione locale. Anche l'impasto è ricorrente (si veda *infra*). Sono purtroppo molto pochi gli esemplari di orlo che conservano l'ansa o la spalla bollata, permettendo di associare un nome ad un tipo preciso di anfora.

Tipo MGS III

Alcuni orli rinvenuti nello scavo di S. Restituta sono riconducibili al tipo MGS III con orlo a quarto di cerchio (o ad echino) e collo cilindrico, documentato nel corso del IV secolo a.C. (Figg. 1.1-1.2). Si tratta probabilmente del tipo più antico di anfora "greco italica" prodotta nelle fornaci di Santa Restituta. Scarti di orli e parete sono stati rinvenuti nell'area della fornace n. 3 e nei pressi della 5 (Fig. 3.4), insieme ad alcuni bolli relativi a nomi greci scritti in greco - ad esempio ΑΡΙΣ nella fornace 3. Altri bolli documentati sono anche: [ΑΡ]Ι*ΣΤΟΚΙ*, ΑΡΙ*ΣΤΟΚ[..]*. Un esemplare con bollo [..]ΥΤΩ è conservato tra i materiali dello scarico Gosetti.

Tipo MGS IV - Will A2

Il tipo in questione ha orlo pronunciato, superiormente piatto e arrotondato nella parte inferiore (oppure a profilo triangolare). Il collo è lungo e cilindrico (ca. 16 cm), leggermente rastremato verso il basso; le anse sono lunghe (ca. cm 18) e diritte.[14] La cronologia proposta dalla bibliografia comprende il IV secolo a.C. e i primi decenni del III (van der Mersch 1994, pp.73-76). E. Will considerava le anfore di questo tipo di possibile origine siceliota (Will 1982, 342-344). C. van der Mersch ha ipotizzato come possibili zone di produzione quelle comprese tra Posidonia-Taranto-Agrigento e in particolare considera certe le produzioni di Hipponion e Gela-Manfria (van der Mersch 1994, p.76).

I dati di Ischia confermano che il tipo è stato prodotto sull'isola, probabilmente in un periodo compreso tra la fine del IV e i primi decenni del III secolo a.C. Nei pressi del forno 5 dell'officina di Santa Restituta sono stati rinvenuti diversi esemplari frammentari riportabili a questo tipo, uno dei quali più conservato degli altri, con bollo ΞΕΝ (Figg. 2.1-2.2), bollo che si ripete anche su decine di anse frammentarie; sempre in questa zona sono documentati alcuni bolli ΞΕΝ ΤΡΕ, costituiti da due nomi, uno greco e uno osco.

In tal modo è possibile collegare un tipo preciso (MGS IV) ad un bollo (ΞΕΝ)[15] e ad un'area precisa di origine. Il tipo in questione è realizzato con l'impasto caratteristico delle anfore greco-italiche di Ischia (*infra*). Le analisi di laboratorio hanno confermato la sua piena appartenenza al gruppo di produzione locale (gruppo chimico 1).

Un altro elemento interessante è dato dalla forte somiglianza - morfologica e di impasto - riscontrata tra le anfore di Ischia appartenenti a questo gruppo e quelle del relitto del Filicudi F[16]. L'esemplare di Ischia più vicino alle anfore del Filicudi F è la MGS IV con *bollo* ΞΕΝ in cartiglio rettangolare. Un ulteriore bollo purtroppo frammentario è costituito da un sigma lunato, rinvenuto accanto al forno 5.

Analisi di laboratorio non sono state eseguite sulle anfore del relitto a causa delle difficoltà che si riscontrano analizzando chimicamente le ceramiche provenienti dal mare, ma un'origine comune dei reperti dei due siti è ugualmente possibile per la somiglianza di forma e impasto.

Sono state invece sottoposte ad analisi di laboratorio alcune anfore della necropoli di Portinenti a Lipari riferibili in un caso al tipo MGS IV, ma per lo più al tipo MGS V, caratterizzate da impasto simile a quello delle anfore dei relitti Filicudi F e Capistello e che, in più, hanno il vantaggio di non provenire da uno scavo subacqueo (si veda *infra*, il paragrafo 5.4).

Una serie di orli/anse frammentari con bolli (ΤΙΝΘ, ΠΑΡ) potrebbe appartenere a questo tipo (Fig. 2.4), anche se non è possibile escludere che si tratti già di MGS V o tipi intermedi.

Tipo MGS V - Will A1

Il tipo MGS V - A1 documentato a Ischia ha il collo a tronco di cono rovesciato e l'orlo a sezione triangolare, leggermente pendente (Figg. 3.1-3.2).[17] Il passaggio tra collo e spalla è sottolineato da un restringimento, quello tra spalla e pancia da una carena appuntita oppure arrotondata. Il puntale è cilindrico/troncoconico, cavo.

Questo tipo, caratteristico della fine del IV e del primo terzo del III secolo a.C. è considerato in bibliografia di origine campana[18], dato che sembra ora confermato dai rinvenimenti di Ischia. Sono documentati i seguenti bolli: ΣΑΤΥΡ•V, [Δ]ΙΟΝΥ, ΔΙ.

5.2. I bolli

Per quanto riguarda i bolli sulle anfore di Ischia - in qualche caso si tratta degli stessi che compaiono su tegole, coppi o pesi da telaio - sono in caratteri greci e comprendono decine di nomi e sono databili tra la metà/fine del IV e il III secolo a.C.[19] Sono impressi in cartiglio rettangolare (in qualche caso ovale) con angoli a spigolo vivo, abbastanza profondo e con le lettere a rilievo marcato. In alcuni casi si tratta di bolli male impressi e forse scartati. Talora si conserva la traccia dell'impressione del punzone nella parte vicina al cartiglio. Alla base delle anse si è riscontrata spesso una "ditata" che sembra essere un elemento caratteristico della produzione di Ischia. Le lettere impresse presentano tratti comuni in età ellenistica, ad esempio l'*alpha* ha la barra centrale interrotta o il sigma è lunato. In molti casi le lettere sono legate tra loro. Significativi sono i bolli che ritraggono una piccola anfora (su ansa) oppure un artigiano mentre fabbrica un'anfora (su di un peso da telaio).

Ancora incerta la pertinenza di tutti i bolli documentati alla produzione locale.

La maggior parte dei bolli reca impressi nomi greci : A, AP, ΑΡΙΣΤ, ΑΡΙΣΤΟ, ΑΡΙΣΤΟΚ (Figg. 1.2, 1.3, 1.4), riferibili forse ad un medesimo nome - ΑΡΙΣΤΟΚΡΑΤΗΣ - presente per intero in un bollo male impresso, forse uno scarto. Altri bolli molto documentati sono: ΠΑΡ (Fig. 2.4) o ΓΑΡ; ΓΛΑΥΚ, ΓΛΑΥΚΟΣ; ΖΩ; ΖΩΙΛ (retrogrado); ΧΑ; ΧΑΡ; ΧΑΡΙΛΑ, ΧΑΡΙΛΕΟΣ; ΧΑΡΜΕ, ΧΑΡΜΕΩ; ΞΕΝ (Figg. 2.1, 2.2); ΞΕΝΩΝ; ΞΕΝ ΤΡΕ (nome greco + nome osco). Almeno quattro esemplari sono riconducibili a ANT, ANTA e ΑΝΤΑΛΛ (retrogradi) (Ανταλλος). Bolli analoghi sono documentati a Lipari, Enserune, Erice e Eraclea Minoa.

Un numero piuttosto significativo è costituito da bolli oschi, scritti in greco: ΤΡΕ (ΒΙΟΣ), ΟΒΙ(ΟΣ), CIBI (su tegola); ΔΕΝΥΨΙ (su tegola, sigla ΔΕ che indica *δημόσιος* (pubblico) o *δημοσία*, più il prenome osco ΝΥΨΙ)[20]; ΜΑΜΑΡΚΟΣ[21].

Ci sono infine alcuni bolli riconducibili forse a nomi etruschi ΤΙΝΘ e C (digamma)ΕΛ (Fig. 2.5).

I pochi bolli in latino, Q. ANTRO, su di un'ansa e due bolli che recano il nome di TR. LOISIO (Fig. 3.5)[22], hanno impasti un po' diversi da quelli della maggior parte delle anfore. L'ultimo bollo, abbreviazione del prenome osco *Tr(ebios)* unito al gentilizio *Loisios*[23], è impresso sull'ansa di un'anfora MGS VI.

5.3. Gli impasti

L'impasto della maggior parte delle anfore di Ischia è molto simile: colore beige chiaro tendente al rosato (Munsell 5YR 7/3) oppure al marroncino (10YR 7/3); in frattura pulita la colorazione tipica è beige tendente al rossiccio (5YR 6/6). Tra le inclusioni visibili ad occhio nudo ci sono granuli di materiale vulcanico e scaglie di mica. Piuttosto inconfondibile anche la tecnica di lavorazione e il modo di trattare le superfici[24].

Una prima verifica ha consentito di stabilire una somiglianza macroscopica tra gli impasti delle anfore greco-italiche di più siti (alcune di quelle rinvenute a Ischia, nei relitti eoliani del Filicudi F e della Secca di Capistello, nella necropoli di Portinenti[25] (si veda *infra*), a Pech Maho, nel sud della Gallia).

Queste prime osservazioni sono alla base della ricerca avviata in alcuni siti e sui materiali di relitti, ricerca affiancata da una serie di analisi di laboratorio tese a verificare un'eventuale origine comune delle anfore.

5.4. I primi dati di laboratorio sulle anfore di Ischia

Volendo indagare il problema dell'origine delle greco-italiche antiche è parso opportuno avviare l'indagine di laboratorio partendo dal centro produttore, cioè da Ischia, sottoponendo ad analisi chimica e mineralogica campioni di scarti, di ceramiche e argille e laterizi rinvenuti nell'area delle fornaci e, in parte, provenienti anche dallo scarico Gosetti.

A questo primo gruppo sono stati affiancati alcuni campioni di greco-italiche simili per morfologia e impasto, provenienti della necropoli di Portinenti a Lipari (tipo MGS V)[26]. Inoltre sono state sottoposte ad analisi anche alcune anse bollate da Ensèrune[27] e da Pech Maho .[28]

Le analisi chimiche eseguite hanno consentito di stabilire che gli scarti delle anfore, l'argilla rinvenuta nel quartiere artigianale e alcuni laterizi facenti parte della struttura delle fornaci, hanno composizioni chimiche e mineralogiche molto simili (Olcese et al. 1996, 18, a cui si rimanda per i dati chimici preliminari). Analoga alla composizione chimica delle anfore è anche quella delle ceramiche di età geometrica di Ischia, fatto che dimostra la continuità nell'approvvigionamento della materia prima nel corso dei secoli.

Le anfore greco-italiche sottoposte ad analisi si suddividono in due gruppi chimici, il primo dei quali di sicura origine locale (*gruppo 1*); comprende infatti scarti di fornace, campioni di argille locali e ceramiche di epoca geometrica prodotte localmente. In questo gruppo sono compresi tra gli altri i bolli : AP, ΑΡΙΣΤ, ΑΡΙΣΤΟ, ΑΡΙΣΤΟΚ, ΓΛΑΥΚΟΣ, ΖΟ, ΖΟΙΛ, ΞΕΝ, ΞΕΝ ΤΡΕ, ΠΑΡ, ΤΙΝΘ, ΧΑΡΙΛΕΩ, ΣΕΛ (con *digamma* iniziale). Sulla base dei pochi campioni riconducibili ad un tipo, sembrano prevalere in questo gruppo le anfore MGS III e IV.

L'altro *gruppo, il 2*, considerata la somiglianza di composizioni con il precedente, potrebbe avere la stessa origine, anche per ora non è possibile escludere che si tratti di altre officine, magari sempre di Ischia e, più in generale, dell'area del Golfo di Napoli. A favore di una origine locale sembra deporre la presenza di qualche scarto all'interno del gruppo, insieme alla ceramica geometrica di produzione locale.

Gli unici frammenti classificabili sono riconducibili al tipo MGS V (con bolli ΔΙ, [Δ]ΙΟΝΥ, ΣΑΤΥΡ•V). Tra i bolli su anse sono documentati: ANT (retrogrado), ΑΝΤΑ[..] (retrogrado), ΔΙ, [Δ]ΙΟΝΥ, [?]ΥΤΩ, ΧΕΝΩΝ, ΠΑΡ corona/sole M (oppure ΓΑΡ corona/sole M), ΠΑΡΗ, ΧΑΡ ΜΕΩ, ΧΑΡ, ΣΑΤΥΡ•V.

I bolli rinvenuti nell'*oppidum* di Ensèrune, sottoposti ad analisi per confronto, data la somiglianza degli impasti e del modo di bollare (bolli: ΑΝΤΑΛ, ΝΥΜΨΙ, ΧΑΡ retrogrado e ΑΙΡΛ) e alcuni di quelli di Pech Maho[29] (bolli: AM, M. LURI) hanno composizioni vicine a quelle del gruppo chimico 2.

I reperti di Lacco Ameno non consentono di acquisire dati nuovi e risolutivi sulla cronologia delle anfore greco-italiche antiche. Il gruppo 1 è piuttosto omogeneo e potrebbe quindi comprendere contenitori prodotti nello stesso periodo. I due gruppi di anfore, formati in base alle analisi chimiche, potrebbero anche corrispondere alla produzione della stessa area produttiva in due momenti cronologici distinti (gruppo 1 anteriore e gruppo 2 successivo?), ma per ora si tratta solo di ipotesi.

Dal punto di vista minero-petrografico le anfore fino ad ora analizzate contengono inclusioni vulcaniche e hanno una matrice carbonatica con microfossili (Thierrin Michael in Olcese et al. 1996); tra i minerali vulcanici individuati prevale nettamente il sanidino rispetto ai clinopirosseni (Fig. 2.3). Sono stati individuati anche vetro vulcanico, plagioclasi, biotite e minerali pesanti. Tra i frammenti di roccia vulcanica prevale la pomice; la massa di fondo è vetrosa con fenocristalli di clinopirosseno e plagioclasi, talora con microliti di plagioclasi.

6. Riepilogo e interpretazione dei dati a disposizione

6.1 L'isola di Ischia, nota dall'epoca della colonizzazione greca per un'intensa attività artigianale, è stata un centro di produzione di anfore del tipo MGS III e di greco-italiche antiche (MGS IV e forse V), nel periodo compreso tra il IV secolo a.C. e il III secolo a.C. Non è attualmente possibile stabilire quando la produzione abbia avuto inizio e fissare una sequenza tipologica precisa. Il quartiere ceramico era attivo già prima dell'epoca ellenistica e la continuità della produzione è un dato certo. Si tratta di anfore con caratteri tipologici e di impasto piuttosto ripetitivi ed omogenei[30]. Le analisi effettuate sulle anfore greco-italiche rivelano l'esistenza di almeno due gruppi chimici, il primo di sicura origine locale, il secondo che potrebbe essere locale, ma per il quale non è possibile escludere un'altra area di origine, forse sempre in Campania (Golfo di Napoli/litorale campano-laziale?). I gruppi individuati sono riportabili alla produzione che potrebbe essere definita, in via ipotetica, *di Ischia e del Golfo di Napoli.* I dati chimici e mineralogici delle anfore di Ischia costituiscono un riferimento utilizzabile per eventuali confronti.[31]

6.2 Le anfore erano destinate forse a contenere il vino dell'isola la cui produzione è molto antica. Non è possibile escludere che le officine di Ischia, conosciuta per la sua vocazione artigianale nel corso dei secoli e per la sua esportazione di ceramiche e laterizi continuata fino ad epoche recenti (Buchner 1994), abbiano prodotto anche contenitori vuoti per le altre importanti aree vinicole del Golfo di Napoli. I numerosi bolli documentati sulle anfore locali, riportabili a nomi greci (di origine ionico-euboica, oschi e etruschi), rivelano una realtà produttiva complessa e intensa, articolata in fasi cronologiche che non è possibile ricostruire completamente.

6.3 Accanto alle anfore greco-italiche probabilmente più antiche, di sicura origine locale (gruppo chimico 1) rinvenute nell'area di Santa Restituta, emerge dalle analisi di laboratorio l'esistenza di un altro gruppo di anfore greco italiche bollate (gruppo chimico 2), provenienti in gran parte dallo scarico Gosetti (al di fuori del quartiere artigianale), pertinenti al tipo MGS V, in qualche caso al tipo MGS VI e quindi più recenti. Questo secondo gruppo comprende anfore greco italiche bollate, talora con bolli documentati anche in altri siti del Mediterraneo[32]. In base alle analisi chimiche non è possibile stabilire se il gruppo chimico 2 sia locale e rimane il dubbio che si tratti di materiali prodotti in officine site a Ischia, oppure in altri centri forse sempre del Golfo di Napoli. Le prime analisi sembrerebbero comunque avvalorare l'ipotesi che si tratti di una produzione di origine campana, consentendo di fare un passo avanti importante nella definizione dell'origine di anfore greco-italiche che più hanno circolato. Composizioni chimiche simili a quelle di questo secondo gruppo hanno anche alcune delle anfore greco italiche rinvenute a Lipari, a Pech Maho e a Ensèrune.

6.4 Ulteriori accertamenti di carattere morfologico, macroscopico, epigrafico e analitico - già programmati - dovrebbero poter stabilire in modo definitivo se le anfore greco-italiche della necropoli di Portinenti (Lipari), quelle del relitto Filicudi F[33] e della Secca di Capistello siano di origine campana. Per ora è emersa la somiglianza di composizione tra i pochi campioni della necropoli di Portinenti e quelle delle anfore del gruppo chimico 2.

6.5 I due bolli di *Tr. Loisio* rinvenuti a Ischia, l'uno attestato su di un anfora MGS VI (Fig. 3.5), la cui datazione è da collocare forse nell'ultimo quarto del III secolo a.C.[34], l'altro su un frammento di ansa, hanno composizioni analoghe a quelle del gruppo chimico 2 di Ischia. Dal punto di vista mineralogico sono caratterizzate da degrassante analogo a quelle delle anfore locali[35], pur distinguendosi da esse per alcuni parametri tessiturali[36].

Composizione chimica simile a quella del gruppo chimico 2 hanno anche alcuni bolli documentati su anfore greco italiche, tra cui ANT, ANTA (retrogrado), ΠΑΡΗ, ΧΑΡ.[37] Ulteriori analisi sono in corso e questo argomento verrà approfondito in un altro lavoro dedicato alle anfore greco-italiche recenti.

Il bollo *M. Luri*, non documentato a Ischia ma a Pech Maho, e il cui contesto di appartenenza è databile tra il 250 e il 210 a.C., sottoposto solo ad analisi chimica e confrontato con i dati di questo lavoro, ha una composizione simile a quella del gruppo chimico 2. Il bollo, che purtroppo non è possibile ricondurre ad un tipo preciso, ha buone probabilità di essere originario della Campania, dove la *gens Luria* è documentata, ad esempio a Pompei e a Ercolano (RE, sv. *Lurius,* 1853-1854).

6.6 Anche se la produzione delle anfore greco-italiche antiche avveniva in più siti, molti esemplari visionati in alcuni siti del Mediterraneo occidentale (pertinenti soprattutto al tipo MGS Ve V/VI), hanno impasti e caratteristiche di lavorazione molto simili tra loro, fatto che fa pensare ad un'area di origine comune; in alcuni casi si tratta di impasti simili a quelli delle anfore rinvenute a Ischia (gruppi chimici 1 e 2).

6.7. Anfore greco-italiche di tipo MGS V e V/VI, con impasti diversi da quelli di Ischia, sono documentate in altri siti, ad esempio a Camarina e a Adria (si veda l'appendice, *infra*). La diversità degli impasti dei tre siti rende ben distinguibili contenitori aventi la stessa tipologia e conferma la presenza di una o più produzioni anche in Sicilia e in area adriatica. Le osservazioni macroscopiche vanno verificate per mezzo di analisi di laboratorio.

6.8. Il quesito scientifico posto più volte dagli archeologi riguardante l'attribuzione delle anfore greco-italiche e soprattutto di alcuni bolli alla Campania o alla Sicilia, appare ridimensionato e di possibile soluzione, se si considerano tutti i criteri distintivi a disposizione (tipologici, epigrafici e di impasto). La produzione della zona Ischia/Golfo di Napoli ha delle caratteristiche di impasto - chimiche e mineralogiche - piuttosto distintive.

Alcune delle anfore greco-italiche di Camarina (tipi MGS V e V/VI), ad esempio, denotano un impasto assimilabile a quello delle produzioni ceramiche definite *di Gela-Agrigento*, diverso e distinguibile da quello delle anfore greco-italiche rinvenute a Ischia.

Nel caso poi il problema venga affrontato con le analisi di laboratorio, va ricordato che confusioni nella separazione tra ceramiche di Campania e Sicilia sono possibili se mai con anfore prodotte nell'area etnea. Il resto della Sicilia presenta argille con caratteristiche geologiche che non dovrebbero generare confusioni con quelle delle argille campane (Thierrin Michael 2000, Montana, comunicazione personale).

7. Le anfore greco-italiche antiche e l'economia della Campania

La fabbricazione delle greco-italiche antiche a Ischia è da connettere alla produzione e alla diffusione del vino campano, che ricevette un impulso determinante grazie alla politica economica di *Neapolis* e ai rapporti di collaborazione del suo ceto dirigente con i Romani in seguito alla stipula del *foedus aequum* del 326 a.C. La prosperità economica e marittima di *Neapolis* e del Golfo nel III secolo a.C., seguita alla consegna della città ai Romani, è dimostrata, già alla fine del IV sec. a.C., dall'intensificarsi dell'attività della zecca napoletana (Lepore 1952, 310). La diffusione delle anfore greco-italiche viene collegata alla politica commerciale dei Romani e ai legami di interesse che si vennero a creare tra famiglie romane influenti da una parte e i dirigenti napoletani e il ceto mercantile greco, dall'altra.[38]

Un ulteriore impulso alla produzione delle anfore, inoltre, è stato visto nella diffusione della coltura intensiva della vite aminea a *Neapolis* e in area vesuviana (Mele in *Neapolis* 1985, pp. 360-361).

L'attività produttiva delle officine ceramiche di Ischia si colloca in questo contesto di prosperità economica del Golfo, precedente le guerre puniche. Le fornaci di Santa Restituta, site su un'isola nota per la fabbricazione ceramica dai tempi della colonizzazione greca e in posizione strategica a poca distanza dal porto, erano destinate a provvedere alla fabbricazione di contenitori per il vino dell'isola e forse anche di altri centri del Golfo (MGS III, IV). Non è esclusa l'esistenza di altri quartieri artigianali a Ischia stessa e nel Golfo di Napoli, la cui probabile esistenza è dimostrata anche dai risultati delle analisi chimiche (MGS V,V/VI). I bolli delle anfore di Ischia riportano nomi per lo più greci, in parte oschi: si tratta con tutta probabilità di napoletani o pitecusani nelle cui officine si producono i contenitori per il vino. Purtroppo non abbiamo molti dati per collegare la produzione delle anfore alla realtà sociale di Ischia e della Campania di età ellenistica e la maggior parte dei bolli contiene nomi comunemente diffusi[39].

La produzione delle anfore greco-italiche sembra continuare nella zona del Golfo di Napoli e in Campania con la fabbricazione del tipo MGS VI.

Per quanto riguarda il notissimo *Trebius Loisios*, le prime analisi di laboratorio eseguite per questo studio sembrano assegnare le anfore greco-italiche recenti (MGS VI) rinvenute a Ischia e bollate con il suo nome (Fig. 3.5) al gruppo chimico 2 , originario forse della Campania.

7.1. La diffusione delle anfore greco-italiche antiche prodotte in Campania

I dati a disposizione, incrociati tra loro, sottolineano ulteriormente il ruolo importante della Campania nella produzione ed esportazione del vino. Tale esportazione, messa in collegamento solito alla II guerra punica, sembra essere in realtà più antica[40]. Le anfore greco-italiche sono importanti indicatori di scambi commerciali e la creazione di una tipologia ben datata, incrociata con i dati epigrafici, appare particolarmente importante[41].

Fondamentale è lavorare in futuro anche sul gruppo chimico 2, individuato grazie alle analisi e comprendente anfore bollate oggetto di circolazione mediterranea, per verificare se sia effettivamente di origine campana.

L'eventuale origine campana dei carichi dei relitti del Filicudi F e della Secca di Capistello, se confermata dalle analisi di laboratorio, proverebbe l'esistenza di esportazioni già ben organizzate tra il Golfo di Napoli e il Tirreno meridionale tra la fine del IV e gli inizi del III secolo a.C.

Un elemento che documenta tali contatti commerciali precoci è dato dalla presenza, per ora sporadica e da verificare, di bolli attestati a Ischia, anche in alcune località della Sicilia meridionale come Selinunte (distrutta durante la I guerra punica), Eraclea Minoa, Gela/Manfria, l'area di Licata e Camarina (distrutta nel 258 a.C.).

Ad una fase di distribuzione commerciale a corto-medio raggio (metà fine IV-III secolo a.C.), che investe soprattutto l'area tirrenica meridionale, segue una fase, forse già a partire dagli inizi del III secolo a.C., con circuiti distributivi più ampi che si intensificano intorno alla metà del secolo e coinvolgono progressivamente il bacino nord-occidentale del Mediterraneo. L'anfora tipo *MGS V - V/VI* è l'indicatore di questa fase di ampia diffusione; la Campania sembra giocare un ruolo importante nelle esportazioni di questo periodo, come sembrerebbero indicare le prime (e ancora insufficienti) analisi mineralogiche eseguite sui materiali di Pech Maho e Ensèrune e sulle anfore rinvenute a bordo di alcuni relitti del Mediterraneo nord-occidentale, come quello della Tour Fondue o quello della Torre della Meloria.[42]

Un programma di analisi mineralogiche sulle anfore greco italiche di alcuni relitti del bacino occidentale del Mediterraneo, datati alla seconda metà del III secolo,[43] può apportare dati nuovi, così come uno studio incrociato con i dati risultanti dallo studio archeologico e archeometrico delle ceramiche a vernice nera di produzione campana.

E' del tutto probabile, infine, e indicazioni in tal senso già esistono, che più centri in Italia - area tirrenica settentrionale, Sicilia, area adriatica - abbiano prodotto tipi molto simili di anfore greco-italiche nello stesso periodo (van der Mersch 1994; Pasquinucci, Menchelli 1999; Toniolo 2000; Thierrin Michael 2000)[44].

I primi dati a disposizione, soprattutto quelli macroscopici e archeometrici, sembrano però documentare per ora una circolazione ampia nel Mediterraneo occidentale di anfore del tipo MGS V e V/VI con caratteristiche piuttosto omogenee di impasto, geologiche e artigianali, la cui area di origine è forse la Campania (Golfo di Napoli?).

8. Prospettive di ricerca in Campania e in alcuni siti di distribuzione nel Mediterraneo

La ricerca avviata a Ischia verrà estesa ai reperti di altri centri della Campania, in modo particolare dell'area del Golfo di Napoli, per verificare la presenza di anfore greco-italiche di Ischia e per individuare eventuali altre produzioni. E' auspicabile poter giungere, in questa come in altre zone, ad una tipologia definita delle anfore greco-italiche, che potrà contribuire a precisare e interpretare meglio fenomeni economici. Contemporaneamente si sottoporranno ad un controllo mirato in laboratorio anche le anfore greco-italiche (antiche e recenti) di altri centri del Mediterraneo per verificarne la composizione, oltre che per conoscere meglio le caratteristiche tecnologiche e di fabbricazione. L'indagine, anche quella di laboratorio, verrà estesa ad altri relitti, in particolare a quelli del Mediterraneo occidentale[45].

I dati di laboratorio ottenuti per questo lavoro costituiscono un buon punto di partenza per continuare le ricerche e per la risoluzione di interrogativi ancora aperti concernenti anche le anfore greco-italiche più recenti (tipo MGS VI) rinvenute a Ischia e in altri siti.

Le analisi di laboratorio, ancora una volta, si sono dimostrate di grande utilità per rispondere a quesiti relativi alla determinazione di origine, soprattutto perché effettuate in stretto collegamento con i dati archeologici ed epigrafici.

APPENDICE:

Le anfore greco-italiche antiche di alcuni siti e relitti : un primo confronto con i reperti di Ischia.

Vengono di seguito elencati alcuni siti terrestri e relitti in cui sono stati effettuati rinvenimenti cospicui di anfore greco-italiche antiche (principalmente tipi Will A1/A2 – MGS V/IV), scelti per un primo confronto con i materiali di Ischia. Anche se le anfore dei siti elencati in questo paragrafo sono state visionate direttamente, le osservazioni vanno considerate come preliminari e necessitano di ulteriori approfondimenti in laboratorio. L'asterisco indica i siti in cui sono state già effettuate analisi di laboratorio di confronto.

El Sec (360 a.C.)
Il relitto di El Sec appartiene ad una nave naufragata intorno al 360 a.C. nelle acque antistanti Palma de Mallorca (Arribas

et Al. 1987; Parker 1992; Olcese 2002). La maggior parte delle anfore a bordo (ne furono recuperate 474, in gran parte disperse) è considerata originaria del Mediterraneo orientale, in particolare all'area egea insulare. Nella pubblicazione di D. Cerdà (Arribas et Al. 1987) compaiono i disegni di alcune anfore greco-italiche e di alcuni tipi di probabile origine magno-greca.

L'esame di ciò che rimane del carico del relitto del Sec - e in particolare delle anfore - ha consentito a chi scrive di stabilire che tra i materiali del Magazzino del Museo di Mallorca non vi sono anfore greco-italiche, solo una MGS III.

La tavola pubblicata nell'articolo del 1987 a cura di Arribas et Al. 1987 (p.440), realizzata con i disegni delle anfore greco-italiche di diversi siti del Mediterraneo (e non del relitto di El Sec), va considerata pertanto come un riepilogo dei tipi delle anfore greco-italiche in generale e non come documentazione delle anfore rinvenute a bordo del relitto[46].

Roghi 1 (325-300 a.C.)(?)

Il relitto Roghi 1, appartenente ad una nave affondata nei pressi dell'isola di Panarea (Le Formiche, Isole Eolie), aveva a bordo anfore greco-italiche del tipo antico, tipo Will A1[47], che appaiono però diverse tra loro, sia nella inclinazione dell'orlo, sia nella forma del corpo più o meno panciuto. Le anfore del relitto Roghi I hanno orlo piano superiormente (e si avvicinano agli orli "a quarto di cerchio"), in qualche caso inclinato verso il basso. Il collo è corto, a tronco di cono rovesciato, le anse medio-corte; presentano inoltre la tipica smussatura che sottolinea il passaggio dalla spalla piana e larga al corpo dell'anfora.

Il relitto è datato al 325-300 a.C. (?) solo sulla base delle anfore che vengono considerate in via ipotetica più antiche di quelle del relitto della Secca di Capistello, senza che sia stato rinvenuto alcun elemento datante in associazione (Cavalier, Livadie 1985, p.9 -71, Campagna 2000, p.450). La datazione, come ha notato L. Campagna, sembrerebbe confermata da altri rinvenimenti, ad esempio da quelli di Taranto piazza Garibaldi, contesto datato tra il 330 e il 300 a.C. (Costamagna 1983, p.108 n.20), mentre recenti rinvenimenti di Lipari paiono però documentare la presenza di anfore greco-italiche simili a quelle del Relitto Roghi tra i materiali di un corredo datato al secondo quarto del III secolo a.C (Campagna 2000, p.450).

Un'analisi morfologica e macroscopica degli impasti delle anfore del relitto Roghi 1 ha evidenziato una somiglianza formale con le greco-italiche documentate a Ischia, anche se ad un primo esame macroscopico, l'impasto sembra un po' diverso. Un esemplare della necropoli di Portinenti, appartenente al tipo MGS V (Bollo MA..) e accostato alle anfore del relitto Roghi di Panarea (Campagna 2000, p.450 n.50), analizzato chimicamente ha una composizione simile a quella delle anfore del gruppo 2 di Ischia.

Secca di Capistello (300-280 a.C.)

Il relitto, recuperato nelle acque di Lipari, è datato sulla base della ceramica a vernice nera (Blanck 1978; Cavalier, Livadie , van der Mersch 1985, pp.53-64)[48]. Oltre a questa ceramica, a bordo si trovavano anfore greco-italiche di tipo MGS V - Will A1, dalle caratteristiche formali e di impasto molto omogenee, tanto da far pensare che fossero originarie di un unico centro produttore. Il corpo dell'anfora, con la tipica forma a trottola, è meno panciuta di quelle del Relitto Roghi I. La smussatura che segna il passaggio dalla spalla al ventre è meno marcata che negli esemplari del relitto Roghi I. L'ansa è piuttosto corta e il collo a imbuto rovesciato, è anche piuttosto corto (se paragonato ad esempio alle anfore del Filicudi F). Si tratta di anfore simili a quelle rinvenute ad Ischia per tipologia, impasto, caratteristiche di lavorazione (ansa con ditata alla base) e come modo di bollare. Le anfore presentano una serie di bolli con nomi greci (ΠΑΡΗ, ΧΑΡΗΣ, ΒΙΩ, ΔΙΩ, ΡΟΡ, ΕΥΞΕΝΟΥ), in alcuni casi documentati anche a Ischia (ΠΑΡΗ, ΒΙΩ, ΔΙΩ).

Capo Graziano - Filicudi F (300-250 a.C.)

Il carico di questo relitto, costituito da anfore greco-italiche tipo MGS IV- Will A2 (che l'Autrice utilizza come prototipo della forma) è ben conservato (Cavalier, Livadie 1985, p.88; Parker 1992, p.118). Per il relitto è stata proposta una datazione intorno al 300 sulla base della ceramica a vernice nera (Morel 1981, p.62; van der Mersch 1994, p.53 e nota 157), a differenza di quanto proposto da M. Cavalier e da C.A. Livadie che lo collocavano nella prima metà avanzata del III secolo a.C. Anfore molto simili a quelle del Filicudi F sono documentate tra i materiali della necropoli in contrada Diana e di Portinenti a Lipari; quelle della contrada Diana sono state rinvenute in tombe databili nel corso del IV a.C. (Campagna 2000, p.449 e nota 53; p.450 nota 58).

Le anfore, più affusolate e lunghe delle MGSV, hanno orlo appiattito superiormente e piuttosto pronunciato, collo e anse decisamente più lunghe di quello delle anfore greco-italiche degli altri relitti. Il passaggio tra spalla e ventre è sottolineato da una riga ma non c'è la smussatura tipica delle anfore greco-italiche tipo Will A1.

L'anfora di Ischia più simile a quella del Filicudi F è bollata XEN ed è stata rinvenuta nei pressi del forno 5 insieme a molti altri frammenti di orlo e puntali (Figg. 2.1-2.2). L'impasto delle anfore del relitto è simile a quello delle anfore della Secca di Capistello e a quello delle anfore di Ischia. I bolli riconosciuti sulle anfore del relitto e documentati anche a Ischia sono: ΠΑ corona/sole M (oppure ΓΑΡ corona/sole M), ΧΑΡ.

Capo Graziano (Filicudi B)

Questo relitto è datato anteriormente alla fine del IV secolo a.C., anche in questo caso sulla base dei caratteri morfologici delle anfore (Cavalier, Livadie 1985, pp.88-89; Parker 1992, p.117). Per quanto possa valere una semplice notazione di colore, l'impasto di queste anfore è di colore più scuro di quello delle anfore di Ischia.

*La Tour Fondue (seconda metà del III secolo a.C.)
La nave naufragata nella zona antistante Marsiglia aveva a bordo alcune anfore greco-italiche di tipo MGS V o V/VI (Dangreaux 1993, 1995). Si tratta di esemplari in qualche caso bollati in greco (tra gli altri: ΠA- o ΓA, XAPM, XAP (bollo circolare). Gli impasti si discostano un po' da quelli di Ischia e sono simili a quelli del relitto Roghi 1 e di alcune anfore greco-italiche più recenti.

*Lipari, Necropoli di Portinenti
La recente pubblicazione dei materiali della necropoli di Portinenti (Lipari) concerne il rinvenimento di 15 esemplari di anfore greco-italiche di tipo antico (Will A1-MGS V), datate alla seconda metà del IV, alcune delle quali bollate (Campagna 2000, p.443 e seguenti).

A ragione l'Autore ha evidenziato un'analogia evidente di impasto tra le anfore MGS V (e pochi esemplari delle MGS IV) della necropoli e le anfore dei relitti eoliani (Roghi 1 e Capo Graziano B, Secca di Capistello) (Campagna 2000, p.450). La somiglianza con le anfore di Ischia dello stesso tipo è notevole. Un bollo [--]NTAΛΛ corrisponde con tutta probabilità al nome documentato anche a Ischia e a Ensèrune, forse a Eraclea Minoa e a Cartagine, riconducibili al nome Aνταλλος, considerato originario della Sicilia per la diffusione in quell'area (van der Mersch 1994, p.162). Non è possibile comunque escludere casi di omonimia già riscontrati.

Sulla base delle analisi di laboratorio, il bollo ha composizioni simili a quelle del gruppo chimico 2, che potrebbe essere campano. Sulle anfore della necropoli (MGS V) sono documentati altri bolli: ΠA[T]P (?), -KΛ[HΣ] (?), M[..]AK[..] (?) e un bollo in latino N.AVLANI. A questi si aggiungono due anse frammentarie con i bolli ΣΩTHP (con impasto differente da quello solitamente documentato nelle greco-italiche antiche).

Napoli, S.Lorenzo Maggiore e P.za Dante
Gli scavi effettuati nella zone di S. Lorenzo a Napoli (Neapolis 1985, p. 235) hanno portato alla luce una serie di frammenti di anfore greco-italiche decontestualizzate, riportabili ai tipi MGS III, IV, V e VI, talora bollate, in corso di studio da parte della Soprintendenza di Napoli e dai suoi collaboratori. Gli impasti di alcune di tale anfore sono simili a quelli della produzione di Ischia.

Tra i materiali di Piazza Dante (Area C, saggio C1, us 487) sono conservate due anfore greco-italiche antiche del tipo MGS VI (?), i cui impasti ricordano quelli di Ischia.

Camarina
Nella città di Camarina, sulla costa sud-orientale della Sicilia è stato rinvenuto, nella zona della stoà ovest, un deposito di anfore, solo in parte scavato, comprendente 800 contenitori circa (Pelagatti 1984-1985, pp.687-692). Dalle notizie esistenti, il deposito di Camarina sembra riferibile alla fase precedente la distruzione della città per opera dei Romani (258 a.C.); ciononostante le anfore sono collocate da C. van der Mersch nel tipo MGS VI, il più recente (come rilevato in Campagna 2000, p.452, nota 76 e da altri Autori). Nel Museo è esposta una ricostruzione parziale del deposito, con otto anfore. Si tratta, a mio parere, di anfore collocabili nei tipi MGS IV e V/VI (?), con almeno tre tipi di impasti. Uno di essi (quello delle MGS VI) è considerato tipico delle ceramiche della zona Gela-Agrigento. Anfore greco italiche con impasto analogo sono documentate a Eraclea Minoa (Antiquarium).

Ad un primo esame macroscopico gli impasti di alcune delle otto anfore greco-italiche di Camarina esposte al Museo non denotano somiglianze con quelli di Ischia, ad eccezione di due esemplari per cui si rende necessario un ulteriore controllo per mezzo di analisi di laboratorio.

Un controllo andrebbe eseguito anche su alcuni frammenti di anse bollate (non riconducibili purtroppo a tipi precisi) con bolli documentati anche a Ischia (BIΩ, XAPIΛA, ΔIΩNY[..]).

Poggio Marcato di Agnone/Monte S.Angelo/Portella di Corso
Il sito ha restituito una serie di anfore del tipo MGS III e IV (un esemplare con bollo ME in cartiglio ovale, ripetuto sull'ansa destra e su quella sinistra) (Barra Bagnasco 1989, Barra Bagnasco 1995). L'impasto di questo esemplare, conservato al Museo di Licata è analogo a prima vista a quello delle anfore di Ischia, anche se sono necessari controlli più accurati e eventuali analisi di laboratorio, soprattutto tenendo conto del fatto che in zona sono documentate attività di produzione ceramica in diversi periodi. Nel Museo di Licata sono conservati anche alcuni bolli su anse non riconducibili a un tipo preciso, tra cui TPE (2654) e ZO. Un dato interessante è che il bollo TPE, che compare anche su materiali di Ischia, si distingue bene dal bollo campano per le lettere (ad esempio la T è grande e i caratteri grossolani), per il modo di bollare e per il tipo di impasto (di colore arancio vivo con grosse inclusioni nere). In diversi siti della Sicilia, come Monte S. Angelo (abitato ellenistico), Eraclea Minoa e Selinunte, è presente lo stesso bollo con le stesse caratteristiche di impasto, ben distinguibile dai bolli di Ischia.

Anfore greco-italiche (tipi recenti) sono state rinvenute a Monte S.Angelo (un esemplare intero è conservato al Museo di Licata, n.1629); da questo sito provengono come si è detto anche alcuni bolli (XAPIΛA, M, anforina). Alcuni hanno uno impasto simile a quelli documentati a Ischia; altri hanno impasti probabilmente caratteristici delle produzioni regionali.

Tra i materiali conservati al Museo di Licata che sarebbe utile ricontrollare e sottoporre ad un controllo accurato, c'è anche l'anfora greco-italica antica della necropoli (tomba 17) di Portella di Corso, di dimensioni piuttosto ridotte.

Il sito, scavato negli anni '70, ha una cronologia compresa tra il VI e il IV secolo a.C.

Gela via Polieno, via Pistillo, Capo Soprano, Manfria (museo di Gela)
Da una prima ricognizione sui materiali conservati al museo di Gela non è stato possibile ricavare indicazioni precise per ricostruire la situazione produttiva e delle importazioni della zona. Esemplari di MGS IV provengono da contesti relativi all'ultima fase di vita della città, prima della distruzione nel 282 a.C. (Adamesteanu, Orlandini 1956, pp.355-357, fig.1b.; Orlandini, 1957 p.166 tav. LXIX, 1); un esemplare bollato ΛΕΠΤΙΝΑ (inv.8315) ha un impasto simile a quello di alcune anfore greco-italiche rinvenute a Ischia.

Nei magazzini del Museo di Gela sono presenti anche anfore di tipo MGS V, simili come morfologia a quelle del relitto Roghi e dall'impasto analogo a quello di Ischia (n.15658 da via Pistillo). Interessante la presenza di alcuni bolli documentati anche a Ischia, forse indicatori di una importazione: ΜΑΜΑΡ (retrogrado) da Capo Soprano; ΧΑΡΜΕΣ (retrogrado), documentato anche a Selinunte (metà III a.C.) e a Eraclea Minoa (fine IV/III secolo a.C.), inoltre il bollo A da Manfria (distrutta verso il 310 a.C.).

*Pech Maho (250 a.C.)
A Pech-Maho, *oppidum* situato tra Narbonne e Perpignan, è stato rinvenuto un cospicuo numero di anfore greco-italiche che appartengono sia ai tipi più antichi che a quelli più recenti (tipi Will A, B, C). Si tratta di materiali che hanno impasti differenti, come risulta da un primo esame macroscopico. Il materiale, oggetto negli anni 70 di uno studio tipologico da parte di Y. Solier (Solier 1979) e di un'indagine archeometrica recente (Thierrin Michael 2000), è ora in corso di riesame da parte di un équipe coordinata da E. Gailledrat (Gailledrat 2002), riesame che dovrebbe portare ad una classificazione completa delle anfore greco-italiche.

Tra le anfore greco italiche, esposte presso il Museo di Sigean e ancora in corso di studio da parte di J. Principal, esistono anfore greco-italiche antiche. Tra i bolli ho avuto modo di riconoscere: ΑΝΔΡΩΝΟΣ (solo ansa); Λ•ΒΙ in cartiglio rettangolare; ΔΙΩΝ; I in cartiglio ovale. In magazzino sono conservati alcuni bolli non riconducibili a tipi precisi: AM in cartiglio ovale; ΧΑΡΙΛΑ; ΧΑΡ; M.LVRI; TETE.
Contando su osservazioni preliminari emerse ad un primo controllo nel Museo di Sigean, un gruppo delle anfore greco-italiche di Pech Maho (tipo Will a) presenta somiglianze, morfologiche, epigrafiche, di impasto e di tecnica artigianale con quelle delle anfore greco-italiche di Ischia (gruppo chimico 2).[49]

Per un'attribuzione corretta delle anfore di Pech Maho è opportuno procedere ad un controllo degli impasti di tutti gli esemplari esposti e dei frammenti conservati nel magazzino. Le analisi chimiche effettuate su alcuni bolli hanno permesso di verificare che essi hanno una composizione chimica molto vicina a quella delle anfore del gruppo 2 di Ischia, la cui origine è da riportare forse all'area Ischia/Golfo di Napoli.

*Ensèrune
Nel Museo di Ensèrune sono esposte alcune anse di anfore greco-italiche bollate, con bolli in qualche caso già noti sulle anfore greco-italiche (ΑΝΤΑΛ, ΑΝΤΑ (retrogrado), ΧΑΡ, ΝΥΜΨΙ, e due di difficile interpretazione).

Gli impasti sono molto simili a quelli di alcune delle anfore greco-italiche di Ischia. Le analisi hanno confermato la che gli esemplari analizzati hanno composizioni chimiche analoghe a quelle del gruppo chimico 2 del materiale rinvenuto a Ischia.

Adria
Una pubblicazione recente ha attirato l'attenzione sui cospicui rinvenimenti di Adria (Toniolo 2000), che insieme a quelli di Spina, pongono il problema dell'origine delle greco-italiche antiche rinvenute in area adriatica (produzioni locali o importazioni ?).

Le anfore greco-italiche antiche rientrano pienamente nella tipologia della Will e nel tipo MGS V di van der Mersch. Già un primo esame macroscopico permette di escludere che la maggior parte delle anfore visionate appartenga al gruppo campano "Ischia/Golfo di Napoli". Gli impasti sono differenti così come le modalità di lavorazione e fanno presumere la produzione di uno o più centri nell'area adriatica.

Ringraziamenti
Questo lavoro non sarebbe stato possibile senza il finanziamento della Fondazione Thyssen di Bonn. Fondamentale è stato anche il sostegno di W.D. Heilmeyer con cui sto preparando la pubblicazione definitiva del quartiere artigianale di S. Restituta, e di Don Pietro Monti, che ha scoperto l'area indagata e ha favorito in ogni modo il nostro lavoro a Ischia.
Si ringrazia anche la Soprintendenza archeologica di Napoli e Caserta e, in modo particolare, C. Gialanella, S. De Caro e F. Zevi, per aver consentito lo studio e le analisi di laboratorio sui materiali di Ischia e per la proficua collaborazione.
V. Thirion Merle e M. Picon hanno più volte discusso con me i problemi archeometrici trattati in questo lavoro, il cui nucleo risale al 1999; proprio la parte archeometrica verrà ripresa e completata con il loro aiuto e con quello di G. Montana (analisi mineralogiche) per il volume in corso di preparazione.
Per le informazioni e per la campionatura dei materiali ringrazio anche M.E. Bellet, S. Buchner, M. Cavalier, F. Cibecchini, B. Dangreaux, A. De Miro, G. Di Stefano, G. Fiorentini, E. Gailledrat, D. Giampaola, L. Guzzardi, M.C. Lentini, J. Principal, L. Pugliese, G. Rossello Bordoy, G. Spagnolo.
I disegni sono di Annalisa Zorzi.

Post scriptum
Ho avuto modo di leggere il nuovo articolo di C. van der Mersch, *Aux sources du vin romain, dans le Latium et la Campania à l'époque médio-républicaine*, pubblicato in *Ostraka 2000,* solo quando avevo consegnato questo lavoro alla stampa e non mi è stato possibile tener conto delle interessanti osservazioni e dei molti spunti di ricerca contenuti in tale studio.

L'introduzione di un ulteriore sistema classificatorio (RMR, production d'amphores ***r****omaines* ***m****edio-***r***epublicaines*) proposto dall'Autore, che affianca quello introdotto dallo stesso Autore nel 1994 (con la definizione MGS, che indica le anfore di Magna Grecia e Sicilia), mi sembra però complicare ulteriormente una situazione di studio di per sé già abbastanza ingarbugliata. Tale definizione rischia di creare confusioni nel campo delle determinazioni di origine delle anfore poiché non è chiaro come si potranno distinguere le greco-italiche MGS dalle RMR, soprattutto quelle prive di bollo. E proprio il campo delle determinazione di origine delle greco italiche è un ambito di ricerca fondamentale se si vogliono utilizzare questi contenitori quali documenti di storia-economica. L'argomento va a mio parere affrontato non tanto introducendo nuove definizioni che inquadrino a priori le anfore, quanto rimettendosi a lavorare direttamente sui materiali archeologici, incrociando dati tipologici, epigrafici e di impasto, creando tipologie organizzate per aree geografiche, formulando infine ipotesi sull'origine, da verificare, se necessario, con analisi di laboratorio.

NOTE

1 Questo articolo è stato estrapolato da una ricerca più ampia sulle fornaci di Ischia in corso di ultimazione e alla cui pubblicazione si rimanda per i dati archeologici e archeometrici in dettaglio (nota 6).
2 L'abbreviazione MGS sta per *Magna Grecia e Sicilia.*
3 Per stabilire con certezza una produzione locale di una determinata classe ceramica, in mancanza dell'officina e di sicuri indizi di produzione, sono necessari diversi approfondimenti non solo di carattere archeologico ma anche macroscopico e tecnologico, tesi a circoscrivere e caratterizzare i materiali prodotti localmente. Senza tale ricerca l'ipotesi formulata resta un'ipotesi di lavoro. Alcune delle utili informazioni che van der Mersch riporta a proposito di ritrovamenti di scarti o esemplari di anfore greco-italiche antiche meritano ulteriori approfondimenti poiché non sempre sono sufficienti a documentare una produzione locale di anfore greco-italiche (van der Mersch 1994, voce "lieux de production", ad esempio per le anfore MGS IV e V, p. 75 e 78).
4 Si è considerato anche il tipo anforico MGS III solitamente incluso nelle anfore magno greche, ma legato alle greco-italiche antiche.
5 Tali rapporti risultano già dalle analisi di laboratorio effettuate su anfore greco-italiche recenti (MGSVI).
6 Dal 1998 è in corso un progetto di studio del vasto quartiere artigianale sito a Lacco Ameno sotto la Chiesa di S. Restituta, alle pendici del Monte Vico (Olcese et Al. 1996; Olcese Hiener 1999), quartiere portato alla luce in più riprese dagli anni '50, dal Rettore della Basilica, Don Pietro Monti. Tale progetto condotto con W.D. Heilmeyer della Freie Universität Berlin, in accordo con la Soprintendenza Archeologica di Napoli (S. De Caro e C. Gialanella), è reso possibile da un finanziamento della Fondazione Thyssen di Bonn. Nonostante manchino precisi dati di scavo, lo studio dei materiali raccolti da Don Pietro Monti ha consentito di ricavare importanti informazioni su alcune questioni aperte, quali la produzione e la diffusione in ambito mediterraneo di classi ceramiche di periodo diversi.
7 I dati emersi dallo studio, che saranno pubblicati in altra sede insieme allo studio delle fornaci, vengono qui utilizzati come occasione di riflessione e confronto con le informazioni attualmente a disposizione sull'origine delle anfore greco-italiche antiche.
8 La raccolta dei dati necessari al completamento di questo articolo è stata possibile grazie ad un finanziamento della Freie Universität Berlin che mi ha permesso di visitare i magazzini e i musei di alcuni centri della Francia meridionale e della Spagna nell'estate del 2000.
9 Si veda oltre, alla nota 14, il problema segnalato per la MGS IV o alcune osservazioni in Asensio, Martin 1998, a proposito della incertezza di definizione del tipo MGS VI.
10 Tra i materiali analizzati ci sono alcuni "bolli greci" e il bollo *M. Lvri* analizzato anche nell'ambito del nostro progetto. Per i materiali di confronto (Megara Hyblaea, Naxos e Siracusa) non vengono forniti dati tipologici o riferimenti bibliografici.
11 Questo fatto conferma ancora una volta la necessità di un'indagine che tenga conto di tutti i dati a disposizione e che parta da una classificazione archeologica definita.
12 Il problema dell'origine delle anfore greco-italiche recenti viene solo accennato in questo articolo e verrà affrontato in un lavoro a parte.
13 Buchner, Rittmann 1948; Monti 1980; Olcese et Al. 1996; Buchner 1997; Olcese 1999.

14 van der Mersch ha inserito nel tipo MGS IV sia l'anfora del relitto Filicudi F che quella di El Sec, probabilmente senza averle viste direttamente. Pur esistendo un'analogia formale, interpretabile forse come derivazione di alcune greco-italiche antiche da prototipi comuni, viste direttamente le due anfore appaiono molto diverse soprattutto per quanto riguarda l'impasto e le modalità di lavorazione, ma anche per la struttura formale e per le dimensioni. Un loro accorpamento appare quindi fuorviante, sia perché le due anfore hanno poco a che vedere, sia perché si crea la difficoltà della citazione - citando il tipo MGS IV mi riferisco alle caratteristiche morfologiche dell'esemplare del Sec o a quello del Filicudi F?

15 Tra i materiali dello scarico Gosetti è conservato un bollo ΞΕΝΩΝ che forse restituisce il nome per intero, Lepore 1952, p. 312, nota 4.

16 Le anfore del relitto del Filicudi F presentano alcuni bolli, solo in parte leggibili per la posizione dell'allestimento o per la presenza di concrezioni (AA.VV. 1985) . Alcuni di questi bolli coincidono con quelli documentati a Ischia.

17 Tali contenitori sono stati prodotti, sempre secondo il van der Mersch, anche in Magna Grecia, nel Golfo di Taranto, in Lucania e in Sicilia centrale e orientale.

18 van der Mersch 1994, p. 79.

19 Lo studio dei bolli di Pithecusa è stato affrontato da S. Buchner per la tesi di dottorato, a cui si rimanda per l'elenco completo dei bolli e per i problemi ad essi connessi.

20 Si tratterebbe dell'indicazione che si tratta di materiale pubblico, fabbricato per conto dello stato (Guarducci 1967, p.488).

21 Per questo bollo, Buchner 1997.

22 Le anfore con il bollo TR. LOISIO hanno precocemente ha attirato l'attenzione degli studiosi per l'ampia diffusione, senza che fosse possibile arrivare ad una determinazione precisa dell'origine.

23 Conosciamo un *meddix tuticus, Seppius Loesius*, a Capua alla fine del III secolo a.C., ricordato da Livio (XXVI,6,13).

24 La Will ha descritto con accuratezza gli impasti delle anfore greco-italiche studiate. Ha notato che il tipo A - sia A1 che A2 - ha un impasto rosato, molto più fine di quello delle greco-italiche recenti. Tale osservazione, confermata anche dall'esame del materiale descritto in questo articolo, è importante in quanto costituisce un criterio ulteriore, insieme a quello tipologico, per la distinzione preliminare di gruppi di anfore.

25 Una somiglianza di impasto è stata sottolineata da L. Campagna tra le anfore della Necropoli di Portinenti a Lipari e quelle dei relitti eoliani che lo studioso riunisce, a ragione, nel medesimo gruppo di impasto (tipo F1) (Campagna 2000 p. 450).

26 Nel caso di Lipari, ad esempio, sono state campionate alcune delle anfore greco-italiche antiche della necropoli di Portinenti che presentano somiglianza evidente - morfologica e di impasto - con le anfore dei relitti delle isole Eolie (e in particolare il relitto Roghi 1, quello della Secca di Capistello e il Filicudi F), tenuto conto della difficoltà di sottoporre ad analisi di laboratorio (soprattutto a quella chimica) materiale che è rimasto lungo tempo nell'acqua del mare.

27 Si tratta di materiale fondamentalmente inedito, nominato da alcuni studi.

28 Nelle clusters effettuate per elaborare i dati chimici, oltre ai bolli campionati per questo lavoro a Sigean, sono state inserite anche le analisi delle anfore greco-italiche di Pech Maho, conservate nella banca dati di Lione (le stesse utilizzate per lo studio di Hesnard et al. 1989).

29 Le anfore greco-italiche di Pech Maho, conservate nel museo di Sigean e costituite da esemplari interi non sono state per ora campionate, sono stati invece campionati materiali frammentari bollati (greco-italiche del tipo Will a), conservati nel magazzino.

30 I tipi MGS III e IV e di qualche MGS V rinvenute Ischia hanno lo stesso tipo di impasto in quanto provenienti da una stessa realtà artigianale, prodotti forse in un lasso di tempo non molto ampio. Ciò spiega anche come già la Will abbia accomunato e considerato insieme i due gruppi di anfore, registrandone la somiglianza morfologica e di impasto.

31 Oltre al gruppo di Ischia individuato e descritto, è stato isolato anche un altro gruppo di anfore del tipo MGS V, dalle caratteristiche macroscopiche un po' diverse (anfore del relitto Roghi 1, del relitto della Tour Fondue e forse alcune del Cabrera 2).

32 Per l'elenco si veda il paragrafo 5.4.

33 Nel caso del relitto Filicudi F, da tempo è stata notata la somiglianza tra la ceramica a vernice nera del relitto (datata al 300 ca. dal Morel) e quella documentata a Ischia (Blanck 1978, p.108).

34 Va ricordato che nello scavo di Santa Restituta è stata rinvenuta una matrice per vasi ad *appliques* firmata MITHRIIS LUSI, Olcese 1986, p.14 nota 28.

35 L'impasto delle anfore bollate Tr. Loisio si presenta macroscopicamente un po' diverso da quello delle anfore locali appartenenti ai tipi più antichi.

36 La lettura delle sezioni sottili è in corso di effettuazione da parte di G. Montana dell'Università di Palermo a cui si devono le informazioni brevemente citate in questo testo, insieme a quelle pubblicate da G. Thierrin Michael in Olcese et al. 1996.

37 Questi dati verranno trattati più approfonditamente nella pubblicazione complessiva delle fornaci.

38 Purcell 1985, 7, nota 27; Frederiksen 1984, p. 232.

39 Il dato in questo senso più interessante, ma da verificare, concerne due bolli, XAP e (ΔΕ)ΝΥΨΙ: Livio (VIII,25,9) ricorda i due *principes civitates*, i capi della cittadinanza, Charilao e Nymfio, che nel 340 aiutarono i Romani ad impadronirsi di Napoli.

40 Osservazioni in questa direzione erano già state formulate da alcuni storici, tra cui F. De Martino 1991, p.201.

41 A favore di una datazione già alla fine del IV a.C. sono le tombe della necropoli della Contrada Diana e i rinvenimenti di Gela che, se non ci consentono sempre di registrare con certezza la presenza di contenitori campani, ci danno comunque informazioni sulla presenza del tipo in contesti ben datati.
42 Si veda l'elenco in appendice. L'analisi mineralogica eseguita nell'ambito di questo lavoro su di un anfora della Tour Fondue, grazie alla disponibilità di B. Dangreaux, sembra indicare la Campania come possibile area di origine (lettura sezione sottile G. Montana che ha in corso di studio le analisi mineralogiche del materiale di Ischia e di quello di confronto nell'ambito del progetto sulle fornaci di S. Restituta). Le anfore del relitto della Torre della Meloria sono state attribuite in base all'analisi mineralogica alla Campania o all'area etnea (possibilità quest'ultima che, in base ai nuovi dati, tenderei però ad escludere).
43 Si veda a questo proposito Cibecchini, Principal 2002.
44 Le anfore greco-italiche antiche di Adria (Toniolo 2000), ad esempio, in base ad un primo esame macroscopico e ai caratteri di lavorazione non hanno nulla in comune con le produzioni campane, a parte la forma. Per contro, gli impasti di alcune di tali anfore mi sono parsi simili a quelli della ceramica comune proveniente dalla stessa zona.
45 In particolare si cercherà di effettuare una verifica sulle greco-italiche di Montecristo, Bon Capo, Torre della Meloria, Cabrera 2 e Tour d'Agnello. Sui relitti di area tirrenica settentrionale è in corso di ultimazione una tesi di dottorato da parte di F.Cibecchini.
46 Pur avendo cercato personalmente e aver intervistato sia Cerdà che altri studiosi locali non mi è stato possibile rintracciare alcuna anfora di tipo greco-italico pertinente al relitto di El Sec; per contro, invece, va segnalata la presenza di un'anfora greco-italica, rinvenuta sul relitto Cabrera 2, ancora visibile nei Bagni Arabi di Palma di Mallorca (devo l'indicazione, verificata personalmente, alla cortesia di Victor Guerrero dell'Università delle Baleari).
47 Ne sono state recuperate 25 di tipo Will A1 /MGS V e una *pelvis* con inclusi vulcanici.
48 Anche C. Albore Livadie ritiene che si tratti di materiali originari di Ischia (AA.VV. 1985, p.61).
49 Sono programmate altre campionature sulle anfore bollate di Pech Maho nell'ambito di un programma di ricerca coordinato da E. Gailledrat.

BIBLIOGRAFIA

AA.VV., 1985, Archeologia subacquea, 2. Isole Eolie, in *Bollettino di Archeologia*, suppl. al n.29, Roma

Alaimo R. *et al.*, 1997, Le ceramiche comuni di Agrigento, Segesta e Termini Imprese: risultati archeometrici e problemi archeologici, in *Il contributo delle analisi archeomentriche allo studio delle ceramiche grezze e comuni: il rapporto forma/funzione/impasto,* Atti della prima giornata di archeometrica della ceramica, Bologna 28 febbraio 1997, 46-69.

Arribas A. *et al.*, 1987, *El barco de El Sec (Costa de Calvia, Mallorca). Estudios de los materiales*, Mallorca.

Asensio i Vilaro D., Martin i Menéndez A., 1998,b El derelicte de Bon Capo (L'Ametlla de Mar): l'inici de l'expansio de vi itàlic a la Peninsula Ibèrica, in *El vi a l'antiguitat. Economia, Produccio i comerc al Mediterrani occidental*, Actes (Badalona 6/9 de Maig de 1998), Badalona 1998.

Bargagliotti S., Cibecchini F., Gambogi P., 1997, Prospezioni subacquee sulle secche della Meloria (LI): alcuni risultati preliminari, in *Atti del Convegno Nazionale di Archeologia Subacquea* (Atti del Convegno Anzio 1996), Bari, 43-53.

Barra Bagnasco M., 1989, Poggio Marcato di Agnone (Licata). Campagna di scavo 1989, *Quaderni dell'Università di Messina 4*, 85-99.

Barra Bagnasco M., 1995, Anfore locresi: documenti a favore di una produzione locale tra VI e IV sec.A.C., in Estudis sobre ceramica antiga, Actes del simposi sobre ceramica antiga (M. Vendrell-Saz, T.Pradell, J.Molera i Maite Garcia, editors), Barcelona 1995

Buchner G., Rittmann A., 1948, Origine e passato dell'isola d'Ischia, Napoli.

Buchner G., 1994, I giacimenti di argilla dell'Isola di Ischia e l'industria figulina locale in età recente, in *Quaderno del Centro studi per la storia della ceramica meridionale*, 17-45.

Buchner S., 1997, *Mamarkos* nell'onomastica greco-italica e i nomi 'italici' del padre di Pitagora, in *AION(archeol)*, n.s. IV, 161-172.

Campagna L., 2000, Le anfore della necropoli in Contrada Pertinenti (proprietà Leone), in *Meligunis Lipara, vol. X, Scoperte e scavi archeologici nell'area urbana e suburbana di Lipari,* (ed. Bernabo Brea L. e Cavalier M.), 443-478.

Cavalier M., 1985, Il relitto A (Roghi) del Capo Graziano a Filicudi, in *BdA 1985*, suppl. al n. 29, Archeologia subacquea **2**, 101-128.

Cavalier, M., Livadie, van der Mersch, 1985, Il relitto della secca di Capistello, in AA.VV. 1985, pp.53-64.

Cibecchini F., Principal J., 2002, Alcune considerazioni sulla presenza commerciale romano-italica nella penisola iberica prima della seconda guerra punica, in *L'Africa romana* XIV, Sassari, Roma, pp. 653-663.

Cibecchini F, Il relitto della Torre della Meloria, Archeologia Subacquea 3, Studi, ricerche e documenti, III, Roma 2002, 209-226

Costamagna L., 1983, Taranto: indagini archeologiche nell'area di Piazza Garibaldi, *Taras* III, 1-2, 101-123.

Dangréaux B., 1993 - 1995, Presqu'île de Giens, Tour Fondue, in *Bilan scientifique du Département des recherches archéologiques sous-marines* 1993, 44-45, Ministère de la Culture et de la Francophonie, Direction du Patrimoine, Sous-Direction de l'Archéologie 1994; 1994, 47, Ministère de la Culture, Direction du Patrimoine, Sous-Direction de l'Archéologie 1995; 1995, 51-52, Ministère de la Culture, Direction du Patrimoine, Sous-Direction de l'Archéologie 1996.

Dangréaux B., 1996, Presqu'île de Giens, épave de la Tour Fondue, in *Bilan scientifique du Département des recherches archéologiques, subacquatiques et sous-marines 1996*, 89-90.

De Martino F., 1991, Attività economica e realtà sociale, in G. Pugliese Carratelli (ed.), *Storia e civiltà della Campania, L'Evo antico*, Napoli, 1993-233.

Desy P., De Paepe P., 1990, Torre San Giovanni (Ugento): les amphores commerciales hellénistiques et républicaines, *Studi di Antichità* **6**, 187-234.

Di Sandro N., 1986, *Le anfore arcaiche dello scarico Gosetti, Pithecusa,* Cahiers CJB, XII, Napoli.

Empereur J.-Y., Hesnard A., 1987, Les amphores hellénistiques, in *Céramiques hellénistiques et romaines,* II, Paris, 9-71.

Gailledrat, E., 2002, Pech Maho, Projet Collectif de Recherche "Etude et mise en valeur du site archéologique de Pech Maho (Sigean, Aude)".

Guarducci M., 1967, Epigrafia greca II, Roma.

Hesnard A., Ricq-de-Bouard M., Arthur P., Picon M., Tchernia A., 1989, Aires de production des gréco-italiques et des DR 1, in *Anfore romane e storia economica: un decennio di ricerche*, Atti del Colloquio di Siena (22-24 maggio 1986), Collection de l'Ecole Française de Rome, **114**, 21-65.

Lepore E.,1952, Per la storia economica e sociale di *Neapolis*, in *Parola del passato*, **7**, 300-332.

Lyko , 2001, *Zur Entwicklung graeco-italischer Amphoren in Velia*, in *Rei Cretarie Fautorum* Acta, 37, 265-268

Manacorda D., 1986, A proposito delle anfore cosiddette 'greco-italiche': una breve nota, in *Recherches sur les amphores grecques* (BCH, Suppl. 13), Paris, 581-586.

Mannoni, T.1984, Caratterizzazioni mineralogico-petrografiche di alcune classi di reperti, in *Ricerche a Pompei: l'insula 5 della regio VI*, Roma 1984, pp.346-351.

Monti P., 1980, *Ischia, archeologia e storia*, Napoli.

Neapolis 1985, Atti del venticinquesimo convegno di Studi sulla Magna Grecia, Taranto 3-7 ottobre 1985, Taranto 1986 (intervento di A. Mele, pp. 360-361).

Olcese, G., 2002, Schiffswracks und Transportamphoren, in Die Griechische Klassik. Idee oder Wirklichkeit. Katalog zur Austellung im Martin Gropius Bau (W.D. Heilmeyer, ed.), Berlin 1 März – 2 Juni 2002, Mainz am Rhein, pp. 111-16.

Olcese G., Picon M., Thierrin Michael G., 1996, Il quartiere ceramico sotto la chiesa di Santa Restituta a Lacco Ameno d'Ischia e la produzione di anfore e di ceramica in età ellenistica, in *Bollettino di Archeologia* **39-40**, 7-29.

Olcese Hiener G., 1999, La produzione di anfore e ceramica a vernice nera a Ischia in età ellenistica: il quartiere artigianale sotto la chiesa di Santa Restituta a Lacco Ameno, in *Proceedings XVth Int. Congress of Classical Archaeology (Proceedings Congress Amsterdam 1998)*, Amsterdam, 290-293.

Adamesteanu, D.,Orlandini P., 1956, *Gela*, in Notizie degli Scavi 10, 203-401.

Orlandini P., 1957, Tipologia e cronologia del materiale archeologico di Gela dalla nuova fondazione di Timoleonte all'età di Ierone II, Parte II, *ArchCl* **9**, 153-173.

Parker A.J., 1992, *Ancient shipwrecks of the Mediterranean and the Roman Provinces*, Oxford.

Pasquinucci M., Menchelli S.,The landscape and economy of the territories of Pisae and Volaterrae (coastal North Etruria), in *JRA*, XII, 1999, 122-141.

Peacock D.P.S., Williams D. 1986, Amphorae and the roman economy: an introductory guide, New York 1986

Purcell N., 1985, Wine and Wealth in Ancient Italy, *JRS* **75**, 1-19.

Ricq De Bouard M., Meille E., Vichy M., Picon M., Les argiles utilisées pour la fabrication des amphores en Italie (Etrurie, Latium, Campanie) in *Anfore romane e storia economica: un decennio di ricerche*, Atti del Colloquio di Siena (22-24 maggio 1986), Collection de l'Ecole Française de Rome, **114**, 257-268.

Riley J.A., 1985, The coarse pottery from Berenice, in *Excavations at Sidi Khrebish Benghazi (Berenice), II*, Tripoli, (Suppl. à Libya Antiqua 5, II), 91-449.

Solier Y., 1979, *Decouvertes d'inscriptions sur plombs en écriture ibérique dans un entrepôt de Pech Maho* (Sigean), RAN 12, 55-123.

Tchernia A.,1986, Le vin de l'Italie romaine. Essai d'histoire économique d'après les amphores, Paris (*BEFAR,* **261**).

Thierrin Michael G., 2000, Amphores gréco-italiques de l'*Oppidum* de Pech-Maho (IIIe siècle avant J.-C.). Détermination d'origine par l'étude pétrographique, in *SFECAG, Actes du Congrès de Libourne (1er-4 juin 2000)*, 225-231.

Toniolo A., Le anfore di Adria (IV-II secolo a.C.), Sottomarina 2000.

Valenza Mele N., Ricerche nella Brettia-Nocera Terinese. Risultati degli scavi e ipotesi di lavoro, Napoli 1991

van der Mersch C., 1994, *Vins et amphores de Grande Grèce et de Sicile, IVe-IIIe s.avant J.-C.,* Centre J. Berard, Etudes I, Napoli.

Will E. L., 1982, Greco-Italic amphoras, *Hesperia* **51**, 338-356.

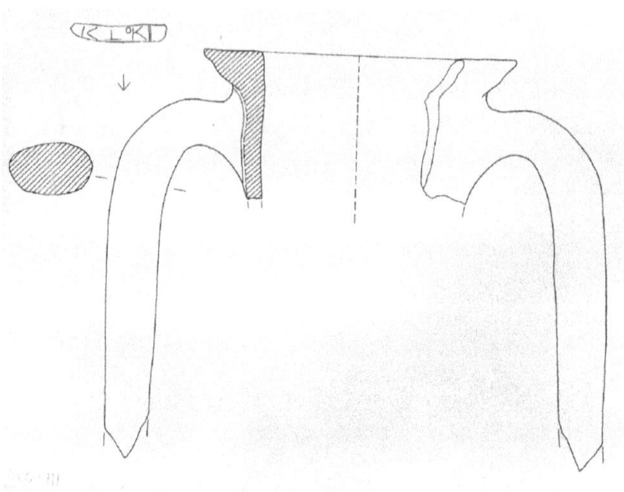

1.1

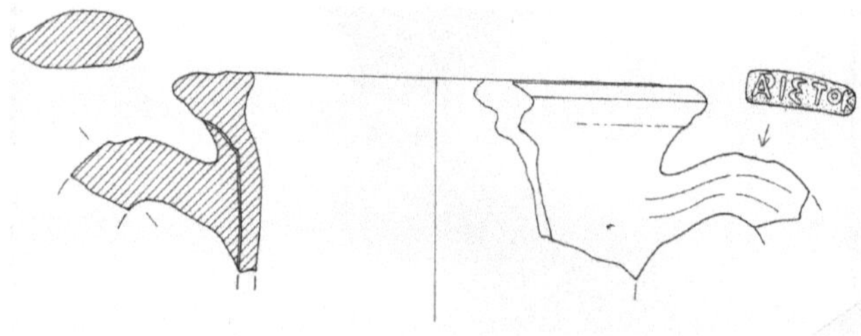

1.2

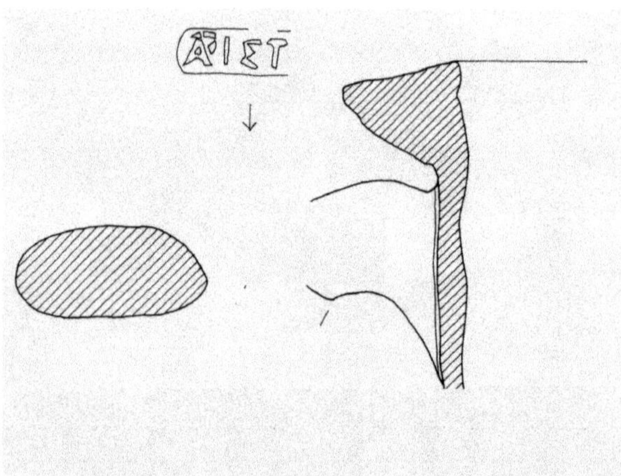

1.3

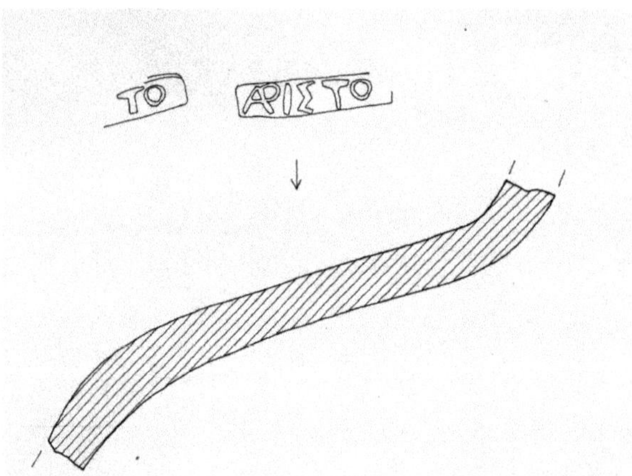

1.4

Figure 1.1-1.4. Anfore greco-italiche antiche di Ischia

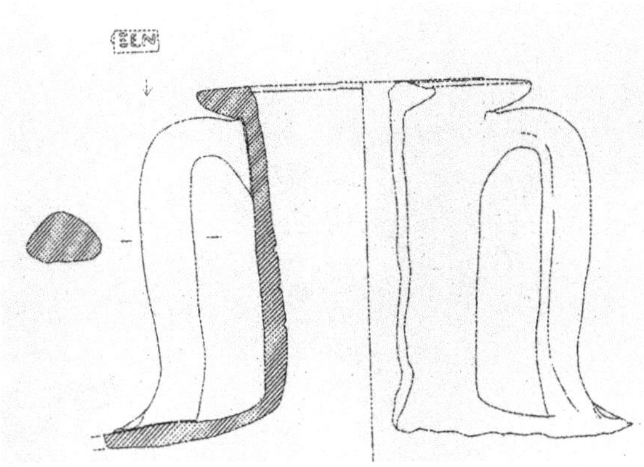

2.1

2.2

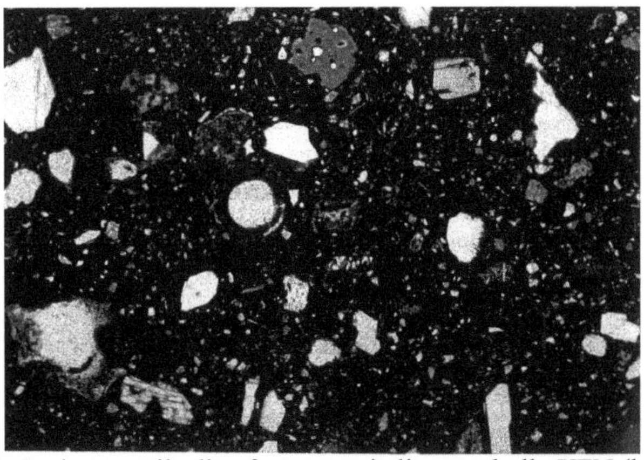

2.3. Sezione sottile di anfora greco-italica con bollo XEN (luce polarizzata, larghezza c. 3,8 mm – da G. Olcese et al. 1996, fig. 14)

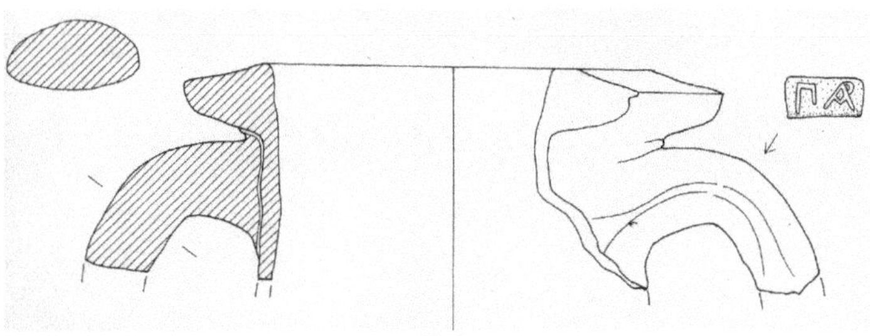

2.4

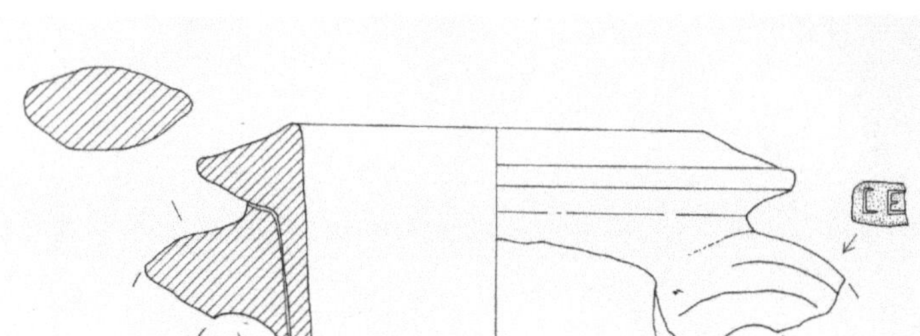

2.5

Figure 2.1-2.5. Anfore greco-italiche antiche di Ischia

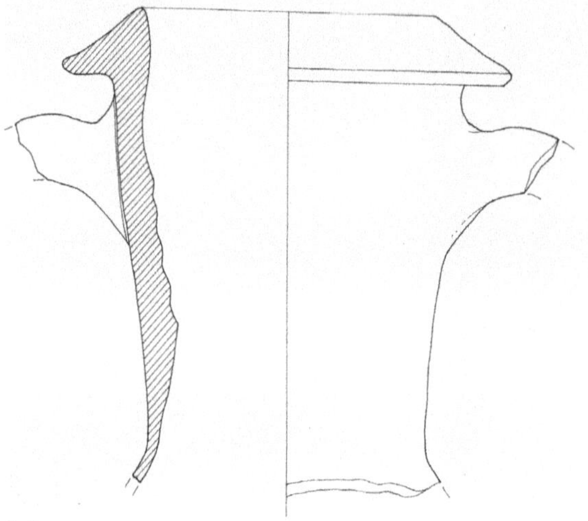

3.1

3.2

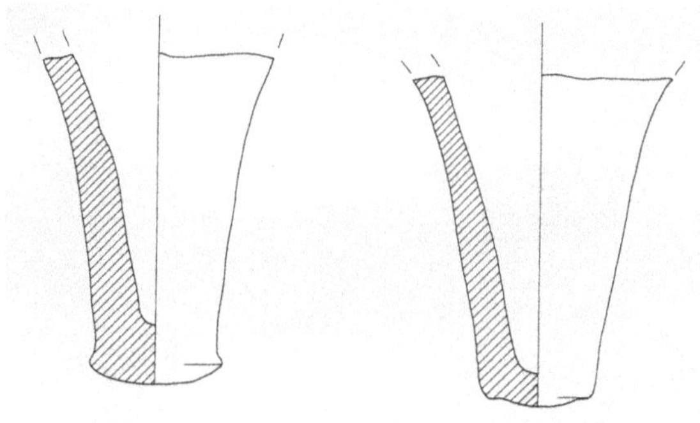

3.3

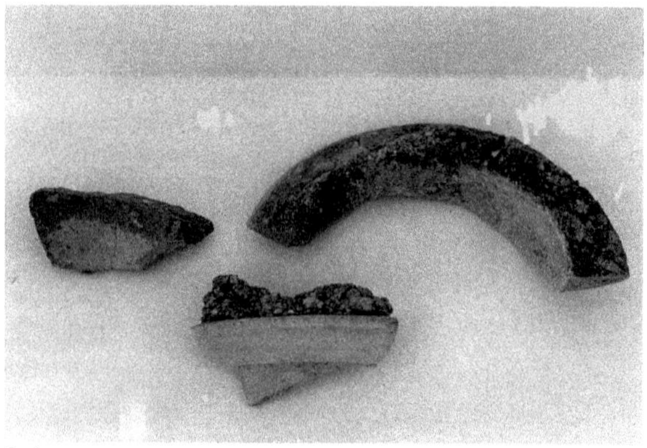

3.4

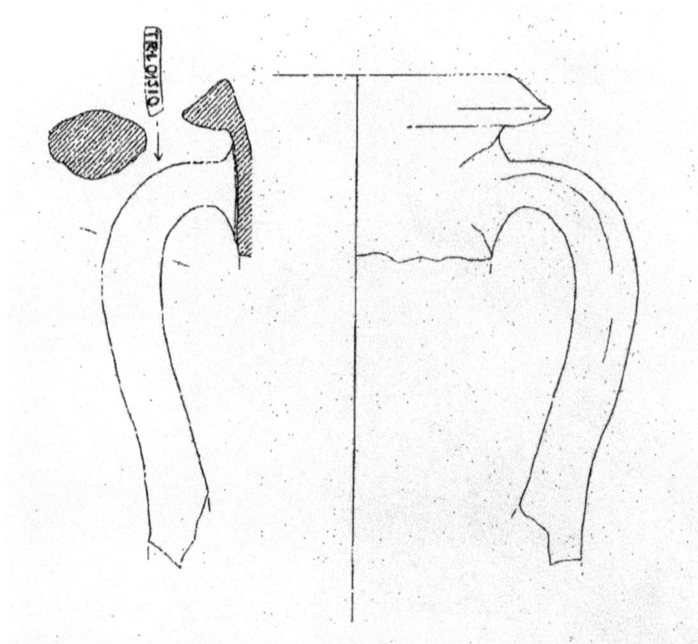

3.5

Figure 3.1-3.2. Anfora greco-italica **3.3** Puntali di anfore greco-italiche; **3.4** Scarti di fornace; **3.5** Anfora greco-italica con bollo TR.LOISIVS.

NOTE PRELIMINARI PER UNA TIPOLOGIA DELLE CERAMICHE COMUCI DELL'ETRURIA MERIDIONALE ("TIBER VALLEY PROJECT")

ALESSANDRA BOUSQUET - SABRINA ZAMPINI
(British School in Rome)

ABSTRACT: The re-examination of material collected during archaeological surveys in South Etruria, 1950-1970 represented the occasion to establish a methodology to follow in the study of common wares. Clearly, the presence of wasters leaves no doubt that pottery was manufactured in South Etruria during the middle Imperial period and certain evidence suggests that this production continued well into the Late Antique phase. The study of the common wares may furnish some answers to this question. The authors chose to approach this study from a typological point of view, whereby objects were grouped according to morphological and technical characteristics, which should have a bearing upon the ceramic chronology. For the study of these artifacts, the authors considered several contexts from South Etruria, Umbria, Campania and Rome which dated between the 4th and 8th centuries AD. This study concludes that during the Late Antique period, the common wares of South Etruria, apart from being quite varied, have completely unique characteristics with respect to the contemporary panorama of Rome.*

LE CERAMICHE COMUNI NEL PROGETTO VALLE DEL TEVERE

Nonostante il maggiore interesse degli ultimi anni, lo studio delle ceramiche comuni costituisce, ancora oggi, uno dei settori meno noti nel panorama ceramico romano. Troppo a lungo, infatti, le ceramiche comuni sono state accantonate a causa della loro scarsa attrattiva estetica e per l'errata convinzione secondo cui, trattandosi essenzialmente di contenitori pratici, non avrebbero seguito criteri di gusto e di moda e pertanto non sarebbero racchiudibili entro un arco di tempo ridotto e dunque cronologicamente significativo. Negli ultimi tempi si sono indubbiamente moltiplicati i contributi nei quali si è iniziato a rettificare e puntualizzare le informazioni relative a questa categoria ceramica, definendo anche per essa centri di produzione, tipologie e aree di diffusione (Olcese 1993, AAVV 1996, Saguì 1998, Pavolini 2000). Questo convegno è sembrata l'occasione opportuna per inserirsi nel dibattito, presentando la metodologia di analisi adottata nell'esame di un cospicua quantità di ceramiche comuni. Nucleo di questo intervento sarà pertanto l'illustrazione del metodo utilizzato mentre per una più puntuale disamina dei risultati ottenuti si rimanda ad altre sedi. (Patterson *et al.* A, Patterson *et al.B.*)

I dati presentati sono soltanto una parte di quelli compresi in una ricerca più ampia e tuttora in corso che è coordinata dalla British School at Rome e prende il nome di "progetto Valle del Tevere". Tale progetto, diretto e seguito da Helen Patterson, si è concentrato sul riesame di tutta la documentazione inerente la South Etruria Survey, ricognizione avvenuta tra il 1950 ed il 1970 e condotta da John Ward-Perkins e dalla sua equipe in un'area di 850 km^2 ca. Il materiale raccolto in quegli anni è risultato di estrema importanza, non solo per l'eccezionale quantità e per il buono stato di conservazione, ma soprattutto perché la zona nella quale si è operato è di grande interesse per i suoi rapporti politici ed economici con Roma nei diversi momenti della sua storia. Proprio per questo motivo, negli ultimi quattro anni, un gruppo di studiosi ha ripreso il lavoro sul materiale ceramico. Il passare del tempo ed il progredire degli studi, con la puntualizzazione di tipologie e cronologie, hanno infatti reso necessario il riesame di tutte le classi ceramiche e tra queste anche delle ceramiche comuni. Il lavoro ha potuto avvalersi anche dell'uso di un sistema GIS - messo a punto da Rob Witcher - grazie al quale è possibile gestire ed analizzare la grande quantità di dati relativi agli oltre 3000 siti identificati, che si articolano in un arco cronologico compreso tra il 1000 a.C. ed il 1300 d.C. circa (Millet e Patterson 1998). Il totale dei frammenti ricogniti databili ammonta a circa 90000 oggetti.

Dato il carattere fortemente eterogeneo delle ceramiche comuni, è opportuno definire, prima di tutto, che cosa si intende in questo contributo con tale definizione. Sono, infatti, state prese in considerazione la ceramica comune da fuoco e quella da mensa e dispensa, con e senza rivestimento. Sono state schedate come ceramiche da fuoco quelle di fattura più grezza con un impasto ricco di inclusi e degrassanti, necessari a rendere tali oggetti refrattari; sono stati invece racchiusi nell'insieme della ceramica comune da mensa e dispensa i frammenti più depurati, privi di inclusi o con inclusi molto piccoli. Tali caratteristiche portano ad escludere l'uso di questi oggetti sul fuoco e permettono di identificarli come contenitori adibiti ai diversi usi della mensa e della dispensa (Olcese e Picon 1994). In questo studio è stato incluso anche l'esame di alcuni contenitori molto poco attestati che sfuggono propriamente ai due gruppi precedenti: le olle perforate, normalmente destinate ad uso agricolo, ed i vasetti ovoidi e piriformi. Sono state invece escluse le produzioni in vernice rossa interna, l'africana da cucina e la vernice rossa romana, il cui studio è stato affrontato da altri specialisti.[1] È opportuno sottolineare che questa divisione in classi è stata effettuata nelle fasi di studio solo per motivi pratici, senza compromettere l'unità del progetto. Durante la ricognizione del South Etruria sono stati raccolti circa 30000 frammenti di ceramiche comuni, il 73 % dei quali è costituito da comune da fuoco, mentre il restante 27% è rappresentato da frammenti di comune da mensa e dispensa, il 3% dei quali presenta una semplice scialbatura poco uniforme (Fig. 1).

Da tali cifre emerge in maniera inequivocabile un grande divario tra le quantità della comune da fuoco e della comune da mensa e dispensa che rappresenta solo un quarto del totale.

Esaminando il materiale identificato (Fig. 2), tale rapporto rimane quasi invariato nel periodo imperiale, mentre sia in epoca repubblicana sia in età tardo antica, il distacco tra le due classi diventa più evidente: se infatti in età medio imperiale, pur rimanendo la comune da fuoco di gran lunga preponderante, è possibile individuare attestazioni abbastanza significative di comune da mensa e dispensa, negli altri due periodi tale classe sembrerebbe quasi sparire. Le spiegazioni di questa discrepanza potrebbero essere diverse: certamente occorre sempre tener presente che si ha a che fare con materiale di ricognizione e dunque passibile di una deformazione informativa di partenza. Sembra comunque difficile immaginare, visto l'attento lavoro svolto dai ricognitori, che proprio alcuni frammenti di comune depurata non siano stati raccolti e che ciò si sia verificato, in maniera più ostinata, soprattutto nei siti di epoca medio repubblicana e tardo antica. D'altra parte si può forse ipotizzare che, a differenza di quanto avveniva a Roma ed Ostia, in queste zone più interne le ceramiche con impasti grezzi venissero impiegate anche per svolgere gli usi normalmente lasciati altrove a quelle più depurate.

Pur avvertendo la necessità di cercare una spiegazione a questo fenomeno in tutte le fasi considerate, allo stato attuale della ricerca l'attenzione si è concentrata maggiormente sul materiale di età tardo antica. In questo periodo, tenendo sempre come riferimento soltanto gli orli identificati, la percentuale di forme depurate arriva appena al 2%. Una differenza così netta richiede una motivazione e per trovarne una, sono stati confrontati questi valori con quelli di diversi contesti databili tra il IV ed il VI secolo d.C. (Fig. 3). È certamente opportuno ricordare la diversa natura dei contesti esaminati e qui messi a confronto. Nel grafico compaiono infatti accanto ai risultati preliminari di questo studio, eseguito come già detto su materiale da ricognizione, quelli derivati dallo studio di contesti scavati. Pur nella consapevolezza di differenze innegabili, si è comunque ritenuto efficace effettuare quest' analisi di confronto almeno a livello così generale.

Lo scavo di Mola di Monte Gelato, tra quelli esaminati, è quello che mostra dati più simili ai nostri (Roberts 1997: 322-323): tra i materiali tardo antichi, databili tra la fine del IV e la metà del VI d.C., la comune da mensa rappresenta appena il 10% delle ceramiche comuni. I risultati sono invece molto diversi se, cercando altri termini di paragone, si prendono in esame i dati di alcuni contesti urbani editi ed inediti. A Roma infatti, sia in un contesto di V secolo a S. Stefano Rotondo (Martin 1991), sia tra materiale ancora inedito della Meta Sudans (oggetto di una tesi di laurea da parte di A. Bousquet), databile nella seconda metà del V con attardamenti nel VI, la quantità di comune da fuoco è maggiore ma non in maniera tanto netta come nel nostro caso. Vedendo invece i dati di un contesto di VI sec., relativo all'Atrio della Casa delle Vestali il rapporto risulta addirittura capovolto in favore della comune da mensa e dispensa (Di Giuseppe *et al.* c.s.). Questo stesso orientamento si mantiene a Portus nel VI, sebbene lo stesso sito faccia registrare un'inversione di tendenza nel VII sec. d.C., quando si assiste ad una preponderanza della comune da fuoco sulla comune da mensa e dispensa. (Coletti 1998). Uscendo poi dall'ambito regionale, gli stessi valori si riscontrano anche in materiali più tardi: nello scavo di Carminiello ai Mannesi, i cui contesti sono compresi tra il tardo V e il tardo VIII secolo, la ceramica comune da mensa e dispensa è sempre più attestata di quella da fuoco (Arthur 1994).
Se continuando ad esaminare il materiale della South Etruria Survey, tale differenza nelle percentuali rimarrà invariata, come già sembra, anche per le epoche precedenti, si potrebbe vedere rafforzata l'ipotesi sopra accennata: in questa zona come altrove in Italia, i contenitori con impasti più grezzi e meno curati esteticamente, erano molto più usati di quelli depurati, dei quali comunque potevano svolgere le funzioni, altrimenti lasciate alle ceramiche fini.

S.Z.

Il materiale esaminato ed il metodo di lavoro: dallo studio dei singoli frammenti alla definizione di gruppi tipologici.

Lo studio del materiale è consistito innanzitutto nell'esame di ogni singolo frammento con l'indicazione delle caratteristiche tecniche quali pesi, diametri e percentuali di conservazione degli orli. Parallelamente, dove possibile, si è cercato un confronto nei repertori editi, infine è stato eseguito un esame macroscopico delle argille di tutti i frammenti, escludendo le pareti. Le forme più conservate – tra cui alcuni pezzi integri o con profilo ricostruito - sono state disegnate ed hanno costituito una preliminare banca dati arricchita dall'aggiunta dei disegni di tutti i frammenti di orli abbastanza conservati ma privi di confronti: attualmente si è arrivati ad un repertorio di 500 disegni.

Il materiale schedato interessa un arco cronologico piuttosto ampio, compreso tra la fine del IV secolo a.C. ed il VI secolo d.C. con alcune attestazioni nel VII d.C. All'interno di questo lungo periodo, i materiali della prima età imperiale sono quelli che hanno causato minori difficoltà. Questa fase è infatti sicuramente più studiata e quindi ricca di confronti nel materiale edito; essa è risultata anche particolarmente significativa grazie all'individuazione, in Etruria meridionale, di alcune fornaci, in parte già note (Duncan 1964, 1965; Peña 1988; Messineo 1991, Patterson *et al.* B). L'attività di questi centri, sembra preferire forme – casseruole con orlo a tesa, olle con orlo appuntito e relativi coperchi – largamente diffuse non solo nel *South Etruria*, ma soprattutto nei più noti contesti romani (Morselli e Tortorici 1989; Messineo 1991) ed ostiensi (Ostia II; Ostia III; Pohl 1970; Carta 1978, Pohl 1978) i quali costituirebbero, dunque, uno dei mercati privilegiati dai centri produttori della media Valle del Tevere. Diversa appare, invece, la situazione sia in epoca repubblicana sia tardo antica perché viene a mancare, per queste classi, l'aiuto delle fornaci che non sono state finora identificate. Nonostante ciò, pur in mancanza di sicuri indicatori di produzione, considerando soltanto le quantità delle attestazioni di vari tipi e le analisi macroscopiche delle argille, è forse possibile attribuire ancora a quest'area la fabbricazione di diverse forme.

Data la preponderanza della comune da fuoco, il lavoro si è concentrato innanzitutto su questi materiali per i quali si è dovuto organizzare un metodo di analisi efficace.

Durante la schedatura ci si è trovati di fronte ad un enorme quantità di tipi diversi: alcuni molto ricorrenti, altri meno; alcuni con confronti sicuri tra il materiale edito ed altri invece privi di un qualsiasi termine di paragone. Si è quindi provato ad ordinare questi dati nel modo che è sembrato più utile e funzionale, anche perché, trattandosi di materiale di ricognizione, mancavano dei sicuri appigli cronologici. Si è tentato, dunque, di arrivare all'individuazione di tipi, illustrati ciascuno in una scheda nella quale sono stati raccolti, oltre alle caratteristiche tecniche (diametri, argille e così via) tutti i confronti trovati in contesti editi. La datazione dei tipi è stata ricavata dalla somma delle datazioni di tutte le attestazioni individuate nei contesti editi. Per i tipi più comuni e meglio identificabili è stato possibile puntualizzare queste datazioni ampie, escludendo tutte le attestazioni sicuramente residue. Attualmente si sta cercando di puntualizzare la cronologia dei tipi, anche attraverso il confronto con materiali inediti.

Anche così ordinato l'insieme dei dati continuava ad essere estremamente frammentario; soprattutto restava invariato il problema rappresentato da quei pezzi disegnati, privi di un confronto e di conseguenza di una possibile datazione. Per ovviare in parte a queste difficoltà, sono stati creati dei "gruppi tipologici" in cui è stato fatto confluire non solo l'identificato, ma anche ciò che ancora non lo è. Ogni gruppo è dunque formato da un tipo noto al quale sono stati avvicinati tutti quei frammenti che, pur non essendo del tutto identici, hanno una morfologia e delle caratteristiche tecniche estremamente simili al tipo in questione (Pavolini 2000: 26-31). Anche in questo caso lo studio ha privilegiato il materiale tardo antico; questo periodo infatti oltre ad essere quello meno studiato e pubblicato, nonostante notevoli eccezioni, è sicuramente quello più vario e ricco di problematiche tra i frammenti esaminati. Si è scelto di presentare qui solo a titolo di esempio due dei gruppi tipologici realizzati.

Il primo gruppo (Fig. 4) è rappresentato da una casseruola con orlo estroflesso ed ingrossato, pareti verticali, distinte esternamente dall'orlo attraverso un piccolo gradino. Gli esemplari considerati hanno un diametro compreso tra i 18 e i 30 cm. Il tipo Fig. 4.1 trova un puntuale confronto nel materiale di Mola di Monte Gelato, in un contesto databile tra la fine del IV e la metà del VI secolo (Roberts 1997: Fig. 236, 178a). Sembra trattarsi di un esemplare abbastanza comune: un ulteriore confronto si può stabilire, infatti, con casseruole frequentemente attestate in uno scavo condotto nei pressi di Rebibbia e relativo alla metà del IV/ metà del V secolo d.C. (Staffa 1986: Fig. 399, 201, 203). Lo stesso tipo è ancora presente alla Meta Sudans intorno alla seconda metà del V/VI sec. d.C. ed ancora nel VI secolo, tra i materiali del Carcere Mamertino a Roma (Di Giuseppe, c.s.). A questo primo oggetto si possono, inoltre, avvicinare una serie di tipi analoghi: la casseruola Fig. 4.2 è assimilabile ad un frammento rinvenuto in un contesto di IV/V secolo a Lugnano in Teverina (Piraino 1999: Fig. 218, 121), ma ha confronti anche a Roma (Staffa 1986: Fig. 399, 199; Di Giuseppe *et al.*). Proseguendo con il resto del gruppo, il tipo Fig. 4.3 è attestato, ancora una volta, a Mola di Monte Gelato (Roberts 1997: Fig. 236, 180a); nel medesimo sito si trovano confronti anche per i tipi Fig. 4.5-6 ed in maniera più generica Fig. 4.4 (Roberts 1997: Fig. 236, 180b).

Il secondo gruppo (Fig. 5) è costituito da un'olla con orlo estroflesso ed ingrossato con profilo esterno arrotondato o squadrato, la parete interna è segnata da un incavo più o meno pronunciato. Anche in questo caso il diametro dei contenitori varia tra i 18 e i 30 cm, fatta eccezione per il tipo (Fig. 5.8) le cui dimensioni non superano i 15 cm. Il primo tipo (Fig. 5.1) è attestato a Mola di Monte Gelato, sia in un contesto di età giustinianea sia in un altro datato tra la fine del IV e la metà del VI secolo d.C. (Roberts 1997: Fig. 231, 138, Fig. 235, 174); olle analoghe ai tipi

Fig. 5.2-3, 5 sono, invece, piuttosto frequenti in un deposito tardo antico di Cosa (Dyson 1976: FC 20-21) che sulla base di un nuovo esame del materiale è stato datato alla prima metà del VI secolo.[2] I tipi Fig. 5.4 e Fig. 5.7-8 sono attestati in Umbria nei contesti tardo antichi di Lugnano in Teverina (rispettivamente Piraino 1999: Fig. 223, 154 e Fig. 224, 155-156).

Non troppo frequenti ma comunque attestate le stesse olle si ritrovano anche nel contesto di metà V/VI secolo della Meta Sudans.

L'uso dei gruppi tipologici dunque, ha permesso di collegare contenitori finora ignoti ad altri noti da confronti editi, proprio sulla base della somiglianza morfologica. Così ad esempio l'olla presentata come tipo fig. 5.6, che non ha un proprio confronto specifico, ma è "tipologicamente assimilabile" agli altri oggetti del secondo gruppo, può essere genericamente individuata come un'olla di epoca tardo antica databile orientativamente tra fine V e metà VI secolo d.C., in quanto vicina alla tradizione tipologica del gruppo 2.

Condizione importante per inserire un oggetto in un gruppo tipologico, oltre alla morfologia simile, è stata la somiglianza di argille: l'analisi di queste ultime è stata fatta come già detto, per il momento, soltanto a livello macroscopico, ma già in questa prima fase è stato possibile isolare un gruppo di impasti che ha grande diffusione nel materiale in esame, mentre si riscontra raramente nel panorama urbano.

I due gruppi tipologici scelti sono molto comuni nell'ambito della ceramica esaminata; ciò si deduce anche dall'esame di una carta di diffusione (Fig. 6) realizzata sovrapponendo le attestazioni dei due gruppi considerati. Essi sono entrambi presenti in buona parte dell'area indagata, con una maggiore concentrazione, dovuta forse anche alla metodologia di raccolta oltre che alla visibilità, nella fascia delimitata dai tracciati della via Cassia e della Flaminia. Il primo gruppo però è più concentrato nell'area a Sud di Veio, verso Roma, l'altro a Nord di Veio ed ancora lungo la via Flaminia, poi, più a Nord, intorno a Sutri.

All'interno dei due gruppi è possibile distinguere almeno due classi dimensionali (una relativa a contenitori con diametro compreso tra i 18 e i 25 cm, l'altra con diametro tra i 25 e i 30 cm). Nel caso del secondo gruppo tipologico sembra probabile ipotizzare anche la presenza di una terza classe dimensionale, relativa a olle più piccole dal diametro non superiore ai 15 cm. La varietà delle dimensioni e la quantità delle attestazioni favorirebbero l'ipotesi di una produzione di tali oggetti proprio nella media Valle del Tevere.

A.B.

Osservazioni conclusive: spunti per il progredire dello studio

Gli esempi appena illustrati dovrebbero aver chiarito sufficientemente il tipo di studio che è stato affrontato ed anche le difficoltà che sono state incontrate. L'individuazione dei gruppi tipologici infatti costituisce solo la fase iniziale di questo lavoro, tuttora in corso. È sembrato comunque opportuno dare una prima comunicazione dello studio intrapreso, soprattutto per esemplificare il metodo d'indagine che è stato seguito. È evidente che c'è ancora molto da fare: ad esempio bisognerebbe approfondire l'esame degli impasti oltre che continuare lo studio di un buon numero di frammenti che non è stato possibile inserire in nessuno dei gruppi tipologici organizzati e per i quali, talvolta, non si ha il minimo appiglio cronologico. A questo proposito un grande ostacolo al progredire del nostro lavoro è costituito dalla penuria di pubblicazioni relative a campagne di scavo e/o ricognizioni nel territorio da noi esaminato. Indubbiamente l'abitudine in lavori di ricognizione ad impegnarsi in pubblicazioni più sistematiche che comprendano anche la presentazione di tavole con i materiali rinvenuti, renderebbe più agevole questo tipo di studi.

Altro approfondimento potrebbe essere lo studio delle forme: degna di osservazione è, ad esempio, la ripresa in età tardo antica di oggetti quali le olle di grandi e medie dimensioni che durante l'epoca medio imperiale avevano subito una flessione, sostituite da piccole olle e da casseruole. La grande diffusione di questi nuovi contenitori, generalmente molto profondi e dall'imboccatura piuttosto ampia, potrebbe essere legata all'entrata vigore di abitudini alimentari nuove.

A.B, S.Z.

Note:

* I nostri ringraziamenti vanno a Helen Patterson che ha seguito questo lavoro, fornendo utili suggerimenti in fase di elaborazione e a Helga Di Giuseppe che ci ha permesso di analizzare eventuali punti di contatto tra il nostro materiale ed alcuni contesti da lei studiati ed ora in corso di stampa. Siamo inoltre grate a Rob Witcher che ha elaborato per noi la curva di diffusione e la carta di distribuzione (rispettivamente Fig. 2 e 6), e a Sally Cann autrice dei disegni. Desideriamo infine ringraziare la cooperativa Parsifal, per conto della quale abbiamo intrapreso lo studio e la prof.ssa C. Panella per averci consentito di utilizzare dati, ancora inediti, dello scavo della Meta Sudans a Roma, da lei diretto.

1 Per maggiore precisione si ricorda che, nell'ambito della ricognizione sono stati raccolti 106 frammenti di vernice rossa interna, 2141 di ceramica africana da cucina e 107 di vernice rossa romana.
2 Si ringrazia S. Fontana per l'informazione.

BIBLIOGRAFIA

AAVV 1996, Les céramiques communes de Campanie et de Narbonnaise (Ier s. av. J. –C – IIe s. ap. J. –C.). La vaisselle de cuisine et de table, *Actes des Journèes d'ètude (Naples, 1994), Coll, CGB,* 14, Naples.

Arthur, P., 1994, Ceramica comune tardo-antica e alto-medievale, in *Il complesso archeologico di Carminiello ai Mannesi, Napoli (Scavi 1983-84)*, id (a cura di), 181-220, Galatina.

Carta, M., 1978, Materiali rinvenuti, in Carta, M., Pohl, I., Zevi, F., *Ostia. La Taberna dell'Invidioso, NSc*, XXXII, Suppl., 46-164.

Coletti, C. M., 1998, Ceramiche comuni dai contesti di Porto (VI e VII secolo), in *Ceramica in Italia: VI – VII secolo. Atti del Convegno in onore di John W. Hayes, Roma 11 – 13 maggio 1995,* Saguì, L. (a cura di), 401-417, Firenze.

Di Giuseppe *et al.*, c.s., Di Giuseppe, H., Filippi, D., De Lussu, F., Ricci, G., La casa delle Vestali: un immondezzaio di VI secolo, in *Contesti tardoantichi e altomedioevalia di Roma,* Paroli, L, (a cura di) con la collaborazione di Vendittelli, L.

Di Giuseppe c.s., Di Giuseppe, H, I contesti ceramici di IV-VII sec. d.C., in *Lo scavo del Carcere Mamertino a Roma*, Fortini, P, (a cura di), *MEFRA*, c.s.

Duncan, G.C., 1964, A Roman pottery near Sutri, *PBSR*, XXXII, n. s. XIX, 38-88.

Duncan, G.C., 1965, Roman republican pottery from the vicinity of Sutri (Sutrium), *PBSR,* XXXIII, n. s. XX, 134-176.

Dyson, S.L., 1976, *Cosa: the utilitarian pottery,* MAAR, XXXIII.

Martin, A., 1991, Sondages under S. Stefano Rotondo (Rome): The Pottery and other Finds, *Boreas*, 14, 157-178.

Messineo, G., 1991, *La via flaminia da Porta del Popolo a Malborghetto,* Roma.

Millet, M. e Patterson, H., 1998, The Tiber Valley Project, *PBSR*, LXVI, 1-20.

Morselli, C. e Tortorici, E., 1989, Curia, Forum Iulium, Forum Transitorium, II, *LSA*, 14, (a cura di), Roma.

Olcese, G., 1993, Le ceramiche comuni di Albintimilium. Indagine archeologica e archeometrica sui materiali dell'area del cardine, Firenze.

Olcese, G. e Picon, M., 1994, Per una classificazione in laboratorio delle ceramiche comuni, in *Ceramica romana e archeometria: lo stato degli studi. Atti delle Giornate Internazionali di Studio, Castello di Montegufoni (Firenze), 26-27 aprile 1993*, (Olcese, G., a cura di), 105-114, Firenze.

Ostia II, Carandini et al., 1970, Studi Miscellanei, 16, 90-101.

Ostia III, Carandini, A., Panella, C, 1973, Studi Miscellanei, 21, (a cura di), 421-451, 454-459.

Patterson *et al.* A, c.s., Patterson, H., Bousquet, A., Fontana, S., Zampini, S., Late Roman common wares and amphorae in the middle Tiber valley, the preliminary results of the Tiber Valley Project, in *1er Congrés Internacional sobre ceràmiques comunes, de cuina i amfores de l'Antiguitat Tardana a la Mediterrània: Arqueologia I Arqueometria (Barcelona, 14-16 de marçde 2002)*, BAR, c.s.

Patterson *et al.* B, c.s., Patterson, H., Bousquet, A., Di Giuseppe, H., Felici, F., Fontana, S., Witcher, R., Zampini, S., Le produzioni ceramiche nella media Valle del Tevere tra l'età repubblicana e tardoantica, Rei Cretariae, c.s.

Pavolini, C., 2000, La ceramica comune. Le forme in argilla depurata dell'Antiquarium. Scavi di Ostia, vol. XIII, Roma.

Peña, J.T., 1988, Roman-period Ceramic Production in Etruria Tiberina: a Geografical and Compositional Study, Doctoral Thesis (Michigan).

Piraino, C., 1999, Ceramica da cucina, in *A roman villa and a late roman infant cemetery. Excavation at Poggio Gramignano, Lugnano in Teverina* (Soren, D., e A., a cura di), 283-315, Roma.

Pohl, I., 1970, Materiali rinvenuti, in Zevi, F., Pohl, I., *Ostia (Roma). Casa delle Pareti Gialle, salone centrale. Scavo sotto il pavimento a mosaico*, *NSc*, XXIV, Suppl. I, 75-234.

Pohl, I., 1978, Materiali rinvenuti, in Carta, M., Pohl, I., Zevi, F., *Ostia. Piazzale delle Corporazioni, Portico Ovest: saggi sotto i mosaici*, *NSc*, XXXII, Suppl., 216-443.

Roberts, P., 1997, The Roman pottery, in *Excavations at the Mola di Monte Gelato, a Roman and Medieval settlement in South Etruria* (Potter, T.W. and King A.C., a cura di), 316-363, Roma.

Saguì, L., 1998, Ceramica in Italia: VI – VII secolo, *Atti del Convegno in onore di John W. Hayes*, Roma 11 –13 maggio 1995, (a cura di), Firenze.

Staffa, A. R., 1986, Località Rebibbia, via S. Cannizzaro. Un punto di sosta lungo la via Tiburtina antica fra l'età di Augusto e la tarda antichità, *Bullettino della Commissione archeologica del comune di Roma,* XCI, fasc. 2, 642-678.

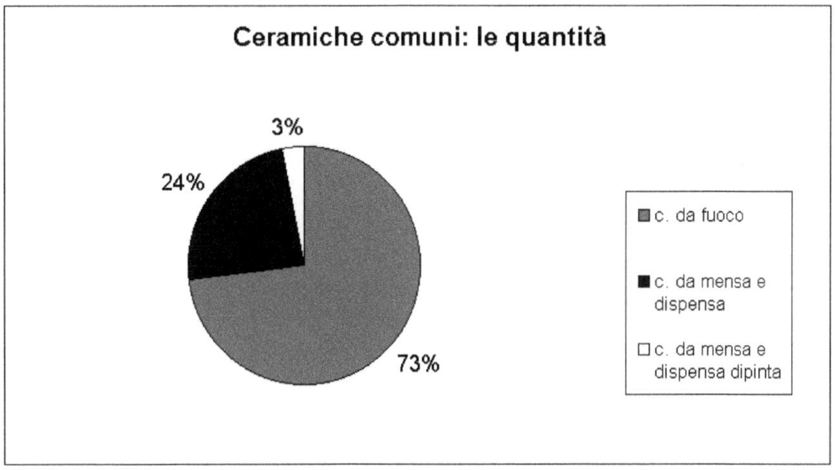

Fig. 1. Le ceramiche comuni della South Etruria Survey (le percentuali sono calcolate in base al totale dei frammenti esaminati).

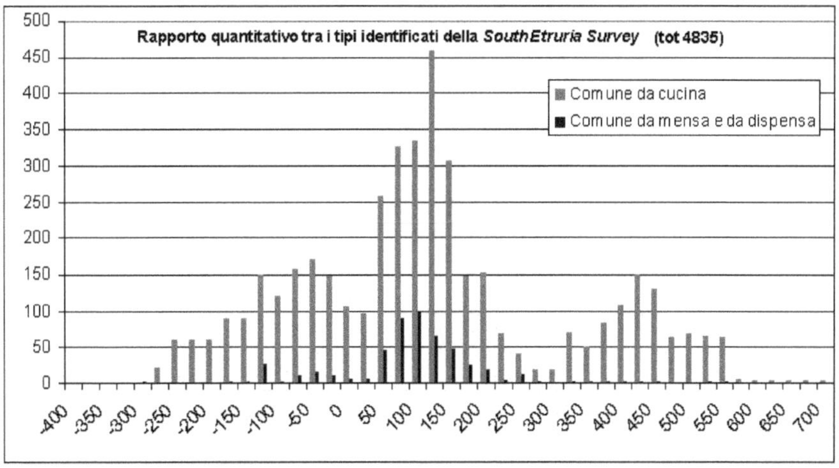

Fig. 2. Attestazioni della ceramica da fuoco e della ceramica comune da mensa e dispensa (dipinta e non): la ceramica comune da fuoco è sempre quella maggiormente attestata (la curva è stata realizzata in base al numero dei frr. databili).

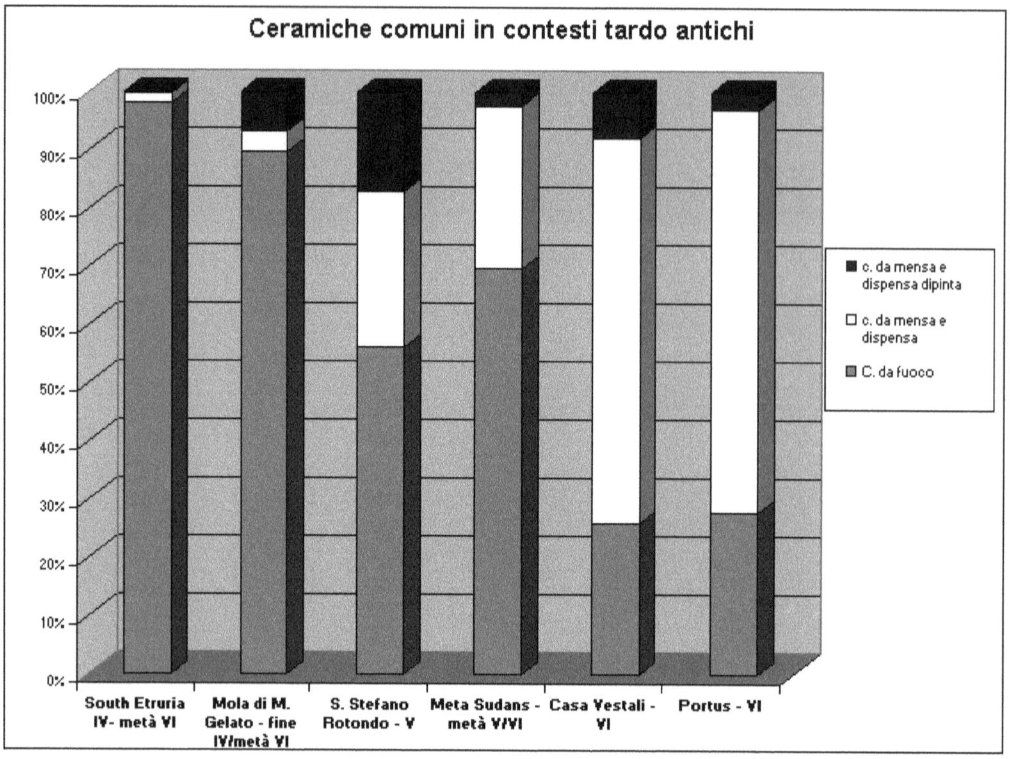

Fig. 3. Differenza tra le attestazioni delle ceramiche comuni in vari contesti compresi tra il IV ed il VIII secolo.

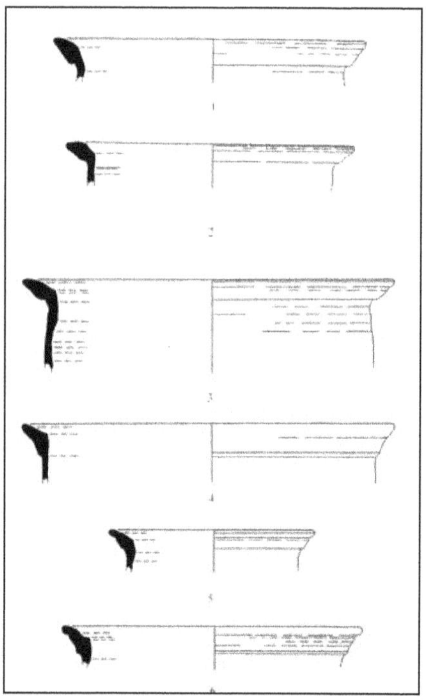

Fig. 4. Gruppo tipologico 1.

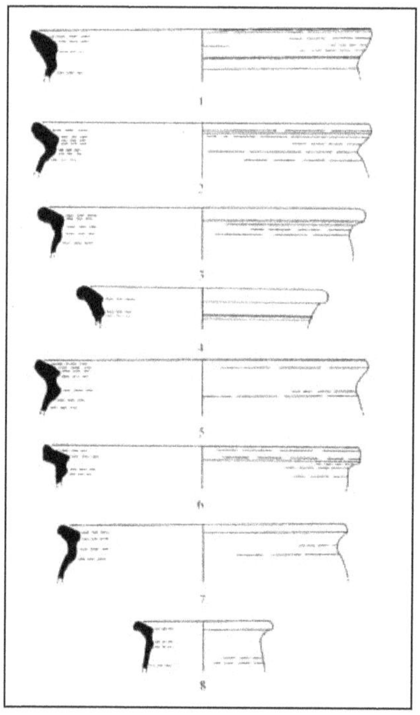

Fig. 5. Gruppo tipologico 2.

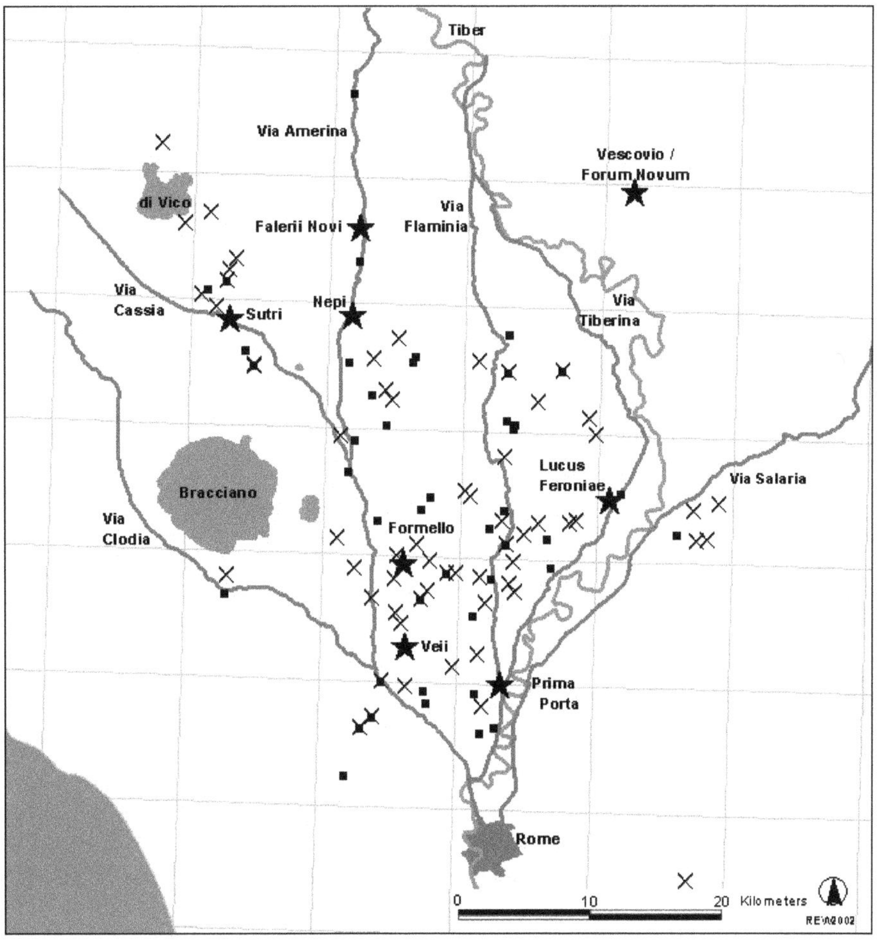

Fig. 6. Diffusione del gruppo tipologico 1 (quadrati) e del gruppo tipologico 2 (croci) nel South Etruria.

CONSIDERAZIONI SU UN CONFRONTO TRA GRUPPI FUNZIONALI IN QUATTRO CONTESTI CERAMICI DEL V SEC. D.C.

ARCHER MARTIN
(American Academy in Rome)

ABSTRACT: This paper compares four 5th century AD pottery assemblages from sites along the Tiber Valley (Ostia, Rome, Lugnano in Teverina and Chianciano Terme), indicating that imports become less frequent farther inland from Ostia and Rome. Whereas amphorae represent the great majority of all pottery in Ostia and Rome, they are all but absent at the inland sites.

Da qualche tempo mi interessano le informazioni che si possono ricavare da complessi ceramici guardati nel loro insieme, oltre a quelle tradizionali fornite dall'osservazione delle singoli classi ceramiche. Si possono pensare a diversi variabili che possono influenzare i complessi ceramici: la datazione, il modo di formazione del contesto, l'ubicazione geografica. Recentemente ho voluto considerare l'ultima con l'esempio di quattro contesti dalla posizione geografica dissimile ma per quanto possibile simili per datazione e formazione con lo scopo di vedere con ciò come varia la composizione di contesti in varie posizione rispetto alle rotte commerciali (Martin, in corso di stampa, a cui rimando per i dati sui contesti, riferimenti bibliografici e confronti). In questa sede vorrei illustrare quest'approccio allo studio della ceramica e riflettere sulle scelte che ho fatto durante il lavoro e sui presupposti che stanno dietro a esso.

Ho scelto quattro contesti che hanno restituito quantità consistenti di materiali (tra 1500 e 2000 frammenti tranne il terzo, che conta ca. 10 000), tutti databili al V secolo (dall'inizio agli anni centrali), su cui ho lavorato io stesso (assieme ad altre persone nel terzo caso, altrimenti da solo) in anni non distanti tra di loro: ciò per minimizzare le divergenze che dipendono dalla competenza del ceramologo. Si tratta di Ostia (riempimento sotto il Casone del Sale), Roma (riempimento sotto la chiesa di S. Stefano Rotondo), Lugnano in Teverina sul tratto ancora navigabile del Tevere a ca.100 km a monte di Roma (riempimento di parte di una villa romana abbandonata per ricavare un cimitero infantile) e Chianciano Terme su una collina sopra un affluente poco o per nulla navigabile del Tevere (obliterazione di una vasca che capta una fonte). Bisogna ammettere che la rassomiglianza nella formazione dei depositi è più calzante nei primi tre casi (strati gettati unitariamente che rialzano il livello del terreno) che nel quarto (scarti che segnano un graduale accumulo nel corso di alcuni anni), ma quest'ultimo sembra comunque riflettere l'approvvigionamento del sito per quanto si può giudicare dal materiale proveniente da altri periodi o da ritrovamenti di superficie.

Molto è stato discusso sui metodi di quantificazione della ceramica, il che non è il mio interesse in questa sede. Il confronto qui si basa sul conteggio dei frammenti e su una stima del massimo numero di individui presenti, che suppone che ogni frammento non attribuito allo stesso vaso di un altro in seguito a attacchi o altri accostamenti possa eventualmente rappresentare un vaso diverso. Non confronto i pesi, perché in seguito a vari spostamenti del materiale non è più stato possibile effettuare la pesatura programmata per il materiale di Chianciano. Altri tipi di quantificazione, quale la stima del numero minimo di esemplari attraverso la percentuale degli orli conservata o il conteggio di parti significanti, semplicemente non erano abituali in Italia negli anni in cui ho fatto il lavoro sui contesti. Il mio discorso non dipende comunque dalla scelta di quantificazione.

I raggruppamenti che ho adoperato riflettono la mia formazione all'Università di Roma nel gruppo sorto che ha indagato le Terme del Nuotatore a Ostia: ceramica fine da mensa, ceramica comune da vari usi domestici, ceramica da fuoco, lucerne e anfore da trasporto. Si tratta essenzialmente di gruppi funzionali, con fattori tecnici che rafforzano la definizione del primo gruppo, che richiede impianti e conoscenze specialistici. Pur volendo mantenere queste distinzioni, mi rendo conto che altre articolazioni sono possibili e effettivamente utilizzate: per esempio, l'associazione della ceramica fine da mensa alla parte ceramica comune eventualmente destinata alla presentazione e consumazione del cibo.

Passando rapidamente al materiale, faccio vedere i grafici sui quattro complessi.

1) A Ostia vediamo che le anfore superano di molto gli altri gruppi messi insieme. La ceramica comune arriva a quasi ¼, seguita da una minore quantità di ceramica da fuoco e da una discreta presenza di ceramica fine. Le lucerne sono pochissime.

2) La situazione cambia di poco a Roma. Scende la ceramica comune e aumentano tutti gli altri gruppi, ma abbiamo sempre una schiacciante percentuale di anfore, poca ceramica fine da mensa e un'esigua quantità di lucerne.

3) A Lugnano cambia decisamente il quadro. Le anfore sono ancora ben presenti ma non più maggioritarie. Anzi vengono superate dalla ceramica da fuoco. La ceramic comune scende notevolmente. La ceramica fine e le lucerne rimangono di limitata importanza.

4) Infine, si vede un ulteriore cambiamento a Chianciano. Le anfore diventano scarse e la ceramica fine e le lucerne si riducono ai minimi termini. Va sottolineato che le anfore risultano scarse malgrado delle attribuzioni generose: sospetto che pure le anfore più riconoscibili tipologicamente abbiano avuto un impiego finale come recipienti per l'acqua dalla fonte e ho avuto dubbi che certi contenitori siano stati prodotti per portare l'acqua, ma ho finito per dare alle anfore tutti i recipienti che presentassero legami con la tradizione anforaria dell'Italia centrale tirrenica medio e tardoimperiale.

Le tendenze vengono riassunti in un grafico sintetico. Qui ho riunito i dati relativi alla ceramica comune e quella da fuoco, perché gli sbalzi reciproci tra di loro mi suggerivano qualche problema: per esempio, l'eventuale utilizzazione a Lugnano di un impasto non distinto da quello da fuoco anche per altri usi domestici. Quindi, si vede il calo delle anfore e l'aumento delle ceramiche comune e da fuoco, ambedue drastici con il passaggio dai siti costieri ben inseriti nelle reti di scambio commerciale al sito interno appartato. Lugnano, integrata nei flussi commerciali ma verso i loro margini, dà valori intermedi.

E' istruttivo confrontare il grafico precedente con uno calcolato senza le anfore. Qui si notano poche differenze tra i quattro siti per quanto riguarda questi gruppi utilizzati in proprio, a differenza delle anfore che servivano solo per il trasporto delle derrate che erano l'oggetto dell'interessamento dei consumatori. La più notevole divergenza viene con la scarsezza della ceramica fine da mensa a Chianciano, forse di difficile reperimento in quella località. Evidentemente queste percentuali rispecchiano le necessità d'uso della ceramica degli abitanti che non cambiano con la diversa posizione geografica. Le anfore si rivelano come qualcosa in più del fabbisogno ordinario.

Accenno soltanto a ulteriori elaborazioni dei dati, in particolare all'incrocio tra i dati sui gruppi funzionali e la provenienza della ceramica. Vediamo che le anfore a Ostia e Roma sono quasi esclusivamente d'oltremare, con niente di produzione locale o regionale e poco dal resto dell'Italia centrale. Lugnano mostra un'aumentata presenza delle anfore regionali e comunque centroitaliche ma ancora la preponderanza di anfore importate. La maggior parte delle poche anfore a Chianciano sono locali, fatti in un impasto indistinguibile dalla ceramica comune d'uso domestico. Per le ceramiche da fuoco si nota che si possono avere notevoli quantità di importazioni a Ostia e a Roma, mentre a monte non arrivano. La ceramica fine mostra una situazione più complessa: quasi esclusivamente importazioni a Ostia e Roma, un'affermazione di prodotti regionali a Lugnano e di nuovo soprattutto importazioni a Chianciano. L'interpreto così: a Ostia e Roma il commercio marittimo è talmente forte che esiste pochissimo spazio per sostituzioni regionali; a Lugnano i flussi commerciali sono abbastanza indeboliti da lasciare posto a succedanei ma ancora sufficientemente forti da permettere la creazione di un mercato regionale a un prodotto che richiede investimenti particolari (es. fornaci a cottura ben controllabile) per la sua produzione; a Chianciano non penetrano nemmeno i flussi che abbiamo visto a Lugnano e la domanda locale non basta per reggere una produzione di ceramica fine, per cui i rari vasi fini rinvenuti sono importati. Il grafico per la ceramica comune evidenzia scarsa importazione a Ostia e Roma e niente a monte.

Può sembrare uno spreco di energia darsi da fare a provare che la presenza delle anfore diminuisce con l'allontanamento dai nodi delle reti commerciali e che cresce inversamente la presenza di prodotti locali: dovrebbero essere cose ovvie. L'utilità è però proprio quello di ottenere parametri da casi sicuri per misurare e valutare quelli meno evidenti. Prendo il caso di un altro sito dove lavoro: Olimpia. E' grande santuario prima e prospero borgo agricolo poi, ubicata a una certa distanza da una costa non ricca di porti. In epoca romana e tardoantica le anfore si attestano tra il 15% e il 35% e si constano la presenza di imitazioni di sigillata accanto a quelle standard e l'assenza di ceramiche comuni e da fuoco importate. Si possono confrontare questi dati con quelli di Lugnano e dire che Olimpia si trovava alquanto in disparte dai flussi commerciali ma non completamente isolata? Credo di sì. Però, quando si cercano altri confronti, sono sorprendentemente rari. Chiaramente sarebbe auspicabile disporre di un banco di dati molto più ampio per poter fare confronti sensati secondo cronologia, ubicazione geografica e modo di formazione del deposito.

In conclusione, mi sono dato due compiti. Il primo era quello di illustrare un approccio metodologico. L'esempio dimostra che l'esame globale di complessi ceramici porta i suoi frutti. In fin dei conti questo è un richiamo a non perdersi nei dettagli, trascurando il quadro d'insieme, che è sempre un rischio tra specialisti. Il secondo compito era quello di riflettere sulle scelte e sui presupposti che stanno dietro il lavoro. Alcuni fatti rispecchiano chiaramente la scuola italiana di studi sulla ceramica romana in cui sono stato allevato. In questo caso non mi sembrano di peso eccessivo. Comunque, non solo la comprensione da parte degli altri ma anche il proprio processo mentale vengono favoriti dalla dichiarazione delle proprie scelte e dal palesamento dei propri presupposti. Tra i vari incontri in cui scambiamo i risultati dei nostri lavori è bene trovare occasioni come questa di confronto su come lavoriamo.

BIBLIOGRAPHY

Martin, A. (c.s.) = Archer Martin, Variation in Ceramic Assemblages as an Indicator of Openness to Trade, in John Pollini (ed.), *TERRA MARIQUE: Studies in Honor of Anna Marguerite McCann on the Receipt of the Gold Medal of the Archaeological Institute of America.*

NOTE SULLA PRESENZA DI BOLLI LATERIZI NEL TERRITORIO DI FONDI (LT)

MASSIMILIANO DI FAZIO
(Università di Roma "La Sapienza")

ABSTRACT: This paper synthesizes a project aimed at studying a series of brick stamps from the area of Fondi in southern Lazio in order to obtain knowledge about the production and distribution of bricks and tiles in the 1st century AD.*

Scopo del presente contributo è di riesaminare gli esemplari di bolli laterizi rinvenuti in tempi più o meno recenti nel territorio di Fondi (LT), al fine di redigere un *corpus* il più completo possibile. Per ottenere questo risultato è sembrato opportuno utilizzare una documentazione ampia: non solo recenti indagini archeologiche ed indagini effettuate in passato, ma anche menzioni di rinvenimenti contenute in opere di antiquari locali del XIX secolo. In particolare, quest'ultimo tipo di approccio ha fornito risultati di un certo interesse, restituendo alla conoscenza storica alcuni esemplari di bolli laterizi altrimenti ignoti. Le fonti antiquarie si sono rivelate utili per ampliare lo spettro dei dati disponibili, rivelando tra l'altro che non sempre le indicazioni confluite nel *Corpus Inscriptionum Latinarum* sono corrette; ma sono state altresì utili per suggerire alcune direzioni di ricerca su questioni di storia economica del territorio oggetto di indagine. Questo metodo è spesso trascurato nell'analisi delle vicende storiche di un territorio, mentre può restituire informazioni preziose su monumenti e rinvenimenti di cui si è ormai persa traccia. In particolare ciò è valido per territori come quello di Fondi, in cui sono carenti indagini archeologiche sistematiche; è evidente che per poter disporre del maggior numero possibile di informazioni è indispensabile procedere all'analisi combinata dei risultati della ricerca sul campo e di quella che si può effettuare nelle pagine di autori del passato, che come vedremo non è peraltro meno costellata di ostacoli e problemi.

L'elenco dei bolli laterizi, comprendente casi dubbi, è il seguente:
Hyacinth(us) / Iuliae / August(ae)
Vinici
M. Arri
Q. Valerius Cato
Figl(inae) Marcian(ae)
Euchri
Hermeros / Ser
Patrobius / Ser
Apolloni Domiti / Lupi
L. Domiti / Lupi - Felix
Eupor Domiti / Lupi
Clari
Caediciae /M.F. Victricis (?)
Bitisus (?)

I primi tre esemplari sono stati individuati durante due recenti interventi archeologici, condotti nel settembre 2001 e nel marzo 2003[1], che hanno interessato l'area di una importante villa di epoca romana nel territorio del Comune di Fondi, in località "Vallaneto" nella contrada nota col nome di "San Raffaele"[2]. I bolli sono stati individuati in settori diversi della villa, ma si è trattato di un recupero effettuato superficialmente nell' *humus*, dunque le posizioni all'interno della struttura non possono essere considerate oltremodo indicative. La condizione frammentaria dei pezzi impedisce di stabilire le caratteristiche dei laterizi sui cui i bolli in questione erano impressi.

Il primo bollo (Fig. 1: *Hyacinth(us) / Iuliae / August(ae)* cartiglio quadrato, cm. 4,8x4,8; altezza lettere cm. 1 ca.) si inserisce in una serie ben nota: esemplari del tutto simili al nostro sono stati rinvenuti in passato (o sono segnalati in musei e collezioni) a Firenze, Capri, Ercolano, Stabia, Pozzuoli, Cuma, Torre del Greco, ed a Ponza e Ventotene[3]. L'unico centro che appare poco coerente con questa distribuzione è in effetti Firenze: ma il pezzo fiorentino apparteneva ad una collezione di un nobile del 1700, Pietro Andrea Andreini[4], e molto probabilmente aveva la stessa provenienza degli altri elementi della collezione, ovvero Miseno, dunque ancora in Campania (Gori 1727: I,255 n.36). La presenza di questi bolli su un'area così ampia ha fatto pensare ad una loro commercializzazione (Morel 1996: 188), e l'esemplare fondano, il più settentrionale[5], parrebbe una conferma in tale direzione.

Il primo nome, *Hyacinthus*, non costituisce un problema: si tratta di uno schiavo di *Iulia*[6], che evidentemente era responsabile della produzione dei laterizi oppure della loro commercializzazione; il nome, di chiara origine greca, è attestato frequentemente nel mondo romano, perlopiù a partire dall'età augustea (Solin 1982: 1107-8). Su *Iulia* invece il discorso è più complesso: già i primi studiosi che hanno avuto a che fare col pezzo si sono interrogati sulla sua identità (vedi *CIL* X,2, 8042,6). Scartata la possibilità che si tratti della figlia dell'imperatore Tito[7], le altre due proposte dipendono dall'integrazione del terzo nome del bollo. Se leggiamo *Augustae*, infatti, abbiamo a che fare con Livia Drusilla (58 a. – 29 d.C.), moglie del principe Augusto e madre di Tiberio, la quale dopo la morte del marito assume il nome di *Iulia Augusta*. In questo caso avremmo anche una forchetta cronologica piuttosto precisa: 14 d.C. (morte di Augusto) - 29 d.C. (morte di Livia). Altri studiosi hanno proposto di integrare come *Augusti*, sottintendendo *filiae*: in tal caso, avremmo a che fare non con la moglie ma con la figlia di Augusto, Giulia Augusta (39 a.C.-14 d.C.) (Jacono 1926). La differenza cronologica evidentemente è ridotta; peraltro, considerati i tempi di stoccaggio, è facile che mattoni prodotti da un'officina imperiale rimanessero in commercio anche per un periodo (ragionevole) dopo la morte del titolare (Thébert 2000: 344 sgg.). Ma i più recenti esemplari rinvenuti a Capri sembrano dire la parola definitiva sulla questione: in uno dei bolli della serie, infatti, si legge, pur se a malapena, un *ae* finale (Miranda 1998: 359, n.E59). Dunque l'integrazione risulta essere obbligata: *Iuliae Augustae*, Livia.

Secondo alcune fonti, come è noto, Livia sarebbe nata da madre fondana (si veda sulla questione Linderski 1974). Questo dato non ci autorizza ovviamente a tirare alcun tipo di conclusioni: non possiamo assolutamente dedurre che la villa fosse di proprietà di Livia o della sua famiglia[8]. Né ci soccorre in qualche modo la carta della distribuzione dei rinvenimenti degli altri esemplari della serie: oltre che in complessi di proprietà imperiale, infatti, il bollo era presente anche in edifici pubblici (Cuma ed Ercolano) o comunque di livello non eccelso. Ma sappiamo, ad ogni buon conto, che una parte del territorio fondano nei primi secoli dell'era cristiana era di proprietà personale della famiglia imperiale (*CIL* VI, 8583; Panciera 1990: 179). Non è escluso che tra i possedimenti imperiali rientrasse anche questo complesso: ne sarebbero buoni indizi, più del bollo, la ricchezza ed il fasto della villa.

Il secondo esemplare rinvenuto (Fig. 2: *Vinic[i]* cartiglio rettangolare, cm. 6,5x1,8; altezza lettere cm. 1,3 ca.) trova anche in questo caso confronti piuttosto precisi, che ci indicano una distribuzione molto simile a quella del pezzo precedente: Capri, Ercolano, Pompei, ed in più Palermo e le isole Lipari[9]. Una variante, *Fortunati / Vinici* è segnalata anche a Ponza (*CIL* X, 8042,53). I *Vinicii* sono una famiglia di origine campana, in particolare di Capua (Castrén 1975: 242 n.462); agli inizi dell'epoca imperiale alcuni membri accedono a cariche importanti del mondo romano, ed in generale possono vantare una certa vicinanza con la corte imperiale[10]. Secondo alcuni studiosi, il bollo si collocherebbe in un generico I secolo d.C. (Miranda 1998: 358), il che sarebbe concorde con la datazione del precedente. Ma gli esemplari delle Lipari, che sono stati rinvenuti in contesti tombali in associazione con materiali piuttosto ben databili quali lucerne e ceramica, hanno fatto propendere gli editori per una datazione agli ultimi decenni del I secolo a.C., o al più fino alla morte di Augusto (Cavalier e Brugnone 1986: 265-267, nn. 155-160). Non a caso in una di queste sepolture, insieme al bollo in questione, era presente un altro bollo con l'indicazione di una liberta di Livia, dunque prima della morte di Augusto. Siamo anche in questo caso nell'ambito più che accettabile di uno scarto di pochi anni.

Un terzo bollo (Fig. 3: *M. Arri* cartiglio rettangolare, cm. 7,5 x 2,5; altezza lettere cm. 1,9 ca.; A e R legate) è in pessimo stato di conservazione, ma la lettura può considerarsi attendibile. Anche in questo caso siamo ampiamente nell'ambito di una produzione a cavallo tra la fine della Repubblica e gli inizi dell'età imperiale. Ed anche in questo caso la distribuzione degli esemplari è pienamente coerente con gli altri due casi: Cuma, Pompei, Ercolano, Lipari, Pollena-Trocchia (Napoli)[11]. Di recente Mario Torelli, occupandosi di produzioni laterizie pompeiane, ha accomunato le produzioni *M. Arri* e *M.Arri Maximi*, entrambe attestate già nel *CIL*, ed ha ricordato che è probabile una relazione con un *M. Arrius Maximus* di *Anagnia* (*CIL* X, 5911; Steinby 1984, 267), concludendo che l'officina poteva essere verosimilmente anagnina. La conferma di questa situazione, sempre secondo Torelli, starebbe nell'assenza del gentilizio nella pur ricca onomastica pompeiana. Ma proprio a Pompei le attestazioni della presenza di Arrii non mancano, anche se in epoca leggermente posteriore; tra questa spicca il riferimento alla casa degli Arrii (*insula Arriana Polliana*), e alla produzione vinicola (*vinum Arrianum*: *CIL* IV, 5572), ed in un documento ercolanense del 63 d.C. si ricordano *in Pompeiano in figlinis Arrianis Poppaeae Aug* (bibliografia in Steinby 1984, 267). Tuttavia, non sono questi elementi che possano far concludere che l'officina fosse pompeiana. Va sottolineato tra l'altro che il gentilizio è attestato anche in prossimità del territorio fondano, per la precisione a Formia. In due lettere del 59 a.C. scritte dalla sua villa formiana, Cicerone ricorda non senza fastidio l'invadente vicino *C. Arrius*, nome noto all'epigrafia formiana (*CIL* X, 6101, 6122, 6136; cfr. Laaksonen 1987: 136). Per quella che potrebbe essere una curiosa coincidenza, in località "Caposele" tra Formia e Gaeta, proprio in quella che nella tradizione locale è sempre stata chiamata (senza evidente motivo) la "villa di Cicerone", venne alla luce la testimonianza epigrafica di *Arrius Salanus*, importante prefetto imperiale in età tiberiana (*CIL* X, 6101; Laaksonen 1987: 137). Ma sono noti *Arrii* anche a *Minturnae*, in Apulia, ed in numerose altre località. Dovremo accontentarci, col Licordari (1982, 34), di concludere una generica origine da un'area compresa tra il Lazio meridionale e la Campania settentrionale (forse più da quest'area).

Un quarto bollo, dato come proveniente dalla villa, è stato segnalato alla locale Soprintendenza Archeologica: si tratta di un bollo di *Q. Valerius Cato*, un nome già noto nell'ambito della produzione laterizia romana (Bloch 1967: nn. 82,83; Steinby 1974: 88). Anche in questo caso saremmo agevolmente all'interno del I secolo d.C., forse intorno alla metà del secolo. Il dato interessante è che, mentre i primi tre esemplari sono certamente di produzione campana, quest'ultimo è di area di produzione urbana.

Nessuno dei quattro esemplari qui presentati trova altri confronti nel territorio fondano; ma la situazione delle nostre conoscenze, come abbiamo già detto, è molto scarsa: rarissimi sono stati in passato gli interventi archeologici, ma rare anche le occasioni in cui materiale venuto occasionalmente alla luce sia stato conservato o ufficializzato. L'unico bollo laterizio edito proveniente da indagini archeologiche prima d'ora è un esemplare rinvenuto durante un intervento nell'area delle terme in Piazza della Repubblica, riferibile alle *Figlinae Marcianae* (Lissi Caronna 1971: 353; il confronto più puntuale è con *CIL* XV,1, 326: *Aur Thall ex figl(inis) Marcian(is)*; su queste figline vedi Steinby 1974-'75, 61-66), la cui datazione sembra da collocarsi ad un periodo più tardo rispetto ai casi finora esaminati (II secolo d.C.)[12]. Va notato che altri laterizi delle figline Marciane circolano in zona: un esemplare pare attestato nell'isola di Ponza (X,2,8042, 71a), riferibile al tipo *Stati.Marci / Statoris*, databile per Bloch al 40 d.C. (Bloch 1967, n.337; Steinby 1974-'75, 63-64).

Altre informazioni sono però conservate in opere di eruditi locali, attivi per lo più nel XIX secolo; ovviamente il problema in questi casi è stabilire l'attendibilità delle informazioni tramandate. Il "capostipite" degli studiosi locali è senza dubbio Francescantonio Notarjanni (1759-1843) (su cui Terella 1939), medico e poligrafo, autore fra le altre opere di un "Viaggio per l'Ausonia" (1814) prodigo di informazioni. Va detto che il Notarjanni non godeva della stima di Mommsen (cfr. *CIL* X, 618), dunque le sue informazioni andranno considerate con cautela. Alcuni esemplari menzionati da Notarjanni furono accolti dal Mommsen senza modifiche, altri con riletture e correzioni. Il primo è *EVCHRI* (con spiga), accolto senza modifiche (*CIL* X,2, 8043, 57) e sembra poter essere confrontato con *T.Flavi / Euchri* (*CIL* XV,1, 1150; Bloch 1967, n.294): in tal caso avremmo a che fare con una produzione urbana, con un esemplare datato ad età flavia; ma l'assenza della spiga (presente invece sugli esemplari *L.Flavi / Philippi*, *CIL* XV,1, 1154 b) invita alla cautela. Il secondo è *HERNEROS / SER*, accolto da Mommsen come *Hermeros / Ser* (*CIL* X,2, 8043, n.61), e sembra essere confrontabile col bollo urbano *Herme[tis?] Servi Fulvi* (*CIL* XV,1, 1184), di cui potrebbe fornire una più corretta integrazione; in questa direzione porta anche la constatazione che l'errata lettura del Notarjanni, *Herneros*, può essere stata indotta dalla legatura di M ed E presente sull'esemplare urbano. Anche in questo caso, dunque, avremmo un bollo di provenienza urbana. Il terzo è *PATROBVS / SER*, accolto come *Patrobius / Ser* (*CIL* X,2, 8043, n.72) grazie anche ad un paio di confronto in zona (*CIL* X,2, 8043, n.56; anche XV,1, 2248); sarebbe interessante accostare *Patrobius* all'omonimo liberto di Nerone, messo a morte da Galba, che ben conosciamo attraverso varie fonti.[13]

Problemi pone un altro esemplare tràdito dal Notarjanni, e non a caso non accolto da Mommsen: un enigmatico *BITISUS* che a quanto si può constatare non solo non risulta come nome, ma neanche come qualsivoglia termine del lessico latino. È difficile stabilire se si tratti di una completa invenzione, oppure di un esemplare di fabbrica locale. Del resto sono molte le lezioni di Notarjanni, non solo per bolli ma anche per epigrafi, che necessitano di correzioni. Un esemplare di bollo fondano letto come *DOMITI APOLLONI PILA*, alla luce di confronti anche di recente rinvenimento diventa *Apolloni Domiti / Lupi* (Notarjanni p. 206: *CIL* X,2, 8043 n. 52; Pesiri 1978: 175). Proprio quest'ultimo esemplare introduce una seconda categoria di bolli, attestati stavolta anche da indagini più recenti ed affidabili: *Apolloni Domiti / Lupi*; *L.Domiti / Lupi – Felix* (con spiga); *Eupor Domiti / Lupi* (Pesiri 1978, 174-5). Si tratta di una serie relativa all'officina di *Lucius Domitius Lupus*, a cui appartengono bolli firmati da diversi nomi: *Apollonius*, *Eupor*, *Felix*, attestati anche in varie zone della Pianura Pontina fino a Velletri (Pesiri 1978: 174-175), a dimostrazione dell'importanza e della complessità organizzativa di questo *atelier*. Non è escluso che alla stessa officina vada riferito il già visto *Patrobius / Ser*, se i confronti con gli esemplari *L. Domiti. Lupi / Patrobius* (*CIL* XV,1, 2248 a-b) sono da considerare validi[14]. Sarebbe interessante a questo punto ricollegare il liberto *Lucius Domitius Lupus* con *Lucius Domitius Phaon*, importante proprietario terriero ed ex-liberto di Domizia Lepida (Gregory 1995; Di Giuseppe 1996). Phaon possedeva terreni in varie località dell'Italia meridionale, tra cui Fondi, come testimoniano i monumentali cippi con epigrafe posti a delimitazione del sepolcro rinvenuti in contrada San Raffaele, a distanza di circa 2,5 km dalla villa oggetto dell'intervento accennato in apertura del presente lavoro (Giglioli 1911; Pesiri 1978: 175 sgg.).

È ancora grazie a ricerche antiquarie ottocentesche che si può recuperare una informazione interessante relativa alla sfera dei traffici: un altro medico, Giovanni Sotis, verso la metà del secolo, nel suo *Memoria sull'antica città di Amicle* (Sotis 1838b: 19-20), racconta che «non ha guari ch'escavando in poca distanza dal casino del sig. Principe dappresso al nuovo vialone che porta sul lido del mare...» si rinvennero alcuni monumenti romani, e nei pressi una sepoltura a cappuccina con grossi tegoloni, due dei quali contenevano le seguenti iscrizioni: *CLARI* e *CAEDICIAE / M.F. VICTRICIS*. Il "casino del Principe" trova probabilmente riscontro in un edificio che in vecchie mappe è indicato come "casale del Principe"[15], nei pressi della strada che dal centro abitato di Fondi porta sul lido del mare (Fig. 4), laddove un misto di fonti malcerte e di tradizioni locali pseudoerudite collocava l'antica città di *Amyclae* (Cébeillac Gervasoni 1984).

Dalla descrizione dunque sembra che il Sotis avesse individuato due bolli laterizi. In effetti il primo, *Clari*, viene inserito come tale dal Mommsen nel *CIL* (X,2, 8043 n.46), e non sembra particolarmente significativo[16]. Il secondo, *Caediciae / M.f. Victricis*, viene invece erroneamente inserito tra le epigrafi (X, 6252). La situazione si complica se si considera che questa iscrizione è tutt'altro che ignota, essendo presente su una serie di bolli, non laterizi ma anforari, di ampia diffusione. La titolare di questi bolli, *Caedicia*, è stata ricollegata alla figura di una nobildonna campana, una ricca proprietaria terriera, che produceva vino di qualità nell'agro Falerno, commerciandolo su largo raggio[17]. Oltre ai mercati italiani (Roma, Tivoli, Firenze) le anfore di Cedicia raggiungevano parecchi luoghi del Mediterraneo, come Cartagine, Corinto, Lione, Tarragona[18]. Con tutta probabilità si tratta della stessa Cedicia che fu esiliata insieme al marito *Flavius Scaevinus* da Nerone nel 65 d.C., come conseguenza della congiura dei Pisoni (Tac., *Ann.*, XV, 71). Questa ricostruzione cronologica è stata messa in discussione di recente: infatti gli esemplari di bolli di Corinto e di Lione sono stati rinvenuti in contesti di II o addirittura forse inizi III secolo d.C., cosa che dovrebbe comportare un abbassamento della datazione tradizionalmente fissata al I secolo (Tchernia 1996). Ma probabilmente queste considerazioni sottovalutano il fenomeno del reimpiego di anfore come materiale da costruzione, per cui il bollo di un'anfora può fornire solo un'indicazione *post quem*. Appare dunque tutto sommato ancora preferibile la ricostruzione di cui sopra.

Se potessimo essere sicuri di quanto scriveva il Sotis, ovvero dell'esistenza di una tegola con lo stesso bollo usualmente presente sulle anfore, avremmo evidentemente una importante testimonianza della versatilità delle officine che facevano capo a Cedicia, e che non si limitavano a prodotti anforacei ma si allargavano anche a laterizi. Ad ampliare ulteriormente lo spettro produttivo c'è da considerare oltretutto la possibilità che l'esemplare fiorentino su menzionato sia riconducibile alla pertinenza di un dolio più che di un'anfora[19]. L'unicità del riferimento in entrambi i casi deve comunque imporre una certa cautela.

Se invece il buon Sotis avesse commesso un errore nella sua descrizione, oppure se (ipotesi più che plausibile) avesse semplicemente riportato maldestramente informazioni di seconda mano[20], l'esemplare fondano rientrerebbe nella casistica. In tal caso potremmo fare con cautela un altro tipo di considerazioni. Sappiamo da Plinio (*NH* XXIII, 35) che il rinomato Cecubo (Tchernia 1986: 324-325) cessò di essere prodotto entro la metà del I secolo d.C.: potrebbe non essere casuale trovare proprio in questo momento nel territorio fondano tracce di importazioni di vino di prestigio dall'agro Falerno. Purtroppo la singolarità del pezzo e le informazioni poco sicure di cui disponiamo non permettono di conferire a queste considerazioni altro valore che quello di pure ipotesi di lavoro. Va sottolineato che proprio nelle vicinanze del luogo indicato da Sotis, in località Sant'Anastasia, è stato proposto di individuare un *atelier* di produzione anforaria (Hesnard 1977); più di recente, per gli stessi rinvenimenti è stata invece prospettata una diversa spiegazione, che chiama in causa interventi di bonifica idraulica (Quilici Gigli 1998). Rinvenimenti di anfore collocate con funzione drenante si susseguono nella piana di Fondi dalla fine del XIX secolo fino ancora a tempi recentissimi (marzo 2003); ma è proprio questa abbondanza di anfore (riscontrabile peraltro su pressoché tutto il territorio) che rende plausibile la presenza di un'officina: le due ipotesi sono ben lungi dall'escludersi a vicenda.

Va sottolineato ancora come questo di *Caedicia* sarebbe l'unico bollo d'anfora, fra quelli individuati nel territorio fondano, databile al I secolo d.C. Altri esemplari infatti sono perlopiù tutti riconducibili all'officina di P. Veveius Papus, e marcano contenitori di tipo Dressel 1a, 1b e 2-4 (Hesnard e Lemoine 1981: 243-295). I confronti con l'eccezionale relitto della Madrague de Giens, col suo carico di anfore con tutta probabilità provenienti dal territorio fondano, permettono una datazione pienamente inquadrata all'interno del I secolo a.C.: il relitto sarebbe affondato intorno al 70 a.C. (Tchernia 1990: 296).

Queste riflessioni potrebbero trovare conferma nei dati della villa in località "Vallaneto" da cui abbiamo preso le mosse. Le indagini hanno infatti avuto avvio con l'auspicio di fornire nuovi dati sull'assetto economico della piana di Fondi in età tardorepubblicana ed imperiale, ovvero in quello che nelle fonti e nelle testimonianze archeologiche appare il momento di maggior fulgore del territorio fondano (si veda per un recente riepilogo Storchi Marino 2002); fulgore che appare decisamente legato alla produzione vinicola, in particolare del Cecubo. Contrariamente alle aspettative, invece, non sono state finora individuate tracce di strutture destinate ad attività produttive, che possano prospettare un collegamento della villa con la grande produzione vinicola per cui il territorio di Fondi era rinomato nel mondo romano[21]. Ovviamente i dati che abbiamo sono del tutto insufficienti per ipotizzare che i produttori locali fossero stati soppiantati agli inizi del I secolo d.C. da "ditte" vinicole radicate in zone di grande produttività e con maggiori possibilità commerciali come l'*ager Falernus*. Ma questo può essere un punto di vista da verificare col prosieguo delle indagini storiche ed archeologiche locali. Per ora sfugge il retroterra sociale che fa da sfondo ai fatti economici che stiamo descrivendo: i dati di cui disponiamo sono troppo esigui per formare un quadro della gestione e del controllo del sistema produttivo come è stato possibile, ad esempio, per il territorio brindisino (Manacorda 1994): troppe incertezze e troppi "se", che si spera possano essere superati nel corso delle ricerche.

In conclusione, se consideriamo i bolli di provenienza sufficientemente sicura (escludendo dunque *Clari*, *Caediciae*, *Bitisus*) abbiamo la seguente situazione: un gruppo di provenienza campano-settentrionale (quello riferito a Livia, i due delle famiglie campane); un gruppo di area urbana (le figline Marciane, *Valerius Cato*, forse *Hermeros* e *Euchrus*); un gruppo presente in un'area delimitata grossomodo tra Velletri e Fondi (quello che fa capo a Domizio Lupo), per il quale, specie se fosse verificabile la relazione con *Domitius Phaon*, non sarebbe fuori luogo proporre una origine fondana. Ciò sembra costituire un'ulteriore conferma della particolare situazione di crocevia del territorio fondano, che si colloca da sempre a metà strada non solo geograficamente ma anche culturalmente ed economicamente fra Roma e la Campania.

NOTE

* Questa relazione prende spunto da un progetto di ricerca condotto nell'ambito del dottorato in Storia Antica presso l'Università La Sapienza di Roma, riguardante la storia economica e sociale del territorio dell'antica *Fundi*, odierna Fondi (LT) Ringrazio i proff. S. Panciera e G.L. Gregori per aver esaminato il testo, dei cui errori ovviamente non sono responsabili.

1 L'intervento è stato condotto sotto la guida della Soprintendenza Archeologica nella persona della dott.ssa N. Cassieri, e coordinato sul campo da chi scrive. Ringrazio per la collaborazione M.C. Biella, a cui va il merito di aver individuato i bolli, e per le foto E. Cappellini; un grazie infine a tutti coloro che hanno partecipato alla campagna.

2 La struttura sorge su una sella fra due alture, ultime propaggini dell'arco collinare che circonda la piana di Fondi, e si affaccia sul lago di San Puoto, a breve distanza dal mare Poche sono le notizie riferite alla villa nella letteratura archeologica recente, che peraltro alla luce dei nuovi interventi andranno riviste (Fasolo 1966; De Rossi 1981: 173-176; Lafon 2001: 259-260 e 377). L'indagine è ancora ad un livello ampiamente preliminare, pur essendo già possibili alcune prime considerazioni. Si tratta sicuramente di un complesso di prestigio, considerando le dimensioni di almeno 100x60 m. ed il materiale raccolto ad una semplice operazione di ripulitura. Ancora non ben precisata è la datazione del complesso, che ad ogni modo restituisce materiale collocabile cronologicamente almeno agli inizi dell'età imperiale; solo ulteriori indagini sistematiche potranno fornire qualche certezza.

3 Stabia, Torre del Greco, dintorni del Mons Tifata, Capri, Napoli, Firenze (*CIL* X, 8042, 6); Capri (Miranda 1998: 357 sgg., nn. E51, E57, E58, E59, e con tutta probabilità anche il lacunoso E72, non riconosciuto dall'Editore); Pozzuoli (Paribeni 1902: 630); Ponza (Jacono 1926: 222 e 230); Ventotene (De Rossi 1986: 191-193); Cuma (Bertoldi 1973: 40; Scatozza Höricht 1991: 355 sgg.); Stabia (Miniero 1999).

4 Il quale, a detta dello stesso Gori, amava raccogliere antichità durante viaggi nel napoletano (Gori 1727: 240: *Petrus Andreas Andreinius Antiquitatum omnium indagator studiosissimus cum Neapoli versaretur anno 1688 summo labore conquisivit, et comparavit*).

5 È difficile valutare la possibile presenza di un altro esemplare a Velletri, testimoniato forse dalle parole del Theuli nel 1644 (cfr. *CIL* X,2, 8043, 106, col commento: *spectare crederem ad laterculum Hyacinthi Iuliae Augustae, si is in Latio inveniretur*). Ma per quali vicende questo bollo potè arrivare a Velletri (ammesso che si trattasse di un esemplare analogo a quelli trattati)?

6 Non menzionato nel Colombario di Livia, dove c'è solo un *...nthus* / *(C)aesar* / *tt* (*CIL* VI, 2, 4096) Ghezzi 1731: 22 n.23), integrato in *(a)nthus* sulla base, presumibilmente, di 4097: *Anthu[* / *Liv[* (Ghezzi 1731: 25, n.29).

7 La figlia di Tito non passò alla storia come un personaggio di spicco, nè conosciamo altre officine col suo nome, per cui questa ipotesi risulta la meno attendibile

8 Per il rapporto tra bolli e proprietà si rimanda alle riflessioni in Steinby 1984.

9 Capri (Miranda 1998: 358, n. E56); Ercolano (Della Corte 1958: 279 n.248); Pompei (*CIL* X, 8042, 108); Palermo (Tusa 1954: 146); Lipari (Cavalier e Brugnone 1986: 265-267, nn. 155-160).

10 Basti citare Lucio Vinicio console nel 5 a.C. e quel Marco Vinicio console nel 30 d.C. a cui era dedicata l'opera di Velleio Patercolo (Cavalier e Brugnone 1986: 267).

11 Cuma (Scatozza Höricht 1991: 356); Puteoli (*CIL* X,2, 8042, 19 b); Pompei (CIL X,2, 8042, 19 a; Steinby 1984: 267, con bibl. precedente), Ercolano (Pagano 1990: 173); Pollena-Trocchia (Della Corte 1932: 313 sgg.); Lipari (Cavalier-Brugnone 1986: 247 sgg., nn. 96-120).

12 Alle *Figlinae Marcianae* non è estraneo *Q. Valerius Cato*, ma in bolli di forma diversa da quello rinvenuto nelle terme fondane (Bloch 1967: n.82; Steinby 1974-'75: 64).
13 Tac. *Hist.* I,49; II,95; Plin. *NH* 35, 168; Plut. *Galba* 17,2; Suet. *Galba* 20,2; Dio *exc.* 63, 3,1; 64, 3,4. Ricordiamo che l'imperatore Galba era nativo della zona tra Fondi e Terracina (Suet. *Galba*, 4, 1). In effetti Solin registra solo quattro personaggi dal nome *Patrobius* noti nel I secolo d.C., due dei quali sono quelli a cui abbiamo fatto riferimento, e dunque l'ipotesi potrebbe essere fondata (Solin 1982: I, 135-6).
14 Data la scarsa attendibilità di Notarjanni, non possiamo escludere che il *SER* sia stato frutto di una assimilazione con *Hermeros / Ser.*
15 In mancanza di documentazione su questo edificio, possiamo limitarci a ricordare che nella storia di Fondi sono tre le famiglie di rango principesco: a partire dal 1591 si succedono i Carafa, i Mansfeld, i Di Sangro; tutti sono coinvolti in opere di bonifica che riguardano anche quella parte del territorio in cui sorge il castelletto.
16 Essendo un nome piuttosto comune, sarebbe imprudente sostenere un confronto col *Clarus* attestato nel Viterbese (Bloch 1967: n.556).
17 L'origine di questa famiglia è stata al centro di discussioni: l'orientamento prevalente individuava nel Massico il centro originario; ma già P. Arthur (1991: 68) avanzava qualche dubbio al riguardo, notando come anche altri territori fossero papabili, fra cui ad esempio Strongoli, dove è attestata una *vinea Caediciana* (*CIL* X, 114). Recenti scoperte dovute a M.L. Lazzarini ci forniscono un importante dato: i Caedicii erano già presenti nel IV sec. proprio a Strongoli (M.L. Lazzarini, *c.s.*). Non è da escludere comunque che almeno un ramo si fosse sviluppato a *Minturnae* (Guidobaldi 1989).
18 Roma (*CIL* XV, 3424); Tivoli (Mari 1983: 380); Firenze (*CIL* X, 6695, 23); Cartagine (*CIL* V, 22637,23); Corinto (Williams e Zervos 1985); Lione (Desbat e Savay Guerraz 1990); Tarragona (dubbio) (*CIL* II, 4973,3).
19 Il bollo si trovava su una «grande olla infranta», e recava oltre al nome l'indicazione *dol* (*CIL* XI, 6695, 23).
20 Va sottolineato che nella stessa opera Sotis cita i bolli già menzionati decenni prima dal Notarjanni come se fossero novità (Sotis 1838b: 19-20); del resto possiamo essere sicuri che conosceva le opere del suo predecessore, dal momento che lo cita più volte nelle sue opere («chiarissimo medico mio amico signor Notarjanni»: Sotis 1838a: 9). Ma il bollo di *Caedicia* non è menzionato da Notarjanni.
21 Non possiamo certo escludere che col prosieguo delle ricerche non venga alla luce anche questo aspetto; ma allo stato attuale dobbiamo sottolineare che il complesso sembra avere caratteristiche più spiccatamente residenziali e di lusso che produttive. Sicuramente alla villa facevano capo terreni coltivati, e dobbiamo supporre qualche forma di produzione almeno per autoconsumo; ma non possiamo al momento sostenere un aspetto commerciale. Gli esemplari di anforacei rinvenuti, ad esempio, si presentano più che altro come materiale di reimpiego all'interno delle strutture murarie, secondo una consuetudine ben conosciuta per il mondo romano.

BIBLIOGRAFIA

Arthur, P., 1991, *Romans in Northern Campania*, London.

Bertoldi, M.E., 1973, Recenti scavi e scoperte a Cuma, *Bollettino di archeologia*, 58, 38-42.

Bloch, H., 1967, *Roman Brick Stamps*, Roma.

Cavalier, M. e Brugnone, A., 1986, I bolli delle tegole nella necropoli di Lipari, *Kokalos*, 32, 181-282.

Castrén, P., 1975, *Ordo Popolusque Pompeianus*, Roma.

Cébeillac Gervasoni, M., 1984, Amicle, in *Bibliografia topografica della colonizzazione greca in Italia e nelle isole tirreniche*, (edd. G.Nenci e G.Vallet), I, 221-223, Pisa-Roma.

De Rossi, G.M., 1981, *Lazio meridionale*, Roma.

De Rossi, G.M., 1986, *Le isole pontine attraverso i tempi*, Roma.

Della Corte, M., 1932, Napoli, *Notizie degli scavi*, 313.

Della Corte, M., 1958, Le iscrizioni di Ercolano, *RAAN*, 33, 239-308.

Desbat, A. e Savay-Guerraz, H., 1990, Note sur la découverte d'amphores Dressel 2/4 italiques tardives, à Saint-Roman-en-Gal (Rhône), *Gallia*, 47, 203-213.

Di Giuseppe, H., 1996, Un'industria tessile di Domizia Lepida in Lucania, *Ostraka*, 5, 31-43.

Fasolo, F., 1966, Presentazione di rilievi di studenti della Facoltà di Architettura di Roma, *Bollettino dell'Istituto di Storia e di Arte del Lazio Meridionale*, 4, 63-69.

Ghezzi, P.L., 1731, *Camere sepolcrali de'liberti e liberte di Livia Augusta*, Roma.

Giglioli, G.Q., 1911, Note archeologiche sul "Latium Novum", *Ausonia*, 6, 39-87.

Gori, A.F., 1727, *Inscriptiones Antiquae in Etruriae Urbibus Exstantes*, Firenze.

Gregory, A.P., 1995, A Study in Survival: the Case of the Freedman L. Domitius Phaon, *Athenaeum*, 83, 401-410.

Guidobaldi, M.P., 1989, in *Minturnae* (ed. F.Coarelli), 70-71, Roma.

Hesnard, A., 1977, Notes sur un atelier d'amphores Dr.1 et Dr.2-4 prés de Terracina, «*MEFRA*», 89, 157-168.

Hesnard, A. e Gianfrotta, P.A., 1989, Les bouchons d'amphore en pouzzolane, in *Amphores romaines et histoire economique, Atti del convegno, Siena 1986*, 393-441, Roma.

Hesnard, A. e Lemoine, Ch., 1981, Les amphores du Cécube et du Falerne, *MEFRA*, 93, 243-283.

Jacono, L., 1926, Ponza, *Notizie degli Scavi*, 219-232.

Lafon, X., 2001, *Villa maritima. Recherches sur les villas littorales de l'Italie romaine*, Paris.

Licordari, A., 1982, Ascesa al senato e rapporti con i territori di origine. Italia: Regio I (Latium), in *Epigrafia e ordine senatorio, Atti colloquio Roma 1981*, II, 9-57, Roma.

Linderski, J., 1974, The Mother of Livia Augusta and the Aufidii Lurcones of the Republic, *Historia*, 23, 463-480.

Lissi Caronna, E., 1971, Fondi. Resti di un impianto termale in piazza dell'Unità, *Notizie degli Scavi*, 330-363.

Manacorda, D., 1994, Produzione agricola, produzione ceramica e proprietà della terra nella Calabria romana tra Repubblica e Impero, in *Epigrafia della produzione e della distribuzione, Roma 1992*, 3-59, Roma.

Mari, Z., 1983, *Tibur III. Forma Italiae I*, Firenze.

Miniero, P. 1999, La produzione laterizia, in *La villa San Marco a Stabia*, (edd. A.Barbet e P.Miniero), 63-71, Napoli-Roma-Pompei.

Miranda, E., 1998, Le iscrizioni latine, in *Capri antica. Dalla preistoria alla fine dell'età romana*, (edd. E.Federico e E.Miranda), 343-371, Capri.

Morel, J.P., 1996, *Élites municipales et manifacture en Italie*, in *Les élites munipales de l'Italie péninsulaire des Gracques à neron, Actes de la table ronde, Clermont-Ferrand 1991* (ed. M.Cébeillac Gervasoni), 181-198, Napoli-Roma.

Notarjanni, F.A., 1814, Viaggio per l'Ausonia, in *Giornale Enciclopedico di Napoli*, 7, 1814.

Pagano, M., 1990, *Tegulae campanae* ad Ercolano, *Cronache Ercolanensi*, 20, 157-176.

Panciera, S., 1990, *Procurator huius praetori*, in *Studia in honorem B. Gerov*, (edd. M.Taceva e D.Bojadziev), 174-189, Sofia.

Paribeni, R., 1902, Pozzuoli, *Notizie degli Scavi*, 629-630.

Pesiri, G., 1978, Iscrizioni di Fondi e del circondario, *Epigraphica*, 40, 162-184.

Quilici Gigli, S., 1998, Sulle bonifiche nell'Italia romana, in *Bonifiche e drenaggi con anfore in epoca romana, atti del convegno, Padova 1995* (ed. S. Pesavento Mattioli), 15-21, Modena.

Scatozza Höricht, L., 1991, Su alcune antefisse romane e bolli da Cuma, *Latomus*, 50, 352-363.

Solin, H., 1982, *Die Griechischen Personennamen in Rom*, Berlin.

Sotis, F. 1838 a, *Cenno istorico della città di Fondi*, Napoli.

Sotis, F., 1838 b, *Memoria sull'antica città di Amicle*, in *Dizionario istorico-geografico del Regno di Napoli*, (ed. F. Mastriani), Napoli.

Steinby, E.M., 1974-'75, La cronologia delle figlinae doliari urbane dalla fine dell'età repubblicana fino all'inizio del III sec., *Bullettino Comunale*, 84, 7-132.

Steinby, E.M., 1984, La produzione laterizia, in *Pompei 79, raccolta di studi, Napoli 1979* (ed. F. Zevi), 265-271, Napoli.

Storchi Marino, A., 2002, Fondi romana: società ed economia, in *Fondi tra antichità e medioevo, atti del convegno, Fondi 2000* (ed. M.T. Piscitelli Carpino), 19-70, Napoli.

Tchernia, A., 1986, *Le vin de l'Italie romaine*, Roma.

Tchernia, A., 1990, Contre les épaves, in *Gaule interne et Gaule méditerranéenne aux IIe et Ier siècles avant J.-C., Actes de la table ronde, Valbonne 1986* (edd. A.Duval, J.-P. Morel, T.Roman), 291-301, Paris.

Tchernia, A., 1996, Maesianus Celsus et Caedicia Victrix sur des amphores de Campanie, in *Les élites munipales de l'Italie péninsulaire des Gracques à neron, Actes de la table ronde, Clermont-Ferrand 1991* (ed. M.Cébeillac Gervasoni), 207-211, Napoli-Roma.

Terella, N., 1939, *Francesco Antonio Notarianni di Lenola*, Roma.

Thébert, Y., 2000, Transport à grande distance et magasinage des briques dans l'Empire romain, in *La brique antique et médiévale, Actes du colloque, Saint-Cloud 1995* (edd. P.Boucheron, H.Broise e Y.Thébert), 341-356, Roma.

Tusa, V., 1954, Palermo, *Notizie degli Scavi*, 146.

Williams, Ch.K. e Zervos, O.H., 1985, Corinth, 1984: east of the Theater, *Hesperia*, 54, 55-96.

Fig. 1. Bollo con cartiglio quadrato : *Hyacinth(us) / Iuliae / August(ae)* (Foto: E. Cappellini)

Fig. 2. Bollo con cartiglio rettangolare : *Vinic[i]* (Foto: E. Cappellini)

Fig. 3. Bollo con cartiglio rettangolare : *M. Arri* (Foto: M. Di Fazio)

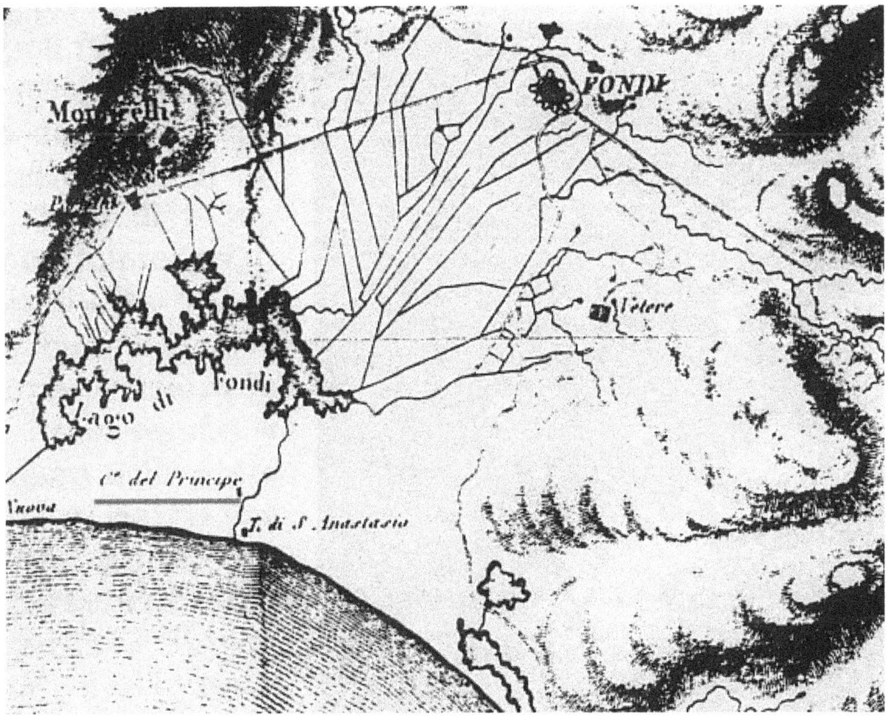

Fig. 4. Pianta del territorio di Fondi (da A.P. Frutaz (c.), Le carte del Lazio, Roma 1972, XLII,5)

L'INDUSTRIA VETRARIA DI SAN VINCENZO AL VOLTURNO TRA IX E XII SEC. : IL BILANCIO DI UN VENTENNIO DI STUDI

FRANCESCA DELL'ACQUA
(Bibliotheca Hertziana, Roma)

ABSTRACT: This paper offers a summary of the work conducted to date, including a study in the 1980's-90's and a more recent re-examination of the exceptional glass finds from San Vincenzo al Voltrno. These finds are of great importance due to their abundance and its high quality and have shed considerable light upon the regional glass industry in the 9th century AD. The study of the glass places the fragments in the context of architectural furnishings and the use of glass in papal Rome, the monastery of Farfa (both with a French influence), and the independent *Langobardia Minor*. Twenty years after the initial study of the glass, this re-examination relies upon different methodologies; thus, allowing a new perspective to the glass from San Vincenzo al Volturno.

Questo breve contributo vuole essere un rendiconto dei percorsi di lavoro seguiti, o a fatica tracciati, nell'affrontare i reperti vitrei del monastero altomedievale di San Vincenzo al Volturno, che rappresentano le tracce di una consistente industria vetraria sviluppatasi nel corso del IX sec. e nuovamente nei secoli seguenti. Si tenterà di soddisfare uno dei principali obiettivi della tavola rotonda, quello di rivelare le modalità di elaborazione del dato archeologico in elemento di ricostruzione storica. Nel quadro del lavoro svolto, verranno anche segnalate due recenti scoperte - una vetrata e una placca di smalto- presentate qui per la prima volta in ambito italiano.

Nel 1984 John Mitchell pubblicava il primo contributo dedicato specificamente ad un oggetto rinvenuto a San Vincenzo nel quale il vetro era protagonista: un frammentario castone in lega di rame dorato, con bordo perlinato, nei cui alveoli venne colato vetro multicolore a formare un motivo floreale che doveva incorniciare ad una o più figure aureolate su una coperta di codice o un reliquiario (Mitchell 1984). Mitchell pensò già allora di legare questo smalto alla produzione vetraria del monastero, perché negli stessi anni stavano venendo allo scoperto officine dalle molteplici specialità, concentrate nei pressi di quella che si sarebbe rivelata la chiesa principale dell'insediamento, il cosiddetto San Vincenzo Maggiore (Marazzi e Francis 1996). Di grande importanza nella storia delle arti suntuarie occidentali per via della scarsità degli smalti *cloisonné* di epoca altomedievale conservati, i tre pezzi vulturnensi sono stati accostati ai pochissimi, eccellenti superstiti di ambito peninsulare, ovvero l'altare d'oro di Sant'Ambrogio a Milano e la stauroteca di Pasquale I a Roma. Uno dei pezzi è ancora inedito, e mostra un elegante motivo ad intreccio, ottenuto versando entro alveoli di rame dorato vetro polverizzato dai colori vivaci, come il giallo, il rosso, l'azzurro, il bianco. Esso apparteneva verosimilmente ad una coperta di codice o ad un reliquario. Il contesto di rinvenimento, nei pressi della chiesa abbaziale maggiore, non ha svelato per ora indizi risolutivi sulla originaria destinazione del pezzo.

Riaperto il dibattito sui centri di manifattura di tali raffinati oggetti, quindi non necessariamente legati a corti civili o ecclesiastiche, San Vincenzo deve riconoscersi anche per altre ragioni teatro di scoperte di primaria importanza a livello europeo. La tipologia dei manufatti è molteplice, dal vasellame da mensa e non, ai monili, al vetro piano da finestra, al vetro "millefiori"; la qualità della miscela vetrosa eccellente; la datazione convenientemente circoscrivibile, senza sbavature sostanziali, in tre fasi: tra la fine dell'VIII sec. e l'anno 881 (anno dell'assalto saraceno che determinò l'abbandono del sito); tra il X-XI sec. (la rioccupazione del sito conseguente l'autoesilio a Capua); tra la fine dell'XI-gli inizi del XII sec. (momento della ricostruzione sulla riva opposta del fiume).

Tuttavia non prima degli ultimi anni la vetraria vulturnense è stata proiettata nel dibattito storico-artistico internazionale. In un consesso del *Corpus Vitrearum Medii Aevi*, tenuto a Cracovia nel 1998 e dedicato alla vetrata come pittura monumentale, vennero presentati i frammenti dipinti a *grisaille* provenienti dal sito della cosiddetta "Abbazia Nuova", fondata dall'abate Gerardo (1076-1109), ex-monaco nella Montecassino di Desiderio. Benché quasi delle briciole se confrontati con l'idea comune di vetrata istoriata, questi piccoli pannelli dipinti suscitarono viva curiosità, essendo tra i primissimi esempi di vetro da finestra decorato dell'Europa mediterranea e avendo un legame -da approfondire- con le testimonianze di poco anteriori inerenti l'abbazia cassinese (Dell'Acqua 1999a).

Due mostre avvenute a brevissima distanza l'una dall'altra, in sottile polemica, hanno portato all'attenzione di un pubblico più vasto la produzione vetraria della fase carolingia. L'occasione del centenario della permanenza di Papa Leone III alla corte di Carlo Magno a Paderborn in Sassonia ha spinto nel 1999 a raccogliere in questa città una miriade di testimonianze su quell'epoca, vista come momento culturale aggregante dell'Europa occidentale. Anche a San Vincenzo è stato riconosciuto un posto significativo, sulla scorta dell'interpretazione di Richard Hodges che aveva visto nella crescita esponenziale delle fortune del monastero a cavallo tra VIII-IX sec. l'intervento economico franco (Hodges 1995: 153-75; Wickman in Hodges 1995: 144). In quella sede la produzione vetraria è stata presentata in una sequenza dall'enfasi transalpina, che partendo dalle evenienze del palazzo reale di Paderborn si spingeva sino alla Francia di Rouen per includere come fatti eccentrici o comunque periferici i più o meno coevi lacerti del rivestimento a foglia d'oro della cappella palatina di Salerno voluta da Arechi II (+787), l'ultimo baluardo della nazione longobarda contro l'espansione franca (Dell'Acqua 1999b). In polemica con quella mostra, nel 2000 a Brescia se ne è inaugurata un'altra, con la quale si rivendicava ai Longobardi l'incubazione della moderna civiltà europea, nella consapevolezza dell'Antico e con un'apertura verso l'Oriente mediterraneo. Anche in questa sede ai reperti in vetro di San Vincenzo -dai pannelli da finestra alla piccola testa di santo imberbe in avorio dalle pupille vitree- hanno avuto il loro posto "al sole", confermandone l'importanza (Mitchell 2001).

Preparatori di questo procrastinato debutto sono stati gli studi inventariali sul vasellame e sul vetro da finestra approdati nel 2001 nel catalogo ufficiale di tutti i reperti mobili della prima fase degli scavi (Mitchell and Hansen 2001). Negli ultimi anni contributi apparsi per mano di Judi Stevenson e della scrivente ne avevano offerto quadri interpretativi (Stevenson 1997; Dell'Acqua 1997). Tuttavia è doveroso ricordare che già un decennio fa, nonostante l'evidenza materiale e i dati scientifici fossero parziali rispetto ad oggi, sia stato tentato con successo da Richard Hodges un precoce quanto provocatoriamente stimolante affondo nella storia della mentalità: l'emulazione e la sottile competizione esistente tra gli abati e le corti laiche o i principali monasteri, in questa fase transitoria tra la dominazione longobarda e quella franca, avrebbe determinato uno scambio non solo a livello regionale di idee e di beni, molti dei quali di materiale vitreo (Hodges 1991).

Come intuibile da quanto esposto, lo spessore culturale del progetto archeologico su San Vincenzo al Volturno si è accresciuto nel tempo, grazie a un fertile coinvolgimento di distinte branche disciplinari, applicate anche allo studio del vetro. Infatti la vasta e varia massa di oggetti, grosso modo divisibile in tre classi principali – vetro cavo, smalti, vetro piano- è stata studiata da specialisti di formazione diversa, ai quali un apporto fondamentale è stato fornito dalle analisi scientifiche. Queste sono state condotte da Ian C. Freestone, chimico presso il British Museum, che da anni coordina un progetto di monitoraggio sul vetro occidentale e mediorientale posteriore all'Antichità romana, dal titolo *Glass after Rome.*

Non mi soffermerò oltre sulle prime due categorie di oggetti, se non per segnalarne l'unicità nell'orizzonte italiano tra VIII-IX sec., desiderando rivolgermi piuttosto al vetro da finestra, sul quale ho avuto un'esperienza diretta reiterata negli anni, che mi può consentire di fornire indicazioni di metodo più specifiche e perciò forse di maggior utilità a chi vi vorrà fare riferimento.

La catalogazione dei singoli frammenti per unità stratigrafica fatta da Deborah James negli anni '80, che li associò ai distinti ambienti scavati, è stato l'imprescindibile presupposto per effettuare una selezione dei frammenti in base a caratteristiche macroscopiche per procedere alla ricomposizione, saltuariamente totale, di numerosi pannelli delle finestre della fase carolingia, nonché di quelle dell'"Abbazia Nuova" nella fase romanica. I criteri selettivi e di riconoscimento delle tecniche impiegate per la forgiatura delle lastre sono stati attinti ad un filone di studi anglosassone, che ha avuto in Donald Harden e Rosemary Cramp i principali esponenti: il primo per le considerazioni di ampia portata sulla tecnologia e l'economia del vetro romano e posteriore; la seconda per il magistrale studio dei resti delle vetrate di Monkwearmouth e Jarrow in Northumbria.

La Cramp nei tardi anni '60 ha pioneristicamente applicato su questi frammenti un rigore classificatorio che l'archeologia aveva spesso disatteso nei confronti del vetro piano, ritenuto di scarsa o nulla importanza. Sorretta da una consapevolezza delle fonti storiche di matrice umanistica e da approfondimenti scientifici sui materiali, la studiosa giungeva ad una sintesi che ha inquadrato quegli schermi vitrei come parte dell'arredo originario dei monasteri fondati da Benedict Biscop[1]. I risultati della sfaccettata analisi rispecchiavano alcuni significativi dettagli del racconto di Beda, che restituiva un ritratto del proprio maestro, di origini aristocratiche, come ardente ammiratore del Cristianesimo romano e perciò desideroso di evocarne la tipica architettura basilicale, votandosi ad organizzare un cantiere che coinvolse artefici da regioni al di là del mare. Questi si dovettero servire di vetro proveniente anch'esso da lontano, addirittura dal Medioriente, come hanno dimostrato le indagini chimico-fisiche, effettuate anche in questo caso da Ian Freestone (Freestone and Hughes, c.s.).

Relazioni a vasto raggio si devono anche supporre nel caso di San Vincenzo, dove il vetro dovette essere importato in rottami o blocchi semilavorati in parte dall'Egitto, in parte da un centro forse peninsulare o comunque di ambito occidentale non ancora identificato, come attesta la lunga gestazione dei dati scientifici, cresciuti in comparazione con altri esempi di vetro nell'ambito territoriale della (ex?) *Langobardia Maior* e *Minor*[2]. Fonti scritte di nessun tipo vengono in soccorso in merito ai probabili contatti sovranazionali, diretti o mediati non è dato dirlo, che rifornirono di materia prima l'impianto vetrario vulturnense, per cui si deve di necessità intessere un'interpretazione di dati di natura diversa, estrapolati dall'analisi dei contesti architettonici, della loro stratigrafia così come della cultura storico-artistica.

Per certo il monastero nel raggio di chilometri era l'unico esempio di architettura dotata di dettagli raffinati come le finestre in vetro, o le pareti dipinte a finto marmo[3], dai quali emergono suggestioni culturali che nella prima fase del monastero (VIII-IX sec.) sembrano avere una matrice laica, forse principesca, come ha riconosciuto Mitchell[4]. Per quanto attiene la provenienza degli artigiani e la loro appartenza o meno alla comunità monastica locale non si può supporre nulla per mancanza di qualsivoglia traccia documentaria o materiale. Si deve però ricordare che, forse non a caso, abili artigiani del vetro hanno lasciato traccia della loro attività presso la corte salernitana di Arechi, dove venne realizzato e messo in opera un magnifico rivestimento ad *opus sectile* in marmi, mosaico e listelli di vetro a foglia d'oro, decorato con una tecnica di origine mediorientale senza paralleli in Occidente nei secoli dell'alto Medioevo.

Del resto a San Vincenzo erano attive anche la lavorazione dei metalli per fare finimenti per cavalcature ad agemina, coperte di codici a smalto, nonché campane; l'intaglio dell'osso e dell'avorio per pettini e lastrine con motivi geometrici o antropomorfi da applicare su arredi mobili e reliquiari; la fabbricazione di eleganti piastrelle pavimentali con venature a finto marmo e di altri elementi di arredo architettonico in terracotta; la scultura di mensole e capitelli da affiancare a quelli di spoglio di età romana; certamente vi fu attiva anche una bottega di pittori, che decorò gran parte degli ambienti della clausura e la chiesa maggiore. La fioritura di queste attività è stata dall'archeologia datata alla fine dell'VIII sec., quindi in coincidenza con le grandi ristrutturazioni del complesso vulturnense volute dall'abate franco Giosué (792-816).

L'interruzione violenta di questa prospera fase della vita del monastero, dovuta all'attacco arabo 'pilotato' dal vescovo-duca di Napoli nell'881, con il subitaneo abbandono del sito, ha consentito di recuperare un'immagine alquanto veridica della situazione delle strutture architettoniche in quel momento, alle quali è legata la recentissima scoperta di una vetrata con transenna lignea a griglia di gusto "all'antica". Lo strato di bruciato dell'incendio appiccato dagli assalitori ha anche 'sigillato' i resti delle attività artigianali in corso presso gli opifici eretti lungo la basilica maggiore, consentendo di ricostruire in alcuni casi le modalità produttive e la gamma dei manufatti (Dell'Acqua 2002). Qui qualcuno stava ancora lavorando alla fusione e all'assemblaggio di monili e di oggetti per uso liturgico con placchette di smalto, piccoli pannelli di vetro colorato uniti da piombi, lastrine di osso e avorio.

Problematico è per ora comprendere se durante l'autoesilio a Capua (881-inizi del X sec.) si fossero perpetuate tra i membri della comunità conoscenze tecniche tali da consentire un primo restauro della strutture architettoniche e dei loro complementi nel corso del X-XI, al momento della rioccupazione del sito. Per ora questa fase intermedia rimane da tutti i punti di vista quella più oscura nella sequenza storica di San Vincenzo. E interessano non solo le modalità di trasmissione delle competenze artigianali ma anche la base economica sulla quale poteva fare affidamento, in questo momento di depressione, la ricerca di materie prime o di prodotti semilavorati con i quali alimentare l'industria monastica. I frammenti di vetro piano emersi lungo i fianchi della basilica maggiore, privi di affinità macroscopiche con quelli della fase carolingia tantomeno con quelli dell'"Abbazia Nuova" di età romanica, fanno credere che una piccola attività dovette pure continuare, forse avvalendosi di vetro riciclato dalle architetture più antiche, sebbene la locazione non sia attualmente chiara. Del resto di tutt'altro tenore appaiono i resti delle menzionate vetrate dell'"Abbazia Nuova", dove compare per la prima volta la pittura temprata a fuoco su vetro dalla tonalità intensissime, per la quale non si può non pensare ad un patronato economico e culturale esterno, verosilmente cassinese. E' stato infinite volte ripetuto un passo della cronaca di Leone di Ostia sul multilingue cantiere desideriano, che forse implicò anche il coinvolgimento di vetrai stranieri[5], ai quali forse attribuire il recupero dell'invetriatura delle finestre, sia tramite piombi che con transenne di stucco pressato[6].

Si ribadisce, in conclusione, che l'eccezionalità della vetraria vulturnense risiede innanzitutto nell'essere sgorgata, e quindi rifiorita, in due diversi momenti caratterizzati da un livello qualitativo diverso ma pur sempre elevato, in un orizzonte storico che appare per ora privo di precedenti strettamente locali.

NOTE

1 Per una rassegna bibliografica aggiornata: Cramp 2001.
2 Dell'Acqua, in c.s. e Freestone, in c.s.: gli interventi sono nati l'uno a commento dell'altro come esito di un comune studio sul vetro adottato a scopi ornamentali nell'architettura altomedievale italiana.
3 Si consideri che ad esempio in una pieve non lontana dal monastero, ma da esso dipendente, sono state trovate alcune lampade vitree per illuminare l'edificio, ma non vetro piano (cfr. Marazzi 2000: 200).
4 Mitchell 1995. Ha scritto sull'ambizione verso il lusso di numerosi fondatori di monasteri, spesso di nobile origine, Brenk 2000.
5 Leone d'Ostia, *Chronica Monasterii Casinensis*, lib. III, cap. 27.
6 Una ricostruzione storica degli sviluppi della vetrata in ambito italiano e occidentale in genere è stata tentata nel volume di Dell'Acqua, 2003, le cui basi sono state poste dagli studi svolti dall'A. sull'industria vetraria vulturnense.

FONTI

Leone d'Ostia, *Chronica Monasterii Casinensis*, lib. III, cap. 27, in *Monumenta Germaniae Historica, Scriptores*, t. XXXIV, a cura di Hoffmann, H., Hannoverae, Impensis Bibliopoli Hahniani, 1980, p. 396.

BIBLIOGRAFIA

Brenk, B., 2000, Klosterbaukunst ersten Jahrtausend: Rhetoric versus Realität, *Annali della Scuola Normale Superiore di Pisa-Classe di Lettere*, s. IV, fasc. 2, 317-42.

Cramp, R., 2001, Window glass from the British Isles, in *La vetrata in Occidente dal IV all'XI secolo. Atti delle giornate di studi, Lucca, Villa Bottini, 23-24-25 Settembre 1999. Il colore nel Medioevo. Arte Simbolo Tecnica. Collana di studi sul colore 3* (a cura di F. Dell'Acqua e R. Silva) Lucca, Istituto Storico Lucchese-Scuola Normale Superiore di Pisa-Corpus Vitrearum Medii Aevi Italia, 67-85.

Dell'Acqua, F., 1997, Ninth-century Window Glass from the Monastery of San Vincenzo al Volturno, (Molise, Italy), *Journal of Glass Studies*, 39, 33-41.

Dell'Acqua, F., 1999 a, Shades of Desiderius. An early example of Italian stained-glass from the Romanesque abbey of San Vincenzo al Volturno (Molise, Italy), in *Corpus Vitrearum Medii Aevi. XIXth International Colloquium, Kraków 1998, 14-16 May, Stained glass as monumental painting, Proceedings*, Kracow, Department for Conservation and Restauration of Works of Art, Academy of Fine Arts, 81-95.

Dell'Acqua, F., 1999 b, Glasherstellung im Kloster San Vincenzo al Volturno, in *799-Kunst und Kultur der Karolingerzeit. Karl der Grosse und Papst Leo III. in Paderborn, Austellung 23. Juli bis 1. November 1999, Paderborn*, cat. Mostra (eds. C. Stiegemann e M. Wemhoff), Mainz am Rhein, Verlag Philipp von Zabern, vol. I, 174-76 e 180-83.

Dell'Acqua, F., 2002, Una vetrata "all'antica" di età carolingia, *Journal of Glass Studies*, 44, 196-99.

Dell'Acqua, F., 2003, *«Illuminando colorat». La vetrata tra la tarda Antichità e l'alto Medioevo attraverso le fonti e l'archeologia. Studi e Ricerche di Archeologia e Storia dell'Arte, 4. Collana diretta da L. Pani Ermini e A. Peroni*, Spoleto, Centro Italiano di Studi per l'Altomedioevo.

Dell'Acqua, F., in c.s., ... Mundus habet noctem, detinet aula diem. Il vetro nelle architetture di Brescia, Cividale, Salerno, San Vincenzo al Volturno, Farfa. Nuovi dati scientifici, in *Atti della Giornata di Studi del Comitato Nazionale Italiano dell'A.I.V.H.-C.I.S.A.M., Spoleto, 20-22 Aprile 2002* (a cura di E. Arslan e D. Ferrari), in c.s.

Freestone, I. C., in c.s., Early Medieval Glass from Brescia, Cividale and Salerno, Italy: Composition and Affinities, in *Atti della Giornata di Studi del Comitato Nazionale Italiano dell'A.I.V.H.-C.I.S.A.M., Spoleto, 20-22 Aprile 2002* (eds. E. Arslan e D. Ferrari), in c.s.

Freestone, I. C. e Hughes, M. J., in c.s., The origins of the glass from Jarrow, in *Jarrow and Wearmouth Monastic Sites* (a cura di R. Cramp), English Heritage.

Hodges, R., 1991, A fetishism for commodities: Ninth century glass-making at San Vincenzo al Volturno, in *Archeologia e storia della produzione del vetro preindustriale* (a cura di M. Mendera), Firenze, All'Insegna del Giglio, 67-90.

Hodges, R. (a cura di), 1995, *San Vincenzo al Volturno 2. The excavations 1980-86. Part II.* London, British School at Rome.

Marazzi, F., 2000, *Colle Sant'Angelo*, in *Il futuro dei Longobardi. L'Italia e la costruzione dell'Europa di Carlo Magno. 18 Giugno-19 Novembre 2000, Brescia, Monastero di Santa Giulia* (a cura di C. Bertelli - G. P. Brogiolo), Milano, Skira, 200.

Marazzi, F. e Francis, K. D., 1996, L'eredità dell'antico. Tecnologia e produzione in un monastero imperiale carolingio: San Vincenzo al Volturno, in *Atti dell'XI Convegno Internazionale su "L'Africa Romana", Cartagine 18-21 Dicembre 1994* (a cura di A. Mastino), Sassari-Ozieri, Edizioni Asfodelo, 1029-45.

Mitchell, J., 1984, Smalto del Nono Secolo proveniente da San Vincenzo al Volturno, *Almanacco del Molise*, Campobasso, Editore Nocera, 201-5.

Mitchell, J., 1995, Arichis und die Künste, in *Für irdischen Ruhm und himmlischen Lohn. Stifter und Auftraggeber in der mittelalterlichen Kunst. Beat Brenk zum 60. Geburtstag* (a cura di H.R. Meier, C. Jäggi, P. Büttner), Berlin, Dietrich Reimer Verlag, 47-64.

Mitchell, J., 2000, *San Vincenzo al Volturno* e *Diffusione dello smalto 'cloisonné'*, in *Il futuro dei Longobardi. L'Italia e la costruzione dell'Europa di Carlo Magno. 18 Giugno-19 Novembre 2000, Brescia, Monastero di Santa Giulia* (a cura di C. Bertelli - G. P. Brogiolo), Milano, Skira, 353-55 e 454-55.

Mitchell, J. e Hansen, I. L. (a cura di), 2001, *San Vincenzo al Volturno 3*, Spoleto, Centro Italiano di Studi per l'Altomedioevo.

Stevenson, J., 1997, Ninth glassware production at San Vincenzo al Volturno, Italy: some new evidence from recent excavations, in *Material Culture in Medieval Europe, Papers of the 'Medieval Europe Brugge 1997' Conference, I.A.P. Rapporten, vol. 7* (a cura di G. De Boe e F. Verhaege), Brugge, Zellik, 125-36.

RECENTI APPROCCI E METODI PER LO STUDIO DELL'EDILIZIA ANTICA : IL CASO DELLA ROMA ARCAICA

GABRIELE CIFANI
(Università di Roma "La Sapienza")

ABSTRACT: The study of ancient architecture in Italy has received considerable attention in recent years, especially in terms of the social and economic aspects of construction. This approach, applied for the case of archaic Rome, allows us to identify important developments that occurred in the 6th century BC, confirming what the ancient literary sources report about Tarquin Rome. In particular the passage from non-specialized building of the 8th and 7th centuries to a highly organized system that developed in the 6th century, with the introduction of *opus quadratum*, systems of vaulting, the use of lime-based plaster. These innovations clearly indicate that construction was one of the most important economic activities of the city.

Nella lunga tradizione di studi sull'architettura romana, accanto alla visione storico artistica ed antiquaria, si profila, già alla fine dell'Ottocento, un approccio analitico di stampo neopositivista, promosso in particolare da archeologi di formazione tecnica, quali ad esempio, i francesi: A. Choisy (1873) e A. Leger (1875), o il tedesco J. Durm (1905).

In Italia nello stesso periodo troviamo ricercatori quali l'ingegnere R. Lanciani (1881; 1897) o l'architetto G. Boni (1900; 1913) pioniere della stratigrafia, seguiti da G. Giovannoni (1928) e G. Cozzo (1928) che impostarono lo studio tecnico dei monumenti antichi, trovando epigoni solo in studiosi di formazione anglosassone, quali le americane E. Van Deman (1912) e M. E. Blake (1947-1973) o in rare figure di formazione letteraria, quali il topografo italiano G. Lugli (1941; 1942; 1957), mentre lo studio analitico del monumento antico a partire soprattutto dal secondo dopoguerra, rimase materia limitata per lo più a figure isolate di architetti come L. Crema (1959) o G. De Angelis D'Ossat (1982).

E' noto infatti come la forte influenza del neoidealismo, affermatasi in Italia a partire dagli anni Venti, soprattutto con gli scritti del filosofo Benedetto Croce, abbia avuto effetti sulla ricerca scientifica e sugli studi umanistici, con un temporaneo disinteresse verso gli aspetti tecnici e materiali della cultura (Barbanera 1998: 124-126 con bibl.), lasciando, nel campo dell'archeologia classica, per molto tempo inalterato il dibattito sull'approccio al monumento antico.

Una prima inversione di tendenza si verifica dalla seconda metà degli anni Sessanta, quando nell'ambito della realizzazione di carte archeologiche, finalizzate allo studio di importanti complessi monumentali minacciati all'espansione edilizia di quegli anni (es. Giuliani 1966; 1970; Quilici 1974), si avvertì la necessità di procedere a forme di documentazione grafica rigorose, effettuate direttamente dagli archeologi e non delegate a tecnici disegnatori (Giuliani 1976; 1989: 11-17).

In quel medesimo periodo ulteriori novità a livello metodologico furono elaborate da studiosi legati per lo più alla rivista *Dialoghi di Archeologia*, fondata da R. Bianchi Bandinelli e da lui diretta tra il 1967 ed il 1975 che, sotto l'influsso delle categorie marxiane, rivalutarono gli aspetti della cultura materiale (es. Carandini 1975) e dello scavo stratigrafico come strumento di ricerca e datazione dei contesti (Carandini 1981), delineando obiettivi e metodologie, fino ad allora, in Italia, appannaggio di pochi studiosi del mondo classico, per lo più estranei all'ambito accademico, come ad esempio A. Lamboglia (1956; 1958).

Da questo contesto, anche in parallelo con quanto si stava sperimentando nell'archeologia medievale, si è sviluppata una nuova attenzione ai resti murari e alle tecniche edilizie quali classi documentarie utili a ricostruzioni di storia economica, con filoni di indagine specifici, connessi soprattutto alla classificazione delle strutture murarie, mediante approcci tipologici, indagini archeometriche sui conglomerati e sulle argille, studio dell'organizzazione dei cantieri e dei materiali impiegati (es. Pani Ermini, De Minicis 1987; Brogiolo 1988 con bibl.; Mannoni 1996 con bibl.).

A partire dagli anni Novanta emerge anche la dizione di "archeologia dell'architettura", in cui sono compresi: l'analisi stratigrafica degli alzati, lo studio delle tecniche costruttive, la mensiocronologia, la ricostruzione dei cicli produttivi e l'approccio etnoarcheologico allo studio dell'edilizia (Brogiolo 1996 con bibl.).

E' ovvio quindi concludere come l'analisi complessiva dell'edilizia di una città o di una regione in un determinato periodo possa fornire importanti dati non solo sul piano storico artistico, ma, anche su quello storico economico, industriale ed ambientale, illuminando su trasformazioni di lunga durata della società e del paesaggio, che costituiscono, al momento in Italia, l'obbiettivo della ricerca archeologica più innovativa e interdisciplinare.

Questo breve excursus di storia degli studi è necessario per comprendere lo stato della ricerca relativa all'edilizia della Roma arcaica, dove il lavoro più impegnativo e sistematico è rappresentato finora dalla sintesi dello svedese Einar Gjerstad, concepita negli anni Cinquanta (Gjerstad 1960).

Si avvertiva quindi l'esigenza di documentare ed interpretare i resti degli edifici della Roma dei Tarquini con un approccio più aggiornato, basato ove possibile, su criteri di archeologia stratigrafica e con l'intento di produrre documenti utili ad una ricostruzione di storia economica, considerando anche la nuova immagine emersa dagli scavi più recenti.

La Roma del VI secolo appare un centro pienamente sviluppato e frutto di una continuità insediativa e culturale che risale alla fine dell'VIII secolo a.C., in un contesto geografico, quale il *Latium vetus*, dove le ricerche condotte dagli anni Settanta hanno evidenziato una vasta diffusione del fenomeno urbano ed una complessa organizzazione sociale (AA.VV. 1980; Roma 1990; Carandini 1997).

Da tale esigenza è stato sviluppato a partire dal 1992 un progetto sull'edilizia romana arcaica condotto da chi scrive in collaborazione con la II Cattedra di Archeologia e Storia dell'Arte Greca e Romana dell'Università di Roma "La *Sapienza*" (prof. A. Carandini), in accordo con la Soprintendenza Archeologica di Roma e il Comune di Roma e proseguita di recente, grazie anche a contributi erogati dall'*Aylwin Cotton Foundation* (UK) e della *Fondazione Pasquali* presso la *Scuola Normale Superiore di Pisa*.

La ricerca è iniziata con una raccolta sistematica di tutte le testimonianze relative ad edifici databili tra il VI ed il V secolo a.C. a Roma, utili ad illuminare sugli aspetti tecnici di realizzazione dei manufatti murari, sui materiali impiegati, sui sistemi di approvvigionamento e su quelli di trasporto.

Tuttavia, anche nel rispetto verso una solida tradizione di studi umanistici relativi alla Roma dei re, è apparso necessario e proficuo combinare questo approccio tecnico con un'analisi sistematica delle fonti letterarie e storico artistiche sul periodo, nella convinzione che solo un'ermeneutica interdisciplinare possa giungere alla comprensione di una struttura socialmente evoluta e complessa quale quella della Roma arcaica.

I risultati scientifici finora conseguiti, anticipati in alcuni articoli preliminari del progetto, interessano sia aspetti tecnici che storico sociali (Cifani 1994; 1998; 2002). Per quanto concerne le origini dell'edilizia a Roma è necessario sottolineare come, alla luce delle più recenti scoperte archeologiche, sia lecito inquadrare una prima attività edilizia già dall'VIII secolo a. C. in concomitanza con i fenomeni della fase protourbana.

L'edificio più importante del periodo è rappresentato dai resti del c.d. "muro di Romolo" ovvero la fortificazione rinvenuta nel 1988 alle pendici settentrionali del Palatino ed indagata in più riprese fino al 1993 (Carandini, Carafa 2000, pp. 139-160). Si tratta di un manufatto in schegge di tufo, largo circa due metri e documentato per una lunghezza di almeno tredici metri, che doveva sostenere una palizzata lignea. La struttura, databile alla fine dell'VIII secolo a. C., costituisce il primo esempio di un'opera collettiva creata nel sito di Roma. Altri edifici compresi tra la seconda metà dell'VIII ed il VII secolo sono stati di recente documentati più ad ovest, nell'area del santuario di Vesta.

Nella fase laziale IV B il dato di maggiore importanza è costituito dall'impiego di rivestimenti fittili; la principale evidenza a riguardo proviene dal riempimento di un pozzo presso la Casa delle Vestali (Gjerstad 1960, p. 359 ss.; Bartoli 1961, c. 19 ss.), dallo strato ventesimo del Comizio (Boni 1900, pp. 327-330, figg. 32-33; Gjerstad 1960, pp. 257-259; Carafa 1998, p. 44 ss.) e, più precisamente per la fine del VII secolo a. C., anche dalla prima fase della Regia (Brown 1975: 22).

Tra la fine del VII e gli inizi del VI secolo a. C. si collocano le prime attestazioni archeologiche dell'opera quadrata a Roma: l'esempio più antico è costituito dalla cisterna sul Palatino, ubicata ad est del tempio della *Magna Mater*. L'edificio mostra una pianta circolare del diametro di m 6 ca, profonda circa m 3; le pareti sono formate da due muri concentrici in opera quadrata di tufo granulare grigio con un'intercapedine di cm 50 ca, riempita di argilla, da cui sono stati recuperati due vasi (una coppa carenata e un'olla biansata di tipo stamnoide con decorazione a fasce serpeggianti) inquadrabili nel periodo laziale IV B (Gjerstad 1960, p. 88 ss. con bibl.; sull'area: Pensabene, Falzone 2001 con bibl.).

Un altro importante caposaldo cronologico dell'edilizia romana arcaica è rappresentato dal segmento di muro nell'area del Foro, sotto il c.d. *Equus Domitiani*, rinvenuto nei sondaggi stratigrafici operati dal Gjerstad. Si tratta di un manufatto in opera quadrata di tufo giallo litoide fondato direttamente sul banco di argilla, con blocchi tagliati sul modulo del piede italico di 27,2 cm; la struttura, probabilmente costruita agli inizi del VI secolo a. C., sembra essere stata distrutta, secondo relazioni stratigrafiche, all'inizio del V secolo a.C. (Gjerstad 1953, pp. 23-29; 1966, pp. 366-369).

L'adozione generalizzata dell'opera quadrata viene infine sancita anche dalla serie delle fortificazioni palatine, dove il muro di III fase, databile in base al contesto stratigrafico intorno al 580 a. C., viene realizzato in opera quadrata di tufo rosso litoide (Carandini, Carafa 2000, pp. 175-181).

Individuata tra la fine del VII secolo a.C. e gli inizi del VI secolo a.C. l'introduzione dell'opera quadrata a Roma, rimane da delineare il passaggio dal legno alla pietra nell'edilizia: questo può essere enucleato, anche in termini economici: intorno alla seconda metà del VII secolo si passa infatti gradualmente da un'edilizia in legno ad un'edilizia con laterizi e materiale lapideo, forse anche per una razionalizzazione nell'impiego dei materiali, secondo fenomeni tipici dell'economia pre-industriale (es. Cipolla 1974, p. 248).

Una crescita del consumo di legname è infatti da addebitarsi allo sviluppo della carpenteria navale, della metallurgia e alla concentrazione demografica in ambito urbano (Cifani 2001 con bibl.). L'aumento della richiesta di legname deve infatti aver portato a progressive deforestazioni del paesaggio con un forte degrado a livello ambientale. Sono riferibili a questa fase i primi impianti di cunicoli di drenaggio nelle campagne, probabilmente legati alla regimazione delle acque e al controllo dell'erosione delle superfici coltivabili (Judson, Kahane 1963; Bergamini 1991).

L'impiego di prodotti geolitici tra i materiali da costruzione di una comunità urbana come Roma alla fine del VII secolo a.C. corrisponde quindi ad una progressiva razionalizzazione delle risorse disponibili, mediante la specializzazione di utilizzo.

Nell'età dei Tarquini, la realizzazione di un circuito di mura urbane dovette rappresentare uno dei più impegnativi cantieri urbani; le fonti ricordano infatti un vasto circuito difensivo di circa 11 km, in opera quadrata di cui sono noti almeno 21 segmenti (Cifani 1998 a, con bibl.). La testimonianza più preziosa a riguardo è fornita da Dionisio di Alicarnasso il quale, a proposito di Tarquinio Prisco, ricorda che " *egli per primo fece costruire con grandi pietre ben lavorate e di forma regolare, le mura della città che in precedenza erano di fattura improvvisata e grossolana"* (Dion. Hal. III.67.4).

Questo ambizioso progetto difensivo è peraltro ben inquadrabile nell'evoluzione urbanistica della città e nel maggior ruolo assunto nel corso del VI secolo dai ceti mercantili presenti nel corpo civico; questi infatti determinano un nuovo assetto di tipo isonomico, in cui le ricchezze vengono investite in opere pubbliche, piuttosto che tesaurizzate dalle aristocrazie del precedente periodo (Ampolo 1984; 1988).

In tale prospettiva si inserisce il progetto dell'edificazione del grande tempio di Giove Capitolino, probabilmente ispirato alla coeva architettura templare ionica e che risalirebbe, secondo la tradizione, agli ultimi anni del regno di Tarquinio Prisco, anche se sarebbe stato realizzato da Tarquinio il Superbo ed inaugurato solo con l'inizio della Repubblica (Colonna 1981; Mura Sommella 1997 e 2000; Mura Sommella *et al.* 2001 con bibl.).

Un altro tipo architettonico di grande importanza attestato alla fine del VI secolo a.C. a Roma è quella della casa ad atrio, documentata nel quartiere residenziale alle pendici settentrionali del Palatino (Carandini, Carafa 2000: 215-282). Si tratta di grandi strutture abitative con *horti* annessi, di circa 900 mq di superficie, che segnano una completa innovazione nel panorama dell'edilizia, introducendo una tipologia che troveremo poi attestata nel V secolo nei contesti urbani di *Regisvillae,* Roselle e Marzabotto.

L'evoluzione dell'edilizia abitativa è dimostrata anche dal grande edificio rurale della fase II dell'Auditorium Flaminio (fine VI-inizi V secolo a.C.) con *pars rustica* e *pars urbana*, prototipo delle ville romane ed esempio della strutturazione in chiave produttiva del suburbio (Carandini *et al.* 1997), che prevedeva anche numerose piccole fattorie sparse nell'agro, realizzate in larga parte con un'edilizia stabile in pietra e tegole (Cifani 2002 con bibl.).

Parallelamente abbiamo importanti innovazioni tecniche quali le attestazioni del sistema ad arco, databili alla fine del VI secolo a.C. (Cifani 1994, pp. 194-197): il primo impiego di tale sistema deve aver trovato luogo nella realizzazione dei grandi condotti sotterranei di drenaggio che hanno caratterizzato l'edilizia del VI secolo a Roma: uno di questi è stato documentato dall'équipe della prof.ssa C. Panella nella valle del Colosseo (Carandini, Carafa 2000, fig. 236) e getta luce sulla complessità dei sistemi di regimazione delle acque realizzati nell'epoca in cui le fonti ricordano la costruzione della *Cloaca maxima.* Tuttavia l'esempio più conservato è costituito dalla cisterna con copertura a volta alle pendici del Palatino, ubicata sotto l'atrio della casa n. 3 e composta da un intradosso a blocchi di tufo cuneati (Carandini, Carafa 2000, pp. 229-231, figg. 199-203).

L'uso di strutture voltate nell'urbanistica tardo arcaica non appare isolato solo a Roma; alcuni scavi a Tarquinia, ancora inediti, condotti dall'Università Statale di Milano, hanno messo in luce una struttura di drenaggio con volta a botte in conci di tufo, sotto un importante asse viario all'interno dell'abitato (comunicazione personale della prof.ssa C. Chiaramonte), mentre la stessa realizzazione di ampi collettori si ricollega ad analoghe opere documentate nelle colonie greche, come si evince anche dai recenti scavi condotti a Cuma (D'Agostino 1996, pp. 35-36).

Per quanto concerne i rivestimenti murari, era noto a Roma l'impiego di intonaci parietali rinvenuti in più punti della città, ma spesso si era pensato ad una elaborazione assai povera, realizzata in argilla, sul modello primitivista dei rivestimenti delle capanne villanoviane e laziali e si era escluso in più casi che per l'età arcaica fossero utilizzati rivestimenti a base di calce quali quelli noti in età medio repubblicana.

Nel corso di questa ricerca, invece, il recupero di numerosi frammenti di intonaco, da un contesto stratigrafico della seconda metà del VI secolo alle pendici settentrionali del Palatino (US 2961), ha permesso di analizzare con maggiore dettaglio la composizione di tali conglomerati.

Questi frammenti, che presentavano anche tracce di un rivestimento decorativo di colore rosso, sono stati sottoposti ad un'analisi termo differenziale effettuata nei laboratori diretti dal prof. Torraca della Facoltà di Ingegneria dell'Università "La Sapienza" ed hanno rivelato una componente di carbonato di calcio pari all'85% del volume, mostrando l'impiego precoce della calce nell'edilizia romana, almeno da epoca tardo arcaica e, con essa, la possibile diffusione di pitture murali all'interno dei maggiori edifici (Cifani 1994, pp. 190-192, nota 45), come conferma anche la notizia del rinvenimento di intonaci dipinti dalla Sacra Via e dall'area del tempio dei Dioscuri (Colonna 1988, pp. 313-314 con bibl.).

Tale dato è inoltre congruente con quello della diffusione di decorazioni architettoniche fittili, attestate fin dal primo quarto del VI secolo a.C. nei contesti della "terza Regia" (Downey 1995 on bibl.).

Riguardo la diffusione dell'opera quadrata a partire dall'inizio del VI secolo a.C., è necessario rilevare come questa comporti un cambiamento non solo nelle tipologie architettoniche, ma soprattutto nell'organizzazione relativa all'edilizia; sostanziali modifiche dovette subire, ad esempio, il sistema degli approvvigionamenti litici: se pensiamo infatti per questa fase alla massiccia richiesta di conci in tufo locale (tufo granulare grigio, c.d. cappellaccio) possiamo ipotizzare come attivi fin già dall'età arcaica una serie di impianti di estrazione.

Il passaggio dalle murature in pietrame a quelle in opera quadrata comporta infatti un impiego di massa delle risorse litiche impensabile senza una precisa coltivazione dei principali depositi geolitici. In particolare il cappellaccio (tufo granulare grigio), trovandosi stratificato per lo più ad una profondità di circa venti metri sotto il livello antico, dovette essere cavato spesso tramite impianti sotterranei o vistosi sbancamenti di superficie, da localizzare necessariamente ai limiti dell'area urbana o nell'immediato suburbio.

A riguardo, possediamo la documentazione diretta di un esempio di cava antica a cielo aperto, vista a fine Ottocento presso Vigna Querini (attuale Città Universitaria), mentre cospicui esempi di impianti in sotterraneo sono noti presso la Stazione Termini e Porta Pia (Cifani 1994, pp. 204-216 con bibl.).

Si tratta di esempi che, indipendentemente dal tipo di datazione proposta per essi (oscillante tra il VI ed il III secolo a. C. in base al materiale cavato ed alle dimensioni dei blocchi tagliati secondo il c.d. piede italico di 27 cm, impiegato a Roma tra il VI ed il III secolo, con un apice nell'età arcaica), valgono comunque come riferimento ad una necessaria organizzazione del territorio suburbano per lo sfruttamento delle risorse geolitiche in funzione edilizia.

Un ultimo aspetto da considerare è quello dei risvolti istituzionali connessi ad una tale "rivoluzione" edilizia. Protagonista di questi imponenti programmi è la popolazione urbana che, spesso insieme ai prigionieri di guerra o di città alleate (es. Palombi 1997) fornisce gratuitamente la manodopera generica, sotto forma di *munia*, una sorta di servizio civile obbligatorio, particolarmente ricordato dagli autori antichi relativamente al periodo di Tarquinio il Superbo, al quale viene ricondotto anche l'introduzione delle condanne *ad metalla* (Liv. I. 56; Plin. *N.H.* VIII. 161; XXXIII. 11; Plut. *Pobl.* 13, su cui Gianfrotta 1996).

Diversamente, lo Stato avoca a sé la conduzione dei lavori con la scelta del personale specializzato (tra cui certamente gli architetti e i coroplasti) ed il monopolio dei principali giacimenti geolitici che, ben attestato nel V secolo ad Atene (Ampolo 1982), può essere ipotizzato anche a Roma, in base al provvedimento preso all'indomani del sacco gallico, nel 390 a.C., quando, per favorire il restauro di vari edifici, venne promossa una distribuzione gratuita di tegole e ai privati fu concesso di cavare liberamente materiale edilizio (Liv. V.45.3).

A livello storico, il nuovo quadro di architettura ed urbanistica che emerge porta a rivalutare il quadro della fonti letterarie sulla Roma dei Tarquini, secondo un filone di studi che, anticipato da un noto articolo del filologo G. Pasquali (1936), poi ripreso nelle ricerche di A. Momigliano, è stato di recente sviluppato da una studioso della sua scuola, quale T. Cornell (1995). A livello di metodo, invece, queste testimonianze dell'edilizia rivelano che, se documentate con un approccio sistematico ed inquadrate come documento di cultura materiale, possono offrire elevate potenzialità di informazione economica e sociale.

L'edilizia del VI secolo a Roma corrisponde infatti al periodo in cui l'attività del costruire si configura per la prima volta come attività specialistica condotta da équipes specializzate di architetti e artigiani, insieme ad una larga partecipazione pubblica nella manodopera generica e non qualificata. Se sul piano sociale e politico le grandi opere del VI secolo a.C. appaiono espressione del regime tirannico ascritto ai Tarquini è anche indubbio che tale struttura organizzativa abbia portato con sé un'accelerazione nello sviluppo e diffusione delle conoscenze tecniche.

E' certamente improprio descrivere questa nuova fase produttiva in termini di "industria", quale quello richiesto dal presente convegno, sia per il quadro ancora limitato della documentazione archeologica, sia soprattutto per l'aspetto esplicitamente capitalistico sotteso al termine che mal si concilia con la complessa e contradditoria realtà socio-economica della Roma arcaica. Questa città, che risulta la più estesa dell'Italia tirrenica e principale scalo commerciale tiberino (da ultimo: Zevi 2002), appare ancora priva di un vero sistema monetale (Zehnacker 1990 con bibl.); è certamente un laboratorio di riforme sociali e istituzionali in chiave isonomica, tramandate dalla tradizione su Servio Tullio (Ampolo 1988), ma dove, ad esempio, le *gentes* difenderanno ancora nel V secolo un proprio ruolo nella proprietà terriera (Capogrossi Colognesi 1988; Torelli 1988; Hermon 2001, pp. 19-138 con bibl).

Ma è anche a partire da questa fase che l'edilizia romana si configura per la prima volta come un complesso ed autonomo settore economico, in grado di assorbire e ridistribuire ampi capitali e di impiegare una notevole forza lavoro, contribuendo all'evoluzione e identità del corpo civico sancita dalla nascita della Repubblica.

BIBLIOGRAFIA

AA.VV. 1980, *La Formazione della Città nel Lazio, Dialoghi di Archeologia* 1980.

Ampolo, C. 1982, Le cave di pietra dell'Attica: problemi giuridici ed economici, *Opus* I.2, 251-260.

Ampolo, C., 1984, Il lusso funerario e la città arcaica, *AION* 6, 71-102.

Ampolo, C., 1988, La città riformata e l'organizzazione centuriata. Lo spazio, il tempo, il sacro nella nuova realtà urbana, A. Momigliano, A. Schiavone (ed.), *Storia di Roma I. Roma in Italia*, Einaudi, 203-239 Torino.

Barbanera, M., 1988, *L'archeologia degli Italiani*, Editori Riuniti, Roma.

Bartoli, A., 1961, I pozzi dell'area sacra di Vesta, *MonAntLincei* 45, 1-144.

Bergamini, M. 1991 (ed.), *Gli Etruschi maestri di idraulica*, Electa Editori Umbri, Perugia.

Blake, M.E., 1947-1973, *Ancient Roman Construction in Italy: I-III,* Carnegie Institution of Washington, Washington-Philadeplphia.

Boni, G., 1900, Roma. Nuove scoperte nella città e nel suburbio, *NotSc* 295-340.

Boni, G., 1913, Il metodo delle esplorazioni archeologiche, "Atti del I Convegno degli Ispettori Onorari dei Monumenti e Scavi", *Boll.Arte* 7, 43-67.

Brogiolo, G. P., 1988, *Archeologia dell'edilizia storica*, Edizioni New Press, Como.

Brogiolo, G. P., 1996, Prospettive per l'archeologia dell'architettura, *Archeologia dell'Architettura* 1, 11-15.

Brown, F. E., 1975, La protostoria della Regia, *RendPontAcc* 47, 15-36.

Capogrossi Colognesi, L., 1988, La città e la sua terra, A. Momigliano, A. Schiavone (ed.), *Storia di Roma I. Roma in Italia*, Einaudi, 263-289 Torino.

Carandini, A., 1975, *Archeologia e cultura materiale*, De Donato, Bari.

Carandini, A. 1981, *Storie dalla terra. Manuale di scavo archeologico*, De Donato, Bari.

Carandini, A., Carafa, P. 2000 (ed.), *Palatium e Sacra Via I. Prima delle mura, l'età delle mura e l'età delle case arcaiche*, Istituto Poligrafico e Zecca dello Stato, Roma.

Carandini, A., 1997, *La nascita di Roma*, Einaudi, Torino.

Carandini, A., Terrenato, N., Ricci, G., De Davide, C., D'Alessio, M.T. 1997, La villa dell'Auditorium, *RM* 104, pp. 117-148.

Carafa, P. 1998, *Il Comizio di Roma dalle origini all'età di Augusto*, «L'Erma»di Bretschneider, Roma.

Choisy, A., 1873, *L'art de bàtir chez les Romains*, Ducher, Paris.

Cifani, G., 1994, Aspetti dell'edilizia romana arcaica, *SE* 60, 185-226.

Cifani, G., 1998, La documentazione archeologica delle mura arcaiche a Roma, *RM* 105, 359-389.

Cifani, G., 2002, Notes on the rural landscape of central Thyrrenian Italy in the 6th-5th c. B.C. and its social significance, in *JRA* 15, 2002, pp.247-260.

Cipolla, C.M., 1974, *Storia economica dell'Europa pre-industriale*, Il Mulino, Bologna

Colonna, G.,1981, Tarquinio Prisco e il tempio di Giove Capitolino, *PP* 36, 41-59.

Colonna, G., 1988, La produzione artigianale, A. Momigliano, A. Schiavone (ed.), *Storia di Roma I. Roma in Italia*, Einaudi, 291-316 Torino.

Cornell, T.J., 1995, *The beginnings of Rome*, Routdlege, London.

Cozzo, G., 1928, *Ingegneria romana*, Mantegazza, Roma.

Crema, L., 1959, *L'architettura romana*, Società editrice internazionale, Torino.

D'Agostino, B., 1996, Cuma (Napoli). Le indagini archeologiche sulle fortificazioni e sulle strade, in *BA* 39-40, pp. 33-41.

Downey, S.B., 1995, *Architectural terracottas from the Regia*, Ann Arbor, 1995.

Durm, J., 1905, *Die Baukunst des Etrusker und Roemer*, A. Kröner Verlag, Stuttgart.

De Angelis d'Ossat 1982, *Realtà dell'architettura: apporti alla sua storia 1933-1978*, ed. Carucci, Roma.

Gjerstad, E.,1953, *Early Rome I. Stratigraphical Researches in the Forum Romanum and along the Sacra Via*, C.W.K. Gleerup,Lund.

Gjerstad, E., 1960, *Early Rome III. Fortifications, domestic architecture, sanctuaries, stratigraphic excavations*, C.W.K. Gleerup, Lund.

Gjerstad, E., 1966, *Early Rome IV. Synthesis of Archaeological evidence*, C.W.K. Gleerup, Lund.

Giovannoni, G., 1928, *La tecnica della costruzione presso i Romani*, Società editrice d'arte illustrata, Roma.

Gianfrotta, P.A., 1996, Plauto (*Captivi* 721-36, 944-5, 998 ss.) e le cave di pietra intorno a Roma, M.G.Picozzi, F. Carinci (ed.), *Studi in onore di Lucia Guerrini*, L'Erma di Bretschneider, 187-189 Roma.

Giuliani, C.F.,1966, *Tibur I*, De Luca, Roma.

Giuliani, C.F., 1970, *Tibur II*, De Luca, Roma.

Giuliani, C.F., 1976, *Archeologia: documentazione grafica*, De Luca, Roma.

Giuliani, C. F., 1989, *L'Edilizia nell'Antichità*, La nuova Italia scientifica, Roma.

Hermon, E., 2001, *Habiter et partager les terres avant les Gracques,* Ecole Française de Rome, Rome.

Judson, S., Kahane, A., 1963, Underground drainageways in southern Etruria and northern Latium, *PBSR* 31, 74-99.

Lanciani, R., 1881, Sulle vicende edilizie di Roma, Bonghi, R. (ed.), *Monografia della città di Roma e della Campagna Romana I*, Tipografia Elzeviriana, Roma, 1-50.

Lanciani, R., 1897, *The Ruins and the excavations of ancient Rome*, MacMillan, London.

Leger, A., 1875, *Les travaux publics et la métallurgie aux temps des Romains*, Impr. J. Dejery & C., Paris 1875.

Lugli, G., 1941, La scienza costruttiva al tempo dei re e dei primi consoli di Roma, *Scienza e Tecnica* V, 413-422.

Lugli, G., 1942, Criteri di massima per la datazione dei più antichi monumenti romani, *RendAccLincei* 1942, 383-390.

Lugli, G., 1957, *La tecnica edilizia dei Romani*, G. Bardi, Roma.

Lamboglia, N., 1956, La datazione stratigrafica dei monumenti di età classica, *Crò nica del IV Congreso Internacional de Ciencias Prehistò ricas y Protohistò ricas* (Madrid 1954), Zaragoza, 903-909.

Lamboglia, N., 1958, Opus Certum, *Riv.Stud.Liguri* 24, 158-170.

Mannoni, T., 1996, *Caratteri costruttivi dell'edilizia storica*, Escum, Genova.

Mura Sommella, A., 1997, Le recenti scoperte sul Campidoglio e la fondazione del Tempio di Giove Capitolino, *RendPontAcc* 70, [2000], 57-79.

Mura Sommella, A., 2000, "La grande Roma dei Tarquini". Alterne vicende di una felice intuizione, *BCAR* 101, 7-26.

Mura Sommella, A., Cazzella, A., De Santis, A., Lugli, F., Rosa, C., Baroni, I., Boccuccia, Micarelli, F., Brincatt, S., Giardino, C., Danti, A., Albertoni, M., 2001, Primi risultati delle indagini archeologiche in Campidoglio nell'area del Giardino Romano e del Palazzo Caffarelli, in *BCAR* 102, pp. 261-364.

Palombi, D., Cic. 2 *Verr.*, V, 19, 48 e *Gloss. Ps. Flac. f5* (= *GL*, IV, p. 61) sulla costruzione del tempio di Giove capitolino, *BCAR* 98, 7-14

Pani Ermini L., De Minicis E., 1987 (ed.), *Archeologia del Medioevo a Roma. Edilizia storica e territorio 1*, Editrice Scorpione, Taranto.

Pasquali, G., 1936, La grande Roma dei Tarquini, *Nuova Antologia*, 16 Agosto, 405-416.

Pensabene, P., Falzone, S., 2001 (ed.), *Scavi del Palatino I: l'area sud occidentale del Palatino tra l'età protostorica e il IV secolo a.C.*, «L'Erma» di Bretschneider, Roma.

Roma 1990, *La grande Roma dei Tarquini* (catalogo della mostra), «L'Erma» di Bretschneider, Roma.

Torelli, M., 1988, Dalle aristocrazie gentilizie alla nascita della plebe, A. Momigliano, A. Schiavone (ed.), *Storia di Roma I. Roma in Italia*, Einaudi, 241-261 Torino.

Van Deman, E.B., 1912, Methods of determining the date of Roman Concrete Monuments, *AJA* 16, 230-251.

Zehnacker, H., 1990, Rome: une societé archaïque au contact de la monnaie (VI-IV siècle) *Crises et transformation des sociétés archaïques de l'Italie antique au V° siècle av. J.C.* (acte table ronde, Rome 1987), Ecole Française de Rome, 307-326 Rome.

Zevi, F., 2002, Origini di Ostia, C. Brunn, A. Gallina Zevi (eds.), *Ostia e Portus nelle loro relazioni con Roma*, Acta Instituti Romani Finlandiae, 3-32 Roma.

LA VILLA DELL'AUDITORIUM E LA QUESTIONE AGRARIA: TRA LE RIFORME DI SERVIO TULLIO E LA SERRATA DEL PATRIZIATO

Maria Teresa D'ALESSIO
(Università di Roma "La Sapienza")

ABSTRACT: Recent archaeological work in the Flaminio district of Rome, where the construction of Renzo Piano's Auditorium has been completed, has revealed a monumental building that was occupied between the 6th century BC and 2nd century AD. The particular state of preservation and a number of unusual details have led scholars to interpret it as a rustic building (villa) that developed into a farm. This paper seeks to present history in three-dimensions based upon the recent archaeological finds. These new data are "read" in light of our knowledge of the historical circumstances of the age as well as literary evidence on agricultural production in ancient Rome.*

Premessa

Nel 1995 sono iniziati nel quartiere Flaminio di Roma, tra Via Maresciallo Pilsudski e Via P. De Coubertin, i lavori per la costruzione dell'Auditorium progettato da Renzo Piano (Fig. 1)[1]. In quest'occasione si sono raggiunti livelli situati circa 5 metri al di sotto del piano di calpestio moderno, su cui sono stati individuati i resti di un antico edificio costruito nella seconda metà del VI secolo a.C. e vissuto fino al II d.C. (Fig. 2). In questo monumento abbiamo proposto di riconoscere un edificio rustico a carattere residenziale (Carandini et al. 1997; Ricci e Terrenato 1998; Terrenato 2001). Data la natura del convegno e il suo preciso riferimento ad aspetti economici e sociali del mondo antico, affronteremo direttamente i problemi posti da tale interpretazione anche alla luce delle nuove scoperte effettuate nell'area circostante, limitandoci - per le dimensioni imposte da questa sede - all'analisi e alle relative ipotesi ricostruttive delle sole fasi iniziali del monumento[2].

Il contesto topografico

Ci troviamo nel suburbio settentrionale di Roma, tra il secondo e il terzo miglio della via Flaminia, in una pianura alluvionale lungo la riva sinistra del Tevere, all'interno della grande ansa subito a monte del Campo Marzio, tra la collina dei Parioli e quella di Villa Glori. Numerose sono le presenze archeologiche individuate in questo settore della città che sembrerebbe caratterizzato da edifici residenziali e sepolcrali noti finora soprattutto per l'età imperiale.

Alla scoperta della cosiddetta villa dell'Auditorium se ne è recentemente affiancata un'altra che ha permesso di aggiungere un nuovo importante elemento alla conoscenza complessiva dell'area. Poco lontano dal nostro edificio infatti, nella zona attualmente corrispondente a Piazza Euclide, la Soprintendenza Archeologica di Roma ha individuato nel 1999 una fonte sacra del bosco di Anna Perenna. Per la vicinanza dei due rinvenimenti oltre che per alcune caratteristiche proprie delle due strutture, Marina Piranomonte, che ha diretto i lavori per conto della Soprintendenza, ha recentemente proposto di interpretare il complesso dell'Auditorium come un annesso di questo santuario destinato ad ospitare banchetti, fornendone così una lettura alternativa a quella qui presentata (Piranomonte 2002a: 62 e Piranomonte 2002b).

Fase 1: La fattoria 550-500 a.C.

Nel sito sopra descritto viene costruita attorno al 550 a.C.[3] una fattoria di circa 300 mq. con ambienti disposti ad "U" sui tre lati di una corte aperta su una strada (Fig. 3). La tecnica edilizia di questo primo impianto è modesta, in scaglie di tufo con elevati in argilla e tetto in tegole. L'interpretazione che viene proposta per la funzione dei singoli ambienti è basata sulla distribuzione dei reperti ceramici che sarà pubblicata assieme al monumento oltre che sul confronto con altri edifici simili coevi. Tra questi si fa in particolare riferimento ad un altro impianto rurale dell'agro romano situato nel suburbio meridionale in località Torrino e databile anch'esso ad età tardo arcaica (Bedini 1984: 86). Sul lato settentrionale del cortile della fattoria dell'Auditorium dovevano trovarsi gli ambienti residenziali, a est la cucina, la stanza con il forno per la cottura degli alimenti e la dispensa e a sud i magazzini (Fig. 4)[4].

Per provare ad interpretare questa piccola struttura tenendo conto di quanto conosciamo dell'organizzazione del territorio intorno a Roma in epoca arcaica soprattutto sulla base delle notizie forniteci dalla tradizione letteraria, dobbiamo rivolgerci alle cosiddette riforme promosse da Servio Tullio durante il proprio regno datato dalla tradizione intorno alla metà del VI secolo a.C. La tradizione letteraria attribuisce infatti a questo re una serie di interventi volti a rinnovare completamente l'organizzazione dello stato romano dal punto di vista sociale, militare e politico. La critica storica più recente (Cornell 1995: 173-179)[5], ritenendo questa tradizione affidabile nella sostanza, fa risalire a Servio Tullio, tra varie istituzioni, anche la creazione delle 4 tribù urbane e delle prime tribù rustiche, cioè quei distretti in cui la terra era divisibile e acquisibile da parte di cittadini liberi al di fuori del controllo delle grandi gentes[6]. Tale divisione delle terre avrebbe comportato, di conseguenza, la nascita della piccola proprietà terriera. È addirittura possibile che grazie a queste "riforme" coloro che in precedenza controllavano le terre per conto dei grandi proprietari in qualità di clienti, riescano ora ad ottenere un piccolo fondo personale gettando così le basi per formare un nuovo gruppo sociale che dal 509 a.C. in poi sarà quello dei plebei.

Potremmo dunque immaginare che la fattoria fosse abitata presumibilmente da un contadino libero, piuttosto agiato, cittadino e soldato di Roma e dalla sua famiglia. Il suo fondo poteva essersi costituito intorno al 550 a.C. proprio grazie alle riforme "democratiche" del re Servio Tullio.

Fase 2: La prima villa (500-300 a.C.)

Questa realtà subisce un drastico mutamento attorno al 500 a.C.[7] quando la fattoria viene rasa al suolo. Al suo posto viene edificato un complesso monumentale che abbiamo definito villa, molto più articolato del precedente e composto da due edifici distinti che testimoniano un evidente cambiamento di scala (Fig. 5). Anche la tecnica edilizia è differente, in opera quadrata di tufo probabilmente ancora con elevati di argilla e tetto in tegole.

L'edificio settentrionale si articola in due settori di diversa funzione. Questi sono stati interpretati come una parte signorile a nord (mq. 338) e una rustica a sud (mq. 240). La parte signorile si sviluppa intorno a una corte circondata su due lati da ambienti disposti in maniera speculare. Spiccano tra questi una grande sala rettangolare al centro del lato nord e due probabili torri alle estremità di ogni lato di ambienti[8]. Sul lato opposto della corte viene allestito, sotto un portico, un torchio oleario di cui si è conservata la base di spremitura collegata alla fossa di decantazione dell'olio. Alle spalle del portico verso est si costruisce invece un piccolo ambiente che rimane separato dal resto dell'edificio e aperto verso la campagna. Sulla base di alcuni indicatori ceramici è stato possibile interpretare questo ambiente come piccolo luogo destinato ad un culto (Fig. 6).

Anche la zona rustica è articolata intorno ad uno spazio scoperto (cortile), con magazzini, una cucina e un ambiente in cui sono state rinvenute due tegole affiancate, ricoperte di cenere e con vasi vicino, che scaldate dovevano servire per cuocere cibi.

Più a sud incontriamo un grande recinto e un secondo edificio (mq. 1455), circondato da un alto muro di recinzione, in cui immaginiamo che vivessero le persone impiegate nelle attività agricole. Gli ambienti sono irregolari e disposti attorno a cortili indipendenti su cui si aprono anche piccole stanzette (cellae), forse adibite ai servi. La tecnica edilizia di questo edificio è meno raffinata rispetto a quella impiegata nella villa settentrionale e ricorda invece quella della fattoria precedente.

Come già anticipato, per identificare la funzione di questo impianto si è scelto di utilizzare il termine "villa". Nonostante questa definizione sia comunemente utilizzata per ben noti edifici rurali databili a partire dall'età tardo-repubblicana possiamo considerare la possibilità che esistessero villae anche in epoca notevolmente più antica. Se è vero che la "villa publica" del Campo Marzio poteva essere una residenza di campagna appartenuta ai Tarquini - così come la "domus publica" ne era stata la dimora regia urbana - secondo quanto recentemente proposto da Filippo Coarelli (1997: 65), avremmo un indizio per ritenere che almeno alcuni edifici rurali, forse particolarmente monumentali o lussuosi, fossero definiti villae fin dall'età tardo-arcaica.

Il cambiamento rispetto alla fattoria è evidente e risulta difficile non pensare che esso rappresenti una soluzione di continuità di un certo rilievo nella vita dell'edificio (cambio di proprietà, cambio/incremento della o delle pratiche agricole nel relativo fundus, etc.). A questo proposito vale la pena di rilevare che nell'arco della generazione che separa la costruzione della fattoria dalla sua distruzione e dalla immediata costruzione della possibile villa, lo stato romano viene completamente rinnovato e si assiste alla nascita della repubblica. La tradizione letteraria ci descrive per questo periodo un rinnovato potere delle famiglie gentilizie ("i patrizi") che sembrerebbero recuperare il controllo della terra dopo la cacciata dell'ultimo re. La prima conseguenza di questa presa di posizione del patriziato è la cancellazione della piccola proprietà contadina nata nell'ultima età regia anche se, naturalmente, non era più possibile cancellare anche l'istituto delle tribù rustiche. In varie occasioni A. Carandini ha ricordato in relazione a questi avvenimenti un famoso passo di Livio (2.23)[9] relativo ad un episodio che sarebbe avvenuto nell'anno 495 a.C. Un piccolo proprietario terriero, ex comandante dell'esercito, è ridotto in rovina per aver perso la propria fattoria mentre combatteva lontano da casa, e vive ora costretto nella condizione di servo (nexus) per poter pagare i debiti contratti per sopravvivere. Il racconto di Livio è ritenuto autentico dalla critica storica più recente (Cornell 1995: 266-267), ed è ragionevole supporre che la sorte del povero soldato dovette essere stata comune a quella di molti altri piccoli proprietari. Solo dopo molto tempo, nel 326 a.C., la lex Poetelia abolirà l'istituzione della servitù per debiti in un clima di ritrovata concordia tra patriziato e plebe[10].

È possibile dunque che il proprietario della villa dell'Auditorium, sorta probabilmente sui fondi di piccoli proprietari caduti in rovina, fosse un patrizio che vi risiedeva stagionalmente mentre la terra poteva essere lavorata - almeno in parte - da persone ridotte in schiavitù in quanto non in grado di far fronte ai propri debiti (nexi). La presenza del torchio in questa fase sembrerebbe indicare la coltura dell'olivo, che Plinio ritiene fosse stata introdotta a Roma al tempo di Tarquinio Prisco e quindi, seguendo la cronologia della tradizione, tra la fine del VII e la prima metà circa del VI secolo a.C. (Plinio, Naturalis Historia, 15.1).

Fasi 3 e 4: dalla villa patrizio-plebea alla villa con atrio (300-80 a.C.).

Passando rapidamente in rassegna le fasi successive, si arriva alla prima ristrutturazione della villa avvenuta alla fine del IV secolo a.C. (Fig. 7). Nonostante le modifiche apportate alla planimetria e alle strutture dell'edificio, sarà sempre rispettata la divisione tra la parte signorile a nord e quella rustica a sud. Il quartiere servile scompare invece sotto un poderoso interro e si conserva in uso solo il recinto esterno. A decorare il tetto della parte signorile della villa di questa nuova fase viene inserita una tegola angolare di gronda con protome di divinità fluviale (forse Acheloo) che poteva richiamare il vicino Tevere, mentre al centro della corte viene allestito un altare forse per il culto della gens[11].

Alla fine del III secolo a.C. l'edificio assume l'aspetto della tipica "villa catoniana" con ambienti disposti attorno ad un atrio tuscanico di tipo canonico e tablino nel quale si conserva a terra la traccia di un possibile armadio per l'archivio della famiglia (Fig. 8).

In seguito a queste trasformazioni, poche saranno le modifiche successive, che non altereranno mai l'aspetto austero della struttura fino al II secolo d.C., quando alcune tombe segnano l'abbandono definitivo della villa in seguito coperta da circa 4 m di accumuli alluvionali.

Conclusioni

Riassumendo la storia fino a qui descritta, si possono isolare almeno due importanti cesure che caratterizzano lo sviluppo di questo monumento. La prima intorno al 500 a.C. quando si assiste ad un colossale cambiamento di scala, soprattutto nelle dimensioni, e una alla fine del IV secolo a.C. quando abbiamo una prima ristrutturazione che segna la distruzione del settore meridionale forse destinato alla manodopera servile.

Tutti questi cambiamenti avvengono in un arco cronologico lungo quasi due secoli in cui si assiste alle importanti trasformazioni storiche - qui solo accennate - che accompagnano la crisi della monarchia, il passaggio alla prima fase della repubblica caratterizzata dagli scontri tra patrizi e plebei, e la nascita dello stato cosiddetto patrizio-plebeo in seguito alle Leggi Licinie Sestie.

Questi gli avvenimenti che influenzano la storia agraria di Roma nel periodo in cui avvengono le prime trasformazioni dell'edificio scavato all'Auditorium. È sembrato suggestivo confrontare le due storie in relazione anche con il resto della documentazione archeologica relativa al territorio suburbano in questo periodo. L'incremento delle presenze relative a insediamenti rurali produttivi intorno a Roma al termine del VI secolo a.C. è stato da tempo messo in relazione con le riforme attribuite a Servio Tullio (Quilici 1974; Quilici e Quilici Gigli 1980, 1986, 1993). Si pensi inoltre, per l'Etruria, al fenomeno della colonizzazione interna riconosciuto da Giovanni Colonna per l'età tardo arcaica (Colonna 1990: 15-16). La nascita della piccola fattoria che sorge intorno al 550 a.C. nell'ansa a nord del Campo Marzio potrebbe essere letta alla luce di questi processi. Analogamente, la grande villa che cancella la fattoria intorno al 500 a.C. sembra rappresentare la forza economica del ricco patrizio che ne avrebbe causato la distruzione, riducendo forse in servitù il suo precedente proprietario. E ancora, la scomparsa dell'edificio che abbiamo interpretato come un quartiere servile destinato ai nexi abbandonato e ridotto a semplice recinto alla fine del IV secolo, potrebbe forse essere la conseguenza di un nuovo rapporto tra il proprietario della villa e la manodopera servile, a sua volta indizio di un nuovo sistema produttivo.

NOTE

* Questo contributo deriva dai seminari effettuati dal 1998 presso l'Università degli Studi di Roma "La Sapienza" sotto la direzione scientifica di Andrea Carandini per l'elaborazione della documentazione prodotta nel corso dello scavo della cosiddetta villa dell'Auditorium. Ringrazio in primo luogo A. Carandini e R. Peroni che mi hanno invitato a prendere parte a questo convegno, e tutte le persone che hanno lavorato al progetto rendendo possibile l'apertura del Museo Archeologico (realizzato dalla Sovraintendenza BB.CC. del Comune di Roma con il coordinamento di P. Virgili nel Foyer dell'Auditorium) e l'edizione complessiva dello scavo al momento in corso di stampa.

1 Dal 1996 la Sovraintendenza ai Beni Culturali del Comune di Roma e la Soprintendenza Archeologica di Roma hanno affidato ad Andrea Carandini il coordinamento dello scavo (realizzato dalla cooperativa Astra) e della ricerca che ne è scaturita.

2 Verranno invece tralasciati gli aspetti più metodologici relativi ai dati di scavo, per i quali si rimanda alla loro edizione preliminare in Carandini *et al.* 1997 e a precedenti interventi presentati in altre sedi (American Academy in Rome, British School at Rome, Velletri, etc.). Per questi motivi non vengono qui presentate piante di scavo né piante di fase della struttura ma solo le immagini ricostruttive realizzate da Consuelo Marras e Alessandra Tronelli per il Museo dell'Auditorium.
3 Ciotole in bucchero tipi Rasmussen 2 e 3 (Rasmussen 1979: 124-125, Tav. 41, 151, 255); olle e bacini in impasto grezzo (per le olle Carafa 1995: 150-156, tipi 364-368 e per i bacini Carafa 1995: 218-224, tipi 603-608) costituiscono il *terminus post quem* per questa cronologia.
4 In uno degli ambienti sul lato orientale della fattoria si è infatti rinvenuto un forno in argilla e tufo coperto a cupola, con pianta circolare e sezione ogivale destinato alla cottura del cibo (Nijboer 1998: 112-113,).
5 Per una diversa interpretazione Fraschetti 1994-1995.
6 Tra queste prime tribù di età arcaica sarebbe da inserire anche la Pollia, la cui estensione territoriale potrebbe comprendere la pianura dove sorge la fattoria dell'Auditorium (Taylor 1960; Alföldi 1965).
7 Devo la cronologia di questa fase ad A. Argento. La datazione si basa su frammenti di bucchero tra cui una kylix tipo Rasmussen 5 (Rasmussen 1979, Tav. 40, 237, 121), ceramica a figure nere (kylix con gorgoneion centrale tipo Bloesch 1940, 1185, Tav. 32, 4a) e d'impasto (Carafa 1995: 238-239 e 243-245, tipi 662-663).
8 La disposizione della grande sala al centro del lato settentrionale risulta molto simile per impianto e cronologia alla sala principale di Acquarossa (Stranbdberg Olofsson 1986: 81-89).
9 Si vedano anche Dionigi di Alicarnasso 6, 26 e Cicerone, *De re publica*, 2,58.
10 Livio, 8, 28; Dionigi di Alicarnasso 16, 5; Cicerone, *De re publica*, 2,34 e Varrone, *Lingua latina*, 7, 105.
11 La disposizione dell'altare al centro della corte ricorda il simile impianto nel santuario in forma di dimora principesca di Montetosto presso Cerveteri (Colonna 1985).

BIBLIOGRAFIA

Alföldi, A., 1965, *Early Rome and the Latins,* Ann Arbor.

Bedini, A., 1984, Scavi al Torrino, *Archeologia Laziale* VI, *QuadAEI* 8, 1984, pp. 84-90.

Bloesch, H., 1940, *Formen attischer Schalen von Exekias bis zum Ende des Strengen Stils.*

Carafa, P., 1995, *Officine ceramiche di età regia. Produzione di ceramica in impasto a Roma dalla fine dell'VIII alla fine del VI secolo a.C.*, Roma.

Carandini, A., D'Alessio, M.T., De Davide, C., Ricci, G. e Terrenato, N., 1997, La villa dell'Auditorium dall'età arcaica all'età imperiale, *RömMitt* 104, 117-148.

Coarelli, F., 1997, *Il Campo Marzio. Dalle origini alla fine della repubblica*, Roma.

Colonna, G., 1985, Il santuario di Montetosto, in S. Stopponi (a cura di), *Case e palazzi d'Etruria* (catalogo della mostra), Milano, 192-195.

Colonna, G., 1990, Città e territorio nell'Etruria meridionale del V secolo, in *Crise et transformation des sociétés archaïques de l'Italie antique au Ve siècle av. J.-C.*, Actes de la table ronde organisée par l'École française de Rome et l'Unité de recherches étrusco-italiques associée au CRNS (UA 1132), Rome 19-21 novembre 1987, 7-21, Roma.

Cornell, T.J., 1995, *The beginnings of Rome*, London.

Fraschetti, A., 1994-1995, Servio Tullio e la partizione del corpo civico, *Metis* 9-10, 129-141.

Nijboer, A.J., 1998, *From household production to workshops*, Groningen.

Piranomonte, M., 2002a, s.v. Annae Perennae Nemus, in *Lexicon Topographicum Urbis Romae. Suburbium*, (a cura di A. La Regina), vol. I, 59-63, Roma.

Piranomonte M. (a cura di), 2002b, *Il santuario della musica e il bosco sacro di Anna Perenna,* Roma.

Pisani Sartorio, G., 1994-1995, Via Maresciallo Pilsudski - Via P. De Coubertin, *BullCom* 96, 276-281.

Quilici, L., 1974, *Collatia*, Firenze.

Quilici, L. e Quilici Gigli, S., 1980, *Crustumerium*, Roma.

Quilici, L. e Quilici Gigli, S., 1986, *Fidenae*, Roma.

Quilici, L. e Quilici Gigli, S., 1993, *Ficulea*, Roma.

Rasmussen, T.B., 1979, *Bucchero Pottery from Southern Etruria*, Cambridge.

Ricci, G. e Terrenato, N., 1998, La villa dell'Auditorium, in M. Tosi e M. Pearce (edd.), *Papers from the EAA Third Annual Meeting at Ravenna 1997*, BAR International Series 718, II, 1998, 45-52, Oxford.

Stranbdberg Olofsson, M., 1986, L'area monumentale di Acquarossa, in *Architettura Etrusca nel Viterbese. Ricerche svedesi a San Giovenale e Acquarossa 1956-1986* (catalogo della mostra), Roma, 81-89.

Taylor, L.R., 1960, *The voting districts of the roman republic*, Roma.

Terrenato, N., 2001,The Auditorium site in Rome and the origins of the villa, *JRA* 14, 5-32.

Wikander, Ch., 1986, (a cura di), *Architettura etrusca nel viterbese* (Catalogo della Mostra, Viterbo 1986), Roma.

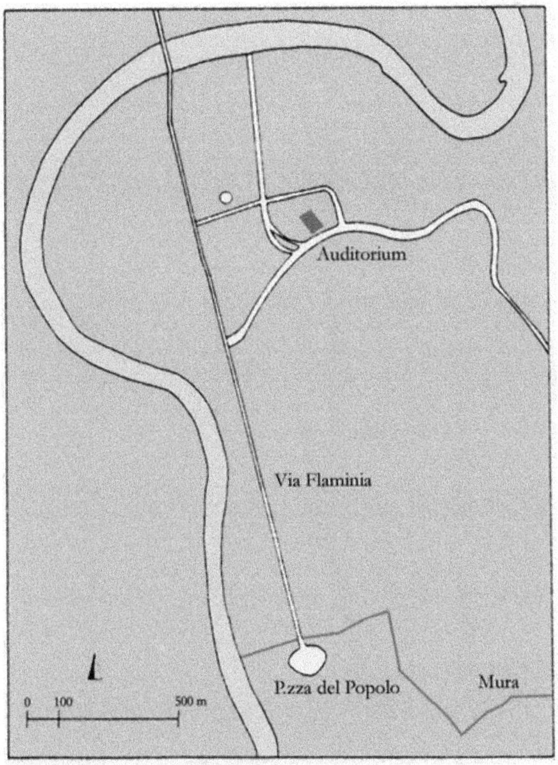

Fig. 1. Localizzazione della villa dell'Auditorium.

Fig. 2. Foto aerea dell'area di scavo (foto di M. Letizia).

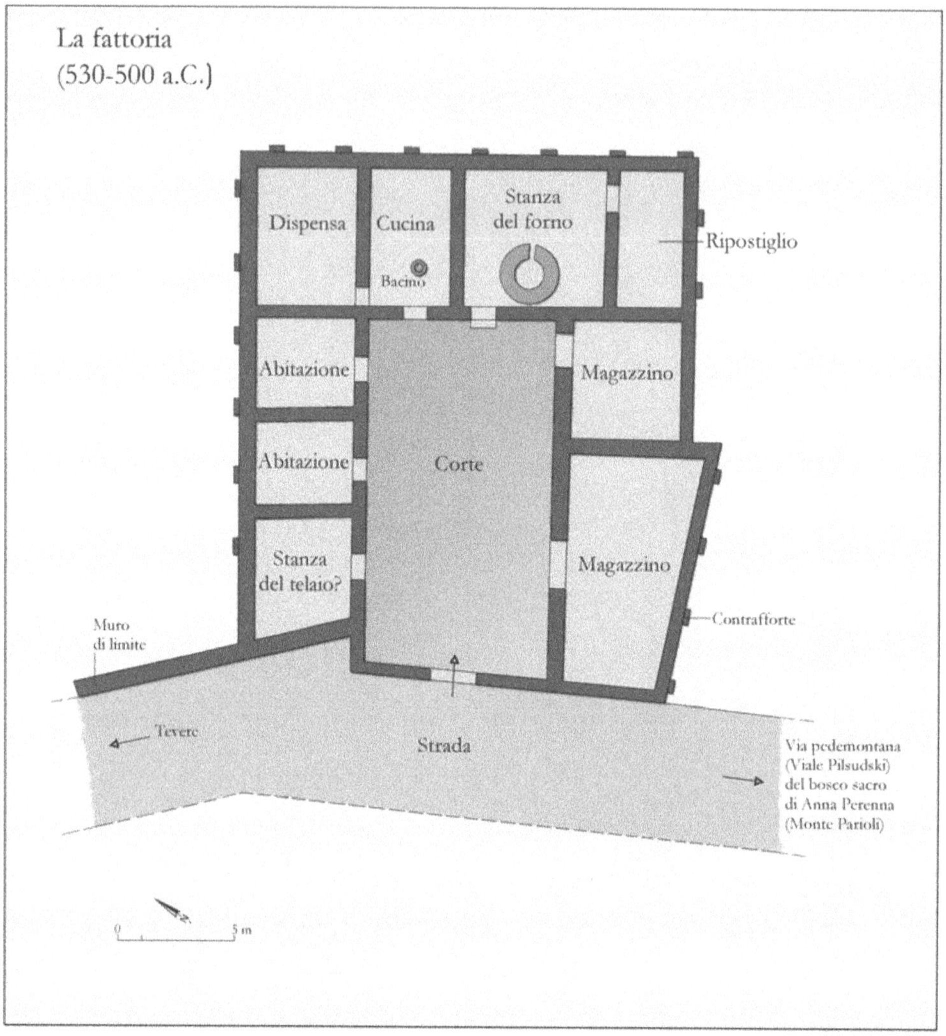

Fig. 3. La fattoria (550-500 a.C.). Pianta ricostruttiva

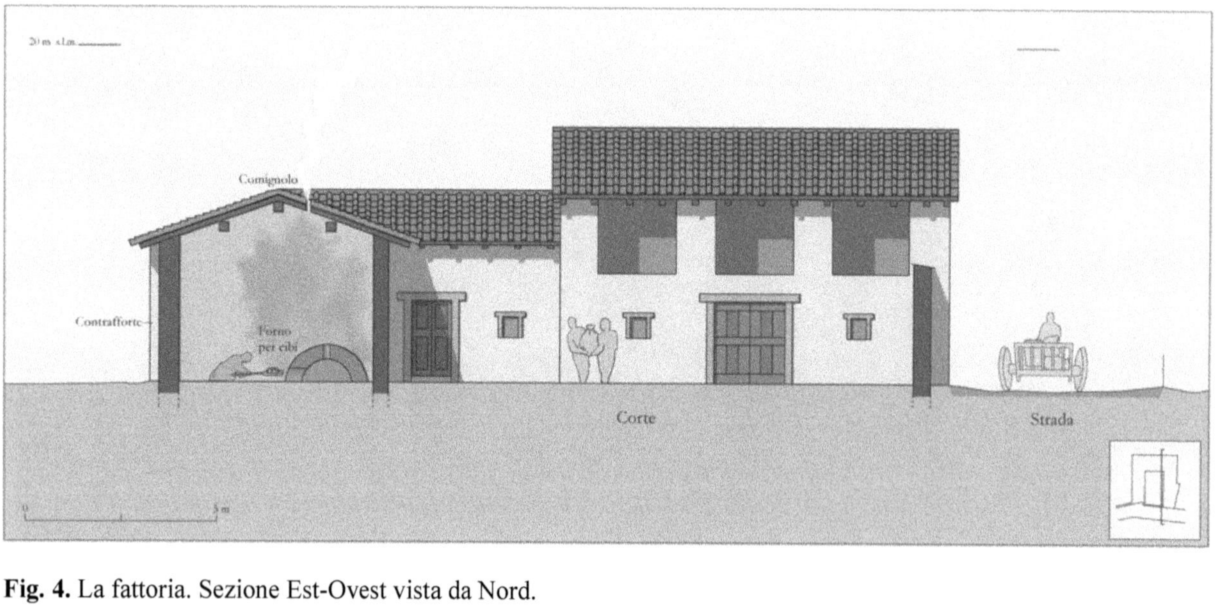

Fig. 4. La fattoria. Sezione Est-Ovest vista da Nord.

Fig 5. La prima villa (500-300 a.C.). Pianta ricostruttiva.

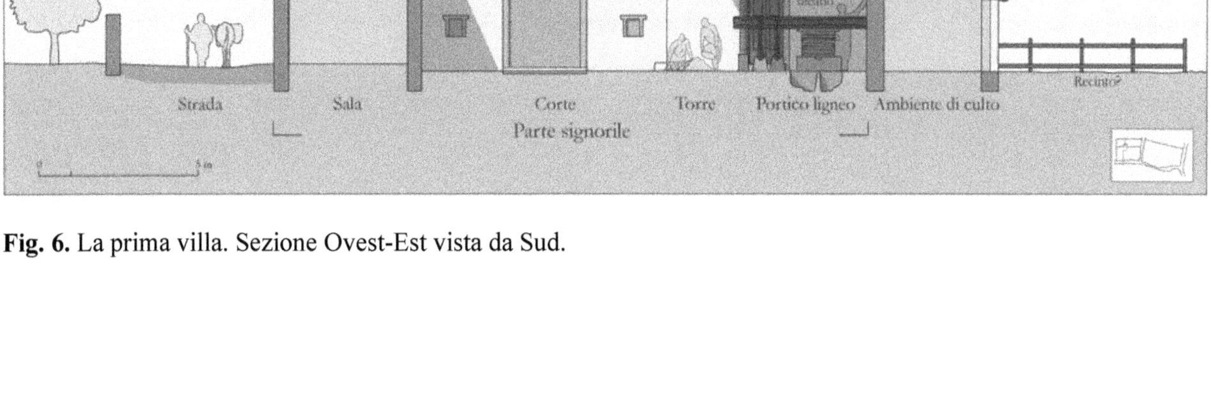

Fig. 6. La prima villa. Sezione Ovest-Est vista da Sud.

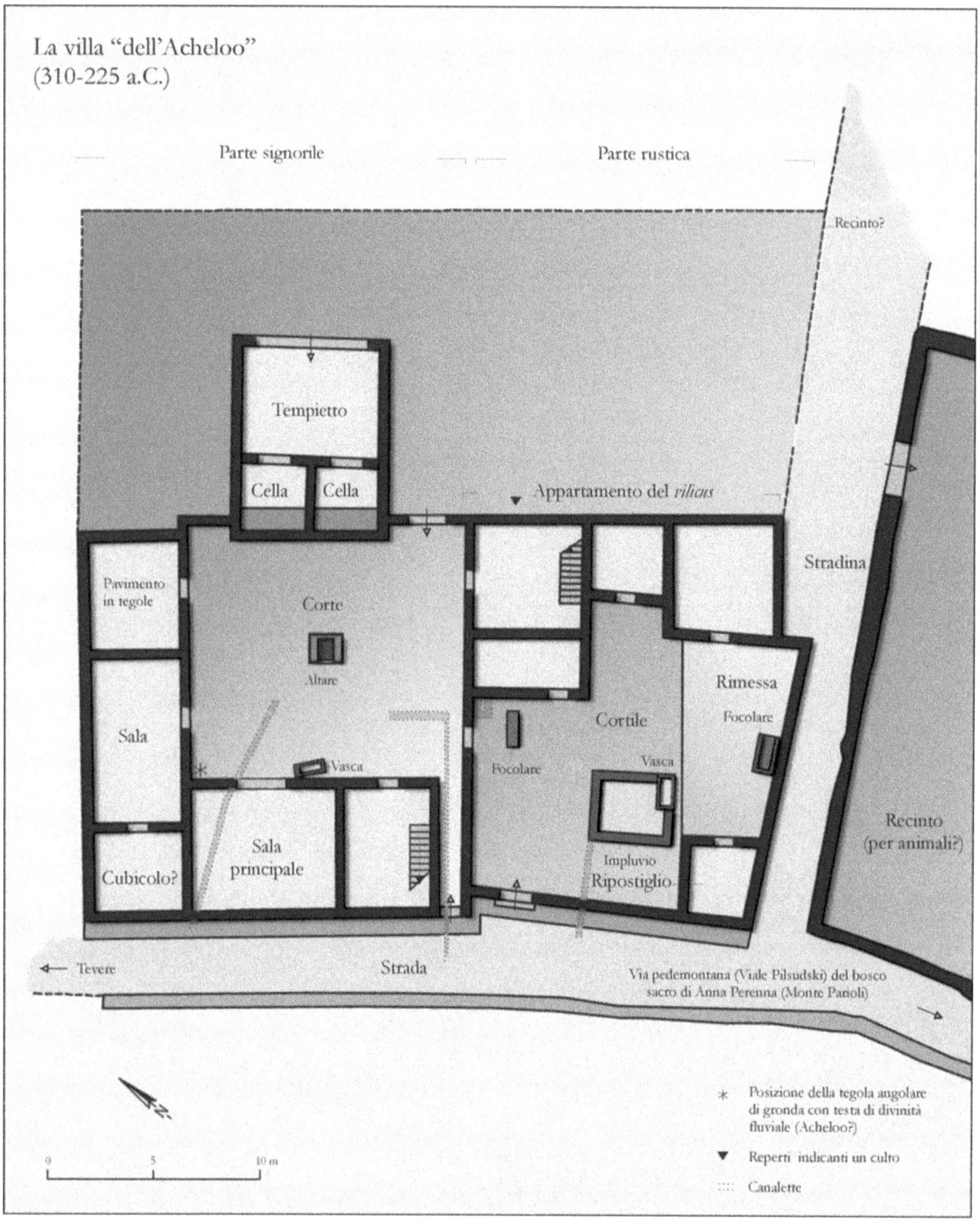

Fig. 7. La villa patrizio-plebea (300-225 a.C.). Pianta ricostruttiva.

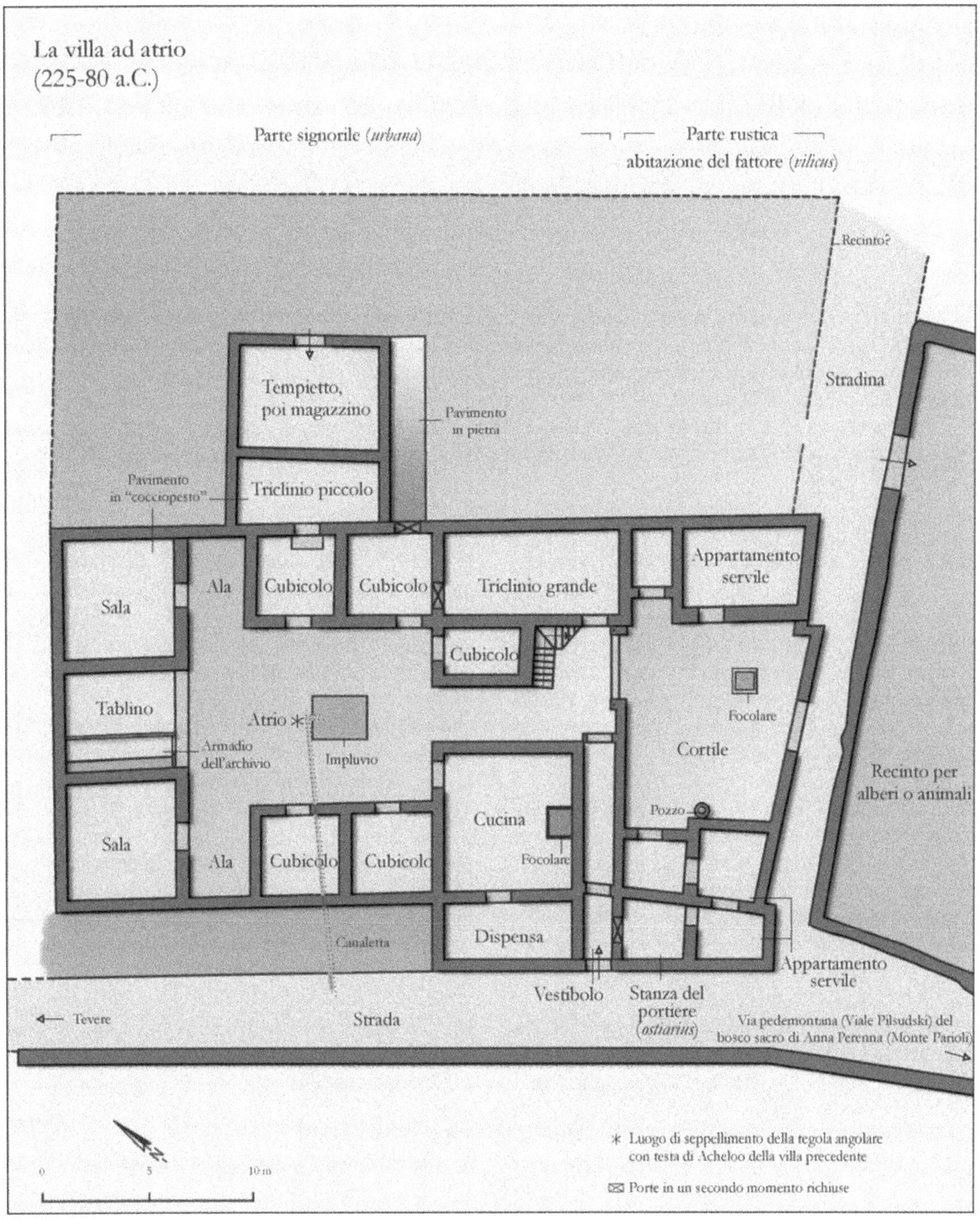

Fig. 8. La villa ad atrio (225-80 a.C.). Pianta ricostruttiva.

RACCOLTA E PROGETTO DI CATALOGO DEI BOLLI ANEPIGRAFICI SU *BESSALES* D'EPOCA IMPERIALE (ROMA ED IL SUO TERRITORIO)

EVELYNE BUKOWIECKI (Université de Provence)
PAOLA CIANCHI (Università di Roma "La Sapienza")

ABSTRACT: By the early imperial period, tiles and brick used in construction were stamped "epigraphic maker's marks", and later, also with "anepigraphic maker's marks". The latter, alsmost completely neglected by scholars are treated here in a presentation of a project involving the systematic recovery and study of anepigraphic maker's marks that will be fully published in the form of a catalogue. This project will allow us to better understand such stamps and, hence, permit researchers to date monument more accurately, and, above all, yield more information about the brick and tile industry and the distribution of a particular type of brick: *bessales*.

Sul territorio di Roma, all'epoca imperiale, il mattone diventa il principale materiale di costruzione e rapidamente, le strutture in *opus testaceum* superano in proporzione tutte quelle costruite con altre tecniche. Questa tecnica, chiamata spesso anche *opus latericium*, utilizza mattoni di varie dimensioni; il *bessales* (circa 20 x 20 cm), il *sesquipedales* (circa 43 x 43 cm) e il *bipedales* (circa 60 x 60 cm).

L'abitudine di bollare i mattoni con un'iscrizione che riporta una serie d'informazioni riguardanti il luogo e la data di produzione di essi, comincia dai primi decenni dell'Impero e a parte alcune interruzioni, perdurerà fino alla sua fine. È chiaro che questi "bolli epigrafi" sono stati e sono ancora molto preziosi per la datazione dei monumenti.

Tuttavia, un altro modo di marcare i mattoni che ha suscitato molto meno l'interesse degli studiosi e che si caratterizza dall'assenza di segno epigrafo appare con il regno d'Adriano, si sviluppa notevolmente all'epoca severiana per sparire del tutto nel Tardo Impero. Stranamente, questi "bolli anepigrafi" non sono stati individuati, per adesso, nelle realizzazioni del resto della dinastia antonina. Queste impronte, realizzate per pressione di una matrice metallica sul mattone nella fase finale della sua essiccazione, sono state rinvenute quasi esclusivamente su *bessales*; o interi, nel rivestimento delle volte o nelle *suspensurae* degli ipocausti, o tagliati, nei paramenti dei muri. Conosciamo due soli casi di bollo anepigrafo su *bipedales*. Gli elementi metallici che formano sul supporto di legno la figura del bollo sono molto vari; i chiodi e le rondelle di tipo e diametro diverso sono i più diffusi, ma sono utilizzati anche dei frammenti di forma più elaborata come per esempio elementi di sistema di serratura o pezzi d'equipaggiamento militare (Fig.1 a-f; Fig.2).

In occasione di queste giornate di studio dedicate ai metodi ed approcci archeologici nei confronti dell'industria e del commercio dell'Italia Antica, vogliamo presentarvi il nostro progetto di raccolta e di catalogazione di questi bolli anepigrafi.

Questa ricerca nasce sotto l'iniziativa di Henri Broise che tuttora continua a seguire da vicino l'avanzamento dei lavori e che, nel 1987, ha per primo realizzato lo studio sistematico di un lotto omogeneo di bolli anepigrafi (Broise and Scheid 1987). Sui 185 frammenti di *bessales* rinvenuti nel *balneum* dei sacerdoti Arvali della Magliana, datato all'inizio del III sec. sono stati individuati 42 forme diverse di bolli anepigrafi. All'epoca, alcune caratteristiche ricorrenti potevano già essere riconosciute:

- i bolli occupano la parte centrale dei *bessales* che hanno dimensioni oscillanti tra 18,5 e 21,5 cm. in larghezza e tra 3 e 3,5 cm. in spessore.

- le matrici metalliche che formano i bolli sono fissate su tavolette di legno che hanno spesso lasciato segni sul *bessales*.

- le tavolette sono probabilmente dotate di un'impugnatura per facilitare il lavoro di marcatura e, data l'estensione di alcuni bolli, forse queste tavolette dovevano avere delle dimensioni vicine a quelle dei *bessales*.

Prima di questo studio, non era mai stato dato il giusto peso a questo materiale; ci troviamo molto spesso in presenza di semplici descrizioni o fotografie (Pfeiffer *et al.* 1905; Steinby 1978) e bisogna risalire alla pubblicazione di Herbert Bloch del 1947 per trovare le prime ipotesi di ricerca.

Durante gli anni successivi al 1987, lo stesso H. Broise ha cominciato ad integrare allo studio altri lotti di materiale provenienti dalle Terme di Caracalla, dall'Anfiteatro Castrense e dal complesso sacro di Vigna Barberini sul Palatino (Broise 1995).

A partire da questi 73 primi bolli anepigrafi cosi individuati, disegnati e catalogati, abbiamo proseguito la raccolta in vari monumenti di Roma (il Palatino[1], le Terme di Caracalla[2] e la collina del Pincio[3]) e anche sul sito di Ostia Antica. Le Terme di Caracalla costituiscono un vero e proprio "serbatoio" di bolli anepigrafi, sia per la quantità sia per la varietà e Ostia Antica dovrebbe permetterci di studiare meglio la loro diffusione e la loro distribuzione. Gli altri monumenti indagati sono soprattutto legati ad altri nostri progetti professionali. In questa raccolta sono considerati anche i *bessales* provenienti da scavi ed isolati per unità stratigrafiche.

Per documentare i bolli sul sito, si procede prima all'individuazione dei *bessales* bollati e dopo una prima pulizia grossolana, si considera la loro quantità e la loro ripetizione nella struttura. Su uno schizzo della volta, del paramento o dell'ipocausto considerato, si localizza ciascuno dei bolli.. Si sceglie poi l'esemplare di migliore qualità e conservazione e si procede alla sua schedatura; si osserva la qualità dell'impressione, lo stato di conservazione, la posizione del bollo sulla superficie del *bessales* e si annotanno le eventuali particolarità. Tutti i *bessales* bollati sono schedati secondo le loro dimensioni, colore, stato di conservazione e vengono menzionati i segni particolare come per esempio quelli lasciati dagli strumenti al momento della fabbricazione. Infine, per rilevare il bollo (Fig. 3, 4, 5) possiamo utilizzare diverse tecniche quali il calco con grafite, il calco con plastilina o il rilievo a contatto; ma ricordiamo che l'obiettivo prioritario è quello di essere in grado, a posteriori, di realizzare un disegno del bollo il più fedele possibile alla realtà. L'ideale è di concludere con una fotografia del bollo ma spesso le condizione di luce in cui si effettuano i rilievi non lo permettono. In laboratorio, si procede poi alla realizzazione dei disegni. Data la quantità di materiale da trattare, abbiamo scelto di utilizzare programmi computerizzati di grafica quale Adobe Illustrator e Autocad.

Ad ogni esemplare di bollo disegnato viene, alla fine, attribuito un numero progressivo d'inventario che prosegue la numerazione cominciata da Henri Broise per i bolli anepigrafi della Magliana. Nell'ambito di questo studio, non abbiamo preso in considerazione, né le tracce di zampe d'animale, né le tracce digitali umane.

Questa "collezione" di bolli raggiunge ormai i 300 esemplari e sentiamo crescere la necessità di trasformarla in uno strumento di lavoro accessibile a tutti perché siamo convinti che un catalogo grafico, il più esaustivo possibile, di tutti i bolli anepigrafi conosciuti, potrebbe veramente essere prezioso per diverse categorie di specialità archeologica: contribuirebbe ad approfondire le conoscenze sulla produzione e la distribuzione di questo materiale di costruzione diffusissimo quale era il *bessales* ed aiuterebbe quelli che s'interessano alle strutture dei periodi considerati.

In effetti, uno dei principali obiettivi di questa ricerca è quello di completare le conoscenze relative alla datazione dei monumenti. Nell'analisi archeologica di un monumento, succede spesso che le relazioni di scavo e la documentazione bibliografica siano molto incompleti o addirittura totalmente assenti. Certo l'applicazione rigorosa del metodo stratigrafico sull'elevato permette spesso di capire la successione delle varie fasi di costruzione, ma purtroppo non sempre è sufficiente a datare i differenti progetti architettonici individuati.

In particolare per il periodo severiano, il passaggio progressivo al monopolio imperiale di tutte le fabbriche di mattoni, interrompe l'utilizzo dei bolli epigrafi dopo il regno di Caracalla (Broise 1987: 145). Di conseguenza, è impossibile contare su questo tipo di datazione per le strutture di quell'epoca.

In assenza di cronologia precisa e per affinare, per quanto possibile, le cronologie proposte, si può fare riferimento ad elementi già sperimentati quali l'individuazione delle varie tecniche costruttive, l'osservazione delle caratteristiche delle costruzioni, o l'identificazione dello stile decorativo, integrandoli con l'analisi dei bolli anepigrafi presenti nelle strutture studiate. In effetti, già adesso, il solo confronto tra i disegni dei diversi siti indagati permette di trovare similitudine o differenze tra le strutture e dunque di dedurne i ravvicinamenti cronologici o no. Per esempio, certi bolli trovati nelle Terme di Caracalla si ritrovano nella *Domus Severiana* o sulla Vigna Barberini, altri, individuati ad Ostia Antica, sono stati individuati anche sul Palatino.

Tuttavia, allo stato attuale delle nostre ricerche, non si può ancora parlare di certezze ma piuttosto d'intuizioni o d'ipotesi che man mano che si vanno scoprendo nuovi bolli acquistano sempre più supporto e validità:

- per il periodo adrianeo, riconosciamo una tipologia piuttosto semplice dei bolli anepigrafi, che siano o meno associati a bolli epigrafi rettangolari; particolarità che svilupperemo più avanti. I *bessales* utilizzati nelle costruzioni di questo periodo sono quasi tutti marcati e di solito, dallo stesso bollo. Nella maggior parte dei casi si tratta d'impronte singole di rondelle, di diametro non superiore ai 3 cm, o di figure, più o meno geometriche, realizzate con dei chiodi, in quantità limitata. Per quest'epoca, i bolli molto complessi che associano chiodi con rondelle o altri elementi metallici non sono stati individuati.

- per il resto della dinastia antonina, anche se il *bessales* era particolarmente utilizzato nelle costruzioni, sia per le volte, sia per i paramenti, non si è ritrovato nelle strutture osservate fino ad ora, nessuno bollo anepigrafo.

- dalla prima età severiana, i *bessales* sono di nuovo marcati, ma solo con bolli anepigrafi. Le matrici comprendono tutti tipi di elementi, con una prevalenza sempre delle rondelle e dei chiodi (Fig. 1b, 1e, 1d). Dopo, man mano che si avanza nel terzo secolo, i bolli sono sempre più complessi e sofisticati (Fig. 1c, 1f, 1a, 2a, 2b). In quest'epoca si riconosce abbastanza spesso un fenomeno che può essere di grande aiuto per la "cronologia relativa" dei monumenti ed è quello dell'evoluzione del bollo. In effetti, la matrice di un bollo, durante la sua utilizzazione, può essere riparata, anche più volte, e può vedere aumentare il numero dei suoi elementi costitutivi. Nel primo caso si riconosce una sola figura con tipi e posizione di chiodi leggermente diversi e nel secondo caso la variazione del bollo può essere accertata solo se lo stato di conservazione e la pulizia del *bessales* sono sufficienti. Tuttavia, per certi bolli, è stato possibile riconoscere fino a tre varianti.

- per quello che riguarda la fine dell'utilizzo del bollo anepigrafo, che in ogni caso copre tutta la dinastia severiana, non abbiamo ancora idee precise, ma sappiamo solo che questa pratica è ormai assente dalle costruzioni massenziane[4].

Un altro obiettivo fondamentale di questa ricerca, che s'inserisce particolarmente nel tema di queste giornate di studio, è quello di comprendere il significato e la funzione di questi bolli e cosi, di riuscire a capire meglio l'organizzazione di un ambiente di lavoro quale una fabbrica di mattoni dove, per un motivo ancora da scoprire, delle "forze-lavoro" erano impegnate a porre dei marchi anepigrafi su dei mattoni.

Un punto ormai fermo è quello di considerare che i bolli anepigrafi non hanno una funzione decorativa come qualche volta è stato affermato (Proietti 1990; Steinby 1986, p. 109), prima perché sono raramente visibili e poi perché la loro diversità in una stessa struttura non lascia intuire nessun concetto estetico. Pensiamo anche che non hanno alcun significato proprio ma che permettono solo di differenziare lotti di mattoni tra loro, in funzione di una suddivisione più articolata nell'organizzazione generale della fabbrica che comprende più unità di produzione organizzate intorno alle singole fornaci. Il personale che componeva ciascuna di queste unità di produzione doveva dividersi tra operai addetti all'impasto dell'argilla, alla preparazione dei mattoni, all'essiccatoio, alla fornace e al magazzino. La nostra ipotesi è che ogni bollo anepigrafo corrisponde ad una sola unità di produzione e dunque identifica, a prima vista, il lavoro di questo singolo gruppo di persone che sembrava operare con una certa indipendenza dal resto della fabbrica. La presenza del bollo anepigrafo sui *bessales* permetteva dunque, sicuramente, un controllo prevalentemente di natura quantitativa e forse anche una verifica qualitativa del mattone da parte del responsabile della fabbrica. Cosi, la variazione del bollo anepigrafo poteva corrispondere ad un cambiamento della squadra, della composizione nella squadra o segnare un momento particolare: una data speciale, una quota di produzione raggiunta, ecc.

Ora, se quanto detto lo applichiamo al periodo adrianeo, sembra più facile comprendere le ragioni della compresenza del bollo anepigrafo insieme a quello epigrafo. In effetti, come aveva già messo in evidenza Herbert Bloch nel 1947 (Bloch 1947: 206-207), sembra che, a quell'epoca, per motivi di controllo, fu introdotto l'uso del bollo personale per ogni operaio. Il bollo anepigrafo poteva cosi distinguere la produzione del singolo operaio o del "capo-operaio" della singola fornace, dalla produzione dell'intera fabbrica, avendo comunque il bollo epigrafo in comune.

Di questi bolli sono state individuate due serie:

- la prima è costituita da bolli molto semplici realizzati con rondelle o con chiodi, sufficientemente distanti dal bollo inscritto per escludere l'ipotesi che si tratti di elementi di fissaggio del bollo epigrafo sulla tavoletta di legno. Di questa serie conosciamo per esempio i bolli dei quaranta operai di Annio Vero dei *Praedia Quintanensia* (Fig. 6), datati del 123 d. C.

- la seconda serie è caratterizzata da bolli realizzati con chiodi disposti in modo tale da formare delle lettere che possono essere interpretate come le iniziali degli operai (Fig. 7). Prendendo in considerazione questi tipi di bolli, sappiamo che ci troviamo sulla linea di confine tra bolli epigrafi e bolli anepigrafi, ma abbiamo scelto comunque di integrarli nel nostro studio, vista l'elaborazione particolarmente approssimativa ed personale di questo tipo di matrice. Possiamo per esempio nominare i bolli che portano il nome di Marco Vinicio Pantagato, il quale lavora nelle Sulpiciane; questo bollo inscritto è accompagnato da 17 varianti di lettere e dunque questo bollo sarebbe stato utilizzato da almeno 17 operai diversi.

Nel periodo severiano, come abbiamo già accennato, la maggior parte delle fabbriche è finita nelle mani dell'imperatore che si è appropriato di questo patrimonio attraverso confische ed eredità (Broise 1995). A questo punto, non è più cosi necessario di marcare i mattoni con bolli epigrafi dal momento che la proprietà, e dunque la produzione, è unica. Tuttavia supponiamo che il controllo interno della produzione era comunque assicurato. Si ipotizza che questo controllo venisse effettuato dall'esercito, come tra l'altro era d'abitudine nelle province dell'impero, perché abbiamo notato che le matrici metalliche dei bolli anepigrafi sono spesso costituite da elementi provenienti dall'equipaggio militare (Broise 1987; Broise 1995; Boube-Piccot 1994). Si tratta certo di materiale di recupero ma l'origine stessa di questo materiale ci sembra la testimonianza di una gestione centralizzata affidata all'esercito. Inoltre coltiviamo la speranza di potere identificare, a partire dalla loro impronta sul mattone, l'origine culturale ma soprattutto l'attribuzione cronologica di ciascuno di questi elementi metallici particolari che compongono le matrice dei bolli (Fig. 2).

Per riprendere l'aspetto più generale del nostro discorso, possiamo dire che la raccolta sistematica dei bolli anepigrafi intrapresa in questi ultimi anni e l'osservazione della loro posizione nelle strutture, ci hanno permesso di formulare alcune ipotesi sulla loro datazione e sulla loro funzione: siamo però ancora lontani da una comprensione globale di questo tipo di pratica. Ci sono rimasti numerosi interrogativi senza risposta e sentiamo comunque il bisogno di confrontare le nostre valutazioni con un numero di bolli raccolti più significativo. In effetti conosciamo per adesso circa 300 bolli diversi ma sospettiamo che possano essere molto più numerosi. Tra i problemi più complessi da considerare c'è quello della disparità dei tipi di bolli anepigrafi severiani presenti in una sola struttura. Per esempio su una volta rivestita da *bessales* è possibile trovare fino a 20 figure di bolli diversi: cosa che non accadeva nel periodo adrianeo. Possiamo ipotizzare una modalità costruttiva che prevedeva di utilizzare in modo proporzionale mattoni di più lotti, tra quelli disponibili nei magazzini, per garantire un livello medio di qualità del materiale impiegato. Questo porterebbe a riscontrare proporzione pressoché identiche dei diversi bolli. Resterebbero da spiegare i casi in cui le diverse quantità non fossero paragonabili: si potrebbe pensare a una ridotta disponibilità di magazzino di un lotto di mattoni rispetto ad un altro al momento del prelievo, ma qui siamo in un campo troppo ipotetico. In alternativa a queste considerazioni, potrebbe anche essere stata una totale casualità nel prelievo e nella distribuzione dei mattoni sui cantieri. Un'altra anomalia è il fatto che non tutti i *bessales* sono marcati. Pensiamo che, come accade anche nel caso dei bolli epigrafi, il numero dei bolli applicati dipendeva dell'organizzazione dell'essiccatoio dove, in assenza di spazi di circolazione interni, solo i mattoni più periferici potevano essere correttamente bollati: quelli centrali non erano raggiungibili. Ci siamo anche chiesti perché il bollo anepigrafo fosse riservato esclusivamente al *bessales* è perché non riguardasse tutti i tipi di mattoni. È vero che per i periodi storici considerati il *bessales* era il tipo di mattone più utilizzato, ma non ci sembra un argomento valido per non bollare i *bipedales* ed i *sesquipedales*. Infine il non utilizzo del bollo anepigrafo per le costruzioni dei regni antonini posteriori a quello di Adriano è per noi un grande enigma per il quale non siamo ancora riusciti a formulare ipotesi.

Ci auguriamo che l'intensificazione della raccolta di questi bolli anepigrafi ci permetta di risolvere al più presto i vari problemi, aprendo cosi la strada alla realizzazione concreta del catalogo che, speriamo, possa soddisfare la curiosità e le esigenze dei vari studiosi.

NOTE

1 *Domus Severiana, Stadio* e Vigna Barberini
2 Gallerie sotterranee
3 Piazzale di Villa Medici, Convento di Trinità dei Monti
4 L'ultima grande fase di costruzione nel cosiddetto "complesso severiano" del Palatino

BIBLIOGRAFIA

Bloch, H., 1947, I bolli laterizi e la storia edilizia romana, Roma.

Boube-Piccot, C., 1994, Les bronzes antiques du Maroc, IV. L'équipement militaire et l'armement, Paris.

Broise, H. and Scheid, J., 1987, Recherches archéologiques à la Magliana. Le balneum des frères Arvales, 130-146, Roma.

Broise H., 1995, Les estampilles anépigraphes sur bessales de la Rome impériale, in La brique antique et médiévale. Production et commercialisation d'un matériau, Collection de l'Ecole Française de Rome 272, 113-125, Roma.

Pfeiffer, G. J., Van Buren, A. W. And Armstrong, H. H., 1905, Stamps on Bricks and Tiles from the Aurelian Wall at Rome, SPASR I, 1-87, Roma.

Proietti, A, 1990, Prodotti laterizi, in Archeologia urbana a Roma: il progetto della Crypta Balbi, 5. L'esedra della Crypta Balbi nel medioevo, Biblioteca di Archeologia Medievale, fig. 165/5 e 168, Roma

Steinby, M., 1978, Lateres signati ostienses, ActaIRF, vol VII, 1-2., Roma.

Fig. 1. Frammenti di bessales con bolli anepigrafici.

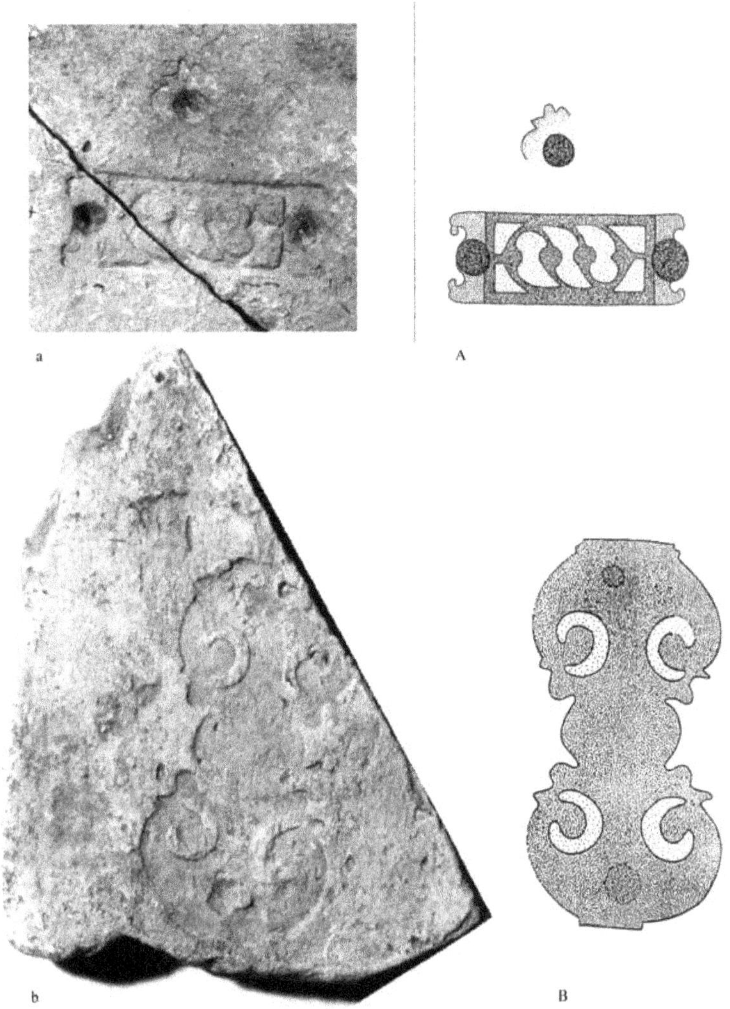

Fig. 2. Esempi di elementi di equipaggio militare utilizzati come matrici di bolli anepigrafici.

Fig 3. Esemplare di bollo anepigrafico.

Fig 4. Calco con plastilina.

Fig 5. Disegno del bollo.

Fig 6. Esemplare del bollo CIL XV 1385

Fig. 7. Esemplare del bollo CIL XV 563

ANFITEATRO FLAVIO DI POZZUOLI, LA DECORAZIONE MARMOREA NELLA STORIA EDILIZIA : TIPOLOGIA E STILE, RESTAURI, OFFICINE E ARTIGIANI

Filippo DEMMA
(Università di Roma "La Sapienza")

ABSTRACT: This paper concerns the stone industry as it pertains to the construction of the Flavian amphitheater in Pozzuoli. Architectural features of this Roman monument have been analyzed in order to elucidate the organization of stone procurement and carving.

Il contributo che segue,[1] unitamente a quello di P. Barresi, insieme al quale fu presentato nell'ultima sessione di questo convegno, rappresenta un tentativo di coordinare metodologie diverse nello studio dell'edilizia romana, allo scopo di esaminare nell'ottica più ampia e completa possibile i numerosissimi dati che si possono ottenere dall'analisi degli elementi architettonici in marmo. Si è affiancato il tradizionale studio stilistico-tipologico all'esame del materiale dal punto di vista della sua lavorazione e dei meccanismi produttivi. Un attento esame ha consentito di identificare tracce di restauri antichi dei pezzi stessi, e quindi di chiarirne la storia dal punto di vista, per così dire, strutturale e funzionale. L'analisi tipologica ha permesso di riconoscere un'articolazione interna dei pezzi in due gruppi e di proporre ipotesi per la cronologia di entrambi. L'applicazione dell'esame stilistico, tradizionalmente riservato a questa classe, non ha esaurito tuttavia la quantità di problematiche proposte dal materiale stesso; per chiarire gli interrogativi che i pezzi continuavano a porre, si è utilizzato l'armamentario critico finora proprio della storia dell'arte e applicato in archeologia per lo studio delle copie scultoree e della pittura vascolare. Come si vedrà, quest'analisi ha consentito di proporre una serie di ipotesi sull'identificazione dell'officina che eseguì gli elementi architettonici, sulla sua articolazione interna, sull'organizzazione del lavoro. In sostanza, si è cercato di trattare una serie di colonne e capitelli come elementi rappresentativi di una cultura materiale, da inserire in un ciclo produttivo, che andava ricostruito, senza fermarsi all'aspetto estetico-decorativo.

Il monumento

L'anfiteatro maggiore di Pozzuoli[2] si sviluppava su due ordini di arcate ed era coronato da un attico porticato (fig. 1). L'impianto originale è stato ricondotto, grazie alle iscrizioni di dedica, all'età Flavia[3]. Le epigrafi chiariscono anche la committenza dell'edificio, dovuto agli sforzi economici della Colonia. Già in antico importanti restauri interessarono l'anello esterno, che presentava un portico voltato impostato su pilastri di trachite con semicolonne addossate. Questi pilastri furono rinforzati in un secondo momento da corpi di fabbrica in laterizio, con relativi sottarchi (fig. 3), che ridussero la luce dei passaggi a circa la metà di quella originaria[4].

Lungo il percorso del portico esterno, ai lati dell'ingresso meridionale, alcuni degli ambienti radiali formati dalle sostruzioni della *cavea* presentano modifiche strutturali che ne segnalano particolari funzioni, connesse con la vita associativa delle corporazioni puteolane: alcuni erano sicuramente utilizzati come *scholae*, per altri la funzione di sede sociale è solo indiziaria[5]. Questi interventi, il rinforzo dei pilastri e la realizzazione delle *scholae*, sono riconducibili alla seconda metà del II secolo, in base allo studio dei pavimenti delle seconde che, in parte, si addossano ai primi[6].

Il loggiato superiore (fig. 2), invece doveva essere largo circa 7.50 m, contava in tutto 72 colonne, scanalate, poste in corrispondenza dei pilastri degli archi della *summa cavea*, alla distanza reciproca di circa 3.90 m, pari a 4 ½ volte il diametro di base[7]. Non è nota la forma delle trabeazioni che dovevano essere in trachite. I fusti delle colonne della *porticus in summa cavea* erano ricavate da un unico blocco, se ne conserva un solo esemplare intero e 127 frammentari[8]. Unica anche la base conservata, di tipo attico semplice[9].

Un'annotazione riguarda il materiale, il marmo proconnesio, che, come dimostrano i nostri materiali, risulta impiegato a Pozzuoli già in epoca Flavia, con notevole anticipo rispetto al periodo della sua grande diffusione, il II secolo d.C., ma in perfetta coerenza con quanto avviene in Campania, dove questo materiale è già noto nel restauro dei monumenti pompeiani dopo il terremoto del 62[10].

Un certo numero di fusti, oltre a 18 capitelli, fu spogliato e ridotto in calce, come del resto numerosissime sculture, in fornaci rinvenute negli stessi locali dell'anfiteatro[11].

Le colonne presentano rapporti non canonici: quello tra il diametro di base e l'altezza del fusto è di 3:16 , pari a quello tra l'altezza del capitello e quella del fusto, di contro ad una consuetudine che prevede rapporti di 2:15; 7:50 e 11:80.[12] Le colonne si presentano, quindi, piuttosto tozze e con un capitello sproporzionatamente alto[13]. Il fatto potrebbe essere messo in relazione con la presenza del velario. Il telo, infatti, era retto da antenne orizzontali appoggiate direttamente sulla trabeazione del portico[14]. In questo caso, quanto maggiore è l'altezza della colonna, tanto maggiore deve essere la lunghezza delle antenne per consentire di coprire la porzione maggiore di spalti sottostanti. Il fusto era, quindi, così tozzo per permettere l'utilizzo di travi orizzontali, lignee, di minore lunghezza; il capitello, invece, era sproporzionatamente alto perché, visto dal basso, non risultasse eccessivamente schiacciato.

Oltre a questi, i materiali conservatisi forniscono un gran numero di dati di ogni tipo: è infatti possibile dedurne indizi cronologici per il completamento dell'opera e per i restauri; una serie di modalità d'intervento nello sviluppo dei restauri stessi - dei quali si hanno tracce su numerosi capitelli e su quasi tutti i fusti conservati; nonché le informazioni utili a ricostruire l'articolazione dell'officina che li produsse.

Esamineremo i vari aspetti dei nostri elementi architettonici separatamente.

Colonne e capitelli: restauri e rilavorazioni

Numerosissimi frammenti presentano tracce di restauri e rilavorazioni riconducibili a tre diverse tipologie: alcuni fusti sono stati suddivisi in sezioni più piccole, nelle quali uno dei piani, quello di posa o quello di attesa, è stato lisciato, e vi è stato ricavato, in genere, un foro rettangolare per un grosso perno (in media 10 x 10 cm). Si conservano 17 esemplari così rilavorati (fig. 4) , che presentano un'altezza minima di 61 cm ed un'altezza massima di 300 cm.

Spesso su uno o più lati sono stati ricavati incassi per la giunzione di un'altra sezione di fusto o, forse, per tasselli di restauro o staffe. La presenza di rilavorazioni per staffe o tasselli è stata riscontrata in nove casi (cfr. fig. 5).
Infine, molto spesso l'imoscapo o il sommoscapo hanno subito rilavorazioni e riadattamenti. In alcuni casi è stata semplicemente tagliata una sezione del cerchio, magari per regolarizzare una frattura; in altri la parte è stata completamente riprofilata.

Non riconducibili alle tipologie sopra descritte è un caso isolato: un frammento di fusto (fig. 6) presenta sul piano d'attesa un profondo incasso a 'V' con le pareti lavorate a subbia e lisciate a gradina, evidentemente per essere incastrato e ricongiunto con un altro (fig. 7).

Anche numerosi capitelli presentano tracce evidenti di rilavorazioni. L'intervento più macroscopico si nota in alcuni casi in cui i capitelli si sono evidentemente spezzati nella caduta. In questi casi i pezzi sono stati rilavorati per essere ricongiunti, come avviene nell'esempio presentato in figg. 8-9. Quando il restauro non è stato così macroscopico le zone più interessate dagli interventi sono, naturalmente: abaco, fiore, elici e volute, caulicoli, ma anche la zona inferiore del *kalathos*.

La caduta delle colonne deve aver causato frequentemente la rottura degli angoli dell'abaco, in questi casi per lo più gli scalpellini si sono limitati a staccare eventuali pezzi lesionati o fratturati (fig 10), come si deduce chiaramente dalle tracce di strumenti, per lo più subbia e, più raramente gradina larga, leggibili sulle fratture[15]. In altri casi l'angolo dell'abaco è stato ridisegnato abbassando la superficie di uno dei lati, come accade nel capitello nr. 25 (fig. 11); oppure interamente ridotto e rilavorato: le misure *standard* del lato dell'abaco, che si aggirano intorno ai 110 cm (3 piedi e ¾),[16] sono state in alcuni casi ridotte di 2/3 di piede, e portate a circa 90 cm,[17] restituendo il profilo rettangolare ai capitelli danneggiati, ma naturalmente riducendo la curvatura dei lati dell'abaco. In questi casi le volute, evidentemente spezzatesi nella caduta, sono state definitivamente eliminate e le fratture normalizzate lisciando la superficie ed abbassandola in modo che risultassero nascoste dietro la cima aggettante delle foglie, o quanto di questa restasse. Numerosi i casi in cui il fiore è stato scalpellato, la superficie che rimane esposta è stata spesso rilavorata con subbia e scalpello, od unghietto.

Anche elici e volute, sia del tipo piatto che di quello con profilo concavo, subiscono rilavorazioni: quando, dopo la frattura, lo scalpellino ha abbastanza marmo a disposizione, regolarizza il profilo degli elementi che rimangono abbassando la superficie e lisciandola. Se gli elementi erano in origine a sezione concava, e l'artigiano ne ha la possibilità, restituisce il profilo originario, altrimenti si limita a lisciare la superficie. Due sono gli esempi migliori: nel capitello nr. 24 (fig. 12) si nota chiaramente che la superficie dell'elice danneggiata è stata abbassata usando una subbia, la cui punta ha lasciato segni evidenti alla base dell'elemento, e lisciata a gradina e scalpello. Nella fattispecie, come si vede chiaramente, il profilo originale era a sezione concava, mentre la rilavorazione lascia la superficie piana. Nel caso del pezzo nr. 2 (fig. 13), volute e foglie dei caulicoli sono state scalpellate, l'elice, molto ridotta, è stata abbassata e l'originario profilo a sezione concava restituito. Anche le fratture delle foglie d'acanto in cima sono state talvolta regolarizzate, ma, tranne che in un caso, non vi è traccia dei tasselli che, solitamente, vengono inseriti per integrare le lacune.

Capitelli tipologia e cronologia

I 54 capitelli attribuibili al portico furono dal Maiuri tutti considerati appartenenti allo stesso tipo e datati al passaggio tra il regno di Domiziano e quello di Traiano. In realtà la serie non è affatto omogenea. Nel gruppo più numeroso (figg.13) 50 pezzi, le foglie d'acanto delle due corone presentano una costolatura centrale ampia e quattro minori, due per lato, che raccolgono i cinque lobi. La costolatura mediana è percorsa al centro, per tutta la sua lunghezza, da un profondo solco, e, in alto, da due piccole scanalature che segnalano l'articolazione delle fogliette della cima. I lobi inferiori si articolano in tre fogliette, quelli superiori in quattro, la cima in sette. Le digitazioni formano, sovrapponendosi, in ogni foglia quattro zone d'ombra ad occhielli stretti ed allungati. Elici e volute sono per lo più a sezione concava, anche se in alcuni pezzi sono lisce, sempre però ricoperte, nel tratto inferiore, dalle foglie dei cauli. Queste presentano le fogliette che si sovrappongono, formando, sotto le volute, zone d'ombra a goccia, sotto le elici la classica sequenza di un occhiello e due triangolini. I caulicoli sono fortemente inclinati, con il corpo ricoperto da tre-quattro fogliette d'acqua. Il collarino può presentarsi in forma di elemento tortile; essere dotato di coroncina di sepali, sia semplice che alternata a fogliette d'acqua, oppure recare un *kyma* lesbio continuo. L'abaco presenta ovolo semicircolare e cavetto molto profondo; l'orlo del *kalathos* è ben distinto ed ha andamento perfettamente circolare. Il fiore dell'abaco si imposta su uno stelo ingrossato che sorge, solitamente, da un calicetto a due foglie. Il tipo in esame si inserisce in una tradizione claudio-flavia di capitelli che presentano caratteri tipologici analoghi e morfologia in evoluzione, a partire dalla metà del I d.C. e terminare in epoca adrianea, il cui modello di riferimento risale, in ultima analisi, all'età augustea. All'interno di questo gruppo i nostri trovano i migliori confronti con esemplari collocabili in piena età domizianea[18].

Quattro capitelli (figg. 14-15), invece, presentano le foglie d'acanto con la costolatura mediana larga ed appiattita, sulla quale, in alto due lunghi solchi paralleli che si prolungano fin oltre alla metà della sua lunghezza. Si tratta dello sviluppo delle piccole incisioni presenti in alcuni tipi cronologicamente precedenti, che segnalavano l'attacco delle fogliette laterali della cima. Le fogliette, tre-quattro per ognuno dei cinque lobi, formano quattro zone d'ombra a triangolino allungato. I cauli verticali, sono appena rilevati dal corpo del *kalathos*, segnati da una profonda scanalatura allargata in alto ad Y, a simulare ai lati le due lunghe fogliette d'acqua. Presentano un fine collarino di sepali, in alcuni casi lavorati in foglioline acantizzanti a cinque lobi, punteggiate di fori di trapano. Volute ed elici sono piatte. L'abaco reca ovolo quasi piatto e cavetto poco profondo. L'orlo del *kalathos* è molto allargato e, talora, non perfettamente circolare. Il fiore è, generalmente, privo di stelo; quando questo è presente è appena accennato, decisamente disorganico, con un calice molto alto, formato da fogliette frastagliate che arrivano all'altezza delle elici. Il tipo al quale appartengono i nostri capitelli è molto diffuso a partire dall'epoca antonina e per tutta l'età severiana[19].

Sembra, dunque, che si possa aggiungere a quanto già noto per le strutture inferiori, anche la notizia di una ristrutturazione della *porticus in summa cavea*, operazione che comportò, come abbiamo visto, il restauro di numerosissimi pezzi, tra colonne e capitelli, e la sostituzione di alcuni capitelli. Quanto alla cronologia di questo intervento, l'esame stilistico dei quattro pezzi più tardi sembra confermare l'ipotesi fatta dal Maiuri per i restauri dei fornici.

Prenderemo di seguito in esame il gruppo più antico e numeroso

I capitelli dell'anfiteatro: proposta per una lettura analitica del segno.

I capitelli del loggiato superiore dell'anfiteatro maggiore di Pozzuoli offrono un'ottima occasione per approfondire l'indagine sulla decorazione architettonica da un punto di vista finora poco sviluppato nella storia degli studi. La circostanza di trovarsi di fronte ad una serie numericamente consistente e tipologicamente omogenea ci consente di analizzare le variazioni formali e stilistiche, nonché i particolari esecutivi dei pezzi e di proporre un quadro interpretativo.

I capitelli del gruppo più antico, se confrontati tra loro, presentano una serie di piccole e grandi differenze. Tenteremo di rendere ragione di queste differenze, proponendo un modello interpretativo in cui speriamo esse possano trovare posto.

Il primo ordine di variazioni riguarda la forma assunta da alcuni elementi ornamentali, innanzitutto **volute ed elici**, inquadrabili nella tipologia che segue, e che tiene conto delle frequenti rilavorazioni subite dai capitelli in questa zona:

Tipo 1: superficie liscia e piana (fig. 13)
Tipo 2: nastro a sezione concava, più o meno angolosa, inquadrata da due listelli (fig. 14)
Tipo 3: superficie originaria abbassata e rilavorata a sezione concava (fig. 13)
Tipo 4: superficie originaria abbassata e rilavorata con andamento liscio e piano (fig. 12)

Ancora, i **caulicoli** possono distinguersi sotto più rispetti. La distinzione più macroscopica riguarda la forma assunta dalla decorazione del collarino, secondo il seguente elenco:

Tipo 1: motivo a treccia
Tipo 2: fila di sepali lisci

Tipo 3: *kyma* di sepali lisci separati da elementi lanceolati (fig. 21)
Tipo 4: *kyma* di foglioline cuoriformi alternate ad elementi lanceolati (figg. 17;18)
Tipo 5: *kyma* capovolto di foglioline cuoriformi alternate ad elementi lanceolati.

Il **calicetto** del fiore dell'abaco è sempre presente, così come lo stelo ed il fiore stesso. Proprio questo elemento decorativo dà luogo alla maggior parte delle variazioni riscontrabili nel repertorio dei nostri capitelli, ma non tutte sono di natura tipologica. Da questo punto di vista, le varianti si limitano a due soli tipi:
Tipo 1: calicetto aperto (cfr. ad es. fig. 17)
Tipo 2: calicetto chiuso.

L'**acanto** si presenta tipologicamente omogeneo; le foglie differiscono però nella decorazione della costolatura centrale, che si articola nelle seguenti varianti:[20]
Tipo a: foglietta lanceolata sovrapposta alla costolatura mediana con digitazioni che formano occhielli circolari interi sul margine, completati dall'indicazione del profilo interno della digitazione ottenuto con un sottile intaglio obliquo.
Tipo a1: semplificazione del precedente, la decorazione si limita all'indicazione degli occhielli circolari sul margine della costolatura centrale, la cui continuità è interrotta dai forellini stessi.
Tipo b: serie di incisioni oblique condotte dalla linea mediana della costolatura centrale al suo margine.
Tipo c: costolatura liscia (fig.18)

Le variazioni morfologiche sopra descritte sono state schematizzate nella Tabella A. Si è preferito indicare la descrizione schematica di tutti i lati leggibili di ognuno dei capitelli, poiché all'interno di ogni singolo pezzo sono evidenti significative variazioni nella forma di singoli elementi. Un semplice sguardo basta a chiarirsi le idee sulla natura delle variazioni sopra descritte. Il ricorrere all'interno di uno stesso capitello, di tipi differenti di caulicoli, calicetti, volute, decorazioni accessorie delle foglie d'acanto chiarisce incontrovertibilmente che le suddette variazioni non dipendono da differenti modelli utilizzati dagli artigiani[21]. Anche l'acanto, pur con le limitazioni sopra indicate, non presenta costanti nelle variazioni della rifinitura della costolatura centrale, se non una comparsa del tipo a1, qualitativamente migliore, solo nei capitelli meglio rifiniti, vale a dire quelli con caulicoli di tipo 4 o, molto più raramente, di tipo 3. In sostanza, è tanto alto il numero delle varianti generate dalle diverse combinazioni delle tipologie dei singoli elementi decorativi, che se si volesse spiegarle con l'esistenza di modelli differenti bisognerebbe supporne un gran numero.

In realtà tutte le variazioni sopra analizzate, sintetizzate, schematizzate sono da imputare a differenti gradi di finitura degli stessi elementi. Pare evidente che, eccezion fatta per il tipo 1, tutti i caulicoli siano una semplificazione del 4, essendo il tipo 3 un tipo 4 con fogliette cuoriformi non rifinite e lasciate lisce; ed il tipo 2 un'ulteriore banalizzazione che non prevede neanche la presenza dei separatori tra i sepali. Così volute ed elici di tipo 1, lisce e piatte, sono una semplificazione di 2, modanate ed a sezione concava; mentre i tipi 3-4 devono essere la restituzione degli originali 2-1 in capitelli danneggiati dalla caduta, anche se abbiamo visto che in alcuni casi elementi in origine con sezione concava vengono restaurati a superficie piana.

Un discorso a parte è necessario per i calicetti del fiore dell'abaco. Questi elementi sono stati raggruppati in due tipi, seguendo l'inquadramento che il Freyberger ha utilizzato per lo studio dei capitelli romani tra Domiziano ed Alessandro Severo[22]. In realtà la distinzione tra gli uni e gli altri, per quanto indubbiamente possibile, nel nostro caso non è nettissima e quelli chiusi sono in realtà dei calicetti aperti in cui la zona di separazione tra le due fogliette è stata peggio sagomata e resa con maggiore semplificazione.

Da queste osservazioni discendono una serie di domande: se il modello alla base di tutte le redazioni doveva essere unico, è possibile ricostruirlo ? Se le variazioni morfologiche che si colgono tra i diversi capitelli, o tra le diverse facce di uno stesso capitello, sono in parte riconducibili a differenti gradi di rifinitura, è possibile che i lati meglio rifiniti siano tali per esigenze dovute alla posizione del pezzo nel portico ? Se, come si è lasciato intendere, alla base di una serie di differenze morfologiche non c'è sempre una semplice banalizzazione del modello, come possono essere spiegate ?

Andiamo con ordine. Sulla base di quanto si è detto, è sicuramente possibile ricostruire il modello base dei nostri capitelli: esso doveva prevedere abaco modanato con ovolo semicircolare e cavetto molto profondo; orlo del *kalathos* ben distinto ed ha andamento perfettamente circolare con volute ed elici a sezione concava; caulicoli inclinati con corpo baccellato e collarino rivestito da un *kyma* lesbio continuo formato da foglie cuoriformi alternate ad elementi lanceolati; fiore e stelo sempre presente, calicetto leggermente aperto; doppia foglia d'acanto con costolatura mediana rivestita da fogliette separate da occhielli d'ombra circolari resi con fori di trapano.

Quanto alla seconda domanda, non sembra possibile connettere automaticamente il maggior grado di rifinitura di alcuni capitelli, o lati di capitelli, con la loro posizione all'interno del portico. Alcuni pezzi uniformemente rifiniti, vale a dire sia con un grado di rifinitura uniforme nei singoli elementi decorativi che con una finitura uniforme di tutti i quattro lati, come ad esempio i nnrr. 6; 12; 16; 22; 23; 50, potevano senz'altro essere tali perché dovevano occupare i posti più prossimi agli accessi, od alle scalinate. Ma nella maggior parte dei casi all'interno di ogni singolo capitello, il grado di rifinitura dei lati è omogeneo per lati contigui. Facciamo un esempio: nei capitelli nr. 21; 33 o 47 due lati contigui presentano un grado di finitura tra loro omogeneo, con collarino dei caulicoli a *kyma* con foglie cuoriformi (tipo 4) ed acanto con costolatura decorata (tipo a1), ma diverso da quello delle altre due facce, peggio rifinite, con caulicoli a sepali e lancette (tipo 3) ed acanto liscio (tipo c). Questo dà luogo a capitelli con lati opposti sempre diseguali, come diseguali tra loro sono due dei lati contigui, per cui non è possibile supporre che il pezzo fosse meglio lavorato nei lati più esposti, quello verso l'arena e quello verso il portico, perché in nessuno di loro due lati opposti si presentano entrambi ben rifiniti. E lo stesso discorso vale, naturalmente, per i lati posti sugli *intercolumni*. Oltre tutto, la circostanza che anche all'interno di ogni singolo lato si presentino differenti gradi di rifinitura nei particolari, come appare evidente dalla circostanza che nello stesso lato di un capitello si trovano caulicoli di tipo differente, vale a scoraggiare una soluzione semplicistica del problema[23]. In realtà la qualità dell'esecuzione è strettamente legata alla competenza ed all'abilità dei singoli scalpellini che, visto il livello dell'officina, non doveva essere mediamente alta. Gli artigiani più abili realizzano alcuni pezzi meglio rifiniti, che, come si è detto, dovevano occupare posti più sensibili nel portico, ma non tengono sotto controllo la qualità di tutti i capitelli.

L'ultima domanda concerne la possibilità di interpretare almeno una parte delle differenze tra i singoli elementi decorativi come l'indice del lavoro di mani differenti su uno stesso modello. Abbiamo finora inquadrato le differenze morfologiche degli elementi decorativi all'interno di uno schema tipologico, cercando di capire fino a che punto le loro variazioni fossero provocate dall'adozione di tipologie differenti. Ma un'analisi attenta consente di ravvisare differenze a volte minime, altre volte più evidenti, all'interno di serie di elementi ornamentali del medesimo tipo. Un ottimo esempio sono i calicetti del fiore dell'abaco. All'interno dei due tipi si possono distinguere calici di almeno sette forme differenti, a volte affini tra loro, altre totalmente diverse. Così avviene pure nei quattro diversi tipi di caulicoli, nonché nella resa delle foglie d'acanto. Nei primi le differenze vanno dal diverso trattamento dei collarini - con fogliette più o meno staccate; uso del trapano maggiore o minore, ovvero più o meno dissimulato – alla differente conformazione delle digitazioni dell'acanto; alla resa diversa delle baccellature che ricoprono il corpo. Nelle seconde la resa di lobi e fogliette cambia in modo da dare luogo ad elementi più o meno lunghi, più o meno appuntiti e, di conseguenza, a zone d'ombra di forma o inclinazione leggermente diversa. Ripetiamo che tutte queste variazioni non sono di natura tipologica, perché non sono varianti morfologiche, vale a dire che sono dovute a differenze nella resa dei singoli elementi. Sono piuttosto assimilabili ai ben noti "elementi morelliani", largamente studiati ed impiegati nel campo della storia dell'arte moderna per stabilire la paternità di opere prive di firma o documenti di accompagnamento, e che, applicati agli studi archeologici, hanno consentito l'approfondimento in particolare della pittura vascolare e della scultura[24]. Nel campo dell'arte decorativa, ed in particolare in quello della decorazione architettonica, i metodi sviluppati dal Morelli nel XIX secolo sono stati recentemente applicati con notevole successo da J. Rohmann nello studio dei capitelli pergameni dell'inizio del II secolo d.C.[25] Lo studioso tedesco si confronta con una serie di pezzi fortemente standardizzati e che, per l'evoluzione tipologica propria della classe alla quale appartengono, presentano nel II secolo ormai alcuni importanti elementi decorativi, come i caulicoli, decisamente atrofizzati ed altri, come le foglie-calicetto, di forma rigidamente codificata. Questo stato del materiale ha costretto il Rohmann a spingere l'analisi ad un grado di profondità tale che gli è stato necessario osservare particolari estremamente minuti per identificare ciò che egli chiama la firma (*Handschrift*) di ciascuno scalpellino. Fortunatamente i nostri pezzi sono, come si è visto, molto meno standardizzati, hanno superfici poco schematizzate in confronto a quelli, orientali e più tardi, studiati dall'archeologo tedesco, presentano caulicoli ben sviluppati e differenze formali a volta ben evidenti nella resa dei singoli elementi decorativi, altre decisamente più difficili da rintracciare. Tutte queste differenze sono senz'altro frutto di diversi modi di utilizzare gli strumenti, così come questi modi sono figli di una formazione differente per ognuno degli artigiani, a cominciare dal maestro dal quale hanno imparato, nel caso dei capi officina, o dallo scalpellino al quale sono stati affiancati, nel caso degli artigiani meno esperti o ancora in formazione, per finire con l'abilità propria di ciascuno di essi.

Nell'esame che segue si sono tenuti in considerazione gli elementi relativi alla resa dei singoli motivi ornamentali, ed è stato possibile individuare alcune zone particolarmente sensibili per l'individuazione di questi particolari, le elenchiamo di seguito: *caulicoli*: la forma delle fogliette interne e le zone d'ombra cui queste danno luogo; il collarino, le baccellature che rivestono il corpo; *calicetto*: le proporzioni e l'apertura; il contatto tra le fogliette ed il rivestimento delle elici; la forma delle fogliette e la rifinitura dell'insenatura centrale tra queste; la base acanto: la forma e l'inclinazione dei lobi e delle fogliette; la sovrapposizione delle fogliette stesse e le zone d'ombra da queste formate.

Descriviamo di seguito le caratteristiche proprie di ciascun artigiano, così come ci è sembrato di poterle individuare.

A (fig. 16)
Scolpisce praticamente sempre volute ed elici a sezione concava; le elici sono leggermente ristrette e sensibilmente rialzate, in modo da incorniciare in alto un ampio spazio bordato ai lati dai caulicoli ed occupato al centro dal calice del fiore dell'abaco.

Lo spazio tra i caulicoli è sempre ben definito ed i contorni degli elementi sono netti e metallici, molto plastici. Il calice del fiore è piccolo, centrato, sempre staccato dalla punta delle elici. Lo scalpellino sagoma bene il solco che divide le due fogliette, sottolineando il punto in cui queste si dipartono con una sorta di tacca orizzontale ben definita e lavorata a scalpello. La base del calicetto è invariabilmente piana; le fogliette sono fortemente ripiegate all'infuori, il loro profilo inferiore è sagomato ad 'S', in modo che la foglietta assuma una forma vagamente cuoriforme e si presenti appuntita.

Le fogliette dei caulicoli si sovrappongono in maniera decisa, in particolare è caratteristico di quest'artigiano il modo accentuato nel quale ripiega la foglietta inferiore dei caulicoli, quasi ad angolo retto, ottenendo occhielli allargati ed abbastanza dritti, sormontati immediatamente da una seconda zona d'ombra triangolare, e da una terza più distanziata ed esterna, con il vertice aperto in alto.

Lo scalpellino 'A' scolpisce caulicoli di forma disorganica: mentre sul lato interno il collare è coerente con il corpo, all'esterno esso non piega, è condotto secondo una linea dritta e riceve la sovrapposizione dei lobi superiori della prima corona di foglie; il corpo in alto è più sottile.

Questo artigiano per lo più rifinisce il collarino del caule con un *kyma* di foglie cuoriformi ed elementi lanceolati. Egli stacca gli elementi col trapano e, poi, ne rifinisce i profili a scalpello, ma non lavora in profondità, il che comporta la presenza di due linee continue orizzontali che inquadrano, in alto ed in basso, il collarino. Le foglioline sono unite in basso da un sottile tratto di marmo, ridotto al minimo da un foro di trapano, che serve anche a definire l'elemento lanceolato, ma ben visibile; ognuna di esse è poi sagomata.

In alcuni casi (capitello nr. 50), il lavoro non è rifinito, i tratti interni e la sagoma esterna delle foglioline cuoriformi non sono delineati, ma anche qui tra i sepali, che vengono a sostituire i cuoricini, l'elemento lanceolato è ben distinto e si nota il lavoro di trapano appena mascherato dallo scalpello.

Il corpo del caulicolo è rivestito di baccellature strette ed allungate, a sezione concava anche negli esemplari meno rifiniti. In alto le baccellature si piegano bruscamente, appoggiandosi all'orlo inferiore del collarino sopra descritto.

Le foglie d'acanto (fig 18), per lo più di tipo a e b, hanno i lobi laterali superiori che piegano bruscamente all'infuori, ne risultano zone d'ombra più strette ed allungate. Le foglioline hanno un profilo fortemente arrotondato.

B (figg. 17)
Questo artigiano scolpisce prevalentemente volute ed elici lisce, pochi i casi in cui queste presentano un profilo a sezione concava, alcuni dei quali sono rilavorazioni. Anche egli restringe e rialza le elici. Lo spazio tra i calulicoli è occupato da un calicetto simile a quello realizzato dallo scalpellino 'A', ma centrato peggio, in genere troppo alto in modo che le fogliette tocchino la parte inferiore delle volute. Anche qui l'artigiano sagoma il solco che divide le due fogliette, sottolineando il punto in cui queste si dipartono con una sorta di tacca orizzontale, ma ha spesso bisogno di un maggior numero di colpi di scalpello e quello che in 'A' è una superficie liscia ed uniforme diviene qui un piano sfaccettato. Le foglioline, ben allargate, non si ripiegano svasandosi, ma restano orizzontali e il profilo inferiore è brusco, non dà luogo alla sagoma a cuore e forma una punta allungata. Le fogliette dei caulicoli sono più oblique, piegano meno decisamente e formano zone d'ombra più piccole ed inclinate. Si tratta di triangolini stretti ed allungati; le fogliette sono praticamente parallele tra loro, così le zone d'ombra, ravvicinate, si dispongono su una verticale leggermente piegata verso l'interno. Il corpo del caule è ingrossato, ma solitamente organicamente descritto, eccezion fatta per il consueto errore nella sovrapposizione con i lobi superiori delle foglie d'acanto della prima corona. Anche l'artigiano 'B' utilizza molto il trapano, ma lo fa con meno maestria di 'A'. Anch'egli rifinisce il collarino del caule con un *kyma* di foglie cuoriformi ed elementi lanceolati, e stacca gli elementi col trapano rifinendone poi il profilo a scalpello, ricavando le due linee continue orizzontali che inquadrano, in alto ed in basso, il collarino. La fogliolina del *kyma* è però raramente sagomata, si allarga parecchio in basso, fatto probabilmente dovuto all'impreciso uso del trapano che ha comportato, nel successivo lavoro a scalpello, l'allargamento della sagoma stessa. I fori del trapano sono spesso ben visibili, e, in proporzione, è maggiore il numero di casi nei quali le fogliette dei *kymatia* non sono lavorate a cuore, ma lasciate allo stadio di semplici sepali. Le fogliette sono staccate tra di loro.

Il corpo del caulicolo si presenta ingrossato, definito da baccellature più allargate, a sezione concava. Il tratto interno delle foglie come del collarino è spesso lasciato liscio, o sommariamente lavorato.

Le foglie d'acanto, di tipo 'a' e 'c', sono più allungate e sembrano più staccate dal *kalathos*, i lobi superiori sono disposti più in diagonale che non dritti e poi svasati; le fogliette dei lobi inferiori toccano i lobi superiori non con la sola punta, ma con tutta la parte superiore del margine laterale; ne risultano zone d'ombra molto strette ed allungate con una sorta di sottile virgola in alto.

C

Questo scalpellino lavora esclusivamente elici e volute lisce, dal profilo pesante, allargate e ribassate. Al centro di ogni lato sta un calicetto ribassato, in alto invariabilmente tangente alle elici, di forma allargata in basso. Le foglioline sono appena sagomate, l'insenatura centrale è dritta, a 'V', e priva del tratto orizzontale in basso. Le foglioline, orizzontali, si piegano appena verso il basso, dove presentano un profilo tondeggiante appena rientrante verso la punta.

Le foglie dei caulicoli, molto ribassate a causa dell'allargamento delle elici, sono semplificate ed appiattite, le digitazioni, arrotondate, si sovrappongono formando in basso piccole gocce con la punta a virgola in alto, sormontate da due triangoli con il vertice chiuso in alto. A causa dell'apertura a ventaglio delle fogliette che le formano, le tre zone d'ombra, distanziate, si dispongono lungo un arco ampio con il culmine rivolto verso il calicetto.

I caulicoli sono di forma ingrossata, il collarino presenta il consueto *kyma* con elementi staccati a trapano, ma rifiniti solo sommariamente a scalpello. La presenza della linea continua orizzontali che inquadra in alto il collarino, notata in precedenza sia per 'A' che per 'B', è estremamente ridotta dall'abitudine di ricavare le lancette definendole semplicemente con due solchi ottenuti col trapano e lisciati con lo scalpello, con andamento a 'Y'. Gli elementi di separazione assumono così la forma semplificata di triangolini col vertice in basso. La fogliolina del *kyma* è molto allargata in basso ed i suoi contorni sono appena definiti, ma ognuna è staccata dall'altra. Quando l'artigiano 'C' tenta di sagomare le foglioline il risultato è una sottile linea continua parallela al margine della fogliolina stessa, che non rende affatto l'inclinazione del piano propria delle realizzazioni di 'A'. Le baccellature sul corpo dei cauli sono più allargate, spesso piatte, sagomate anche in alto, dove piegano bruscamente verso l'esterno e sono staccate l'una dall'altra, fatto che provoca l'assenza della linea continua che bordava il collarino in basso sia nei capitelli scolpiti da 'A' che in quelli di 'B'.

Nei lobi dell'acanto le fogliette, dalla punta appena sfaccettata, si aprono a ventaglio dando luogo a zone d'ombra più dritte e triangolari sottolineate da profonde incisioni orizzontali.

D (figg. 18-19)

Lo scalpellino 'D' scolpisce elici e volute prevalentemente lisce. Lo stelo del fiore dell'abaco è generalmente storto, inclinato verso la destra di chi guarda; il calicetto ha forma allungata, più stretta in basso rispetto a quelli scolpiti dai precedenti. L'insenatura tra le foglioline è, in genere, leggermente inclinata, ed è indicata con una semplice scanalatura rettilinea non sagomata. Le foglioline si piegano verso il basso solo in punta, e spesso quella a destra è più in basso della sinistra, cosicché il calicetto dà la sgradevole impressione di essere leggermente inclinato a destra.

Le fogliette dei caulicoli sono strette ed appuntite, accorciate rispetto alle precedenti si appoggiano ai lobi accanto solo con la punta formando piccole zone d'ombra triangolari, la prima con il vertice rivolto verso il calicetto, le altre con il vertice in alto, ravvicinate ed allineate lungo uno stretto arco con il culmine verso il centro del lato. Anche il corpo ed il collarino del caule sono lavorati sommariamente e danno l'impressione di essere estremamente schiacciati. Il collarino è per lo più ribassato, di dimensioni ridotte che lasciano l'impressione di una certa disorganicità; le foglioline cuoriformi risultano da una sorta di linea sinusoidale continua definite da profonde incisioni a 'V' aperte alternativamente in basso (al centro di ogni fogliolina), ed in alto (tra due foglioline), dove il vuoto è riempito dai triangolini che costituiscono la semplificazione delle lancette. Il procedimento è simile a quello adottato da 'C' il quale però scolpisce solchi interni alle foglioline più stretti, e le separa con incisioni ad 'Y', non a 'V', staccando così più decisamente le foglioline l'una dall'altra ed attenuando l'impressione del *kyma* continuo. I caulicoli sono rivestiti dalle consuete baccellature, per lo più dritte e con i margini in alto bruscamente ripiegati verso l'esterno.

Anche le foglie d'acanto (fig.19) sono estremamente semplificate: le fogliette, appuntite, sono descritte sommariamente da incisioni nella parte inferiore, formano occhielli d'ombra triangolari, verticali, stretti ed allungati.

E (figg. 20-21)

Scolpisce volute ed elici indifferentemente lisce o a sezione concava. Il calicetto presenta lo stelo sempre perfettamente centrato, è di forma ingrossata. La linea che divide le fogliette scende in basso fino alla base. Le foglie sono fortemente estroflesse e ripiegate, presentano un profilo semplificato ed un punta allungata.

L'acanto dei caulicoli presenta fogliette allungate e dalla punta pronunciata. Quelle più interne sono fortemente ripiegate e formano in basso una zona d'ombra a goccia allargata, mentre, allargandosi a ventaglio, le fogliette superiori formano piccoli triangoli aperti in alto.

I caulicoli, pur con i difetti generalizzati, hanno un collarino abbastanza coerente, ornato generalmente da coroncine di sepali separati dal trapano, che incide profondi segni ad 'Y' lasciando in alto triangolini pieni che sostituiscono le lancette. I sepali hanno forma quasi ovale, l'artigiano lavora usando il trapano obliquamente, per definire l'intero profilo degli elementi, non si limita a forare il marmo e poi a rifinire a scalpello. Quando le foglie sono lavorate a cuore la linea interna è stretta, e la forma dei separatori del *kyma* resta identica a quella che assumono nel *kyma* liscio.

Il collarino presenta in basso una linea continua alla quale si appoggiano le baccellature.

Le foglie d'acanto delle due corone presentano lobi che si aprono a ventaglio verso l'esterno; i due laterali superiori salgono dritti, paralleli alla costolatura mediana, per poi piegare all'esterno. Le digitazioni sono lavorate in modo che le fogliette si sovrappongano non solo con le punte, ma si appoggino anche in parte di lato. Si formano così zone d'ombra a goccia stretta in alto ed allargata in basso, leggermente inclinate.

F

Scolpisce elici preferibilmente piatte. I calicetti sono bassi, stretti in basso, con le foglie molto allargate, separate al centro da un breve tratto a 'V', dal quale sorge, sempre lievemente spostato a sinistra, lo stelo.
L'acanto dei caulicoli presenta fogliette corte ed appuntite che, all'interno, formano una sola zona d'ombra a goccia, in alto leggermente inclinate all'interno.

I caulicoli sono piuttosto appiattiti, le linee che inquadrano i collarini scolpiti da 'A' e 'B' sono completamente scomparse. I sepali sono delineati chiaramente, assumono un profilo lanceolato, definito ai lati ed in basso da una serie di fori di trapano spesso non cancellati con lo scalpello. Gli elementi di separazione sono appuntiti. Quando i sepali sono lavorati in forma di cuore lo scalpellino produce un solco allargato e dritto che separa i due lobi della foglietta, con un effetto di piatto schematismo. Le baccellature sono ben separate da solchi di trapano allargati e ben evidenti.

Anche le foglie d'acanto sono piuttosto piatte, aderenti al *kalathos* e poco aggettanti. Le fogliette sono strette ed appena distinte, le punte arrotondate formano zone d'ombra oblunghe, strette e diritte.

G (figg. 14; 22)

Questo scalpellino predilige forme semplificate che rende con molta approssimazione. Volute ed elici, per lo più lisce, sono ribassate; al centro del lato il calicetto è alto, stretto in basso, dove la linea di contorno piega definendo un profilo bombato. La linea mediana è stretta e talora non si ferma, raggiungendo la base. Le foglioline sono piegate all'infuori, una delle due, solitamente la destra, è più alta ed ingrossata dell'altra. Lo stelo è decentrato, non sorge dal centro del calicetto, ma poggia sulla fogliolina di sinistra e si piega a destra.

Il caulicolo è estremamente semplificato: le fogliette dell'acanto sono allungate ed appuntite, si aprono a raggiera; quella più bassa ed interna risulta obliqua e forma una zona d'ombra bassa e tondeggiante. La mancata definizione degli elementi vegetali più interni ai quali si sovrappongono le fogliette superiori, e la lunghezza di queste, non consentono la formazione dei consueti triangoli, ma danno luogo a semplici punti scuri aperti in alto.

Il collarino è asimmetrico ed obliquo, più stretto all'esterno si allarga sensibilmente all'interno, dove la parte non lavorata è più estesa rispetto a quella riscontrata nelle esecuzioni degli altri artigiani. Nel conformare il collarino l'artigiano dà la precedenza alla definizione delle fogliette, che tende a staccare e delineare, ma rifinisce raramente in forma di cuore. In questi casi, quando cioè la foglietta è lasciata allo stadio di semplice sepalo, l'elemento di separazione non compare. All'opposto, nei collarini più rifiniti la lancetta si riduce ad una piccola punta ricavata scavando il marmo dall'esterno verso l'interno e non dall'alto verso il basso. Le baccellature che rivestono il corpo del caule sono allargate e rettilinee, e piegano bruscamente verso l'asterno; presentano la punta non arrotondata, ma quasi quadrata.

Le foglie d'acanto presentano la decorazione della costolatura mediana anch'essa semplificata, l'artigiano G si limita ad incidere la decorazione sulla superficie della costolatura, non crea l'effetto di un elemento sovrapposto alla foglia d'acanto stessa. Le fogliette sono corte ed appena distinte da scanalature, mentre le punte accorciate formano, incontrando i lobi superiori, zone d'ombra a forma di triangolo isoscele molto appuntito e dritto.

L'organizzazione dell'officina

I sette artigiani individuati organizzano il lavoro in maniera peculiare. Il caso di un capitello dovuto ad una sola mano è un *unicum* (nr. 49). Nel 98 % dei casi, invece, i pezzi sono realizzati ognuno da due artigiani, che lavorano, di regola per facce contigue, come appare abbastanza naturale, dal momento che, in questo modo, essi possono attaccare due lati opposti, poi spostarsi e lavorare rimanendo uno di fronte all'altro. Le zone di confine che vengono a trovarsi sotto uno degli spigoli dell'abaco sono lavorate da uno dei due, senza una regola fissa.

Il caso inverso, vale a dire quello in cui un artigiano realizza due lati opposti tra loro implica che i due scalpellini lavorino affiancati contemporaneamente su due facce tra loro contigue. Questo si verifica in undici casi: nella produzione dei capitelli nnrr. 2; 3; 5; 11; 22; 24; 26; 34; 38; 39; 50 sono coinvolti tutti i sette artigiani senza un ordine preferenziale.

In realtà, essendosi conservati 50 capitelli su 72, essendo leggibili 154 facce su 288 (le 88 dei 18 capitelli mancanti più 46 illeggibili dei capitelli conservati), e tenendo conto dell'abitudine degli artigiani a lavorare in coppia, possiamo supporre che in totale gli scalpellini potessero essere anche otto, e che e che nei 134 lati perduti potessero essere compresi i 36 scolpiti da un'ipotetica Mano 'H'. Alla Tabella B schematizziamo i risultati quantitativi della nostra indagine.

Il discorso appena accennato ci conduce ad affrontare due ulteriori questioni: la qualità del lavoro dei singoli scalpellini ed i rapporti di natura gerarchica tra di loro; la qualità e la formazione dell'officina. Il modello alla base delle singole realizzazioni, così come è stato da noi ricostruito, viene reso fedelmente da due soli artigiani, quelli che abbiamo chiamato 'A' e 'B'. Tra questi il primo deve essere il capo-officina, il secondo, forse, un suo aiutante.

Per ciò che attiene ai rapporti reciproci, sembra di poter dire che 'A' venga "imitato" da 'C' e da 'E'. Si deduce dalla forma delle fogliette nel calicetto, estroflesse e ripiegate, sempre sagomate a cuore e con le punte chiaramente distinte; nonché dal trattamento della zona di separazione tra le fogliette, condotta fin quasi alla base ed accuratamente sagomata da 'A'. Inoltre affine è il modo in cui sono conformate le digitazioni dell'acanto, sia nei caulicoli, con la prima foglietta interna allungata e bruscamente ripiegata; sia nelle foglie che rivestono il *kalathos*, con le fogliette che toccano i lobi contigui con tutta la parte superiore del profilo interno. Le differenze nella resa sono parimenti evidenti: le fogliette del calice sono sproporzionate, troppo piccole e dritte ('C'), oppure troppo grandi e curve ('E'); il calicetto stesso è troppo largo ('C') o troppo stretto ('E') alla base. Le fogliette dei lobi dell'acanto sono ben staccate, plasticamente rese e lievemente appuntite in 'A', mentre, pur imitando forma ed andamento, 'C' le appiattisce e le arrotonda; 'E' dà loro un rilievo eccessivo, non le piega abbastanza e ne appuntisce eccessivamente le estremità, oltre a limitarsi a descriverne il tratto inferiore tramite semplici incisioni sui lobi.

Il modello di 'D', 'G' ed 'F' sembra invece essere stato il lavoro di 'B'. Identiche le zone diagnostiche: 'B' scolpisce calici con le foglie allargate, ma abbastanza orizzontali, le stacca con una linea più corta, così pure 'D' ed 'F', mentre 'G' ingrossa leggermente una delle due foglie nel tentativo di rendere il profilo cuoriforme ed indicare bene la punta. Direttamente confrontabili le fogliette dell'acanto, accorciate ed oblique, non ripiegate, nei caulicoli, tangenti con poco più che la punta nel rivestimento del *kalathos*, danno luogo a zone d'ombra dal contorno più netto, triangolare e meno inclinate rispetto a quelle dell'altro gruppo. 'B' scolpisce caulicoli dall'orlo ingrossato, con fogliette cuoriformi segnate da incisioni profonde ed allargate verso il basso, particolare che ritroviamo imitato dai suoi "allievi". Tra questi 'F' è quello che scolpisce in maniera più chiara ed organica, ma anche stilisticamente più piatta e schematica.

Il livello generale dell'officina non pare, tutto sommato, particolarmente elevato. Numerosi sono gli errori, alcuni dei quali certamente presenti già in fase di sbozzatura. In tutti i capitelli, infatti, i lobi superiori delle foglie d'acanto della prima corona si sovrappongono invariabilmente all'orlo dei caulicoli che presenta, costantemente, il profilo esterno rettilineo, non circolare come sarebbe normale, e completamente nascosto dalla foglia. Nei prodotti migliori delle officine di buon livello il contatto tra i due elementi può verificarsi, ma entrambi sono sempre organicamente definiti. Inoltre frequenti sono errori di rifinitura, come la dissimmetria nella lavorazione delle foglie del calice; l'andamento inclinato dello stelo che non sorge esattamente dal centro del calice *etc.* Si è detto, però, che alcuni prodotti di questi scalpellini raggiungono un buon livello; da questi si può tentare di partire per ricostruire i modelli, e le ascendenze culturali dei capi-officina e, conseguentemente, dell'officina stessa. I capitelli senz'altro più prossimi ai nostri sono da ricercare tra quelli della villa di Domiziano a Castel Gandolfo e della *domus Flavia*. Con questi pezzi è possibile spingere il confronto fin nei particolari: il tipo dei calicetti scelti è il medesimo, e spesso è possibile confrontare direttamente la forma delle foglie dei calicetti, talora, come a Pozzuoli, lievemente asimmetriche ed inclinate, e con profilo cuoriforme e punta praticamente identici. Così pure l'orlo dei caulicoli ha un trattamento identico a quello di alcuni pezzi puteolani, come raffrontabile è l'uso di appoggiare i lobi laterali della foglia centrale superiore all'orlo del caule. Infine, la conformazione di lobi e digitazioni dell'acanto che riveste il *kalathos* è del tutto analoga.

Per riassumere, da un lato l'imprecisione estrema di numerosi pezzi puteolani non consente di pensare ad un impiego dell'officina di Castel Gandolfo nell'anfiteatro flegreo; dall'altro i punti di contatto sono evidenti. Si potrebbe allora pensare che i modelli da cui i capitelli puteolani sono derivati siano arrivati direttamente da Roma e siano stati i medesimi impiegati dalle officine della *domus Flavia* e della villa domizianea di Castel Gandolfo.

NOTE

1 Il lavoro è parte della più ampia ricerca realizzata da chi scrive sull'architettura e la decorazione dei monumenti pubblici di Pozzuoli, per il dottorato di ricerca in Archeologia Classica dell'Università degli Studi di Roma "la Sapienza". Si ringrazia la Soprintendenza Archeologica di Napoli e Caserta che ha consentito la pubblicazione dei dati, in particolare la dott.ssa C. Gialanella, per l'affettuoso interessamento e la cordiale disponibilità nei confronti dell'intero progetto. Al prof. F. Zevi sono riconoscente per la consueta attenzione ed il costante incoraggiamento con il quale ha voluto accompagnare anche questo, come tutti i miei studi, arricchendolo di stimolanti suggerimenti e preziosi consigli. Questo lavoro in particolare deve molto a P. Pensabene, che ne ha discusso con me, con la pazienza e la competenza di sempre, lo ringrazio per quanto ha voluto insegnarmi.

2 La letteratura sul nostro munumento è molto vasta, si citano di seguito solo gli studi degli ultimi cento anni: Dubois 1907, p.315 sgg.; Maiuri 1928, p. 520 sgg.; Idem 1955; D'Ambrosio 1976; Sommella 1978, nr. 37 p.58 sgg.; Camodeca 1979; Graefe 1979, 78 sgg.; Sabbatini Tumolesi 1980, 57; Golvin 1988, p.180 sgg.; Gialanella,Sampaolo 1987, 190-2; *Campi Flegrei* 1990, p.86 sgg.; Gialanella 1993, p.91 sgg.; Johannowsky 1993, p.101 sgg.; Wilson Jones 1993; Fora 1996, pp.19-30; Steuernagel 1999, 150 sgg.

3 Una recente ipotesi formulata dal Camodeca (1996, 96), che riprende in realtà un'idea già avanzata dal Le Glay (1977, 102 sgg.), retrodata ad età neroniana la costruzione del monumento. Le premesse sulle quali si basa questa ipotesi ci sembrano poco salde. Non è certo questa la sede per una discussione in merito; le argomentazioni relative sono state svolte da chi scrive nella propria tesi di dottorato (Demma 2002, 51 sgg.), e sono di prossima pubblicazione.

4 I pilastri in trachite misurano in media cm 181 x 123; la luce dei passaggi del portico fu ridotta dall'aggiunta dei rinforzi in laterizio (in edia 180 x 125 cm) da 4.97 a 2.42 m - cfr. fig. 3

5 Sulle *scholae* cfr. Maiuri 1955, 44 sgg.; Golvin 1988, 181; Steuernagel 1999, 150 sgg.; Demma 2002, 23 sgg.; Demma 2003

6 Cfr. Demma 2003

7 Il rapporto indicato da Vitruvio (V, 9, 4-5) per il dimensionamento degli *intercolumni* nei portici ionici e corinzi è di 1:5 ½ tra diametro di base e spazio tra le colonne, e risulta doppio rispetto alla ratio da utilizzare nei portici dorici (2:5 ½). Questo rapporto si riscontra nella nostra *porticus* tra il diametro di base e l'interasse.

8 I fusti delle colonne della *porticus in summa cavea* erano ricavate da un unico blocco di marmo proconnesio, alte circa 473 cm (16 piedi), con un diametro di base di cm 86-8 (3 piedi). L'imoscapo (diam. cm 90) è modanato con una stretta fascia liscia (h 6-7 cm) ed il piano di posa presenta, solitamente, tre fori per perni di 5 cm di lato. Il sommoscapo (diam. cm 80) presenta un basso listello ed un quarto di cerchio, sul piano d'attesa è solitamente un solo foro per perno, per la connessione con il capitello, di dimensioni variabili tra 8 x 8 e 9 x 12 cm, fornito di canaletta. Il fusto è scandito da 24 scanalature larghe 6 cm al sommoscapo, 9 cm all'imoscapo, profonde 3.4 cm, separate da listelli lisci larghi 3 cm.

9 La base è alta 47 cm per un diametro superiore di 97, ed ha un plinto lungo 120 cm. Sul piano d'attesa sono tre fori quadrati, da perno, di 8 x 8 cm, dotati di canalette per la colatura.

10 Jacobelli, Pensabene 1995-6

11 Durante gli scavi del 1939 alcune statue furono rinvenute nell'arcata XXIII del settore NW, sotto una delle scale della cavea, affiancate sul terreno e raggruppate per essere cotte, se i resti rinvenuti nell'ambiente attiguo, come sembra verosimile, vanno attribuiti alle strutture di una calcara (cfr. Maiuri 1955, p.78 e Tav. XVII)

12 Wilson Jones 1989, pp. 39 e sgg.

13 Con un fusto del genere ci si sarebbe aspettati un capitello alto tra 55 e 60 cm; mentre, viceversa, un capitello alto circa 90 cm si accompagna normalmente a fusti tra i 590 ed i 620 cm; cfr.Wilson Jones 1989, pp. 42-4

14 Cfr. Graefe 1979, 79 e fig. 98

15 Cfr. per esempio i nnrr. 1; 3; 5 e 26

16 Cfr. ad es. nnrr. 7 e 16, che conserva l'abaco praticamente intatto.

17 Cfr. nr. 12

18 Capitelli di questa tradizione paragonabili ai nostri si collocano generalmente a partire dalla metà del I d.C.; ci riferiamo a quelli da Nemi (Valle Giardino, oggi MNR I/11, nnrr. 4-5, metà I d.C.), attribuiti alla metà del I d.C. ; Ostia, portico dell'edificio fuori porta marina (Pensabene 1973, nr. 230) ultimi decenni I d.C.; Ostia, Sinagoga (Pensabene 1973, nnrr. 232-233), fine I d.C. ; Museo Nazionale Romano, già a Villa Savoia (MNR I/3, nr. I,1, tardo flavio); ma anche Verona, Museo Archeologico (Sperti 1983, nnrr. 43-47), fine I d.C. All'interno di questa tradizione, i confronti più prossimi ai nostri capitelli sono al Foro di Cesare (Heilmeyer 1970 tav. 46, 3 "preflavio"); a Milano, Museo Archeologico (Belloni 1958, nr.11, 60-70 d.C.); al Museo Nazionale Romano (MNR I/3, nr.I,1, già a villa Savoia, Flavio: confronto ottimo, differisce solo nella foglietta d'acqua al posto del calice del fiore dell'abaco e nelle volute a sezione concava); al Tempio di Romolo (capitello di fine I d.C. - Flaccomio *et al.* p. 108 sgg. nr.4); ma, soprattutto a Castelgandolfo (Freyberger 1990,nr.38, tav.6c; Magi 1973/4, 63 sgg., fig.2; Hesberg 1978/9, p.313, figg. 6-10, pressoché identico); all'antiquario comunale (domizianeo, confrontabile in particolare per il trattamento del collare del caulicolo, Freyberger 1990, nr. 68, tav.8g). L'acanto, oltre che negli esempi già citati trova confronti in capitelli di età flavia, caratterizzati da elementi tipologici differenti: ad Ostia, Basilica (Freyberger 1990, nnrr.40-1 tav. 10d-e; Pensabene 1973, nnrr. 236 e 250); Tempietto del Foro delle Corporazioni (Pensabene 1973, nr. 225) e Roma, area della Curia (Freyberger 1990, nr.51 tav.10f; Pensabene 1973, p.64; Heilmeyer 1970, p.162 nota 691) contemporanei. Fuori dall'Italia sono abbastanza simili i capitelli della scena del teatro di Merida, traianeo (Diaz Martos 1985, nnrr. D2-3)

19 Buoni esempi appartenenti alla seconda metà del II d.C., e molto simili ai nostri sono a Roma, presso il Portico d'Ottavia (Freyberger 1990, nr.226b, antonino: acanto e cauli simili, a Roma è presente lo stelo); e ad Ostia, R. IV, Is. IV,15 – (Pensabene 1973, nr. 295); R. IV, Is. V,2 (Pensabene 1973, nr. 296); presentano acanto praticamente identico; elici più distanziate, a Pozzuoli piatte. Il tipo continua in età severiana: è ben attestato a Roma, presso la Biblioteca del Palatino, e ad Ostia, capitello presso il tempio rotondo (Pensabene 1973, nr 302). Un tipo di acanto molto simile si ritrova nei capitelli compositi dell'arco ostiense di Caracalla. Un

ulteriore confronto, in questo ambito, ci sembra istituibile con un pezzo del Museo Nazionale Romano del quale non si conosce la provenienza (MNR 1/3, nr.I,16) a Roma c'è in più lo stelo del fiore.
20 Questo tipo di variazioni nella decorazione superficiale è stato individuato, dal momento che in numerosi casi esse sono del tutto evidenti. D'altra parte, però, le pessime condizioni di conservazione di molti pezzi, non consentono una piena lettura di tutti i particolari, e non lasciano quindi discernere se una foglia di tipo 'c' non sia in realtà stata in origine ornata da un motivo tipo 'a' oppure 'b'.
21 Qualche esempio: per quanto riguarda volute ed elici, solo per limitarsi ai tipi 1 e 2, vale a dire a quelli sicuramente originali e non risultanti da una rilavorazione, esistono casi (nnrr. 5; 9), in cui entrambi i tipi compaiono nello stesso capitello. Nei capitelli nnrr. 1; 2; 3; 4; 10; 11; 12; 13; 14 troviamo l'alternanza di calicetti aperti (tipo 1) e chiusi (tipo 2); in particolare, nel nr. 2 la stessa alternanza tra i calicetti si affianca ad una differente scelta anche nel tipo dei caulicoli, tipo 2 con calice 1 e tipo 3 con calice 2. Corrispondenza che, d'altra parte, non è affatto da intendersi in senso vincolante: i calici di tipo 1 si trovano accostati a tutti i tipi di caulicoli, così come, del resto, quelli di tipo 2. Oltre tutto, in più occasioni, nello stesso lato di un capitello si trovano caulicoli di tipo differente: 6; 7; 8 presentano un caule tipo 3 ed uno tipo 4 nello stesso lato. Ancora a proposito dei caulicoli, il tipo1, con treccia sul collarino, compare solo ed esclusivamente nel lato b del capitello nr.13, e va interpretato, probabilmente, come una riparazione introdotta in un caso in cui un errore dello scalpellino non deve aver lasciato abbastanza marmo per ripetere il motivo consueto dei sepali. Così come un errore, malamente rimediato, deve essere occorso nel nr.1, lato 'a', dove il *kyma* è di dimensioni ridotte e appare estremamente schiacciato.
22 Freyberger 1990, Beil. VI
23 Come si è detto, il lato 'b' del nr. 24; il lato 'a' del 25 nonché il lato 'b' del 26 presentano un caule tipo 3 ed uno tipo 4.
24 G. Morelli sviluppò un metodo di studio della pittura moderna basandosi sulla constatazione che ogni artista ha un cifrario personale che adopera nei particolari secondari, che assumono nelle sue opere sempre la stessa forma, ad esempio una pennellata mossa in un determinato modo, un orecchio o il muso di un cavallo rappresentati in una maniera caratteristica. Questi particolari furono definiti nella storia degli studi "elementi morelliani", e adoperati nell'attribuire opere non firmate, o non riconducibili ad artisti determinati in base a documentazioni esterne. Il Morelli pubblicò le sue opere alla fine del XIX secolo, in tedesco e sotto lo pseudonimo di I. Lermolieff, basta citare qui i due volumi dei *Kunstkritiche Studien über italienische Malerei*, rispettivamente dedicati alle Gallerie Borghese e Doria Pamphili ed alle raccolte di Monaco e Dresda (Lermolieff 1890-1). In campo archeologico frutti particolarmente copiosi sono stati ottenuti applicando i metodi del Morelli nello studio della pittura vascolare greca, dal Beazley in poi; e nell'esame della scultura greca e delle copie romane, a partire dal Lippold. Cfr. Bianchi Bandinelli 1978, p. 12 sgg.; Beazley 1956; *Id.* 1963
25 Rohmann 1998, in part. pp. 21-5

BIBLIOGRAFIA

Beazley, J.D. , 1956, *Attic Black-figure Vase-painter.*, London

Beazley, J.D. , 1963, *Attic Red-figure Vase-painter.*, London

Belloni, G.G., 1958, *I capitelli romani di Milano.* Roma

Bianchi Bandinelli, R., 1978, *Introduzione all'archeologia*, Bari-Roma

Camodeca, G., 1979, La carriera del Prefetto del Pretorio *Sex. Cornelius Repentinus* in una nuova iscrizione puteolana - *Puteoli* 3, 41-76

Camodeca, G., 1996, L'élite municipale di Puteoli fra la tarda Repubblica e Nerone - *Les élites municipales de l'Italie péninsulaire des Gracques à Néron.* Atti Conv. Clairmont Ferrand 1991 [1996], p. 91 sgg.

Campi Flegrei , 1977, AA.VV., *I Campi Flegrei nell'Archeologia e nella Storia.* Roma

Campi Flegrei , 1987, AA.VV., *I Campi Flegrei.* Napoli

Campi Flegrei, 1990, AA.VV., *I Campi Flegrei. Un itinerario archeologico.* Venezia

Campi Flegrei, 1992, AA.VV., *Civiltà dei Campi Flegrei.* Napoli

D'Ambrosio, A., 1976, *La cappella di S. Gennaro nell'anfiteatro di Pozzuoli.* Pozzuoli

Demma, F., 2002, *I monumenti pubblici urbani di* Puteoli *tra i Flavi ed i Severi: architettura e decorazione.* Roma

Demma, F., 2003, Pavimenti e mosaici dagli edifici pubblici di Pozzuoli - *Atti del IX convegno dell'A.I.S.C.O.M.* - Aosta, Febbraio 2003. In corso di stampa

Dubois, C., 1907, *Pouzzoles antique, histoire et topographie.* BEFAR 98, Paris.

Flaccomio, G. et. al., 1979, *Il "Tempio di Romolo" al Foro Romano.* (Roma. Quaderni dell'Istituto di storia dell'architettura, Ser.26, Nr.157-162)

Fora, M., 1996, *I* Munera Gladiatoria *in Italia. Considerazioni sulla loro documentazione epigrafica.* Milano

Freyberger, K.S., 1990, *Stadtrömische Kapitelle aus der Zeit von Domitians bis Alexander Severus.* Mainz

Gialanella, C., 1993, La topografia di *Puteoli* - Puteoli 1993, 38 e ss.

Gialanella, C., Sampaolo, V., 1980-1, *Note sulla topografia di Puteoli* , - Puteoli 4-5, 133-61

Gialanella, C.; Sampaolo, V., 1987, Pozzuoli, Campi Flegrei 1987, 183-97

Golvin, J.C., 1988, *L'Amphitéâtre romain.* Paris

Graefe, R., 1979, *Vela Erunt.* Mainz am rhein.

Heilmeyer, W.D., 1970, *Korinthische Normalkapitelle. Studien zur Geschichte der römischen Architekturdekoration.* (Heidelberg. 195. Mitteilungen des Deutschen Archäologischen Instituts. Römische Abteilung, Ergönzungsheft 16)

Hesberg, 1978-80 Zur Datierung des Theatres in der Domitiansvilla von Castel Gandolfo – *RendPontAc* 51-52, 305-324

Jacobelli, L., Pensabene, 1995-1996, La decorazione architettonica del Tempio di Venere a Pompei: contributo allo studio e alla ricostruzione del santuario. – *RivStPomp* 7, p. 45 sgg.

Johannowsky, W., 1993, *I monumenti maggiori – Puteoli,* 1993

Le Glay, M., 1977, Nouvelles inscriptions relatives au règne de Néron – *BullSocNatAntFr* 1977, 102 sgg.

Lermolieff, I., 1890-1, *Kunstkritiche Studien über italienische Malerei.* Dresden vol. I 1890; II 1891

Maiuri, A., 1928, Lavori di restauro della Soprintendenza alle Antichità nel biennio 1927-28, *BdA*, 520 sgg.

Maiuri, A., 1955, *Studi e ricerche sull'anfiteatro flavio puteolano.* MemNap III

Diaz Martos, A., 1985, *Capiteles Corintios Romanos de Hispania.* Madrid.

MNR, I-XII, *Museo Nazionale Romano. Le sculture* Vol.I,1-12: Le sculture. Roma,1979-1995

Pensabene, P., 1973, *Scavi di Ostia 7. I capitelli.* Roma

Pueoli, 1993, AA.VV., *Puteoli.* Napoli

Rohmann, J., 1998, *Die Kapitellproduktion der römischen Kaiserzeit in Pergamon.* Berlin - New York

Sabbatini Tumolesi, P., 1980, *Gladiatorium Paria. Annunci di spettacoli gladiatori a Pompei.* Roma

Sommella, P., 1966, Stadi, EAA VII, s.v., 464 ss.

Sommella, P., 1978, *Forma e urbanistica di Pozzuoli romana. Puteoli* 2, 1-98

Sperti, L., 1983 *I capitelli romani del Museo Archeologico di Verona.* Roma

Steuernagel, D., 1998, <Corporate Identity>. Über Vereins-, Stadt- und Staatskulte im kaiserzeitlichen Puteoli – *RM* 106, p. 149 sgg.

Wilson Jones, M., 1989, Designing the Roman Corinthian Order – *JRA* 2, 35 sgg.

Wilson Jones, M., 1993, Designing Amphiteatres – *RM* 100, 391 sgg.

Wilson Jones, M., 2000, *Principles of Roman Architecture.* New Haven- London

TABELLA A

Numero	Lato	Scalpellinoo	Caulicoli	Volute	Acanto
1	a	C	4	1	a1
	b	D	4	1	a1
	c	D	4	1	a1
	d	C	4	1	a1
2	a	B	3	3	c
	b	C	4	3	c
	c	B	//	2	//
	d	C	4	3	b
3	a	B	2	4	c
	b	D	3	4	c
	c	B	2	4	c
	d	D	3	4	c
4	a	A	3	2	c
	b	A	2	2	c
	c	B	4	2	c
5	a	C	4	4	c
	b	E	4	4	c
	c	C	4	4	c
	d	E	?	4	?
6	a	A	4	2	c
	b	B	3	2	c
	c	B	3	2	c
	d	A	4	2	c
7	a	F	3	1	c
	b	C	4	1	c
	c	C	4	1	c
	d	F	3	1	c
8	a	D	3	1	c
	b	G	4	1	c
	c	G	4	1	c
	d	D	3	1	c
9	a	F	3	2	a1
	b	?	?	2	a1
	c	?	?	2	a1
	d	G	4	2	a1
10	a	F	2	2	c
11	a	F	2	3	a
	b	E	3	3	a
	c	F	?	3	?
	d	E	3	3	a
12	a	F	4	2	b
	b	B	4	2	b
	c	B	4	2	b
	d	F	?	2	?
13	a	A	2	2	c
	b	A	3	2	c
	c	?	2	2	c
	d	B	?	2	c
14	a	F	4	1	b
	b	F	4	1	c
	c	C	4	1	c
15	a	C	4	1	a
	b	A	5	4	a
16	a	C	4	1	a
	b	D	4	1	a
	c	D	4	1	a
	d	C	4	1	a
17	a	G	3	2	c
	b	?	?	2	?
	c	A	4	2	c
	d	A	4	2	c
18				3	
19	a	C	4	1	a
	b	C	4	1	b
	c	D	4	1	b
	d	D	4	1	c
20	a	C	4	1	c
	b	G	4	1	c
	c	G	4	1	c
	d	C	4	1	c
21	a	F	4	1	a1
	b	G	3	1	c
	c	G	3	1	c
	d	F	4	1	c
22	a	C	4	1	a?
	b	D	4	1	c
	c	C	4	1	c
	d	D	4	1	a
23	a	B	4	2	a1
	b	C	4	1	a1
	c	C	4	2	a1
	d	B	4	1	a1
24	a	G	3	4	b
	b	D	3; 4	4	c
	c	G	3	4	c
	d	?	?	4	?
25	a	G	3; 4	2	c
	b	G	3	2	c
26	a	A	3	2	c
	b	E	3; 4	2	c
	c	A	4	2	c
27	a	E	3	2	b
	b	E	3	2	b

28	a	E	2	2	b
	b	E	2	2	b
29	a	G	3	4	c
	b	G	3	4	c
	c	E	?	4	c
	d	E	?	1	?
30		?	?	1	?
31	a	D	3	1	a
	b	D	3	1	al
	c	G	3	1	al
32	a	B	4	1	b
	b	C	?	1	?
	c	C	4	1	al
	d	B	4	1	al
33	a	F	3	1	a
	b	G	4	1	a
	c	G	4	1	c
	d	F	4	1	a
34	a	C	2	3	a
	b	G	2	3	a
	c	?	?	3	?
	d	G	2	3	c
35	a	E	4	2	b
	b	?	?	2	?
	c	E	2	2	c
36	a	E	2	2	b
	b	?		2	
	c	E	2	1	b
	d	?	?	1	
37	a	E	3	2	b
	b	E	?	2	?
	c	C	3	2	b
38	a	E	?	2	b
	b	C	?	2	b
	c	E	3	2	b
	d	C	3	2	b
39	a	G	2	4	b
	b	E	2	4	b
	c	?	?	4	?
	d	E	2	4	?
40		E	2	3	b
41	a	C	4	1	c
	b	C	4	1	//
	c	E	4	1	//
	d	E	4	1	//
42	a	E	4	1	c
	b	E	4	1	al
	c	F	4	1	al
	d	F	4	1	al
43	a	A	4	2	c
	b	B	3	2	c
44	a	B	4	1	c
	b	E	4	1	C
	c	E	3	1	C
	d	B	3	1	c
45	a	C	3	1	c
	b	E	1	1	c
	c	E	4	3	A
	d	C	4	4	C
46	a	C	3	2	C
	b	F	4	2	C
47	a	B	4	2	B
	b	//	//	2	//
	c	//	//	2	//
	d	B	4	2	B
48	a	G	3	1	A
	b	G	4	1	A
	d	F	2	1	A
49	a	A	4	2	B
	b	A	4	2	B
	c	A	4	?	B
	d	A	4	?	B
50	a	F	3	1	al
	b	G	4	1	C
	c	F	3	1	al

TABELLA B

Scalpellino	Lati *	Semi-capitelli **	Capitelli interi
A	17	7	1
B	18	9	//
C	31	16	//
D	15	8	//
E	30	15	//
F	20	10	//
G	23	12	//

* Dati effettivamente rilevati

** Numero minimo ipotizzabile

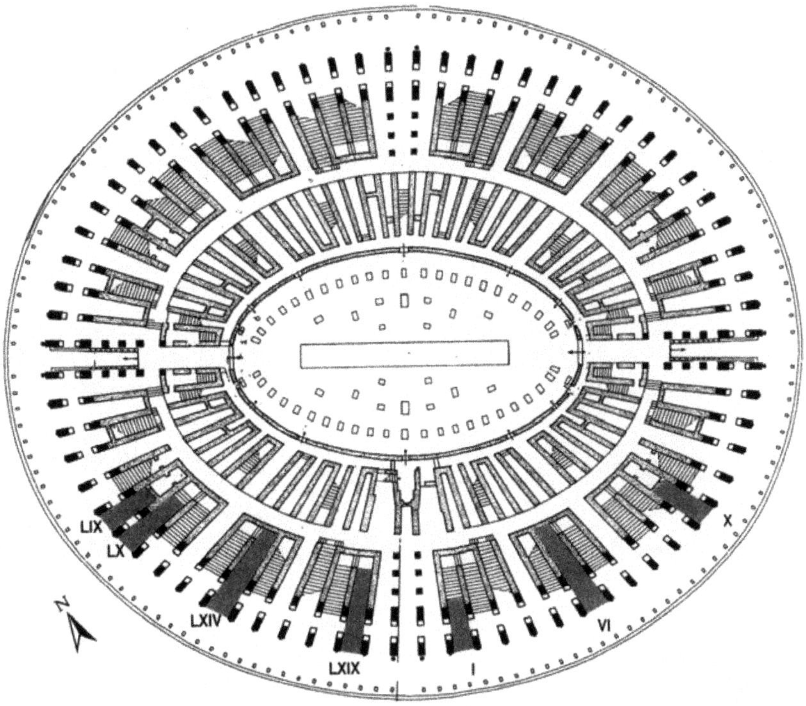

Fig. 1. Anfiteatro maggiore di Pozzuoli, pianta (da Steuernagel 1999)

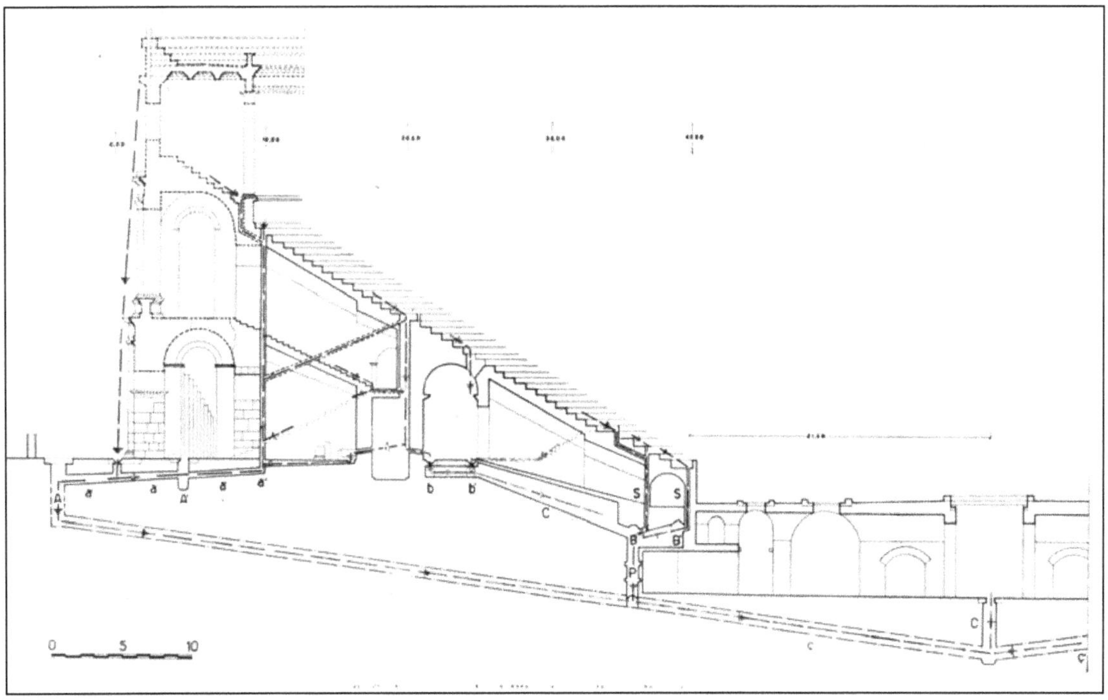

Fig. 2. Anfiteatro maggiore di Pozzuoli, sezione (da Maiuri 1955)

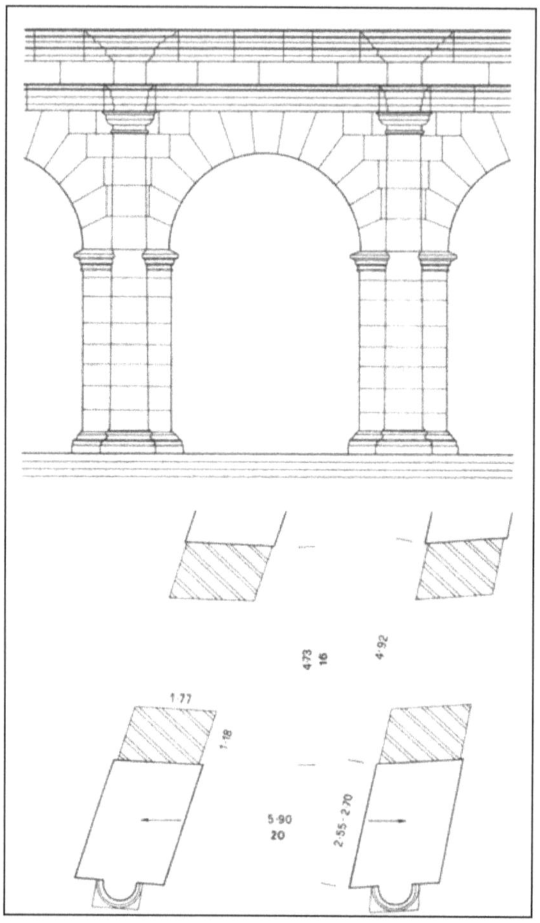

Fig. 3. Anfiteatro maggiore di Pozzuoli, portico pilastrato, pianta dei restauri (da Wilson Jones 1993)

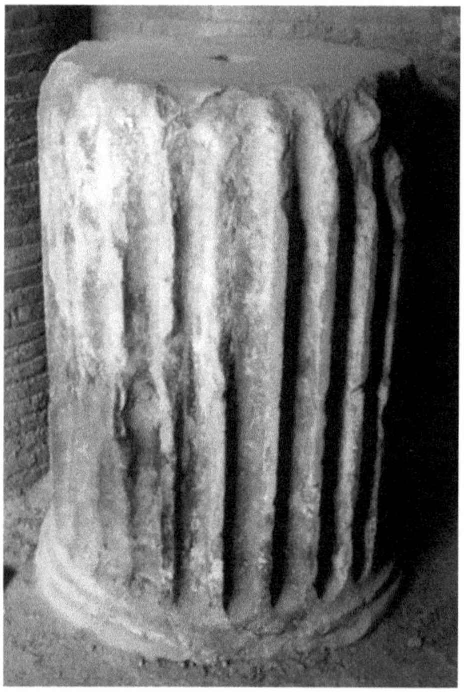

Fig. 4. Colonna, particolare del restauro

Fig. 5. Colonna, particolare del restauro

Fig. 6. Colonna, particolare del restauro

Fig. 7. Colonna, particolare del restauro

Fig. 8. : Capitello nr. 39

Fig. 9. Capitello nr. 39, particolare

Fig. 10. Capitello nr. 26, particolare

Fig. 11. Capitello nr. 25, particolare

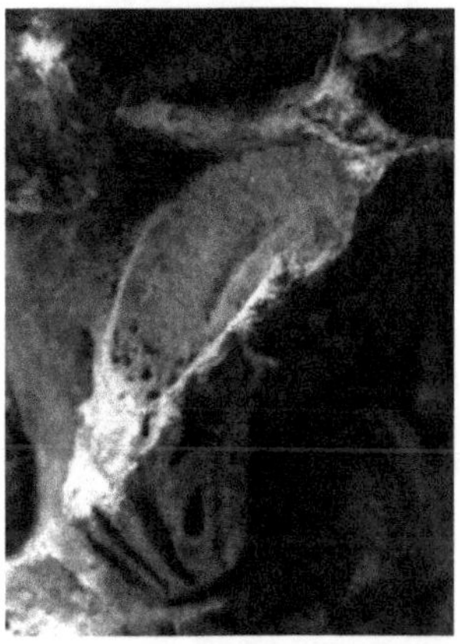

Fig. 12. Capitello nr. 24, particolare

Fig. 13. Capitello nr. 25

Fig. 14. Capitello della seconda fase, epoca antonina.

Fig. 15. Capitello della seconda fase, epoca antonina

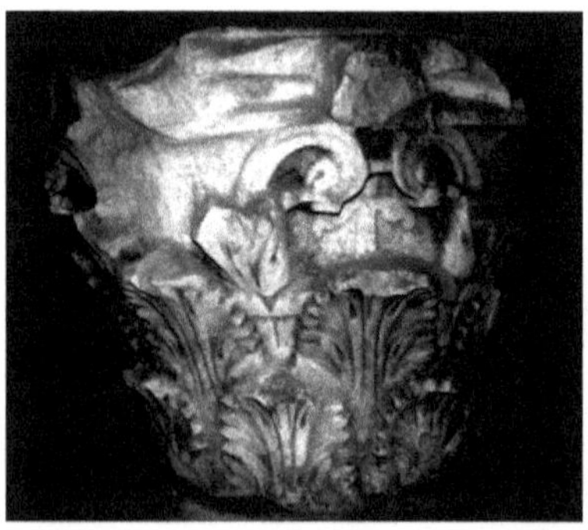

Fig. 16. Scalpellino 'A': capitello nr. 49

Fig. 17. Scalpellino 'B': acanto; capitello nr. 4

Fig. 18. Scalpellino 'D', capitello nr. 8

Fig. 19. Scalpellino 'D', acanto; capitello nr. 16

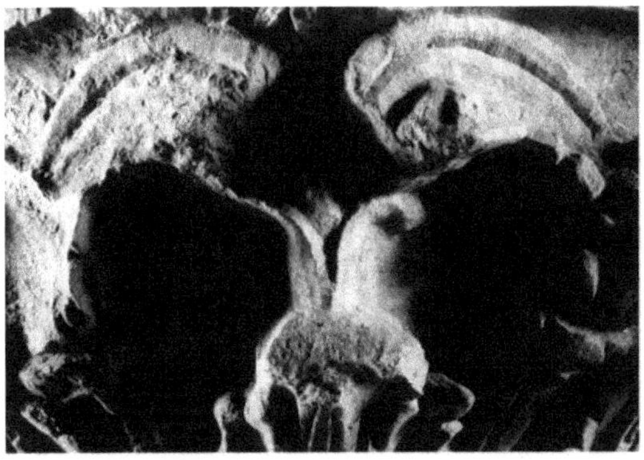

Fig. 20. Scalpellino 'E', capitello nr. 35

Fig. 21. Scalpellino 'E', capitello nr. 25

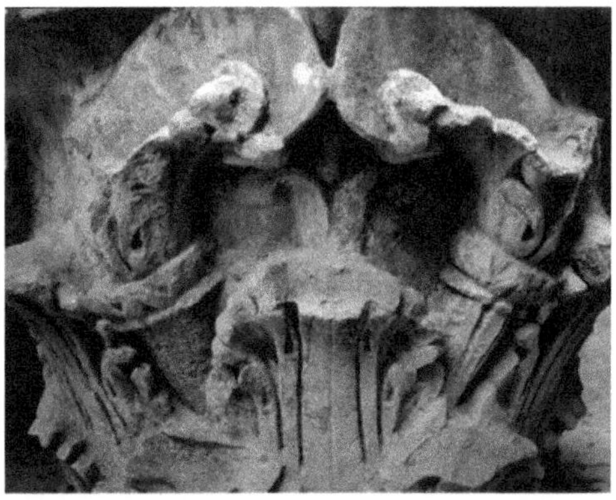

Fig. 22. Scalpellino 'G', capitello nr. 26

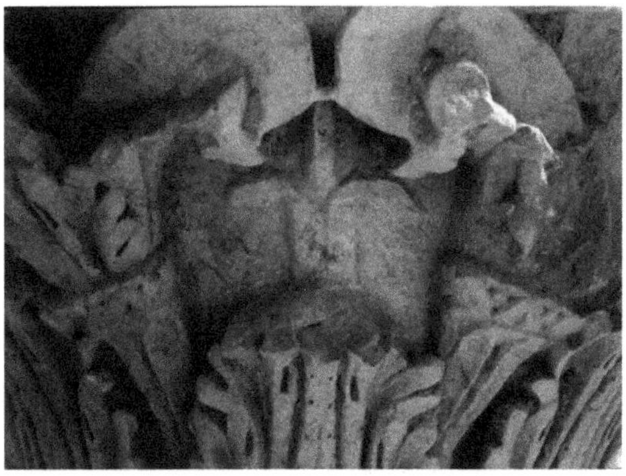

Fig. 23. Scalpellino 'G', acanto; capitello nr. 31

ANFITEATRO FLAVIO DI POZZUOLI, PORTICO *IN SUMMA CAVEA* : UNA STIMA DEI COSTI

PAOLO BARRESI
(Università di Roma "La Sapienza")

ABSTRACT: Beginning with the study by Filippo Demma on the *porticus in summa cavea* of the Flavian amphitheater in Pozzuoli, this paper reconstructs construction costs, calculating the amount of labor needed to carved bases, capitels and columns and considering the sums reported in a 19th century building-registry. The methods of construction employed during the Roman period were not significantly different from the early modern period. The cost of marble as building material and its transport have been studied by Janet de Laine; the only difference applied here is based upon the Price Edict of Diocletian, where the measure of cubic feet, and not square feet, is used.

Il calcolo dei costi nell'architettura antica è un problema di grande interesse, non solo per motivi inerenti alla storia dell'architettura, ma anche per le sue implicazioni storiche ed economiche. Per raggiungere tale obbiettivo si dispone certo di un gran numero di fonti sull'argomento, a partire dalle iscrizioni edilizie sugli appalti dei templi di età classica ed ellenistica in Grecia, fino ai prezzi dell'Editto di Diocleziano, e alle iscrizioni su manufatti in marmo che ne documentano il costo (Duncan Jones 1974, p. 119, n. 394; Pensabene 1983, 59-61) ; tuttavia, occorre ammettere che non è facile pervenire a ricostruzioni valide, a causa delle molte incognite che si incontrano. E' vero, infatti, che siamo abbastanza ben informati sui costi della manodopera e dei materiali, specialmente in determinati contesti, ma serie difficoltà sorgono al momento in cui tali dati si devono calare nei casi concreti: resteranno sempre celati, infatti, alcuni aspetti, come il rapporto numerico tra manodopera libera e servile, e soprattutto il costo della vita nelle singole regioni e nei diversi periodi (Hellmann 2002, 56), che potrebbero far oscillare anche di molto le stime basate sui pochi dati parziali a noi noti.

Le difficoltà aumentano se si prendono in esame determinati periodi, come quello romano, in cui le fonti sull'edilizia sono piuttosto scarse, se paragonate ad esempio con quelle sull'architettura greca di età classica ed ellenistica, per la quale si può contare su numerose iscrizioni relative agli appalti e alle spese per i materiali, anche confrontabili con gli edifici esistenti (Burford 1969; Hellmann 2002, 56-60).

Per ovviare in parte a tali difficoltà, si può allora elaborare un metodo di calcolo dei costi basato su criteri empirici, che valuti anzitutto il lavoro necessario a costruire un edificio e poi lo traduca in termini monetari, in modo da orientare almeno la stima su un ordine di grandezza plausibile. Ciò è stato ultimamente tentato da J. De Laine riguardo ad un caso concreto, quello delle Terme di Caracalla (De Laine 1997). Se ci si concentra sull'architettura marmorea, poi, occorre mettere in conto che si trattava di un materiale pregiato, il cui costo non doveva solo basarsi sul lavoro necessario a estrarlo e trasportarlo, ma doveva anche fondarsi su criteri di gradimento e difficoltà di estrazione e trasporto.

Tenendo conto di tali premesse, intendiamo studiare qui la ricostruzione dei costi del portico *in summa cavea* dell'anfiteatro flavio di Pozzuoli, esaminato da F. Demma in un intervento pubblicato in questa stessa sede: riteniamo di poterlo proporre come caso emblematico per la ricostruzione dei costi in un edificio marmoreo romano, sia perché è stato appunto oggetto di una ricerca esauriente che ha determinato numero e dimensione dei elementi architettonici, oltre a vari aspetti relativi alla sua realizzazione, sia perché impiegava marmo importato dal Proconneso, e può diventare così indicativo del livello di costi di simili complessi edilizi diffusi nel bacino del Mediterraneo tra I e II sec. d.C. (Pensabene 2001 per i problemi relativi alla circolazione di vari tipi di marmo bianco importato in un importante contesto come la Tripolitania; e da ultimo Pensabene 2002 sulla diffusione del marmo proconnesio nell'architettura romana). Ci sembra che una sede come quella del presente convegno sia la più adatta per proporre l'applicazione generalizzata di un tale metodo, che consente un approccio nuovo nei confronti del calcolo dei costi edilizi, e che non sembra abbia avuto l'attenzione che meritava al momento della sua presentazione, da parte di J. De Laine.

La fonte principale per il prezzo del marmo in età imperiale è l'Editto di Diocleziano (Giacchero 1974) (Tab. 1), che però presenta degli aspetti di controversa interpretazione: in particolare, ci si interroga se il "piede" che costituisce l'unità di misura per i prezzi dell'Editto sia da considerare quadrato o cubico; occorre poi chiedersi se i prezzi fossero relativi al materiale in cava, oppure acquistato presso i magazzini imperiali di Porto (dunque, comprendendo nel prezzo il trasporto dalle cave); infine, bisogna stabilire se e fino a che punto si possano applicare quei prezzi alla situazione economica e storica dell'Impero di uno o due secoli prima, che è il periodo di massima diffusione del marmo e nel quale si colloca anche la costruzione dell'anfiteatro di Pozzuoli.

Per quanto riguarda la prima questione, ritengo che il piede usato nell'Editto di Diocleziano fosse cubico: non solo in quanto alcune iscrizioni delle cave di granito del Foro nel Mons Claudianus descrivono il volume di un blocco in piedi cubici (Peacock, Maxfield 1997, 212 sgg.; Pensabene 1999, 726), ma anche perché un gromatico del II secolo d.C. (Balbus, *Expositio et ratio omnium formarum*, p. 97 ll. 1-13) afferma: *Solidum est quod Graeci stereon appellant, nos quadratos pedes appellamus; cuius longitudinem et latitudinem et crassitudinem metimur, ut parietum structuras, pilarum pyramidum aut lapidum materias, et his similia* dove l'espressione *quadratos pedes* si riferisce ai piedi cubici, *constratos pedes* ai piedi quadrati. La seconda questione è più difficile da affrontare, anche perché richiederebbe un approfondito esame sul problema della diffusione del marmo nel mondo romano. Mi limiterò qui ad alcuni accenni.

Propongo che i prezzi dell'Editto fossero quelli negoziati presso depositi situati nelle città provinciali più vicine alle cave di provenienza: qui si trovavano infatti le strutture adeguate alle transazioni e alla conservazione del materiale, che poi poteva essere direttamente spedito verso la destinazione finale. L'acquisto dei marmi imperiali da parte di privati o di città era infatti possibile, anche se richiedeva somme ingenti; e se un committente ad Efeso voleva utilizzare colonne in marmo frigio, non poteva farle arrivare da Porto. Penso poi che la differenza tra i diversi prezzi dell'Editto non derivasse semplicemente dalla maggiore o minore lontananza delle cave dalle vie di comunicazione, o dalla difficoltà di trasporto, perché, in tal caso, il granito del Mons Claudianus sarebbe dovuto costare all'incirca quanto il porfido (in quanto le due cave si trovano ambedue nel Deserto Orientale egiziano), e invece vi è una differenza di 150 denari tra i due; il *marmor lacaedemonicum*, d'altro canto, le cui cave sono disposte nel Peloponneso, costa quanto il porfido. Ne consegue che i prezzi dell'Editto devono intendersi, a mio parere, come relativi a marmi acquistati nel luogo di smistamento (ovvero la città provinciale più vicina alle cave); i prezzi del trasporto dovevano dunque cambiare a seconda della destinazione finale.

Si potrebbe obiettare che in tal modo si toglie validità al prezzo imposto dall'Editto, che non sarebbe allora valido in tutto l'Impero; ma l'Editto stesso fornisce i prezzi dei trasporti marittimi e terrestri, e in base a questi, si poteva calcolare il costo calmierato dei marmi in ogni città.

Riguardo al terzo problema, mi sembra logico partire dall'ipotesi che i prezzi dell'Editto rispecchiassero i rapporti reciproci tra i valori delle diverse qualità di marmo: e questi valori dovevano essere rimasti gli stessi per tutta l'età imperiale. Infatti, se il costo del marmo nell'Editto non dipendeva in grande misura dal trasporto, doveva dipendere da altri fattori, legati alla natura stessa dei vari tipi di marmo e alla preferenza degli acquirenti.

Poiché le fonti antiche sono spesso carenti sulle questioni di costi edilizi, per ricostruire il sistema con cui era calcolato il costo dei marmi, ritengo adeguato l'approccio ultimamente riproposto da Janet De Laine, ovvero rivolgersi a prontuari edili (Pegoretti 1869, I, 278) del XIX secolo, che riflettono esperienze di un'epoca in cui le modalità di lavorazione degli elementi decorativi architettonici non erano ancora radicalmente cambiate rispetto al periodo romano imperiale; quello scritto da Pegoretti nel 1869, afferma tra l'altro che i prezzi dei vari tipi di marmo (come materiale da scultura o decorazione architettonica) erano costituiti dal prezzo "ai depositi, cave o fucine più prossime al luogo di lavoro, più le spese di trasporto, dazi, pedaggi, e altre accessorie"; inoltre, dopo aver stabilito che il prezzo del marmo deriva dal costo del lavoro necessario a cavarlo e lavorarlo, precisa che "non in tutti i tipi di marmi si hanno gli stessi rapporti tra i tempi occorrenti per i diversi lavori; infatti, la facilità di segatura dipende dalla regolarità delle fibre, mentre la manodopera per sbozzatura o intaglio varia secondo la tessitura, omogeneità, grossezza dei grani" (Pegoretti 1869,I, p. 361).

I costi dei marmi in cava potevano allora variare in relazione alla dimensione e al tipo dei pezzi estratti, specialmente se si tratta di grandi lastre o colonne; alla rarità di pezzi voluminosi estraibili dalla cava, che dipende dal tipo di marmo o dalle vene; alla durezza e difficoltà di lavorazione, in relazione con la grana e con le qualità mineralogiche del marmo. In grandi cave romane, come quelle di cipollino nell'Eubea o del Mons Claudianus in Egitto, la quantità di fusti monolitici scartati fa capire che per ogni grosso elemento cavato occorreva preventivare una certa percentuale di lavoro perduto nel cavare elementi rivelatisi poi inadatti alla spedizione, perché difettosi in origine o cavati in modo errato (Pensabene 1999). Tale percentuale doveva dipendere dal tipo e dalla granatura del marmo, dalle condizioni della cava, o da altri fattori non sempre determinabili.

Inoltre, occorre considerare la preferenza degli acquirenti verso certi tipi di marmo, in relazione alla loro quantità disponibile sul mercato; se alcune qualità erano preferite, nonostante le eventuali difficoltà di cavatura e di trasporto, il prezzo non poteva che lievitare: era probabilmente il caso del porfido.

Il problema della traduzione in denari di I-II secolo dei prezzi in denari dioclezianei è stato ultimamente risolto ancora da Janet De Laine, che ha proposto di valutare in 0,5 "modii castrensi" di farina ogni giornata di lavoro, ancora in base all'Editto di Diocleziano (De Laine 1997, 209: in tal modo si risolvono le difficoltà relative all'inflazione e al diverso valore della moneta nel tempo): l'equivalenza tra i prezzi dioclezianei e quelli della media età imperiale si può dunque ottenere recuperando il prezzo di un modio castrense di farina nel periodo che si vuole esaminare: nel nostro caso, equivale a 2 sesterzi di I-II secolo (1/2 denario), e poiché sappiamo che 1 modio castrense è valutato 50 denari dioclezianei, abbiamo la possibilità di valutare i prezzi dei marmi dell'Editto in denari di I-II secolo.

In cava, il tempo attribuito ai lavori necessari per l'estrazione del blocco si può attribuire come segue (Tab. 2): 4 g/mc per la semplice cavatura del blocco solo sgrossato; 7,5 g/mc per la squadratura dello stesso blocco; 0,5 g/mc per la lizzatura. Il totale è di 12 g/mc.

Inoltre, possiamo contare su un altro dato: sappiamo che nelle cave di Carrara del XVI secolo il puro materiale valeva 1/3 del prezzo finale in cava De Laine 1997, 119), e tale modello potrebbe utilmente essere applicato anche al marmo antico. Se calcoliamo allora il lavoro occorrente per un metro cubo di marmo in cava, e vi aggiungiamo un terzo di questo valore, secondo il modello "materiale : lavoro = 1 : 3" notato in età moderna a Carrara, abbiamo la situazione quale doveva presentarsi in cava per un blocco. Ipotizzando allora un rapporto "prezzo del blocco in cava : prezzo del materiale grezzo" di 3:1, si devono aggiungere 4 g/mc, per quantificare il valore del materiale. Ne risulta un prezzo teorico di cava di 16 g/mc.

Come si è detto, però, le differenze tra i vari prezzi dell'Editto derivavano dalle diverse difficoltà di cavatura e dalla relativa abbondanza di pezzi di grandi dimensioni estraibili: dunque, occorre moltiplicare i risultati derivanti dal calcolo della manodopera, per un coefficiente derivato dalla proporzione reciproca tra i vari prezzi (ottenuto dividendo ogni prezzo dioclezianeo per 20: Porfido e serpentino = 12,5; Frigio e Numidico = 10; Africano = 7,5; Assuan e Cipollino = 5; Proconnesio = 2). Tale coefficiente rende conto dei molteplici fattori che rendevano più o meno pregiati i vari marmi.

Se si moltiplica allora il risultato precedente in g/mc per i quozienti relativi ai diversi tipi di marmo, e si traducono poi le g/mc così ottenute in denarii dioclezianei, si dovrebbero così essere ricostruiti i prezzi dell'Editto; e difatti vediamo che i valori risultanti sono molto vicini a quelli documentati dall'Editto:

a) porfido e lacedemone: 12,5 x 16 = 200 g/mc = 5,2 g/pc = 260 denarii (250 Editto);
b) Frigio e numidico: 160 g/mc = 4,15 g/pc = 208 den/pc (200 Editto);
c) Africano: 120 g/mc = 3,1 g/pc = 155 den/pc (150 Editto);
d) Assuan e cipollino: 80 g/mc = 2 g/pc = 100 denarii (100 Editto);
e) proconnesio: 32 g/mc = 0,83 g/pc = 41 denarii (40 Editto).

Si è introdotto anche il dato sulle giornate di lavoro per piede cubo (g/pc)[1] al fine di fornire un dato che fosse in linea con l'unità di misura utilizzata in antico, e che poteva forse essere effettivamente utilizzato per calcolare il lavoro occorrente. Nella tabella 2 si riassumono i dati sopra esposti.

I valori per cavatura e squadratura sono quelli proposti dalla De Laine; si è aggiunto il valore in g/mc della lizzatura, ossia il trasporto dei blocchi cavati a valle, considerato partendo dai valori riportati per le cave di Carrara: 15 persone per tre carichi da 20 tonnellate al giorno (Dolci 1980, 197).
Bisogna ora affrontare brevemente il problema del costo del trasporto, che a mio parere non era compreso nel valore dato dall'Editto. Janet De Laine ha proposto che, per motivi connessi alla pesantezza del carico, le *naves lapidariae* dovessero essere riempite solo per un 25-30% della loro capacità: il prezzo andava allora calcolato in unità di peso, e il tasso di 16 denari dioclezianei per modio castrense per miglio, che è il prezzo medio dell'Editto di Diocleziano per il trasporto via mare, va tradotto in 0,0124 denarii (di Diocleziano) per tonnellata per miglio, e ciò conduce a un costo piuttosto basso, di 0,00012 denarii di II secolo, per tonnellata / miglio romano.

Tuttavia, credo che il costo del trasporto marittimo dovesse essere calcolato in unità di volume, come pensa anche Jean Rougé (Rougé 1966, 369-370) : infatti, da un lato la disposizione dei carichi nelle navi lapidarie naufragate (Punta Scifo, Giardini Naxos, Isola delle Correnti), fa pensare che tali navi viaggiassero con la stiva piena, forse grazie ad uno scafo sagomato in modo da consentire la navigazione anche con carichi pesanti; dall'altro, il marmo poteva servire come zavorra commerciabile (McGrail 1989, 353-358), in modo da essere imbarcato non solo su speciali navi lapidarie, ma anche su navi di tipo normale, che in tal modo avrebbero utilizzato anche lo spazio destinato alla zavorra.

Nel caso del viaggio da Alessandria a Roma, che, secondo l'Editto, costava 16 denarii dioclezianei per modio castrense (= 0,0128 mc), il costo per 1 mc (= 78 MK) era di 1248 denarii di Diocleziano, ovvero circa 12,5 denarii di I-II secolo per mc; nel caso di una colonna alta 36 piedi, di volume 14,8 mc, abbiamo un costo di 185 denarii.

Dopo il trasporto, il materiale veniva sbozzato, passava poi per un ulteriore stadio di lavorazione (definito "rustico" dal Pegoretti), collocato in opera e infine rifinito: ognuna di queste operazioni aveva un costo in ore di lavoro, traducibili in giornate e quindi in denarii.

Passiamo dunque al calcolo dei costi del portico *in summa cavea* nell'anfiteatro flavio di Pozzuoli (Tab. 3). Esso era costituito da 72 colonne in marmo proconnesio, con fusti lisci alti m 4,73 (16 piedi), capitelli alti cm 90 (3 piedi), basi alte cm 47 (1,5 piedi): in tutto, la colonna era alta m 6,10 = 20 1/2 piedi.

I. Prima calcoliamo il costo del materiale. Il volume del fusto era di mc 2,75; in base al costo del proconnesio dell'Editto, di 15,5 denarii di I-II secolo al mc, abbiamo un costo unitario di 42,5 denarii per fusto, per un totale di 3060 denari. Per i capitelli (mc 0,7), 11 denarii l'uno, e 792 denarii in totale; per le basi, calcolate come 1/3 circa dei capitelli, 3,75 denarii l'una e 270 denari in tutto, per un costo totale di 57,25 denarii per colonna e 4122 denarii in tutto.

II. A tale costo va aggiunta la spesa della sbozzatura preliminare, calcolata, in base al testo del Pegoretti, in 300 ore di lavoro per mc. Per i fusti, il costo era di 300 ore x mc 2,75 = 41,5 denari; per i capitelli, sempre in base al Pegoretti, il lavoro di sbozzatura risulta di 210 ore/mc, ovvero 147 ore = 14,7 giornate = 7,5 denari. Per semplificare, il costo delle basi è valutato sempre 1/3 di quello dei capitelli, dunque 2,5 denarii.

III. Per quanto riguarda il trasporto, si ritiene che il proconnesio fosse ammassato presso il porto di Nicomedia, da cui poi raggiungeva Porto o le altre destinazioni (Pensabene 2002). Il costo del viaggio da Proconneso a Nicomedia, e da Nicomedia a Pozzuoli, paragonabile a quello da Alessandria a Roma (che costava 16 denarii per modio castrense, nell'Editto; equivalente a 12,5 denarii di I-II secolo per mc), era: fusti: mc 2,75 x 12,5 = 34,5 denarii; capitelli: mc 0,7 x 12,5 = 9 denarii; basi: 3 denari.

IV. Seguiva poi una lavorazione più approfondita, definita "rustico" dal Pegoretti, destinata a togliere le scabrosità dalla superficie, ma ancora non definitiva. Per i fusti di proconnesio, a grana grossa, la formula a (2 + 0,5 / x) che esprime le ore di lavoro per mq, tiene conto sia del materiale che del diametro inferiore del fusto (x), mediante la costante a = 8. Per i capitelli, la formula è a (1 + 0,25 / x), con il valore in funzione del diametro del capitello (x) e del fattore a, che cambia a seconda della grana del marmo: per il proconnesio è a = 5,8. Le basi vengono stimate 1/3 del costo del capitello.
Abbiamo così i seguenti valori: fusti: 20,65 x mq 13,93 = 287,65 ore = 14,5 den.; capitelli: 7,87 x mq 2,75 = 21,64 ore = 1,5 den.; basi: 1/3 capitelli = 0,5 den.

V. In seguito, le colonne e i capitelli venivano collocati nell'edificio. Nel caso dell'anfiteatro, ciò comportava un'elevazione di circa m 18 per basi e fusti, di m 23 per i capitelli, e il lavoro necessario può essere calcolato mediante una formula, ancora di Pegoretti: (Ore di lavoro per tonnellata di peso) = *0,20 (imbracatura) + 0,33 x m di distanza (avvicinamento) + 0,2 x m di altezza (elevazione) + 0,1 (posizionamento) + 1 (grappe)*.

Presupposti in media 100 metri di avvicinamento dei pezzi, e un peso specifico medio di 2,7 ton / mc per il marmo, abbiamo i seguenti risultati:

fusti: t 7,42 x 38 = 281,96 ore = 14 den.
capitelli: t 0,7 x 39 = 27,3 ore = 1,5 den.
basi: t 0,23 x 37,9 = 8,71 ore = 0,5 den.

VI. Dopo aver montato i pezzi, si procedeva alla rifinitura finale: scanalatura dei fusti, cesellatura di basi e capitelli. La scanalatura dei fusti è valutata dal Pegoretti, per marmi a cristalli grandi (Proconnesio / Tasio): 18,67 (sbozzo) + 16 (finitura) = 34,67 ore/mq (la superficie laterale del fusto è mq 12,77): Scanalatura fusto: mq 12,77 x 34,67 = 442,73 ore = 22 den.

La finitura di capitelli corinzi di dimensioni simili, per Pegoretti, richiedeva 1351,75 ore, con marmi a frattura scheggiata, come il proconnesio (Pegoretti 1869, I, 398). Si hanno dunque valori di: h 1351,75 = 67,5 den.

Per le basi, la cesellatura di sagome richiedeva 8,67 ore a mq con marmi a grana grossa; la superficie laterale delle basi si può calcolare come mq 1,32, dunque si hanno valori di mq 1,32 x 8,67 = 11,44 ore = 0,5 den. Da tutti i dati precedenti, si può trarre la tabella riassuntiva (tab. 3).

I valori relativi alla sbozzatura, "rustico" e finitura dei capitelli possono essere collegati a quanto sappiamo sul numero di operai al lavoro sui capitelli stessi, che, secondo lo studio di Filippo Demma qui pubblicato, dovevano essere da 7 a 8. Per quanto riguarda la finitura, se ogni capitello richiedeva 1351,75 ore, il totale dei 72 capitelli avrà richiesto 97326 ore, ovvero 9732,5 giornate/uomo da 10 ore; con 8 operai, la finitura di tutti i capitelli avrebbe dunque richiesto 1216,5 giorni; con 7 operai, 1390 giorni. Sbozzatura e "rustico" avrebbero invece richiesto, assieme, 1214 giornate/uomo: ipotizzando che tali lavorazioni fossero state effettuate dagli stessi scalpellini che scolpirono le foglie di acanto, per le prime due operazioni sarebbero stati necessari 152 giorni con 8 operai, e 175 giorni con 7 operai. In tutto, 1368,5 o 1565 giorni (4 - 5 anni).

Nella stima non si è tenuto conto del costo di trasporto dal luogo di attracco al luogo di messa in opera, visto che l'anfiteatro non era molto distante dal porto di Pozzuoli, e che in parte tale fattore è stato incluso nel calcolo della messa in opera; tuttavia, non è da escludere che le spese di trasporto dalla nave al cantiere potrebbero essere state un fattore non trascurabile, anche in considerazione di eventuali rotture o danneggiamenti che potrebebro aver avuto luogo in questa delicata fase. Riteniamo, su basi totalmente empiriche e non dimostrabili, che tali fattori potrebbero aver influito per un 1%, da aggiungere quindi come supplemento al prezzo finale.

Queste cifre andrebbero confrontate con prezzi noti di elementi architettonici di età romana, che però le fonti o le iscrizioni non forniscono frequentemente. Un'iscrizione di Smirne di II secolo d.C. (*IvSmyrna* 697) parla di una colonna in marmo *kymbellites* costata 200 denarii, ma non vengono precisate né le dimensioni né il tipo di marmo. Il numero di colonne finanziate, nel complesso, era però di 52: dunque si trattava di un'ampia fornitura di colonne, paragonabile alle 72 dell'anfiteatro di Pozzuoli, e il prezzo di 200 denarii sembra paragonabile al nostro risultato.

Con tali considerazioni non si intende preconizzare la nascita di una sorta di prontuario per calcolare i prezzi di ogni edificio romano, del quale si possa calcolare il volume del materiale lapideo usato; piuttosto, sul piano metodico, si auspica che nello studio dell'architettura romana si presti

.

maggiore attenzione agli aspetti economici e organizzativi della costruzione, alla quantificazione delle risorse mobilitate, agli investimenti della committenza. La nostra proposta, basata sul metodo di J. De Laine, fornisce appunto un sistema per avvicinarsi ad una stima realistica del lavoro e del conseguente finanziamento che richiesero i grandi programmi edilizi in marmo di importazione, diffusi in tutte le province romane a partire dall'età augustea e per tutta l'età severiana.

NOTE

1 I valori espressi in "giornate per metri cubi" = g/mc sono trasformati in "giornate per piedi cubi" = g/pc mediante divisione per 38,5.

BIBLIOGRAFIA

Burford, A. , 1969, The Greek temple builders at Epidauros. Liverpool.

De Laine, J., 1987, The Baths of Caracalla. A study in the design, construction and economics of large-scale building projects in Imperial Rome (JRA Suppl. 25), Portsmouth.

Dolci, E. , 1980, Carrara, cave antiche, Carrara.

Duncan Jones, R., 1974, The Economy of Roman Empire. Quantitative Studies, Cambridge.

Giacchero, M., 1974, Edictum Diocletiani et Collegarum de pretiis rerum venalium, Genova.

Hellmann, M.-Ch., 2002, Paris.

Mc Grail, S. , 1989, The Shipment of Traded Goods and of Ballast in Antiquity, in OJA, 8, 353-358.

Monna, D., Pensabene, P., 1977, Marmi dell'Asia Minor, Roma.

Peacock, D.P.S., Maxfield, V., 1997, Mons Claudianus. Survey and Excavation. Vol. I, Topography and Quarries (Documents de fouilles de l'Institut Français d'Archéologie Orientale 37), Le Caire.

Pegoretti, G., 1869, Manuale pratico per l'estimazione dei lavori architettonici (II ed.), Milano.

Pensabene, P., 1983, Osservazioni sulla diffusione dei marmi e sul loro prezzo nella Roma imperiale, in DdA, 1, 1983, 55-63.

Pensabene, P., 1999, Le cave del Mons Claudianus: conduzione statale, appalti, e distribuzione, in JRA, 12, 721-736.

Pensabene, P. , 2001, Pentelico e proconnesio in Tripolitania: coordinamento o concorrenza nella distribuzione? Contributo ad una nuova discussione dei modelli di Ward Perkins sulla circolazione del marmo, in ArchClass, 52, 63-127.

Pensabene, P., 2002, Le principali cave di marmo bianco. 1. Marmo proconnesio, in I marmi colorati della Roma imperiale, Catalogo della mostra, Venezia, 203-205.

Rougé, J., 1966, Recherches sur l'organisation du commerce maritime dans le Méditerranée, Paris.

TABELLA 1		
Prezzo Editto	Tipi di marmo	
250 denarii	*Porphyrites* (porfido rosso egiziano)	*Lakedaimonion* (*serpentino* spartano)
200 denarii	*Noumedikon* (*giallo antico* numidico)	*Dokimenon* (*pavonazzetto* di Docimium in Frigia)
150 denarii	*Loukoullion* (marmo *africano*, da Teos)	*Thessalon* (*verde antico* di Tessaglia)
100 denarii	*Pyrropoikilon* (granito di Assuan)	*Klaudianon* (granito *del Foro*, dal Mons Claudianus)
	Karystion (*cipollino* dall'Eubea)	
75 denarii	*Tripontikon* (marmo non identificato)	*Alabastresion* (forse alabastro egiziano)
	Herakleiotikon (da Eraclea al Latmo)	
60 denarii	*Euthydemianon* (marmo non identificato)	
50 denarii	*Thasion* (marmo di Taso)	*Lesbion* (marmo grigio di Lesbo)
40 denarii	*Potamogallenon* (marmo non identificato, forse bitinico: Monna, Pensabene 1977, 172)	*Skyrianon* (da Sciro: marmo bianco?)
	Prokonnesion (marmo proconnesio)	*Anakastenon* (marmo non identificato)

TABELLA 2							
TIPI DI MARMO	Giornate di lavoro	Materiale (1:3)	Quoziente	G/mc	G/pc	Costo	EDITTO
Porfido	12	4	12,5	200	5,2	260	250
Lacedemone	12	4	12,5	200	5,2	260	250
Frigio	12	4	10	160	4,15	208	200
Numidico	12	4	10	160	4,15	208	200
Africano	12	4	7,5	120	3,1	155	150
Assuan	12	4	5	80	2	100	100
Cipollino	12	4	5	80	2	100	100
Proconnesio	12	4	2	64	0,83	41	40

TABELLA 3								
	Fusti		Capitelli		Basi		Tot.	
	#1	#72	#1	#72	#1	#72	#1	#72
I. Materiale	42,5	3060	11	792	3,75	270	*57,25*	*4122*
II. Sbozzatura	41,5	2988	7,5	540	2,5	180	*51,5*	*3708*
III. Trasporto	34,5	2484	9	648	3	216	*46,5*	*3348*
IV. "Rustico"	14,5	1044	1,5	108	0,5	36	*16,5*	*1188*
V. Montaggio	14	1008	1,5	108	0,5	36	*16*	*1152*
VI. Finitura	22	1584	67,5	4860	0,5	36	*90*	*6480*
Totali	**169**	**12168**	**98**	**7056**	**10,75**	**774**	***277,75***	***19998***

PRODUZIONI LATERIZIE E CANTIERI EDILIZI TRAIANEI

ELISABETTA BIANCHI
(Sovraintendenza ai Beni Culturali del Comune di Roma)

ABSTRACT: The study of 551 brick stamps discovered a century ago in the excavations of the Forum and Baths of Trajan demonstrates that the brick industry in Rome between the mis 1st and early 2nd centuries AD was highly standardized. The *figlinae* producers of brick for the Forum have been identified in *Regio* VI. The results of this study suggest that there was an industrial type of organization in place that was capable of supplying vast amounts of materials necessary for the construction of massive public works projects. The analysis of the distribution of the various types of bricks in the different sectors of the monments and the information contained in the inscriptions has allowed us to deepen our knowledge of the building industry and related aspects of economic history. XRD analyses have revealed differences between the clays and in the techniques in clay preparation.

Gli ingenti lavori di scavo e di restauro che a Roma, nell'ultimo decennio, hanno interessato il Foro e le Terme di Traiano, due dei principali complessi architettonici di età traianea, offrono la possibilità di fare il punto sulla produzione laterizia destinata ai cantieri imperiali. I bolli laterizi rinvenuti nel secolo scorso in modo episodico nei due monumenti, non erano finora mai stati messi a confronto. Questa relazione rappresenta un primo tentativo di riordinare il materiale notevolmente arricchito grazie alle nuove indagini.

Alla luce dei nuovi numerosi esemplari rilevati, l'intero complesso dei marchi di fabbrica su mattoni rinvenuti in tempi diversi è stato riesaminato, sia per completare il quadro già delineato da H.Bloch, che per cercare di comprendere se, fra le varie parti di ciascuno dei due complessi, potesse essere stabilita una cronologia relativa e la sua conformità o meno rispetto alle datazioni tradizionali.

Il mattone è l'unico tra i materiali da costruzione che abbia restituito un repertorio completo di nomi di produttori. Accanto a personaggi meno noti ne compaiono altri molto più conosciuti alla prosopografia doliare e ciò rientra in un panorama più ampio costituito da altri esempi dell'edilizia della media e poi tarda età imperiale, come la Villa Adriana di Tivoli o le Terme di Caracalla. Avendo l'opportunità di esaminare l'insieme dei bolli laterizi conosciuti in un edificio traianeo di così vaste dimensioni nel centro di Roma, è stato avviato il confronto dei dati desunti dai vari tipi presenti nel Foro[1] con materiali rinvenuti in contesti traianei vicini. Dalle pendici del Quirinale e del Campidoglio al Colle Oppio si realizzarono nello stesso periodo, le Terme, i Mercati e i restauri del Foro di Cesare, incluso l'integrale rifacimento del Tempio di Venere Genitrice, dedicato nel 113 d.C. insieme alla Colonna di Traiano[2].

Le informazioni contenute nelle iscrizioni dei tipi, che in certi casi attestano l'attività in questi "antichi cantieri" di generazioni successive di officinatori operanti per la stessa fabbrica, hanno permesso di considerare aspetti storici ed economici, mai esaminati prima per i due monumenti.

Ciascun contesto presenta, come si vedrà, un diverso schema di compartecipazione alla fornitura dei materiali da parte di diversi importanti proprietari di fondi, membri dell'alta società romana (Steinby 1982), ad uno stesso programma costruttivo ed è possibile immaginare quali profitti siano potuti derivare dal possesso delle risorse naturali e dalla loro lavorazione per fini industriali. In sostanza, i lineamenti di questa impresa rispecchiano un'organizzazione produttiva tale da giustificare qui più che altrove la definizione di quella che la Steinby chiama "grande industria" (Steinby 1993a, 143).

Si sta tentando di formulare un quadro provvisorio delle concordanze, in vista del riordino dei bolli finora rinvenuti nei complessi traianei sopra citati. Obiettivo di un simile lavoro, è quello di poter delineare i caratteri della produzione laterizia a Roma tra la metà del I e la metà del II secolo d.C., utilizzando un *corpus* dei bolli rinvenuti nei grandi edifici pubblici, edificati contemporaneamente e in un'area ristretta.

Era ovvio chiedersi quanto la realizzazione di progetti monumentali di questa portata dovesse prevedere in termini di pianificazione e organizzazione del cantiere costruttivo e secondo quali regole.

Nell'ambito di uno studio più ampio sul Foro, ci si è posti l'interrogativo di quali fossero gli strumenti per l'ottenimento del flusso dei materiali necessari per la realizzazione del progetto e come il marmo, il travertino, il tufo o il legname, anche per i laterizi la ricerca è stata orientata verso l'individuazione dei canali di provenienza, risalendo alle aree geografiche connesse con l'attività delle fabbriche (Bianchi e Meneghini 2002).

I ritrovamenti all'interno del Foro di Traiano

Il Foro di Traiano è oggi in gran parte visibile grazie agli scavi susseguitisi nell'arco di circa due secoli **(Fig. 1)**. Buona parte della Basilica Ulpia era stata scoperta tra il 1812 e il 1813 e successivamente, tra il 1929 e il 1933 (Amici 1982, 1-4), quando venne liberato anche il portico orientale della piazza. Più recentemente, tra il 1991 e il 2000, sono state esplorate le parti centrale e meridionale della piazza (Meneghini 1998, 2001b), mentre è tuttora in corso, anche a cura di chi scrive, un tentativo di ricostruzione delle fasi di cantiere del Foro (Bianchi e Meneghini 2002).

I primi ritrovamenti di bolli laterizi nel Foro di Traiano, risalgono al 1932 e H. Bloch per primo ne elaborò una classificazione (Bloch 1947, 49-61).

Gli scavi condotti tra il 1991 e il 1997 hanno riguardato il settore meridionale del portico orientale, in prossimità dell'esedra settentrionale del Foro di Augusto, rivelando la planimetria delle strutture, ormai scomparse, come la gran parte degli ordini architettonici e dei rivestimenti marmorei (Meneghini 1998, 127-148). Qui è stato possibile, analizzare le cortine laterizie di alcune canalette fognarie sottostanti la pavimentazione della piazza e disposte lungo le fondazioni degli elevati, nonché i resti dei primi gradini e del muro di spina di una scala che serviva gli ambienti superiori del portico. Questi muri hanno restituito bolli noti soltanto in parte al Bloch per quest'area, già indagata durante i lavori degli anni Trenta.

Il grande scavo realizzato tra il 1998 e il 2000, realizzato in occasione del Grande Giubileo, ha invece interessato una superficie ben più vasta (Meneghini 2001b).

Sono state scoperte l'intera estensione della piazza forense e le fosse di fondazione del muro di recinzione meridionale "trisegmentato"e di un'ampia area porticata, laddove si credeva fosse collocato un arco di trionfo, tradizionalmente ipotizzato come accesso al foro, al centro di un muraglione semicircolare.

Nel cortile porticato posto a sud della grande galleria tripartita, l'intero sistema fognante e i crolli degli elevati dei muri, hanno restituito un discreto numero di laterizi bollati.

Immediatamente a nord, si conservano i maestosi resti del colonnato con fusti rudentati di Giallo Antico che, addossato al muro trisegmentato fronteggiava scenograficamente l'estremità meridionale della piazza del foro. Dell'attico, che probabilmente si trovava al di sopra di questo ordine architettonico, resta, allo stato di crollo, uno spezzone di opera laterizia di grandi dimensioni. Il suo nucleo presenta su due lati opposti una cortina che ha restituito, sia pure nei pochi filari conservati, ben tre laterizi bollati.

Nel mese di febbraio 2002, è stata rilevata la presenza di due nuovi tipi di età adrianea da parte di R. Meneghini e di chi scrive, durante una nuova ricognizione dei resti che si trovano a nord della Colonna Traiana.

I due bolli laterizi, mai individuati prima, nè in queste strutture, nè in tutto il resto del foro di Traiano, rivestono allo stato attuale delle ricerche particolare importanza per la comprensione delle diverse fasi costruttive del foro (Meneghini 2002; Bianchi 2001b, App. II.

Su un totale di 141 bolli ora conosciuti nell'area del Foro, 95 sono quelli osservati da Bloch negli anni Trenta (dei quali 47 sicuramente riferibili al Foro di Traiano) e 46 quelli individuati con gli scavi realizzati tra il 1998 e il 2000 e con nuove ricognizioni. Su un totale di 27 tipi finora identificati, 9 erano quelli già noti dal catalogo di Bloch per il periodo traianeo, ai quali se ne sono aggiunti 16[3], oltre ai 2 adrianei rinvenuti *in situ*.

I ritrovamenti all'interno delle Terme di Traiano

Sulle Terme di Traiano già A. De Romanis nel 1822 pubblicò i primi dati relativi all'analisi delle cortine laterizie dei ruderi allora visibili del complesso termale, riconoscendo differenti <<marche o bolli de' mattoni>>**(fig. 2)**. Questi dati furono raccolti e completati da Bloch con le osservazioni di Weege, Hülsen e soprattutto di Dressel sui materiali della grande esedra pubblicati nel *Corpus* (Bloch 1947, 36-49).

Nel 1968, durante alcuni lavori di consolidamento della c.d. Biblioteca, ovvero l'abside L, fu possibile osservare alcuni bolli laterizi *in situ* nella sommità della struttura (Romeo 1974-75).

Negli anni Settanta e Ottanta del XX secolo, K. De Fine Licht (1974, 1990) analizzò, le murature delle absidi L, H e D, quelle delle Sette Sale, e i condotti fognari connessi con la cisterna e l'edificio a ovest.

Più recentemente, in occasione di un intervento di restauro dell'abside D del recinto esterno, realizzato tra il 1997 e il 1998[4], circa 12 bolli laterizi identificabili sono stati individuati sui bipedali degli archi e delle piattabande posti a copertura delle nicchie.

In quegli stessi anni, gli scavi condotti da G. Caruso e R. Volpe[5] all'interno del c.d. "Criptoportico", una galleria delle Terme che corre lungo il lato occidentale del recinto esterno, hanno rivelato nella sua parte terminale i resti di arcate pertinenti ad un edificio preesistente all'impianto termale. Tali arcate risultano chiuse da una struttura in laterizio in fase con i muri della galleria. Su queste murature sono stati individuati tre bolli laterizi, dei tipi già rinvenuti nelle strutture della soprastante abside.

Dei bolli laterizi pubblicati da Bloch (1947, 45, n. 47), 158 recavano indicazioni topografiche precise nell'ambito del monumento.

Attualmente si può calcolare che su un totale di 410 esemplari localizzabili, ancora in corso di studio, 73 sono i tipi identificati[6]. Nel considerare questi numeri, nel confronto con quelli indicati per il Foro, si deve tenere conto di due fattori: la diversa estensione originaria dei due complessi e la notevole sproporzione nei volumi totali delle parti realizzate in laterizio nell'uno e nell'altro.

***Figlinae, Domini* e *officinatores* presenti nel Foro e nelle Terme di Traiano**

Nel II secolo le strutture produttive dell'industria laterizia prevedevano la figura dei *domini,* proprietari delle terre dove venivano fabbricati i mattoni e quella degli *officinatores*, capi-officina (Steinby 1993a, 139), persone nelle cui *officinae* venivano prodotti i mattoni.

Nelle **Tabelle 1-2** sono riportati i nomi delle fabbriche e i nomi dei proprietari con quelli degli officinatori, in corsivo, rispettivamente produttori per il Foro e per le Terme.

Tali dati riguardano le figline note impegnate nella costruzione dei due complessi, otto nel Foro e 15 nelle Terme, e i tipi della catena di produzione di ciascuna fabbrica utilizzati all'interno dei diversi settori.

Sono presenti, in ambedue i monumenti, laterizi prodotti dalle *figlinae* Domiziane, Bruziane, Cepioniane, Marciane e di Plotina; Tempesine, Geniane, Macedoniane solo nel Foro; Caniniane, Tonneiane, Oceane, Medulliane, Subortane e soprattutto Salaresi e Sulpiciane solo nelle Terme.

Sono quasi tutte figline "maggiori" che tra la fine del I secolo e i primi due decenni del II operavano, si può dire esclusivamente, per il mercato di Roma (Steinby 1993b, 10). Risulta possibile calcolare approssimativamente il quantitativo di mattoni fornito da ciascuna fabbrica, e il numero totale delle figline impegnate nell'impresa, sulla base di due parametri fondamentali: i metri quadri complessivi di cortine da eseguire e i tempi di realizzazione previsti per il completamento delle opere (vedi *infra*, p. 000). Pertanto, i motivi di un numero così alto di *figlinae* nelle Terme, in confronto a quelle documentate nel Foro, devono risiedere unicamente nella superficie enormemente più estesa di cortine da realizzare.

Sia per il Foro che per le Terme, nelle Tabelle 1-2 sono indicati, nella prima colonna i nomi delle *figlinae*, nella seconda il tipo di bollo identificato con il numero corrispondente nel *CIL*XV,1[7]. I numeri evidenziati in neretto corrispondono ai tipi presenti in ambedue i contesti. Accanto si trova l'indicazione del totale dei tipi presenti per ciascuna fabbrica seguito dal numero complessivo degli esemplari rinvenuti. Nella quarta colonna si riportano i nomi dei proprietari, o *domini* (in tondo), e degli eventuali officinatori, *officinatores* (in corsivo), presenti nelle iscrizioni dei vari tipi.

Confrontando le due tabelle è possibile visualizzare quali differenti "catene di produzione", individuabili nei diversi tipi, per ciascuna figlina, siano state destinate all'uno o all'altro complesso. Le datazioni tra parentesi offrono una indicazione di massima della data di produzione del tipo, ove questo si discosti cronologicamente dagli altri inquadrabili nella piena età traianea.

Nelle **Tabelle 3-4** le figline e i loro produttori sono suddivisi per i settori dei due complessi all'interno dei quali sono stati individuati (Bianchi 2001b, Tab. II).

Dei tipi di laterizi utilizzati nel Foro di Traiano **(Tabella 1)**, i bipedali, furono forniti esclusivamente dalle officine Domiziane, di Camidieno Atimeto e di Anterote Severiano, mentre delle Bruziane, delle Cepioniane e delle Tempesine sono state rinvenute, e probabilmente non è un caso, soltanto tegole. Questo dato corrisponde perfettamente a quanto esposto da M. Steinby riguardo alla specializzazione nella gamma di produzione verso la quale fu orientata l'attività delle fabbriche maggiori, nel periodo della massima espansione dell'industria laterizia (Steinby 1993b, 11).

Naturalmente il numero totale dei bolli individuati nei vari settori del Foro di Traiano corrisponde a una percentuale esigua rispetto a quella originaria, tuttavia, è possibile delineare un quadro distributivo dei materiali forniti dalle diverse fabbriche piuttosto omogeneo, che non dovrebbe discostarsi di molto da quello reale.

I diversi tipi vanno circoscritti a un arco cronologico di circa 40 anni che va dalla fine dell'età domizianea al 123-125 d.C. Appare evidente una uniforme distribuzione dei bolli di piena età traianea, ma se ne notano di più antichi nelle fogne del settore sud orientale della piazza. Qui si riscontra l'impiego di materiali attribuibili ad un periodo compreso tra la fine dell'età domizianea e la prima età traianea.

Della *Gens* Domizia, dominante nell'industria doliare durante il I sec. d. C., nel Foro di Traiano sono presenti materiali prodotti da tre dei quattro *domini* succedutisi nella proprietà delle figline: Lucano, Tullo e Domizia Lucilla, complessivamente attivi dal 59 d.C. all'età adrianea[8] **(Fig. 3)**.

Tra gli officinatori dei due fratelli troviamo il nome del servo Primigenio, su un tipo collocabile cronologicamente prima del 93 d.C.. Successivi sono i bolli degli officinatori di Tullo, Agatobulo[9] **(Fig. 3.2)** e dei servi di questo, Aprile e Trofimo, ma anche di alcuni liberti Arignoto, Evaristo e Criserote.

Dei due bolli di età adrianea recentemente rinvenuti *in situ,* il 1033 reca i nomi dei consoli Petino e Aproniano del 123 d.C. **(Fig. 3.7)**. In esso compare il nome di Domizia Lucilla nuova proprietaria delle figline Domiziane e madre del futuro imperatore Marco Aurelio, con il suo servo e officinatore Doriforo.

La Basilica e l'ossatura delle c.d. biblioteche, di recente interpretate da R. Meneghini come aule di culto del *Templum Divi Traiani* (Meneghini 2002), presentano materiali coevi prodotti da tutte le figline impegnate nell'impresa, non oltre il 110, ciò che confermerebbe la tradizionale datazione, fornita dai Fasti Ostiensi, al 112-113 per il blocco Basilica-Colonna.

Tuttavia la presenza, in particolare del secondo bollo adrianeo,1209b, prodotto da Giulio Stefano, con qualche probabilità *dominus* delle Geniane, e recante la data dei due consoli Asiatico e Aquilino del 125 d.C., fa slittare inequivocabilmente, a una data posteriore alla fabbricazione del tipo, la costruzione *a fundamentis* del settore monumentale di ingresso, come opera di completamento del complesso forense, e quindi delle due aule di culto.

Delle figline Bruziane **(Fig. 4)**, un bollo (32) fu rinvenuto *in situ* da Bloch nella c.d. biblioteca occidentale. Lo scavo 1998-2000, sul lato opposto del complesso, ha invece restituito altri due tipi (29d e 29g). Si tratta in tutti i casi della produzione del proprietario M. Rutilio Lupo (Bloch 1947, 316-320). Questi fu sotto Traiano prima *Praefectus Annonae* e poi *Praefectus Aegypti* dal 113 al 117 e, specialmente tra il 105 e il 125, attivissimo fornitore per opere pubbliche, specialmente a Ostia. La sua presenza in Egitto iniziò nel 110 e da questo anno egli avviò una produzione di laterizi caratterizzata dalla presenza della datazione consolare. Gli esemplari dei tipi 29c e 32 rinvenuti rispettivamente nell'area meridionale e nelle murature della c.d. biblioteca occidentale, ne sono privi e quindi vanno fatti risalire agli anni precedenti questa data. Il 29g (De Fine Licht 1990, Fig. 118,2) **(Fig. 4.3)**, invece, va attribuito agli anni 118-120 (Steinby 1974-75, 27-28), ad un periodo cioè successivo al termine della prefettura di R. Lupo.

Delle Tempesine compaiono i bolli del *dominus* Vismazio Successo, databili al 100-110 d.C. In un secondo tipo lo stesso Vismazio Successo compare come *patronus* di Felice, officinatore anche di M. Rutilio Lupo proprietario delle Bruziane.

Nel settore centrale del Foro durante i nuovi scavi è stato rinvenuto un bollo delle figline Macedoniane di Antonia Manliola, la cui produzione inizia nei primi anni di Traiano e prosegue fino al 110 d.C.

Quantitativamente molto ben rappresentata è poi la produzione delle figline Cepioniane **(Fig. 5)**, che deve essere attribuita in parte alla piena età traianea e in parte alla fine di essa. Si tratta dei materiali di Curiazio Cosano *dominus*, dal primo decennio del II secolo, fino al 123, delle due sezioni chiamate *ab Euripo* e *a Pila Alta* **(Fig. 5.2)**.

Proprietaria di un'altra sezione delle stesse figline era Plozia Servilia Isaurica (Setälä 1977, 164), che nel Foro compare con diversi suoi officinatori: Lucio Gellio Prudente, Tito Rausio Pamfilo e Stazio Marco Lucifero.

Accanto a questo materiale, databile al 100-110 d.C., se ne riscontra altro più recente, quale i sigilli degli stessi Stazio Marco Lucifero **(Fig. 5.3)** e di Tito Rausio Pamfilo, divenuti già officinatori di Arria Fadilla, madre di Antonino Pio, succeduta a Plozia Isaurica come proprietaria delle figline intorno al 115 (Helen 1975, 76), nonchè quelli di Curiazio Cosano (97c) riferibili, invece, al 117.

L'esame dei materiali rinvenuti nel settore centrale e meridionale, ai confini con il Foro di Augusto, già prima del ritrovamento *in situ* dei due tipi adrianei aveva del resto rivelato la presenza, insieme al già citato bollo di R. Lupo databile al 118, di esemplari più recenti.

E' evidente che sia per questo settore, che per quello a nord della Colonna, la cronologia va oltre la data tradizionale di costruzione del Foro e che, per il suo completamento si sia dovuto ricorrere ad una nuova fornitura di materiale che quindi le stesse figline, soprattutto Bruziane, Domiziane e Cepioniane, devono essersi impegnate a fabbricare.

Passando a esaminare i materiali impiegati nelle Terme, è necessario premettere, come già accennato, che laterizi delle stesse figline recanti diversi tipi di bolli sono attestati in ambedue i contesti. Nelle Terme, infatti, come nel Foro, sono documentati due tipi sia delle Cepioniane che delle Domiziane e uno delle Bruziane **(Tabelle 1-2)**.

Delle Bruziane di Rutilio Lupo si trovano, oltre a molti esemplari del tipo 18 **(Fig. 4.1)** nelle Sette Sale e nel muro della grande esedra due varianti del 29g (Steinby 1977-78, n. 52, tav. 11) **(Fig. 4.2)**. I bolli laterizi delle Cepioniane nelle Terme offrono un repertorio molto più articolato di quanto non si sia riscontrato nel Foro. *Plozia Servilia Isaurica,* i cui bolli si incontrano nella grande esedra e nelle costruzioni davanti a essa, come nelle absidi B,D, compare qui con tutti i suoi officinatori (tranne *L. Gellius Prudens*) compresi *Eucharus*, *Peculiaris* e *Statius Marcius Bassus* (Steinby 1977-78, n. 91, tav. 17) **(Fig. 5.1)**. Tra questi, *Statius Marcius Lucifer* è presente con lo stesso tipo visto nel Foro (59b), mentre di *T. Rausius Pamphilus* si trovano impiegati mattoni recanti tipi differenti da quello del Foro (67a, 67b, 68d). Nelle Terme, i mattoni di *Curiatius Cosanus* si trovano nella grande esedra con quelli di Plozia Servilia Isaurica. Al tipo 97b, visto nel Foro (cfr. **Fig.5.2**), si affiancano il 98 (Steinby 1977-78, n. 137, tav. 26) **(Fig. 5.4)** e il 99, recanti la data consolare del 123 d.C., nei quali compare Sesto Alfio Amando come officinatore. Mancano del tutto i materiali di Arria Fadilla, *domina* delle figline che, come si è visto, alla fine del regno di Traiano fornì i materiali per le ultime fasi edilizie del Foro.

Riguardo alle Domiziane, presenti un po' ovunque nelle Terme, accanto a bolli più antichi quali quelli degli officinatori di Domizio Tullo, Nicomaco (De Romanis 1822, tav.5,5) **(Fig.3.3)**, Primitivo[10] **(Fig.3.4)**, Agatobulo o addirittura dei due Domizi Lucano e Tullo con L. Rutilio Sosia e Q. Oppio Verecondo (Steinby 1977-78, n. 999, tav. 172) **(Fig. 3.1)**, si trovano materiali della nuova proprietaria Domizia Lucilla con Nicomaco e Agatobulo divenuti suoi officinatori, anche se i rinvenimenti riguardano il settore delle Sette Sale e non il vero e proprio complesso termale. Tra i materiali dei liberti, molti esemplari del tipo di Domizio Clemente (De Romanis 1822, tav.5,9) **(Fig.3.5)**, sono stati trovati nelle absidi L,D, nel gruppo di ambienti denominato M[11] e nei resti della costruzione centrale; il 1096a di Domizio Evaristo[12] **(Fig.3.6)**, variante di quello rinvenuto nel Foro, nella grande esedra e nelle absidi D e H.

Delle *figlinae* che non producono laterizi per il Foro, nelle Terme si trova il bollo di *Cn. Domitius Amoenus* divenuto liberto di Tullo e riferibile alle figline Caniniane (Steinby 1974-75, 34; Steinby 1977-78, n. 864, tav. 152) **(Fig. 6)**.

Come qui di seguito esposto, si sono voluti inserire in questa descrizione alcuni bolli provenienti dall'area delle Terme ma non strettamente connessi con la sua fase costruttiva, come la fila di taberne costruite in età adrianea davanti alla grande esedra, al solo scopo di evidenziare quali differenze di fornitura possono essere occorse in pochi anni dopo il completamento del complesso termale.

In opera nelle taberne di fronte alla grande esedra si trova un tipo appartenente a Q. Abumio Cediciano, sotto il quale si era avviata l'attività delle figline Furiane, tra la fine del regno di Traiano e l'inizio di quello di Adriano (Steinby 1974-75, 43) oltre a uno dei *Praedia Mammeiana* di Giulia albana. Ancora qui, tra i materiali dei *Praedia Quintanensia* (Steinby 1974-75, 78), situate probabilmente, *ad Quintanas* o nella *Res Publica Lavicanorum,* il bollo 1496a, rinvenuto insieme a quelli di Cornelio Severo e Trebicia Tertulla, si riferisce a *D. Veturius Cerdo*, che troveremo nel 123 al servizio di *M. Annius Verus* (Steinby 1974-75, 79).

Adrianeo è anche un bollo di Q. Asinio Marcello delle officine Medulliane e della sua officinatrice Appia Piramide (Steinby 1974-75, 66, n.11), rinvenuto nel riempimento del collettore delle Sette Sale.

Nel primo ordine di nicchie dell'abside L del recinto esterno si trovano per la prima volta i bolli delle *Oceanae* divenute di proprietà imperiale proprio dall'età traianea **(Fig. 7)**. Il nome dell'officinatore, del quale De Romanis notò sedici bolli laterizi, per la sezione *Minores* è quello *L. Bruttidius Augustalis* (De Romanis 1822, tav.5,8) **(Fig. 7.1)**, che iniziò la sua attività nei primi anni di Traiano e che sarà nei decenni seguenti una figura preminente tra i figuli[13].

Nel bollo 709b, delle *Oceanae Maiores* (Steinby (1977-78, n. 608) **(Fig. 7.2)**, databile al primo decennio del II secolo, *Aprilis* compare come servo di Aquilia Sozomena, officinatrice imperiale. Più tardi questo operaio, manomesso dalla padrona, entrerà al servizio di Traiano, verso la fine del suo governo, come *C. Aquilius Aprilis* e rimarrà sotto Adriano uno dei principali figuli imperiali.

Tra i materiali della prima età traianea delle fabbriche denominate Opus Salarese, rinvenuti nella grande esedra e nelle absidi I e L c'è il bollo 954 di *Cn.Pinarius Cornelius Severus,* console suffetto nel 112 (Bloch 1947, 48).

E' notevole anche la presenza, di un bollo di *Trebicia Tertulla* **(Fig. 8)** (Steinby 1977-78, n. 462) databile alla prima età adrianea e notato, oltre che in numerosi esemplari della stessa variante nelle taberne davanti alla grande esedra, insieme al tipo citato di *Cornelius Severus,* anche nell'abside B. In questa stessa struttura si trova il bollo traianeo di *Marcius Firmus* figulo imperiale delle f. Subortane (Steinby 1977-78, n. 478) **(Fig. 9)**.

Molto consistente è la presenza dei materiali delle figline Sulpiciane. Si tratta per lo più di mattoni triangolari. Il bollo 566 del primo decennio del II secolo, è di *M. Vinicius Pantagathus.* Il tipo è rappresentato in diverse varianti, i cui esemplari si ritrovano in molte parti del complesso termale, nelle incassature per gli architravi del secondo ordine dell'abside L del recinto esterno, nel corpo centrale e nelle Sette Sale. Dello stesso periodo, rinvenuti in opera nelle murature delle absidi I, H, L, sono i bolli di *Rufus* e di *T. Claudius Zosimus.* Recentemente, quest'ultimo, nella variante 582b, insieme al 591a e al 574 **(Cfr.Tabella 2)** è stato rilevato anche nelle pareti della galleria che corre al di sotto dell'abside L (Caruso-Volpe 2000, 48; Volpe 2002, 515, n. 12). Ancora delle Sulpiciane, nei condotti fognari delle Sette Sale, insieme ai materiali di Vinicio Pantagato e di Rufo sono stati rinvenuti molti bolli di *Claudius Herodotus* (De Fine Licht 1990, Fig. 114).

Delle figline Tonneiane, si riscontra la presenza delle tegole di Giulia Procula e della nuova proprietaria Pedania Quintilla, con i bolli dell'officinatore Nonio Clemente e di Sesto Vismazio Nerito databili agli anni 104-109 d.C.

Compaiono tra gli altri anche nomi di figuli non riferibili alle figline note. Nell'abside L, tipicamente traianei sono i bolli di *C. Milasius Cupitus* (1305), nel corpo centrale si trovano i bolli di C. Flavio Abascante (1143) e quello di M. Erennio Pollione (De Fine Licht 1990, Fig. 116; De Romanis 1882, tav. 5,4) **(Fig.10.1-2)** che compaiono anche come fornitori per i materiali nelle Sette Sale e dell'edificio a ovest della cisterna. Infine, nella grande esedra si trova T. Flavio Corinto, figulo imperiale con il 710b.
Occorre, a questo punto, accennare alla vistosa assenza nel Foro di Traiano dei bolli delle f. Marciane. Nelle **Tabelle 1-4** i materiali di Anterote Severiano sono stati inseriti come prodotti delle Marciane, poiché sembra strano che queste figline, di proprietà dello stesso Traiano e utilizzate per il restauro traianeo del Foro di Cesare, per le Terme[14] e per i

Mercati, siano proprio quelle mancanti in un quadro così completo di presenze di produttori per la fornitura dei materiali necessari alla costruzione del Foro.

Tuttavia, sulla base di alcuni elementi, è possibile ipotizzare un collegamento tra le f. Marciane e i due officinatori T. Camidieno Atimeto e Anterote Severiano.

Al primo personaggio appartiene il tipo 696 **(Fig. 11.2)**, rinvenuto durante gli scavi del 1932 in un elevato numero di esemplari e il 697 di recente rilevato in una fogna nell'area meridionale.

Come testimoniato dal bollo 695 (De Romanis (1882): tav.5,7) **(Fig. 11.1)**, rinvenuto sia nelle absidi B, H, L delle Terme che nelle Sette Sale, oltre che nei Mercati di Traiano, l'officinatore in questione era un agente dell'imperatrice Plotina[15] e nel suo *cognomen Atimetus* resta traccia della sua originaria condizione servile.

Il gentilizio Camidieno derivatogli dal primo *patronus*, è piuttosto raro e pochissime sono le iscrizioni nelle quali si trova attestato. Tutte inducono a risalire a un'origine umbra dello stesso patrono[16] del quale, in via ipotetica, Atimeto può aver continuato a svolgere l'attività, per qualche tempo forse indipendentemente e poi, per ragioni che non conosciamo, sotto l'imperatrice. Non si conosce l'esatta localizzazione dei *praedia* di Plotina, ma non si deve escludere che i maggiori produttori, pur lavorando per conto della coppia imperiale, potessero continuare a svolgere la loro attività nei loro possedimenti. In tal modo, sarebbe possibile ricondurre questi bolli, secondo quanto esposto nel paragrafo seguente, a una provenienza analoga a quella del resto dei materiali del Foro di Traiano.

Riguardo l'ipotesi del collegamento con le Marciane, essi si collocherebbero tra il 105, anno del conferimento a Plotina del titolo di "Augusta" (Lancaster 1995, 31), che appare sulla variante del bollo rinvenuta nei Mercati, e il 110, anno in cui, secondo Bloch, il nome di Traiano compare sui bolli delle Marciane (Steinby 1974-75, 65).

Non del tutto sicura è inoltre la zona di fabbricazione dei bipedali prodotti da Anterote Severiano (811d), servo di Traiano, e quindi officinatore imperiale[17] ma, sulla base del ritrovamento di scarti di fabbricazione recanti lo stesso tipo di bollo a *Lucus Feroniae* (Filippi e Stanco c.s.), si può ipotizzare con una certa sicurezza una provenienza dall'alta Valle del Tevere. I suoi bolli, CIL XV, 811, in due varianti, all'interno del Foro[18] **(Fig.12.1-2)**, furono trovati sia nell'area della Basilica Ulpia e *in situ* nella c.d. biblioteca orientale[19], che in opera anche nella scala posta alla terminazione sud del portico orientale della piazza. Il bollo è caratteristico dell'età di Traiano; nella variante 811e-g si trova sovente con altri già visti di Curiazio Cosano e di Trofimo ed è presente anche nei Mercati (Bloch 1947, 52) e nel Foro di Cesare (Bloch 1947, 61-63). Nelle Terme (Bloch 1947, 50-58; De Fine Licht 1990, 93; Filippi e Stanco c.s.) si trovano ambedue le varianti 811d e 811f, impiegate nella grande esedra, nell'arco di una nicchia dell'abside D, nell'edificio M e nel collettore delle Sette Sale.

Il nome di Anterote Severiano, nei principali repertori di bolli editi sia da Bloch che dalla Steinby non appare mai in connessione con una delle grandi figline. Si dovrebbe accettare l'ipotesi che un servo imperiale potesse gestire in assoluta autonomia una produzione vastissima, quale quella testimoniata dall'enorme diffusione dei suoi prodotti nella maggior parte dei monumenti traianei di Roma. Tuttavia alcune osservazioni aprono uno spiraglio su un suo possibile collegamento con le figline imperiali. Innanzitutto, la sua condizione di servo imperiale lo pone sullo stesso piano di un officinatore imperiale di condizione libertina come T. Camidieno Atimeto. In secondo luogo, la forma del bollo *versibus falcatis*, nonchè la disposizione, per così dire, ad archi concentrici e non circolare del testo dell'iscrizione denunciano una stretta somiglianza tipologica con i tipi 312-313 **(Fig. 12.3)** di *Calpetanus Favor* delle f. Marciane. Con il 313, in particolare, e con i laterizi di Camidieno Atimeto, entrambi i bolli in questione si ritrovano associati nelle Terme[20] e nei Mercati di Traiano, nella Basilica Argentaria e nella forica sopra il Foro di Cesare (Bloch 1947, 17 e 55).

Un'ultima nota riguarda i dati delle analisi svolte su un campione di argilla dei prodotti di ambedue i figuli, secondo i quali risultano analogie di qualità della materia prima e di trattamento dell'impasto (Morbidelli 2001).

Nuove evidenze archeologiche e nuove analisi di laboratorio potranno confermare o meno questa ipotesi ma, se a Camidieno Atimeto e ad Anterote Severiano si potessero attribuire con certezza due sezioni della vasta produzione delle f. Marciane, nel quadro delle presenze delle fabbriche produttrici di materiali per il Foro, queste figline risulterebbero coinvolte, come è logico aspettarsi, nell'approvvigionamento dei materiali necessari per la realizzazione del progetto, e a esse andrebbe riferita, se usiamo per proporzione le quantità note, la maggioranza dei bipedali.

Dal punto di vista strettamente economico-produttivo, questo dato potrebbe essere interpretato come un segnale forte, anche per Roma, di quel processo che altrove, come a Ostia, proprio in questi anni stava conducendo alla concentrazione della produzione laterizia nelle mani della famiglia imperiale.

Nelle Terme tale segnale appare meno significativo perché all'interno della più complessa articolazione della fornitura, quella di proprietà imperiale, sia pure comprendendo qui anche i laterizi delle Oceane, si confonde con un numero maggiore di prodotti derivanti da fabbriche private.

Localizzazione geografica delle figline

A proposito della provenienza del materiale laterizio, grazie a un recente e fondamentale studio ancora inedito di E.

Stanco e G. Filippi, è oggi possibile individuare con una certa approssimazione i siti delle fabbriche che hanno prodotto laterizi per il Foro di Traiano. Esse vanno localizzate tutte nella VI *Regio*, con una particolare concentrazione nel territorio dell'antica *Ameria* (odierna Giove), sulla riva sinistra del Tevere e in quello di *Statonia* (odierna Bomarzo) sulla riva destra **(Fig. 13)**. Più esattamente, i siti di produzione che sono stati individuati sono: *Statonia* per le figline Domiziane, l'*Ager Amerinus*, per le Tempesine, le Bruziane, le Macedoniane da localizzarsi queste ultime immediatamente a nord delle Tempesine e, con sicurezza, Penna in Teverina per le Cepioniane.

Questa ristretta area va inserita in un più ampio panorama di centri di produzione dislocati lungo tutto il corso del Tevere. A partire da nord, dall'impianto portuale di Pagliano (Morelli 1957, 3-60), dopo la confluenza del Paglia e della Chiana, fino a *Crustumerium* alle porte di Roma, si trovava una notevole quantità di fabbriche che sfruttavano la naturale disponibilità di argilla e di legname. Da quel porto il fiume diveniva una grande via navigabile per il materiale laterizio che, caricato su chiatte, veniva trasportato fino a Roma.

La notevole quantità di laterizi rinvenuti nello scavo degli anni Ottanta condotto presso il porto sul Tevere a sud di Roma, presso Lungotevere Testaccio, in corso di studio da parte di chi scrive, potrà risultare molto interessante anche per comprendere le modalità di stoccaggio dei laterizi prima della definitiva destinazione d'uso.

Note tecniche sulla fabbricazione dei laterizi

Per le procedure di fabbricazione del laterizio ci si può riferire da un lato alla grande produzione romana sulla quale si hanno significative testimonianze dal Rinascimento in poi (Giustini 1997), oltre che ai metodi in uso ancora oggi nelle moderne fornaci che hanno mantenuto viva la tradizione artigianale.

Per esempio, in una delle moderne fornaci di Castel Viscardo[21], presso Orvieto, si fabbricano mattoni, destinati ad usi particolari, secondo le tecniche del passato innovate soltanto dall'introduzione di impastatrici meccaniche e di forni a gas. Dopo la stagionatura e una serie di operazioni che ne accrescono la plasticità, l'argilla **(Fig.14.a)** viene impastata **(Fig.14.b)** poi battuta entro forme di legno delle varie dimensioni. **(Fig.14.c)** Prima di cuocere i laterizi nella fornace, al fine di evitarne la frantumazione per repentina essiccazione, questi vengono ordinatamente disposti a terra su un piazzale, come accadeva nella lavorazione antica, su uno strato di sabbia fine, spolverati con sabbia, "a stagionare" perché non si asciughino troppo in fretta e si frantumino. Per estendere il periodo dell'anno utile per la fabbricazione, durante i mesi più freddi, oggi i mattoni vengono distesi su un terreno "riscaldato" da tubazioni di acqua calda, allo scopo di abbreviare i tempi di essiccatura.

In questa fase della lavorazione un operaio da solo può formare al giorno dai 150 ai 180 mattoni delle stesse misure di quelli antichi, es. 40x40 cm e circa 100 delle dimensioni di 60x60 cm[22].

I primi richiedono 3-4 giorni per l'asciugatura, i secondi dai 20 ai 25 giorni, venendo rifilati e poi girati sull'altra faccia a circa metà dei periodo. I laterizi vengono infine impilati prima di essere cotti in uno dei forni moderni **(Fig.14.d)**.

Le fornaci romane per mattoni erano, in Italia, generalmente di forma quadrata o rettangolare (De Laine 1997: 115) e potevano avere una capacità variabile dai 20 agli oltre 100 mc (*Cato*, *Agr*., 38; Fontana 1995).

J. DeLaine (1997, 117-118, tav. 9) ha calcolato, per un modello di fornace di 100 mc, una capacità di cottura di 65 mc di mattoni, un carico pari a 52.000 bessali, o 9.600 sesquipedali o 4.750 bipedali equivalenti, ciascun gruppo, a un volume di argilla cruda, pari a 93 mc. Considerando un modello ideale di produzione, la studiosa ha ipotizzato, per ogni stagione di attività, che doveva estendersi da metà aprile a metà ottobre (circa 180 giorni), un impiego di 7 uomini per 8 carichi ogni stagione[23].

Nell'impianto di Castel Viscardo vi è una fornace di forma ovale, costruita secondo le antiche tecniche, delle dimensioni interne di m 5,40x4,50 e dell'altezza di 6,5 m (inclusa la camera di combustione sottostante), per un totale di circa 90 mc, che può cuocere circa 30.000 pezzi di un formato medio a cotta. Ciascuna di queste richiede, 1-2 settimane con il lavoro di 5-6 operai e può essere ripetuta in genere per non più di 3-4 volte a stagione.

Al di là della certificazione di proprietà contenuta negli stessi bolli si è voluto procedere all'analisi della materia prima, l'argilla, cavata nei grandi fondi di senatori e cavalieri.

A questo proposito, le analisi svolte dalla geologa P. Morbidelli, dell'Istituto di Scienze della Terra dell'Università di Roma La Sapienza, hanno fornito importanti informazioni riguardo alla qualità e alle tecniche di lavorazione dell'argilla dei mattoni del Foro di Traiano (vedi Appendice).

Per le analisi di laboratorio sono stati selezionati reperti rappresentativi di una campionatura più ampia e provenienti da diversi settori dell'area archeologica in questione.

Le analisi diffrattometriche hanno evidenziato: che si tratta di due gruppi di impasti argillosi: al gruppo A appartengono i materiali o meglio gli impasti delle f. Domiziane, delle Macedoniane, delle Tempesine, di Camidieno Atimeto e di Anterote Severiano, mentre al gruppo B afferiscono sia quelli delle f. Cepioniane (di tutte e tre le sezioni), che delle Bruziane. La mineralogia degli impasti è molto simile suggerendo una comune provenienza del materiale con la possibilità che si possa trattare di officine di produzione diverse che utilizzavano miscele argilla/degrassante differenti. A questo proposito i risultati delle analisi chimiche e petrografiche, che non è stato ancora possibile eseguire, saranno fondamentali per un'adeguata e corretta interpretazione delle tecnologie di produzione di questi materiali.

La presenza di minerali e/o associazioni di minerali (calcite, quarzo, ecc.) fornisce indicazioni sulla temperatura di cottura dei mattoni. Ad esempio, è stato possibile accertare che i laterizi prodotti dalle figline del gruppo A sono stati cotti a temperature vicine ai 950°C, mentre per quelli delle officine del gruppo B la temperatura di cottura deve essere stata molto più bassa (intorno ai 600°).

A differenza delle Terme e dei Mercati, l'opera laterizia fu adoperata nel Foro su scala molto minore e con essa furono realizzati, come già detto, soltanto l'intero impianto fognante, le c.d. biblioteche con i numerosi vani scala connessi (Bianchi 2001a)[24] e alcuni settori dell'architettura meridionale della piazza.

L'inizio del II secolo corrisponde a Roma a un aumento progressivo delle costruzioni in laterizio ed è singolare notare invece come questa tecnica nella costruzione del Foro di Traiano corrisponda solo al 9% del totale dei materiali utilizzati (Bianchi e Meneghini 2002).

Si può calcolare che per la costruzione delle parti in laterizio del Foro siano stati utilizzati circa 1.305.000 mattoni, per un peso totale di circa 2000 tonnellate.

Il materiale utilizzato nel Foro di Traiano risulta, sulla base dell'evidenza disponibile, costituito da tegole spezzate e da bipedali in rapporto quantitativo non precisabile; allo scopo di ottenere un numero definito di mattoni prodotti si può adottare il sesquipedale come simbolica unità di misura con riferimento ai parametri quantitativi calcolati dalla DeLaine.

Per una fornace, ogni infornata poteva contenere 9.600 sesquipedali. Se il numero di cotte annue corrispondeva a 8, un impianto come quello di Castel Viscardo avrebbe potuto produrre in un anno un quantitativo pari a 76.000 mattoni. Per fabbricare il milione e trecentocinquemila mattoni necessari per il Foro, utilizzando una sola fornace sarebbero occorsi 17 anni. Ciò spiega, inequivocabilmente il motivo del coinvolgimento di un così alto numero di produttori. Dividendo, pertanto, il numero complessivo dei mattoni per sette, il numero delle figline produttrici finora accertate per la fase traianea del Foro, si ottiene una fornitura media totale di 187.000 mattoni prodotti da ciascuna, 76.000 ogni anno, in un arco di tempo di 2,5 anni di attività esclusivamente dedicata a questo progetto.

L'organizzazione dei cantieri

Riguardo all'organizzazione per la costruzione del Foro, si deve pensare che una normativa consolidata e un numero imprecisato di figure preposte debbano aver regolato sia l'appalto dei lavori che quello per la fornitura dei materiali, nonché lo svolgimento delle varie fasi della costruzione.

Conosciamo dalle fonti la figura di un *curator operum publicorum* il quale sotto gli Antonini, fu incaricato di pagare i *redemptores*[25]. Questi com'è noto erano appaltatori o fornitori privati. Molte iscrizioni ricordano inoltre l'esistenza di *mensores aedificiorum* (Lancaster 1998, 306, n.61), periti o misuratori, addetti probabilmente al controllo delle varie fasi dei lavori.

L'ipotesi della probabile presenza di un'associazione di *redemptores* che possono aver negoziato separatamente il lavoro di costruzione delle varie parti del complesso fu già formulata da L. Lancaster per i Mercati di Traiano e per i contemporanei restauri al Foro di Cesare (Lancaster 1998, 306). Nel Foro di Traiano, la complessa pianificazione necessaria per l'organizzazione di un cantiere di tali dimensioni, deve aver previsto per le parti in laterizio qualcosa di molto simile a quanto ipotizzato per i Mercati, sia per ciò che riguarda la convergenza sul luogo di costruzione di mattoni di diversa produzione, che per la realizzazione dei singoli edifici.

Anche se le evidenze per associazioni tra i costruttori contraenti sono rare nel mondo romano, casi analoghi sono documentati in diversi settori dell'economia, tra i quali proprio quello dell'industria laterizia (Helen 1975, 113-115).

L'analisi dei laterizi di ambedue i complessi sembra fornire una risposta al quesito che si poneva Bloch trattando delle Terme: "Soprattutto due problemi richiedono dunque una chiarificazione: prima se e in quanto i singoli bolli si conciliano con la data accertata dell'edificazione e poi se i timbri nel loro complesso rispecchiano la rapidità con cui l'opera grandiosa fu compiuta".

Sia per il Foro che per le Terme, la gran parte dei materiali conferma le datazioni tradizionali (inaugurazione del Foro nel 112 d.C., costruzione delle Terme tra il 104 e il 109)[26], soltanto nel Foro molti materiali attestano che il completamento di alcuni settori andò ben oltre queste date. Qui infatti la presenza di materiali della tarda età traianea, se non della prima età adrianea (Cepioniane di Arria Fadilla e Rutilio Lupo), nel settore meridionale e i due bolli adrianei nelle costruzioni a nord della Colonna Traiana non lasciano dubbi a riguardo.

Nell'edificio a ovest delle Sette Sale la presenza del tipo 29g di Rutilio Lupo costituisce la prova per una datazione alla tarda età traianea di questo edificio sorto tra la Terme e la sua grande cisterna. Nelle Terme non compaiono i laterizi di Arria Fadilla e la produzione delle Cepioniane si ferma a quelli di Plozia Servilia Isaurica, tuttavia nella grande esedra furono impiegati laterizi con bolli della più tarda produzione della sezione *ab Euripo* (97b) prima che su di essi comparisse la datazione consolare[27]. Non sembra superfluo sottolineare l'importanza del contemporaneo impiego del bollo 97b, nei sistemi fognari dei settori orientale e meridionale del Foro e nelle strutture dei Mercati che si trovano ai piedi della Torre delle Milizie.

Adrianeo è invece sicuramente il tipo 525cI di Trebicia Tertulla, probabilmente notato dal Dressel nei resti dell'Abside B, ma lo stesso Bloch, pur avendolo inserito nell'elenco relativo a quel settore, espresse il dubbio sulla sua effettiva presenza (Bloch 1947, 48).

Riguardo alla cronologia della costruzione, dunque, secondo quanto su esposto, si deve concludere che se nel Foro, nonostante la cubatura relativamente modesta delle parti realizzate in laterizio, le informazioni contenute nei bolli rivelano che il completamento delle opere dovette andare oltre gli anni 112 e 113 d.C., indicati dalle fonti, il complesso dei bolli laterizi rinvenuti nelle Terme, diversamente, sembra confermare che qui, nonostante la mole delle opere da eseguire, i tempi della realizzazione del progetto furono realmente quelli dichiarati dalle stesse fonti, con la chiusura dei lavori nel 109 d.C. (De Fine Licht 1990).

Tuttavia, il dato più significativo che emerge da questo studio riguarda l'aspetto economico, legato alla produzione laterizia del periodo compreso tra la fine del I e i primi decenni del II secolo.

Come sosteneva Bloch, da quest'epoca <<il libero artigiano perde la sua indipendenza; i piccoli proprietari di fornaci diventano impiegati dei grandi latifondisti privati o dell'imperatore>> (Bloch 1947, 334-335). L'incremento dell'industria laterizia doveva, sempre secondo Bloch (1947, 338), essere dipeso, come si desume da una lettera di Plinio (Ep., VI, 19), da disposizioni impartite da Traiano ai candidati per i pubblici uffici di investire un terzo dei loro capitali in beni stabili italiani. Si trattava di terre all'interno delle quali si trovavano, talvolta, ricchi giacimenti di argilla. Va da sé che il migliore sfruttamento di queste terre non poteva che consistere nell'incrementare la produzione dei mattoni per il mercato edilizio e dal momento che Roma, proprio da questo periodo, vedeva crescere vistosamente il numero delle opere pubbliche, si può dire che la produzione fu programmata soprattutto, e in taluni casi esclusivamente, finalizzandola alle esigenze della capitale. Naturalmente, se lo spaccato che si presenta, relativamente alle fabbriche prese in esame, offre il quadro di una produzione quasi del tutto condizionata dal mercato di Roma, esisteva pur sempre una molteplicità di fabbriche di dimensioni minori in grado di soddisfare i progetti edilizi locali su tutto il territorio italico.

Per tornare all'argomento in questione e sempre con riguardo all'attività delle figline in esame, come conseguenza del progressivo sfruttamento di risorse derivate dalle proprietà terriere e poi del crescente ruolo di "industriali" dei personaggi di alto rango, appare ovvio immaginare l'esistenza, e la concentrazione in un periodo ristretto (forse la fine del I secolo), di uno smisurato quantitativo di laterizi pronti che andavano necessariamente smaltiti, perché rapidamente producessero quei forti guadagni che costituivano l'obiettivo di tanta organizzazione da parte dei produttori.

Il controllo stretto sulle forniture pubbliche di laterizi, dovette inizialmente essere esercitato da un'èlite di produttori legati alla vita pubblica e alla dinastia imperiale e successivamente, in via esclusiva, da parte della casa imperiale, dapprima ufficiosamente (sino al 110) e poi ufficialmente.

A questo proposito è anche importante comprendere esattamente i rapporti tra proprietari e officinatori e se, nei casi di dipendenza diretta da officine di proprietà imperiale, il ruolo di questi ultimi godesse di effettiva autonomia nella produzione. Per esaminare il caso del Foro di Traiano, i ritrovamenti ci presentano, allo stato attuale delle conoscenze e inclusi i tipi adrianei rinvenuti *in situ*, 2 tipi di bolli laterizi con l'indicazione del *dominus*, dell'officinatore e del servo, 14 con l'indicazione del *dominus* e dell'officinatore, 7 tipi recanti soltanto il nome del *dominus* e 4 con il nome dell'officinatore da solo, esattamente quelli prodotti da CamidienoAtimeto e Anterote Severiano.

Dove sia certa l'esistenza di una struttura che sovrasti il singolo *officinator,* come per le figline di proprietà di personaggi altolocati, di rango equestre e senatorio, non è possibile considerare indipendente la figura dell'imprenditore, proprio a motivo della presenza sui bolli del riferimento alla proprietà dei *praedia.*

All'apparenza invece, Camidieno Atimeto e Anterote Severiano, rappresentanti di un ceto più modesto, avrebbero prodotto, per conto proprio, la parte qualitativamente migliore del materiale laterizio utilizzato per la costruzione del Foro (i mattoni bipedali) .

Ciò è difficile, sia a causa della tipologia del materiale, che rappresentava probabilmente anche la percentuale più costosa della fornitura, sia per la comprovata partecipazione dei due officinatori a produzioni afferenti alla stessa Plotina (Atimeto) e forse, attraverso le Marciane, a Traiano in persona (Anterote Severiano).

Il processo che, come si è visto, condusse alla concentrazione della produzione nelle mani della classe senatoria, compirà dunque, di lì a poco, un passo irreversibile verso il monopolio nell'uso di materiali di manifattura imperiale con la conseguenza di lauti profitti da parte dell'imperatore stesso, come si evince dalla "ingombrante" presenza, proprio nel Foro, di materiali prodotti dalle officine imperiali. Senza dubbio, come dimostrato da Bloch in numerosi esempi di edifici del periodo immediatamente successivo, si continuano a trovare impegnate numerose fabbriche private che dovevano essere sottoposte, probabilmente, ad uno stretto controllo imperiale.

Il panorama che sembra delinearsi evidenzia un possibile, forte condizionamento nella scelta del laterizio, quale materiale da costruzione privilegiato, come risultato del suo stesso incremento produttivo.

In altre parole, la volontà politica che indirizza le scelte dell'architettura di età traianea nella realizzazione di grandi complessi pubblici, tiene indubbiamente conto della necessità di smaltire, quanto più possibile, l'enorme massa di materiali derivati dal nuovo impulso dato all'industria laterizia. Il "motore" che muove questo meccanismo, come è ovvio, è di natura squisitamente economica ed è costituito dai lauti profitti ricevuti in cambio delle forniture di mattoni. A tale meccanismo non è estraneo lo stesso Traiano, anche se il suo nome, come si è visto, in un primo momento non compare sui marchi di fabbrica a dimostrare che il processo di monopolizzazione è ancora in corso. La linea di confine può essere individuata nella data del 110; a partire da quell'anno infatti, come sottolineato dal Bloch, il nome del sovrano appare nei bolli delle figline Marciane e, si può ipotizzare, anche in quelli delle Oceane, divenute di proprietà imperiale proprio sotto Traiano.

I dati sin qui offerti in via preliminare, si riferiscono soltanto a due dei complessi architettonici di età traianea tra quelli previsti per il completamento dello studio. I risultati dell'esame dei materiali di altri edifici coevi, quali i Mercati, i restauri traianei del Foro di Cesare, e l'ingente aliquota di laterizi, pure traianei, rinvenuti nello scavo del Lungotevere Testaccio, ai quali si sta applicando la stessa metodologia di indagine, potrà fornire nuove e interessanti informazioni per un ulteriore sviluppo delle ipotesi delineate nel presente studio.

NOTE

1 I dati relativi al Foro di Traiano, presentati sinteticamente in questa comunicazione, sono stati esposti da chi scrive in un catalogo completo dei bolli del Foro di Traiano, in Bianchi (2001b).

2 Fasti Ostienses I.I.XIII.1. n. 3: *Id*(us) *Mai*(as) *Imp. Traianus*/ [templum Ve]*neris in for Caesaris et*/ [columna]*m in foro suo dedicavit.*

3 Per i Mercati di Traiano, il catalogo elaborato da Lancaster (1995) include 68 esemplari, riferibili a 15 tipi differenti, sei dei quali mai trovati prima.

4 L'analisi architettonica è stata svolta da D. Cirone per conto del IV dipartimento del Comune di Roma.

5 Caruso e Volpe (2000): p. 48; Volpe (2002). Ringrazio particolarmente R. Volpe non solo per avermi messo a disposizione tutta la documentazione in suo possesso relativa ai bolli laterizi delle Terme di Traiano, ma per la disponibilità e l'amicizia con le quali ha conversato con me sull'argomento.

6 E' possibile calcolare che nei magazzini, oltre a molti altri esemplari dei tipi rinvenuti in opera, sono presenti anche esemplari per un totale di altri 17 tipi.

7 Le concordanze indicate in alcuni casi fanno riferimento al Supplemento (= S) di Bloch.

8 La produzione della *Gens* Domizia, dominante nell'industria doliare durante il I sec. d. C. può essere distinta in quattro periodi. Agli anni precedenti il 59 d. C. si riferisce l'attività di Domizio Afro. Nel Foro di Traiano sono presenti materiali prodotti da tutti e tre i suoi successori: Lucano e Tullo compaiono insieme sui bolli insieme ai nomi dei loro schiavi, a partire da quella data e fino al 93 d.C., anno della morte di Lucano. Il nome di Tullo compare da solo fino al 107 d.C., anno della sua morte. Al periodo posteriore appartengono i laterizi prodotti da Domizia Lucilla, nipote di Tullo.

9 Il bollo 258a di Agatobulo, databile a agli anni prima del 107, anno della morte di Domizio Tullo, fu già segnalato dalla Lancaster (1995) nei Mercati di Traiano ed è stato di recente rilevato da chi scrive nella copertura della fogna assiale che corre a nord della Colonna Traiana. Per la rappresentazione di questo bollo (Fig. 3.1) si usa qui la figura del tipo pubblicata da Lancaster (1995): 28, Fig. 1.

10 La figura 3.4 raffigura il bollo 262 rinvenuto nelle absidi H e D delle Terme durante gli scavi del 1997-1998.

11 A questo proposito la Fig. 2, tratta da De Fine Licht (1974) è stata modificata rinominando con la lettera M l'edificio posto all'angolo con l'abside L, come indicato da Bloch (1947): 37, Fig. 13.

12 La figura 3.6 rappresenta il bollo 1096a rinvenuto nelle absidi H e D delle Terme durante gli scavi del 1997-1998.

13 Si deve considerare questa datazione poiché secondo Bloch (1947: 267), l'attività del figulo iniziò intorno al 100 d.C., il tipo 377b non è tra i primi da lui fabbricati, come risulta invece per il tipo 378 e var., ed è stato rinvenuto in opera anche nel Pantheon. In questo caso deve essersi trattato dell'impiego di vecchie rimanenze, ma nelle Terme deve essere stato adoperato come materiale di nuova fabbricazione.

14 313 e 904 f. I tipi di Anterote Severiano, secondo quanto esposto in questo paragrafo sono stati inseriti nella Tabella 2 tra i mattoni delle Marciane.

15 Nelle Terme come officinatore di Plotina compare anche P. Ocio Antioco (698, 700).

16 Un Camidieno si ritrova a Bevagna (CIL XI, 5095). In un'altra iscrizione, relativa ad un'urna già conservata a Cave (CIL XIV, 3394) da *Praeneste*, un certo *Camidienus Plocamus* rivolge una dedica alla moglie Ulpia Smirna. Infine, un Camidieno liberto di Commodo si trova in un'iscrizione da *Pistia/Plestia* nella VI *Regio* (od. Colfiorito) (CIL XI, 5625).

17 Anterote Severiano, usò il suo nome per esteso nei laterizi fabbricati sotto questo imperatore, mentre dal 123 comparve come *Anteros Caesaris nostri servus.* Bloch (1947): 15-18, 112-113.

18 Il tipo 811d proviene sia dalla c.d biblioteca orientale del Foro, dall'abside D, dall'edificio M delle Terme e dalle Sette Sale; il tipo 811f proviene da vari settori del Foro e sia dal collettore delle Sette Sale che dall'edificio M.
19 La misurazione dello spessore dei ricorsi di bipedali visibili sulla parete sud della scala C (Fig. 1), dietro la parete nord della c.d. biblioteca occidentale (cm 4,5 sul muro che sostiene la scala e cm 5,7-5,00 immediatamente a sinistra), rivela che tali bipedali sono, con buona probabilità del tipo 811d di Anterote Severiano. La stessa misura si riscontra per il bipedale ancora *in situ* sullo spigolo della parete sud della c.d. biblioteca orientale.
20 In una fogna si trova anche il bollo 904f di *Hermes* servo di *Calpetanus Favor.*
21 Ringrazio i Signori Stefano Stefani e Gianfranco Cattoni delle Fornaci Stefani di Castel Viscardo (TR) per la disponibilità e per le informazioni avute e il sig. Luigi Stefani per essersi fatto fotografare durante il suo lavoro.
22 De Laine (1997): 116, riporta l'ipotesi di una tavola di valori per fare mattoni di misure differenti, molti dei quali sono equivalenti ai tipi romani imperiali. Il modello include il tempo impiegato per preparare l'argilla, raggiunge un numero di 1000 al giorno per un operaio che fabbrica mattoni con un assistente e può valere per 1000 bessali; 167 mattoni grandi al giorno (sono più piccoli se confrontabili con i bipedali romani). Il volume totale di argilla preparata e lavorata al giorno corrisponde circa a 1,25-1,38 mc, leggermente di più se si considerano i bipedali. Si calcola che si potessero produrre circa 220 bipedali al giorno.
23 Comprensivi delle fasi di carico della fornace, della cottura vera e propria, della fase di raffreddamento e dello scarico dei mattoni.
24 Per il calcolo si è tenuto conto della presenza, ovunque in questo settore, di cortina interna ed esterna, tranne che lungo i muri sud delle Biblioteche, entrambi costruiti a diretto contatto con il muro perimetrale nord della Basilica Ulpia.
25 Cod. Iust.: Dig.50.8.11; 50.10.2.1.; per la figura di un *redemptor operum Caesarum* vedi Pearse (1974): 38, n. 54 e Lancaster (1998): 305, n.52.
26 Per il Foro: *Fasti Ostienses* I.I.XIII.1. n. 22, p.200:K(alendis) ia] *nuar* (iis) *imp. Traianus Forum suum et/* [Bas]*ilicam Ulpiam dedicavit.* L'incendio che distrusse nel 104 la Domus Aurea creò l'area libera per l'innalzamento delle Terme di Traiano, affidato a Apollodoro (Cass. Dio., 69. 4.1) (Bloch (1947): 45, n. 46). La data della dedica, il 109 d.C. è nota da una tavola dei Fasti Ostienses scoperta dal Calza nel 1932 (Degrassi, *Inscr.It.* 13., p. I, N.5): *X K(alendas) Iul(ias) Imp.nerva Traianus caes. Aug. Germ(anicus) Dacicus thermas suas dedicavit et publicavit.*
27 I bolli adrianei di Curiazio Cosano e del suo officinatore Sesto Alfio Amando saranno utilizzati negli edifici costruiti davanti alla grande esedra.

BIBLIOGRAFIA

Amici, C. M., 1982, Foro di Traiano: Basilica Ulpia e biblioteche, Roma.

Bianchi, E., 2001a, Sistemi scalari nel Foro di Traiano, Appendice II, a R. Meneghini, 2001, Il Foro di Traiano - Ricostruzione architettonica e analisi strutturale, *RM*, 108.

Bianchi, E., 2001b, I Bolli laterizi del Foro di Traiano. Il catalogo del Bloch e i rinvenimenti delle campagne di scavo 1991-1997 e 1998-2000, *BCom,* 102, c.s.

Bianchi, E. e Meneghini, R., 2002, Il Cantiere costruttivo del Foro di Traiano, *RM,* 109, c.s.

Bloch, H., 1947, I bolli laterizi e la storia edilizia romana. Contributi all'archeologia e alla storia. Ristampa da *BCom,* 64, 1936 - 66, 1938 e 71, 1943-1945, Roma.

Bloch, H., 1948, Supplement to Volume XV, 1 of the Corpus Inscriptionum Latinarum, *Harv.Cl.St.*, 56-59, Cambridge.

Caruso, G. e Volpe, R., 2000, Preesistenze e persistenze delle Terme di Traiano, in *Romanization and the city, creation, transformations, and failures* (ed. Fentress, E.), *JRA*, Suppl. 38, 43-71, Portsmouth, Rhode Island.

De Fine Licht, K., 1974, Untersuchungen an den Trajansthermen zu Rom, *Analecta Romana Instituti Danici*, Suppl., 7, 5-48.

De Fine Licht, K., 1990, Untersuchungen an den Trajansthermen zu Rom, 2, Sette Sale, *Analecta Romana Instituti Danici*, Suppl. 19, 9-103.

DeLaine, J., 1997, The Baths of Caracalla, *JRA,* Suppl. 25.

De Romanis, A., 1822, Le antiche camere esquiline delle Terme di Tito, 48 e ss., Roma.

Filippi, G. e Stanco, E.A., c.s., Epigrafia e toponomastica della produzione laterizia nella valle del Tevere: l'Umbria e la Sabina tra Tuder e Crustumerium; l'Etruria tra Volsinii e Lucus Feroniae, in *Atti del Convegno "Interpretare i bolli laterizi", IRF*, c.s.

Fontana, S., *Un impianto per la produzione di calce presso Lucus Feroniae*, in *N. Christie* (ed.) *Settlemet and economy in Italy 1500 BC to AD 1500*, Oxford 1995: 563-570.

Giustini, L., 1997, Fornaci e laterizi a Roma dal XV al XVI secolo, in *Museo della città e del territorio,* Roma.

Helen, T., 1975, The organization of Roman Brick Production in the First and Second Centuries A.D.: An Interpretation of Roman Brick Stamps, in *Annales Academiae Scientiarum Fennicae. Diss. Hum. Litt.*, 5, Helsinki.

Lancaster, L., 1995, The date of Trajan's Markets: an assessment in the light of some unpublished brick stamps, *BSR* 63:25-44.

Lancaster, L., 1998, Building Trajan Markets, *AJA*, 102, 2, 283-308.

Lugli, G., 1952-1969, Fontes ad topographiam veteris urbis Romae pertinentes, 8, Roma.

Meneghini, R., 1998, L'architettura del Foro di Traiano attraverso i ritrovamenti archeologici più recenti, *RM,* 105, 127-148.

Meneghini, R., 2001, Il Foro di Traiano - Ricostruzione architettonica e analisi strutturale, *RM*, 108.

Meneghini, R., 2001b, La nuova immagine architettonica del Foro di Traiano, in *L'architettura di Apollodoro nella cultura classica* (a cura di G. Calcani et al.), 48-65, Roma.

Meneghini, R., 2002, La Colonna di Traiano, le Biblioteche e il Templum Divi Traiani: dati per una nuova lettura architettonica, *MEFRA*, c.s.

Morbidelli, P., 2001, Appendice I, a Bianchi, E., 2001b, I Bolli laterizi del Foro di Traiano. Il catalogo del Bloch e i rinvenimenti delle campagne di scavo 1991-1997 e 1998-2000, *BCom,* 102, c.s.

Morelli, C., 1957, Gli avanzi portuali di Pagliano presso Orvieto, *Boll. dell'Istituto Storico Artistico Orvietano,* 13, 3-60.

Pearse, J.L.D., 1974, The Organization of Roman Building during the Late Republic and Early Empire, Cambridge.

Romeo, P., 1974-1975, Restauro delle Terme di Traiano (Anno 1967-1968), *BCom,* 84, 249-259.

Setälä, P., 1977, Private Domini in Roman Brick Stamps of the Empire. A Historical and Prosopographical Study of Landowners in the District of Rome, *Annales Academiae Scientiarum Fennicae. Diss. Hum. Litt.,* 10, Helsinki.

Steinby, M., 1974-1975, La cronologia delle "figlinae" doliari urbane dalla fine dell'età repubblicana fino all'inizio del III secolo, *BCom*, 84, 7-132.

Steinby, M., 1977-78, Lateres signati ostienses, *ActaIRF,* 7, 1-2.

Steinby, M., 1982, I Senatori e l'industria laterizia urbana, in *Epigrafia e ordine senatorio, Atti del Colloquio Internazionale AIEGL,* I, 227-237, Roma

Steinby, M., 1987, Indici complementari ai bolli doliari urbani (CIL XV,1)*, ActaIRF,* 11.

Steinby, M.,1993a, L'organizzazione produttiva dei laterizi: un modello interpretativo per l'instrumentum in genere?, *JRA Suppl.6,* 139-143.

Steinby, M.,1993b, Ricerche sull'industria doliare nelle aree di Roma e Pompei: un possibile modello interpretativo, in *I Laterizi di età romana nell'area nordadriatica* (a cura di C. Zaccaria), 9-14, Roma.

Volpe, R., 2002, Paesaggi urbani tra Oppio e Fagutal, *MEFRA,* 112, 2, 511-556.

APPENDICE: BOLLI DEL FORO DI TRAIANO: ANALISI PETROGRAFICHE, DIFFRATTOMETRICHE E CHIMICHE

Paola MORBIDELLI
(Università degli Studi di Roma "La Sapienza")

Sono stati selezionati 10 reperti rappresentativi di una campionatura più ampia e provenienti da diversi settori dell'area archeologica del Foro di Traiano. In particolare, sono stati prelevati campioni in numero di cinque tra i laterizi recanti i tipi principali di bolli rinvenuti nell'area della Basilica Ulpia e altrettanti dai laterizi rinvenuti nel settore meridionale.

Campione	Sigla	Provenienza
Cat. 4/ CIL XV, 1003	B1	Area della Basilica Ulpia
Cat. 18bis/ CIL XV, 59b	B2	Settore meridionale
Cat. 10/ CIL XV, 612	B3	Area della Basilica Ulpia
Cat. 3/ CIL XV, 1094	B4	Area della Basilica Ulpia
Cat. 14/ CIL XV, 811d	B5	Area della Basilica Ulpia
Cat. 5/ CIL XV, 696	B6	Area della Basilica Ulpia
Cat. 23/ CIL XV, 29g	B7	Attico del muro di fondo della piazza
Cat. 22/ CIL XV, 83b	B8	Settore meridionale
Cat. 8/ CIL XV, 822.1	B9	Settore meridionale
Cat. 21/ CIL XV, 97c	B10	Settore meridionale

Il criterio scelto per tale selezione è stato quello di verificare eventuali differenze nella materia prima utilizzata e sulle tecniche di produzione di ciascuna delle principali fabbriche presenti sul sito:

Metodologie analitiche

I campioni sono stati prelevati rispettando le Doc NORMAL 3/80 (1980) e sono stati sottoposti ad analisi diffrattometriche a raggi X, petrografiche e chimiche.

L'analisi qualitativa in diffrattometria a raggi X (XRD) su polveri, ottenute mediante un mortaio d'agata, è stata eseguita con un diffrattometro PHILIPS PW 1830 (radiazione CuK□; 40 KV, 20 mA). I dati sono stati registrati nell'intervallo 3°-70° 2□, con una velocità di 1°/min ed un passo di scansione pari a 2s/step, slitta divergente di 1°, slitta convergente di 0.1 mm e slitta antiscatter di 2°. Le analisi petrografiche sono state eseguite su sezioni sottili dello spessore di circa 35 m.

Le analisi chimiche sono state effettuate in fluorescenza a raggi X (XRF) mediante un SIEMENS con tubo ad anticatodo al Cr e potenza di 3000 W. I risultati delle analisi sono stati normalizzati con i valori della perdita totale a 900° C per calcinazione.

Risultati

Analisi petrografiche

L'analisi su sezione sottile ha messo in evidenza che la campionatura risulta sostanzialmente omogenea. Particolare attenzione è stata rivolta ai due elementi fondamentali dell'impasto: il degrassante e la matrice.

La matrice di colore giallastra e rossastra è di natura carbonatica e risulta finissima senza uno scheletro. Nei campioni B1, B3, B4, B5, B6 e B9 essa è più compatta, criptocristallina e con rare tracce di relitti di forme minerali indice di una probabile cottura dei manufatti a temperature maggiori come confermato dalle analisi diffrattometriche.

Il degrassante, costituito da elementi da subarrotondati ad arrotondati, di dimensioni dell'ordine dei 50 □m e minori e piuttosto scarso, è rappresentato, in ordine decrescente di abbondanza, da: cristalli di quarzo, k-feldspato, pirosseno (diopside), rare lamelle di biotite (campioni B1, B6 e B8), rara Cc nei campioni B2, B7, B8 e B10 e scarsi ossidi. Rarissime lamelle di gesso. La componenente litica del degrassante è data dagli ARFs (Rock Argillaceous Fragments), da frammenti di leucititi (campioni B4 e B5), lave tefritico/fonolitiche, e qualche frammento di *chamotte* (campioni B2, B7 e B8). Nel campione B5 si possono osservare alcuni fossili dispersi nella matrice.

Analisi diffrattometriche

I campioni presentano una composizione mineralogica (**Tabella 1**) relativamente omogenea e prevalentemente data da: quarzo, k-feldspato, pirosseno (diopside), biotite/illite. La presenza e/o assenza di wollastonite permette di suddividere in gruppi i materiali campionati in quanto indice di temperature di cottura alle quali sono stati soggetti i laterizi. Infatti le variazioni mineralogiche indotte dall'aumento di temperatura rappresentano un buon parametro per discriminare in gruppi.

Su queste basi possono farsi le seguenti considerazioni:

- La variazione sia del contenuto delle fasi nella miscela che dei reciproci rapporti quantitativi, rende plausibile l'ipotesi che si possa trattare di officine di produzione diverse che utilizzavano miscele in cui il rapporto argilla/degrassante era differente. Tuttavia, la mineralogia degli impasti risulta molto simile suggerendo una comune provenienza del materiale;

- la presenza di calcite nei manufatti B2, B7, B8 e B10 indica che le temperature dei forni non hanno superato la decarbonatazione di questo minerale; infatti, la reazione $CaCO_3 \tau CaO + CO_2$ inizia a circa 750°C a P_{atm} in assenza di CO_2 nella fase fluida (Maggetti, 1982; Duminuco et al., 1996). La stabilità della calcite viene diminuita dalla presenza di quarzo a causa della reazione

$$CaCO_3 + SiO_2 \tau CaSiO_3 + CO_2$$

Wollastonite

che inizia, a pressione atmosferica ed in assenza di CO_2 nella fase fluida, a circa 550°C. L'associazione di calcite e quarzo e l'assenza di wollastonite negli impasti studiati, potrebbe indicare che le temperature non hanno raggiunto i 600°C (Skippen, 1972). Quest'ultima temperatura potrebbe però anche essere stata raggiunta tenendo in considerazione il probabile incremento della frazione molare di CO_2 all'interno del forno dovuta al contributo di materiale vegetale usato come combustibile.

Per i campioni B1, B3, B4, B5, B6 e B9, si possono supporre, invece temperature superiori ai 600°C data la presenza di wollastonite ma, almeno per i campioni B1 e B6, inferiori ai 950°C data la presenza di miche. La calcite in questo caso va considerata come minerale secondario (come confermato dalle analisi petrografiche su sezioni sottili).

- Queste prime osservazioni hanno permesso di suddividere i bolli laterizi in due gruppi: A) campioni B1, B3, B4, B5, B6 e B9; si tratta di materiali o meglio gli impasti delle f. Domiziane, delle Macedoniane, delle Tempesine, di C. Atimeto e di A. Severiano; B) campioni B2, B7, B8 e B10 che afferiscono sia a quelli delle f. Cepioniane (di tutte e tre le sezioni), che a quelli delle f. Bruziane.

Analisi chimiche

I risultati delle analisi sono riportati in **Tabella 2**.

I campioni mostrano un medio alto contenuto in CaO soprattutto nei campioni B1, B4, B5, B6 B9 e B10, mentre la SiO_2 risulta superiore al 53% in peso nei campioni B2, B3, B7 e B8. Plottando i risultati chimici nel diagramma triangolare SiO_2- $(CaO+MgO)$-Al_2O_3 si delineano due campi, per altro molto vicini, in cui cadono i campioni.

Campione	Qz	Kf	Dp	Mica	Woll	Cc	Gypsum
4/1003 (B1)	XX	XXX	XX	X	X	XX	X
18bis/59b (B2)	XXXX	XXX	X	-	-	X	-
10/612 (B3)	XXX	XX	X	-	X	X	-
3/1094 (B4)	XXX	XX	XX	-	X	X	X
14/811d (B5)	XX	X	X	-	X	X	X
5/696 (B6)	XXX	XXX	XXX	X	X	X	X
23/29g (B7)	XXXX	XX	X	-	-	XX	-
22/83b (B8)	XXXX	XX	XX	X	-	XX	-
8/822.1 (B9)	XXX	XX	XX	-	X	XX	X
21/97c (B10)	XXXX	XX	X	-	-	X	-

Tabella 1. Risultati delle analisi qualitative. Qz = quarzo; Kf = K-feldspato; Dp = diopside; Woll = wollastonite; Cc = calcite; - = al di sotto del limite di rilevabilità; X = scarso; XX= frequente; XXX = abbondante; XXXX = molto abbondante.

	B1	B2	B3	B4	B5	B6	B7	B8	B9	B10
SiO_2	47,28	54,64	53,86	50,38	47,32	51,77	53,46	55,64	50,27	50,57
TiO_2	0,65	0,70	0,73	0,65	0,71	0,66	0,71	0,71	0,70	0,66
Al_2O_3	13,71	14,91	15,03	13,52	14,71	13,4	14,99	15,04	14,76	13,82
P_2O_5	0,16	0,23	0,35	0,15	0,21	0,16	0,34	0,89	0,19	0,28
Fe_2O_3	5,37	5,82	5,96	5,41	6,21	5,67	5,78	6,01	5,88	5,66
MgO	4,61	4,03	3,49	4,25	3,8	4,24	3,45	4,33	4,33	3,85
MnO	0,11	0,12	0,11	0,12	0,12	0,12	0,1	0,11	0,11	0,12
CaO	17,34	11,43	11,73	16,07	16,39	16,24	11,41	10,14	14,92	15,09
Na_2O	1,56	1,68	1,47	1,28	1,75	1,60	1,47	1,52	1,58	1,28
K_2O	2,3	2,43	2,62	3,06	2,37	2,26	2,57	2,46	2,42	2,38
LOI	6,91	4,01	4,65	5,11	6,41	3,88	5,72	3,15	4,84	6,29

Tabella 2. Analisi chimiche in fluorescenza a raggi X (XRF). Elementi maggiori (% in peso).

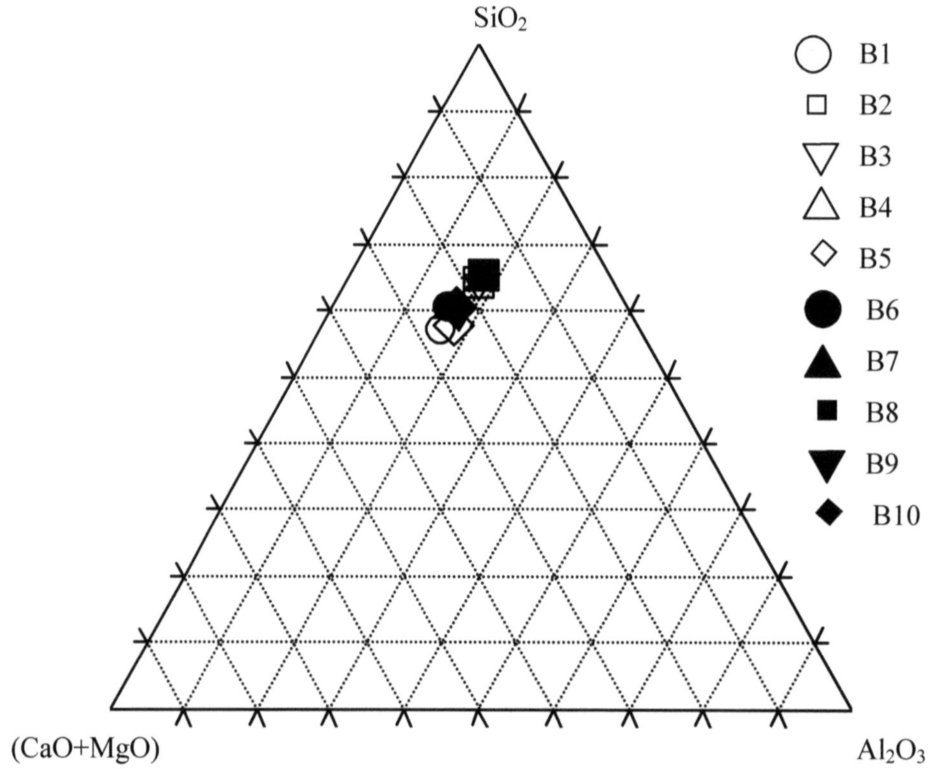

Tabella 3. I raggruppamenti sembrano ricalcare, tranne per i campioni B2 e B10, quelli delineati in via preliminare attraverso l'analisi diffrattometrica: Bolli laterizi B1, B4, B5, B6, B9 e B10; Bolli laterizi B2, B3, B7, B8. Le differenze dei due gruppi sono da imputare, molto probabilmente, alla natura del degrassante ed ad un diverso trattamento degli impasti in fase di lavorazione piuttosto che ad una diversa materia prima utilizzata.

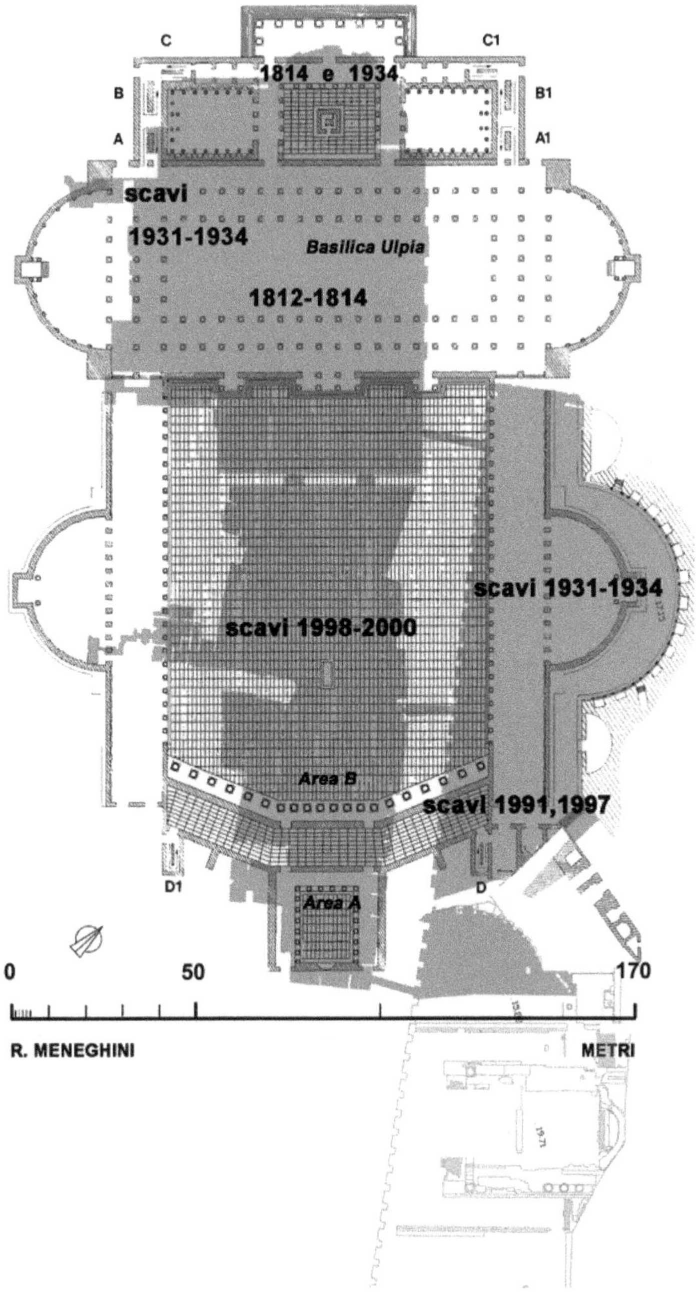

Fig. 1. Pianta del Foro di Traiano con anni di scavo [da Meneghini 2001b].

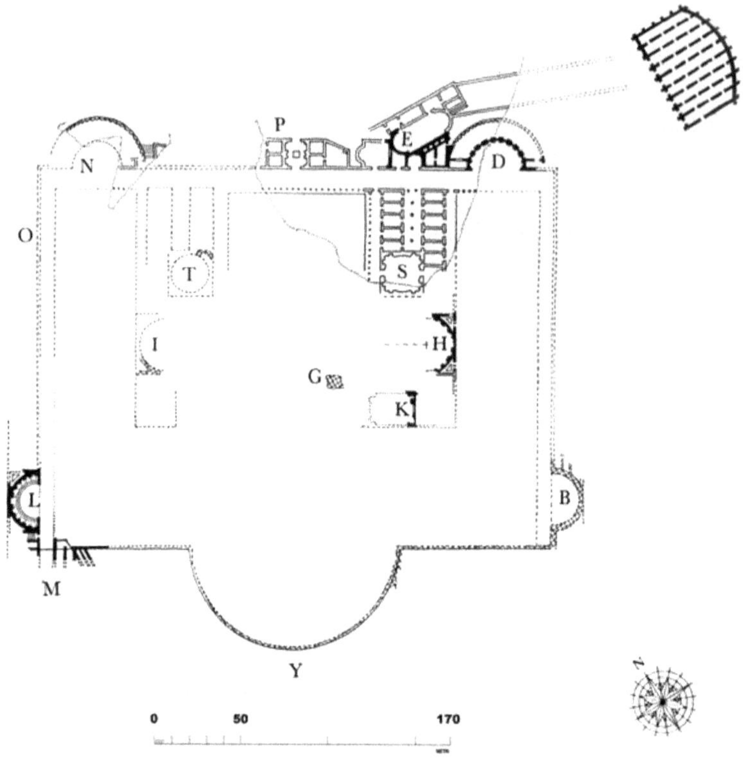

Fig. 2. Pianta delle Terme di Traiano [da De Fine Licht 1974].

Fig. 3. Bolli laterizi delle figline Domiziane [Fig. 3.7 = Bianchi 2001b, fig. 27].

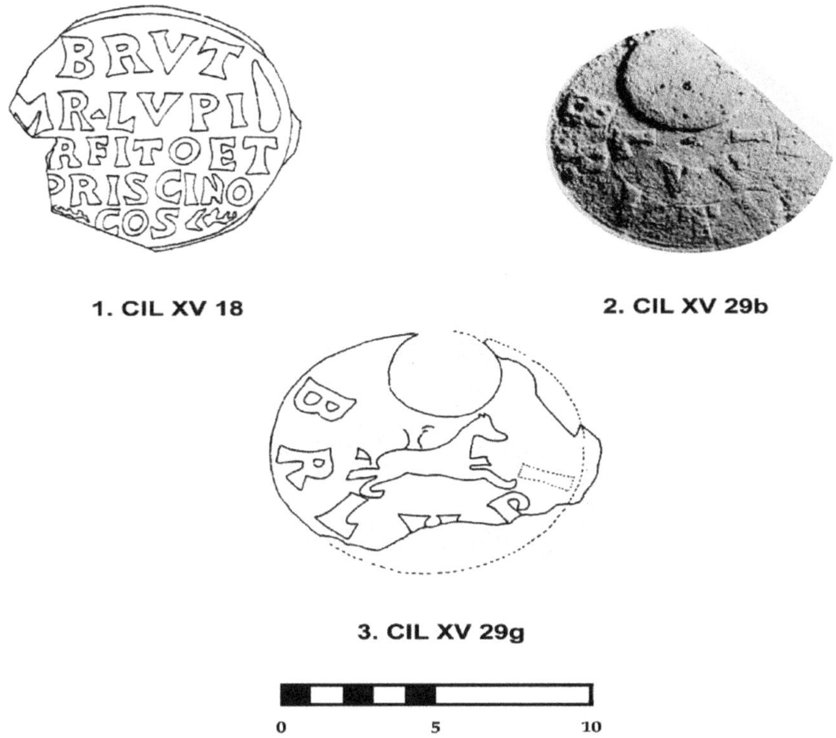

Fig. 4. Bolli laterizi delle figline Bruziane [Fig. 4.1 da De Fine Licht 1990, fig. 113,4].

Fig. 5. Bolli laterizi delle figline Cepioniane [Fig. 5.2 = Bianchi 2001b, fig. 18; Fig. 5.3 = Bianchi 2001b, Fig. 21].

CIL XV 1100

0 5 10

Fig. 6. Bollo laterizio delle figline Caniniane.

1. CIL XV 377b

2. CIL XV 709b

0 5 10

Fig. 7. Bolli laterizi delle figline Oceane.

CIL XV 525cl

0 5 10

Fig. 8. Bollo laterizio delle figline Salaresi.

CIL XV 545b

0 5 10

Fig. 9. Bollo laterizio delle figline Subortane.

1. CIL XV 1179

2. CIL XV 1181

0 5 10

Fig. 10. Bolli laterizi dell'officinatore M. Erennio Pollione.

1. CIL XV 695 2. CIL XV 696

0 5 10

Fig. 11. Bolli laterizi dell'imperatrice Plotina. [Fig. 11.2 = Bianchi 2001b, fig. 8].

1. CIL XV 811d 2. CIL XV 811f 3. CIL XV 313

0 5 10

Fig. 12. Bolli laterizi delle figline Marciane [Figg. 12.1-2 = Bianchi 2001b, figg. 13a, 14b; Fig. 12.3 da De Romanis 1822, tav.5,3].

Fig. 13. Localizzazione geografica delle figline fornitrici di laterizi per il Foro di Traiano.

14.a

14.c

14.b

14.d

Fig. 14 a-d. Le fasi di fabbricazione dei laterizi nella moderna fornace di Castel Viscardo (TR) [foto E. Bianchi].

AMEDEO MAIURI ET LES BOUTIQUES D'HERCULANUM : APPROCHE HISTORIOGRAPHIQUE

NICOLAS MONTEIX
(Université de Provence – Centre Camille Jullian)

ABSTRACT: This paper addresses the ideas developed by Amedeo Maiuri regarding commerce and the ancient craftsman with a focus on Herculanum. Following a summary of his ideas, their origin and evolution, is a survey of the many directions taken in the written tradition about Herculanum and the writing of history in the 1920's. The methods applied to archaeological sources by this Italian scholar are then discussed. The theoretical foundation of A. Maiuri's work indicates that he applied critical analysis in his reflections on the shops and craft workshops on Campanian villas.

Amedeo Maiuri (1886-1963) a été surintendant des fouilles et directeur du Musée National de Naples de 1924 à 1961. A partir d'avril 1927, il a dirigé, en plus de ses autres activités, la reprise des fouilles d'Herculanum, abandonnées depuis 1875. En préambule à cette reprise, il a annoncé des publications régulières des résultats de fouille, sous forme d'articles scientifiques et d'ouvrages de vulgarisation (Maiuri 1928). En effet, entre 1927 et 1961, il a eu un monopole quasi exclusif des publications sur Herculanum. En 1958, A. Maiuri publie le premier volume d'une série, inachevée, consacrée aux fouilles qu'il a dirigées : les *Nuovi Scavi.* Il s'agit alors de la première et unique synthèse développant les acquis de plus de deux siècles de fouilles sur le site.

Durant ces trente années de fouille, A. Maiuri s'est formé une idée personnelle du site, de sa nature socio-économique et de son évolution topographique et édilitaire. Il tend à démontrer le caractère envahissant et indésirable des boutiques et ateliers. Nous ne pouvons que nous interroger sur les raisons de sa condescendance pour les activités commerciales et artisanales sur un site qui, par ses qualités de conservation, aurait pu constituer un terrain d'investigation optimal pour des recherches sur ce sujet. Malgré quelques révisions (Guadagno 1993 ; Łoś 1992, 1995 ; Mouritsen 1996 ; Wallace-Hadrill 1994 : 118-131), ses idées restent fréquemment reprises sans examen critique. Leur évolution, liée à l'extension des fouilles, est perceptible. Il semble qu'elles mêlent les traditions historiographiques d'Herculanum avec les recherches du moment, tout en intégrant des données nouvelles issues des fouilles menées au XXe siècle. Seule une enquête approfondie, reprenant non seulement ses sources bibliographiques – souvent implicites – mais explorant également son usage des données archéologiques, peut permettre de comprendre comment une des plus importantes figures de l'archéologie italienne du XXe siècle a perçu le commerce et l'artisanat antiques et a influencé leur image.

Dans un ouvrage publié en 1932, puis dans son guide de 1936, A. Maiuri expose la différence ayant existé entre Herculanum et Pompéi. Proche de Naples, la première de ces deux villes, coincée entre le Vésuve et la mer ne peut pas se développer économiquement, au contraire de Pompéi (Maiuri 1932 : 46-47 ; 1936 : 16). Cité de culture, Herculanum serait également une cité de détente pour les élites romaines et napolitaines désireuses de se reposer loin du tumulte des grandes villes, populeuses et rendues bruyantes par les commerçants (Maiuri 1932 : 48). Son caractère principal serait donc un faible tissu commercial. Les boutiques et ateliers spécialisés (mosaïstes, sculpteurs, marbriers, ébénistes) mis au jour se caractériseraient par une apparence moins vulgaire que ceux de Pompéi (Maiuri 1936 : 16-18). A. Maiuri décrit une ville résidentielle dont la société ne comporte que deux strates : d'une part des riches séjournant dans de somptueuses maisons, de l'autre une masse populaire vivant des ressources maritimes.

L'avancée des fouilles vers le *decumanus maximus* et la mise au jour de la *Casa del Bicentenario* (Maiuri 1940) vont transformer la vision d'A. Maiuri sur Herculanum. Il examine désormais cette ville avec le même schéma interprétatif que celui appliqué à Pompéi. Pour cette dernière cité, il décrit une " invasion " du tissu urbain par des commerçants, affranchis et nouveaux riches, qui expulsent les élites traditionnelles de la ville (Maiuri 1927 : 81 *sq.* ; 1942 : 216-217). A. Maiuri reformule ses opinions dans sa synthèse de 1958. Herculanum apparaît désormais moins comme une ville " de villégiature " dont la société aurait deux strates. Le contraste culturel et socio-économique avec Pompéi est fortement atténué. Vers les années 55-60 ap. J.-C., une grande mutation interviendrait dans les habitudes économiques de la cité, due essentiellement à l'accroissement des courants commerciaux d'outre-mer. Le forum s'ouvrirait alors au commerce et le *decumanus maximus* deviendrait la principale artère économique de la cité. Conséquence sociale de cette transformation de l'économie de la ville, de nombreuses maisons auraient subi des changements de propriétaires et des transformations architecturales (création de boutiques ou de structures " industrielles ", profonds remaniements de parcelles dans les *insulae*). Cette évolution socio-économique se traduirait surtout par le remplacement des élites traditionnelles, " *le più vecchie famiglie patrizie ercolanesi* ", par des nouveaux riches, " *libert(i) arricchit(i)* ", " *liberti mercanti o artigiani* ". Les membres de l'élite se réfugieraient dans leurs domaines, laissant la ville être envahie les marchands (Maiuri 1958 : 40, 198, 207, 223-224, 248, 377, 393, 422, 431, 443). Tout laisse à croire que seul le commerce était une activité lucrative, ceux qui ne s'y adonnaient pas étant condamnés à vivre dans de piètres conditions (Maiuri 1958 : 253). De plus, les boutiquiers montreraient un luxe ostentatoire : par l'utilisation de pavements de marbre, par les boutiques qui donnent à voir l'atrium, et même par leur comptoir de vente (Maiuri 1958 : 224, 253, 433-434, 437). Enfin, la simple présence de marchands en devanture corrompait l'aspect général des maisons, qui passerait d'une forme " *signorile* " et " noble " à un aspect plus " populaire " et " rustique " (Maiuri 1958 : 223, 248, 261-263, 422, 426, 435, 443-444, 446, 454). Toutefois, certains exemples s'écartent de ce schéma évolutif. Ainsi, l'équation entre le niveau social perceptible à travers la décoration et l'activité supposée de l'occupant n'est pas toujours valable. L'exemple de la *Casa di Nettuno e Anfitrite* (V, 6-7) sort tellement du cadre de sa théorie que, pour tenter de l'y réinsérer, A. Maiuri est obligé de proposer une interprétation anachronique, considérant son occupant comme un " *mercante del Rinascimento* ", amateur d'art (Maiuri 1958 : 393). Ce discours reste un cadre théorique à vocation normative. Les interprétations d'A. Maiuri brouillent l'image du rapport entre l'habitat et les activités commerciales. La stricte séparation entre les élites de la cité et les activités commerciales semble erronée. Ses propos sont teintés d'une forte nostalgie face aux transformations advenues à la maison " traditionnelle ". Il faut alors déterminer les origines de ces idées : tradition des recherches, contexte historiographique, idéologie ?

Les premières théories d'A. Maiuri reprennent sans doute la vulgate qui s'est progressivement développée sur Herculanum. Toutefois, la faiblesse de l'apparat critique dans ses ouvrages empêche de déterminer l'origine exacte de ses idées. Même dans sa synthèse de 1958, il cherche à donner l'impression que seules les données archéologiques ont servi de fondement à sa rédaction, citant fréquemment ses prédécesseurs, C. Bonucci (1835) et M. Ruggiero (1885). La reprise permanente de certaines idées traditionnellement attachées à Herculanum et l'absence de renvois bibliographiques dans les ouvrages du XIXe siècle empêchent de retracer facilement leur gestation. L'origine de quelques éléments récurrents peut toutefois être mise en évidence.

Selon C. Grell (1982 : 81-82), on ne doit pas chercher les origines de ces idées dans les descriptions des voyageurs du XVIIIe siècle. Au début du XIXe siècle, les comparaisons entre Herculanum et Pompéi restent rares. En 1833, B. Quaranta met en parallèle l'ensemble des connaissances alors disponibles sur les deux villes en utilisant essentiellement des sources textuelles. Il souligne le caractère mercantile de Pompéi et considère les deux villes comme jumelles (Quaranta 1833 : 59-60). Il affirme, à partir de la lecture erronée d'une inscription trouvée en façade des *Praedia Iuliae Felicis* (*C.I.L.* IV, 1136), que Pompéi devait comporter " *nientemeno che novecento botteghe colle pergole* (...) " (Quaranta 1833 : 52). Nous pouvons supposer que la croyance en un tel nombre de boutiques à louer par un même propriétaire a dû jouer un grand rôle dans la différenciation qui s'est progressivement instaurée entre les deux villes.

Une fois que des vestiges ont pu être visités à Herculanum, et malgré leur surface réduite, les comparaisons avec Pompéi se sont multipliées. Ainsi, les livres publiés sur Pompéi au XIXe siècle consacrent tous au moins un chapitre à Herculanum. A partir des années 1860, sous l'impulsion de l'archéologie allemande, les recherches se détachent des seules considérations antiquaires. Les interprétations concernant l'urbanisme et les conditions socio-économiques d'Herculanum commencent alors à se fixer, grâce à la reprise des fouilles à ciel ouvert en 1869. L'ouvrage écrit en 1871 par Ch.-E. Beulé est caractéristique de cette période. Cet auteur décrit Pompéi comme une cité uniquement tournée vers le commerce (Beulé 1872 : 333-334). Il considère qu'Herculanum est propre au repos grâce à l'air vif de la mer (Beulé 1872 : 48-49). Herculanum aurait été une importante enclave de la culture grecque, où la population, dont " les Romains les plus riches ", s'adonnait à loisir aux arts et aux lettres (Beulé 1872 : 281-282). Il semble être le premier à avoir théorisé cette vision devenue ensuite traditionnelle d'Herculanum. L'analyse des objets d'art mis au jour dans la Villa des Papyri constitue le fondement essentiel de ses interprétations.

Quelques années plus tard, J. Beloch parvient aux mêmes conclusions. Etudiant le pavement des rues d'Herculanum, il déduit que l'activité commerciale devait y être moins importante qu'à Pompéi. Son étude onomastique lui permet de conclure que de riches familles avaient migré à Herculanum, amenant avec elles le patrimoine artistique retrouvé. Son ouvrage, qui utilise le résultat des fouilles, l'épigraphie et les textes antiques, va servir de référence pour les études du début du siècle suivant. Il a figé l'image d'Herculanum ville de villégiature, " *zur Villegiatur einladenden Lage* " (Beloch 1890 : 224). Il est le premier à avoir utilisé un passage de la lettre de Pline à Tacite (*Epist.*, VI, 16, 9) pour caractériser Herculanum. Pourtant, rien n'indique que Pline ait cherché à définir Herculanum quand il mentionne les agréments de la côte. Au contraire, le manque de précision des termes employés laisse supposer qu'il a voulu caractériser l'ensemble du golfe de Naples plutôt qu'une seule cité. Cette théorie de J. Beloch est devenue l'interprétation courante donnée à la ville, reprise dans de nombreuses publications consacrées à Herculanum. Sa démonstration laisse supposer une parenté entre le plan d'Herculanum et celui de Naples. Cette idée critiquable (Guadagno 1993 : 83-87), fondée sur l'utilisation d'un plan schématique et incomplet, est ensuite reprise intégralement par A. Maiuri.

En 1908, pour encourager la reprise des fouilles, C. Waldstein reprend l'interprétation qui fait d'Herculanum une ville fortement teintée de culture grecque. Il extrapole les découvertes faites dans la Villa des Papyri au reste de la cité (Waldstein-Shoobridge 1908 : 85). L'ensemble de sa démonstration suit les propos de Ch.-E. Beulé et de J. Beloch, fréquemment cités. C. Waldstein refuse toutefois de généraliser l'absence de boutiques dans la zone fouillée à l'ensemble de la ville. Il décrit le matériel de pêche comme seule trace d'activité " industrielle " (Waldstein-Shoobridge 1908 : 95). A. Maiuri (1932) reprend cet exposé dans son intégralité. Waldstein caractérise le peuplement d'Herculanum comme plus " *aristocratic* " que celui de Pompéi (Waldstein-Shoobridge 1908 : 96). Cette synthèse a ouvert la voie à A. Maiuri. Aussi, les premières théories qu'il défend dans ses ouvrages reprennent ces idées : Herculanum aurait été une ville fortement liée dès ses origines à Naples ; ville de villégiature, elle aurait essentiellement accueilli de riches personnages, venus y trouver le repos et s'imprégner de culture grecque ; les faibles activités commerciales de la cité la distingueraient fortement de Pompéi. Autant d'idées dont les fondements sont soit les textes antiques sur la Campanie, soit les objets d'art mis au jour dans la Villa des Papyri.

Avec l'avancée des fouilles, A. Maiuri a trouvé une nouvelle source d'inspiration dans l'historiographie de son temps. Traditionnellement, on estime que les considérations d'A. Maiuri sur le développement commercial des villes campaniennes prennent leur origine dans les écrits de M. Rostovtseff. Bien que pertinente, cette idée cache mal une influence plus complexe. En effet, l'usage par A. Maiuri des thèses du savant russe relève plus de la transformation que de l'acceptation pure et simple.

D'après M. Rostovtseff, l'urbanisation se développe en Italie dans les deux derniers siècles de la République. Une nouvelle bourgeoisie aisée, constituée de boutiquiers et de propriétaires terriens est à l'origine de ce phénomène (Rostovtseff 1926 : 21-22 ; 1957 : 21-22). Un des représentants de cette élite économique serait Trimalcion, même si M. Rostovtseff considère que son statut d'affranchi n'est pas représentatif des milieux d'affaires de son temps (Rostovtseff 1926 : 58-59 ; 1957 : 57-58). Peu après la dictature de Sylla, et plus encore pendant le règne d'Auguste, l'ensemble de l'Italie s'industrialise. A Pompéi, un nouveau type d'habitations entourées de boutiques apparaîtrait alors (Rostovtseff 1926 : 72 ; 1957 : 73). Dans le chapitre III de son ouvrage, M. Rostovtseff estime que l'étude détaillée de Pompéi améliorerait les connaissances de l'histoire économique du Ier siècle ap. J.-C. Dans la suite de ce chapitre, il décrit l'amorce, sous les Julio-Claudiens, du développement économique des provinces. A l'inverse de la situation décrite pour l'Italie, l'urbanisation entraînerait la constitution d'une nouvelle bourgeoisie d'affaires (Rostovtseff 1926 : 88-90 ; 1957 : 90-93). Durant cette période, dans l'ensemble de l'empire, émergerait une nouvelle classe de bourgeois, les affranchis (Rostovtseff 1926 : 100 ; 1957 : 104). Enfin, M. Rostovtseff estime que l'Italie, à la fin de la période julio-claudienne, connaît des difficultés croissantes sur le plan économique (Rostovtseff 1926 : 177-178 ; 1957 : 187-190).

Ces idées sont reprises par A. Maiuri, bien qu'il n'ait pas suivi le schéma de développement économique de Pompéi développé dans la *SEHRE*. Il a en fait utilisé certaines des idées développées par M. Rostovtseff à propos des provinces pour les appliquer aux cités campaniennes. Il a en outre exagéré certains aspects, comme la croissance du nombre d'affranchis. Il n'est donc pas possible de considérer que les théories d'A. Maiuri sont l'application stricte au cas d'Herculanum des idées développées par M. Rostovtseff. Par ailleurs, dans aucun de ses livres sur cette ville, A. Maiuri ne cite l'ouvrage du savant russe. Il n'en reste pas moins que ce livre était connu et apprécié d'A. Maiuri (Maiuri 1948 : 13). De plus, les relations entre les deux hommes sont amplement attestées. Ainsi, c'est M. Rostovtseff (1932) qui a réalisé le compte-rendu laudatif du premier livre d'A. Maiuri sur Herculanum. Par ailleurs, les deux savants ont été en contact épistolaire, A. Maiuri signalant à M. Rostovtseff certaines découvertes à Herculanum ou Pompéi (Iezzi-Scafati 1984 : 269-270 ; Buonocore 1999 : 425).

A. Maiuri s'est vraisemblablement inspiré des idées du savant russe. Toutefois, certaines de ces théories sont caractéristiques des courants historiographiques des années 1920. Ainsi, plusieurs auteurs soulignent le rôle des affranchis dans la vie commerciale de Pompéi (Frank 1920 : 190-218 ; Gordon 1927). Il reste donc difficile de définir avec exactitude les emprunts effectués par A. Maiuri à M. Rostovtseff. De plus, A. Maiuri force le trait de son analyse, dans un sens souvent très condescendant, à la différence de T. Frank et M. Rostovtseff. Ceux-ci mentionnent le rôle important des affranchis dans la vie économique au Ier siècle de notre ère, mais ne parlent pas d'éviction brutale des anciennes élites.

Il nous reste à examiner si l'idéologie fasciste a pu exercer une certaine influence sur la pensée d'A. Maiuri. En effet, ayant été nommé Surintendant en 1924, il peut être considéré comme un archéologue du régime mussolinien. Toutefois, il n'est pas possible, comme l'a montré D. Manacorda (1982 : 451), de classer les archéologues de cette période en trois catégories (fascistes, anti-fascistes et non fascistes).

La période la plus intense d'activité archéologique à Herculanum se situe entre 1927 et 1941. En effet, avec l'aide de M. Castelli, Haut Commissaire à Naples, des crédits très importants sont débloqués pour permettre l'expropriation de terrains situés au-dessus du site. Après le débarquement des Alliés, les fouilles sont momentanément arrêtées en 1943, puis reprennent jusqu'à la fin des années 1950, à un rythme bien moins soutenu. Les *Nuovi Scavi* ont indéniablement été des fouilles voulues et largement financées par le régime fasciste : le 9 avril 1927, dans son discours de réception à la *Società Romana di Storia Patria*, B. Mussolini offre à ceux qu'il nomme ses « confrères » la reprise des fouilles à Herculanum. Il reprend très exactement les théories d'A. Maiuri, accentuant les différences entre Pompéi, adonnée au commerce, et Herculanum, cité de la culture (cit. in Cagnat 1927 : 102-103). Selon D. Manacorda (1982 : 449-450), un des effets du conditionnement fasciste a été de transformer le mode de rédaction des archéologues et des historiens de l'Antiquité : ces derniers ont abandonné l'écriture scientifique au profit de formules " esthétisantes ". Tant que dure le régime fasciste, A. Maiuri exprime ses analyses sur l'éviction de l'élite traditionnelle par les affranchis dans un style épique et très précieux (Maiuri 1927 : 81 sq.). Après guerre, les mêmes idées sont présentées de façon plus scientifique et plus sobre (Maiuri 1958 : 248).

Toutefois, si ces faits pourraient laisser supposer une proximité d'A. Maiuri avec le fascisme, il faut nuancer ce jugement. L'influence exercée sur un discours de B. Mussolini, le financement de ses fouilles en Campanie et quelques considérations stylistiques ne permettent pas de considérer A. Maiuri comme un homme-lige du régime. Ainsi, seuls 6 des 59 articles de vulgarisation écrits entre 1927 et 1942 sur Herculanum et Pompéi ont été publiés dans des revues ayant vocation de propagande (*Roma*, *Il giornale d'Italia*). A la libération, A. Maiuri a été nommé *Direttore Generale delle Antichità e Belle Arti* par Omedeo, ministre du gouvernement Badoglio. Sa nomination n'a pas été suivie d'effet, car il s'est trouvé sur la liste des personnes à épurer. L'appui de Benedetto Croce lui a permis de voir son cas réexaminé, puis de réintégrer l'*Accademia dei Lincei* (Iezzi-Sacaffati 1984 : 281), ce qui permet de supposer qu'il ne s'est pas compromis dans des épisodes condamnables, selon F. Zevi (2001 : 74). N'aurait-il pas cherché à s'insérer partiellement dans le moule du fascisme dans le seul but de pouvoir développer ses travaux archéologiques, financés par le nouveau régime ? Le fascisme ne paraissant avoir eu qu'une influence très limitée sur les idées d'A. Maiuri, il ne faut absolument pas en faire une clé de lecture unique.

Il faut à présent cerner la part prise, dans les raisonnements d'A. Maiuri sur la société d'Herculanum, par les données archéologiques, en nous appuyant sur sa synthèse de 1958. L'un des points sur lesquels A. Maiuri a fait oeuvre de pionnier à Herculanum reste l'utilisation de l'archéologie du bâti. Il a cherché à retracer les différentes périodes d'occupation de la ville en dressant une typologie des modes de construction, ce qui n'avait pas été fait auparavant (Maiuri 1958 : 62-74). L'établissement de cette typo-chronologie permet à A. Maiuri d'esquisser, pour certaines maisons, le schéma de leur évolution, ou bien de dater leur construction. Plus fréquemment, A. Maiuri se contente de quelques remarques sur les changements survenus dans les maisons. Lorsque des transformations amènent à de grands bouleversements au sein d'un îlot, ses explications veulent être plus complètes. Il énumère alors les différentes composantes architecturales de la maison en indiquant leur datation et décrit particulièrement les éléments décoratifs. L'interprétation la plus poussée est faite pour la *Casa Sannitica* (V, 1-2), dont les transformations ont amené à la création de la *Casa del Gran Portale* (V, 34-35) et de la *Casa con Giardino* (V, 32-33) (Maiuri 1958 : 197-199, 377-378, 431). Malgré la possibilité d'esquisser l'évolution de chaque maison, A. Maiuri fonde la majeure partie de ses raisonnements sur des observations stylistiques. De la sorte, comme dans le cas de la *Casa del Tramezzo di Legno* (III, 4-9.11-12) (Maiuri 1958 : 207), au lieu de présenter des phases de transformation claires et détaillées, il n'indique que certains de leurs éléments. En raison de son aversion pour les transformations qu'il constate, et malgré sa parfaite maîtrise des données architecturales, A. Maiuri ne décrit l'évolution des boutiques et des maisons d'Herculanum que par petites touches.

Un autre élément aurait pu être pris en compte pour interpréter boutiques et ateliers : les objets qui y ont été mis au jour. Toutefois, A. Maiuri y fait peu allusion dans son ouvrage. Ils auraient dû être décrits dans un second volume qui n'est jamais paru (Maiuri 1958 : V-VI). Malgré la volonté de briser le mythe faisant d'Herculanum une mine de bronzes et de marbres, nous pouvons supposer que le second volume aurait eu une approche fortement antiquaire, comme l'indique son titre : *Ercolano. I nuovi scavi (1927-1958). La decorazione - Le opere d'arte* (Maiuri 1958 : VI, 239, 464). Les objets mis au jour sont parfois mentionnés dans le texte, essentiellement pour interpréter les ateliers. Ainsi, la découverte de nombreuses intailles en Or. II, 10 permet à A. Maiuri d'interpréter ce local comme celui d'un *gemmarius* (Maiuri 1958 : 463-464). Cette utilisation reste cependant exceptionnelle. La majorité des boutiques et des ateliers a été interprétée soit en se fondant sur les structures maçonnées, soit sur la seule présence d'un seuil à rainure.

Au-delà de ces rares considérations sur l'architecture et les objets, A. Maiuri ne détaille son raisonnement que dans le cas de la *Casa del Bicentenario* (V, 15-16) (Maiuri 1958 : 222-224). Cette maison servirait, à elle seule, à justifier l'argumentation sur l'invasion de la maison traditionnelle par des affranchis s'adonnant au commerce. Ainsi, A. Maiuri montre que cette *domus* a d'abord été plus grande, communicant avec les *Case del Bel Cortile* (V, 8) et *dell'Apollo Citaredo* (V, 9-12). Il décrit ensuite la manière dont elle a été transformée par la proximité du *decumanus maximus*. Après une étude des différents types de maçonnerie constituant les murs, il conclut, malgré la présence d'éléments remontant à la période samnite, que la maison a été intégralement reconstruite entre 10 av. J.-C. et 5 ap. J.-C.

Vers les années 55-60 de notre ère, d'importantes transformations auraient eu lieu. Des boutiques seraient créées à ce moment dans trois des pièces de façade. L'une d'elles (V, 16-17) deviendrait indépendante de la maison. Dès lors, le nouveau propriétaire serait contraint d'habiter non plus autour de l'atrium et du péristyle, mais dans l'appartement qui se développe au-dessus des boutiques. De plus, le faible nombre d'objets mis au jour dans les pièces entourant l'*atrium* témoignerait de leur utilisation réduite par le dernier propriétaire. La description de la pièce 7 montrerait parfaitement cet abandon du rez-de-chaussée. En effet, fermée par un panneau coulissant et repliable, cette pièce aurait abrité, en des temps plus nobles, soit des archives, soit les *imagines maiorum*. Cette interprétation est discutable, toutes les archives mises au jour à Herculanum, notamment dans la *Casa del Bicentenario*, ayant été découvertes à l'étage (Maiuri 1958 : n. 49 p. 472 ; *Giornali degli Scavi di Ercolano* [*GS*] *1938* : 10 ottobre). La décadence dans laquelle serait tombée la maison serait également perceptible en examinant la fresque qui orne le côté ouest du *tablinum*. Le cadre central représente Dédale et Pasiphae. Une réparation ampute une partie de cette figuration mythologique (Fig. 1-2). Elle a été faite avec un enduit rouge qui ne reprend pas le dessin et qui est d'un rouge différent de celui utilisé pour le reste du panneau. L'observation attentive de cette fresque permet d'entrevoir une autre explication. Ainsi, les bords inférieurs et supérieurs du fragment ajouté correspondent parfaitement avec la ligne de fracture qui s'est produite lors de la chute du panneau durant l'éruption. Tout laisse à penser que la restauration supposée antique par A. Maiuri a en fait été effectuée par les ouvriers du chantier peu après la mise au jour du *tablinum*. Dans la description des étages, A. Maiuri expose une autre série d'arguments (Maiuri 1958 : 234-239). Tout d'abord, il note que l'appartement de façade serait beaucoup plus soigné que celui auquel on accédait par le péristyle. Ceci renforcerait son hypothèse d'une occupation de l'étage donnant sur la rue par le dernier propriétaire de la maison. Enfin, la supposée " croix " mise au jour à l'étage est le dernier point de son argumentation. Grâce à cette découverte, A. Maiuri considère que l'étage était loué à une famille de *peregrini*, de foi chrétienne (Maiuri 1958 : 236-237). La mise au jour, dans la villa de Boscoreale, d'une étagère fixée au mur selon le même principe et présentant un aspect similaire à la « croix » (De Caro 1994 : 31-35, tav. 2b) permet de considérer cette dernière au mieux comme un autel mural.

L'étude détaillée des arguments présentés autour de la *Casa del Bicentenario* par A. Maiuri montre son mode de raisonnement. L'ensemble est cohérent, mais les arguments présentés pris séparément sont souvent discutables. A. Maiuri n'a pas bâti sa théorie de l'évolution des implantations commerciales à partir des données recueillies dans cette maison. Au contraire, son interprétation est un préalable à l'utilisation des données issues de la fouille. Celles-ci sont ramenées de force vers sa théorie. De ce fait, nous devons considérer que son utilisation des données archéologiques est orientée.

Pour compléter cette recension critique, il est nécessaire de s'interroger sur la façon dont A. Maiuri a écrit sa synthèse de 1958. Son rôle de Surintendant lui interdisait une présence permanente à Herculanum. Il inspectait les fouilles de temps en temps et venait également lorsque des objets ou des structures mis au jour nécessitaient une décision que lui seul pouvait prendre. Selon les journaux de fouille, la " croix " de la *Casa del Bicentenario* est découverte le 28 janvier 1938. Dans son article consacré à la publication de cette découverte, A. Maiuri écrit que la " croix " a été mise au jour le 3 février 1938, selon ses notes personnelles (Maiuri 1940 : 193). Lors de ses visites, il consignait ses observations sur un carnet dont seuls quelques extraits ont été publiés (Iezzi-Scafati 1984). Il utilisait beaucoup plus ce dernier que les journaux de fouille. S'il les avait utilisés, la date réelle de découverte de la " croix " aurait été mentionnée.

La préférence accordée à ses carnets personnels a des conséquences importantes sur les données publiées par A. Maiuri. L'exemple du métier à tisser de la *Casa del Telaio* (V, 3-4) (fouillée entre le 2 février 1931 et le 21 janvier 1933) et de son devenir entre la fouille et la publication est à ce titre édifiant. Dans les journaux de fouilles, seule une brève mention indique la découverte de cet instrument dans la partie est du péristyle, au détour de la description finale de la maison, rédigée à la fin de janvier 1933. Dans la relation quotidienne des fouilles, le métier à tisser n'apparaît jamais. Le 18 janvier 1933, un dessin en est dressé par R. Oliva (Fig. 3-4). Le *Giornale dei Lavori* mentionne le début de la restauration du métier à tisser à partir du 8 février 1933, par les restaurateurs d'enduits. Dans son livre, A. Maiuri signale trois métiers à tisser : dans la boutique VII, 1a (Maiuri 1958 : 449), dans la *Casa del Telaio* (V, 3-4) (Maiuri 1958 : 430) et dans la " chambre de la brodeuse " (Or. II, 10). A cet endroit, il donne une description de la pièce qui correspond à la photographie qui agrémente le texte (Maiuri 1958 : 463, fig. 420 ; Fig. 5). L'analyse des journaux de fouille permet de décrypter ce cliché : des différents objets censés provenir de cette pièce, seuls le lit et les ossements y ont été effectivement trouvés (*GS 1936* : 8 ottobre) ; le métier à tisser n'apparaît jamais lors de la fouille de cette boutique ou d'une autre maison sur le site ; le seul métier à tisser jamais mis au jour à Herculanum est celui qui a donné son nom à la *Casa del Telaio* (V, 3-4). Il faut donc considérer que le métier de la " brodeuse " a été découvert en V, 3-4.

Partant de ces données, il est possible de retracer le parcours du métier à tisser entre le moment où il a été trouvé, en V, 3-4, et sa description en Or. II, 10. Le 18 janvier 1933, il est dessiné par R. Oliva, alors qu'il a été découvert plusieurs jours auparavant. Immédiatement après, l'architecte réfléchit à une hypothèse de restitution. Sur son dessin, il représente les rares éléments conservés qu'il a observés. Le 8 février 1933, les ouvriers chargés des enduits peints commencent à restaurer le métier à tisser, sans suivre la restitution proposée par R. Oliva. Quelques années plus tard, il est installé en Or. II, 10, avec d'autres objets de provenances diverses. A. Maiuri a-t-il ensuite fait une confiance trop grande à ses assistants chargés de la mise en valeur du site ? A-t-il accordé trop d'importance aux intailles mises au jour dans ce local pour noter le détail des autres objets retrouvés ? Lors de sa rédaction, fort de ses notes et d'une visite de contrôle sur le site, il décrit ce qu'il voit après la mise en valeur de cette pièce et invente l'histoire de la jeune brodeuse. La mise en parallèle des journaux de fouilles avec les textes d'A. Maiuri dans d'autres cas montrerait qu'il s'est contenté de décrire des situations mises en scène pour les visiteurs.

A l'issue de cet examen des méthodes de travail d'Amedeo Maiuri, plusieurs conclusions s'imposent. Ses idées sur les transformations du tissu commercial à Herculanum ont fortement évolué. Ainsi, un changement radical s'opère dans ses interprétations à la fin des années 1930, en lien avec l'avancée des fouilles. Il abandonne alors l'idée d'une ville de villégiature pour tenter de montrer le nombre croissant des boutiques à compter des années 55-60 ap. J.-C. De multiples influences lui ont permis de développer ces deux théories. Elles ont d'abord été fondées sur " l'hérédité de culture " existant à Herculanum. Les écrits de J. Beloch semblent y avoir joué un rôle non négligeable. La seconde théorie d'A. Maiuri, proche de celle développée pour Pompéi, se fonde sur les écrits de M. Rostovtseff, notablement remaniés, et sur l'historiographie des années 1920. L'idéologie fasciste ne paraît avoir eu qu'une influence très limitée sur ses œuvres scientifiques. La place prise par les données archéologiques dans l'œuvre d'A. Maiuri est paradoxale. Il cherche à donner l'impression que ces raisonnements ne se fondent que sur ces dernières. Pourtant, il n'utilise pas directement les comptes-rendus de fouille, mais se réfère exclusivement à ses observations personnelles faites généralement après restauration.

Cette pratique l'a ainsi amené à commettre des erreurs et à mettre en scène le site. Le principal problème reste que son utilisation des données archéologiques est fortement biaisée par ses présupposés théoriques. De ce fait, l'utilisation de ces données reste très mécanique et souvent erronée. Sur d'autres sujets, il ne faut pas écarter les écrits d'A. Maiuri, souvent remarquables par la justesse de leurs observations. En revanche, son interprétation normative de l'évolution des boutiques à Herculanum doit être abandonnée. Pour mieux cerner le rôle et la place des implantations artisanales et commerciales dans les villes campaniennes, il est désormais nécessaire de reprendre l'ensemble des données disponibles pour les exploiter sans a priori théorique.

BIBLIOGRAPHIE

Beloch, J., 1890, *Campanien, Geschichte und Topographie des antiken Neapel und seiner Umgebung,* 2e édition, Studia Historica, 11, E. Morgenstern, Breslau.

Beulé, Ch.-E., 1872, *Le drame du Vésuve*, 2e édition, Lévy frères, Paris.

Bonnuci, C., 1835, *Ercolano,* Napoli.

Buonocore, M., 1999, Rostovzev e l'epigrafia, in *Rostovtzeff e l'Italia,* (A. Marcone), 419-437, Incontri perugini di storia della storiografia antica e sul mondo antico, 11, Ed Scientifiche Italiane, Napoli.

Cagnat, R., 1927, Les fouilles d'Herculanum, in *En pays romain,* Collection d'études d'histoire et d'archéologie, De Boccard, Paris, p. 88-105.

De Caro, S., 1994, *La villa rustica in località Villa Regina a Boscoreale*, Giorgio Breitschneider, Roma.

Frank, T., 1920, *An Economic History of Rome to the end of the Republic,* J. Hopkins press, Baltimore.

Gordon, M., 1927, The ordo of Pompeii, *JRS,* 17, 165-183.

Grell, Ch., 1982, *Herculanum et Pompéi dans les récits des voyageurs français du XVIIIe siècle*, Mémoires et documents sur Rome et l'Italie méridionale, 2, Centre J. Bérard, Naples.

Guadagno, G., 1993, Ercolano. Eredità di cultura e nuovi dati, in *Ercolano 1738-1988. 250 anni di ricerca archeologica,*(L. Franchi dell'Orto), 73-98, Monografie Soprintendenza Archeologica di Pompei, 6, L'Erma di Bretschneider, Roma.

Iezzi, B., Scafati, N., 1984, " Amedeo Maiuri. Vita e contatti di archeologo ", in *Pompei Ercolano Stabiae Oplontis. LXXIX - MCMLXXIX, Mostra bibliografica*, 255-288, Napoli, 1984.

ŁoŚ, A., 1992, *Quibus patet curia municipalis.* Remarques sur la structure de la classe dirigeante de Pompei, *Cahiers du Centre Gustave Glotz*, 3, 259-297.

ŁoŚ, A., 1995, La condition sociale des affranchis au 1er siècle après J.-C., *Annales HSS,* 5, 1011-1043.

Maiuri, A., 1927, *Pompei,* Istituto Geografico De Agostini, Novara.

Maiuri, A., 1928, La ripresa degli scavi di Ercolano, *RendNap*, n.s. 41, 45-52.

Maiuri, A., 1932, *Herculanum*, Ed. Alpina, Paris.

Maiuri, A., 1936, *Herculaneum*, Itinéraires des musées et monuments de l'Italie, 53, Libreria dello Stato, Roma.

Maiuri, A., 1940, La croce di Ercolano, *RendPontAcc*, 15, 193-218.

Maiuri, A., 1942, *L'ultima fase edilizia di Pompei*, Campania Romana, 2, Istituto di Studi Romani, Spoleto.

Maiuri, A., 1948, Gli studi pompeiani nel II° centenario degli scavi, *Accademia nazionale dei Lincei, Problemi attuali di scienza e di cultura*, 9, Bardi, Roma.

Maiuri, A., 1958, *Ercolano. I nuovi scavi. (1927-1958)*, vol. 1, Libreria della Stato, Roma.

Manacorda, D., 1982, Per un'indagine sull'archeologia italiana durante il ventennio fascista, *Archeologia Medievale*, 9, 443-470.

Mouritsen, H., 1996, Order and disorder in Late Pompeian politics, *Les élites municipales de l'Italie péninsulaire des Gracques à Néron. Actes de la table ronde de Clermont Ferrand (28-23 novembre 1991)*, (Cébeillac-Gervasoni M.), 139-144, Coll. CJB, 13 / CEFR 215, Rome-Naples.

Quaranta, B., 1833, Origini, vicende e scavazioni di Ercolano e Pompei, *Annali Civili del Regno delle Due Sicile*, 1, fasc. 1, 52-64.

Rostovtzeff, M., 1926, *The social and economic history of the Roman empire*, Clarendon press, Oxford.

Rostovtzeff, M., 1932, Compte-rendu de Maiuri 1932, *AJA*, 36, 585-587.

Rostovtzeff, M., 1957, *The social and economic history of the Roman empire. 2nd edition revised by P.M. Fraser*, Clarendon press, Oxford.

Ruggiero, M., 1885, *Storia degli Scavi di Ercolano*, Napoli.

Waldstein, Ch., Shoobridge, M.A., 1908, *Herculaneum. Past present & future. With appendixes*, MacMillan, London.

Wallace-Hadrill, A., 1994, *Houses & society in Herculaneum & Pompei,* Princeton University Press, Princeton.

Zevi, F., Aspetti dell'archeologia pompeiana nel Novecento : gli scavi del Maiuri a Pompei, in *Pompei. Scienza e Società, Atti del Convegno internazionale di Napoli (25-27 novembre 1998) per il 250° Amiversario degli Scavi di Pompei,* (P.G. Guzzo), 73-79, Electa, Napoli.

Fig. 1. *Casa del Bicentenario*, panneau du côté ouest du *tablinum* représentant Dédale et Pasiphae (Cliché N.M.).

Fig. 2. *Casa del Bicentenario*, détail de la réparation du panneau représentant Dédale et Pasiphae (Cliché N.M.).

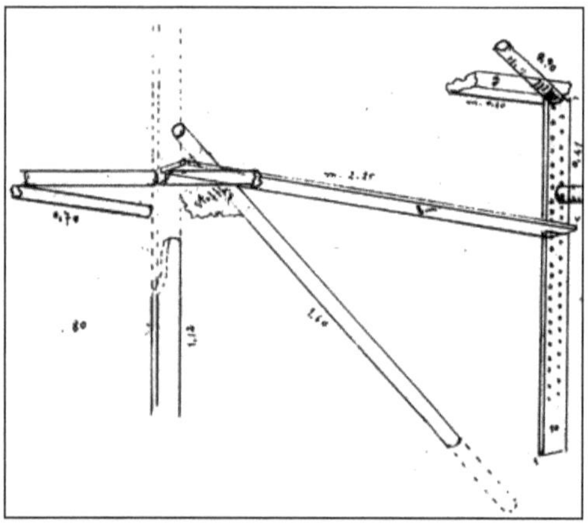

Fig. 3. Représentation en perspective du métier à tisser de la *Casa del Telaio* (V, 3-4) peu après sa mise au jour (Dessin R. Oliva ; *Archivio Disegni SAP*, P 658 f°3 ; 18/01/1933).

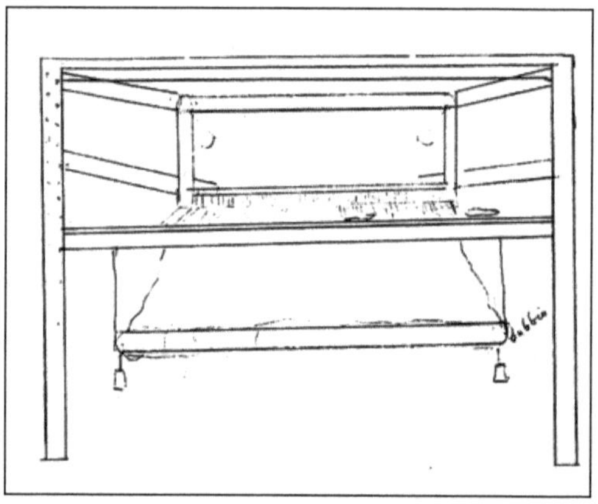

Fig. 4. Proposition de restitution du métier à tisser de la *Casa del Telaio* (V, 3-4) (Dessin R. Oliva ; *Archivio Disegni SAP*, P 658 f°4 ; s.d.).

Fig. 5. " *Camera della ricamatrice* ". Mise en scène de la pièce annexe de l'atelier Ins. Or. II, 10 (Nég. SAP E/B 56 ; 1957).

TRA CONTINUITÀ E ROTTURA: LE ASSOCIAZIONI MEDIEVALI DI MESTIERE NEL PENSIERO STORICO E POLITICO TRA FINE DEL XIX E XX SECOLO

PAOLO GULL
(Università della Tuscia)

ABSTRACT: Vocational guilds in Medieval Italy have raised the attention of historians on many occasions and have even been considered by scholars of other disciplines (economic history and, especially, the social sciences). Readings were strongly influenced by the political trends of moment and, more generally, by the vicissitudes of the contemporary world. Between the end of the 19th century and the period of Fascism, Italy witnessed the construction of an anti-modern and anti-socialist perception of the Middle Ages, assuming an ironic stereotype of a society lacking inter-class conflicts. The same Fascist culture, although strongly infused by Roman Imperial myth, was instrumental in this vision thanks in part to the convergence of some sectors of the Catholic world. Following the Second World War additional and equally ideological readings of this phenomenon developed from Marxist thought, while the anti-modernism of Christian culture, which faced new global tendencies, especially after the fall of the Berlin Wall, would find other unexpected "companions".

La storiografia sulle organizzazioni di mestiere nell'Italia medievale è un tema che ha frequentemente attirato l'attenzione degli studiosi per il carattere multiforme di questo filone di studi che è arrivato anche a configurarsi come ambito di ricerca specifico, divenendo, nel clima fortemente ideologizzato delle generazioni tra la fine del XIX e l'inizio del XX secolo, territorio di frontiera fra diversi saperi.

Mentre sotto la lente degli storici del diritto il problema si è per esempio ridotto alla questione della continuità o meno dell'istituto giuridico rispetto al mondo romano, nelle riflessioni di sociologi e storici dell'economia il tema è stato talvolta dilatato sulla scorta di spiegazioni globali del mondo.

In realtà la questione delle associazioni di mestiere è stato assunto a metafora o a momento costitutivo e centrale dell'intera civiltà comunale, simbolo di un medioevo cattolico nella sua prassi, corporativo nella sua struttura istituzionale e popolare in quella sociale; ora strumentalmente tirato per un verso ora per l'altro, esso risulta così costituito essenzialmente da queste tre grandi componenti che sono il riflesso di altrettante posizioni ideologiche che si dividono la torta del dibattito culturale.

Questo tema ha così prodotto una vasta letteratura di cui esistono numerose sintesi, ognuna delle quali offre un punto di vista diverso anche in considerazione del materiale bibliografico esaminato, scelto fra un'ampia produzione intellettuale; ovviamente di molti di questi studi sono profondamente debitore[1].

La parabola di questo tormentato percorso critico offre ancora oggi numerosi spunti di riflessione, in particolare se si osserva come il regime riuscì, sotto il segno del corporativismo, ad egemonizzare un problema che aveva sollecitato letture radicalmente diverse perfino in seno alla stessa nascente cultura fascista. Se questo secondo punto è facilmente interpretabile pensando alla molteplicità degli apporti culturali e politici alle origini del movimento fascista, occorre leggere più fra le righe per rendersi conto di come gli studi sul corporativismo non si limitarono a riproporre una lettura "continuista" dell'istituto giuridico rispetto al diritto romano (esigenza tuttavia mai sopita nell'ideologia del regime) ma cercarono di costruire una interpretazione fascista del medioevo o meglio una delle possibili interpretazioni fasciste del medioevo.

In due importanti saggi, Daniele Manacorda (1982a, 1982b) aveva puntato il dito sul peso della cultura fascista nel campo delle scienze archeologiche, proponendo una lettura che, seppur ancor oggi pienamente convincente, rivela solo un lato (oscuro) del problema. L'impatto della cultura legata al mito della Roma imperiale fu infatti talmente ampio da permeare vaste espressioni della società esibendo le sue manifestazioni più vistose in urbanistica ed architettura.

Nell'ambito della cultura egemone di quegli anni, il medioevo ebbe un'eco meno vistosa ma come vedremo altrettanto significativa. Il medioevo non fu così assente dalla cultura fascista anche se è chiaro che nelle scienze archeologiche venne relegato ai margini pur con eccezioni, tutte significative.
Le ragioni della oggettiva modestia dei risultati scientifici di quegli anni sono probabilmente più da ricercarsi in un arretramento metodologico (Manacorda 1982b: 103) che nella scelta ideologica di ignorare un certo periodo storico, arretramento figlio della sconfitta di quei germi di

positivismo che tra Otto e Novecento a fatica si facevano strada nella cultura italiana. Germi contro i quali più filoni seppero congiurare, preparando oggettivamente il terreno al regime di Mussolini.

Per comprendere questa evoluzione è così necessario risalire molto più indietro nel tempo, prendendo le mosse almeno dalla svolta che il pensiero cattolico compì negli ultimi anni dell'Ottocento.

IL PENSIERO CATTOLICO: LA STORIA

Sebbene la più importante e durevole espressione della storiografia tra fine Ottocento e inizi del Novecento sul tema delle corporazioni sia stata senz'altro sviluppata da quella scuola di pensiero che Benedetto Croce definì "economico-giuridica", il pensiero storiografico di quegli anni non si esaurì in questi pur essenziali apporti: sulla lunga durata, infatti, il suo percorso tormentato, con una periodizzazione scandita dai due conflitti mondiali, mostra bene i punti di svolta che punteggiano un'indagine nata e rimasta ideologicamente connotata.

Va anzitutto sottolineato come gli studi sulle organizzazioni di mestiere siano stati, fin dall'inizio, intimamente connessi ad un'ondata di interesse nei confronti del medioevo che investì, a più riprese e con diversi accenti, la società italiana pre e postunitaria; se è vero che questo interesse si poneva nel solco di più vasti movimenti o "mode" intellettuali, anche di lunga durata, occorre ricordare che in questa fase ad esso, almeno in Italia e Francia, non fu estraneo il rinnovato impegno sociale della Chiesa che ebbe, come momento di sintesi, il messaggio della *Rerum novarum* (1891).

L'enciclica leoniana è uno snodo che probabilmente va considerato come il crocevia da cui muovere in questo percorso: l'epoca del pontificato di Leone XIII (1878-1903) fu il terreno di coltura delle riflessioni di Giuseppe Toniolo prima e Agostino Gemelli poi. Quest'ultimo, del resto, è l'autore di *Medioevalismo*, manifesto del primo numero della rivista "Vita e pensiero" (1914), che rappresenta ancor oggi probabilmente la sintesi ideologica più efficace di questo clima culturale.

Il pensiero di Toniolo e l'enciclica leoniana appaiono intimamente connessi: da un lato il richiamo del pontefice alla corporazione medievale come modello per tutti gli operatori del mondo del lavoro, nel segno di una più fervida vita religiosa, diventò un tema ricorrente del pensiero cattolico moderno; dall'altro è proprio Toniolo che, prima ancora di Max Weber e con accenti ben diversi, riconobbe il nesso umanesimo-rinascimento-protestantesimo come radice dello sviluppo del capitalismo[2]. Il pensiero cattolico sposò, così, una visione della storia in cui il modello organicistico della società medievale era alla base di una radicale critica alla società moderna che collocava riforma protestante e rivoluzione industriale su una medesima linea di progressivo abbandono dei valori cristiani.

Gli eventi sociopolitici che, dopo la rivoluzione francese ed il sovvertimento definitivo dell'*Ancient Régime*, avevano segnato il XIX secolo furono così all'origine di una ridefinizione della dottrina sociale della Chiesa che, dietro le posizioni antisocialiste, disponeva il suo arsenale di polemica antimoderna: il modello di società proprio del medioevo comunale venne in tal modo assunto a paradigma idealizzato di una società compiutamente cristiana.

Questa visione rigorosa tuttavia andò sfumandosi e articolandosi tra la fine del XIX secolo e i primi anni del Novecento quando, di fronte alla difficoltà di costruire una vera corporazione che riunisse lavoratori e datori di lavoro, la dottrina sociale cristiana dovette riconoscere giocoforza la necessità di optare per le associazioni sindacali semplici, il cosiddetto sindacato confessionale o "bianco".

E' un momento di pausa negli studi: gli storici cattolici perdettero progressivamente interesse nei confronti del tema dell'associazionismo medievale alle cui caratteristiche, vere o presunte, si ispirava il modello corporativo cattolico e di questo mutamento di rotta pare cogliere un'eco nelle vicende della fondazione della Società Cattolica Italiana per gli Studi scientifici. La storia della costituzione della Società getta anche una luce significativa sulla mancata presa del pensiero di Toniolo sulla storiografia italiana. Nel suo *entourage*, infatti, mancavano storici di professione, come Cinzio Violante sottolinea (1961: 739-741), e questo ne rendeva debole e poco incisiva la peculiare visione unitaria ed organica della cultura.

Toniolo aveva proposto una strutturazione dell'istituzione in quattro cattedre (storia delle dottrine filosofiche, storia delle dottrine sociali, storia delle scienze naturali e storia e discipline ausiliarie) fortemente integrate fra loro; nel 1899, invece, al momento della costituzione effettiva, le cinque sezioni in cui fu suddivisa la società (religiosa, filosofica ed apologetica; sociale-economica e giuridico-politica; fisico-naturale e matematica; storica; filologico-letteraria e artistica) imboccarono strade autonome e indipendenti. La autorevole presidenza assunta dal Prefetto della Biblioteca Vaticana Francesco Ehrle nella sezione di storia spostò, in particolare, l'orientamento culturale da una linea che perseguisse grandi sintesi di valore apologetico ad una più stretta severità scientifica nella convinzione che "il trionfo della verità sarebbe venuto di per sé quando fossero state scoperte ed esaminate tutte le fonti disponibili e conosciuti tutti i fatti conoscibili" (Violante 1961: 746). Ciò comportò una chiusura degli studi storici in un ambito filologico erudito.

IL PENSIERO CATTOLICO: LA SCIENZA

Malgrado questa obiettiva battuta d'arresto, la volontà di costruire sintesi culturali all'altezza delle sfide dell'epoca non venne tuttavia meno, ma si spostò su un nuovo fronte, quello delle scienze naturali.

Fin dai primi anni del secolo, infatti, Agostino Gemelli aveva invitato a più riprese i cattolici ad affrontare in modo adeguato il rapporto fra religione e scienza (Gemelli 1906, 1907) elaborando contemporaneamente la sua idea di un istituto superiore cattolico di studi filosofici che sottopose a Toniolo. Questo progetto è alla base della costituzione della Università Cattolica che avvenne alcuni anni più tardi, proprio assieme a seguaci e collaboratori di Toniolo.

Ciò avvenne dopo la guerra, quando Gemelli trovò un terreno adatto per la costituzione nel 1919, assieme a Filippo Meda, dell'Istituto di Studi superiori G. Toniolo, che aprì i suoi corsi nel 1921 con le facoltà di Filosofia e Scienze sociali.

Il corpo docente di quest'ultima facoltà era costituito come si è detto in gran parte da collaboratori di Toniolo ed era proprio di quello spirito che discendeva dagli anni della *Rerum novarum* che Gemelli si era fatto interprete intransigente con lo scritto *Medievalismo* (1914). In questo testo, vero "manifesto" di un'epoca, la cultura moderna è definita "un aggregato meccanico di parti… messe insieme senza connessione organica" (p.2) e riconosciuta come il "principale nemico della vita cristiana" (p.11).

Ormai al di fuori dei binari della riflessione storiografica ufficiale, il medioevo ritorna in questo modo ad essere il modello di una società il cui cardine sono le istituzioni corporative.

Il pensiero cattolico: stato e società

Oltre che nella fondazione dell'Università cattolica, il pensiero di Toniolo ebbe un'altra ricaduta, forse la più originale e feconda. Nelle sue riflessioni, infatti egli identificava nel sindacato (cioè nell'unità organica professionale) e nella corporazione (cioè nella sintesi di tutti i sindacati) quegli organi destinati a rimediare all'insufficienza dell'individuo e a frenare il prepotere dello stato. Di questi organismi, Toniolo, trovava ampi esempi proprio nelle associazioni di mestiere, le "società intermedie" del medioevo (Violante 1961: 725). Non è certamente un caso che anni più tardi, sulla stessa rivista in cui Gemelli aveva lanciato il suo manifesto, Filippo Meda avesse ripreso in modo vigoroso e programmatico questa visione riconoscendo proprio nella corporazione un "ente intermedio" fra stato e cittadino (Meda 1916: 347).

La radice comune del pensiero di Toniolo, delle iniziative di Gemelli e delle riflessioni di Meda mostra in modo molto chiaro come i diversi temi nei quali si sviluppa il pensiero cattolico degli anni anteriori al 1920 si tenessero saldamente l'un l'altro. Da un lato Gemelli identificava nel rapporto con le scienze naturali il momento di più aspra polemica con la cultura moderna, positivista, dall'altro Meda riconosceva l'esigenza di frenare il prepotere dello stato sui cittadini. Entrambi indugiavano nel vagheggiamento del medioevo come modello di società compiutamente cristiana, in perfetta linea con la ricostruzione storica di Toniolo: sono infatti lo stato liberale, erede della Riforma e della Rivoluzione francese, e la cultura positivistica che esso esprime gli avversari da cui difendersi e da battere.

Gli echi nella storiografia di mestiere

Gli storici di mestiere, legati come si è detto soprattutto alla scuola economico-giuridica, reagiscono a queste "mode" culturali in maniera contrastata andando così incontro ad una frattura molto forte.

La sociologia cattolico-sociale di Toniolo, come anche la storia economica di Achille Loria, altra componente nuova nel panorama delle scienze umane del tempo, pur nelle profonde differenze, sembrano infatti in quegli anni gli ambiti scientifici che colgono i mutamenti in atto con maggiore immediatezza e dinamismo. La visione organicistica di Toniolo influenzò così una schiera di giovani intellettuali alla ricerca di spiegazioni globali del mondo, tra cui spiccavano Antonio Boggiano-Pico, più orientato all'azione sociale in campo sindacale e Nicolò Rodolico, nella cui opera giovanile (1899) si avvertono gli echi delle tensioni sociali del suo tempo. I temi loriani, invece, ebbero forse un'eco meno vasta ma di una fertilità più duratura. Tra i primi, Salvemini, superando la visione strettamente organicistica, trasferì sul piano del conflitto economico il motivo delle "antitesi" più di quanto avesse fatto Pasquale Villari stesso (Artifoni 1984: 372-373; 1988: 19-21).

L'incontro tra diversi saperi, tuttavia, non avvenne in questi termini fecondi: la vicenda più significativa di quegli anni è costituita infatti dalla polemica tra Gioacchino Volpe e Gino Arias, colpevole secondo il primo di aver accolto in modo acritico le posizioni, giudicate eccessivamente schematizzanti, di Loria. Questa spaccatura, come ben evidenziato da Edoardo Artifoni (1988: 23-34), influenzerà in modo pesante tutto il destino della scuola economico giuridica.

Al di là delle qualità speifiche degli studi di Arias, si può probabilmente parlare a tutti gli effetti di un'occasione perduta di confronto tra diverse scuole scientifiche: da un lato il sociologismo cristiano di Toniolo, anche per il mutato indirizzo della militanza cattolica, si andava progressivamente orientando verso l'azione sociale, abbandonando così il terreno della riflessione storica; dall'altro la storia economica di matrice loriana, già passata sotto il pesante maglio della scomunica di Croce venne definitivamente messa fuori gioco da Volpe con la sua stroncatura di Arias. Ma poiché in quella sede Volpe dichiarò di parlare da ***storico***, ciò sanzionò molto più che la semplice recensione negativa (sia pur pesantissima) di un libro: da quel momento gli storici di mestiere abbandonarono progressivamente lo sguardo unitario che scaturiva dal confronto, pur conflittuale, tra le diverse scuole, per rinchiudersi nel campo delle storie speciali. Gli studi sulle organizzazioni di mestiere si ridurranno così in gran parte a ricerche sull'origine dell'istituto corporativo e sui problemi della sua continuità rispetto al mondo romano.

La polemica Volpe-Arias preluse dunque ad una svolta che si completerà, come si è accennato, nel clima mutato del primo dopoguerra.

L'ENTRATA IN SCENA DEL FASCISMO

Questa evoluzione della nostra storiografia ha senza dubbio una sua precisa logica interna: efficaci pagine di Artifoni (1988: 30-34) ne sintetizzano bene il percorso; tuttavia il suo sviluppo non si sottrasse all'influsso delle convulse vicende della politica degli anni che vanno dalla fine della prima guerra mondiale alla marcia su Roma. Nel clima di forti tensioni sociali che videro nascita ed affermazione del fascismo, gli intellettuali che più prontamente vi aderirono colsero infatti al balzo la palla della riflessione storica sulle corporazioni di mestiere per proporre una loro peculiare lettura con forte valenza politica.

Abbiamo già sottolineato come la storiografia del primo Novecento contenesse in gran parte dei suoi filoni robuste dosi di dura polemica antisocialista che gli intellettuali fascisti trovarono per così dire bell'e pronta ed è probabilmente un accorto uso di questi temi che permise conversioni apparentemente ardite in seno ad un nutrito gruppo di intellettuali cattolici. Di fronte a questa forte affinità culturale, molti di essi provvedettero semplicemente ad abbandonare il principale elemento che li avrebbe distinti da un troppo stretto connubio col pensiero fascista, la diffidenza nei confronti dello statalismo, arrivando a posizioni convergenti altrimenti inconcepibili.

Anche in questo caso i fenomeni non sono del tutto lineari. L'interesse del fascismo nei confronti della storia sociale del medioevo italiano assume infatti dei toni molto diversi in conseguenza del carattere magmatico dell'elaborazione teorica dei primi anni. E' estremamente indicativo il richiamo ai visionari programmi di Gabriele d'Annunzio per la reggenza del Quarnaro (Alatri 1980: 224-243): nel pensiero dello scrittore traspare esplicitamente il medioevo comunale come modello che nutre il suo concetto di spiritualità del lavoro; questo principio, chiaramente ereditato dal pensiero cattolico, venne forzato da d'Annunzio fino ad assumere toni talmente oscuri da risultare quasi caricaturali. Più pragmatica ma destinata ad essere progressivamente assorbita dal regime la posizione di Sergio Panunzio: sebbene in modo confuso, egli rivendicava l'autonomia delle entità sindacali contro l'onnipotenza dello stato, un concetto come abbiamo visto non troppo lontano dal pensiero di Toniolo, come lo era molta parte della sua visione fortemente organicistica del medioevo. Se questa resta comunque una posizione di preciso carattere antimoderno, la sua componente antistatalista risulterà sostanzialmente incompatibile con le posizioni progressivamente più centralistiche dello stato fascista (De Angelis 1988).

Nel 1923, infatti, la marcia su Roma marcò una definizione più precisa della visione corporativa dello stato: il motivo dell'opposizione alle spinte classiste che avevano attraversato tragicamente gli anni dell'immediato dopoguerra egemonizzò progressivamente gran parte della cultura politica del tempo ed il suo influsso sul pensiero storico non tarda a farsi palese. Con l'insediamento nel 1925 della "commissione dei diciotto" presieduta da Giovanni Gentile il processo si compì con la cooptazione degli storici Gioacchino Volpe, Pier Silvio Leicht, Gino Arias e Francesco Ercole.

Questa operazione riunificò paradossalmente antichi avversari, promossi a "corporativisti di stato" (la bella definizione è sempre di Artifoni, 1988: 34) istradando decisamente questa storiografia (d'ora innanzi avara di novità di rilievo) nei binari del regime. Ed è proprio in questo punto che avverrà l'incontro con il pensiero cattolico: la convergenza dei clerico-moderati sulle posizioni antisocialiste taglia progressivamente fuori tutta la cultura non legata al fascismo.

LA STORIOGRAFIA DI REGIME

Si realizzò così in questi anni un blocco di posizioni fortemente omogeneo in cui il dibattito, anche apparentemente vivace, rimase un elemento superficiale destinato a non incidere sulle strutture profonde della cultura del tempo. Due temi in particolare vennero sviluppati in maniera vistosa e forse sproporzionata, due temi apparentemente non connessi fra loro in modo diretto ma entrambi concatenati funzionalmente nella logica del pensiero degli intellettuali fascisti. Il primo riprendeva un tema già noto: quello della continuità o meno dell'istituto corporativo tra l'età romana e il medioevo, laddove le sostanziali differenze tra le due epoche erano state già ampiamente messe in luce ed il problema già definito e parzialmente risolto da Volpe. Con la scoperta nel 1920 delle *Honorantiae civitatis Papiae*, si riaprì fra gli studiosi una discussione, unanimemente riconosciuta come piuttosto caduca, che si protrasse fino alla seconda guerra mondiale[3]. Fu un dibattito in cui molti contributi sembrano oggi più il tentativo di trovare a tutti i costi un elemento di continuità con la romanità che non delle elaborazioni scientifiche originali, ed infatti troviamo con frequenza digressioni di carattere storico sull'origine delle corporazioni in ogni scritto di diritto corporativo.

Di gran lunga più incisivo è invece il secondo elemento della questione. Sulla scorta delle analisi economico-sociali della civiltà medievale, e dell'età comunale in particolare, era evidente agli studiosi del tempo una sostanziale diversità tra corporazione medievale (l'"ente intermedio" di Toniolo e Meda) e il nascente sistema corporativo fascista in cui lo stato aveva un preciso ruolo unificatore. Come già tratteggiato dai cattolici, l'istituto medievale sembrava soprattutto un elemento di difesa dallo strapotere delle istituzioni statali, cosa che disegnava così un medioevo comunale sostanzialmente libero all'interno di un quadro istituzionale fondamentalmente diverso rispetto alla costituzione dello stato fascista corporativo.

Tuttavia, nel clima politico ormai mutato, la prospettiva cambia in modo deciso. Questi elementi di libertà che ai cattolici del primo Novecento apparivano come una fondamentale virtù del mondo comunale sembrano ora, non solo agli intellettuali più legati al fascismo ma a gran parte della cultura del tempo, elemento negativo, segno di quella stessa potenziale instabilità sociale che aveva portato l'italia sul baratro del bolscevismo. Essi disegnano così un ardito nesso logico: come la tendenza all'autonomia dei vari istituti della società è sfociata nella crisi delle istituzioni comunali[4] così, fino all'avvento del fascismo, la demagogia classista ha messo a repentaglio l'ordine della società. Compito dello stato fascista è dunque quello di porre rimedio a questi rischi ancora attuali fondando un sistema ispirato sì ai modelli della società medievale, ma più perfetto, che tra l'altro trova un esempio proprio nel tardo medioevo, nell'organizzazione della Repubblica di Venezia, che è forse l'esempio in cui lo stato, in sintonia con l'insegnamento della Chiesa, sembra avere un controllo più forte sulla società (Arias 1928: 443-444).

In questa importante parte della cultura fascista il medioevo non cessa di esercitare il fascino di un modello positivo, pur nel riconoscimento di questi limiti. Si esce così dallo stereotipo irenico del cattolicesimo sociale di fine Ottocento per costruirne un altro, funzionale al nuovo momento politico.

L'impegno a costruire un tipo di società che nega l'esistenza del conflitto di classe incontrò così il consenso di settori sempre più ampi del mondo cattolico, anche fra quegli intellettuali che, superata la diffidenza iniziale legata alle riserve nei confronti di un eccessivo potere dello stato trovarono, specie dopo i Patti lateranensi, un certo spazio ed una voce in capitolo[5].

Il cerchio di questa vicenda intellettuale si chiude così nel segno dell'antisocialismo e la temperie culturale che ne risultò si avvia verso la conclusione col secondo conflitto mondiale. Una nuova cesura sarà così evidente negli anni successivi a questo quando la parabola della bibliografia sul tema delle corporazioni di arti e mestieri imboccherà una fase quantitativamente discendente.

L'analisi di questo nuovo clima intellettuale è ancora in gran parte da fare. Nell'Italia postbellica l'interpretazione marxista del fenomeno si affermò come è ovvio con rapidità, esercitando una forte egemonia sull'interpretazione economico-sociale del medioevo e sviluppando un orientamento storiografico che spostò in modo deciso l'attenzione sul mondo della produzione. La sintesi più eloquente di questo momento culturale è forse quella contenuta nella voce apparsa sull'Enciclopedia Einaudi a firma di Viktor Rutenburg (1973), significativamente redatta con ampio uso di bibliografia sovietica. E' un momento di grande tensione ideologica in cui le posizioni della storiografia marxista non incontrano un consenso unanime come ad esempio testimonia la dura polemica fra Rutenburg stesso, "arcigno custode dell'ortodossia", e Federigo Melis sul ruolo del salariato nell'economia laniera fiorentina[6]. Posizioni come quelle di Melis sono significativamente minoritarie in quegli anni, ma queste discussioni hanno comunque l'innegabile merito di riportare con decisione l'asse delle riflessioni verso problemi di carattere storico-economico.

Nel frattempo, e siamo ormai alla fine del XX secolo, un altro snodo storico segna un possibile mutamento nel dibattito scientifico, riflesso di un'evidente trasformazione della sensibilità politico-sociale: la crisi dei sistemi socialisti genera importanti e convulsi rivolgimenti ideologici nei quali, in un quadro segnato da nuove instabilità a livello mondiale, una parte del pensiero della sinistra anche marxista si incontra, nel segno di una nuova polemica antimoderna, coi temi più tradizionali del cristianesimo di matrice sociale.

Al di là delle interpretazioni "mitiche" del medioevo, per lo più ai margini della storiografia di mestiere, è da comprendere come questo clima culturale, di grande momento, influenzerà nuove letture della storia italiana ed europea.

NOTE

1 Fra i contributi ormai classici ricordiamo Dagmar Flascassovitti 1975-76 che si sofferma soprattutto sui testi apparsi nella Rivista internazionale di scienze sociali, il periodico fondato da Giuseppe Toniolo nel 1893; Greci 1988 che intreccia questi temi con quelli della "storiografia delle antitesi"; l'incisivo Artifoni 1988 che sottolinea gli aspetti di frattura tra le due correnti storiografiche e, attraverso la crisi della scuola economico-giuridica punta il dito sull'approdo comune nella storiografia fascista; il documentatissimo Occhipinti 1990, infine, che, chiamando in causa Agostino Gemelli, adombra una prima spiegazione culturale delle convergenze tra fascisti e cattolici sul tema della storia corporativa.
2 Toniolo 1893a, 1893b, 1893c, 1984; su questo cf. per primo Vigna 1918: 435, poi le decisive riflessioni di Cinzio Violante 1961: 733-739.
3 Un riassunto in Occhipinti 1990: 103-121
4 Un concetto, questo, chiaramente espresso da Solmi (1923: 878); cf. anche Ercole 1928: 23-27.
5 P.es. Pagano 1929, in part. p.278; Ercole 1929.

6 Una sintesi in Del Treppo 1978

BIBLIOGRAFIA

Alatri, P. (ed.), 1980, *Scritti politici di Gabriele d'Annunzio*, Milano.

Arias, G., 1928, Stato fascista e stato corporativo, *Gerarchia* 8, 439-444.

Artifoni, E, 1988, Forme del potere e organizzazione corporativa in età comunale: un percorso storiografico, in *Economia e corporazioni. Il governo degli interessi nella storia d'Italia dal medioevo all'età contemporanea* (ed. C. Mozzarelli), Milano, 9-34.

Artifoni, E., 1984, Medioevo delle antitesi, *Nuova Rivista Storica* 68, 367-380.

Dagmar Flascassovitti, C., 1975-76, La medievistica italiana tra otto e novecento e il problema delle corporazioni medioevali. 1. L'ambiente culturale della Rivista Internazionale di scienze sociali, *Annali dell'Università di Lecce. Facoltà di lettere e Filosofia* 7, 173-193.

De Angelis, S., 1980, Sergio Panunzio: rivoluzione e/o stato dei sindacati, *Storia Contemporanea* 11, 969-987.

Del Treppo, M., 1978, Federigo Melis, storico, in *Studi in memoria di Federigo Melis*, I, Napoli (http://www.istitutodatini.it/schede/melis/htm/melis3.htm)

Ercole, F., 1928, Le origini del corporativismo fascista, *Politica* 10, 5-36.

Ercole, F., 1929, Il trattato ed il concordato del laterano, *Gerarchia* 8, 337-343.

Gemelli, A. 1914, Medioevalismo, *Vita e pensiero* 1, 1-24

Gemelli, A., 1906, Il progresso delle scienze biologiche innanzi al pensiero cattolico, *Studium* 1, 1-28.

Gemelli, A., 1907, Per il progresso degli studi scientifici fra i cattolici italiani, *Studium* 2, 662-673.

Greci, R., 1988, *Corporazioni e mondo del lavoro nell'Italia padana medievale*, Bologna.

Manacorda, D., 1982a, Per un'indagine sull'archeologia italiana durante il ventennio fascista, *Archeologia medievale* 8, 443-470

Manacorda, D., 1982b, Cento anni di ricerche archeologiche italiane: il dibattito sul metodo, *Quaderni di storia* 8, 85-119

Meda, F., 1916, La riabilitazione cristiana del corporativismo, *Vita e pensiero* 2, 343-350

Occhipinti, E., 1990, Quarant'anni di studi italiani sulle corporazioni medievali tra storiografia e ideologia, *Nuova Rivista Storica* 74, 101-174 .

Pagano, A., 1929, Dalla idea cristiana alla idea fascista, *Politica* 9, 241-279.

Rodolico, N., 1899, *Il popolo minuto. Note di storia fiorentina (1343-1378)*, Bologna.

Rutenburg, V.I., 1973, Arti e Corporazioni, in Storia d'Italia, 5, *I documenti* 1, Torino, 613-642.

Solmi, A., 1923, Corporativismo medievale e sindacalismo moderno, *Gerarchia* 2, 871-879.

Toniolo, G., 1893a, La genesi storica dell'odierna crisi sociale ed economica, *Rivista Internazionale di Scienze sociali* 1, 39-68, 223-253.

Toniolo, G., 1893b, L'economia capitalistica moderna, *Rivista Internazionale di Scienze sociali* 1, 529-605.

Toniolo, G., 1893c, L'economia capitalistica moderna, *Rivista Internazionale di Scienze sociali* 2, 402-419.

Toniolo, G., 1894, L'economia capitalistica moderna, *Rivista Internazionale di Scienze sociali* 4, 26-37.

Vigna, L., 1918, Giuseppe Toniolo, un maestro di cattolicesimo sociale, *Vita e Pensiero* 8, 451-458.

Violante, C., 1961, Il significato dell'opera storiografica di G. Toniolo nell'età di Leone XIII, in *Aspetti della cultura cattolica nell'età di Leone XIII.* Atti del convegno. Bologna, 27-29 dicembre 1960 (ed. G. Rossini), Roma, 707-767

www.ingramcontent.com/pod-product-compliance
Lightning Source LLC
LaVergne TN
LVHW072250300926
849160LV00018B/1626
* 9 7 8 1 8 4 1 7 1 6 2 0 6 *